Lecture Notes in Computer Science 5984

Commenced Publication in 1973
Founding and Former Series Editors:
Gerhard Goos, Juris Hartmanis, and Jan van Leeuwen

Donghoon Lee   Seokhie Hong (Eds.)

Information Security and Cryptology – ICISC 2009

12th International Conference
Seoul, Korea, December 2-4, 2009
Revised Selected Papers

 Springer

Volume Editors

Donghoon Lee
Seokhie Hong
CIST (Center for Information Security Technologies)
Korea University
5-1 Anam, Sungbuk Gu, Seoul, 136-713, Korea
E-mail: donghlee@korea.ac.kr, hsh@cist.korea.ac.kr

Library of Congress Control Number: 2010930429

CR Subject Classification (1998): E.3, K.6.5, C.2, D.4.6, G.2.1, E.4

LNCS Sublibrary: SL 4 – Security and Cryptology

ISSN   0302-9743
ISBN-10   3-642-14422-5 Springer Berlin Heidelberg New York
ISBN-13   978-3-642-14422-6 Springer Berlin Heidelberg New York

springer.com

© Springer-Verlag Berlin Heidelberg 2010
Printed in Germany

Typesetting: Camera-ready by author, data conversion by Scientific Publishing Services, Chennai, India
Printed on acid-free paper   06/3180

Preface

ICISC 2009, the 12th International Conference on Information Security and Cryptology, was held in Seoul, Korea, during December 2–4, 2009. It was organized by the Korea Institute of Information Security and Cryptology (KIISC) and the Ministry of Public Administration and Security (MOPAS). The aim of this conference was to provide a forum for the presentation of new results in research, development, and applications in the field of information security and cryptology. It also served as a place for research information exchange. The conference received 88 submissions from 22 countries, covering all areas of information security and cryptology. The review and selection processes were carried out in two stages by the Program Committee (PC) comprising 57 prominent researchers via online meetings. First, at least three PC members blind-reviewed each paper, and papers co-authored by the PC members were reviewed by at least five PC members. Second, individual review reports were revealed to PC members, and detailed interactive discussion on each paper followed. Through this process, the PC finally selected 25 papers from 15 countries. The acceptance rate was 28.4%. The authors of selected papers had a few weeks to prepare for their final versions based on the comments received from more than 80 external reviewers. The conference featured one tutorial and one invited talk. The tutorial was given by Amit Sahai from the University of California and the talk was given by Michel Abdalla from École normale supérieure. There are many people who contributed to the success of ICISC 2009. We would like to thank all the authors who submitted papers to this conference. We are deeply grateful to all 57 members of the PC, especially to those who shepherded conditionally accepted papers. It was a truly nice experience to work with such talented and hard-working researchers. We wish to thank all the external reviewers for assisting the PC in their particular areas of expertise. We would like to thank all the participants of the conference who made this event an intellectually stimulating one through their active contribution. The support given to the ICISC 2009 workshop by the following sponsors is greatly appreciated: National Security Research Institute (NSRI), Electronics and Telecommunications Research Institute (ETRI), National Institute for Mathematical Sciences (NIMS), Korea Internet and Security Agency (KISA), Korea University BK21 Information Security in Ubiquitous Environment, Seoul National University Research Institute of Mathematics (SNU RIM), Korean Federation of Science and Technology Societies (KOFST), Chungnam National University Internet Intrusion Response Technology Research Center (IIRTRC), MarkAny, SG Advantech, AhnLab, LG CNS, and Korea University.

December 2009

Donghoon Lee
Seokhie Hong

Organization

ICISC 2009 was organized by the Korea Institute of Information Security and Cryptology (KIISC) and Ministry of Public Administration and Security (MOPAS)

Executive Committee

General Chair   Kwangjo Kim (KAIST, Korea)
Program Chair   Donghoon Lee (CIST, Korea University, Korea)
                       Seokhie Hong (CIST, Korea University, Korea)
Organizing Chair   Taekyoung Kwon (Sejong University, Korea)

Program Committee

Joonsang Baek   I2R, Singapore
Alex Biryukov   University of Luxembourg, Luxembourg
Liqun Chen   HP Labs, UK
Jung Hee Cheon   Seoul National University, Korea
Paolo Milani Comparetti   Vienna University of Technology, Austria
Nicolas T. Courtois   University College London, UK
Frédéric Cuppens   Telecom Bretagne, France
Paolo D'Arco   University of Salerno, Italy
Bart De Decker   Katholieke Universiteit Leuven, Belgium
David Galindo   University of Luxembourg, Luxembourg
Philippe Golle   Palo Alto Research Center, USA
Vipul Goyal   UCLA, USA and MSR, India
Louis Granboulan   EADS Innovation Works, France
Matthew Green   Independent Security Evaluators, USA
Dong-Guk Han   Kookmin University, Korea
Martin Hell   Lund University, Sweden
Deukjo Hong   Attached Institute of ETRI, Korea
Jin Hong   Seoul National University, Korea
Nick Hopper   University of Minnesota, USA
David Jao   University of Waterloo, Canada
Jaeyeon Jung   Intel Labs, USA
Seungjoo Kim   Sungkyunkwan University, Korea
Xuejia Lai   Shanghai Jiao Tong University, China
Byoungcheon Lee   Joongbu University, Korea
Mun-Kyu Lee   Inha University, Korea
Pil Joong Lee   Pohang University of Science and Technology,
                               Korea
Yingjiu Li   Singapore Management University, Singapore

Subreviewers

Taeyoon Han
Jeongdae Hong
Xinyi Huang
Emeline Hufschmitt
Sebastiaan Indesteege
Daisuke Inoue
Hugo Jonker
Jeonil Kang
Emilia Käsper
Takeshi Kawabata
Dmitry Khovratovich
HyunMin Kim
Jangseong Kim
Jihye Kim
Kitae Kim
Minkyu Kim
So Jeong Kim
Sungkyung Kim
Woo Chun Kim
Youn Kyu Kim
Bonwook Koo
Barbara Kordy
Jung Keun Lee
Jin Li
Peter van Liesdonk
Hsi-Chung Lin
Joseph K. Liu
Yali Liu
Hans Loehr
Nicky Mouha
Sandra Marcello
Sascha Müller

Kris Narayan
Ching Yu Ng
Ivica Nikolic
Kazumasa Omote
Wolter Pieters
Saša Radomirović
Minoru Saeki
Teruo Saito
Thomas Schneider
Jae Woo Seo
Masaaki Shirase
Siamak F. Shahandashti
Maki Shigeri
HyunDong So
Jeong Eun Song
Masakazu Soshi
Takahiko Syouji
Toshiaki Tanaka
Isamu Teranishi
Etsuko Tsujihara
Frederik Vercauteren
Christian Wachsmann
Jhih-Wei Wang
Jian Weng
Chi-Dian Wu
Zhongming Wu
Yanjiang Yang
Yeon-Hyeong Yang
Tsz Hon Yuen
Jinmin Zhong
Zayabaatar
Bo Zhu

Table of Contents

Key Management and Key Exchange

Public Key Cryptography

Algebraic Cryptanalysis and Stream Cipher

Security Management and Efficient Implementation

Side Channel Attack

Privacy Enhanced Technology

Cryptographic Protocol

Cryptanalysis of Hash Function

Network Security

Generic One Round Group Key Exchange in the Standard Model

M. Choudary Gorantla[1], Colin Boyd[1],
Juan Manuel González Nieto[1], and Mark Manulis[2]

[1] Information Security Institute, Faculty of IT, Queensland University of Technology
GPO Box 2434, Brisbane, QLD 4001, Australia
mc.gorantla@isi.qut.edu.au, {c.boyd,j.gonzaleznieto}@qut.edu.au
[2] Cryptographic Protocols Group, Department of Computer Science
TUDarmstadt & CASED, Germany
mark@manulis.eu

Abstract. Minimizing complexity of group key exchange (GKE) protocols is an important milestone towards their practical deployment. An interesting approach to achieve this goal is to simplify the design of GKE protocols by using generic building blocks. In this paper we investigate the possibility of founding GKE protocols based on a primitive called *multi key encapsulation mechanism (mKEM)* and describe advantages and limitations of this approach. In particular, we show how to design a one-round GKE protocol which satisfies the classical requirement of authenticated key exchange (AKE) security, yet without forward secrecy. As a result, we obtain the first one-round GKE protocol secure in the standard model. We also conduct our analysis using recent formal models that take into account both outsider and insider attacks as well as the notion of key compromise impersonation resilience (KCIR). In contrast to previous models we show how to model both outsider and insider KCIR within the definition of mutual authentication. Our analysis additionally implies that the insider security compiler by Katz and Shin from ACM CCS 2005 can be used to achieve more than what is shown in the original work, namely both outsider and insider KCIR.

Keywords: Group Key Exchange, Key Encapsulation Mechanism, Key Compromise Impersonation.

1 Introduction

The computation of a common secret key among a group of members communicating over a public network is usually performed through a group key exchange (GKE) protocol. The secrecy (indistinguishability) of the established group key is modelled through the requirement called *authenticated key exchange (AKE) security* [1,2,3]. The classical AKE-security notion comes in different flavours depending on whether the protocol provides forward secrecy or not. Informally, a protocol with forward secrecy ensures that the secrecy of the group key is preserved despite possible user corruptions in the future. The user corruptions also

D. Lee and S. Hong (Eds.): ICISC 2009, LNCS 5984, pp. 1–15, 2010.
© Springer-Verlag Berlin Heidelberg 2010

have different flavours depending on whether only long-lived secrets are leaked (weak corruption [1,4]) or the ephemeral, session-dependent information from the internal states can be revealed as well (strong corruption [5]). Bresson et al. [1] also define mutual authentication (MA) security as a desired notion of security for GKE protocols. The notion of MA-security requires that parties who complete the protocol should output identical session keys and that each party should be ensured of the identity of the other participating parties

However, as discussed by Katz and Shin [6] and Bohli et al. [7] the above security notions are not adequate if the GKE protocol should resist misbehaviour of its participants; in particular, preventing honest users from computing different keys and from having distinct views on the identities of other participants. Bresson and Manulis [5] merged the insider security requirements defined by Katz and Shin into their notion of MA-security in the presence of malicious insiders, improving upon the notion of MA-security from Bresson et al. [1]. This stronger MA-security can be obtained for any AKE-secure GKE protocol using Katz and Shin's compiler, which we refer to as the KS-compiler.

Recently, AKE- and MA-security notions have been further extended by Gorantla et al. [8] considering outsider and insider *key compromise impersonation resilience* (KCIR). Informally, a GKE protocol with KCIR ensures that an honest party cannot be impersonated by an adversary which has access to the private keys of other parties. The notion of outsider KCIR was modelled within AKE-security and insider KCIR was embedded into MA-security [8]. However, these notions defy the natural expectation that insider KCIR should imply outsider KCIR. It also remains unclear whether the KS-compiler can be used to achieve the additional insider KCIR or not.

KEY ENCAPSULATION MECHANISMS. Cramer and Shoup [9] formalised the concept of hybrid encryption which securely merges public and symmetric encryption techniques to encrypt messages. In short, the public key part called *key encapsulation mechanism (KEM)* is used to generate and encrypt a random session key, while *data encryption mechanism (DEM)* based on symmetric techniques is used to encrypt the actual message using that session key. The KEM primitive has been further extended to *multi KEM (mKEM)* by Smart [10]. mKEM is useful in scenarios where a single message should be encrypted for multiple recipients.

It is evident from their properties, especially by generating a random session key, that KEMs can also be utilized for the establishment of secure shared keys. In fact, the question of constructing key establishment protocols from KEMs has been investigated in the two-party setting: Gorantla et al. [11] provided generic constructions in both the directions based on signcryption KEMs, whereas Boyd et al. [12] presented a generic one-round protocol using plain encryption KEMs. The natural question is, thus, whether mKEMs in turn can be utilized for the design of GKE protocols? The non-triviality of the problem, in contrast to what one may think after having [11,12], is the consideration of insider attacks which are not present in the two party case.

1.1   Our Contributions

In this paper, we extend the technique of Boyd et al. [12] to the group setting and present a generic one-round GKE protocol using mKEM as a building block which we prove AKE-secure in the standard model, yet without forward secrecy. The main reason for lack of forward secrecy is that mKEMs known today are not forward secure. Since forward secrecy is a desirable goal for some applications we also discuss the modified two-round version of the protocol based on one-time mKEM and digital signatures.

We enrich KCIR notions for GKE by including a definition of outsider KCIR into MA-security. In this way we achieve the natural implication between insider and outsider KCIR. We demonstrate the usefulness of the new notion by showing that the generic transformation of Bresson et al. [1] to achieve outsider MA-security is not sufficient for outsider KCIR.

Our new definition also highlights the separation between AKE-security and KCIR. As observed by Boyd and Mathuria [13, §5.5, p.166] two-party protocols can always achieve KCIR if each party encrypts its ephemeral pubic key with the partner's long-term public key. This holds also for the generic two-party protocol of Boyd et al.[12]. However, when we move to the group setting this observation does not hold any more with respect to AKE-security. As an example, we show that our one-round GKE protocol does not achieve AKE-security with outsider KCIR. Nevertheless, we show that our protocol still achieves MA-security with outsider KCIR. Thanks to the implication from insider KCIR to outsider KCIR we can show this by proving that our protocol when compiled with the KS-compiler achieves MA-security with insider KCIR.

Katz and Shin [6] informally mentioned that the KS-compiler could provide KCIR. Gorantla et al. [8] also speculated that when the KS-compiler is applied to the protocol of Boyd and González Nieto [14] it would result in a GKE protocol secure under both AKE-security and MA-security with KCIR. However, we observe that the KS-compiler does not necessarily guarantee AKE-security with outsider KCIR.

1.2   Related Work

Boyd [15] presented three classes of one round key exchange protocols, which may be seen as a different paradigm to the classical Diffie-Hellman key exchange. In Class 1, the parties exchange random nonces in clear as their contributions towards the session key. A long-term shared symmetric key is then used to derive the session key. Constructing concrete GKE protocols in this class is not very interesting as the assumption that all the parties in the group initially share a common symmetric key seems unrealistic [16]. In Class 2, only one party uses confidential and authentication channels to send its nonce while all other parties send their nonces in clear. Concrete protocols in the Class 2 can be constructed using public key encryption and signature schemes. The protocol of Boyd and González Nieto [14] falls into this class. In Class 3, all the parties use confidential channels to send their nonces. Our proposed protocol falls into this class. A major drawback of protocols in all the three classes is that they cannot provide forward secrecy. However, a distinctive feature of Class 3 protocols is that they can be proven secure under the AKE-security notion without employing public key signatures. Hence, Class 3 protocols seem suitable to construct efficient deniable GKE protocols [17]. We do not formally explore this possibility in this paper.

Bohli et al. [7] defined *contributiveness* as another desired security notion for GKE protocols. This notion demands that a proper subset of insiders should not predetermine the resulting session key. Bresson and Manulis [5] strengthened this notion by considering strong corruptions where the ephemeral session state of an instance might also be revealed in addition to the long-term private key of the party. They also proposed compilers to achieve contributiveness in both weak and strong corruption models [18].

1.3   Organization

Section 2 reviews existing notions of AKE-security and MA-security with insider KCIR and also presents a new notion of MA-security with outsider KCIR. In Section 3, we describe our one-round GKE protocol based on mKEM and prove it AKE-secure without forward secrecy. Additionally, we mention how to extend this protocol with an additional round and obtain forward secrecy. In Section 4, we prove that the compiler by Katz and Shin [6] if executed with our protocol provides MA-security with outsider and insider KCIR. Section 5 gives security and efficiency comparison of existing GKE protocols. Appendix A describes the background concepts that serve as building blocks in our paper.

2   Security Model for GKE Protocols

In this section, we review existing notions of AKE-security and MA-security considered for GKE protocols. We also present our new notion of MA-security with outsider KCIR.

Let $\mathcal{U} = \{U_1, \ldots, U_N\}$ be a set of N parties. The protocol may be run among any subset of these parties. Each party U_j for $j \in [1, N]$ is assumed to have a pair of long-term public and private keys, (pk_j, sk_j) generated during an initialization phase prior to the protocol run. A GKE protocol π executed among $n \leq N$ users is modelled as a collection of n programs running at the n different parties in $\mathcal{U}$. Each instance of π within a party is defined as a session and each party may have multiple such sessions running concurrently.

Let π_U^i be the i-th run of the protocol π at party $U \in \mathcal{U}$. Each protocol instance at a party is identified by a unique session ID. We assume that the session ID is derived during the run of the protocol. The session ID of an instance π_U^i is denoted by sid_U^i. We assume that each party knows who the other participants are for each protocol instance. The partner ID pid_U^i of an instance π_U^i, is a set of identities of the parties with whom π_U^i wishes to establish a common group key. Note that pid_U^i includes the identity of U itself.

An instance π_U^i enters an *accepted* state when it computes a session key sk_U^i. Note that an instance may terminate without ever entering into an accepted state. The information of whether an instance has terminated with acceptance or without acceptance is assumed to be public. Two instances π_U^i and $\pi_{U'}^j$ at two different parties U and U' respectively are considered *partnered* iff (1) both the instances have accepted, (2) $\mathsf{sid}_U^i = \mathsf{sid}_{U'}^j$, and (3) $\mathsf{pid}_U^i = \mathsf{pid}_{U'}^j$.

The communication network is assumed to be fully controlled by an adversary $\mathcal{A}$, which schedules and mediates the sessions among all the parties. $\mathcal{A}$ is allowed to insert, delete or modify the protocol messages. If the adversary honestly forwards the protocol messages among all the participants, then all the instances are partnered and output identical session keys. Such a protocol is called a correct GKE protocol. In addition to controlling the message transmission, $\mathcal{A}$ is allowed to ask the following queries.

- Execute(pid) prompts a complete execution of the protocol among the parties in pid with a unique session ID sid. $\mathcal{A}$ is given all the protocol messages, modelling passive attacks.
- Send(π_U^i,m) sends a message m to the instance π_U^i. If the message is pid, the instance π_U^i is initiated with partner ID pid. The response of π_U^i to any Send query is returned to $\mathcal{A}$.
- RevealKey(π_U^i) If π_U^i has accepted, $\mathcal{A}$ is given the session key sk_U^i established at π_U^i.
- Corrupt(U_j) The long-term secret key sk_j of U_j is returned to $\mathcal{A}$. Note that this query returns neither the session key (if computed) nor any session specific internal state.
- RevealState(π_U^i) The ephemeral internal state of π_U^i is returned to $\mathcal{A}$. We assume that the internal state is erased once π_U^i has accepted.
- Test(π_U^i) A random bit b is secretly chosen. If $b = 1$, $\mathcal{A}$ is given $\kappa_1 = sk_U^i$ established at π_U^i. Otherwise, a random value κ_0 chosen from the session key probability distribution is given. Note that a Test query is allowed only once that too on an accepted instance.

Corrupted Parties, Corrupted Instances and Insiders. We call a *party* U corrupted if it has been issued a Corrupt query, while a *protocol instance* π_U^i is called corrupted if a RevealState(π_U^i) query has been asked. Note that there exist uncorrupted protocol instances at corrupted parties when the session specific ephemeral secrets are not revealed. A party is called an *insider* in a particular protocol run if both the party and the protocol instance are corrupted or if the adversary issues a Corrupt query to the party and then impersonates it i.e. when the adversary issues a Send query on behalf of π_U^i with a message m not previously output by π_U^i.

2.1 AKE-Security

The notion of freshness is central to the definition of AKE-security. Informally, a session is considered *fresh* if the session key established in that session is not trivially compromised. In Figure 1, we review different notions of freshness defined for GKE protocols in the literature. The first notion is a slightly revised notion from Katz and Yung [4], considering RevealState queries. This notion does not capture either forward secrecy or KCIR. Hence, the adversary is not allowed to corrupt any party associated with the test session. The second notion considers forward secrecy and may be seen as a stronger notion than that of Bresson and Manulis [5], where the corruption of a party U' is allowed after the session π_U^i has accepted. This differs from the notion of Bresson and Manulis, where the adversary is not allowed to issue a corrupt query until π_U^i and all its partners have accepted. The second notion may also be seen as a revised notion from Katz and Shin [6] considering RevealState queries. The third notion, which was recently defined by Gorantla et al. [8], considers both forward secrecy and outsider KCIR.

The basic notion of freshness (not considering forward secrecy or KCIR) [4]

An instance π_U^i is fresh if the following conditions hold:

1. the instance π_U^i or any of its partners has not been asked a RevealKey after their acceptance
2. the instance π_U^i or any of its partners has not been asked a RevealState before their acceptance
3. there has not been a Corrupt(U') query for any $U' \in$ pid$_U^i$ (including $U' = U$)

The notion of freshness with forward secrecy [6,5]

An instance π_U^i is fs-fresh if the following conditions hold:

1. the instance π_U^i or any of its partners has not been asked a RevealKey after their acceptance
2. the instance π_U^i or any of its partners has not been asked a RevealState before their acceptance
3. there has not been a Corrupt(U') query for any $U' \in$ pid$_U^i$ (including $U' = U$) before π_U^i has accepted

The notion of freshness with outsider KCIR and forward secrecy [8]

An instance π_U^i is kcir-fs-fresh if the following conditions hold:

1. the instance π_U^i or any of its partners has not been asked a RevealKey after their acceptance
2. the instance π_U^i or any of its partners has not been asked a RevealState before their acceptance
3. If $\pi_{U'}^j \in$ pid$_U^i$ and $\mathcal{A}$ asked Corrupt(U'), then any message that $\mathcal{A}$ sends to π_U^i on behalf of $\pi_{U'}^j$ must come from $\pi_{U'}^j$, intended to π_U^i .

Fig. 1. Notions of Freshness

Definition 1 (AKE-Security). An adversary $\mathcal{A}^{AKE}$ against the AKE-security notion is allowed to make Execute, Send, RevealState, RevealKey and Corrupt queries in Stage 1. $\mathcal{A}^{AKE}$ makes a Test query to an instance π_U^i at the end of Stage 1 and is given a challenge key κ_b as described earlier. It can continue asking queries in Stage 2. Finally, $\mathcal{A}^{AKE}$ outputs a bit b' and wins the AKE security game if (1) $b' = b$ **and** (2) the instance π_U^i that was asked Test query remained fresh(or fs-fresh/kcir-fs-fresh correspondingly) till the end of $\mathcal{A}^{AKE}$'s execution. Let $\mathsf{Succ}_{\mathcal{A}^{AKE}}$ be the success probability of $\mathcal{A}^{AKE}$ in winning the AKE security game. The advantage of $\mathcal{A}^{AKE}$ in winning this game is $\mathsf{Adv}_{\mathcal{A}^{AKE}} = |2 \cdot \Pr[\mathsf{Succ}_{\mathcal{A}^{AKE}}] - 1|$. A protocol is called AKE-secure if $\mathsf{Adv}_{\mathcal{A}^{AKE}}$ is negligible in the security parameter k for any polynomial time $\mathcal{A}^{AKE}$.

Remark 1. It is clear that if a GKE protocol does not have forward secrecy, the AKE-security of the session key can be compromised by revealing the long-term key of a protocol participant. An adversary can perform a KCI attack on GKE protocols without forward secrecy by replaying messages of past successful executions or even by relaying messages from an honest party. The KCI attacks of Gorantla et al. [8] on Boyd and González Nieto [14] and Bresson et al. [19] protocols work in the same way. As the AKE-security notion with outsider KCIR implies that at most $n - 1$ corruptions are allowed, it is necessary for a protocol realizing this notion to have at least (partial) forward secrecy when $n - 1$ parties are corrupted or (full) forward secrecy. However, as evident by Gorantla et al.'s KCI attack on Al-Riyami and Paterson's protocol [20], having forward secrecy alone is not sufficient for a GKE protocol to have AKE-security with outsider KCIR. We leave it an open problem to define AKE-security notion with outsider KCIR and partial forward secrecy and to construct a GKE protocol realizing it.

2.2 MA-Security

We present two notions of MA-security with KCIR, one in the presence of only outsiders and another in the presence of insiders. The notion of MA-security with KCIR in the presence of insiders was defined by Gorantla et al. [8], while the notion of MA-security with outsider KCIR is new.

Definition 2 (MA-Security with Outsider KCIR). An adversary $\mathcal{A}^{MA}$ against the MA-security of a correct GKE protocol π is allowed to ask Execute, Send, RevealState, RevealKey and Corrupt queries. $\mathcal{A}^{MA}$ violates the MA-security of the GKE protocol if at some point during the protocol run, there exists an uncorrupted instance π_U^i that has accepted with a key sk_U^i and another party $U' \in \mathsf{pid}_U^i$ that is uncorrupted at the time π_U^i accepts such that there are no insiders in pid_U^i and

1. there exists no instance $\pi_{U'}^j$ with $(\mathsf{pid}_{U'}^j, \mathsf{sid}_{U'}^j) = (\mathsf{pid}_U^i, \mathsf{sid}_U^i)$ **or**
2. there exists an instance $\pi_{U'}^j$ with $(\mathsf{pid}_{U'}^j, \mathsf{sid}_{U'}^j) = (\mathsf{pid}_U^i, \mathsf{sid}_U^i)$ that has accepted with $sk_{U'}^j \neq sk_U^i$.

The above definition implies that $\mathcal{A}^{MA}$ must be passive for any corrupted party in pid_U^i. Note that in a protocol execution with n parties, the above definition also implies that $\mathcal{A}^{MA}$ is allowed to corrupt up to $n - 1$ parties.

Let $\mathsf{Succ}_{\mathcal{A}^{MA}}$ be the success probability of $\mathcal{A}^{MA}$ in winning the above security game. A protocol is said to provide MA-security with outsider KCIR if $\mathsf{Succ}_{\mathcal{A}^{MA}}$ is negligible in the security parameter k for any polynomial time $\mathcal{A}^{MA}$.

Definition 3 (MA-Security with Insider KCIR). An adversary $\mathcal{A}^{MA}$ against the MA-security of a correct GKE protocol π is allowed to ask Execute, Send, RevealState, RevealKey and Corrupt queries. $\mathcal{A}^{MA}$ violates the MA-security of the GKE protocol if at some point during the protocol run, there exists an uncorrupted instance π_U^i (although the party U may be corrupted) that has accepted with a key sk_U^i and another party $U' \in \text{pid}_U^i$ that is uncorrupted at the time π_U^i accepts such that

1. there is no instance $\pi_{U'}^j$ with $(\text{pid}_{U'}^j, \text{sid}_{U'}^j) = (\text{pid}_U^i, \text{sid}_U^i)$ **or**
2. there is an instance $\pi_{U'}^j$ with $(\text{pid}_{U'}^j, \text{sid}_{U'}^j) = (\text{pid}_U^i, \text{sid}_U^i)$ that has accepted with $sk_{U'}^j \neq sk_U^i$.

Note that this notion implies that there can be up to $n-2$ insiders (i.e. except U and U'). Let $\text{Succ}_{\mathcal{A}^{MA}}$ be the success probability of $\mathcal{A}^{MA}$ in winning the above security game. A protocol is said to provide MA-security with insider KCIR if $\text{Succ}_{\mathcal{A}^{MA}}$ is negligible in the security parameter k for any polynomial time $\mathcal{A}^{MA}$.

3   One Round GKE Protocol from mKEM

Smart [10] formalised the notion of mKEM by extending the concept of KEM. Using an mKEM scheme, a user who wants to encrypt a large message to n parties can encapsulate a single session key to all the parties at once and then apply a DEM with the session key to encrypt the actual message. Smart also defined the notion of indistinguishability under chosen ciphertext attacks (IND-CCA) for mKEM. The definition and security model for mKEM have been reviewed in Appendix A.1.

In Figure 2, we present a generic construction of GKE protocol based on mKEM. The parties can establish the group session key by executing an mKEM in parallel. Let $\mathcal{U} = \{U_1, U_2, \cdots, U_n\}$ be the set of protocol participants. The protocol uses an mKEM scheme (KeyGen, Encap, Decap). Let (pk_i, sk_i) be the public-private key pair of the party U_i, generated using the KeyGen algorithm. Each party starts the protocol by running the Encap algorithm and then broadcasts the encapsulation C_i to the other parties in the group. Upon receiving the encapsulations each party runs the Decap algorithm for each encapsulation intended for it and retrieves the symmetric keys. The session ID is defined as the concatenation of all the encapsulations along with the group identity $\mathcal{U}$.

The session key is finally computed by each party from the symmetric key it has generated during the Encap algorithm and all the symmetric keys decapsulated. A pseudo random function (PRF) f is used to derive the session key. Note that the session key derivation in our protocol is slightly different from the approach used in Boyd et al. [12]. In Boyd et al.'s protocol a randomness extraction function is first applied to the symmetric keys K_i's before using them as seeds to a PRF to derive the session key. In our protocol, we directly use the symmetric keys generated by the IND-CCA secure mKEM as seeds to f to simplify the protocol design. As shown in the proof below this does not effect the security of the protocol.

Computation

Each U_i executes an mKEM with public keys $\{pk_j | 1 \leq j \leq n; j \neq i\}$ as input and obtains the symmetric key and encapsulation pair (K_i, C_i)

$$(K_i, C_i) \leftarrow \mathsf{Encap}(\{pk_j | 1 \leq j \leq n; j \neq i\})$$

Broadcast

Each U_i broadcasts the computed encapsulation C_i along with its identity.

$$U_i \rightarrow \mathcal{U} \setminus \{U_i\} : \quad C_i, U_i$$

Key Computation

1. Each U_i executes the decapsulation algorithm using its private key sk_i and on each of the incoming encapsulations C_j and obtains the symmetric keys K_j, where $1 \leq j \leq n$, $j \neq i$.

$$K_j \leftarrow \mathsf{Decap}(sk_i, C_j) \text{ for each } 1 \leq j \leq n, \ j \neq i$$

2. Each U_i then computes the session ID as the concatenation of all the outgoing and incoming messages exchanged i.e. $\mathsf{sid} = (C_1 \| \cdots \| C_n \| \mathcal{U})$, where $\mathcal{U}$ is the set of identities of all the n users.
3. The session key κ is then computed as

$$\kappa = f_{K_1}(\mathsf{sid}) \oplus f_{K_2}(\mathsf{sid}) \oplus \cdots \oplus f_{K_n}(\mathsf{sid})$$

where f is a pseudo random function.

Fig. 2. A generic GKE protocol from mKEM

3.1   Proof of Security

Theorem 1. *The protocol in Figure 2 is AKE-secure without forward secrecy as per Definition 1 assuming the underlying mKEM is IND-CCA secure. The advantage of $\mathcal{A}^{AKE}$ is given as $Adv_{\mathcal{A}^{AKE}} \leq n \cdot \frac{q_s^2}{|\mathcal{C}|} + n \cdot q_s \cdot (Adv_{\mathcal{A}^{CCA}} + n \cdot Adv_{\mathcal{A}^{PRF}})$, where $n \leq N$ is the number of parties in the protocol, N is the number of public keys in the system, q_s is the number of sessions $\mathcal{A}^{AKE}$ is allowed to activate, $|\mathcal{C}|$ is the size of the ciphertext space, $\mathcal{A}^{CCA}$ is a polynomial adversary against the IND-CCA security of the underlying mKEM and $\mathcal{A}^{PRF}$ is a polynomial adversary adversary against the pseudo random function.*

The proof of above theorem is given in the full version [21].

3.2   Instantiating the Protocol

Smart [10] presented an efficient IND-CCA secure mKEM based on ElGamal encryption scheme. However, it has been proven secure in the random oracle model. Although our generic construction does not assume random oracles, a concrete realization with this mKEM will only be secure in the random oracle model.

Smart also proposed a generic mKEM from any public key encryption scheme. This construction was proven IND-CCA secure assuming that the underlying encryption scheme was IND-CCA secure [10, Theorem 2]. Hence, generic mKEMs in the standard model can be constructed from public key encryption schemes which are also secure in the standard model [22,9,23]. This means that our protocol can be realized in the standard model by using the generic mKEM construction. However, note that the security in the standard model comes at the price of additional computational efficiency and longer message size. Nevertheless, this instantiation will result in the first concrete GKE protocol which has only one round of communication.

3.3 Achieving Forward Secrecy

Our one-round protocol in Figure 2 does not provide forward secrecy. However, it can be used as a building block for a two-round GKE protocol that achieves this additional goal. This protocol runs as follows: In the first round, each user U_i chooses an *ephemeral* asymmetric key pair (pk_i, sk_i) for mKEM and broadcasts pk_i to the group. In the second round users perform the one-round protocol in Figure 2 using asymmetric mKEM keys from the first round. It is easy to see that such construction involving one-time mKEMs results in an unauthenticated GKE protocol with forward secrecy. The AKE-security of this protocol can be achieved using digital signatures similar to [4]; in particular, one can treat one-time pk_i as a nonce of U_i and require the additional signature of U_i on $C_i|pk_1|\dots|pk_n$ in the second round.

4 Achieving MA-Security with KCIR

Bresson et al. [1] proposed a generic transformation that turns an AKE-secure GKE protocol π into a protocol π' that provides MA-security in the presence of an outsider adversary. Yet, their notion of MA-security did not consider KCIR. The transformation uses the well known technique of constructing an "authenticator" using the shared session key established in π. It works as follows: Let κ_i be the session key computed by U_i in protocol π. The protocol π' requires an additional round in which each party U_i computes a message $auth_i = \mathcal{H}(\kappa_i, i)$, where $\mathcal{H}$ is a hash function (modelled as random oracle in the proof) and broadcasts it to all other parties. Each party verifies the incoming messages using the session key established at their end. If the verification is successful, π' terminates with each party U_i accepting the session key $\kappa_i' = \mathcal{H}(\kappa_i, 0)$.

We show that the above transformation does not necessarily guarantee MA-security with outsider KCIR. For example, consider a protocol π which does not have forward secrecy like the protocol of Boyd and González Nieto [14] or our one-round protocol in Figure 2. Definition 2 implies that an adversary against MA-security with outsider KCIR can issue up to $n - 1$ Corrupt queries but must then remain passive on behalf of corrupted users. As the protocol π does not have forward secrecy, corrupting a single party U_i is enough to obtain the session key κ_i. The adversary can now easily impersonate an uncorrupted party U_j in protocol π' by computing $auth_j = \mathcal{H}(\kappa_i, j)$. Hence, transformations based on shared keys cannot be used to obtain MA-security with outsider KCIR.

Instead, we show that the KS-compiler [6] when applied to our protocol achieves MA-security with both outsider and insider KCIR. Katz and Shin [6] proved that this compiler when applied to an AKE-secure GKE protocol provides MA-security in the presence of insiders, yet without considering KCI attacks. Here, we show that their technique is also sufficient to obtain MA-security with outsider and insider KCIR. It is easy to see that MA-security with insider KCIR implies MA-security with outsider KCIR, i.e. given an adversary against MA-security with outsider KCIR, one can construct an adversary against MA-security with insider KCIR. Hence, we only need to prove that the compiled protocol guarantees MA-security with insider KCIR.

Theorem 2. *If we apply the KS-compiler to our protocol in Figure 2, the resulting protocol provides MA-security with insider KCIR. The success probability of the adversary $\mathcal{A}^{MA}$ is given as $n^2 \cdot Adv_{\mathcal{A}^{CMA}} + n \cdot \frac{q_s^2}{|\mathcal{C}|} + Adv_{\mathcal{A}^{coll}}$, where n is the number of parties in the protocol, q_s is the number of sessions $\mathcal{A}^{MA}$ is allowed to activate, $|\mathcal{C}|$ is the size of the ciphertext space, $\mathcal{A}^{CMA}$ is a polynomial adversary against the unforgeability of the signature scheme under chosen message attack and $\mathcal{A}^{coll}$ is a polynomial adversary adversary against the collision resistance of the pseudo-random function F in the KS-compiler.*

The proof of above theorem is given in the full version [21].

Remark 2. Note that the protocol obtained after applying Katz and Shin's compiler to our one-round GKE protocol still does not achieve forward secrecy. Hence, as discussed in Remark 1, it cannot achieve AKE-security with KCIR. However, from Theorem 2 it is evident that forward secrecy is not necessary for a GKE protocol to achieve MA-security with insider KCIR.

5 Conclusion

Table 1 compares the security of some of the existing GKE protocols. The column "Rounds" shows the number of communication rounds required to complete the protocol. The terms "AKE", "AKE-FS" and "AKE-KCIR" refer to AKE-security, AKE-security with forward secrecy and AKE-security with KCI resilience respectively. Similarly, "MA" refers to mutual authentication and "MA-Out" and "MA-In" refer to mutual authentication with outsider and insider KCIR respectively. The entry "Yes*" indicates that the corresponding protocol appears to be secure under the notion but there is no formal proof. The last column in the table says whether the protocol is proven in the random oracle model or in the standard model.

It can be observed from the table that our protocol is the only one-round GKE protocol secure in the standard model. Although the protocol of Bohli et al. satisfies all the desired notions of security, it requires two-rounds of communication

Table 1. Security and efficiency comparison among existing GKE protocols

	Rounds	AKE	AKE-FS	AKE-KCIR	MA	MA-Out	MA-In	Model
Boyd and González Nieto [14]	1	Yes	No	No	No	No	No	ROM
Katz and Yung [4]	3	Yes	Yes	Yes*	honest	Yes*	No	Std.
Bohli et al. [7]	2	Yes	Yes	Yes	Yes	Yes	Yes	ROM
Bresson and Manulis [5]	3	Yes	Yes	Yes*	Yes	Yes	Yes*	Std.
Furukawa et al. [24]	2	Yes	Yes	Yes*	Yes	Yes	Yes*	Std.
Our Protocol	1	Yes	No	No	No	No	No	Std.
Our Protocol + KS-compiler	2	Yes	No	No	Yes	Yes	Yes	Std.

and moreover proven secure only in the random oracle model. Of the other protocols which are proven secure in the standard model, the protocols of Bresson and Manulis and Furukawa et al. [24] appear to satisfy all the desired notions, but they require three and two communication rounds respectively. Applying the KS-compiler to our protocol results in a two-round GKE protocol that satisfies the MA-security notion with insider KCIR. However, the resulting protocol still cannot provide forward secrecy or AKE-security with KCIR. The approach outlined in Section 3.3 with the combination of the KS-compiler results in a GKE protocol that appears to satisfy all the desired notions of security. However, this protocol will have three rounds of communication.

Although our one-round GKE protocol cannot achieve all the security notions, it will be very useful in scenarios where communication efficiency highly desired. Unlike the previously known one-round GKE protocol, our protocol has been proven secure in the standard model. We have also discussed generic techniques with which the security of the protocol can be enhanced. However, as expected this additional security guarantee comes at the price of extra number of rounds. We leave it an open problem to construct an efficient mKEM in the standard model, which can in turn be used to construct a one-round GKE protocol using our approach.

References

1. Bresson, E., Chevassut, O., Pointcheval, D., Quisquater, J.J.: Provably authenticated group Diffie-Hellman key exchange. In: CCS 2001: Proceedings of the 8th ACM conference on Computer and Communications Security, pp. 255–264. ACM, New York (2001)
2. Bresson, E., Chevassut, O., Pointcheval, D.: Provably Authenticated Group Diffie-Hellman Key Exchange - The Dynamic Case. In: Boyd, C. (ed.) ASIACRYPT 2001. LNCS, vol. 2248, pp. 290–309. Springer, Heidelberg (2001)

3. Bresson, E., Chevassut, O., Pointcheval, D.: Dynamic Group Diffie-Hellman Key Exchange under Standard Assumptions. In: Knudsen, L.R. (ed.) EUROCRYPT 2002. LNCS, vol. 2332, pp. 321–336. Springer, Heidelberg (2002)
4. Katz, J., Yung, M.: Scalable Protocols for Authenticated Group Key Exchange. In: Boneh, D. (ed.) CRYPTO 2003. LNCS, vol. 2729, pp. 110–125. Springer, Heidelberg (2003)
5. Bresson, E., Manulis, M.: Securing Group Key Exchange against Strong Corruptions. In: Proceedings of ACM Symposium on Information, Computer and Communications Security (ASIACCS 2008), pp. 249–260. ACM Press, New York (2008)
6. Katz, J., Shin, J.S.: Modeling insider attacks on group key-exchange protocols. In: Proceedings of the 12th ACM Conference on Computer and Communications Security CCS 2005, pp. 180–189. ACM, New York (2005)
7. Bohli, J.M., Gonzalez Vasco, M.I., Steinwandt, R.: Secure group key establishment revisited. Int. J. Inf. Sec. 6(4), 243–254 (2007)
8. Gorantla, M.C., Boyd, C., González Nieto, J.M.: Modeling Key Compromise Impersonation Attacks on Group Key Exchange Protocols. In: Jarecki, S., Tsudik, G. (eds.) PKC 2009. LNCS, vol. 5443, pp. 105–123. Springer, Heidelberg (2009)
9. Cramer, R., Shoup, V.: Design and analysis of practical public-key encryption schemes secure against adaptive chosen ciphertext attack. Technical report (2002), http://shoup.net/
10. Smart, N.P.: Efficient Key Encapsulation to Multiple Parties. In: Blundo, C., Cimato, S. (eds.) SCN 2004. LNCS, vol. 3352, pp. 208–219. Springer, Heidelberg (2005)
11. Gorantla, M.C., Boyd, C., Nieto, J.M.G.: On the Connection Between Signcryption and One-Pass Key Establishment. In: Galbraith, S.D. (ed.) Cryptography and Coding 2007. LNCS, vol. 4887, pp. 277–301. Springer, Heidelberg (2007)
12. Boyd, C., Cliff, Y., González Nieto, J.M., Paterson, K.G.: One-Round Key Exchange in the Standard Model. International Journal of Applied Cryptography 1(3), 181–199 (2009)
13. Boyd, C., Mathuria, A.: Protocols for Authentication and Key Establishment. Information Security and Cryptography. Springer, Heidelberg (August 2003)
14. Boyd, C., González Nieto, J.M.: Round-Optimal Contributory Conference Key Agreement. In: Desmedt, Y.G. (ed.) PKC 2003. LNCS, vol. 2567, pp. 161–174. Springer, Heidelberg (2002)
15. Boyd, C.: Towards a classification of key agreement protocols. In: The Eighth IEEE Computer Security Foundations Workshop CSFW 1995, pp. 38–43. IEEE Computer Society, Los Alamitos (1995)
16. Boyd, C.: On Key Agreement and Conference Key Agreement. In: Mu, Y., Pieprzyk, J.P., Varadharajan, V. (eds.) ACISP 1997. LNCS, vol. 1270, pp. 294–302. Springer, Heidelberg (1997)
17. Bohli, J.M., Steinwandt, R.: Deniable Group Key Agreement. In: Nguyên, P.Q. (ed.) VIETCRYPT 2006. LNCS, vol. 4341, pp. 298–311. Springer, Heidelberg (2006)
18. Bresson, E., Manulis, M.: Contributory Group Key Exchange in the Presence of Malicious Participants. IET Information Security 2(3), 85–93 (2008)
19. Bresson, E., Chevassut, O., Essiari, A., Pointcheval, D.: Mutual Authentication and Group Key Agreement for Low-Power Mobile Devices. In: Proc. of MWCN 2003, October 2003, pp. 59–62 (2003)
20. Al-Riyami, S.S., Paterson, K.G.: Tripartite Authenticated Key Agreement Protocols from Pairings. In: Paterson, K.G. (ed.) Cryptography and Coding 2003. LNCS, vol. 2898, pp. 332–359. Springer, Heidelberg (2003)

21. Gorantla, M.C., Boyd, C., Nieto, J.M.G., Manulis, M.: Generic One Round Group Key Exchange in the Standard Model. Cryptology ePrint Archive, Report 2009/514 (2009), http://eprint.iacr.org/
22. Cramer, R., Shoup, V.: A Practical Public Key Cryptosystem Provably Secure Against Adaptive Chosen Ciphertext Attack. In: Krawczyk, H. (ed.) CRYPTO 1998. LNCS, vol. 1462, p. 13. Springer, Heidelberg (1998)
23. Canetti, R., Halevi, S., Katz, J.: Chosen-Ciphertext Security from Identity- Based Encryption. In: Cachin, C., Camenisch, J.L. (eds.) EUROCRYPT 2004. LNCS, vol. 3027, pp. 207–222. Springer, Heidelberg (2004)
24. Furukawa, J., Armknecht, F., Kurosawa, K.: A Universally Composable Group Key Exchange Protocol with Minimum Communication Effort. In: Ostrovsky, R., De Prisco, R., Visconti, I. (eds.) SCN 2008. LNCS, vol. 5229, pp. 392–408. Springer, Heidelberg (2008)

A   Preliminaries

We first review the definition and notion of security considered for mKEM and then briefly describe Katz and Shin's compiler.

A.1   Multi KEM

An mKEM takes the public keys of n parties as input and outputs a session key K and an encapsulation of K under all the n public keys. It is formally specified by three algorithms as described below:

KeyGen: This is a probabilistic algorithm that takes the domain parameters as input and outputs a public-private key pair (pk, sk).

Encap: This is a probabilistic algorithm that takes the domain parameters, the public keys of n receivers $(pk_1, \ldots, pk_n)$ and outputs a session key $K \in \{0, 1\}^k$ and an encapsulation C of K under the public keys $(pk_1, \ldots, pk_n)$.

Decap: This is a deterministic algorithm that takes the domain parameters, an encapsulation C and a private key sk_i as input and outputs either a key K or $\perp$.

For an mKEM to be considered valid it is required that for all key pairs (pk_i, sk_i), $i \in [1, n]$ if $(K, C) = \mathsf{Encap}(\{pk_1, pk_2, \ldots, pk_n\})$ then $\mathsf{Decap}(C, sk_i) = K$ for each $i \in [1, n]$.

The IND-CCA notion of security for mKEM is defined in a similar way to the traditional KEMs as below.

Definition 4. An mKEM is IND-CCA secure if the advantage of any probabilistic polynomial time adversary in the following game is negligible in the security parameter k.

Setup: The challenger runs the KeyGen algorithm and obtains n key pairs (pk_i, sk_i) for $1 \leq i \leq n$. All the public keys $\mathcal{P} = \{pk_1, \cdots, pk_n\}$ are given to the adversary.

Phase 1: The adversary is allowed to issue decapsulation queries as below:

Decap: The adversary issues this query with input $\mathcal{P}' \subseteq \mathcal{P}$ and an encapsulation C. The challenger returns either a key K or $\perp$ after executing the Decap algorithm on C using the private keys corresponding to $\mathcal{P}'$. Note that if Decap on input C produces different symmetric keys for two different private keys of users in $\mathcal{P}'$, then the encapsulation C is deemed invalid and the adversary is returned $\perp$.

Challenge: The adversary gives a set of keys $\mathcal{P}^* \subseteq \mathcal{P}$ to the challenger. The challenger first chooses $b \in \{0, 1\}$. It then runs the Encap algorithm using $\mathcal{P}^*$ and generates $(\mathcal{K}_b, C^*)$. It then sets $\mathcal{K}_{1-b}$ to be a random key drawn uniformly from the key space i.e., $\mathcal{K}_{1-b} \xleftarrow{R} \{0, 1\}^k$. Both the keys $\{\mathcal{K}_0, \mathcal{K}_1\}$ are given to the adversary along with the challenge encapsulation C^*.

Phase 2: The adversary is allowed to issues queries to challenger as in Phase 1 with the following restriction: A decapsulation query on an encapsulation C' (includes $C' = C^*$) that trivially reveals the session key $\mathcal{K}_b$ is not allowed.[1]

Guess: The goal of the adversary is to guess which one of the two keys $\{\mathcal{K}_0, \mathcal{K}_1\}$ is encapsulated in C^*. It finally outputs a guess bit b' and it succeeds if $b' = b$. The advantage of the adversary is given as $Adv_{ACCA} = |2 \cdot \Pr[b' = b] - 1|$.

---

[1] This restriction is necessary to address benign malleability [10].

Modeling Leakage of Ephemeral Secrets in Tripartite/Group Key Exchange

Mark Manulis[1], Koutarou Suzuki[2], and Berkant Ustaoglu[2]

[1] Cryptographic Protocols Group, TU Darmstadt & CASED, Germany
mark@manulis.eu
[2] NTT Information Sharing Platform Laboratories
3-9-11 Midori-cho Musashino-shi Tokyo 180-8585, Japan
{suzuki.koutarou,ustaoglu.berkant}@lab.ntt.co.jp

Abstract. Recent advances in the design and analysis of secure two-party key exchange (2KE) such as the leakage of ephemeral secrets used *during* the attacked sessions remained unnoticed by the current models for group key exchange (GKE). Focusing on a special case of GKE — the tripartite key exchange (3KE) — that allows for efficient one-round protocols, we demonstrate how to incorporate these advances to the multi-party setting. From this perspective our work closes the most pronounced gap between provably secure 2KE and GKE protocols.

The proposed 3KE protocol is an implicitly authenticated protocol with one communication round which remains secure even in the event of ephemeral secret leakage. It also significantly improves upon currently known 3KE protocols, many of which are insecure. An optional key confirmation round can be added to our proposal to achieve the explicitly authenticated protocol variant.

1 Introduction

Bellare and Rogaway [2] and Blake-Wilson, Johnson and Menezes [3] independently proposed models for analyzing security of two-party key exchange (2KE) protocols in the shared and public key settings, respectively. In their approach an adversary is given the ability to interact with parties and controls the communication with the simple goal of distinguishing a test session key from a random key. Motivating with the signed variant[1] of the classical unauthenticated Diffie-Hellman [13] protocol, Canetti and Krawzcyk [10] argued that it is desirable to augment the 2KE adversary with the ability to learn session-specific and protocol-defined ephemeral information that is not related to the test session. LaMacchia, Lauter and Mityagin [25] allowed leakage of some test session specific ephemeral information under certain conditions. Menezes and Ustaoglu [31] extended the timing of the information leakage. All these developments were within the framework of two-party key exchange.

---

[1] In the signed Diffie-Hellman protocol users sign outgoing ephemeral public keys with their static keys.

D. Lee and S. Hong (Eds.): ICISC 2009, LNCS 5984, pp. 16–33, 2010.

Group key exchange (GKE) protocols are essentially the generalization of 2KE protocols to the group case. However, this generalization brings additional problems both in the design and the analysis of the protocols. The first formal model for GKE protocol was described by Bresson et al. [5] inspired by the two-party approach in [2]. Many modifications and improvements appeared thereafter, see the survey in [30]. GKE models mainly focus on the *outsider security* which is modeled through the requirement of AKE-security, e.g. [5,4,21,9], as this requirement deals explicitly with the secrecy of the established keys, which becomes meaningless if the adversary is an insider. Yet, several models, e.g. [20,6,8,15,14], consider the optional *insider security* aiming to prevent attacks by which insiders force parties to complete either with different keys (usually modeled as MA-security) or with keys that have some biased distribution (usually modeled as contributiveness). Several compilers have been proposed to augment AKE-secure protocols with security against insider attacks, e.g. [20,6,7]. Beside consideration of outsider and insider security GKE models differ in the treatment of corruptions. Earlier GKE models, e.g. [5,21], considered *weak corruptions* allowing the adversary to obtain users' static keys, but not their ephemeral session secrets. Later models, e.g. [9,8,14] assumed *strong corruptions* allowing the adversary to learn both static private keys and session specific secrets through a single query. Manulis and Bresson [8], inspired by the two-party approach in [10] refined the notion of strong corruptions in GKE allowing the adversary to obtain static keys independently from ephemeral session secrets; yet, restricting the leakage of ephemeral secrets to sessions for which the adversary does not need to distinguish the key. The reason is that GKE protocols known today become insecure if ephemeral secrets used to compute a group key leak, in other words leaking ephemeral secrets of one session affects the security of other non-partnered sessions. As a result many GKE protocols are insecure if parties for better performance pre-compute their ephemeral secrets off-line. Gorantla et. al. [14] subsequently strengthened [8] by considering key compromise impersonation attacks.

Despite of their significant improvement over the years GKE models remain incomparable to the 2KE models in terms of security guarantees they provide. In contrast to the 2KE models such as [23,31], GKE models do not consider leakage of ephemeral secrets for the session which is to be proven AKE-secure. In this paper we aim to fix the gap between 2KE and GKE models. Focusing on AKE-security we first revise the latest GKE models to accommodate leakage of ephemeral secrets against the attacked session. In order to illustrate that our model is reasonable and practical for our analysis we focus on three-party key exchange (3KE), which is a special class of GKE protocols and come up with a provably secure solution that resists these stronger leakage attacks.

Notation. Let $\hat{e} : \mathbb{G} \times \mathbb{G} \mapsto \mathbb{G}_T$ be a non-degenerate bilinear map from a group $\mathbb{G}$ to a group $\mathbb{G}_T$ both of prime order q. Let P be a generator of $\mathbb{G}$; for a user U_A we set U_A's static and ephemeral keys $S_A = s_A P$ and $X_A = x_A P$, respectively. The lowercase letters are the private keys.

2   Three vs. Two Party Key Establishment

Antoine Joux [17,18] used properties of pairings to extends the classical (unauthenticated) two-party Diffie-Hellman protocol [13] to the case of three parties, preserving the optimal one-round communication complexity. Since then tripartite key exchange as a special form of group key exchange has gained attention of the research community and several attempts have been made to improve the original protocol in order to enlarge the class of attacks it can resist.

2.1   Authenticating Outgoing Messages

Shim [32] argued that Joux's protocol fails to a variant of the well know person-in-the-middle attack against the (unauthenticated) Diffie-Hellman protocol. To address that shortcoming Shim proposed a protocol where Alice broadcasts

$$T_A = x_A s_A P. \tag{1}$$

Upon exchanging these ephemeral public keys the parties compute $t = \hat{e}(P,P)^{s_A s_B s_C}$ and the session key

$$k = \text{H}(\hat{e}(P,P)^{x_A x_B x_C s_A s_B s_C t}, U_A, U_B, U_C). \tag{2}$$

Shim's protocol fails to key compromise impersonation attack [33,29]. Suppose Malice sends two ephemeral public keys uP and vP to Alice on behalf of Bob and Charlie respectively. With the knowledge of Alice's static private key Malice can compute t; with the knowledge of u Malice can also compute $k = \hat{e}(vP, T_A)^{ut}$, which is the key Alice computes. Lin and Lin [29] observe that the attack is possible since Shim's protocol does not authenticate the T_A's origin. To resolve such issues one venue is introducing new elements into the communicated messages: along the ephemeral public key a user could append extra information that identifies messages' origin or provides evidence for following protocol specifications. For example [11] requires that along the message in Shim's protocol Alice also computes and broadcasts $X_A = x_A P$; the suggested session key is

$$k = \hat{e}(P,P)^{x_A x_B x_C s_A s_B s_C}.$$

Suppose, however, that an adversary Malice can obtain a certificate for an ephemeral public key X_A used by Alice. Malice can then send $X_M = S_A$, $T_M = T_A$, and the certificate to Bob and Charlie. As a result Bob and Charlie will believe the session key is shared with Malice, whereas the key is shared with Alice, who correctly identifies all session peers. This example resembles Kaliski's on-line unknown key share (UKS) attack [19] on the MQV protocol [26]. It is plausible [22, §7.3], that the ephemeral public keys pre-computed for efficiency reasons are not as securely stored as the ephemeral private keys. In that case the UKS attack can be made off-line implying that timing information leakage has important security consequences.

The modification to Shim's protocol in [29] requires that in addition to T_A, Alice also computes and broadcasts

$$m_A = \text{H}(s_A, x_A) \tag{3}$$

$$u_A = (s_A x_A)^{-1}(m_A + s_A) \bmod q. \tag{4}$$

Bob and Charlie verify Alice's message by computing $t_A = u_A^{-1} \bmod q$, $z_A = t_A m_A \bmod q$, and checking that

$$T_A \overset{?}{=} z_A P + t_A S_A. \tag{5}$$

The session key (as computed by Alice) is

$$k = \text{H}(\hat{e}(S_B + T_B, S_C + T_C)^{s_A + s_A x_A}, U_A, U_B, U_C)$$
$$= \text{H}(\hat{e}(P, P)^{(s_A + s_A x_A)(s_B + s_B x_B)(s_C + s_C x_C)}, U_A, U_B, U_C). \tag{6}$$

Malice can easily circumvent the verification by selecting a random integer m_B, setting $T_B = -m_B P - S_B$, $u_B = -1 \bmod q$ and sending these values on Bob's behalf to Alice and Charlie; see also [28, §4.1]. Alice (as well as Charlie) compute $t_B = -1^{-1} = -1 \bmod q$, $z_B = -m_B \bmod q$ and verify Equation 5 namely,

$$T_B = z_B P + t_B S_B = -m_B P - S_B.$$

Subsequently, Alice computes the key

$$k = \text{H}(\hat{e}(S_B + T_B, S_C + T_C)^{s_A + s_A x_A}, U_A, U_B, U_C)$$
$$= \text{H}(\hat{e}(S_B - m_B P - S_B, S_C + T_C)^{s_A + s_A x_A}, U_A, U_B, U_C)$$
$$= \text{H}(\hat{e}(P, P)^{(s_A + s_A x_A)(-m_B)(s_C + s_C x_C)}, U_A, U_B, U_C). \tag{7}$$

With the knowledge of m_B Malice can compute the same session key.

Lim et al. [28] further propose a "fix" to the above problem that requires additional information in the messages and further verification procedures. However, as observed in [27, §4.2], u_A relates the static and ephemeral key such that given the static private key s_A an adversary can derive the ephemeral private key x_A and thereafter recover the session key, so protocols with u_A as in Equation 4 do not provide forward secrecy. As an alternative [27] suggests $W_A = x_A \text{H}(x_A)(S_A)$, $n_A = \text{H}(T_A, W_A, p_A)$ for a time stamp p_A, and

$$s_A = (s_A x_A \text{H}(x_A))^{-1}(m_A + s_A n_A) \bmod q. \tag{8}$$

The above examples aimed to provide certain assurances about incoming messages without allegedly sacrificing security. Compilers can be viewed as an abstraction to such approach, at the expense of overhead like complicated messages or more communication rounds. A more rigorous analysis of that approach can be found in [21,16].

Ephemeral key leakage has been motivated for two party key agreement protocols [10,23,34], but so far we did not include it in our analysis. In Equation 8 if s_A is leaked the adversary cannot obtain x_A, but if x_A is leaked, then the adversary can easily obtain the static secret s_A. Furthermore, in [24] authors observed that within a party cryptographic primitives can share the source of randomness; if the source is weak then signature schemes such as DSA can leak static private keys. Therefore, in the presence of leakage of ephemeral private information compilers' based solutions are non-trivial to adopt.

2.2   Al-Riyami and Patterson Protocols

Al-Riyami and Patterson [1] proposed four one round three party key agreement protocols. The design aims to "avoid the use of expensive signature computations". The protocols broadcast a message consisting of a single ephemeral public key along with necessary certificates, but differ in the key derivation procedures which are inspired by two-party protocols. These protocols inherit vulnerabilities from the underlying two-pass protocols, but suggest that lessons from two-party protocols should be applied to three-party protocols. In the TAK-4 protocol, akin to MQV [26] and HQMV [23], Alice, Bob and Charlie after exchanging static-ephemeral key pairs (S_A, X_A), (S_B, X_B) and (S_C, X_C), respectively, compute the session key

$$k = \hat{e}(P,P)^{(x_A + \mathrm{H_e}(X_A,S_A)s_A)(x_B + \mathrm{H_e}(X_B,S_B)s_B)(x_C + \mathrm{H_e}(X_C,S_C)s_C)}.$$

Given, the complicated HMQV security argument it is not surprising that no security argument for TAK-4 is provided. In fact as described in [1] TAK-4 fails to the following UKS attack in which Alice and Bob will falsely think that they share a key with Malice, whereas Charlie correctly identifies his peers as Alice and Bob. In the attack Malice, who owns a certificate for the public key $1_G{}^2$, intercepts all public keys and computes $X_M = X_C + \mathrm{H_e}(X_C, S_C)S_C$, implicitly defining $x_M = x_C + \mathrm{H_e}(X_C, S_C)s_C$. Note that

$$k = \hat{e}(P,P)^{(x_A + \mathrm{H_e}(X_A,S_A)s_A)(x_B + \mathrm{H_e}(X_B,S_B)s_B)(x_C + \mathrm{H_e}(X_C,S_C)s_C)}$$
$$= \hat{e}(P,P)^{(s_A + \mathrm{H_e}(S_A,S_A)s_A)(x_B + \mathrm{H_e}(X_B,S_B)s_B)(x_C + \mathrm{H_e}(X_C,S_C)s_C + \mathrm{H}(X_M,1_G)0)}$$
$$= \hat{e}(P,P)^{(s_A + \mathrm{H_e}(S_A,S_A)s_A)(x_B + \mathrm{H_e}(X_B,S_B)s_B)(x_M + \mathrm{H}(X_M,1_G)0)}.$$

Therefore, by sending (S_M, X_M) instead of (S_C, X_C) to Alice or Bob, Malice successfully mounts a UKS attack on TAK-4. The possibility of such attacks is acknowledged in [1], which also offers two alternatives to prevent them. The requirements in [1] do not prevent the adversary from mounting the above attack thus the more sound approach is to include identities in the key derivation as typically done in two party key agreement. In general fewer assumptions and primitives are better as they leave less room for security vulnerabilities.

---

[2] The element 1_G is the identity element in $\mathbb{G}$.

2.3 Ephemeral Information Leakage

In general, the security considerations important for two-party protocols are also relevant for multi-party protocols. Motivation for ephemeral information leakage is independent from number of users involved in a key agreement protocol. Primitives used in compilers often assume no ephemeral key leakage. Thus, it is worth considering implicitly authenticated key exchange protocols.

Ephemeral keys introduce further security aspects. For example, in Shim's protocol leaking static keys does not reveal the past session keys, but an adversary that can access one ephemeral and one static private key from different users can compute the session key. So, for a party concerned with forward secrecy with respect to its own static key, there is a difference if its peer static or ephemeral private key is leaked: the session key is still secure in the former case but no longer in the latter.

3 Implicitly Authenticated Tripartite Protocol

Informally, in our proposed protocol P parties exchange ephemeral and static keys and derive the keying material as described bellow. Optionally, there can be a key confirmation round.

Initialization. User U_i performs:
1. Select an ephemeral private key $x_i \in_R [1, q]$ and compute $X_i = g^{x_i}$.
2. Create a session state, identified by (P, U_i, X_i) that contains only (x_i, X_i).

Communication. Upon receiving request: $(P, U_i, U_{i+1}, U_{i+2}, \mathtt{rl})$, user U_i broadcasts $(1|P, U_0, U_1, U_2, \mathtt{rl}, X_i)$.

Derivations. Upon receiving the first round of messages U_i does the following:
1. Verify that $X_{i+1}, X_{i+2} \in \mathbb{G}^*$.
2. Compute $\mathtt{sid}^i = P|U_0|X_0|U_1|X_1|U_2|X_2$.
3. Compute KeyDer$(U_i, \mathtt{rl}, \mathtt{sid}^i, x_i, s_i)$.

Completion. To complete the session U_i does:
1. Destroy the session state.
2. Accept the session key k.

Key material. On input $(U_i, \mathtt{rl}, \mathtt{sid}^i, x_i, s_i)$ the auxiliary key derivation KeyDer computes:

1. Compute $\mathtt{F_0} = \mathtt{H_e}(X_0)$, $\mathtt{F_1} = \mathtt{H_e}(X_1)$ and $\mathtt{F_2} = \mathtt{H_e}(X_2)$.
2. Compute

$$\sigma_0 = \begin{cases} (\hat{e}(X_1 + S_1, X_2 + S_2))^{x_0 + \mathtt{F_0}s_0} & \text{if } \mathtt{rl} = 0 \\ (\hat{e}(X_0 + \mathtt{F_0}S_0, X_2 + S_2))^{x_1 + s_1} & \text{if } \mathtt{rl} = 1 \\ (\hat{e}(X_0 + \mathtt{F_0}S_0, X_1 + S_1))^{x_2 + s_2} & \text{if } \mathtt{rl} = 2 \end{cases} \quad (9)$$

3. Compute

$$\sigma_1 = \begin{cases} (\hat{e}(X_1 + \mathtt{F_1}S_1, X_2 + S_2))^{x_0 + s_0} & \text{if } \mathtt{rl} = 0 \\ (\hat{e}(X_0 + S_0, X_2 + S_2))^{x_1 + \mathtt{F_1}s_1} & \text{if } \mathtt{rl} = 1 \\ (\hat{e}(X_0 + S_0, X_1 + \mathtt{F_1}S_1))^{x_2 + s_2} & \text{if } \mathtt{rl} = 2 \end{cases} \quad (10)$$

4. Compute

$$\sigma_2 = \begin{cases} (\hat{e}(X_1 + S_1, X_2 + \text{F}_2 S_2))^{x_0 + s_0} & \text{if } \texttt{rl} = 0 \\ (\hat{e}(X_0 + S_0, X_2 + \text{F}_2 S_2))^{x_1 + s_1} & \text{if } \texttt{rl} = 1 \\ (\hat{e}(X_0 + S_0, X_1 + S_1))^{x_2 + \text{F}_2 s_2} & \text{if } \texttt{rl} = 2 \end{cases} \qquad (11)$$

5. Compute

$$\sigma_3 = \begin{cases} (\hat{e}(X_1 + \text{F}_1 S_1, X_2 + \text{F}_2 S_2))^{x_0 + \text{F}_0 s_0} & \text{if } \texttt{rl} = 0 \\ (\hat{e}(X_0 + \text{F}_0 S_0, X_2 + \text{F}_2 S_2))^{x_1 + \text{F}_1 s_1} & \text{if } \texttt{rl} = 1 \\ (\hat{e}(X_0 + \text{F}_0 S_0, X_1 + \text{F}_1 S_1))^{x_2 + \text{F}_2 s_2} & \text{if } \texttt{rl} = 2 \end{cases} \qquad (12)$$

6. Return $k = \text{H}(\sigma_0, \sigma_1, \sigma_2, \sigma_3, \texttt{sid}^i)$.

Instances with the same session id $\texttt{sid}$, and hence with the same ephemeral public keys and partners, compute the same output since

$$\text{H}(\sigma_0, \sigma_1, \sigma_2, \sigma_3, \texttt{sid}^i) = \text{H}\big((\hat{e}(P, P))^{(x_0 + \text{F}_0 s_0)(x_1 + s_1)(x_2 + s_2)},$$
$$(\hat{e}(P, P))^{(x_0 + s_0)(x_1 + \text{F}_1 s_1)(x_2 + s_2)},$$
$$(\hat{e}(P, P))^{(x_0 + s_0)(x_1 + s_1)(x_2 + \text{F}_2 s_2)},$$
$$(\hat{e}(P, P))^{(x_0 + \text{F}_0 s_0)(x_1 + \text{F}_1 s_1)(x_2 + \text{F}_2 s_2)}, \texttt{sid}^i\big). \qquad (13)$$

A special attention should be paid to the content of the internal state which by definition contains only the ephemeral private keys used by session throughout the protocol execution. Neither the static private key s_i, nor the values $\sigma_0 \ldots \sigma_3$, nor the derived key material become part of the session state. This is different from the definition used in [12], where the model allows the adversary to learn the complete state of the Turing machine. Our formulation is similar to the more common approach for two party Diffie-Hellman protocols, see for example [10,23,34], where the session state consists only of the ephemeral private key x_i used by U_i.

To include key confirmation, the output of H is modified to (k_m, k). Furthermore, after Derivation and before Completion users perform the following:

Confirmation. To execute key confirmation U_i does:

1. Compute tags $T_0 = \text{H}_3(k_m, U_0, X_0, \texttt{sid}^i)$, $T_1 = \text{H}_3(k_m, U_1, X_1, \texttt{sid}^i)$, and $T_2 = \text{H}_3(k_m, U_2, X_2, \texttt{sid}^i)$.
2. Record[3] T_{i+1} and T_{i+2}, and delete k_m.
3. Broadcast $(2|\text{P}, T_i, U_i, \texttt{sid}^i, \texttt{rl})$

Verification. U_i verifies that the incoming T_{i+1} and T_{i+2} are equal to the tags stored in the session state.

---

[3] To prevent leakage of these confirmation tags, U_i can store fingerprint of these tags. Upon obtaining tags from the alleged peers U_i computes and compares fingerprints of incoming tags with the fingerprints stored in the session state. Thus we can assume that the confirmation tags do not become part of the session state.

In the analysis of many two-party protocols ephemeral public and private keys can be obtained by the adversary only during the session execution. Thus such arguments do not cover pre-computed ephemeral key pairs. In some cases the adversary may be able to recover past ephemeral keys. For this reason in our protocol description the ephemeral key pairs are pre-computed and the adversary can access them before event the session is initialized. Indeed the Initialization stage can be performed long before the Communication stage. Similarly, the protocol description does not explicitly destroy the ephemeral private key (but should be done in practice) to allow the possibility that the adversary obtain the ephemeral key after observing some subsequent actions of the parties. These modifications only increase the power of the adversary and does not decrease it relative to the usual approach where ephemeral keys can be obtained only during the session execution.As mentioned in the introduction, Bresson and Manulis [8] considered leakage of ephemeral secrets from the internal states prior to the execution of a session, thus incorporating pre-computations into the model, and also after the completeness of the session, thus implicitly requiring the erasure of ephemeral secrets from the state. However, their approach disallows leakage of ephemeral secrets during the execution of the session.

4   The Model and Security Definitions

Our model can be seen as an extension of the strong authenticated key exchange model for two-party protocols from [31] to the group setting. It is described using the classical notations and terminology from previous models for GKE protocols, in particular those in [21,8,14].

Protocol Participants and Initialization. Let $\mathcal{U} := \{U_1, \ldots, U_N\}$ be a set of potential protocol participants and each user $U_i \in \mathcal{U}$ is assumed to hold a static private/public key pair (s_i, S_i) generated by some algorithm $Gen(1^\kappa)$ on a security parameter 1^κ during the initialization phase.

Protocol Sessions and Instances. Any subset of $\mathcal{U}$ can decide at any time to execute a new protocol session and establish a common group key. Participation of some $U \in \mathcal{U}$ in multiple sessions is modeled through an number of *instances* $\{\Pi_U^s \mid s \in [1 \ldots n], U \in \mathcal{U}\}$, i.e. the Π_U^s is the s-th session of U. Each instance is invoked via a message to U with a *partner id*[4] $\mathtt{pid}_U^s \subseteq \mathcal{U}$, which encompasses the identities of all the intended session participants (note that $\mathtt{pid}_U^s$ also includes U). We say that U owns the instance Π_U^s. In the invoked session Π_U^s *accepts* if the protocol execution was successful, in particular Π_U^s holds then the computed *group key k_U^s.*

Session state. During the session execution each participating Π_U^s creates and maintains a *session id* $\mathtt{sid}_U^s$ and an associated internal state $\mathtt{state}_U^s$ which in

---

[4] Invocation may also include other public information such as the protocol name that is invoked, the order of user and so on.

particular is used to maintain ephemeral secrets used by Π_U^s during the protocol execution. We say that U *owns* session sid_U^s if the instance Π_U^s was invoked at U. Note that the integer s is only a tool to describe the model. The users do not keep track of s, instead sessions are identified via the vector sid_U^s. At the onset of the instance the user that owns the instance may not have enough information to create sid_U^s; until sid_U^s is created the instance is identified via pid_U^s and the outgoing ephemeral public key[5] which is unique per user except with negligible probability. Furthermore, we assume that instances that accepted or aborted delete all information in their respective states.

Partnering. Two instances Π_U^s and $\Pi_{U_*}^t$ are called *partnered* or *matching* if $\mathrm{sid}_U^s \subseteq \mathrm{sid}_{U_*}^t$ or $\mathrm{sid}_{U_*}^t \subseteq \mathrm{sid}_U^s$ and $\mathrm{pid}_U^s = \mathrm{pid}_{U_*}^t$. The first condition models the fact that if session ids are computed during the protocol execution, e.g. from the exchanged messages, then their equality should be guaranteed only at the end of the protocol, i.e. upon the acceptance of Π_U^s and $\Pi_{U_*}^t$.

Note also that the notion of partnering is self-inclusive in the sense that any Π_U^s is partnered with itself. If the protocol allows a user U to initiate sessions with U, then the equality $\mathrm{pid}_U^s = \mathrm{pid}_{U_*}^t$ is a multi-set equality.

Adversarial Model. The adversary $\mathcal{A}$, modeled as a PPT machine, can schedule the protocol execution and mount own attacks via the following queries:

- *AddUser*(U, S_U): This query allows $\mathcal{A}$ to introduce new users. In response, if $U \notin \mathcal{U}$ (due to the uniqueness of identities) then U with the static public key S_U is added to $\mathcal{U}$; Note that $\mathcal{A}$ is not required to prove the possession of the corresponding secret key s_U[6].
- *Send*(Π_U^s, m): With this query $\mathcal{A}$ can deliver a message m to Π_U^s whereby U denotes the identity of its sender. $\mathcal{A}$ is then given the protocol message generated by Π_U^s in response to m (the output may also be empty if m is not required or if Π_U^s accepts). A special invocation query of the form *Send*($U, ('start', U_1, \ldots, U_n)$) with $U \in \{U_1, \ldots, U_n\}$ creates a new instance Π_U^s with $\mathrm{pid}_U^s = \{U_1, \ldots, U_n\}$ and provides $\mathcal{A}$ with the first protocol message.
- *RevealKey*(Π_U^s): This query models the leakage of session group keys and provides $\mathcal{A}$ with k_U^s. It is answered only if Π_U^s has accepted.
- *RevealStaticKey*(U): This query provides $\mathcal{A}$ with the static private key s_U.
- *RevealState*(Π_U^s): $\mathcal{A}$ is given the ephemeral secret information contained in state_U^s at the moment the query is asked. Note that the protocol specifies what the state contains.
- *Test*(Π_U^s): This query models the indistinguishability of the session group key according to the privately flipped bit τ. If $\tau = 0$ then $\mathcal{A}$ is given a random session group key, whereas if $\tau = 1$ the real k_U^s. The query is requires that Π_U^s has accepted.

---

[5] Implicitly, this assumes that the first outgoing message contains the ephemeral public key. If necessary this can be modified to accommodate other types of protocols.

[6] In our security argument we will only assume that S_U chosen by $\mathcal{A}$ is checked to be an element of $\mathbb{G}$.

Correctness. A GKE protocol is said to be *correct* if, when in the presence of benign[7] adversary all instances invoked for the same protocol session accept with the same session group key.

Freshness. The classical notion of freshness of some instance Π_U^s is traditionally used to define the goal of AKE-security by specifying the conditions for the $Test(\Pi_U^s)$ query. For example, the model in [21] defines an instance Π_U^s that has accepted as fresh if none of the following is true: (1) at some point, $\mathcal{A}$ asked *RevealKey* to Π_U^s or to any of its partnered instances; or (2) a query $RevealStaticKey(U_*)$ with $U_* \in \mathtt{pid}_U^s$ was asked before a *Send* query to Π_U^s or any of its partnered instances.

Unfortunately, these restrictions are not sufficient for our purpose since Π_U^s becomes immediately unfresh if the adversary gets involved into the protocol execution via a *Send* query after having learned the static key s_{U_*} of some user U_* those instance participates in the same session as Π_U^s. We fairly remark that [21] does not address (strong) corruptions of ephemeral secrets.

The recent model in [8] defines freshness using the additional *AddUser* and *RevealState* queries as follows. According to [8], an instance Π_U^s that has accepted is fresh if none of the following is true: (1) $\mathcal{A}$ queried $AddUser(U_M, S_{U_M})$ with some $U_* \in \mathtt{pid}_U^s$; or (2) at some point, $\mathcal{A}$ asked *RevealKey* to Π_U^s or any of its partnered instances; or (3) a query $RevealStaticKey(U_*)$ with $U_* \in \mathtt{pid}_U^s$ was asked before a *Send* query to Π_U^s or any of its partnered instances; or (4) $\mathcal{A}$ queried *RevealState* to Π_U^s or any of its partnered instances at some point after their invocation but before their acceptance.

Although this definition is already stronger than the one in [21] it is still insufficient for the main reason that it excludes the leakage of ephemeral secrets of instances in the period between the protocol invocation and acceptance. Also this definition of freshness does not model key compromise impersonation attacks.

The recent update of the freshness notion in [14] addressed the lack of key compromise impersonation resilience. In particular, it modifies the above condition (3) by requiring that if there exists an instance $\Pi_{U_*}^t$ which is partnered with Π_U^s and $\mathcal{A}$ asked $RevealStaticKey(U_*)$ then all messages sent by $\mathcal{A}$ to Π_U^s on behalf of $\Pi_{U_*}^t$ must come from $\Pi_{U_*}^t$ intended for Π_U^s. This condition should allow the adversary to obtain static private keys of users prior to the execution of the attacked session while requiring its benign behavior with respect to the corrupted user during the attack.

Yet, this freshness requirement still prevents the adversary from obtaining ephemeral secrets of participants during the attacked session. What is needed is a freshness condition that would allow the adversary to corrupt users and reveal the ephemeral secrets used by their instances in the attacked session at will for the only exception that it does not obtain both the static key s_{U_*} *and* the ephemeral secrets used by the corresponding instance of U_*; otherwise security can no longer be guaranteed. In the following we give the combined definition of freshness taking into account the previously described problems.

---

[7] Benign adversary executes an instance of the protocol and faithfully delivers messages without any modification.

Definition 1. *An instance Π_U^s that has accepted is fresh if none of the following is true:*

1. *$\mathcal{A}$ queried AddUser(U_*, S_{U_*}) with some $U_* \in \text{pid}_U^s$; or*
2. *$\mathcal{A}$ asked RevealKey to Π_U^s or any of its accepted partnered instances; or*
3. *$\mathcal{A}$ queried both RevealStaticKey(U_*) with $U_* \in \text{pid}_U^s$ and RevealState($\Pi_{U_*}^t$) for some instance $\Pi_{U_*}^s$ partnered with Π_U^s; or*
4. *$\mathcal{A}$ queried RevealStaticKey(U_*) with $U_* \in \text{pid}_U^s$ prior to the acceptance of Π_U^s and there exists no instance $\Pi_{U_*}^t$ partnered with Π_U^s.*

Note that since $U \in \text{pid}_U^s$ and since the notion of partnering is self-inclusive Condition 3 prevents the simultaneous corruption of static and ephemeral secrets for the corresponding instance Π_U^s as well. In case when users are allowed to own two partnering instances i.e., they can initiate protocols with themselves the last condition should be modified to say that the number of instances U equals the number of times U appears in pid_U^s. Note also that the above definition captures key-compromise impersonation resilience through Condition 4: $\mathcal{A}$ is allowed to corrupt participants of the test session in advance but then must ensure that instances of such participants have been honestly participating in the test session. In this way we exclude the trivial break of security where $\mathcal{A}$ reveals static keys of users prior to the test session and then actively impersonates that users during it. On the other hand, as long as $\mathcal{A}$ remains benign with respect to such users their instances will still be considered as fresh.

AKE-Security. We are ready to generalize the strong AKE-security definition from [25,31] to a group setting.

Definition 2. *Let P be a correct GKE protocol and τ be a uniformly chosen bit. We define the adversarial game $\text{Game}_{\mathcal{A},\text{P}}^{\text{ake}-\tau}(\kappa)$ as follows: after initialization, $\mathcal{A}$ interacts with instances via queries. At some point, $\mathcal{A}$ queries Test(Π_U^s), and continues own interaction with the instances until it outputs a bit τ'. If Π_U^s to which the Test query was asked is fresh at the end of the experiment then we set $\text{Game}_{\mathcal{A},\text{P}}^{\text{ake}-\tau}(\kappa) = \tau'$.*

$$\text{We define:} \qquad \text{Adv}_{\mathcal{A},\text{P}}^{\text{ake}}(\kappa) := |2\Pr[\tau = \tau'] - 1|$$

and denote with $\text{Adv}_{\text{P}}^{\text{ake}}(\kappa)$ the maximum advantage over all PPT adversaries $\mathcal{A}$. We say that a GKE protocol P provides strong AKE-security if this advantage is negligible.

5   Security Arguments

In this section, we provide security arguments of the proposed implicitly authenticated tripartite protocol. We need the gap BDH(Bilinear Diffie-Hellman) assumption, where one tries to compute BDH(U, V, W) accessing the BDDH oracle. Here, we denote BDH(U, V, W) = $\hat{e}(P, P)^{\log U \log V \log W}$, and the BDDH oracle on input $(uP, vP, wP, \hat{e}(P, P)^x)$ returns the bit 1 if $uvw = x$ and the bit 0 otherwise.

Theorem 1. *If $\mathbb{G}$ is a group where gap Bilinear Diffie-Hellman assumption holds and H and $\mathsf{H_e}$ are random oracles, the proposed implicitly authenticated tripartite protocol in Section 3 is secure in the sense of Definition 2.*

Outline of proof of Theorem 1 is provided in Appendix A. Here, we give an intuition of the proof. We denote by $(S_0, X_0), (S_1, X_1), (S_2, X_2)$ the static and ephemeral public keys of users U_0, U_1, U_2 in the test session sid^t. Consider the case, where user U_0 is honest, ephemeral public key X_0 is not revealed, and static public keys S_1 and S_2 are not revealed. In this case, solver $\mathcal{S}$ embeds instance (U, V, W) of gap BDH problem as $X_0 = U, S_1 = V, S_2 = W$. Since H is random oracle, adversary $\mathcal{A}$ need to ask $\sigma_0, \sigma_1, \sigma_2, \sigma_3$ to H, s.t. $\mathrm{BDDH}(X_0 + \mathrm{F_0}S_0, X_1 + S_1, X_2 + S_2, \sigma_0) = 1$, $\mathrm{BDDH}(X_0 + S_0, X_1 + \mathrm{F_1}S_1, X_2 + S_2, \sigma_1) = 1$, $\mathrm{BDDH}(X_0 + S_0, X_1 + S_1, X_2 + \mathrm{F_2}S_2, \sigma_2) = 1$, and $\mathrm{BDDH}(X_0 + \mathrm{F_0}S_0, X_1 + \mathrm{F_1}S_1, X_2 + \mathrm{F_2}S_2, \sigma_3) = 1$, to distinguish the session key. Since user U_0 is honest, solver $\mathcal{S}$ knows $s_0 = \log(S_0)$. By using s_0, solver $\mathcal{S}$ can compute four independent terms w.r.t. $s_1 = \log(S_1)$ and $s_2 = \log(S_2)$: $\sigma_0' = \hat{e}(X_1 + S_1, X_2 + S_2)^{-\mathrm{F_0}s_0}\sigma_0 = \hat{e}(P, P)^{x_0(x_1 + s_1)(x_2 + s_2)}$, $\sigma_1' = \hat{e}(X_1 + \mathrm{F_1}S_1, X_2 + S_2)^{-s_0}\sigma_1 = \hat{e}(P, P)^{x_0(x_1 + \mathrm{F_1}s_1)(x_2 + s_2)}$, $\sigma_2' = \hat{e}(X_1 + S_1, X_2 + \mathrm{F_2}S_2)^{-s_0}\sigma_2 = \hat{e}(P, P)^{x_0(x_1 + s_1)(x_2 + \mathrm{F_2}s_2)}$, and $\sigma_3' = \hat{e}(X_1 + \mathrm{F_1}S_1, X_2 + \mathrm{F_2}S_2)^{-\mathrm{F_0}s_0}\sigma_3 = \hat{e}(P, P)^{x_0(x_1 + \mathrm{F_1}s_1)(x_2 + \mathrm{F_2}s_2)}$. By using these four independent terms, solver $\mathcal{S}$ can compute answer of gap BDH problem $((\sigma_0'^{-1}\sigma_1')^{-1}\sigma_2'^{-1}\sigma_3')^{1/((\mathrm{F_1} - 1)(\mathrm{F_2} - 1))} = \mathrm{BDH}(X_0, S_1, S_2)$. This is why the proposed protocol uses four terms $\sigma_0, \sigma_1, \sigma_2, \sigma_3$.

6 Conclusion

We presented a new 3KE protocol and a more general GKE model that takes into account ephemeral key leakage. In this way we closed the outstanding gap in the modeling of AKE-security for 2KE and GKE protocols. Our implicitly authenticated 3KE protocol does not make use of compilers and proceeds in one round achieving this desired higher level of security. As such it is the first one-round tripartite key exchange protocol having these security properties without complicating the messages of the original protocol by Joux [17,18].

We did not take into account malicious insiders in GKE protocols [8,14] and did not consider the possibility of invoking sessions with destination addresses as done in the so called post-specified peer model [10,31]. It is an interesting open problem to formally consider the post-specified peer setting. Furthermore, it is of independent worth to provide methods for key confirmation and contributiveness for implicitly authenticated protocols that tolerate malicious insiders.

References

1. Al-Riyami, S.S., Paterson, K.G.: Tripartite Authenticated Key Agreement Protocols from Pairings. In: Paterson, K.G. (ed.) Cryptography and Coding 2003. LNCS, vol. 2898, pp. 332–359. Springer, Heidelberg (2003)
2. Bellare, M., Rogaway, P.: Entity Authentication and Key Distribution. In: Stinson, D.R. (ed.) CRYPTO 1993. LNCS, vol. 773, pp. 232–249. Springer, Heidelberg (1994)

3. Blake-Wilson, S., Johnson, D., Menezes, A.: Key Agreement Protocols and their Security Analysis. In: Darnell, M.J. (ed.) Cryptography and Coding 1997. LNCS, vol. 1355, pp. 30–45. Springer, Heidelberg (1997)

4. Bresson, E., Chevassut, O., Pointcheval, D.: Dynamic Group Diffie-Hellman Key Exchange under Standard Assumptions. In: Knudsen, L.R. (ed.) EUROCRYPT 2002. LNCS, vol. 2332, pp. 321–336. Springer, Heidelberg (2002)

5. Bresson, E., Chevassut, O., Pointcheval, D., Quisquater, J.-J.: Provably Authenticated Group Diffie-Hellman Key Exchange. In: Proceedings of the 8th ACM conference on Computer and Communications Security (CCS 2001), pp. 255–264. ACM Press, New York (2001)

6. Bresson, E., Manulis, M.: Malicious Participants in Group Key Exchange: Key Control and Contributiveness in the Shadow of Trust. In: Xiao, B., Yang, L.T., Ma, J., Muller-Schloer, C., Hua, Y. (eds.) ATC 2007. LNCS, vol. 4610, pp. 395–409. Springer, Heidelberg (2007)

7. Bresson, E., Manulis, M.: Contributory Group Key Exchange in the Presence of Malicious Participants. IET Information Security 2(3), 85–93 (2008)

8. Bresson, E., Manulis, M.: Securing Group Key Exchange against Strong Corruptions. In: Proceedings of ACM Symposium on Information, Computer and Communications Security (ASIACCS 2008), pp. 249–260. ACM Press, New York (2008); Full version in Intl. J. Applied Cryptography in 2008

9. Bresson, E., Manulis, M., Schwenk, J.: On Security Models and Compilers for Group Key Exchange Protocols. In: Miyaji, A., Kikuchi, H., Rannenberg, K. (eds.) IWSEC 2007. LNCS, vol. 4752, pp. 292–307. Springer, Heidelberg (2007)

10. Canetti, R., Krawczyk, H.: Analysis of Key-Exchange Protocols and Their Use for Building Secure Channels. In: Pfitzmann, B. (ed.) EUROCRYPT 2001. LNCS, vol. 2045, pp. 453–474. Springer, Heidelberg (2001)

11. Cheng, Z., Vasiu, L., Comley, R.: Pairing-based one-round tripartite key agreement protocols. Cryptology ePrint Archive, Report 2004/079 (2004)

12. Cremers, C.: Session-state reveal is stronger than ephemeral key reveal: Attacking the NAXOS key exchange protocol. In: Abdalla, M., Pointcheval, D., Fouque, P.-A., Vergnaud, D. (eds.) ACNS 2009. LNCS, vol. 5536, pp. 20–33. Springer, Heidelberg (2009)

13. Diffie, W., Hellman, M.E.: New Directions in Cryptography. IEEE Transactions on Information Theory IT-22(6), 644–654 (1976)

14. Gorantla, M.C., Boyd, C., González-Nieto, J.M.: Modeling Key Compromise Impersonation Attacks on Group Key Exchange Protocols. In: Jarecki, S., Tsudik, G. (eds.) Public Key Cryptography – PKC 2009. LNCS, vol. 5443, pp. 105–123. Springer, Heidelberg (2009)

15. Gorantla, M.C., Boyd, C., González-Nieto, J.M.: Universally Composable Contributory Group Key Exchange. In: Proceedings of the 4th International Symposium on Information, Computer, and Communications Security (ASIACCS 2009), pp. 146–156. ACM Press, New York (2009)

16. Hitchcock, Y., Boyd, C., Nieto, J.M.G.: Tripartite Key Exchange in the Canetti-Krawczyk Proof Model. In: Canteaut, A., Viswanathan, K. (eds.) INDOCRYPT 2004. LNCS, vol. 3348, pp. 17–32. Springer, Heidelberg (2004)

17. Joux, A.: A one round protocol for tripartite Diffie–Hellman. In: Bosma, W. (ed.) ANTS 2000. LNCS, vol. 1838, pp. 385–393. Springer, Heidelberg (2000)

18. Joux, A.: A one round protocol for tripartite Diffie–Hellman. Journal of Cryptology 17(4), 263–276 (2004)

19. Kaliski Jr., B.S.: An unknown key-share attack on the mqv key agreement protocol. ACM Transaction on Information and System Security 4(3), 275–288 (2001) doi:10.1145/501978.501981
20. Katz, J., Shin, J.S.: Modeling Insider Attacks on Group Key-Exchange Protocols. In: Proceedings of the 12th ACM Conference on Computer and Communications Security (CCS 2005), pp. 180–189. ACM Press, New York (2005)
21. Katz, J., Yung, M.: Scalable protocols for authenticated group key exchange. In: Boneh, D. (ed.) CRYPTO 2003. LNCS, vol. 2729, pp. 110–125. Springer, Heidelberg (2003), http://eprint.iacr.org/2003/171
22. Krawczyk, H.: HMQV: A high-performance secure Diffie-Hellman protocol. Cryptology ePrint Archive, Report 2005/176. Full version of [23]
23. Krawczyk, H.: HMQV: A high-performance secure Diffie-Hellman protocol. In: Shoup, V. (ed.) CRYPTO 2005. LNCS, vol. 3621, pp. 546–566. Springer, Heidelberg (2005)
24. LaMacchia, B., Lauter, K., Mityagin, A.: Stronger security of authenticated key exchange. Cryptology ePrint Archive, Report 2006/073 (2006)
25. LaMacchia, B., Lauter, K., Mityagin, A.: Stronger Security of Authenticated Key Exchange. In: Susilo, W., Liu, J.K., Mu, Y. (eds.) ProvSec 2007. LNCS, vol. 4784, pp. 1–16. Springer, Heidelberg (2007)
26. Law, L., Menezes, A., Qu, M., Solinas, J., Vanstone, S.: An efficient protocol for authenticated key agreement. Designs, Codes and Cryptography 28(2), 119–134 (2003)
27. Lim, M.-H., Lee, S., Lee, H.: Cryptanalysis on improved one-round Lin-Li's tripartite key agreement protocol. Cryptology ePrint Archive, Report 2007/411
28. Lim, M.-H., Lee, S., Park, Y.-H., Lee, H.-J.: An enhanced one-round pairing-based tripartite authenticated key agreement protocol. In: Gervasi, O., Gavrilova, M.L. (eds.) ICCSA 2007, Part II. LNCS, vol. 4706, pp. 503–513. Springer, Heidelberg (2007)
29. Lin, C.-H., Lin, H.-H.: Secure one-round tripartite authenticated key agreement protocol from Weil pairing. In: Shibata, Y., Shih, T.K. (eds.) 19th International Conference on Advanced Information Networking and Applications – AINA 2005, vol. 2, pp. 135–138. IEEE, Los Alamitos (2005)
30. Manulis, M.: Survey on Security Requirements and Models for Group Key Exchange. Technical Report 2006/02, Horst-Görtz Institute, Network and Data Security Group (January 2008)
31. Menezes, A., Ustaoglu, B.: Comparing the Pre- and Post-specified Peer Models for Key Agreement. In: Mu, Y., Susilo, W., Seberry, J. (eds.) ACISP 2008. LNCS, vol. 5107, pp. 53–68. Springer, Heidelberg (2008)
32. Shim, K.: Efficient one round tripartite authenticated key agreement protocol from Weil pairing. IET Electronics Letters 39(2), 208–209 (2003)
33. Sun, H.-M., Hsieh, B.-T.: Security Analysis of Shim's Authenticated Key Agreement Protocols from Pairings. Cryptology ePrint Archive, Report 2003/113 (2003)
34. Ustaoglu, B.: Comparing SessionState Reveal and EphemeralKeyReveal for Diffie-Hellman protocols. To appear in ProvSec 2009 (2009)

A Outline of Proof of Theorem 1

In this section, we provide outline of proof of Theorem 1, because of page limitation. We need the gap BDH(Bilinear Diffie-Hellman) assumption, where one tries to compute $\mathrm{BDH}(U, V, W)$ accessing the BDDH oracle. Here, we denote $\mathrm{BDH}(U, V, W) = \hat{e}(P, P)^{\log U \log V \log W}$, and the BDDH oracle on input $(uP, vP, wP, \hat{e}(P, P)^x)$ returns the bit 1 if $uvw = x$ and the bit 0 otherwise.

Let κ denote the security parameter, and let $\mathcal{A}$ be a polynomially (in κ) bounded adversary. We assume that $\mathcal{A}$ succeeds in an environment with n users $\{U_i\}$, activates at most s instances $\{\Pi_{U_i}^j\}$ within a user U_i. We use $\mathcal{A}$ to construct a gap BDH solver $\mathcal{S}$ that succeeds with non-negligible probability. The adversary $\mathcal{A}$ is said to be successful with non-negligible probability if $\mathcal{A}$ wins the distinguishing game with probability $\frac{1}{2} + p(\kappa)$, where $p(\kappa)$ is non-negligible, and the event M denotes a successful $\mathcal{A}$.

Let Π^t be the test instance with session id $\mathtt{sid}^t = (\mathtt{P}, U_A, S_A, X_A, U_B, S_B, X_B, U_C, S_C, X_C)$. Let Π be any completed instance owned by an honest user with session id $\mathtt{sid}$ such that $\mathtt{sid} \neq \mathtt{sid}^t$. Let H^* be the event that $\mathcal{A}$ queries $(\sigma_0, \sigma_1, \sigma_2, \sigma_3, \mathtt{sid}^t)$ to $\mathtt{H}$, where $\sigma_0, \sigma_1, \sigma_2, \sigma_3$ are correctly formed. Let $\overline{H^*}$ be the complement of event H^*. Since $\mathtt{sid}$ and $\mathtt{sid}^t$ are distinct, the inputs to the key derivation function $\mathtt{H}$ are different for $\mathtt{sid}$ and $\mathtt{sid}^t$. Since $\mathtt{H}$ is a random oracle, $\mathcal{A}$ cannot obtain any information about the session key of test instance Π^t from the session key of instance Π. Hence $\Pr(M \wedge \overline{H^*}) \leq \frac{1}{2}$ and $\Pr(M) = \Pr(M \wedge H^*) + \Pr(M \wedge \overline{H^*}) \leq \Pr(M \wedge H^*) + \frac{1}{2}$, and we have $\Pr(M \wedge H^*) \geq p(\kappa)$. Henceforth the event $M \wedge H^*$ is denoted by M^*.

We will consider the not exclusive classification of all possible events in the following tables. In the tables, we denote by $(A, X), (B, Y), (C, Z)$ the static and ephemeral public keys of users U_A, U_B, U_C in the session id $\mathtt{sid}^t$ of the test instance Π^t. Events can be classified not exclusively as in Table 1 when A, B, C are distinct, as in Table 2 when $A = B \neq C$, as in Table 3 when $A = C \neq B$, as in Table 4 when $A \neq B = C$, and as in Table 5 when $A = B = C$. Since the classification covers all possible events, at least one event $E_{xy} \wedge M^*$ in the tables occurs with non-negligible probability, if event M^* occurs with non-negligible probability. Thus, the gap BDH problem can be solved with non-negligible probability, and that means we shows that the proposed protocol is secure. We will investigate each of these events in the following subsections.

A.1   Event $E_{1a} \wedge M^*$

Setup. The algorithm $\mathcal{S}$ begins by establishing n honest users that are assigned random static key pairs. $\mathcal{S}$ embed instance (U, V, W) of gap BDH problem as follows. $\mathcal{S}$ randomly selects three users U_A, U_B, U_C and integer $j \in_R [1, s]$. $\mathcal{S}$ selects static and ephemeral key pairs on behalf of honest users with the following exceptions. The j-th ephemeral public key X selected on behalf of U_A is chosen to be U, the static public key B selected on behalf of U_B is chosen to be V, and the static public key C selected on behalf of U_C is chosen to be W, $\mathcal{S}$ does not possess the corresponding static and ephemeral private keys.

Simulation. $\mathcal{S}$ activates $\mathcal{A}$ on this set of users and awaits the actions of $\mathcal{A}$. $\mathcal{S}$ simulate oracle queries as follows.

1. $Send(U_i, ('start', \text{P}, U_i, U_j, U_k))$: $\mathcal{S}$ selects ephemeral private key x_i randomly, computes ephemeral public key $X_i = g^{x_i}$, returns $(\text{P}, U_i, U_j, U_k, X_i)$, and records it.

2. $Send(\Pi_{U_i}^l, (\text{P}, U_i, U_j, U_k, X_j, X_k))$: If $(\text{P}, U_i, U_j, U_k, X_i)$ is recorded, $\mathcal{S}$ records instance $\Pi_{U_i}^l$ is completed. Otherwise, $\mathcal{S}$ records instance $\Pi_{U_i}^l$ is not completed.

3. $RevealKey(\Pi_{U_i}^l = (\text{P}, U_i, S_i, X_i, U_j, S_j, X_j, U_k, S_k, X_k))$: $\mathcal{S}$ maintains list L_S of query $\Pi_{U_i}^l$ and answered session key K.

   (a) If instance $\Pi_{U_i}^l$ is not completed, $\mathcal{S}$ returns error.

   (b) Else if instance $\Pi_{U_i}^l$ is recorded in L_S, $\mathcal{S}$ returns recorded session key K.

   (c) Else if $(\sigma_0, \sigma_1, \sigma_2, \sigma_3, \text{sid})$ is recorded in L_H, where sid is the session id of instance $\Pi_{U_i}^l$, and $\text{BDDH}(X_i + \text{F}_iS_i, X_j + S_j, X_k + S_k, \sigma_0) = 1$, $\text{BDDH}(X_i+S_i, X_j+\text{F}_jS_j, X_k+S_k, \sigma_1) = 1$, $\text{BDDH}(X_i+S_i, X_j+S_j, X_k+\text{F}_kS_k, \sigma_2) = 1$, $\text{BDDH}(X_i+\text{F}_iS_i, X_j+\text{F}_jS_j, X_k+\text{F}_kS_k, \sigma_3) = 1$, $\mathcal{S}$ returns recorded session key K and records it in L_S.

   (d) Otherwise, $\mathcal{S}$ returns random session key K, and records it in L_S.

4. $\text{H}(\sigma_0, \sigma_1, \sigma_2, \sigma_3, \text{sid} = (\text{P}, U_i, S_i, X_i, U_j, S_j, X_j, U_k, S_k, X_k))$: $\mathcal{S}$ maintains list L_H of query $(\sigma_0, \sigma_1, \sigma_2, \sigma_3, \text{sid})$ and answered hash value K.

   (a) If sid is the session id of the test instance $\Pi^t = (\text{P}, U_A, A, X = U, U_B, B = V, Y, U_C, C = W, Z)$, and $\text{BDDH}(X + DA, Y + B, Z + C, \sigma_0) = 1$, $\text{BDDH}(X + A, Y + EB, Z + C, \sigma_1) = 1$, $\text{BDDH}(X + A, Y + B, Z + FC, \sigma_2) = 1$, $\text{BDDH}(X + DA, Y + EB, Z + FC, \sigma_3) = 1$, and U_A is honest, i.e., $\mathcal{S}$ knows $a = \log(A)$, then $\mathcal{S}$ stops and is successful by outputting answer of gap BDH problem $((\sigma_0'^{-1}\sigma_1')^{-1}\sigma_2'^{-1}\sigma_3')^{1/((E-1)(F-1))} = \text{BDH}(X, B, C)$, where $\sigma_0' = \hat{e}(Y + B, Z + C)^{-Da}\sigma_0$, $\sigma_1' = \hat{e}(Y + EB, Z + C)^{-a}\sigma_1$, $\sigma_2' = \hat{e}(Y + B, Z + FC)^{-a}\sigma_2$, $\sigma_3' = \hat{e}(Y + EB, Z + FC)^{-Da}\sigma_3$, and $D = \text{F}_A = \text{H}_e(X), E = \text{F}_B = \text{H}_e(Y), F = \text{F}_C = \text{H}_e(Z)$.

   (b) Else if $(\sigma_0, \sigma_1, \sigma_2, \sigma_3, \text{sid})$ is recorded in L_H, $\mathcal{S}$ returns recorded hash value K.

   (c) Else if instance $\Pi_{U_i}^l$ is recorded in L_S, where $\Pi_{U_i}^l$ is an instance with session id sid, and $\text{BDDH}(X_i+\text{F}_iS_i, X_j+S_j, X_k+S_k, \sigma_0) = 1$, $\text{BDDH}(X_i+S_i, X_j+\text{F}_jS_j, X_k+S_k, \sigma_1) = 1$, $\text{BDDH}(X_i+S_i, X_j+S_j, X_k+\text{F}_kS_k, \sigma_2) = 1$, $\text{BDDH}(X_i + \text{F}_iS_i, X_j + \text{F}_jS_j, X_k + \text{F}_kS_k, \sigma_3) = 1$, $\mathcal{S}$ returns recorded session key K and records it in L_H.

   (d) Otherwise, $\mathcal{S}$ returns random hash value K, and records it in L_H.

5. $\text{H}_e(X_i)$: $\mathcal{S}$ simulates random oracle in the usual way.

6. $RevealState(\Pi_{U_i}^l)$: If ephemeral public key of instance $\Pi_{U_i}^l$ is U, then $\mathcal{S}$ aborts with failure, otherwise responds to the query faithfully.

7. $RevealStaticKey(U_i)$: If static public key of user U_i is V or W, then $\mathcal{S}$ aborts with failure, otherwise responds to the query faithfully.

8. $AddUser(U_i, S)$: $\mathcal{S}$ responds to the query faithfully.

9. $Test(\Pi_{U_i}^l)$: If ephemeral public key of the owner is U and static public keys of the other users are V, W in instance $\Pi_{U_i}^l$, then $\mathcal{S}$ responds to the query faithfully, otherwise $\mathcal{S}$ aborts with failure.

10. If $\mathcal{A}$ outputs a guess γ, $\mathcal{S}$ aborts with failure.

Analysis. The simulation of $\mathcal{A}$ environment is perfect except with negligible probability. The probability that $\mathcal{A}$ selects the instance, where ephemeral public key of the owner is U and static public keys of the other users are V, W, as the test instance Π^t is at least $\frac{1}{n^3 s}$. Suppose this is indeed the case, $\mathcal{S}$ does not abort as in Step 9, and suppose event $E_{1a} \wedge M^*$ occurs, $\mathcal{S}$ does not abort in Step 7 and Step 6.

Under event M^* except with negligible probability, $\mathcal{A}$ queries H with $\mathrm{BDH}(X + DA, Y + B, Z + C)$, $\mathrm{BDH}(X + A, Y + EB, Z + C)$, $\mathrm{BDH}(X + A, Y + B, Z + FC)$, and $\mathrm{BDH}(X + DA, Y + EB, Z + FC)$. Therefore $\mathcal{S}$ is successful as described in Step 4a and does not abort as in Step 10.

Hence, $\mathcal{S}$ is successful with probability $Pr(S) \geq \frac{p_{1a}}{n^3 s}$, where p_{1a} is probability that $E_{1a} \wedge M^*$ occurs.

A.2   Other Events

Event $E_{1b} \wedge M^*$. Same as the event $E_{1a} \wedge M^*$ in Subsection A.1, except the following points. In Setup, $\mathcal{S}$ embeds gap BDH instance (U, V, W) as $A = U, B = V, C = W$. In Simulation of H, $\mathcal{S}$ extracts $\mathrm{BDH}(U, V, W)$ as follows: $((\sigma_0'^{-1}\sigma_1')^{-1}\sigma_2'^{-1}\sigma_3')^{1/((E-1)(F-1))} = \mathrm{BDH}(A, B, C)$, where $\sigma_0' = (\hat{e}(Y + B, Z + C)^{-x}\sigma_0)^{1/D}$, $\sigma_1' = \hat{e}(Y + EB, Z + C)^{-x}\sigma_1$, $\sigma_2' = \hat{e}(Y + B, Z + FC)^{-x}\sigma_2$, $\sigma_3' = (\hat{e}(Y + EB, Z + FC)^{-x}\sigma_3)^{1/D}$.

Event $E_{2a} \wedge M^*$. Same as the event $E_{1a} \wedge M^*$ in Subsection A.1, except the following points. In Setup, $\mathcal{S}$ embeds gap BDH instance (U, V, W) as $X = U, Y = V, Z = W$. In Simulation of H, $\mathcal{S}$ extracts $\mathrm{BDH}(U, V, W)$ as follows: $((\sigma_0'^E\sigma_1'^{-1})^F(\sigma_2'^E\sigma_3'^{-1})^{-1})^{1/((E-1)(F-1))} = \mathrm{BDH}(X, Y, Z)$, where $\sigma_0' = \hat{e}(Y + B, Z + C)^{-Da}\sigma_0$, $\sigma_1' = \hat{e}(Y + EB, Z + C)^{-a}\sigma_1$, $\sigma_2' = \hat{e}(Y + B, Z + FC)^{-a}\sigma_2$, $\sigma_3' = \hat{e}(Y + EB, Z + FC)^{-Da}\sigma_3$.

Event $E_{2b} \wedge M^*$. Same as the event $E_{1a} \wedge M^*$ in Subsection A.1, except the following points. In Setup, $\mathcal{S}$ embeds gap BDH instance (U, V, W) as $A = U, Y = V, Z = W$. In Simulation of H, $\mathcal{S}$ extracts $\mathrm{BDH}(U, V, W)$ as follows: $((\sigma_0'^E\sigma_1'^{-1})^F(\sigma_2'^E\sigma_3'^{-1})^{-1})^{1/((E-1)(F-1))} = \mathrm{BDH}(A, Y, Z)$, where $\sigma_0' = (\hat{e}(Y + B, Z + C)^{-x}\sigma_0)^{1/D}$, $\sigma_1' = \hat{e}(Y + EB, Z + C)^{-x}\sigma_1$, $\sigma_2' = \hat{e}(Y + B, Z + FC)^{-x}\sigma_2$, $\sigma_3' = (\hat{e}(Y + EB, Z + FC)^{-x}\sigma_3)^{1/D}$.

Event $E_{3a} \wedge M^*$. Same as the event $E_{1a} \wedge M^*$ in Subsection A.1, except the following points. In Setup, $\mathcal{S}$ embeds gap BDH instance (U, V, W) as $X = U, B = V, Z = W$. In Simulation of H, $\mathcal{S}$ extracts $\mathrm{BDH}(U, V, W)$ as follows: $((\sigma_0'^{-1}\sigma_1')^F(\sigma_2'^{-1}\sigma_3')^{-1})^{1/((E-1)(F-1))} = \mathrm{BDH}(X, B, Z)$, where $\sigma_0' = \hat{e}(Y + B, Z + C)^{-Da}\sigma_0$, $\sigma_1' = \hat{e}(Y + EB, Z + C)^{-a}\sigma_1$, $\sigma_2' = \hat{e}(Y + B, Z + FC)^{-a}\sigma_2$, $\sigma_3' = \hat{e}(Y + EB, Z + FC)^{-Da}\sigma_3$.

Event $E_{3b} \wedge M^*$. Same as the event $E_{1a} \wedge M^*$ in Subsection A.1, except the following points. In Setup, $\mathcal{S}$ embeds gap BDH instance (U, V, W) as $A = U, B = V, Z = W$. In Simulation of H, $\mathcal{S}$ extracts $\mathrm{BDH}(U, V, W)$ as follows: $((\sigma_0'^{-1}\sigma_1')^F(\sigma_2'^{-1}\sigma_3')^{-1})^{1/((E-1)(F-1))} = \mathrm{BDH}(A, B, Z)$, where $\sigma_0' = (\hat{e}(Y + B, Z + C)^{-x}\sigma_0)^{1/D}$, $\sigma_1' = \hat{e}(Y + EB, Z + C)^{-x}\sigma_1$, $\sigma_2' = \hat{e}(Y + B, Z + FC)^{-x}\sigma_2$, $\sigma_3' = (\hat{e}(Y + EB, Z + FC)^{-x}\sigma_3)^{1/D}$.

Event $E_{3'a} \wedge M^*$ and $E_{3'b} \wedge M^*$. Event $E_{3'a} \wedge M^*/E_{3'b} \wedge M^*$ can be handled same as event $E_{3a} \wedge M^*/E_{3b} \wedge M^*$ in Subsection A.2/A.2, because of symmetry of B and C.

A.3   Other Cases

In the case of $A = B \neq C$, events $E^1_{1b}, E^1_{2a}, E^1_{3b}, E^1_{3'a}$ in Table 2 can be handled same as events $E_{1b}, E_{2a}, E_{3b}, E_{3'a}$ in Table 1, with condition $A = B \neq C$.

In the case of $A = C \neq B$, events $E^{1'}_{1b}, E^{1'}_{2a}, E^{1'}_{3a}, E^{1'}_{3'b}$ in Table 3 can be handled same as events $E_{1b}, E_{2a}, E_{3a}, E_{3'b}$ in Table 1, with condition $A = C \neq B$.

In the case of $A \neq B = C$, events $E^2_{1a}, E^2_{1b}, E^2_{2a}, E^2_{2b}$ in Table 4 can be handled same as events $E_{1a}, E_{1b}, E_{2a}, E_{2b}$ in Table 1, with condition $A \neq B = C$.

In the case of $A = B = C$, events E^3_{1b}, E^3_{2a} in Table 5 can be handled same as events E_{1b}, E_{2a} in Table 1, with condition $A = B = C$.

Table 1. Classification of events, when A, B, C are distinct. "ok" means the static key is not revealed, or a partnered instance exists and its ephemeral key is not revealed. "r" means the static or ephemeral key may be revealed. "r/n" means the ephemeral key may be revealed if the corresponding partnered instance exists, or no corresponding partnered instance exists. "succ. prob." row shows the probability of success of solver $\mathcal{S}$, where $p_{xy} = Pr(E_{xy} \wedge M^*)$ and n and s are the number of users and instances.

	A	X	B	Y	C	Z	succ. prob.
E_{1a}	r	ok	ok	r/n	ok	r/n	$p_{1a}/n^3 s$
E_{1b}	ok	r	ok	r/n	ok	r/n	p_{1b}/n^3
E_{2a}	r	ok	r	ok	r	ok	$p_{2a}/n^3 s^3$
E_{2b}	ok	r	r	ok	r	ok	$p_{2b}/n^3 s^2$
E_{3a}	r	ok	ok	r/n	r	ok	$p_{3a}/n^3 s^2$
E_{3b}	ok	r	ok	r/n	r	ok	$p_{3b}/n^3 s$
$E_{3'a}$	r	ok	r	ok	ok	r/n	$p_{3'a}/n^3 s^2$
$E_{3'b}$	ok	r	r	ok	ok	r/n	$p_{3'b}/n^3 s$

Table 2. Classification of events, when $A = B \neq C$

	A	X	B = A	Y	C	Z	succ. prob.
E^1_{1b}	ok	r	ok	r/n	ok	r/n	p^1_{1b}/n^3
E^1_{2a}	r	ok	r	ok	r	ok	$p^1_{2a}/n^3 s^3$
E^1_{3b}	ok	r	ok	r/n	r	ok	$p^1_{3b}/n^3 s$
$E^1_{3'a}$	r	ok	r	ok	ok	r/n	$p^1_{3'a}/n^3 s^2$

Table 3. Classification of events, when $A = C \neq B$

	A	X	B	Y	C = A	Z	succ. prob.
$E^{1'}_{1b}$	ok	r	ok	r/n	ok	r/n	$p^{1'}_{1b}/n^3$
$E^{1'}_{2a}$	r	ok	r	ok	r	ok	$p^{1'}_{2a}/n^3 s^3$
$E^{1'}_{3a}$	r	ok	ok	r/n	r	ok	$p^{1'}_{3a}/n^3 s^2$
$E^{1'}_{3'b}$	ok	r	r	ok	ok	r/n	$p^{1'}_{3'b}/n^3 s$

Table 4. Classification of events, when $A \neq B = C$

	A	X	B	Y	C = B	Z	succ. prob.
E^2_{1a}	r	ok	ok	r/n	ok	r/n	$p^2_{1a}/n^3 s$
E^2_{1b}	ok	r	ok	r/n	ok	r/n	p^2_{1b}/n^3
E^2_{2a}	r	ok	r	ok	r	ok	$p^2_{2a}/n^3 s^3$
E^2_{2b}	ok	r	r	ok	r	ok	$p^2_{2b}/n^3 s^2$

Table 5. Classification of events, when $A = B = C$

	A	X	B = A	Y	C = A	Z	succ. prob.
E^3_{1b}	ok	r	ok	r/n	ok	r/n	p^3_{1b}/n^3
E^3_{2a}	r	ok	r	ok	r	ok	$p^3_{2a}/n^3 s^3$

Efficient Certificateless KEM in the Standard Model*

Georg Lippold, Colin Boyd, and Juan Manuel González Nieto

Information Security Institute, Queensland University Of Technology,
GPO Box 2434, Brisbane QLD 4001, Australia
{g.lippold,c.boyd,j.gonzaleznieto}@qut.edu.au

Abstract. We give a direct construction of a certificateless key encapsulation mechanism (KEM) in the standard model that is more efficient than the generic constructions proposed before by Huang and Wong [9]. We use a direct construction from Kiltz and Galindo's KEM scheme [10] to obtain a certificateless KEM in the standard model; our construction is roughly twice as efficient as the generic construction.

1 Introduction

CERTIFICATELESS ENCRYPTION introduced by Al-Riyami and Paterson [1] is a variant of identity based encryption that limits the key escrow capabilities of the key generation centre (KGC), which are inherent in identity based encryption [3]. Dent [8] published a survey of more than twenty certificateless encryption schemes that focuses on the different security models and the efficiency of the respective schemes. In certificateless cryptography schemes, there are three secrets per party:

1. The key issued by the key generation centre (Dent [8] calls it "partial private key"). We assume in the following that this key is ID-based, although it does not necessarily have to be ID-based.
2. The user generated private key x_{ID} (Dent calls it "secret value").
3. The ephemeral value chosen randomly for each session.

KEY ENCAPSULATION MECHANISMS (KEM) provide efficient means to communicate a random key from a sender to a designated receiver. Messages used with public key encryption schemes are usually limited in length or have to belong to a specific group. Contrariwise, key encapsulation mechanisms encrypt only a key that is then usually used in a symmetric *data encapsulation mechanism* (DEM) and thus provide increased efficiency over public key encryption. The resulting scheme is then called a *hybrid encryption* scheme [7,6]. Efficient constructions for a certificateless encryption scheme in the standard model can be obtained from our scheme using the KEM-DEM construction [6,2].

* Research funded by the Australian Research Council through Discovery Project DP0666065.

D. Lee and S. Hong (Eds.): ICISC 2009, LNCS 5984, pp. 34–46, 2010.

PREVIOUS WORK has identified both identity based key encapsulation mechanisms (IB-KEM) [10,5] (see [11] for a comparison) and certificateless key encapsulation mechanisms (CL-KEM) [2,9]. However, the known constructions for CL-KEM schemes are all generic constructions: they involve running a public key based encryption scheme and an ID-based KEM in parallel and are thus not very efficient. In this work we propose the first direct CL-KEM construction from an efficient IB-KEM in the standard model and prove the construction secure.

THE SECURITY MODEL for our CL-KEM construction is similar to that of previous work by Bentahar et al. [2] and Huang and Wong [9]. We consider a "weak" certificateless adversary that can replace public keys, but cannot request decapsulations of a ciphertext under a replaced public key unless the corresponding *user secret value* is disclosed to the simulator. This is a realistic notion as in real life one cannot expect a user to successfully decrypt ciphertexts that do not correspond to the user's private key. For a full discussion of the security model see Section 3 on the following page.

THE MAIN CONTRIBUTIONS of this work are:

- First efficient direct construction for a CCA secure certificateless key encapsulation mechanism proven secure in the standard model.
- Simplified proof strategy for certificateless KEM constructions.
- Direct efficient constructions for certificateless CCA secure encryption [2] and key agreement [4] follow from our construction.
- Approximately twice as efficient as the generic construction by Huang and Wong.
- Improved security model for certificateless KEM

2   Definitions

2.1   Target Collision Resistant Hash Function

Let $\mathcal{F} = (\mathsf{TCR}_s)_{s \in S}$ be a family of hash functions for security parameter k and with seed $s \in S$ where S is parametrized by the security parameter k. $\mathcal{F}$ is said to be *collision resistant* if, for a hash function $\mathsf{TCR} = \mathsf{TCR}_s$ with $s \xleftarrow{\$} S$, it is infeasible for an efficient adversary to find two distinct values $x \neq y$ such that $\mathsf{TCR}(x) = \mathsf{TCR}(y)$.

The notion of a *target collision resistant hash function*(TCR) is strictly weaker. The adversary against a target collision resistant hash function is supplied with a randomly drawn hash function $\mathsf{TCR} = \mathsf{TCR}_s$ and a randomly chosen element x. The task of the adversary is to find a y such that $\mathsf{TCR}(x) = \mathsf{TCR}(y)$. Note that the adversary may not select x, and is thus limited with respect to collision resistant hash functions. Target collision resistant hash functions are sometimes also called *universal one-way hash functions*. Naor and Yung [13] and Rompel [14] give efficient constructions for target collision resistant hash functions from arbitrary one-way functions. In the following we assume that TCR's exist and define the advantage of any efficient polynomial time adversary $\mathcal{M}$ against a randomly chosen hash function $\mathsf{TCR} = \mathsf{TCR}_s$ as

$$\mathbf{Adv}^{\text{hash-tcr}}_{\mathsf{TCR},\mathcal{M}}(k) = \Pr[y \xleftarrow{\$} \mathcal{M}(\mathsf{TCR}(\cdot), x) | \mathsf{TCR}(y) = \mathsf{TCR}(x)]$$

The hash function TCR is said to be *target collision resistant* if the advantage for all $\mathcal{M}$ against TCR is negligible in k.

2.2   Admissible Bilinear Pairing

Let $\mathbb{G}$ and $\mathbb{G}_T$ be groups of prime order p. A bilinear pairings map $e : \mathbb{G} \times \mathbb{G} \to \mathbb{G}_T$ between the groups $\mathbb{G}$ and $\mathbb{G}_T$ satisfies the following properties:

Bilinear. We say that a map $e : \mathbb{G} \times \mathbb{G} \to \mathbb{G}_T$ is *bilinear* if $e(g^a, g^b) = e(g, g)^{ab}$ for all $g \in \mathbb{G}$ and $a, b \in \mathbb{Z}_p$.

Non-degenerate. We say that e is non-degenerate if it does not send all pairs in $\mathbb{G} \times \mathbb{G}$ to the identity in $\mathbb{G}_T$. Since $\mathbb{G}$ and $\mathbb{G}_T$ are groups of prime order p, it follows that if $g \in \mathbb{G}$ is a generator of $\mathbb{G}$, then $e(g, g)$ is a generator of $\mathbb{G}_T$.

Computable. There is an efficient algorithm to compute $e(g, h)$ for any $g, h \in \mathbb{G}$.

2.3   Decisional Bilinear Diffie-Hellman Problem

The decisional Bilinear Diffie-Hellman assumption states that given $\{g^a, g^b, g^c\} \in \mathbb{G}^3$ it is hard to distinguish $e(g, g)^{abc} \in \mathbb{G}_T$ from a random element $R \xleftarrow{\$} \mathbb{G}_T$. Let $\mathcal{Z}$ be an algorithm that takes as input a triple $\{g^a, g^b, g^c, T\} \in \mathbb{G}^3 \times \mathbb{G}_T$, and outputs a bit $b \in \{0, 1\}$ indicating $T \stackrel{?}{=} e(g, g)^{abc}$. We define the dBDH advantage of $\mathcal{Z}$ to be

$$\mathbf{Adv}^{\text{dBDH}}_{\mathcal{Z}} = \left| \Pr\left[a, b, c \xleftarrow{\$} \mathbb{Z}_p : Z(g^a, g^b, g^c, T) = \left(T \stackrel{?}{=} e(g, g)^{abc} \right) \right] - 1/2 \right|$$

3   Security Model

3.1   Types of Certificateless Adversaries

In certificateless cryptography it is common to distinguish between two types of adversaries:

Type I: A Type I adversary represents an outsider adversary that does not have access to the secret master key of the key generation centre (KGC).

Type II: A Type II adversary represents an insider adversary that has access to the master secret key (e.g. a malicious KGC).

The security of the scheme is then further classified by the type of decryption oracle access that the adversary has:

Strong security: The adversary has access to a *strong decryption oracle*. This means that the oracle can decrypt ciphertexts even if it does not know the private key that matches the public key used for encryption. Thus it can decrypt a ciphertext $C \in \mathcal{C}$ even if the adversary replaced the certificateless public key that was used to generate the ciphertext and does not disclose the matching private key to the decryption oracle.

Weak security: The adversary has access to a *weak secret value decryption oracle* (Weak SV Decrypt oracle). The oracle can decrypt ciphertexts only if it is given all private keys necessary for decryption. If the adversary replaced a public key, then decryption is only possible if the adversary submits the private key matching the public key along with the decryption request.

In his survey on certificateless encryption schemes, Dent [8] remarks that "the Weak [...] [security] model seems to most realistically reflect the potential abilities of an attacker." All published CL-KEM schemes [9,2] focus on the *weak security* model. We will use this model for our work as well.

3.2 Certificateless Key Encapsulation Mechanism

We use the definition by Huang and Wong [9] for a *certificateless key-encapsulation mechanism (CL-KEM)*. A certificateless KEM consists of the following algorithms:

CL-KEM IBE Setup: On input 1^k where $k \in \mathbb{N}$ is a security parameter, it generates a master public/private key pair (mpk, msk).

CL-KEM IBE KeyDerivation: On input msk and a user identity $\mathsf{ID} \in \{0,1\}^*$, it generates a user partial key / ID-based private key sk_{ID}.

CL-KEM User KeyGen: On input mpk and a user identity ID, it generates a user public/private key pair $(\beta_{\mathsf{ID}}, x_{\mathsf{ID}})$.

CL-KEM Encapsulation: takes as input $(mpk, \beta_{\mathsf{ID}}, \mathsf{ID})$ and outputs an encapsulation key pair $(K, C) \in \mathcal{K} \times \mathcal{E}$ where C is called the encapsulation of the key K and $\mathcal{K}$ and $\mathcal{E}$ are the key space and the encapsulation space respectively.

CL-KEM Decapsulation: takes as input $((sk_{\mathsf{ID}}, x_{\mathsf{ID}}), \mathsf{ID}, C)$ and decapsulates C to get back a key K, or outputs the special symbol $\perp$ indicating invalid encapsulation.

3.3 The Security Game for CL-KEM

To model the security guarantees of a certificateless scheme correctly, we introduce the following model that merges the requirements by Dent [8] and Huang & Wong [9]. The adversary $\mathcal{M}$ has access to the following oracles:

Reveal master key: The adversary is given access to the master secret key.

Reveal ID-based key(ID): The adversary extracts the ID-based private key of party ID.

Get user public key(ID): The adversary obtains the certificateless public key for ID. If the certificateless key for the identity has not yet been generated, it is generated with the *user key gen* algorithm.

Replace public key(ID, pk): Party ID's certificateless public key is replaced with pk chosen by the adversary. All communication (encryption, encapsulation) for Party ID will use the new public key.

Reveal secret value(ID): The adversary extracts the secret value x_{ID} that corresponds to the certificateless public key for party ID. If the adversary issued a *replace public key* query for ID before, $\perp$ is returned.

Decapsulate(ID, C): The adversary learns the decapsulation of C under ID or $\perp$ if C is invalid or if the adversary replaced the public key of ID.

Decapsulate(ID, C, x): The adversary learns the decapsulation of C under ID using the secret value x. The special symbol $\perp$ will be returned if C is invalid.

Get challenge key encapsulation(ID*): The adversary requests a challenge key encapsulation and thus marks the transition from **Oracles$_1$** to **Oracles$_2$** in Experiment 1. The simulator returns a challenge key encapsulation as described in Experiment 1.

The security game for a CL-KEM scheme is associated with the following experiment:

$$\textbf{Experiment Challenge}_{\text{CL-KEM}\mathcal{M}}^{cl-kem-cca}(k):$$

$$(mpk, msk) \xleftarrow{\$} \textbf{CL-KEM IBE Setup}(k)$$

$$(\text{ID}^*, state) \xleftarrow{\$} \mathcal{M}^{\textbf{Oracles}_1}(find, mpk)$$

$$K_0^* \xleftarrow{\$} \mathcal{K}; (C^*, K_1^*) \xleftarrow{\$} \textbf{CL-KEM Enc}(pk, \text{ID}^*) \qquad (1)$$

$$\gamma \xleftarrow{\$} \{0,1\}; K^* = K_\gamma^*$$

$$\gamma' \xleftarrow{\$} \mathcal{M}^{\textbf{Oracles}_2}(guess, K^*, C^*, state)$$

$$\text{Return } \gamma == \gamma'$$

The advantage an adversary $\mathcal{M}$ has against a CL-KEM scheme is therefore expressed by

$$\textbf{Adv}_{\mathcal{M}}^{\text{CL-KEM}}(k) = \left| \Pr\left[\textbf{Experiment Challenge}_{\text{CL-KEM}\mathcal{M}}^{cl-kem-cca}(k)\right] - 1/2 \right|$$

For a *Type 1* adversary $\mathcal{M}$, **Oracles$_1$** and **Oracles$_2$** mean access to all oracles listed above with the following limitations:

1. No *reveal master key* queries.
2. C^* must not be submitted to a *decapsulate* oracle under ID*.
3. Not both (*reveal secret value* OR *replace public key*) AND *reveal ID-based key* oracles may be asked for ID*.

For a *Type 2* adversary $\mathcal{M}$, **Oracles$_1$** and **Oracles$_2$** are subject to the following limitations:

1. **Oracles$_1$** and **Oracles$_2$** now includes *reveal master key* as allowed query,
2. C^* must not be submitted to a *decapsulate* oracle under ID*.
3. *reveal secret value* must never be asked for ID*,
4. **Oracles$_1$** must not include *replace public key* for ID*.

4   The CL-KEM Scheme

We describe the phases of our certificateless key encapsulation mechanism in this section. Our protocol consists of five phases: *setup, identity based key derivation, user key generation, key encapsulation,* and *key decapsulation.* The algorithms *setup,* and *identity based key derivation* are exactly the same as in Kiltz and Galindo's KEM [11]. In the following, we first recapitulate the parameters needed for the Kiltz-Galindo KEM and continue then to describe the differences needed to obtain a certificateless KEM. We will use *bilinear pairings* and *Waters hash* in the scheme, which we describe shortly.

4.1   Waters' Hash

To prove our scheme, we use Waters' hash function $H : \{0,1\}^n \to \mathbb{G}$ as described in Waters' identity based encryption scheme [15]. On input of an integer n, the randomized hash key generator $\mathsf{HGen}(\mathbb{G})$ chooses $n+1$ random group elements $h_0, h_1, \ldots, h_n \in \mathbb{G}$ and returns $h = (h_0, h_1, \ldots, h_n)$ as the public description of the hash function. The hash function $H : \{0,1\}^n \to \mathbb{G}^*$ is evaluated on a string $\mathsf{ID} = (\mathsf{ID}_1, \ldots, \mathsf{ID}_n) \in \{0,1\}^n$ as the product $H(\mathsf{ID}) = h_0 \prod_{i=1}^n h_i^{\mathsf{ID}_i}$.

4.2   CL-KEM Algorithms

Setup. On input of the security parameter k, the key generation center picks suitable bilinear pairing parameters $(e(\cdot, \cdot), p, \mathbb{G}, \mathbb{G}_T, g)$ and uses $\mathsf{HGen}(\mathbb{G})$ to obtain a suitable Waters' hash function. The KGC also publishes system parameters $(u_1, u_2, z) \in \mathbb{G}$. See Algorithm **CL-KEM IBE Setup** in Figure 1 on the next page for details.

Identity-based Key Derivation. To generate an ID-based key for an identity $\mathsf{ID} \in \{0,1\}^n$, the key generation centre follows the Algorithm **CL-KEM IBE KeyDerivation** in Figure 1 on the following page.

User key generation. To obtain a certificateless KEM, we introduce the new algorithm *user key generation* into the Kiltz-Galindo KEM. The user generates a certificateless key pair from the system parameters as outlined by Algorithm **CL-KEM User Keygen** in Figure 1 on the next page. After key generation, the user publishes β_{ID} and keeps x_{ID} private.

Certificateless Key Encapsulation. We modify the Kiltz-Galindo encapsulation mechanism by using β_{ID} instead of z for encryption. Thus we get a very efficient encapsulation mechanism, outlined by Algorithm **CL-KEM Enc** in Figure 1 on the following page. The key K is used for encryption, C is the certificateless encapsulation of K.

CL-KEM IBE Setup(k) :

$$u_1, u_2, \alpha \xleftarrow{\$} \mathbb{G}^*; z \leftarrow e(g, \alpha)$$

$$H \xleftarrow{\$} HGen(\mathbb{G})$$

$$mpk \leftarrow (u_1, u_2, z, H); msk \leftarrow \alpha$$

$$\text{Return}(mpk, msk)$$

CL-KEM IBE KeyDerivation(msk, ID) :

$$s \xleftarrow{\$} \mathbb{Z}_p^*$$

$$sk_{\mathsf{ID}} \leftarrow (\alpha \cdot H(\mathsf{ID})^s, g^s)$$

$$\text{Return}(sk_{\mathsf{ID}})$$

CL-KEM User Keygen(mpk, ID) :

$$(u_1, u_2, z, H) \leftarrow mpk$$

$$x_{\mathsf{ID}} \xleftarrow{\$} \mathbb{Z}_p^*$$

$$\beta_{\mathsf{ID}} \leftarrow z^{x_{\mathsf{ID}}}$$

$$\text{Return}(\beta_{\mathsf{ID}}, x_{\mathsf{ID}})$$

CL-KEM Enc$(mpk, \beta_{\mathsf{ID}}, \mathsf{ID}, M)$:

$$r \xleftarrow{\$} \mathbb{Z}_p^*$$

$$c_1 \leftarrow g^r$$

$$c_2 \leftarrow H(\mathsf{ID})^r, t \leftarrow \text{TCR}(c_1)$$

$$c_3 \leftarrow (u_1^t \cdot u_2)^r; z \leftarrow mpk$$

$$K \leftarrow \beta_{\mathsf{ID}}{}^r = (z^x)^r \in \mathbb{G}_T$$

$$C \leftarrow (c_1, c_2, c_3) \in \mathbb{G}^3$$

$$\text{Return}(K, C)$$

CL-KEM Dec(sk_{ID}, x, C) :

$$c_1, c_2, c_3 \leftarrow C$$

$$d_1, d_2 \leftarrow sk_{\mathsf{ID}}$$

$$r_1, r_2 \xleftarrow{\$} \mathbb{Z}_p^*$$

$$t \leftarrow TCR(c_1)$$

$$K \leftarrow \left(\frac{e(c_1, d_1 \cdot (u_1^t u_2)^{r_1} \cdot H(\mathsf{ID})^{r_2})}{e(c_2, d_2 \cdot g^{r_2})e(g^{r_1}, c_3)} \right)^{x_{\mathsf{ID}}}$$

$$\text{Return}(K)$$

Fig. 1. Our CCA secure CL-KEM

Certificateless Key Decapsulation. Decapsulation is also very efficient as it needs only one additional exponentiation over the Kiltz-Galindo KEM decapsulation algorithm. The Algorithm **CL-KEM Dec** in Figure 1 describes the decapsulation.

This concludes the description of the certificateless KEM construction.

5   Efficiency Comparison

When compared to the only other CL-KEM in the standard model by Huang and Wong [9], we note that both key generation and encapsulation are twice as efficient, we save one exponentiation during decapsulation, key size is smaller and ciphertext size is approximately halved. For a detailed comparison see Table 1 on the facing page.

6   Proof of Security for the CL-KEM

Theorem 1. *Assume* TCR *is a target collision resistant hash function. Under the decisional Bilinear Diffie-Hellman assumption relative to the generator G, the CL-KEM from Section 4 on the previous page is secure against chosen ciphertext attacks.*

Table 1. Comparison of the Huang-Wong scheme with our scheme

Scheme	KeyGen	Enc	Dec	Keysize pk	Ciphertext overhead
	#pairings + #[multi,regular,fixed-base]-exp				
IB-KEM [11]	0 + [0,2,0]	0 + [1,3,1]	3 + [1,0,2]	n+4	3l
+ PKE [12]	0 + [0,4,0]	0 + [0,4,0]	0 + [0,2,0]	4	2l
= CL-KEM [9]	0 + [0,6,0]	0 + [1,7,1]	3 + [1,2,2]	n+8	5l
Ours	0 + [0,3,0]	0 + [1,3,1]	3 + [1,1,2]	n+4	3l

We instantiate the Huang & Wong [9] scheme with the most efficient CCA2 secure PKE scheme by Kurosawa & Desmedt [12] and the most efficient CCA2 secure ID-based KEM by Kiltz & Galindo [11] and compare it to our direct construction from the Kiltz & Galindo KEM.

Proving the protocol is easier if we do not treat *Type I* and *Type II* adversaries separately. Essentially, there are two strategies for dealing with an adversary:

- Embed the challenge into the ID-based part. Then the adversary may learn the secret value or replace the certificateless public key. This is generally not applicable for *Type II* adversaries.
- Embed the challenge into the CL-based part. Then the adversary may learn the ID-based secret key. This is applicable for both *Type I* and *Type II* adversaries.

For Type I adversaries that want to learn the CL-key, we use the proof from Kiltz and Galindo [11] unmodified and hand over the *user secret value* x_{ID} to the adversary. The original proof does still hold in this setting.

For Type II adversaries and Type I adversaries that want to learn the ID-based key, we have to modify the proof. The simulator $\mathcal{B}$ gets the dBDH challenge (g, g^a, g^b, g^c, T) from its challenger. Given that the adversary $\mathcal{M}$ has an advantage in the CL-KEM game, $\mathcal{B}$ uses the adversary $\mathcal{M}$ to get an advantage in solving the dBDH challenge. This strategy simplifies proving the security of the scheme: a well known proof in the ID-based setting is expanded only with what is necessary for the certificateless setting. As it turns out, the proof for the CL-part of the scheme is easier to understand as it does not have to deal with artificial aborts.

We rewrite the proof by Kiltz and Galindo to get a proof for the CL-KEM scheme for Type II adversaries. As in Kiltz & Galindo's paper, the main idea is again that the simulator knows a back door for the hash function H. Knowing the back door for H allows the simulator to let H "vanish" for the target identity. To achieve this, we have to embed the challenge slightly differently from the original proof by Kiltz and Galindo [11]. We also use a game based approach. The simulator $\mathcal{B}$ starts with knowing the discrete logarithms of g^a, g^b, g^c and "forgets" the discrete logarithms during modifications of the game.

Game 0. (Forget b) The simulator $\mathcal{B}$ picks $(a, b, c) \xleftarrow{\$} \mathbb{Z}_p^*$, computes g^c and $t^* = \mathsf{TCR}(g^c)$ and additionally picks $d \xleftarrow{\$} \mathbb{Z}_p^*$. The *CL-KEM IBE Setup* algorithm is modified as follows:

CL-KEM IBE Setup(k) :

$$\gamma \xleftarrow{\$} \mathbb{Z}_p, u_1 = g^a, u_2 = (g^a)^{-t^*} g^d, \alpha = g^b; z \leftarrow e(g, \alpha) = e(g, g^b)$$

$$H \xleftarrow{\$} HGen(\mathbb{G}) \tag{2}$$

$$mpk \leftarrow (u_1, u_2, z, H); msk \leftarrow \alpha$$

$$\text{Return}(mpk, msk)$$

We assume that the adversary $\mathcal{M}$ makes no more than q_0 queries for distinct identities. One of these identities will be used to create the challenge ciphertext. We enumerate these queries. The simulator $\mathcal{B}$ guesses the index of the target identity ID^* that the adversary will use in the test query by selecting $q^* \xleftarrow{\$} \mathbb{Z}_{q_0}$. We also assume that the adversary does not make more than q decapsulation queries. B sets the target identity's public key to $\beta_{\mathsf{ID}^*} = e(g^a, g^b) = z^a$. Both the KGC public key and the master secret key $\alpha = g^b$ can be given to the adversary at the start of the game.

FIND PHASE. During its execution, $\mathcal{M}$ makes a number of *reveal master key, reveal ID-based key, reveal secret value, replace public key,* and *decapsulate* requests. The simulator deals with the adversary's queries in the following way:

Get master key: $\mathcal{B}$ returns α.

Get user public key(ID)**:** If these requests target an identity that has not been initialized before, there are two possibilities: If it is the q^*th distinct query, the simulator returns $\beta_{\mathsf{ID}^*} = z^a$ as discussed above. Otherwise, the simulator generates a new certificateless key $(\beta_{\mathsf{ID}}, x_{\mathsf{ID}})$ on the fly, publishes the ID's certificateless public key β_{ID} in the directory of certificateless public keys and records the certificateless private key x_{ID} along with the ID in a table (later referred to as the *table of certificateless private keys*).

Replace user public key$(\mathsf{ID}, \beta'_{\mathsf{ID}})$**:** The simulator inserts the new certificateless public key β'_{ID} into the table of certificateless public keys and inserts $\perp$ into the *table of certificateless private keys* at position ID.

Reveal ID-based key(ID)**: (only Type I)** As the simulator knows $\alpha = g^b$ these queries can always be answered throughout the game for Type I adversaries. For Type II adversaries, α can be passed to the adversary at the start of the game. Then it is not necessary to provide this functionality to the adversary (the adversary may compute the keys on its own).

Decapsulation(C, ID)**:** The simulator returns the decapsulation of C under ID query using the entry from the *table of certificateless private keys* or $\perp$ if the certificateless public key was replaced by the adversary or C is an invalid encapsulation.

Decapsulation(C, ID, x)**:** The simulator returns the decapsulation of C under ID query using x as the user secret value or $\perp$ if C is an invalid encryption.

Eventually, the adversary returns a target identity ID^*. The simulator chooses a random key K_0^* and runs the encapsulation algorithm to create a key K_1^* together with the challenge ciphertext $C^* = (c_1^*, c_2^*, c_3^*)$. The challenge ciphertext is computed as

$$c_1^* \leftarrow g^c, t^* \leftarrow \mathsf{TCR}(g^c), c_2^* = H(\mathsf{ID}^*)^c, c_3^* = (u_1^{t^*} u_2)^c$$

Then, the simulator chooses a random bit b and the challenge ciphertext C^* is returned together with the key $K^* = K_b^*$ to the adversary.

GUESS PHASE. The adversary continues to query the oracles provided by the simulator under the condition that he may not request a decapsulation of C^* under ID^* and may not request the *user secret value* x_{ID^*}. Finally, the adversary returns a bit b'. If $b' = b$ then the simulator returns 1, else he returns 0. This completes the description of the simulator. Let X_i denote the event that the adversary $\mathcal{M}$ wins game i. Thus we have for the advantage of the adversary against the CL-KEM scheme: $\mathbf{Adv}_{CL-KEM,\mathcal{M}}^{cl-kem-cca} = |\Pr[X_0] - 1/2|$.

Game 1.(Eliminate hash collisions): The simulator fixed $c_1^* = g^c$ and $t^* = \mathsf{TCR}(g^c)$ at the start of the game and aborts if a decapsulation query is made for any ciphertext $C = (c_1, c_2, c_3)$ for that $\mathsf{TCR}(c_1) = t^*$ and $c_1 \neq c_1^*$. Otherwise, Game 0 and Game 1 are identical. This event happens only with negligible probability as otherwise $\mathcal{M}$ could be used as an efficient adversary against TCR. Thus we have

$$|\Pr[X_1] - \Pr[X_0]| \leq \mathbf{Adv}_{\mathsf{TCR},\mathcal{M}}^{\text{hash-tcr}}(k)$$

Game 2.(Change of hash keys): The game continues as in Game 1 except that the simulator changes the way the hash keys $\boldsymbol{h} = (h_0, h_1, \ldots, h_n)$ are generated. Set $m = 2q$ (where q is the upper bound on the decapsulation queries) and randomly choose

$$x_0, x_1, \ldots, x_n \xleftarrow{\$} \{0, \ldots, p-1\}; \quad y_0', y_1, \ldots, y_n \xleftarrow{\$} \{0, \ldots, m-1\} \tag{3}$$

$$k \xleftarrow{\$} \{0, \ldots, n\}$$

and set $y_0 \leftarrow p - km + y_0'$.

$\mathcal{B}$ redefines the public hash keys $\boldsymbol{h} = \{h_0, \ldots, h_n\}$ as $h_i = g^{x_i} u_1^{y_i} = g^{x_i}(g^a)^{y_i}$ for $0 \leq i \leq n$. Thus, the public hash function H evaluated at identity $\mathsf{ID} \in \{0, 1\}^n$ is given by

$$H(\mathsf{ID}) = h_0 \prod_{i=1}^n h_i^{\mathsf{ID}_i} = g^{x(\mathsf{ID})} u_1^{y(\mathsf{ID})} = g^{x(\mathsf{ID})}(g^a)^{y(\mathsf{ID})}$$

with $x(\mathsf{ID}) = x_0 + \sum_{i=1}^n \mathsf{ID}_i x_i$ and $y(\mathsf{ID}) = y_0 + \sum_{i=1}^n \mathsf{ID}_i y_i$ (where $x()$ and $y()$ are only known to the simulator). As this does not change the distribution of the hash keys, the probability of success for the adversary does not change:

$$\Pr[X_2] = \Pr[X_1]$$

Game 3.(Abort for wrong challenge identity): The simulation proceeds as in Game 2. Once the simulator is being asked the *challenge ciphertext* query, it checks the ID^* is the q^*th distinct identity and aborts otherwise. The simulator also aborts if $y(\mathsf{ID}^*) \neq 0$.

As we do not need to change the key derivation oracle during the sequence of games (as Kiltz and Galindo do), we can simplify the proof significantly. We especially do not have to deal with artificial aborts, as the abort probability for the simulator can be estimated directly using results from Kiltz and Galindo [11, Section A.2]. From Equation 3 on the preceding page we have that

$$y(\mathsf{ID}^*) = 0 = p - km + y_0' + \sum_{i=1}^{n} \mathsf{ID}_i^* y_i$$

and from the distribution of the y_i we get that

$$0 \le y_0' + \sum_{i=1}^{n} \mathsf{ID}_i^* y_i < (n+1)m$$

Thus if $y(\mathsf{ID}^*) = 0 \bmod m$, then there is a unique $0 \le k < n+1$ such that $y(\mathsf{ID}^*) = 0$ over the integers. Since k is uniformly and independently distributed over the integers, we get:

$$\Pr[y(\mathsf{ID}^*) = 0] = \Pr[y(\mathsf{ID}^*) = 0 \bmod p] \ge \Pr[y(\mathsf{ID}^*) = 0 \bmod m]/(n+1)$$

Thus for a fixed k and $b \in \mathbb{Z}_m$ we have that $\Pr[y(\mathsf{ID}) = b \bmod m] = 1/m$. So we conclude with

$$\Pr[y(\mathsf{ID}^*) = 0] \ge \frac{1}{n+1} \Pr[y(\mathsf{ID}^*) = 0 \bmod m] = \frac{1}{n+1} \cdot \frac{1}{m} = \frac{1}{m(n+1)}$$

Thus, the probability that Game 3 succeeds is given by the probability that $y(\mathsf{ID}^*) = 0$ and that ID^* is the q^*th distinct identity. As there are at most q_0 distinct ID queries by the adversary we have

$$\Pr[X_3] \ge \Pr[X_2]/(q_0 m(n+1))$$

Game 4.(Change of decapsulation oracle / Forget a): The simulator knows all *user secret keys* except for those the adversary replaced with a *replace certificateless public key* request. Regarding decapsulation queries, the simulator does not have to answer requests for identities that were issued a *replace certificateless public key* query unless the adversary supplies the *user secret key* matching the replaced certificateless public key. As the simulator can derive *ID-based private keys* from the master parameters, answering decapsulation queries for all identities except ID^* is easy, as all secret information to do this is readily available using the standard **CL-KEM Dec** algorithm as described in Figure 1 on page 40.

The simulator established in Game 3 that $y(\mathsf{ID}^*) = 0$. This enables the simulator to answer decapsulation queries for ID^* in the following way: instead of answering the decapsulation as in **CL-KEM Dec** in Figure 1 on page 40, the simulator computes the decapsulations for ID^* as follows: with $u_1 = g^a, u_2 = (g^a)^{-t^*} g^d$ and $c_1 = g^r$ we have

$$c_3 = (u_1^t u_2)^r = ((g^a)^t g^{-t^* a} g^d)^r = ((g^{a(t-t^*)} g^d)^r = (c_1^a)^{t-t^*} \cdot c_1^d.$$

To decapsulate the correct key K, we would like to compute $e(g^a, g^b)^r$. Thus knowing g^b and computing $c_1^a = (g^r)^a = g^{ra}$ will allow us to compute K by computing $e(g^{ra}, g^b) = e(g, g)^{rab}$:

$$\left(c_3/c_1^d\right)^{\frac{1}{t-t^*}} = \left((c_1^a)^{t-t^*} \cdot c_1^d/c_1^d\right)^{\frac{1}{t-t^*}} = (c_1^a)^{\frac{t-t^*}{t-t^*}} = c_1^a = g^{ra}$$

As $K = \beta_{\text{ID}^*}^r = e(g^a, g^b)^r = e(g, g)^{abr}$, knowing $t = TCR(g^r)$ we can recompute K with

$$K = e\left(g^b, (c_3/c_1^d)^{\frac{1}{t-t^*}}\right) = e(g^b, g^{ar}) = e(g, g)^{abr}$$

As this behaviour does not alter the adversary's view of the game we have

$$\Pr[X_4] = \Pr[X_3]$$

Game 5. (Modify the challenge / Forget c): The simulator changes its answer to the *get challenge key encapsulation* query. Game 3 established that $y(\text{ID}^*) = 0 \bmod p$, thus the challenger can compute the challenge ciphertext $C^* = (c_1^*, c_2^*, c_3^*)$ as

$$c_1^* = g^c, c_2^* = (g^c)^{x(\text{ID}^*)}, c_3^* = (g^c)^d, K = T$$

where g^c and T are given by the challenger before the game starts. Now the answer of the adversary to the challenge ciphertext is directly related to the challenge, and thus the simulator has an advantage in solving the dBDH challenge if the adversary has an advantage in winning the game:

$$\mathbf{Adv}_{CL-KEM,\mathcal{M}}^{cl-kem-cca} = \left|\Pr[X_0] - \frac{1}{2}\right| \leq \left|\frac{1}{q_0 m(n+1)}\mathbf{Adv}_{\mathcal{M}}^{\text{dBDH}}(k) + \mathbf{Adv}_{\text{TCR},\mathcal{M}}^{\text{hash-tcr}}(k) - \frac{1}{2}\right|$$

7 Conclusion

We show how to construct an efficient CL-KEM scheme from an existing ID-based KEM scheme in the standard model. Our construction requires only one additional exponentiation during the construction of the certificateless key and one additional exponentiation during the decapsulation compared to the original ID-based KEM scheme and is thus more efficient than any generic construction that has been published before. By modifying the Kiltz-Galindo KEM scheme [11] which is one of the most efficient ID-based KEM schemes in the standard model, we obtain the most efficient CL-KEM scheme in the standard model today.

References

1. Al-Riyami, S.S., Paterson, K.G.: Certificateless Public Key Cryptography. In: Laih, C.-S. (ed.) ASIACRYPT 2003. LNCS, vol. 2894, pp. 452–473. Springer, Heidelberg (2003), http://eprint.iacr.org/2003/126.pdf
2. Bentahar, K., Farshim, P., Malone-Lee, J., Smart, N.P.: Generic Constructions of Identity-Based and Certificateless KEMs. J. Cryptology 21(2), 178–199 (2008)
3. Boneh, D., Franklin, M.: Identity based encryption from the Weil pairing. SIAM Journal of Computing 32(3), 586–615 (2003), http://crypto.stanford.edu/~dabo/papers/bfibe.pdf
4. Boyd, C., Cliff, Y., González Nieto, J.M., Paterson, K.G.: Efficient one-round key exchange in the standard model. In: Mu, Y., Susilo, W., Seberry, J. (eds.) ACISP 2008. LNCS, vol. 5107, pp. 69–83. Springer, Heidelberg (2008)

5. Boyen, X., Mei, Q., Waters, B.: Direct chosen ciphertext security from identity-based techniques. In: Atluri, V., Meadows, C., Juels, A. (eds.) ACM Conference on Computer and Communications Security, pp. 320–329. ACM, New York (2005)
6. Cramer, R., Shoup, V.: Design and analysis of practical public-key encryption schemes secure against adaptive chosen ciphertext attack. SIAM J. Comput. 33(1), 167–226 (2004)
7. Dent, A.W.: A Designer's Guide to KEMs. In: Paterson, K.G. (ed.) Cryptography and Coding 2003. LNCS, vol. 2898, pp. 133–151. Springer, Heidelberg (2003)
8. Dent, A.W.: A survey of certificateless encryption schemes and security models. International Journal of Information Security 7(5), 349–377 (2008)
9. Huang, Q., Wong, D.S.: Generic Certificateless Key Encapsulation Mechanism. In: Pieprzyk, J., Ghodosi, H., Dawson, E. (eds.) ACISP 2007. LNCS, vol. 4586, pp. 215–229. Springer, Heidelberg (2007)
10. Kiltz, E., Galindo, D.: Direct Chosen-Ciphertext Secure Identity-Based Key Encapsulation Without Random Oracles. In: Batten, L.M., Safavi-Naini, R. (eds.) ACISP 2006. LNCS, vol. 4058, pp. 336–347. Springer, Heidelberg (2006)
11. Kiltz, E., Galindo, D.: Direct Chosen-Ciphertext Secure Identity-Based Key Encapsulation without Random Oracles. Cryptology ePrint Archive, Report 2006/034 (2006), http://eprint.iacr.org/2006/034
12. Kurosawa, K., Desmedt, Y.: A new paradigm of hybrid encryption scheme. In: Franklin, M. (ed.) CRYPTO 2004. LNCS, vol. 3152, pp. 426–442. Springer, Heidelberg (2004)
13. Naor, M., Yung, M.: Universal One-Way Hash Functions and their Cryptographic Applications. In: STOC, pp. 33–43. ACM, New York (1989)
14. Rompel, J.: One-Way Functions are Necessary and Sufficient for Secure Signatures. In: STOC, pp. 387–394. ACM, New York (1990)
15. Waters, B.: Efficient Identity-Based Encryption Without Random Oracles. In: Cramer, R. (ed.) EUROCRYPT 2005. LNCS, vol. 3494, pp. 114–127. Springer, Heidelberg (2005)

Accelerating Twisted Ate Pairing with Frobenius Map, Small Scalar Multiplication, and Multi-pairing

Yumi Sakemi, Shoichi Takeuchi, Yasuyuki Nogami, and Yoshitaka Morikawa

Graduate School of Natural Science and Technology, Okayama University
3-1-1, Tsushima-naka, Okayama, Okayama 700-8530, Japan
{sakemi,takeuchi,nogami,morikawa}@trans.cne.okayama-u.ac.jp

Abstract. In the case of Barreto-Naehrig pairing-friendly curves of embedding degree 12 of order r, recent efficient Ate pairings such as R-ate, optimal, and Xate pairings achieve Miller loop lengths of $(1/4)\lfloor \log_2 r \rfloor$. On the other hand, the twisted Ate pairing requires $(3/4)\lfloor \log_2 r \rfloor$ loop iterations, and thus is usually slower than the recent efficient Ate pairings. This paper proposes an improved twisted Ate pairing using Frobenius maps and a small scalar multiplication. The proposal splits the Miller's algorithm calculation into several independent parts, for which multi-pairing techniques apply efficiently. The maximum number of loop iterations in Miller's algorithm for the proposed twisted Ate pairing is equal to the $(1/4)\lfloor \log_2 r \rfloor$ attained by the most efficient Ate pairings.

Keywords: *twisted* Ate pairing, Miller's algorithm, Frobenius map, *multi–pairing, thread computing.*

1 Introduction

Recently, pairing–based cryptographic applications such as ID-based cryptography [3] and group signature schemes [23] have received much attention. In order to make these applications practical, the efficient parallelization of pairing calculations which seems to be inherently sequential is one of the main open problems. For sequential pairing calculations with ordinary curves, various improvements such as Ate [7], *twisted* Ate [21], *subfield–twisted* Ate [8], *R*–ate [20], *optimal* [27], and Xate [24] pairings have been proposed. In general, pairing calculations consist of two parts. One part is Miller's algorithm and the other is the so–called *final exponentiation*. In the case of the Ate pairing, let r, t, and k be the order, Frobenius trace, and embedding degree, respectively. The calculation is denoted as

$$\alpha(Q, P) = f_{t-1,Q}(P)^{(p^k-1)/r}, \tag{1}$$

where $P \in \mathbb{G}_1$, $Q \in \mathbb{G}_2$, and $f_{t-1,Q}(\cdot)$ is a certain rational function that is calculated by Miller's algorithm. The number of calculation loops of Miller's algorithm, given by $\lfloor \log_2(t-1) \rfloor$ in the case of Eq.(1) for example, has played an important role in the development of faster pairings. On the other hand,

D. Lee and S. Hong (Eds.): ICISC 2009, LNCS 5984, pp. 47–64, 2010.

some recent processors such as Core 2 Duo^{TM} have several computation cores. If the Miller's algorithm calculation, specifically the above $f_{t-1,Q}(P)$, is *efficiently* split into several independent calculation parts, *multi–pairing* techniques, *thread computing*, or some other techniques can be *efficiently* applied. Then, pairing calculations will become much faster. This paper tries to achieve the above for *twisted* Ate pairings by using Frobenius maps and a precomputed *small* scalar multiplication. In what follows, $f_{t-1,Q}(P)$ is abbreviated as $f_{t-1,Q}$.

Barreto–Naehrig (BN) [2] curves with embedding degree 12 form one of the most important families of ordinary pairing-friendly curves because sextic twists are available. This paper mainly deals with the case of BN curves. Lee et al. [20] have proposed an idea that applies R–ate pairing techniques to *twisted* Ate pairing, yielding *twisted R*–ate pairings. In the case of BN curves with embedding degree 12, where the parameters are given with a certain integer χ as

$$p(\chi) = 36\chi^4 - 36\chi^3 + 24\chi^2 - 6\chi + 1, \tag{2a}$$

$$r(\chi) = 36\chi^4 - 36\chi^3 + 18\chi^2 - 6\chi + 1, \tag{2b}$$

$$t(\chi) = 6\chi^2 + 1, \tag{2c}$$

the *twisted R*–ate pairing calculates

$$R(P,Q) = f_{a_1,P}(Q)^{p^{10}} \cdot f_{a_2,P}(Q) \cdot l_{[a_1]p^{10}P,[a_2]P}(Q), \tag{3}$$

where $a_1 = 2\chi + 1$ and $a_2 = 6\chi^2 + 4\chi$. In what follows, let $[s]P$ denote the scalar multiplication of a rational point P with a scalar s. From Eq.(3), twisted R–ate pairings need two Miller's algorithm calculations with a Frobenius map, thus *multi–pairing* technique or *thread computing* can be efficiently applied. In addition, as shown above, one has $2\lfloor \log_2 \chi \rfloor$ calculation loops which is two times larger than the $\lfloor \log_2 \chi \rfloor$ of the latter. It is quite important in the context of accelerating techniques to bound the maximum number of loop iterations. In the cases of *optimal*, R–ate, and Xate pairings, though they differ from Eq.(3) in that they have only one Miller's algorithm calculation, the number of loop iterations is $\lfloor \log_2 \chi \rfloor$.

This paper proposes an improved twisted Ate pairing using not only Frobenius maps but also a precomputed *small* scalar multiplication. The proposed *twisted* Ate pairing has two Miller's algorithm calculations. In addition, its *maximum* number of loop iterations is bounded by $\lfloor \log_2 \chi \rfloor$.

First, we introduce a simple idea that efficiently splits Miller's algorithm calculation into several independent calculation parts together with a Frobenius map and a precomputed *small* scalar multiplication. In the case of BN curves, according to Eqs.(2), first we show

$$p \equiv (2\chi - 1)p^{10} + 2\chi \bmod r. \tag{4}$$

Then, as shown in Eq.(5a), the Miller's algorithm calculation $\hat{f}_{\chi,P}(Q)$ of the proposed *twisted* Ate pairing is split into two Miller's algorithm calculations F_1 and F_2 for which the number of loop iterations is bounded by $\lfloor \log_2 \chi \rfloor$.

$$\hat{f}_{\chi,P}(Q) = F_1{}^p \cdot F_2, \tag{5a}$$

where, setting $P_p = [p]P$, F_1 and F_2 are respectively given as

$$F_1 = \{f_{2\chi,P} \cdot g_{[2\chi]P,-P}\}^{p^{10}} \cdot f_{2\chi,P} \cdot g_{[(2\chi-1)p^{10}]P,[2\chi]P}, \tag{5b}$$

$$F_2 = \{f_{2\chi,P_p} \cdot g_{[2\chi]P_p,-P_p}\}^{p^{10}} \cdot f_{2\chi,P_p} \cdot g_{[(2\chi-1)p^{10}]P_p,[2\chi]P_p}. \tag{5c}$$

In the above equations, $g_{[a]P,[b]P}$ is given by $l_{[a]P,[b]P}/v_{[a]P+[b]P}$. $l_{[a]P,[b]P}$ denotes the line passing through two rational points $[a]P$ and $[b]P$. $v_{[a]P+[b]P}$ denotes the vertical line passing through $[a]P + [b]P$.

This paper proposes an idea that makes the Miller's algorithm calculations for F_1 and F_2 *independent* by using a Frobenius map and a small scalar multiplication. First, calculate a rational point $P_p = [p]P$. This makes the calculations of F_1 and F_2 independent. Then, using this *precomputed P_p, multi–pairing* techniques are efficiently applied for the calculation of Eq.(5a). Although it is not our main contribution, *thread computing* also works efficiently. In this case, the number of calculation loops becomes $\lfloor \log_2 \chi \rfloor$ for each thread. This paper also shows another example of embedding degree 8. After that, this paper shows some experimental results with *multi–pairing* techniques and *thread computing* on Core2 Duo^TM. It is shown that the Miller's algorithm calculation part of the proposed *twisted* Ate pairing with *multi–pairing* techniques and that with *thread computing* become faster than the original *twisted* Ate pairing by 55.6% and 70.3%, respectively. Although this paper mainly improves *twisted* Ate pairings, the proposed idea can be also applied to *twisted R–*ate pairings which also become more efficient.

2   Fundamentals

This section reviews Barreto–Naehrig curves, twists, *twisted* Ate pairings, divisor theory, *twisted R–*ate pairings [20], Xate pairings [24], *skew* Frobenius maps, and *multi–pairings*.

2.1   Elliptic Curves and BN Curves

Let $\mathbb{F}_p$ be prime field and E be an elliptic curve over $\mathbb{F}_p$. $E(\mathbb{F}_p)$ is the set of rational points on the curve, including the *infinity point* $\mathcal{O}$. It forms an additive Abelian group. Let $\#E(\mathbb{F}_p)$ be its order, and consider a large prime number r that divides $\#E(\mathbb{F}_p)$. The smallest positive integer k such that r divides $p^k - 1$ is called the *embedding degree*. One can consider a pairing such as the Tate or Ate pairing on $E(\mathbb{F}_{p^k})$. Usually, $\#E(\mathbb{F}_p)$ is written as

$$\#E(\mathbb{F}_p) = p + 1 - t \tag{6}$$

where t is the Frobenius trace of $E(\mathbb{F}_p)$. The characteristic p and Frobenius trace t of Barreto–Naehrig (BN) curves [2] are given by using an integer variable χ as in Eqs.(2). In addition, a BN curve E has equation

$$E : y^2 = x^3 + b, \ b \in \mathbb{F}_p \tag{7}$$

whose embedding degree is 12. In this paper, let $\#E(\mathbb{F}_p)$ be a prime number r. As introduced in [2], this paper focuses on ordinary pairing–friendly curves as given in Eqs.(2).

2.2   Twist Technique

Let E be an ordinary elliptic curve and E' be the twisted elliptic curve of E. When the embedding degree k is equal to de, where e is a positive integer and d is the twist degree such as $2, 3, 4$, and 6, the following isomorphism is given between $E'(\mathbb{F}_{p^e})$ and $E(\mathbb{F}_{p^e})$.

$$\psi_d : \begin{cases} E'(\mathbb{F}_{p^e}) & \to E(\mathbb{F}_{p^{de}}), \\ (x, y) & \mapsto (xv^{2/d}, yv^{3/d}), \end{cases} \tag{8}$$

where x and y are x–coordinates and y–coordinates of a rational point, respectively. Corresponding to the twist degree d, v is chosen as a quadratic non residue, a cubic non residue, or a quadratic and cubic non residue in $\mathbb{F}_{p^e}$. Thus, when the twist degree d is even, the x–coordinate $xv^{2/d}$ belongs to the proper subfield $\mathbb{F}_{p^{k/2}}$ because $v^{2/d} \in \mathbb{F}_{p^{k/2}}$. In addition, when $d = 2$ or 4, the coefficient of x of the twisted curve is written as $E' : y^2 = x^3 + av^{-4/d}x + b$ or $y^2 = x^3 + av^{-4/d}x$, respectively. When one uses Barreto–Naehrig curves that belong to the class of *pairing–friendly* curves, one can apply quadratic/cubic/sextic twists because its embedding degree is 12. Of course, sextic twists are the most efficient for pairing calculations and rational point compression. In what follows, the curve E' specifically means the twisted elliptic curve of E such that $\#E'(\mathbb{F}_{p^e})$ is divisible by r.

2.3   Twisted Ate Pairing with BN Curves

This section briefly reviews *twisted* Ate pairings [21] on BN curves, which are what we mostly deal with. Let ϕ be Frobenius endomorphism, i.e.,

$$\phi : E(\mathbb{F}_{p^{12}}) \to E(\mathbb{F}_{p^{12}}) : (x, y) \mapsto (x^p, y^p), \tag{9}$$

Then, in the case of BN curves, let $\mathbb{G}_1$ and $\mathbb{G}_2$ be

$$\mathbb{G}_1 = E(\mathbb{F}_{p^{12}})[r] \cap \mathrm{Ker}(\phi - 1), \quad \mathbb{G}_2 = E(\mathbb{F}_{p^{12}})[r] \cap \mathrm{Ker}([\zeta_6]\phi^2 - [1]), \tag{10}$$

where $E(\mathbb{F}_{p^{12}})[r]$ denotes the subgroup of rational points of order r in $E(\mathbb{F}_{p^{12}})$ and ζ_6 is the primitive 6-th root of unity such that $[\zeta_6] : (x, y) \mapsto (\zeta_6^2 x, \zeta_6^3 y)$. Let $P \in \mathbb{G}_1$ and $Q \in \mathbb{G}_2$. The *twisted–Ate* pairing $\alpha(\cdot, \cdot)$ is defined as

$$\alpha(\cdot, \cdot) : \begin{cases} \mathbb{G}_1 \times \mathbb{G}_2 & \to \mathbb{F}_{p^{12}}^* / (\mathbb{F}_{p^{12}}^*)^r \\ (P, Q) & \mapsto f_{s,P}(Q)^{(p^{12}-1)/r}. \end{cases} \tag{11}$$

$A = f_{s,P}(Q)$ is usually calculated by Miller's algorithm[8], followed by the so–called *final exponentiation* $A^{(p^{12}-1)/r}$. The number of calculation loops in Miller's algorithm for the *twisted*–Ate pairing with BN curves is determined by $\lfloor \log_2 s \rfloor$, where the parameter s in the case of BN curves is given by

$$s = (t-1)^2 = 36\chi^3 - 18\chi^2 + 6\chi - 1 \bmod r. \tag{12}$$

Note that, in the case of BN curves, since the number of calculation loops of Miller's algorithm for the *twisted* Ate pairing is larger than those of recent efficient Ate pairings such as the *optimal* [27]. R–ate [20], and Xate [24] pairings, the *twisted*–Ate pairing is usually slower than the recent efficient Ate pairings. However, in contrast to these efficient Ate pairings, the twisted Ate pairing mainly uses rational points in $\mathbb{G}_1$ defined over a prime field $\mathbb{F}_p$. Thus, *twisted* Ate pairing has the possibility to become faster than the recent efficient Ate pairings. This paper tries to achieve that potential by using *multi-pairing* techniques.

2.4 Divisors

Let D be the principal divisor of $Q \in E$. For scalars $a, b \in \mathbb{Z}$, let aD and bD be written as

$$aD = (aQ) - (\mathcal{O}) + \mathrm{div}(f_{a,Q}), \quad bD = (bQ) - (\mathcal{O}) + \mathrm{div}(f_{b,Q}), \tag{13}$$

where $f_{a,Q}$ and $f_{b,Q}$ are the rational functions for aD and bD, respectively. Then, we have the following relations.

$$f_{a+b,Q} = f_{a,Q} \cdot f_{b,Q} \cdot g_{aQ,bQ}, \tag{14a}$$
$$f_{ab,Q} = f_{b,Q}^a \cdot f_{a,bQ} = f_{a,Q}^b \cdot f_{b,aQ}, \tag{14b}$$

where $g_{aQ,bQ} = l_{aQ,bQ}/v_{aQ+bQ}$. $l_{aQ,bQ}$ denotes the line passing through the two points aQ and bQ. v_{aQ+bQ} denotes the vertical line passing through $aQ + bQ$. Miller's algorithm calculates $f_{s,Q}$ efficiently.

2.5 Twisted R–Ate Pairing with BN Curves

Lee et al. [20] have proposed an efficient Ate pairing called the R–ate pairing. According to [20], the basic idea is finding $w = a_1 t + a_2$ with small coefficients a_i where w and t are the parameters for bilinear pairings such as r or t_i, where $t_i = p^i \pmod{r}$. Then, the R-ate pairing calculates $f_{a_i,Q}$ by Miller's algorithm. In the case of BN curves, the R–ate technique is efficiently applied for *twisted* Ate pairings, where it uses $2r = a_1 t_{10} + a_2$, where $a_1 = 2\chi + 1$ and $a_2 = 6\chi^2 + 4\chi$. Let $P \in \mathbb{G}_1$ and $Q \in \mathbb{G}_2$, where $\mathbb{G}_1$ and $\mathbb{G}_2$ are defined as in Eqs.(10). The *twisted* R–ate pairing is defined as

$$R(P,Q) = f_{a_1,P}(Q)^{p^{10}} \cdot f_{a_2,P}(Q) \cdot g_{[a_1]p^{10}P,[a_2]P}(Q)^{(p^{12}-1)/r}. \tag{15}$$

2.6   Xate Pairing with BN Curves

Recent efficient Ate pairings such as *optimal*, R–ate, and Xate pairings achieve $\lfloor \log_2 r \rfloor / \varphi(k)$ calculation loops in Miller's algorithm, where $\varphi(\cdot)$ is the Euler's function. For comparison in **Sec.**4, this paper briefly refers to the Xate pairing [24] using the cross–twisted (Xt) technique [1].

In the case of BN curves, let $\mathbb{G}_1$ and $\mathbb{G}_2$ be

$$\mathbb{G}_1 = E(\mathbb{F}_{p^{12}})[r] \cap \mathrm{Ker}(\phi - 1), \quad \mathbb{G}_2 = E(\mathbb{F}_{p^{12}})[r] \cap \mathrm{Ker}(\phi - [p]), \qquad (16)$$

and let $P \in \mathbb{G}_1$ and $Q \in \mathbb{G}_2$, The Xate pairng $\beta(\cdot, \cdot)$ is defined as

$$\beta(\cdot, \cdot) : \begin{cases} \mathbb{G}_2 \times \mathbb{G}_1 & \to \mathbb{F}_{p^{12}}^* / (\mathbb{F}_{p^{12}}^*)^r \\ (Q, P) & \mapsto \tilde{f}_{\chi, P}(Q)^{(p^{12}-1)/r}, \end{cases} \qquad (17)$$

where

$$\tilde{f}_{\chi, P}(Q) = \{f_{\chi, Q}^{1+p} \cdot l_{\chi Q, p\chi Q}\}^{1+p^3} \cdot l_{\chi Q + p\chi Q, p^3\chi Q + p^4\chi Q}. \qquad (18)$$

According to Eq.(18), the number of calculation loops of Miller's algorithm is determined by $\lfloor \log_2(\chi) \rfloor$, that is $(1/4)\lfloor \log_2 r \rfloor$. Applying the cross–twisted (Xt) technique [1], let $P' = \psi_d(P)$ and $Q' = \psi_d(Q)$, The Xt–Xate pairing is given by $\beta(Q', P')$.

2.7   Skew Frobenius Maps for a Rational Point $P \in \mathbb{G}_1$

For an arbitrary rational point $P \in \mathbb{G}_1 \subset E(\mathbb{F}_{p^k})$, as previously introduced, consider $P' = \psi_d^{-1}(P) \in \mathbb{G}_1' \subset E'(\mathbb{F}_{p^k})$. Note that P' satisfies the following relation [16]

$$(\phi_e - [p^e])\, P' = \mathcal{O}, \quad \phi_e(P') = (x_{P'}^{p^e}, y_{P'}^{p^e}), \qquad (19)$$

where $e = k/d$ and P' be $(x_{P'}, y_{P'})$. Then, $\forall P(x_P, y_P) \in \mathbb{G}_1$, the skew Frobenius map $\tilde{\phi}_e$ is defined as [26].

$$\tilde{\phi}_e : \begin{cases} \mathbb{G}_1 & \to \mathbb{G}_1, \\ (x, y) & \mapsto (x^p / v^{2(p^e-1)/d}, y^p / v^{3(p^e-1)/d}). \end{cases} \qquad (20)$$

Let $[s]P$ denote the scalar multiplication of a rational point P with scalar s. Then, for an arbitrary rational point $P \in \mathbb{G}_1$, the following relation holds.

$$\left(\tilde{\phi}_e - [p^e]\right) P = \mathcal{O} \text{ and thus } \tilde{\phi}_e(P) = [p^e]P. \qquad (21)$$

This relation is sometimes useful for accelerating a scalar multiplication in $\mathbb{G}_1$. The authors [26] have exhibited an efficient scalar multiplication for a pairing–friendly elliptic curve $E(\mathbb{F}_p)$ with the skew Frobenius endomorphism $\tilde{\phi}_e$.

In the case of BN curves, since $k = 12$, $d = 6$, and $e = k/d = 2$, the skew Frobenius map $\tilde{\phi}_2$ becomes

$$\tilde{\phi}_2 : \begin{cases} \mathbb{G}_1 & \to \mathbb{G}_1, \\ (x, y) & \mapsto (x/v^{(p^2-1)/3}, y/v^{(p^2-1)/2}). \end{cases} \tag{22}$$

In practice, note that $1/v^{(p^2-1)/3}$ and $1/v^{(p^2-1)/2}$ become a primitive third root of unity and -1 in $\mathbb{F}_p$, respectively.

2.8   Multi–pairing

For the following sets of rational points,

$$S_P = \{P_1, P_2, \cdots, P_N \in \mathbb{G}_1\}, \ S_Q = \{Q_1, Q_2, \cdots, Q_N \in \mathbb{G}_2\}, \tag{23}$$

consider the following product of N pairings.

$$M_N = \prod_{i=1}^{N} \alpha(P_i, Q_i)^{(p^k-1)/r}. \tag{24}$$

Granger et al. [13] have proposed an efficient algorithm for calculating the above product, namely the *multi–pairing* algorithm. As shown in **Algorithm 1**, squarings are unified at Step 5. In what follows, **Algorithm 1** is called MMA. In addition, the well–known Montgomery's trick [6] is efficiently applied for inversions at Step 7 and Step 11. Note that the following rational points are also obtained through the calculation flow.

$$S_R = \{R_1, R_2, \cdots, R_N \in \mathbb{G}_1\}, \text{where } R_i = [s]P_i. \tag{25}$$

In what follows, denote the calculation result of MMA(s,N,S_P,S_Q) by $F_{s,S_P}(S_Q)$ or simply F_{s,S_P}. Then, one *final exponentiation* is carried out as

$$M_N = F_{s,S_P}^{(p^k-1)/r}. \tag{26}$$

In this paper, the *multi–pairing* technique is applied for calculating *just one pairing*.

3   Main Idea

In this section, using BN curves of embedding degree 12, we construct an improved *twisted* Ate pairing that efficiently works together with the *multi–pairing* technique. This pairing is based on the relation given by Eq.(4). A secondary benefit is that *thread computing* will also work efficiently. First, we show how to obtain Eq.(4), and then an efficient bilinear map is proposed. Then, it is shown that the *multi–pairing* technique can be applied.

Algorithm 1. Miller's Algorithm for Multi–pairing

<table>
<tr><td colspan="2" align="center">MMA(s, N, S_P, S_Q)</td></tr>
<tr><td>Input:</td><td>s, N, $S_P = \{P_1, P_2, \cdots, P_N \in \mathbb{G}_1\}$, $S_Q = \{Q_1, Q_2, \cdots, Q_N \in \mathbb{G}_2\}$</td></tr>
<tr><td>Output:</td><td>$\prod\limits_{i=1}^{N} f_{s,P_i}(Q_i)$, $S_R = \{[s]P_1, [s]P_2, \cdots, [s]P_N\}$</td></tr>
</table>

1. $f \leftarrow 1$.
2. For $i = N$ downto 1.
3. $R_i \leftarrow P_i$.
4. For $j = \lfloor \log_2(s) \rfloor$ downto 1:
5. $f \leftarrow f^2$.
6.   For $i = N$ downto 1.
7. $f \leftarrow f \cdot g_{R_i,R_i}(Q_i)$.
8. $R_i \leftarrow 2R_i$.
9.   If $s[j] = 1$,then:
10.   For $i = N$ downto 1.
11. $f \leftarrow f \cdot g_{R_i,P_i}(Q_i)$.
12. Return f

*$s[j]$ denotes the j–th bit of the loop parameter s from the lower.

3.1 How to Obtain Eq.(4)

First, the following relation holds.

$$36\chi^4 - 36\chi^3 + 18\chi^2 - 6\chi + 1 \equiv 0 \bmod r. \tag{27}$$

Since $p \equiv t - 1 \equiv 6\chi^2 \bmod r$ from Eq.(2c),

$$p^2 - 6\chi p + 3p - 6\chi + 1 \equiv 0 \bmod r$$
$$(-6\chi + 3)p \equiv -p^2 + 6\chi - 1 \bmod r. \tag{28}$$

Squaring both sides of Eq.(28) leads to

$$(6\chi - 3)^2 p^2 \equiv (p^2 - 6\chi + 1)^2 \bmod r$$
$$36\chi^2 p^2 - 36\chi p^2 + 9p^2 \equiv p^4 - 12\chi p^2 + 2p^2 + 36\chi^2 - 12\chi + 1 \bmod r. \tag{29}$$

From $p^4 + 1 \equiv p^2 \bmod r$,

$$36\chi^2 p^2 - 36\chi p^2 + 9p^2 \equiv -12\chi p^2 + 3p^2 + 36\chi^2 - 12\chi \bmod r,$$
$$36\chi^2 (p^2 - 1) \equiv (24\chi - 6)p^2 - 12\chi \bmod r,$$
$$6\chi^2 (p^2 - 1) \equiv (4\chi - 1)p^2 - 2\chi \bmod r. \tag{30}$$

Multiplying Eq.(30) by $(p^2 - 1)^{-1}$,

$$6\chi^2 \equiv -(4\chi - 1)p^4 + 2\chi p^2 \bmod r, \tag{31}$$

where using $p^4 - p^2 + 1 \equiv 0 \bmod r$ and based on

$$\gcd(p^4 - p^2 + 1, p^2 - 1) \equiv 1 \bmod r, \tag{32}$$

$(p^2 - 1)^{-1}$ is given as

$$p^4 - p^2 + 1 \equiv 0 \bmod r,$$
$$-p^2(p^2 - 1) \equiv 1 \bmod r,$$
$$(p^2 - 1)^{-1} \equiv -p^2 \bmod r. \tag{33}$$

From $p^2 \equiv p^4 + 1 \bmod r$,

$$6\chi^2 \equiv -(4\chi - 1)p^4 + 2\chi(p^4 + 1)$$
$$\equiv -(2\chi - 1)p^4 + 2\chi. \tag{34}$$

Finally, since $p \equiv t - 1 \equiv 6\chi^2 \bmod r$ and $p^6 \equiv -1 \bmod r$, Eq.(4) is obtained.

3.2 Proposal

In the case of BN curves of order r, the number of calculation loops of Miller's algorithm for the Ate pairing is $(1/2)\lfloor \log_2 r \rfloor$. Those of the R–ate, Xate, and *twisted* Ate pairings are $(1/4)\lfloor \log_2 r \rfloor$, $(1/4)\lfloor \log_2 r \rfloor$, and $(3/4)\lfloor \log_2 r \rfloor$, respectively. In the case of the *twisted R*–ate pairing, Eq.(15) has two Miller's algorithm calculations and the *maximum* length of their calculation loops is $(1/2)\lfloor \log_2 r \rfloor$. The proposed *twisted* Ate pairing achieves the *maximum* $(1/4)\lfloor \log_2 r \rfloor$ as follows. According to the divisor theorem, specifically Eq.(14b), the Miller's algorithm calculation of the *twisted* Ate pairing with BN curves is given by

$$f_{(t-1)^2,P}(Q)^{(p^{12}-1)/r} = \{f_{(t-1),P}(Q)^{t-1} \cdot f_{(t-1),[t-1]P}(Q)\}^{(p^{12}-1)/r},$$
$$= \{f_{6\chi^2,P}(Q)^p \cdot f_{6\chi^2,[p]P}(Q)\}^{(p^{12}-1)/r}, \tag{35}$$

where $p = t - 1 \bmod r$. Let $P \in \mathbb{G}_1$, $Q \in \mathbb{G}_2$, and $P_p = [p]P$. Applying the relation Eq.(4) to Eq.(35), the proposed *twisted* Ate pairing is given as follows.

$$\zeta(\cdot, \cdot) : \begin{cases} \mathbb{G}_1 \times \mathbb{G}_2 & \to \mathbb{F}^*_{p^{12}}/(\mathbb{F}^*_{p^{12}})^r \\ (P, Q) & \mapsto \hat{f}_{\chi,P}(Q)^{(p^{12}-1)/r}, \end{cases} \tag{36a}$$

where

$$\hat{f}_{\chi,P}(Q) = (\{f_{2\chi,P} \cdot l_{[2\chi]P,-P}\}^{p^{10}} \cdot f_{2\chi,P} \cdot l_{[(2\chi-1)p^{10}]P,[2\chi]P})^p$$
$$\cdot \{f_{2\chi,P_p} \cdot l_{[2\chi]P_p,-P_p}\}^{p^{10}} \cdot f_{2\chi,P_p} \cdot l_{[(2\chi-1)p^{10}]P_p,[2\chi]P_p}. \tag{36b}$$

The bilinearity of $\hat{f}_{\chi,P}(Q)$ is shown in **App.** A. When the embedding degree k is an even number such as in the case of BN curves, it is well known that the vertical line $v_{aP+bP}(Q)$ of $g_{aP,bP}(Q)$ can be ignored by the *final exponentiation*. Thus, in the case of BN curves, note that the calculations of vertical lines are not required. Let F_1 and F_2 be

$$F_1 = \{f_{2\chi,P} \cdot l_{[2\chi]P,-P}\}^{p^{10}} \cdot f_{2\chi,P} \cdot l_{[(2\chi-1)p^{10}]P,[2\chi]P}, \tag{37a}$$
$$F_2 = \{f_{2\chi,P_p} \cdot l_{[2\chi]P_p,-P_p}\}^{p^{10}} \cdot f_{2\chi,P_p} \cdot l_{[(2\chi-1)p^{10}]P_p,[2\chi]P_p}. \tag{37b}$$

Eq.(36b) is written as $\hat{f}_{\chi,P}(Q) = F_1^p \cdot F_2$. In general, F_1 is first calculated, then F_2 is calculated because the rational point P_p needed for the calculation of F_2 is obtained through the calculation of F_1. Though the total number of calculation loops is given by $(1/2)\lfloor \log_2 r \rfloor$ as shown in Eq.(36b), if $[p]P$ is efficiently precomputed, the calculation of Eq.(36b) will be accelerated by *multi–pairing* techniques or *thread computing* from the viewpoints of software and hardware, respectively. Then, the maximum of the calculation loops theoretically reaches $(1/4)\lfloor \log_2 r \rfloor$. Note that, as introduced in **Sec.3.3**, $[p]P$ is efficiently calculated with the skew Frobenius map $\tilde{\phi}_2$ as in Eq.(43).

3.3 Multi–pairing Technique

First, suppose that the rational point $[p]P$ is precomputed as P_p. Then Eq.(36b) is calculated as

$$
\hat{f}_{\chi,P}(Q) = \{f_{2\chi,P}^p \cdot f_{2\chi,P_p} \cdot l_{[2\chi]P,-P}^p \cdot l_{[2\chi]P_p,-P_p}\}^{p^{10}}
$$
$$
\cdot f_{2\chi,P}^p \cdot f_{2\chi,P_p} \cdot l_{[(2\chi-1)p^{10}]P,[2\chi]P}^p \cdot l_{[(2\chi-1)p^{10}]P_p,[2\chi]P_p}. \tag{38}
$$

Then, apply the *multi–pairing* technique to the calculation of $A = f_{2\chi,P}^p \cdot f_{2\chi,P_p}$. First, let $Q_p = [p]Q$. Since $Q \in \mathbb{G}_2$ has the following property,

$$
f_{s,P}(Q)^p = f_{s,P}(Q_p), \tag{39}
$$

$A = f_{2\chi,P}^p \cdot f_{2\chi,pP}$ is calculated by

$$
A = f_{2\chi,P}(Q_p) \cdot f_{2\chi,P_p}(Q). \tag{40}
$$

Thus, for the proposed *twisted* Ate pairing calculation, the *multi–pairing* technique is efficiently applied as **Algorithm 2**. After that, one *final exponentiation* follows.

$$
\hat{f}_{\chi,P}(Q) = \{F_{2\chi,S_P}(S_Q) \cdot l_{[2\chi]P,-P}^p \cdot l_{[2\chi]P_p,-P_p}\}^{p^{10}}
$$
$$
\cdot F_{2\chi,S_P}(S_Q) \cdot l_{[(2\chi-1)p^{10}]P,[2\chi]P}^p \cdot l_{[(2\chi-1)p^{10}]P_p,[2\chi]P_p}, \tag{41}
$$

where $S_P = \{P, \; P_p\}$ and $S_Q = \{Q_p, \; Q\}$. For an arbitrary rational point $P \in \mathbb{G}_1$, according to Eq.(4), the scalar multiplication $P_p = [p]P$ is carried out by

$$
P_p = [(2\chi - 1)p^{10}]P + [2\chi]P. \tag{42}
$$

In the above calculation, $[p^{10}]P$ is easily determined by the skew Frobenius map for the rational point in $\mathbb{G}_1$ that was introduced in **Sec.2.7**. Therefore, note that $\lfloor \log_2 \chi \rfloor \approx (1/4)\lfloor \log_2 r \rfloor$ and Eq.(42) becomes

$$
P_p = [2\chi - 1]\tilde{\phi}_2^5(P) + [2\chi]P. \tag{43}
$$

In the case of BN curves, the integer parameter χ can be optimized so as to have small Hamming weight [24]. Thus, compared to a general scalar multiplication, Eq.(43) is quite efficiently calculated. On the other hand, Q_p is easily determined by the Frobenius endomorphism ϕ as Eq.(9).

Algorithm 2. Miller's algorithm for the proposed *twisted* Ate pairing with *multi–pairing* technique in the case of BN curves

---

Input : $P \in \mathbb{G}_1, Q \in \mathbb{G}_2, 2\chi, p$

Output : $f = \hat{f}_{\chi,P}(Q)$

Procedure :

    1. $P_1 \leftarrow [2\chi]P$

    2. $P_2 \leftarrow P_1 - P$

    3. $P_2 \leftarrow \tilde{\phi}_2^5(P_2)$

    4. $P_p \leftarrow P_2 + P_1$ $//P_p \leftarrow [p]P$

    5. $Q_p \leftarrow \phi(Q)$ $//Q_p \leftarrow [p]Q$

    6. $A \leftarrow \text{MMA} (2\chi, 2, S_P, S_Q)$ $//A \leftarrow F_{2\chi,S_P}(S_Q),$

                                                  $//S_P = \{P, P_p\}, S_Q = \{Q_p, Q\}$

    7. $B \leftarrow l_{[2\chi]P,-P}$

    8. $C \leftarrow l_{[2\chi]P_p,-P_p}$

    9. $f \leftarrow B^p \cdot C$

   10. $B \leftarrow l_{\tilde{\phi}_2^5([2\chi-1]P),[2\chi]P}$

   11. $C \leftarrow l_{\tilde{\phi}_2^5([2\chi-1]P_p),[2\chi]P_p}$

   12. $f \leftarrow f^{p^{10}} \cdot A \cdot B^p \cdot C$

   13. Return f

3.4 Other Pairing–Friendly Curves

As another example, this section considers a pairing–friendly curve of embedding degree 8 that has a *quartic twist*, as introduced in [10]. In this case, the parameters are given as follows.

$$p(\chi) = (81\chi^6 + 51\chi^5 + 45\chi^4 + 12\chi^3 + 13\chi^2 + 6\chi + 1)/4, \tag{44a}$$

$$r(\chi) = 9\chi^4 + 12\chi^3 + 8\chi^2 + 4\chi + 1, \tag{44b}$$

$$t(\chi) = -9\chi^3 - 3\chi^2 - 2\chi. \tag{44c}$$

Corresponding to Eq.(4), the following relation is obtained.

$$p^3 = p^2 + 3\chi + 1 \bmod r. \tag{45}$$

In this case, since $k = 8$, $d = 4$, and $e = k/d = 2$, $[p^2]P$ for an arbitrary rational point $P \in \mathbb{G}_1$ is efficiently calculated by the skew Frobenius map $\tilde{\phi}_2$ as

$$[p^2]P = \tilde{\phi}_2(P). \tag{46}$$

Then, in this case, the proposed *twisted* Ate pairing is given as follows.

$$\hat{f}_{\chi,P}(Q) = F_{3\chi,S_P} \cdot \{l_{[3\chi]P,P} \cdot l_{\tilde{\phi}_2(P),[3\chi+1]P}\}^{p^3}$$

$$\cdot l_{[3\chi]P_{p^3},P_{p^3}} \cdot l_{\tilde{\phi}_2(P)_{p^3},[3\chi+1]P_{p^3}}, \tag{47}$$

where we set $P_{p^3} = [p^3]P$ and $Q_{p^3} = [p^3]Q$. Note that the vertical line $v_{aP+bP}(Q)$ of $g_{aP,bP}(Q)$ can be ignored by *final exponentiation* since it has a *quartic twist*. This case employs $S_P = \{P, P_{p^3}\}$ and $S_Q = \{Q_{p^3}, Q\}$ for *multi–pairing*. In this context, $[p^3]P$ is calculated with the skew Frobenius map $\tilde{\phi}_2$ by Eq.(45) and $[p^3]Q$ is easily determined by the Frobenius endomorphism ϕ.

As with the twisted R–ate pairing [20], the proposed *twisted* Ate pairing is based on the original *twisted* Ate pairing [21]. Therefore, the target pairing–friendly curves on which the proposed *twisted* Ate and also *twisted* R–ate pairings become more efficient than the original *twisted* Ate pairing are restricted. For example, Freeman curves [9] do not belong to such families of pairing–friendly curves.

4   Experimental Result

This section discusses the implementation of the proposed *twisted* Ate pairing with BN curves of embedding degree 12 and shows some *experimental* results.

4.1   Comparison

Using the following positive integer χ of Hamming weight 3 [24],

$$\chi = 2^{62} + 2^{35} + 2^{24}, \tag{48}$$

accordingly the order r becomes a 254–bit prime number and the size of $\mathbb{F}_{p^{12}}$ becomes 3048–bit. We implemented the proposed twisted Ate pairing together with the multi-pairing technique and thread computing. Table 1 and Table 2 show the computational environment and the experimental result, respectively. For constructing $\mathbb{F}_{p^{12}}$, Kato et al.'s work [18] and the tower field technique for $\mathbb{F}_{(p^4)^3}$ [25] were used. For comparison, Xt–Xate, *twisted* Ate, *twisted* R–ate pairings, and the proposed *twisted* Ate pairing given by Eq.(36) were implemented and their results were shown in Table 2. Note that the implementation of the proposed *twisted* Ate pairing did not use techniques to parallelize lower–level functions such as SIMD or SWAR shown in [14] and [15]. In the case of BN curves, the total numbers of calculation loops of the *twisted* Ate pairing, the proposed *twisted* Ate pairing with *multi–pairing* technique, and that with *thread computing* are $(3/4)\lfloor \log_2(r) \rfloor$, $(1/2)\lfloor \log_2(r) \rfloor$, and $(1/4)\lfloor \log_2(r) \rfloor$, respectively. Since the calculation time of Miller's algorithm depends on this number, the reduction of the number directly contributes to the efficiency of Miller's algorithm calculation. As shown in Table 2, the Miller's part of the proposed *twisted* Ate pairing with *multi–pairing* technique and that with *thread computing* become faster than the original *twisted* Ate pairing by 55.6% and 70.3%, respectively. The proposed technique can also be applied to the *twisted* R–ate pairing. Though the efficiency of the proposed techniques for the *twisted* R–ate pairing is described in **App**. C, the calculation time of the Miller's part will become about two times faster. In the Miller's algorithm calculation for Xt–Xate pairing, elliptic curve additions and doublings are calculated over $\mathbb{F}_{p^2}$. On the other hand, in the case of the *twisted* Ate pairing, they are calculated over $\mathbb{F}_p$. Thus, as shown in Table 2, the proposed *twisted* Ate pairing with thread computing was slightly faster than

Table 1. Computational environment

CPU	Core^{TM} 2 Duo* 2.53GHz
Cache size	6144KB
OS	Fedora 8 2.6.26
Compiler	gcc 4.2.2
Library	GNU MP 4.1.2 [12], pthread

*Core 2 Duo is a registered trademark of Intel Corporation.

Table 2. Comparison of timings of pairings with BN curves of 254–bit prime order (The Hamming weight of integer variable χ is 3.)

[unit:ms]

	pairing	Miller's part	final exp.	total
normal[†]	Xt–Xate	4.38		9.00
	twisted R–ate	7.64		12.3
	twisted Ate	13.9	4.62	18.5
multi–pairing[†]	**proposed** *twisted* **Ate**	6.17		10.8
thread computing		4.12		8.74

Remark : Core 2 Duo (2.53GHz), C language, and GMP [12] are used.

[†] Only single (thread) core is used.

the Xt–Xate pairing, even though their numbers of calculation loops in Miller's algorithms are the same. This paper does not take the overheads of making and closing *threads* into account because they are negligible and closely related to the concerned *processor* and *kernel* of the operating system. Of course, the number of data transmissions between the cores is preferred to be small as the proposed method achieves.

For comparison, using another integer of large Hamming weight for χ, the proposed *twisted* Ate and other pairings were also implemented. In this case, the following 63–bit integer χ of Hamming weight 32 is used.

$$\chi = 4825411341445627382. \tag{49}$$

The experimental results are summarized in Table 3. As shown in Table 3, the proposed ideas can substantially accelerate *twisted* Ate pairing even when the Hamming weight of χ is increased.

4.2   Thread Computing

Although it does not represent our main contribution, *thread computing* also works efficiently.

Consider applying *thread computing* to the calculation of Eq.(36b). Fig.1 in **App**. B shows the calculation flow of the proposed method with BN curves and *thread computing*. According to Eq.(37), the calculation of F_2 does not depend on that of F_1 for which $[p]P$ of course needs to be precomputed. Thus, not only *multi–pairing* techniques but also *thread computing* with two calculation cores

Table 3. Comparison of timings of pairings with BN curves of 254–bit prime order (The Hamming weight of integer variable χ is 32.)

[unit:ms]

	pairing	Miller's part	final exp.	total
normal[†]	Xt–Xate	5.5		12.0
	twisted R–ate	9.3		15.8
	twisted Ate	13.8	6.5	20.3
multi–pairing[†]	**proposed** *twisted* **Ate**	**8.3**		**14.8**
thread computing		**5.4**		**11.9**

Remark : Core 2 Duo (2.53GHz), C language, and GMP [12] are used.
[†] Only single (thread) core is used.

shown in Fig.1 will efficiently work for the proposed *twisted* Ate pairing. Note here that $[p]P$ is efficiently calculated by the skew Frobenius endomorphism $\tilde{\phi}_2$ as introduced in Sec.3.3. In this case, the number of calculation loops of Miller's algorithm for the proposed *twisted* Ate pairing with *thread computing* practically becomes $(1/4)\lfloor \log_2 r \rfloor$.

5   Conclusion and Future Work

This paper proposed an idea for splitting Miller's algorithm and then applying the *multi–pairing* technique to just one pairing calculation. As introduced in **App.** C, in the case of BN curves, the Miller's part of the twisted R–ate pairing with the proposed idea and *thread computing* becomes about two times faster. For the recent efficient Ate pairings such as *optimal* pairing, a similar technique with *multi–pairing* and *thread computing* should be considered. Then, as shown in Table 2, the *final* exponentiation should be improved.

Merely splitting up the Miller's algorithm calculation is not so difficult. However, as in the proposed method, it is not always possible to combine an efficient split together with an efficient multi–pairing technique. Such an efficient parallelization of Miller's algorithm calculation for other pairings will be an important area for future work.

References

1. Akane, M., Nogami, Y., Morikawa, Y.: Fast Ate Pairing Computation of Embedding Degree 12 Using Subfield–Twisted Elliptic Curve. IEICE Trans. Fundamentals E92-A(2) (2009) (to appear)
2. Barreto, P.S.L.M., Naehrig, M.: Pairing–Friendly Elliptic Curves of Prime Order. In: Preneel, B., Tavares, S. (eds.) SAC 2005. LNCS, vol. 3897, pp. 319–331. Springer, Heidelberg (2006)
3. Boneh, D., Lynn, B., Shacham, H.: Short signatures from the Weil pairing. In: Boyd, C. (ed.) ASIACRYPT 2001. LNCS, vol. 2248, pp. 514–532. Springer, Heidelberg (2001)
4. Boneh, D., Boyen, X., Shacham, H.: Short group signatures. In: Franklin, M. (ed.) CRYPTO 2004. LNCS, vol. 3152, pp. 41–55. Springer, Heidelberg (2004)

5. Boneh, D., Boyen, X., Goh, E.-G.: Hierarchical identity based encryption with constant size ciphertext. In: Cramer, R. (ed.) EUROCRYPT 2005. LNCS, vol. 3494, pp. 440–456. Springer, Heidelberg (2005)
6. Cohen, H.: A course in computational algebraic number theory. In: GTM, vol. 139. Springer, Heidelberg (1993)
7. Cohen, H., Frey, G.: Handbook of Elliptic and Hyperelliptic Curve Cryptography. In: Discrete Mathematics and Its Applications. Chapman & Hall CRC, Boca Raton (2005)
8. Devegili, A.J., Scott, M., Dahab, R.: Implementing Cryptographic Pairings over Barreto-Naehrig Curves. In: Takagi, T., Okamoto, T., Okamoto, E., Okamoto, T. (eds.) Pairing 2007. LNCS, vol. 4575, pp. 197–207. Springer, Heidelberg (2007)
9. Freeman, D.: Constructing Pairing-Friendly Elliptic Curves with Embedding Degree 10. In: Hess, F., Pauli, S., Pohst, M. (eds.) ANTS 2006. LNCS, vol. 4076, pp. 452–465. Springer, Heidelberg (2006)
10. Freeman, D., Scott, M., Teske, E.: A taxonomy of pairing-friendly elliptic curves. preprint (2006), http://math.berkeley.edu/~dfreeman/papers/taxonomy.pdf
11. Galbraith, S.D., Scott, M.: Exponentiation in pairing-friendly groups using homomorphisms. In: Galbraith, S.D., Paterson, K.G. (eds.) Pairing 2008. LNCS, vol. 5209, pp. 211–224. Springer, Heidelberg (2008)
12. GNU MP, http://gmplib.org/
13. Granger, R., Smart, N.P.: On computing products of pairings. Cryptology ePrint Archive: Report 2006/172
14. Grabher, P., Großschädl, J., Page, D.: On Software Parallel Implementation of Cryptographic Pairings. In: Avanzi, R.M., Keliher, L., Sica, F. (eds.) SAC 2008. LNCS, vol. 5381, pp. 34–39. Springer, Heidelberg (2009)
15. Hankerson, D., Menezes, A., Scott, M.: Software Implementation of Pairings. In: Identity–Based Cryptography, IOS Press, Amsterdam (2008), http://www.math.uwaterloo.ca/~ajmeneze/research.html
16. Hess, F., Smart, N., Vercauteren, F.: The Eta Pairing Revisited. IEEE Trans. Information Theory, 4595–4602 (2006)
17. Itoh, T., Tsujii, S.: A Fast Algorithm for Computing Multiplicative Inverses in $GF(2^m)$ Using Normal Bases. Inf. and Comp. 78, 171–177 (1988)
18. Kato, H., Nogami, Y., Yoshida, T., Morikawa, Y.: Cyclic Vector Multiplication Algorithm Based on a Special Class of Gauss Period Normal Basis. ETRI Journal 29(6), 769–778 (2007), http://etrij.etri.re.kr/Cyber/servlet/BrowseAbstract?paperid=RP0702-0040
19. Knuth, D.: The Art of Computer Programming: Seminumerical Algorithms, vol. 2. Addison-Wesley, Reading (1981)
20. Lee, E., Lee, H., Park, C.: Efficient and Generalized Pairing Computation on Abelien Varieties. To appear in IEEE transactions on Information Theory (2009)
21. Matsuda, S., Kanayama, N., Hess, F., Okamoto, E.: Optimised Versions of the Ate and Twisted Ate Pairings. In: Galbraith, S.D. (ed.) Cryptography and Coding 2007. LNCS, vol. 4887, pp. 302–312. Springer, Heidelberg (2007)
22. Mitsunari, S.: A Fast Implementation of η_T Pairing in Characteristic Three on Intel Core 2 Duo Processor. IACR ePrint archive, 2009/032.pdf
23. Nakanishi, T., Funabiki, N.: Verifier-Local Revocation Group Signature Schemes with Backward Unlinkability from Bilinear Maps. In: Roy, B. (ed.) ASIACRYPT 2005. LNCS, vol. 3788, pp. 443–454. Springer, Heidelberg (2005)
24. Nogami, Y., Akane, M., Sakemi, Y., Kato, H., Morikawa, Y.: Integer Variable χ-based Ate Pairing. In: Galbraith, S.D., Paterson, K.G. (eds.) Pairing 2008. LNCS, vol. 5209, pp. 178–191. Springer, Heidelberg (2008)

25. Nogami, Y., Morikawa, Y.: A Fast Implementation of Elliptic Curve Cryptosystem with Prime Order Defined over F_{p^8}. Memoirs of the Faculty of Engineering Okayama University 37(2), 73–88 (2003)
26. Sakemi, Y., Nogami, Y., Okeya(Hitachi), K., Kato, H., Morikawa, Y.: Skew Frobenius Map and Efficient Scalar Multiplication for Pairing-based Cryptography. In: Franklin, M.K., Hui, L.C.K., Wong, D.S. (eds.) CANS 2008. LNCS, vol. 5339, pp. 226–239. Springer, Heidelberg (2008)
27. Vercauteren, F.: Optimal Pairings. IACR ePrint archive,
http://eprint.iacr.org/2008/096

A   Bilinearity and Nondegeneracy of the Proposed *twisted* Ate Pairing

First, Eq.(4) becomes

$$p \equiv (2\chi - 1)p^{10} + 2\chi \bmod r$$
$$\equiv (2\chi + p^6)p^{10} + 2\chi \bmod r. \tag{50}$$

Then, let $6\chi^2 = (2\chi + p^6)p^{10} + 2\chi + cr$, where c is a certain integer, the following relation holds.

$$f_{(t-1)^2,P}^{(p^{12}-1)/r}$$

$$= \left\{ f_{(2\chi+p^6)p^{10}+2\chi,P}^{p} \cdot f_{(2\chi+p^6)p^{10}+2\chi,[p]P} \cdot f_{cr,P}^{p} \cdot f_{cr,[p]P} \right\}^{(p^{12}-1)/r}$$

$$= \left\{ f_{(2\chi+p^6)p^{10}+2\chi,P}^{p} \cdot f_{(2\chi+p^6)p^{10}+2\chi,[p]P} \cdot f_{r,P}^{2cp} \right\}^{(p^{12}-1)/r}, \tag{51a}$$

where note that $g_{[(2\chi+p^6)p^{10}+2\chi]P,[cr]P}$ becomes 1. In the above equation,

$$f_{(2\chi+p^6)p^{10}+2\chi,P}^{(p^{12}-1)/r}$$

$$= (f_{2\chi+p^6,P}^{p^{10}} \cdot f_{p^{10},[2\chi+p^6]P} \cdot f_{2\chi,P} \cdot g_{[(2\chi+p^6)p^{10}]P,[2\chi]P})^{(p^{12}-1)/r}$$

$$= \left\{ (f_{2\chi,P} \cdot f_{p^6,P} \cdot g_{[2\chi]P,[p^6]P})^{p^{10}} \cdot f_{p^{10},P}^{2\chi+p^6} \cdot f_{2\chi,P} \cdot g_{[(2\chi+p^6)p^{10}]P,[2\chi]P} \right\}^{(p^{12}-1)/r}. \tag{51b}$$

$f_{(2\chi-1)p^{10}+2\chi,[p]P}^{(p^{12}-1)/r}$ is also developed in the same way of Eq.(51b). Then,

$$f_{(t-1)^2,P}(Q)^{(p^{12}-1)/r} = \{\hat{f}_{\chi,P}(Q) \cdot A\}^{(p^{12}-1)/r}, \tag{52a}$$

where

$$A = (f_{p^6,P}^{p^{10}} \cdot f_{p^{10},P}^{2\chi+p^6})^{p} \cdot f_{p^6,[p]P}^{p^{10}} \cdot f_{p^{10},[p]P}^{2\chi+p^6} \cdot f_{r,P}(Q)^{2cp} \tag{52b}$$

and

$$\hat{f}_{\chi,P}(Q) = \{ (f_{2\chi,P} \cdot g_{[2\chi]P,[p^6]P})^{p^{10}} \cdot f_{2\chi,P} \cdot g_{[(2\chi+p^6)p^{10}]P,[2\chi]P} \}^{p}$$

$$\cdot (f_{2\chi,[p]P} \cdot g_{[2\chi p]P,[p^6 p]P})^{p^{10}} \cdot f_{2\chi,[p]P} \cdot g_{[(2\chi+p^6)p^{10}p]P,[2\chi p]P}. \tag{52c}$$

In Eq.(52b), $f_{(t-1)^2,P}^{(p^{12}-1)/r}$ is the original *twisted* Ate pairing and $f_{r,P}^{(p^{12}-1)/r}$ is Tate pairing. In addition, $f_{p^e,P}^{(p^{12}-1)/r}$ has a bilinearity that is shown in the same of Appendix A in [24] with Eq.(21). Thus, based on these bilinearities, the right–hand side of the following equation gives a bilinear map.

$$\hat{f}_{\chi,P}(Q)^{(p^{12}-1)/r} = \{f_{(t-1)^2,P}(Q) \cdot A^{-1}\}^{(p^{12}-1)/r}. \tag{53}$$

In the same way of Xate pairing [24], according to Eqs.(51), the non–degeneracy of the proposed *twisted* Ate pairing is given by combining those of *twisted* Ate, Tate pairings [21], and $f_{p^e,P}(Q)^{(p^k-1)/r}$.

B Calculation Flow of the Proposed *twisted* Ate Pairing with BN Curve and *thread computing*

In the case of BN curve, the calculation flows of Miller's algorithm for the proposed *twisted* Ate pairing with *thread computing* on two cores are shown in Fig.1.

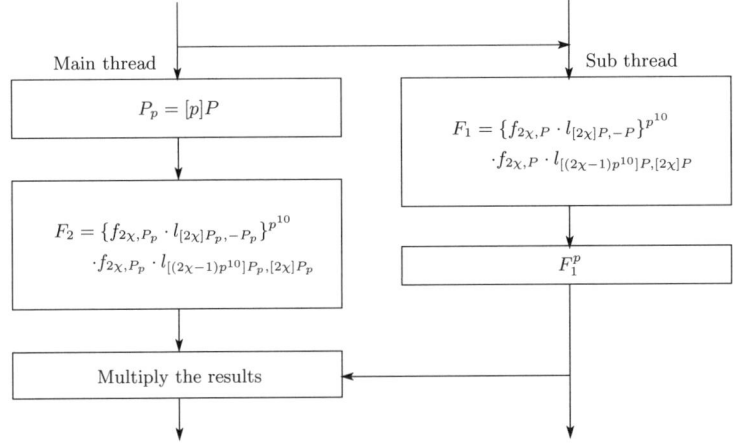

Fig. 1. Calculation flow of the proposed method with BN curves and *thread computing*

C Twisted R–Ate Pairing with *thread computing*

The proposed techniques are applicable to *twisted* R–ate pairing. Precomputing a rational point $[\chi]P$, *twisted* R–ate pairing becomes as

$$\begin{aligned}
R(P,Q) &= \{f_{2\chi+1,P}^{p^{10}} \cdot f_{6\chi^2+4\chi,P} \cdot g_{[2\chi+1]p^{10}P,[6\chi^2+4\chi]P}\}^{(p^{12}-1)/r} \\
&= \{f_{2\chi,P}^{p^{10}} \cdot g_{[2\chi]P,P}^{p^{10}} \cdot f_{\chi,P}^{6\chi} \cdot f_{6\chi,[\chi]P} \cdot f_{4\chi,P} \\
&\quad \cdot g_{[6\chi^2]P,[4\chi]P} \cdot g_{[2\chi+1]p^{10}P,[6\chi^2+4\chi]P}\}^{(p^{12}-1)/r} \\
&= \{f_{2\chi,P}^{p^{10}} \cdot f_{\chi,P}^{1+p+p^3+p^{10}} \cdot f_{4\chi,P} \cdot f_{6\chi,[\chi]P} \cdot g_{[2\chi]P,P}^{p^{10}} \\
&\quad \cdot g_{[6\chi^2]P,[4\chi]P} \cdot g_{[2\chi+1]p^{10}P,[6\chi^2+4\chi]P}\}^{(p^{12}-1)/r}, \tag{54}
\end{aligned}$$

where $6\chi = 1 + p + p^3 + p^{10} \bmod r$. Let F_1 and F_2 be

$$F_1 = f_{\chi,P}, \tag{55a}$$
$$F_2 = f_{6\chi,[\chi]P}, \tag{55b}$$

Eq.(54) becomes as

$$\begin{aligned}
R(P,Q) = &\{F_1^{2p^{10}} \cdot g_{P,P}^{p^{10}} \cdot F_1^{1+p+p^3+p^{10}} \cdot F_1^4 \cdot g_{P,P} \cdot g_{[2]P,[2]P} \cdot F_2 \cdot g_{[2\chi]P,P}^{p^{10}} \\
&\cdot g_{[6\chi^2]P,[4\chi]P} \cdot g_{[2\chi+1]p^{10}P,[6\chi^2+4\chi]P}\}^{(p^{12}-1)/r}, \\
= &\{F_1^{5+p+p^3+3p^{10}} \cdot F_2 \cdot g_{P,P}^{(p^{10}+1)} \cdot g_{[2]P,[2]P} \cdot g_{[2\chi]P,P}^{p^{10}} \\
&\cdot g_{[6\chi^2]P,[4\chi]P} \cdot g_{[2\chi+1]p^{10}P,[6\chi^2+4\chi]P}\}^{(p^{12}-1)/r}.
\end{aligned} \tag{56}$$

According to Eq.(56), the calculations of F_1 and F_2 are independent for which $[\chi]P$ needs to be precomputed. For this calculation, *thread computing* with two calculation cores is efficiently applied. Then, the calculation time of the Miller's part will become about two times faster.

On the other hand, *multi–pairing* technique can be also applied to the *twisted R*–ate pairing. In this case, $R(P,Q)$ is given by

$$R(P,Q) = \left(F_1^{5+p+p^3+3p^{10}} \cdot F_2\right)^{(p^{12}-1)/r}. \tag{57}$$

Therefore, since the exponent of F_1 is not simple, *multi–pairing* technique will not efficiently work as the proposed *twisted* Ate pairing with *multi–pairing*.

Factoring Unbalanced Moduli with Known Bits

Eric Brier[1], David Naccache[2], and Mehdi Tibouchi[1,2]

[1] Ingenico
1, rue Claude Chappe, BP 346, F-07503 Guilherand-Granges, France
eric.brier@ingenico.com
[2] École normale supérieure
Équipe de cryptographie, 45 rue d'Ulm, F-75230 Paris CEDEX 05, France
{david.naccache,mehdi.tibouchi}@ens.fr

Abstract. Let $n = pq > q^3$ be an RSA modulus. This note describes a LLL-based method allowing to factor n given $2 \log_2 q$ contiguous bits of p, irrespective to their position. A second method is presented, which needs fewer bits but whose length depends on the position of the known bit pattern. Finally, we introduce a somewhat surprising *ad hoc* method where two different known bit chunks, totalling $\frac{3}{2} \log_2 q$ bits suffice to factor n.

The technique underlines the danger of using unbalanced moduli on leaky hardware implementations.

1 Introduction

The problem of factoring using partial information was introduced by Rivest and Shamir [11] in 1986. Factoring using partial information relates both to the (very theoretical) *oracle complexity* of factoring and to the (very practical) *side channel* analysis of public-key implementations.

In most past works [11,5,6,7,12] the attacker knows some of the bits of one of the factors, usually the most significant bits (MSBs) or chunks of bits spread over one of the factors [8]. In other settings (*e.g.* [9]), the opponent is given access to an oracles answering yes/no questions. Recently, May and Ritzenhofen considered the factoring of integers whose factors feature a common, yet unknown, bit-pattern [10]. Finally, [3] tackles the factorization of numbers of the form $p^r q$.

In this note we show that for unbalanced RSA moduli $n = pq > q^3$ (as considered for example in [13], see figure 1), one can factor n given $2 \log_2 q$ contiguous bits of p. The technique is interesting because it does not appear to relate directly to other LLL-based results. Furthermore, the amount of bits to be known does not depend on the size of n but rather of the size of its smaller factor q.

Conventions: Throughout this paper, capital letters will denote the bit-size of lowercase variables. In addition, we will illustrate the different factoring techniques using black rectangles for known (given) bit blocs and white rectangles for unknown bit blocks.

D. Lee and S. Hong (Eds.): ICISC 2009, LNCS 5984, pp. 65–72, 2010.

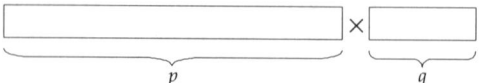

Fig. 1. The factoring problem: Hard

2   An Initial Observation

Factoring given $p' = p \bmod 2^Q$, the Q least significant bits (LSBs) of p, is trivial:

$$\frac{n}{p'} \bmod 2^Q = q \bmod 2^Q = q$$

Similarly, it is trivial to factor given the Q most significant bits (MSBs) of p by Euclidean division.

Fig. 2. Factoring knowing the Q LSBs (or MSBs) of p: Easy

It is easy to observe that factoring unbalanced moduli is also easy when p presents a pattern of Q zeros at positions $[2Q - 1, Q]$.

If p is of the form $p = u2^{2Q} + y$ where $Y \le Q$ then:

$$\gcd\left(n, n \bmod 2^{2Q}\right) = \gcd\left(pq, yq \bmod 2^{2Q}\right) = \gcd\left(pq, yq\right) = q$$

Fig. 3. Factoring knowing that bits $[2Q - 1, Q]$ of p are zeros: Easy

The previous equation $p = u2^{2Q} + y$ is a particular case of the general form $p = u2^{W+L} + v2^W + y$ where v is a known L-bit pattern. Given v and setting $a = v2^W$, $b = n \bmod 2^{W+L}$ and $q = x$, factoring n boils down to solving the equation:

$$b = x(a + y) \bmod 2^{W+L} \tag{1}$$

for $\{x, y\}$, with x of size Q and y of size W. The two following sections focus on solving this equation.

3   Applying Lattice Reduction

The most straightforward approach to solve equation (1) is to set $z = xy$. The new variable z being of size $Q + W$. The equation becomes:

$$b = ax + z \bmod 2^{W+L}$$

which is a bivariate linear modular equation. In [6], Coppersmith gives an LLL-based heuristic algorithm, to solve such equations when the sum of the sizes of variables is less than the modulus divided by the equation's degree. In our case, this means that:

$$Q + (Q + W) < W + L$$

The solution is thus found as soon as $L > 2Q$. This means that n can be factored as soon as $2Q$ contiguous bits of p are known, no matter where their position is (figure 4).

Fig. 4. Factoring given any $2Q$-bit block of p: Easy

4   Using Fewer Bits

We also notice that this equation is very similar to Boneh and Durfee's *Small Inverse Problem* (section 4 of [4]). This problem amounts to solving the equation:

$$1 = x(a + y) \bmod e.$$

Replacing 1 by an arbitrary integer b does not change anything in the algorithm's analysis, since the diagonal of the triangular basis of the lattice used to solve the equation is independent of b.

The main difference is that [4] handles only the case $2Y = E$, which is not necessarily the case in our setting.

We will focus on solving $b = x(a + y) \bmod e$ for $\{x, y\}$ with $X = e^{\delta}$ and $Y = e^{\alpha}$. The lattice is built as in section 4 of [4] but the choice of the optimizing parameter t will differ.

For convenience, we set $t := \tau m$. In the inequality $\det(L) < e^{mw}$, we consider only dominant terms, *i.e.* terms in m^3, we get the inequality:

$$3\alpha\tau^2 + 3(\alpha + \delta - 1)\tau + \alpha + 2\delta - 1 < 0.$$

Solutions to this inequality exist if and only if the discriminant of the quadratic equation in τ is positive. The condition on α and δ is:

$$3\delta^2 - \alpha^2 - 2\alpha\delta - 6\delta - 2\alpha + 3 > 0.$$

This result is of independent interest, generalizing [4].

In our initial problem, the parameters are as follows:

$$e = 2^{W+L}, \quad \delta = \frac{Q}{W+L}, \quad \text{and} \quad \alpha = \frac{W}{W+L}.$$

Then, the length L of the known bit pattern must satisfy

$$3L^2 + (4W - 6Q)L + 3Q^2 - 8QW > 0.$$

This quadratic admits two solutions, the smaller of which corresponds to parameters $\delta > 1$, which makes no sense. Taking the larger solution into account, the final result is:

$$L > Q + \frac{2}{3}(\sqrt{W^2 + 3QW} - W).$$

In other words, as the position of the known bit block slides from the LSBs to the MSBs (i.e. when W increases from 0 to ∞), the amount of known bits increases from Q to $2Q$ (figure 7).

This method is always better than the one presented in section 3. Furthermore, since the equation solved in this case is of Boneh-Durfee type, the results of Bauer and Joux [1,2] ensure that the algorithm provably terminates if the given bound is satisfied (contrary to more general, heuristic variants of Coppersmith's algorithm).

Fig. 5. Factoring given progressively bigger chunks of p: Easy

5   *Ad Hoc* Configurations

In addition to the previously presented techniques, it appears possible to obtain better results in a number of specific cases. We illustrate two such instances in this section.

5.1   Disjoint LSB Blocks

We first turn our attention to the case, very similar to the observation in the introduction, where we know a pattern of Q bits in the prime factor p starting from the Q-th bit. As per the previous section's results, this is not enough since we would need $5Q/3$ bits to factor. Thus, we suppose that we also know the L LSBs of p. Evidently, we can now get the L LSBs of q as well by division modulo 2^L. In other words, we have the following representation of the factors:

$$p = u2^{Q+L} + v2^Q + y2^L + w$$
$$q = x2^L + w',$$

where v, w and w' are known and $ww' = n \bmod 2^L$.

Expand the equation $pq = n$ and reduce it modulo 2^{2Q}. Obviously, one can factor 2^L since we properly selected w'. We get a quadratic bivariate equation in the variables x and y. The variables are of size 2^{Q-L} and the equation must be satisfied modulo 2^{2Q-L}. Note that the only quadratic term is $xy2^L$, hence the equation becomes linear modulo 2^L (and easy to solve). We use lattice reduction techniques to present the general solution under the form:

$$x = x_0 + rx_1 + sx_2$$
$$y = y_0 + ry_1 + sy_2,$$

where r and s are unknown integers. The linear equation is to be understood modulo 2^L and thus the numbers x_i and y_i can be chosen of approximate size $2^{L/2}$. Since x and y are of size 2^{Q-L}, we infer that r and s are of size $2^{Q-3L/2}$. We now plug the parameterizations of x and y into our original equation and get a quadratic equation in the variables r and s. It is clear that we can factor 2^L and get an equation modulo 2^{2Q-2L}. Again, we use Coppersmith's algorithm for bivariate equations to compute r and s. For this to be possible, the sum of the sizes of the variables must be less than half the modulus size:

$$2(Q - \frac{3L}{2}) \le Q - L,$$

which is easily transformed into $Q \ge 2L$. From the values of r and s, we get back to the values of x and y and subsequently find q.

All in all, if we know a pattern of Q bits of p in the range $[2Q - 1, Q]$ and the $Q/2$ LSBs of p (or q), we can factor n in polynomial time (figure 6). Note that the number of bits needed in this section is less than the number claimed by the previous section. This stems from the fact that p's LSBs of p leak direct knowledge on q's LSBs.

5.2   Particular n Formats

We now adapt to our purpose the finer analysis of [4], section 5 (instead of section 4). For the sake of conciseness, we adopt the terminology and notational

Fig. 6. Factoring given bits $[2Q - 1, Q]$ and $[Q/2, 0]$ of p: Easy

conventions introduced in that paper, to which we refer the reader. Consider again:

$$b = x(a + y) \bmod e$$

with $|x| \leq X = e^{\delta}$ and $|y| \leq Y = e^{\alpha}$, where α and δ are such that $\alpha + \delta < 1$.

Unfortunately, in general, the resulting matrix M_y of y-shifts is not geometrically progressive in Boneh-Durfee's sense.

However, M_y does become geometrically progressive if we further assume that $|b| \leq e^r$ for some constant $r \in \mathbb{R}$ satisfying:

$$0 < r < \alpha + \delta \quad \text{and} \quad r < 2 - \frac{1 - \delta}{\alpha}$$

The implications of this assumption will be examined at the end of this section.

We can readily verify that, under this additional assumption, M_y is geometrically progressive with parameters $(4^m, e, m, \alpha + \delta - r, \alpha - 1, r - 1, 1, (1 - r)/(\alpha + \delta - r))$.

Setting the parameter t to $(1 - \alpha - \delta)m/\alpha$, we find that $\det(L_1)e^{-mw} = e^{u(m)}$ with

$$u(m) = \left[2 + \alpha + 2\delta + \frac{1}{\alpha}(1 - \alpha - \delta)(2 + \alpha + \delta) \right] \frac{m^3}{6} - \frac{1 - \delta}{2\alpha} m^3 + o(m^3)$$

$$= \left(\alpha - (1 - \delta)^2 \right) \frac{m^3}{6\alpha} + o(m^3)$$

It follows that lattice reduction can be applied for large enough m as soon as:

$$(1 - \delta)^2 > \alpha$$

This result may, yet again, be of independent interest.

Returning to our particular setting in which

$$e = 2^{W+L}, \quad \delta = \frac{Q}{W + L}, \quad \text{and} \quad \alpha = \frac{W}{W + L}$$

we see that the length L must satisfy $(L + W - Q)^2 > W(L + W)$, which gives the following bound:

$$L > Q + \frac{1}{2}(\sqrt{W^2 + 4QW} - W)$$

Although this bound also increases from Q to $2Q$ as W grows, it is always (slightly) tighter than the bound obtained it section 4. To assess the best possible improvement we denote $W = \lambda Q$ and seek to maximize:

$$f(\lambda) = \frac{2}{3}(\sqrt{\lambda^2 + 3\lambda} - \lambda) - \frac{1}{2}(\sqrt{\lambda^2 + 4\lambda} - \lambda)$$

We have $f'(\lambda_0) = 0$ for $\lambda_0 \approx 0.716$, the positive root of the polynomial $\lambda^4 + 7\lambda^3 + 12\lambda^2 - 9$ corresponding to a maximal gain of $f(\lambda_0) \approx 0.049$.[1]

However, this 5% improvement is only obtained under a very costly assumption: the condition on b implies that n has pattern of $Q + L/W$ zero bits before position $W + L$. Note that:

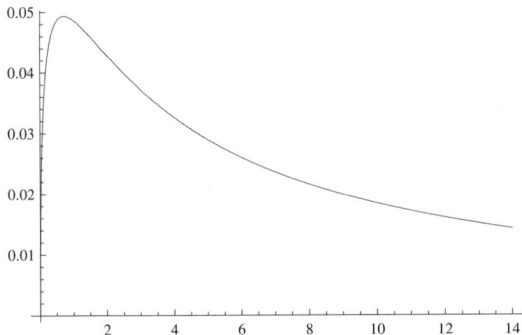

Fig. 7. A plot of $f(\lambda)$. Note that $\lim_{\lambda \to \infty} f(\lambda) = 0$

The technique will therefore only apply to n values having this special form.

6   Conclusion

This paper showed that the knowledge of a pattern of contiguous bits in the larger factor of an unbalanced modulus is sufficient to factor as soon as the length of this pattern is twice the size of the smaller factor.

A deeper analysis showed that fewer bits are required, depending on the known bit-chunk's position.

The existence of a variety of *ad hoc* configurations, of which we gave two examples seems to indicate that a systematic exploration of topic is an interesting further research direction.

Acknowledgements

We would like to thank anonymous referees for helpful comments and suggestions.

---

[1] E.g. for $Q = 400$ bits the attack requires ≈ 20 fewer bits.

References

1. Bauer, A.: Toward a rigorous generalization of Coppersmith's methods for finding small roots of multivariate polynomial equations, Ph.D. thesis, Université de Versailles Saint-Quentin (September 2008)
2. Bauer, A., Joux, A.: Toward a rigorous variation of Coppersmith's algorithm on three variables. In: Naor, M. (ed.) EUROCRYPT 2007. LNCS, vol. 4515, pp. 361–378. Springer, Heidelberg (2007)
3. Boneh, D., Durfee, G., Howgrave-Graham, N.: Factoring $N = p^r q$ for large r. In: Wiener, M. (ed.) CRYPTO 1999. LNCS, vol. 1666, pp. 326–337. Springer, Heidelberg (1999)
4. Boneh, D., Durfee, G.: Cryptanalysis of RSA with private key d less than $n^{0.292}$. IEEE Transactions on Information Theory 46, 1339–1349 (1999)
5. Coppersmith, D.: Factoring with a hint, IBM Research Report RC 19905 (1995)
6. Coppersmith, D.: Finding a small root of a univariate modular equation. In: Maurer, U.M. (ed.) EUROCRYPT 1996. LNCS, vol. 1070, pp. 155–165. Springer, Heidelberg (1996)
7. Crépeau, C., Slakmon, A.: Simple backdoors for RSA key generation. In: Joye, M. (ed.) CT-RSA 2003. LNCS, vol. 2612, pp. 403–416. Springer, Heidelberg (2003)
8. Herrmann, M., May, A.: Solving linear equations modulo divisors: On factoring given any bits. In: Pieprzyk, J. (ed.) ASIACRYPT 2008. LNCS, vol. 5350, pp. 406–424. Springer, Heidelberg (2008)
9. Maurer, U.: Factoring with an Oracle. In: Rueppel, R.A. (ed.) EUROCRYPT 1992. LNCS, vol. 658, pp. 429–436. Springer, Heidelberg (1993)
10. May, A., Ritzenhofen, M.: Implicit Factoring: On polynomial time factoring given only an implicit hint. In: Jarecki, S., Tsudik, G. (eds.) PKC 2009. LNCS, vol. 5443, pp. 1–14. Springer, Heidelberg (2009)
11. Rivest, R., Shamir, A.: Efficient factoring based on partial information. In: Pichler, F. (ed.) EUROCRYPT 1985. LNCS, vol. 219, pp. 31–34. Springer, Heidelberg (1986)
12. Santoso, B., Kunihiro, N., Kanayama, N., Ohta, K.: Factorization of square-free integers with high bits known. In: Nguyên, P.Q. (ed.) VIETCRYPT 2006. LNCS, vol. 4341, pp. 115–130. Springer, Heidelberg (2006)
13. Shamir, A.: RSA for paranoids. RSA Laboratories CryptoBytes 1(3), 1–4 (1990)

Algebraic Cryptanalysis of SMS4: Gröbner Basis Attack and SAT Attack Compared

Jeremy Erickson[1], Jintai Ding[2,3], and Chris Christensen[4]

[1] The University of North Carolina at Chapel Hill, Chapel Hill, NC 27514
jerickso@cs.unc.edu*
[2] The University of Cincinnati, Cincinnati, OH 45221
jintai.ding@uc.edu
[3] South China University of Technology, Guangzhou, China
[4] Northern Kentucky University, Highland Heights, KY 41099
christensen@nku.edu

Abstract. The SMS4 block cipher is part of the Chinese WAPI wireless standard. This paper describes the specification and offers a specification for a toy version called simplified SMS4 (S-SMS4). We explore algebraic attacks on SMS4 and S-SMS4 using Gröbner basis attacks on equation systems over GF(2) and GF(2^8), as well as attacks using a SAT solver derived from the GF(2) model. A comparison of SAT and Gröbner basis attacks is provided.

1 Introduction

Algebraic cryptanalysis is a relatively new field of cryptology. The basic idea is to model a cipher using a system of polynomial equations over a finite field. This approach has gained attention since Nicolas Courtois claimed that it could be used to attack AES, which has a simple algebraic structure [1]. This attack has also been attempted on other ciphers such as DES [2]. Algebraic cryptanalysis has been shown very effective for families of stream ciphers.

The SMS4 cipher was designed by the Chinese government as part of their WAPI standard for wireless networks. The best currently known attacks on SMS4 are the 14-round rectangle attack and 16-round impossible differential attack discussed by Jiqiang Lu in [3]. However, as shown in [4], SMS4 itself has a simple algebraic structure, similar to AES. Thus, we have attempted to attack it with algebraic attacks over GF(2). Wen Ji and Lei Hu have also attempted to attack SMS4 with an algebraic attack over both GF(2) and GF(2^8), as shown in [5] and [6], but their papers present only theoretical results, not any experimental results. We have found our experimental results contradictory to their analysis.

In this paper we present an attempt to attack SMS4 with algebraic attacks over GF(2), including several potential alterations. We also present preliminary

---

* Much of this work was done while Jeremy Erickson was an undergraduate at Taylor University, Upland, IN 46989.

D. Lee and S. Hong (Eds.): ICISC 2009, LNCS 5984, pp. 73–86, 2010.
© Springer-Verlag Berlin Heidelberg 2010

results of attacks based on $GF(2^8)$ as in [5]. Both types of attacks were implemented using the Magma computer algebra system ([7]), as well as using the MiniSAT boolean satisfiability solver in some cases. Preliminary results indicate that Magma is more effective than MiniSAT for the full cipher, while MiniSAT outperforms Magma in the simplified version of the cipher created for our experiments. No effective guess-and-determine attack strategy was found, but some preliminary results were determined. We found evidence that the results in [5] and [6] are very inaccurate. This casts serious doubt about the their theoretical analysis and the previous analysis they relied on.

This paper begins with a description of the SMS4 algorithm itself, including a description of the simplified variant. We also describe implementation details for the attack itself, as well as experimental results. At the end we discuss the implications of these results.

2   Structure of SMS4

SMS4 is an unbalanced Feistel cipher with a block size of 128 bits and a key size of 128 bits. Each block is divided into four 32-bit blocks, referred to as "words", which in turn consists of four 8-bit bytes. An English translation of the official specification is provided at [8]. We also describe the cipher here. There are several fundamental components to the cipher.

2.1   The SMS4 S-Box

The official definition of the SMS4 S-box is based on a table of values (See Table 1.)

However, as shown in [4], the S-box can also be represented as an affine transformation over $GF(2)$, followed by an inversion over $GF(2^8)$, followed by another affine transformation over $GF(2)$. The system is thus written as

$$s(x) = I(x \cdot A + C) \cdot A + C, \tag{1}$$

where I indicates inversion over $GF(2^8)$ (with the inverse of 0 defined as 0) and the necessary field conversion. The values are given as

$$A = \begin{bmatrix} 1\,1\,1\,0\,0\,1\,0\,1 \\ 1\,1\,1\,1\,0\,0\,1\,0 \\ 0\,1\,1\,1\,1\,0\,0\,1 \\ 1\,0\,1\,1\,1\,1\,0\,0 \\ 0\,1\,0\,1\,1\,1\,1\,0 \\ 0\,0\,1\,0\,1\,1\,1\,1 \\ 1\,0\,0\,1\,0\,1\,1\,1 \\ 1\,1\,0\,0\,1\,0\,1\,1 \end{bmatrix},$$

$$C = (1, 1, 0, 0, 1, 0, 1, 1).$$

To convert from $GF(2)$ to $GF(2^8)$, we use the irreducible polynomial

$$f(x) = x^8 + x^7 + x^6 + x^5 + x^4 + x^2 + 1$$

Table 1. The SMS4 S-box, with the first input nibble as the row index and the second as column index

	0	1	2	3	4	5	6	7	8	9	a	b	c	d	e	f
0	d6	90	e9	fe	cc	e1	3d	b7	16	b6	14	c2	28	fb	2c	05
1	2b	67	9a	76	2a	be	04	c3	aa	44	13	26	49	86	06	99
2	9c	42	50	f4	91	ef	98	7a	33	54	0b	43	ed	cf	ac	62
3	e4	b3	1c	a9	c9	08	e8	95	80	df	94	fa	75	8f	3f	a6
4	47	07	a7	fc	f3	73	17	ba	83	59	3c	19	e6	85	4f	a8
5	68	6b	81	b2	71	64	da	8b	f8	eb	0f	4b	70	56	9d	35
6	1e	24	0e	5e	63	58	d1	a2	25	22	7c	3b	01	21	78	87
7	d4	00	46	57	9f	d3	27	52	4c	36	02	e7	a0	c4	c8	9e
8	ea	bf	8a	d2	40	c7	38	b5	a3	f7	f2	ce	f9	61	15	a1
9	e0	ae	5d	a4	9b	34	1a	55	ad	93	32	30	f5	8c	b1	e3
a	1d	f6	e2	2e	82	66	ca	60	c0	29	23	ab	0d	53	4e	6f
b	d5	db	37	45	de	fd	8e	2f	03	ff	6a	72	6d	6c	5b	51
c	8d	1b	af	92	bb	dd	bc	7f	11	d9	5c	41	1f	10	5a	d8
d	0a	c1	31	88	a5	cd	7b	bd	2d	74	d0	12	b8	e5	b4	b0
e	89	69	97	4a	0c	96	77	7e	65	b9	f1	09	c5	6e	c6	84
f	18	f0	7d	ec	3a	dc	4d	20	79	ee	5f	3e	d7	cb	39	48

and let the first term represent the constant term in a polynomial of degree 7, the second term represent the x coefficient, etc.

However, calculation shows that these results do not match the table provided in the SMS4 specification without modification. If the input to and output from the S-box are each reversed, then the output is correct. Thus, we propose the alternate model of the S-box

$$s(x) = A_2 \cdot I(A_1 \cdot x + C_1) + C_2 \qquad (2)$$

with parameters

$$A_1 = \begin{bmatrix} 1 & 0 & 1 & 0 & 0 & 1 & 1 & 1 \\ 0 & 1 & 0 & 0 & 1 & 1 & 1 & 1 \\ 1 & 0 & 0 & 1 & 1 & 1 & 1 & 0 \\ 0 & 0 & 1 & 1 & 1 & 1 & 0 & 1 \\ 0 & 1 & 1 & 1 & 1 & 0 & 1 & 0 \\ 1 & 1 & 1 & 1 & 0 & 1 & 0 & 0 \\ 1 & 1 & 1 & 0 & 1 & 0 & 0 & 1 \\ 1 & 1 & 0 & 1 & 0 & 0 & 1 & 1 \end{bmatrix},$$

$$A_2 = \begin{bmatrix} 1 & 1 & 0 & 0 & 1 & 0 & 1 & 1 \\ 1 & 0 & 0 & 1 & 0 & 1 & 1 & 1 \\ 0 & 0 & 1 & 0 & 1 & 1 & 1 & 1 \\ 0 & 1 & 0 & 1 & 1 & 1 & 1 & 0 \\ 1 & 0 & 1 & 1 & 1 & 1 & 0 & 0 \\ 0 & 1 & 1 & 1 & 1 & 0 & 0 & 1 \\ 1 & 1 & 1 & 1 & 0 & 0 & 1 & 0 \\ 1 & 1 & 1 & 0 & 0 & 1 & 0 & 1 \end{bmatrix},$$

$$C_1 = (1, 1, 0, 0, 1, 0, 1, 1)^T,$$
$$C_2 = (1, 1, 0, 1, 0, 0, 1, 1)^T.$$

Compared to the original model, this model uses right multiplication, reverses the columns of A for A_1, reverses the rows of A for A_2, uses C^T for C_1 and reverses C_1 for C_2. This achieves reversing the input and output, compared to (1). Calculations reveal that this model matches the table.

When the S-box is used in SMS4, it is applied 4 times in parallel, to an entire word. Thus, $X \in GF(2)^{32}$ is split into $(x_1, x_2, x_3, x_4) \in (GF(2)^8)^4$, and

$$S(X) = (s(x_1), s(x_2), s(x_3), s(x_4)).$$

2.2 The Linear Diffusion Transformation

SMS4 uses two linear diffusion transformations, one for the round function and one for the key schedule. Here the notation $\lll$ represents circular left shifting. Each function operates on $x \in GF(2)^{32}$. For the round function, we use

$$L(x) = x \oplus (x \lll 2) \oplus (x \lll 10) \oplus (x \lll 18) \oplus (x \lll 24). \tag{3}$$

For the key schedule, we use

$$L'(x) = x \oplus (x \lll 13) \oplus (x \lll 23). \tag{4}$$

2.3 The SMS4 Key Schedule

We define a vector $(Y_i, Y_{i+1}, Y_{i+2}, Y_{i+3}) \in (GF(2)^{32})^4$ as the key schedule input to round i.

Denote the input key as (K_0, K_1, K_2, K_3). Then

$$Y_0 = K_0 \oplus 0xa3b1bac6,$$
$$Y_1 = K_1 \oplus 0x56aa3350,$$
$$Y_2 = K_2 \oplus 0x677d9197,$$
$$Y_3 = K_3 \oplus 0xb27022dc.$$

Also denote $CK_i = (ck_{i,0}, ck_{i,1}, ck_{i,2}, ck_{i,3}) \in (\mathbb{Z}_2^8)^4$ where $ck_{i,j} = 28i + 7j$ mod 256, represented in binary.

Then

$$RK_i = Y_{i+4} = Y_i \oplus L'(S(Y_{i+1} \oplus Y_{i+2} \oplus Y_{i+3} \oplus CK_i)). \tag{5}$$

2.4 The SMS4 Round Function

We define a vector $(X_i, X_{i+1}, X_{i+2}, X_{i+3}) \in (GF(2)^{32})^4$ as the input to round i, numbering the rounds from 0. Thus, (X_0, X_1, X_2, X_3) represents the plaintext. Then,

$$X_{i+4} = X_i \oplus L(S(X_{i+1} \oplus X_{i+2} \oplus X_{i+3} \oplus RK_i)). \tag{6}$$

The output of the last four rounds is reversed (at the word level) to generate the ciphertext. Thus, the ciphertext is $(X_{35}, X_{34}, X_{33}, X_{32})$.

3   Simplified SMS4

To provide for some basic exploration of the behavior of algebraic attacks over a larger number of rounds, as well as to provide a form of SMS4 that can be worked out by hand, we propose a simplified SMS4 algorithm, which will be referred to from here as S-SMS4.

The basic operations of S-SMS4 are identical to full SMS4, except that all operations on 128-bit blocks become operations on 32-bit blocks, operations on 32-bit words become operations on 8-bit "words", and operations on 8-bit bytes become operations on 4-bit nibbles.

3.1   The S-SMS4 S-Box

The S-box of SMS4 was designed from the description of the full SMS4 S-box in [4]. The new S-box is designed to transform a 4-bit vector to another 4-bit vector, but otherwise follows (1) plus reversing input and output. Thus, a smaller cyclic matrix is the basic A with its bottom row as the row vector for C. Thus,

$$A = \begin{bmatrix} 1\,1\,1\,0 \\ 0\,1\,1\,1 \\ 1\,0\,1\,1 \\ 1\,1\,0\,1 \end{bmatrix},$$

$$C = (1, 1, 0, 1).$$

Accounting for the reversal and using the form of (2), however, we derive the following matrices in a similar manner:

$$A_1 = \begin{bmatrix} 0\,1\,1\,1 \\ 1\,1\,1\,0 \\ 1\,1\,0\,1 \\ 1\,0\,1\,1 \end{bmatrix},$$

$$A_2 = \begin{bmatrix} 1\,1\,0\,1 \\ 1\,0\,1\,1 \\ 0\,1\,1\,1 \\ 1\,1\,1\,0 \end{bmatrix},$$

$$C_1 = (1, 1, 0, 1)^T,$$

$$C_2 = (1, 0, 1, 1)^T.$$

The inversion step is similar to full SMS4, except that we use $\mathrm{GF}(2^4)$ with an irreducible polynomial of

$$f(x) = x^4 + x^3 + x^2 + x + 1.$$

This S-box can also be written as a table, see Table 2.

Table 2. S-SMS4 S-box, in the same form as Table 1

	00	01	10	11
00	1001	0001	1011	0010
01	1111	0110	1000	1101
10	0111	1100	0011	1110
11	0100	0000	1010	0101

Because the S-SMS4 S-box only accepts one byte as input, which is two nibbles, we split $X \in (GF(2))^8$ into $(x_1, x_2) \in (GF(2)^4)^2$ and write:

$$S(X) = (s(x_1), s(x_2)).$$

These parameters were chosen in attempt to model the properties of the full SMS4 S-box, providing a small field size over which inversion remains non-trivial. The A matrix is simply a cyclic matrix with the same first row as the beginning of the first row in full SMS4. This first row seemed as appropriate as any.

3.2 The S-SMS4 Linear Diffusion Transformation

S-SMS4, like full SMS4, uses two linear diffusion transformations. Each function operates on $x \in GF(2)^8$. For the round function,

$$L(x) = x \oplus (x \lll 2) \oplus (x \lll 6). \tag{7}$$

For the key schedule,

$$L'(x) = x \oplus (x \lll 3) \oplus (x \lll 5). \tag{8}$$

The specific parameters in these equations are fairly arbitrary; the attack could be generalized to use different numbers. We attempted to attain the essence of the full SMS4 transformations. In $L(x)$, the parameters have a GCF of 2, as in full SMS4. In $L'(x)$, the factors are prime numbers, as in full SMS4. The longer length of $L(x)$ could not be effectively preserved, due to the smaller vectors.

3.3 The S-SMS4 Key Schedule

The key schedule for S-SMS4 is analogous to full SMS4, except that we must use shorter initial keys and CK values. The initial keys are as follows:

$$Y_0 = K_0 \oplus 0xa3,$$

$$Y_1 = K_1 \oplus 0xb1,$$

$$Y_2 = K_2 \oplus 0xba,$$

$$Y_3 = K_3 \oplus 0xc6.$$

This initialization vector is simply the beginning of the full SMS4 initialization vector; however, the specific numbers cannot alter the difficulty of breaking the cipher. We could always solve the equations with any initialization vector (including 0) and then adjust the results at the end by adding the appropriate constant.

Denote $CK_i = (ck_{i,0}, ck_{i,1}) \in (\mathbb{Z}_2^4)^2$ where $ck_{i,j} = 11i + 3j \mod 16$, represented in binary. Then (5) holds. Note that we could have written $ck_{i,j} = si + tj \mod 16$ with other values of s and t; our choice was arbitrary. However, this choice will hopefully generate similar mixing. In the original cipher $s = 4t$, but both s and t are much smaller than 256, so no directly analogous relationship exists.

3.4   The S-SMS4 Round Function

With the notations in this section, (6) holds for simplified SMS4. We denote S-SMS4 to have eight rounds, thus the ciphertext is $(X_{11}, X_{10}, X_9, X_8)$.

4   Gröbner Basis and SAT Solver Attacks over GF(2)

The primary attempt to attack SMS4 in this paper is based on solving a system of equations over GF(2). The equations are divided into two groups, one representing the key schedule for the entire cipher, and one with a representation of the round function process for each plaintext/ciphertext pair. The Magma code is written in such a way that full and simplified SMS4 can easily be compared by changing which predefined functions are loaded.

4.1   Modelling the Key Schedule

The key schedule is modelled separately from the rounds, because it only needs to be modelled once for any key to be broken, even if there is more than one plaintext/ciphertext pair. The following system of equations is used for each round r (indexed starting from 0) and byte (full)/nibble (simplified) index i (also indexed from 0). The model of the S-box inversion is excluded, as the system was tested using several representations. The real system has a set of equations indicating that $ZK_{r,i}$ and $WK_{r,i}$ correspond to inverses in $\mathrm{GF}(2^8)$ or $\mathrm{GF}(2^4)$. (These equations are derived from $XY - X = 0$ and $YX - Y = 0$, so that they work correctly when inverting zero).

A single subscript (e.g. BK_r) indicates a word in $\mathrm{GF}(2)^{32}$ or $\mathrm{GF}(2)^8$, and a double subscript (e.g. $BK_{r,i}$) indicates a byte or nibble within the word.

$$BK_r = Y_{r+1} \oplus Y_{r+2} \oplus Y_{r+3} \oplus CK_r,$$
$$ZK_{r,i} = A_1 \cdot BK_{r,i} \oplus C_1,$$
$$DK_{r,i} = A_2 \cdot WK_{r,i} \oplus C_2,$$
$$EK_r = L'(DK_r),$$

$$Y_{r+4} = Y_r \oplus EK_r.$$

When this system of equations is actually implemented in Magma, each variable in GF(2) (with the exception of WK variables) has its own equation. Vectors are used here for simplicity of explanation.

This system shows intermediate variables for every step of the operation. In practice, faster times were obtained by combining several linear steps (by substituting the expression from the previous result rather than variables.) The best times were obtained using intermediate variables for DK and Y variables, substituting in expressions in all other cases.

4.2   Modelling the Round Function

The model for the round function is similar to the model of the key schedule. However, there is now a separate equation for each plaintext/ciphertext pair p. Thus, in this case, a double subscript indicates a word and a triple subscript indicates a nibble or byte. As in the case of the key schedule, the model also has a set of equations indicating that $Z_{p,r,i}$ and $W_{p,r,i}$ correspond to inverses in the appropriate extension field.

$$B_{p,r} = X_{p,r+1} \oplus X_{p,r+2} \oplus X_{p,r+3} \oplus Y_{r+4},$$

$$Z_{p,r,i} = A_1 \cdot B_{p,r,i} \oplus C_1,$$

$$D_{p,r,i} = A_2 \cdot W_{p,r,i} \oplus C_2,$$

$$E_{p,r} = L(D_{p,r}),$$

$$X_{p,r+4} = X_{p,r} \oplus E_{p,r}.$$

As with the key schedule, when this system is actually implemented in Magma, each variable in GF(2) (with the exception of W variables) has its own equation.

Also as with the key schedule, fewer intermediates are actually needed to solve the system. Only the X variables were left as intermediates in the final representation, and inverses of the last three equations were used so that we could still use the implicit representation of inversion.

4.3   SAT Solver Attacks

In addition to Gröbner Basis attacks, some attacks over GF(2) were also attempted using MiniSAT. To convert the polynomials generated by Magma into the proper input form, we wrote a Perl script using the method of [9]. Our conversion system did not attempt to reorder or rewrite the equations to change the random seed, and we used a cutting size of 6 as the paper suggested. The script allowed us to convert our equations to MiniSAT format, run the MiniSAT solver, and verify that the solution contained the correct key.

5   Results of GF(2)-Based Attacks

These attacks were tested on an Intel®Xeon®dual-core CPU running at 2.00 GHz. The system had 32 GB of RAM and ran 64-bit CentOS 5. Magma 2.15-10 and MiniSAT 2.0 were used.

For small numbers of rounds, we tested Magma and MiniSAT both with the same systems of equations. We discovered that SAT solvers did not finish within several hours. However, we have previous test data from the system with more intermediate variables running on a Core^{TM}2 Duo system running at 2.40 GHz with 16 GB of RAM, running Ubuntu 8.0.4.1. These systems actually had fewer intermediate variables when converted into SAT form, due to the intermediate variables created converting long sums into SAT. All tests were done using two plaintext/ciphertext pairs, which experiments demonstrated to be clearly optimal for Magma. Results are in Table 3 and graphed in Fig. 1.

Table 3. Typical test results

	Magma		MiniSAT	
Rounds	Time (s)	Mem (MB)	Time (s)	Mem (MB)
SMS4				
4	2.370	100.20	235.575	70.74
5	7.720	207.68	>6000	-
S-SMS4				
4	0.030	8.86	0.032002	16.28
5	0.070	10.66	0.100006	17.07
6	11.650	128.15	0.364022	18.36
7	81.780	555.34	6.044380	24.33

5.1   Magma vs. SAT Solver

The results for S-SMS4 seemed to indicate that the SAT solver could provide a more efficient solution, but this was not true for full SMS4. Also, as verified in several tests, the SAT solver did not finish within 100 minutes with 5 rounds of SMS4. Thus, Magma holds more promise for real attacks on SMS4. We believe that the most likely explanation for this result is that while SAT works primarily through guessing, which is effective when there are a small number of variables, F4 works through structured algebraic methods, which have higher initial cost but are better amortized by larger, more complicated sets of equations.

The computational complexity of the operations on full SMS4 cannot reliably be determined from two data points. However, our hope is that the data from simplified SMS4 is representative of the asymptotic complexity. The complexity of the F4 attack seems to be exponential, with a large jump between 5 and 6 rounds of the cipher. For four rounds we expect the result to be obtained quickly, because the entire state vector X is known. It seems that the gap in the state vector becomes large enough to be highly significant when we reach

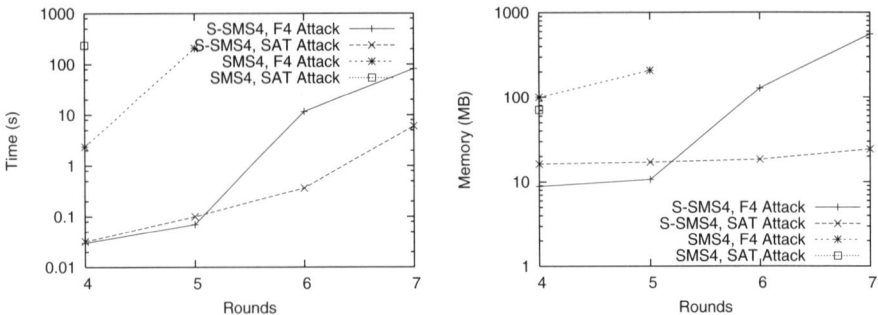

Fig. 1. Typical test results

6 rounds. This is likely the reason that full SMS4 could not be broken for 6 or more rounds on our system. The complexity of the SAT attack seems to be more directly exponential, without the significant gap.

6   Guess-and-Determine Attack

A common technique for algebraic cryptanalysis is to guess some of the variables, and then using algebraic cryptanalysis to solve others. If guessing n variables reduces runtime by a factor greater than 2^n, then the attack can save time, provided that an incorrect guess solves as quickly as a correct guess.

In order to test the guess-and-determine attack on SMS4, we decided to use 7 rounds of simplified SMS4. Using 6 or more rounds of full SMS4 would have been more ideal, but we were not able to break this many rounds in a reasonable amount of time for the tests. Table 4 in the appendix provides results from guess attacks.

As might be expected, no significant benefit was gained from guessing any single bit. Even testing guessing with multiple bits, no attempt at guessing n bits gained an improvement factor of greater than 2^n in either time or memory. However, there were appreciable differences between guessing different values. It appears that guessing the first and/or last round keys achieve the most significant speedup.

From this data, no evidence indicates that guess-and-determine attacks can be effective against SMS4. However, the behavior may be different for significant numbers of rounds in the full cipher. For these systems, these tests indicate that guessing from the first and last round keys probably offers the most promise.

7   GF(2^8) Attacks

Using the method of [4], which was repeated in [5], we wrote a Magma program to test the attack over GF(2^8). As discussed in [10], [11], and [12], XSL would not be expected to outperform a good Gröbner basis algorithm such as F4. Thus, Magma's builtin F4 algorithm is used, rather than XSL. The equation system from [5] is used almost unaltered. However, there is an off-by-one error in their indexing of all X variables (resulting in the use of X_{-1} in the first round), and their model of the S-box is taken from [4] unaltered and does not take reversal into account. Thus, we increased the index of the X variables by one and utilized our corrected S-box model from section 2.1. This resulted in a system that produced correct results for 4 rounds. Performance was consistent with a GF(2) system tested without the field equations, but with all intermediate variables, which is significantly slower than the GF(2) system with field equations or with fewer intermediate variables. Runtimes were consistently between 240 and 250 seconds, and using 283.53MB of RAM each time. Because this attack used only one plaintext/ciphertext pair, and it has a time measurement between the values for one and two pairs with the similar GF(2) attack (187.120 and 325.910 s, respectively, when the field equations are removed), with similar results for memory, the $GF(2^8)$ attack seems to have similar efficiency to the GF(2) attack with all intermediate variables, at least for four rounds. However, upon testing with more rounds on our system, Magma runs out of memory. This likely indicates that the complexity increase from increasing the number of rounds greatly exceeds what is predicted in [5]. We also see that their complexity prediction of 2^{59} for the attack on four rounds is far too high, which also demonstrates a flaw in their model. Thus, experiments contradict their predictions. However, to determine the actual behavior of the system for larger numbers of rounds, further experimentation on a system with more RAM is necessary.

The authors of [5] have updated their analysis in [6], including adding an analysis of SMS4 over GF(2). Their complexity prediction of 2^{90} for the four round attack over $GF(2^8)$ is even higher, and their estimates for GF(2) attacks at 4 rounds (2^{102}) and 5 rounds (2^{121}) show drastically higher complexity, and higher increase in complexity, than we observed in our experiments. Also, unlike their claim, the growth does appear from our experiments to be exponential for simplified SMS4, so we suspect it is indeed exponential for full SMS4 over GF(2). Thus, the equations used to analyze the behavior of XL seem not to line up with the actual running time of the faster F4 algorithm at all.

8   Conclusion and Discussion

At this point, we have not demonstrated any practical attack on SMS4 which has great promise of efficiency for the full cipher. However, we still discovered useful results. It appears that F4 or a similar algorithm is likely to be more useful than a SAT solver for the full cipher. For the simplified algorithm, the SAT solver does appear to be more feasible. However, it could be that Magma's additional overhead to compute a Gröbner basis becomes less significant and could have better asymptotic complexity. Few intermediate variables are needed, but the round keys should be intermediate variables. Guess-and-determine attacks have not been shown to be effective, but may be effective if round key bits are guessed.

Also, breaking the system over $GF(2^8)$ does not appear to provide any benefit over solving over $GF(2)$. Specifically, the claims of [5] and [6] are contradicted by our experimental results. This casts very serious doubts about the basis of their theoretical analysis.

There are many possible improvements which we have not had time to explore. There exist improved methods for converting equations into SAT solver input. In addition, not all methods and adjustments in [9] such as improving the optimal cutting number have been attempted. Thus, it is possible that the SAT solver attack could become more feasible with improved conversion.

Further work on the $GF(2^8)$ attack is possible. Experiments could be performed with sufficient RAM to test several numbers of rounds, so that the increase in complexity can be measured. This would allow a more substantial comparison of $GF(2)$ and $GF(2^8)$ implementations.

Overall, we believe any existing direct algebraic analysis will not work well in attacking SMS4 and new methods that could fully utilize the hidden algebraic structures need to be developed to attack SMS4 more efficiently in terms of algebraic cryptanalysis.

Acknowledgments

This work is a result of the 2008 and 2009 National Science Foundation-sponsored Research Experience for Undergraduates (REU) in Mathematical Cryptology jointly offered by Northern Kentucky University and the University of Cincinnati. Thanks to the United States Air Force Office of Scientific Research for funding the REUs and to the Computational Algebra Group within the School of Mathematics and Statistics of the University of Sidney for supplying Magma for the REUs and for this project. The first author was also supported by AT&T, IBM, and Sun Corps.; NSF grants CNS 0834270 and CNS 0834132; ARO grant W911NF-09-1-0535; and AFOSR grant FA9550-09-1-0549. The second author would also like to thank partial support of Grant-60973131 from NSF China and the support of Taft Foundation. We also worked with Amber Rogers of Northern Kentucky University on creating SAT solver conversion code, and portions of the code used in creating SMS4 equations were written by Brian Nixon of the University of Michigan.

References

1. Courtois, N., Pieprzyk, J.: Cryptanalysis of block ciphers with overdefined systems of equations. In: Zheng, Y. (ed.) ASIACRYPT 2002. LNCS, vol. 2501, pp. 267–287. Springer, Heidelberg (2002)
2. Courtois, N., Bard, G.V.: Algebraic cryptanalysis of the data encryption standard. In: Galbraith, S.D. (ed.) Cryptography and Coding 2007. LNCS, vol. 4887, pp. 152–169. Springer, Heidelberg (2007)
3. Lu, J.: Attacking reduced-round versions of the sms4 block cipher in the chinese wapi standard. In: Qing, S., Imai, H., Wang, G. (eds.) ICICS 2007. LNCS, vol. 4861, pp. 306–318. Springer, Heidelberg (2007)

4. Liu, F., Ji, W., Hu, L., Ding, J., Lv, S., Pyshkin, A., Weinmann, R.P.: Analysis of the sms4 block cipher. In: Pieprzyk, J., Ghodosi, H., Dawson, E. (eds.) ACISP 2007. LNCS, vol. 4586, pp. 158–170. Springer, Heidelberg (2007)
5. Ji, W., Hu, L.: New description of sms4 by an embedding over gf(2^8). In: Srinathan, K., Rangan, C.P., Yung, M. (eds.) INDOCRYPT 2007. LNCS, vol. 4859, pp. 238–251. Springer, Heidelberg (2007)
6. Ji, W., Hu, L., Ou, H.: Algebraic attack to sms4 and the comparison with aes. In: International Symposium on Information Assurance and Security, vol. 1, pp. 662–665 (2009)
7. Bosma, W., Cannon, J.J., Playoust, C.: The magma algebra system i: The user language. J. Symb. Comput. 24(3/4), 235–265 (1997)
8. Diffie, W., Ledin, G. (translators): Sms4 encryption algorithm for wireless networks. Cryptology ePrint Archive, Report 2008/329 (2008),
http://eprint.iacr.org/
9. Bard, G.V., Courtois, N.T., Jefferson., C.: Efficient methods for conversion and solution of sparse systems of low-degree multivariate polynomials over gf(2) via sat-solvers. Cryptology ePrint Archive, Report 2007/024 (2007),
http://eprint.iacr.org/
10. Cid, C., Leurent, G.: An analysis of the xsl algorithm. In: Roy, B. (ed.) ASIACRYPT 2005. LNCS, vol. 3788, pp. 333–352. Springer, Heidelberg (2005)
11. Yang, B.Y., Chen, J.M., Courtois, N.: On asymptotic security estimates in xl and gröbner bases-related algebraic cryptanalysis. In: López, J., Qing, S., Okamoto, E. (eds.) ICICS 2004. LNCS, vol. 3269, pp. 401–413. Springer, Heidelberg (2004)
12. Ars, G., Faugère, J.C., Imai, H., Kawazoe, M., Sugita, M.: Comparison between XL and gröbner basis algorithms. In: Lee, P.J. (ed.) ASIACRYPT 2004. LNCS, vol. 3329, pp. 354–371. Springer, Heidelberg (2004)

Appendix: Guess-and-Determine Attack Results

Table 4 contains results for the guess-and-determine attack on 7 rounds of simplified SMS4.

Table 4. Results of guess-and-determine attacks

Attack	# Bits	Time (s)	RAM (MB)	Speedup	RAM Reduc.
No guessing	0	83.210	556.43	1.00	1.00
Entire key	32	0.350	45.92	237.74	12.12
First key bit	1	84.940	552.74	0.98	1.01
Key bit 12 (0)	1	81.790	553.85	1.02	1.00
Key bit 13 (1)	1	81.160	551.19	1.03	1.01
Last key bit	1	81.340	545.80	1.02	1.02
First two key bits	2	81.400	549.32	1.02	1.01
First and 12 key bits	2	81.080	549.45	1.03	1.01
First and 13 key bits	2	80.440	546.67	1.03	1.02
First and last key bit	2	80.050	540.07	1.04	1.03
First three key bits	3	80.410	540.99	1.03	1.03
First four key bits	4	79.650	537.08	1.04	1.04
First eight key bits	8	90.560	580.41	0.92	0.96
First and last four	8	78.820	511.29	1.06	1.09
RK2 bit 1	1	81.090	554.57	1.03	1.00
RK2 bits 1, 2	2	78.150	556.41	1.06	1.00
RK2 bit 1, RK4 bit 1	2	77.820	532.19	1.07	1.05
RK1 (all bits)	8	19.980	152.00	4.16	3.66
RK2 (all bits)	8	57.290	429.42	1.45	1.30
RK3 (all bits)	8	57.210	384.42	1.45	1.45
RK4 (all bits)	8	46.890	304.93	1.77	1.82
RK5 (all bits)	8	50.440	333.27	1.65	1.67
RK6 (all bits)	8	56.590	364.54	1.47	1.53
RK7 (all bits)	8	21.940	173.77	3.79	3.20
RK1, RK7 (all bits)	16	0.270	45.92	308.19	12.12
RK1 bit 1	1	69.110	531.79	1.20	1.05
RK1 bits 1, 2	2	65.760	476.22	1.27	1.17
RK1 bits 1, 8	2	64.019	471.69	1.30	1.18
RK1 bit 1, RK7 bit 1	2	68.989	512.97	1.21	1.08
RK1 bits 1-2, 7-8	4	46.920	365.62	1.77	1.52
RK1 bits 1-4	4	22.460	156.08	3.70	3.57
RK1 bits 5-8	4	26.710	234.14	3.12	2.38
RK7 bits 6-8	3	27.940	181.75	2.98	3.06
R1 intermediates	8	72.140	495.74	1.15	1.12
R7 intermediates	8	39.140	294.49	2.13	1.89
RK1-7 bit 1	7	50.729	400.43	1.64	1.39
RK1-2, RK6-7 bit 1	4	64.510	483.45	1.29	1.15
RK1, RK7 bits 1-2	4	50.909	385.66	1.63	1.44

MXL₃: An Efficient Algorithm for Computing Gröbner Bases of Zero-Dimensional Ideals

Mohamed Saied Emam Mohamed[1], Daniel Cabarcas[2], Jintai Ding[2],
Johannes Buchmann[1], and Stanislav Bulygin[3]

[1] TU Darmstadt, FB Informatik
Hochschulstrasse 10, 64289 Darmstadt, Germany
{mohamed,buchmann}@cdc.informatik.tu-darmstadt.de
[2] Department of Mathematical Sciences, University of Cincinnati,
South China University of Technology
cabarcd@email.uc.edu, jintai.ding@uc.edu
[3] Center for Advanced Security Research Darmstadt (CASED)
Stanislav.Bulygin@cased.de

Abstract. This paper introduces a new efficient algorithm, called MXL₃,
for computing Gröbner bases of zero-dimensional ideals. The MXL₃ is
based on XL algorithm, mutant strategy, and a new sufficient condition
for a set of polynomials to be a Gröbner basis. We present experimental results comparing the behavior of MXL₃ to F₄ on HFE and random
generated instances of the MQ problem. In both cases the first implementation of the MXL₃ algorithm succeeds faster and uses less memory
than Magma's implementation of F₄.

Keywords: Multivariate polynomial systems, Gröbner basis, XL algorithm, Mutant, MutantXL algorithm.

1 Introduction

The standard way to represent the polynomial ideals is to compute a Gröbner
basis of it. One of the most useful applications of Gröbner bases is to compute
efficiently the variety of the ideal. This leads to solving the polynomial system
induced by the ideal.

The Buchberger algorithm [4] was the first algorithm for computing Gröbner
bases. It is based on the computation of Gröbner bases using s-polynomials.
F₄ [11] is an algorithm that uses linear algebra and Buchberger's s-polynomial
techniques to compute Gröbner bases.

XL was introduced in [6] as an efficient algorithm for solving polynomial
equations in case only a single solution exists. The MutantXL algorithm was
proposed as a variant of XL that is based on the mutant strategy [9,8]. The
MXL₂ algorithm [16] is an improvement to MutantXL that uses the partial
enlargement technique [16] and a necessary number of mutants to solve.

As explained in [13,17] the XL algorithm calculates the reduced Gröbner basis
in the case of a single solution. So, we wonder if a variant of the XL algorithm
can compute Gröbner bases in a more general case.

D. Lee and S. Hong (Eds.): ICISC 2009, LNCS 5984, pp. 87–100, 2010.

The comparison of XL and F_4 in [13,17] concluded that F_4 computes a Gröbner basis faster and uses less memory resources than XL. By combining the mutant strategy with the XL algorithm, it was shown in [9] that MutantXL outperforms XL in all cases. Moreover the results presented in [16] showed that MXL_2 outperforms F_4 for all the random systems and 57% of the HFE cases that are considered in that paper. Another indicator for the fact that a variant of MutantXL outperforms F_4 is in [15]. So this variant of the XL algorithm is a good candidate to be adapted for computing Gröbner bases.

In this paper we introduce a new efficient algorithm for computing Gröbner bases of zero-dimensional ideals that we call MXL_3. The MXL_3 algorithm uses the MutantXL strategy, MXL_2 improvements, and a new efficiently checkable condition to test whether a set of polynomials is a Gröbner basis. We give an experimental comparison between the first implementation of the MXL_3 algorithm and Magma's implementation of the F_4 algorithm on some HFE cryptosystems and some randomly generated instances of the MQ problem. We show that for the HFE systems MXL_3 can solve systems of univariate degree 288 that have number of variables up to 49 while Magma's F_4 can not solve any system with more than 39 variables under the same memory constraints. Moreover, we show that MXL_3 solves the HFE challenge 1 using a smaller matrix dimensions than Magma's F_4.

This paper is organized as follows. In Section 2 we give an overview of Gröbner bases and present the new condition to test whether a set of polynomials is a Gröbner basis. In Section 3 we review the XL algorithm, mutant strategy, and the MXL_2 improvements. In Section 4 we describe the MXL_3 algorithm. In Section 5 we give our experimental results on random and HFE systems and finally we conclude the paper in Section 6.

2   Gröbner Bases

We adopt the notation and use some of the results from [2]. Let K be the ground field, and let the polynomial ring $K[x_1, \ldots, x_n]$ over K be denoted by $K[\underline{x}]$. A term in the indeterminates $x_1, \ldots, x_n$ is a power product of the form $x_1^{e_1} \cdots x_n^{e_n}$ with $e_i \in \mathbb{N}$. We denote by T the set of all terms. A monomial is any product of a field element and a term. Let $\leq$ denote a term order on T. The degree of $t = x_1^{e_1} \cdots x_n^{e_n} \in T$ is defined by $\deg(t) := \sum_{i=1}^{n} e_i$. For $f = \sum_{t \in T} c_t t \in K[\underline{x}]$, where $c_t \in K$ is the coefficient of t in f, we define the terms of f by $T(f) := \{t \in T \mid c_t \neq 0\}$, the degree of f by $\deg(f) := \max\{\deg(t) \mid t \in T(f)\}$, the head term of f by $\mathrm{HT}(f) := \max_{\leq} T(f)$, the head coefficient of f, denoted by $\mathrm{HC}(f)$, is the coefficient of the head term, and the head monomial of f is $\mathrm{HM}(f) := \mathrm{HC}(f)\,\mathrm{HT}(f)$. If $f, g \in K[\underline{x}]$ the s-polynomial of f and g is defined as $\mathrm{spol}(f, g) = \frac{t}{\mathrm{HM}(f)} f - \frac{t}{\mathrm{HM}(g)} g$, with $t := \mathrm{lcm}(\mathrm{HT}(f), \mathrm{HT}(g))$.

Given a subset P of $K[\underline{x}]$, we denote by $\langle P \rangle$ the ideal generated by P, and by $\mathrm{HT}(P)$ the set of head terms from elements in P. We denote by $\mathrm{span}_K(P)$ the K-linear span of P. We will denote by $P_{(op)d}$ the subset of all the polynomials of degree $(op)d$ in P, where (op) is any of $\{=, <, >, \leq, \geq\}$.

Definition 1. *A finite subset G of an ideal I of the polynomial ring $K[\underline{x}]$ is called a Gröbner Basis for I (w.r.t the term order $\leq$) if*

$$\langle \mathrm{HT}(G) \rangle = \langle \mathrm{HT}(I) \rangle .$$

A finite subset $\widetilde{H}$ of $K[\underline{x}]$ is a row echelon form of H w.r.t. $\leq$ if $span(\widetilde{H}) = span(H)$ and elements of $\widetilde{H}$ have pairwise different leading terms.

Definition 2. *Let P be a finite subset of $K[\underline{x}]$, $0 \neq f \in \langle P \rangle$ and $t \in T$. A representation*

$$f = \sum_{i=1}^{s} a_i t_i p_i$$

with $a_i \in K$, $t_i \in T$, and $p_i \in P$ is called a t-representation of f w.r.t. P (and $\leq$) if $\mathrm{HT}(t_i p_i) \leq t$ for $i = 1, \ldots, s$. A $\mathrm{HT}(f)$-representation of f w.r.t. P is called a standard representation.

Proposition 1. *[2] Let G be a finite subset of $K[\underline{x}]$ with $0 \notin G$, and assume that for all $g_1, g_2 \in G$, $\mathrm{spol}(g_1, g_2)$ equals zero or has a standard representation w.r.t. G. Then G is a Gröbner basis.*

We recall a result commonly known as Buchberger's second criterion. We paraphrase it in the following proposition.

Proposition 2. *[5,2] let F be a finite subset of $K[\underline{x}]$ and $g_1, p, g_2 \in K[\underline{x}]$ be such that $HT(p) \mid \mathrm{lcm}(\mathrm{HT}(g_1), \mathrm{HT}(g_2))$, and for $i = 1, 2$ $\mathrm{spol}(g_i, p)$ has a standard representation w.r.t. F, then $\mathrm{spol}(g_1, g_2)$ also has a standard representation w.r.t. F.*

In the rest of this paper we will be working with the total-degree orderings of terms. So by "order" we mean "total-degree order" here. In the total-degree orderings, we compare total degree first. In case of the equality, there are many different orderings that can break the ties. The most commonly used are the graded lexicographic and the graded reverse lexicographic orderings.

Now we present our new result that establishes a sufficient condition for a finite set to be a Gröbner basis.

Proposition 3. *Let G be a finite subset of $K[\underline{x}]$ with D being the highest degree of its elements. Let $<$ be an order on $K[\underline{x}]$. Suppose that the following holds:*

1. *G contains all the terms of degree D as leading terms; and*
2. *if $H := G \cup \{t \cdot g \mid g \in G, t$ a term and $\deg(t \cdot g) \leq D + 1\}$, there exists $\widetilde{H}$, a row echelon form of H, such that $\widetilde{H}_{\leq D} = G$,*

then G is a Gröbner basis.

Note that condition 1 implies $\langle G \rangle$ is a zero-dimensional ideal. From now on we concentrate on zero-dimensional ideals.

Proof. Let $G = \{g_1, \ldots, g_s\}$ with $g_i \neq g_j$ for $i \neq j$. Suppose that the highest degree in G is D and that conditions 1 and 2 above hold. We want to show that for $i, j \in \{1, \ldots, s\}$, with $i \neq j$, $f := \mathrm{spol}(g_i, g_j)$ has a standard representation w.r.t. G. without loss of generality, it suffices to show it for $\mathrm{spol}(g_1, g_2)$.

If $d := \deg(\mathrm{lcm}(\mathrm{HT}(g_1), \mathrm{HT}(g_2))) \leq D + 1$, then by condition 2

$$f \in \mathrm{span}_K(H) = \mathrm{span}_K(\widetilde{H}) = \mathrm{span}_K(G) \oplus \mathrm{span}_K(\widetilde{H}_{=D+1}).$$

If $\deg(f) < D + 1$ then it is trivial to see that $f \in \mathrm{span}_K(G)$ and hence has a standard representation w.r.t. G. Suppose that $\deg(f) = D + 1$. By condition 1, every term of degree $D + 1$ appears as a head term in H. Choose $h_1 \in H$ such that $\mathrm{HT}(h_1) = \mathrm{HT}(f)$ and define f_1 by

$$f_1 := f - \frac{\mathrm{HC}(f)}{\mathrm{HC}(h_1)} h_1.$$

It is easy to see that $f_1 \in \mathrm{span}_K(\widetilde{H})$ and that $\mathrm{HT}(f_1) < \mathrm{HT}(f)$. If $\deg(f_1) = D + 1$ we can repeat the same argument for f_1 and by iterating the argument a finite number of times m, we obtain an expression

$$f = \sum_{i=1}^{m-1} a_i h_i + f_m \qquad (1)$$

with $a_i \in K$, $h_i \in H$, for $1 \leq i < m-1$ $\mathrm{HT}(h_i) > \mathrm{HT}(h_{i+1})$ and $\deg(f_m) < D+1$. Since $f_m \in \mathrm{span}_K(\widetilde{H})$ and $\deg(f_m) < D + 1$, $f_m \in \mathrm{span}_K(G)$ thus clearly (1) yields a standard representation of f w.r.t G.

For $d > D + 1$, we proceed by induction. Suppose that $d > D + 1$ and that for $i \neq j$, if $\deg(\mathrm{lcm}(\mathrm{HT}(g_i), \mathrm{HT}(g_j))) < d$ then $\mathrm{spol}(g_i, g_j)$ has a standard representation w.r.t. G. Assume, without loss of generality, that $\deg(g_1) \geq \deg(g_2)$ and note that $\deg(g_1) > (D + 1)/2$. Let $t := \mathrm{lcm}(\mathrm{HT}(g_1), \mathrm{HT}(g_2))$ and let t_1, t_2 be terms such that for $i = 1, 2$, $t = t_i \mathrm{HT}(g_i)$. Note that $\deg(t_i) \geq 2$ and that t_1 and t_2 are disjoint. Choose any terms $t_{11}, t_{12}, t_{21}, t_{22}$ such that for $i = 1, 2$, $t_i = t_{i1} t_{i2}$ and $\deg(g_1) + \deg(t_{12}) = D + 1$ and $\deg(t_{21}) = 1$. These choices are possible because $(D + 1)/2 < \deg(g_1) \leq D$ thus $1 \leq D + 1 - \deg(g_1) < D + 1 - (D + 1)/2 = (D + 1)/2 < deg(g_1)$ and because $\deg(t_2) \geq 2$. It follows that $\deg(t_{11}), \deg(t_{12}), \deg(t_{21})$ and $\deg(t_{22})$ are all greater than or equal to 1. Also, if we let $t^* := \frac{t}{t_{11} t_{21}}$, by construction, for $i = 1, 2$, $\mathrm{lcm}(t^*, \mathrm{HT}(g_i)) = t/t_{i1}$ divides t properly, $\deg(t^*) = D$ and since t_1 and t_2 are disjoint, t^* is different from both $\mathrm{HT}(g_1)$ and $\mathrm{HT}(g_2)$. Then, by condition 1, there exist $g \in G \setminus \{g_1, g_2\}$ with $\mathrm{HT}(g) = t^*$. Also, for $i = 1, 2$, since $\deg(\mathrm{lcm}(\mathrm{HT}(g), \mathrm{HT}(g_i))) < \deg(t)$, by the inductive hypothesis, $\mathrm{spol}(g, g_i)$ has a standard representation w.r.t. G. Moreover, $\mathrm{HT}(g)$ divides t and therefore, by the Buchberger's second criterion, $\mathrm{spol}(g_1, g_2)$ has a standard representation w.r.t. G.

3   From XL to MXL₂

The MXL₃ algorithm adapts MXL₂ which in turn adapts XL [6]. Below we present a brief overview of the XL algorithm, the mutant strategy [8,9] and the MXL₂ improvements [16].

Let P be a finite set of polynomials in $K[\underline{x}]$. Given a degree bound D, the XL algorithm is simply based on extending the set of polynomials P by multiplying each polynomial in P by all the terms in T such that the resulting polynomials have degree less than or equal to D. Then, by using linear algebra, XL computes $\widetilde{P}$, a row echelon form of the extended set P. Afterwards, XL searches for univariate polynomials in $\widetilde{P}$.

In [8,9], it was pointed out that during the linear algebra step, certain polynomials of degrees lower than expected appear. These polynomials are called mutants. The mutant strategy aims at distinguishing mutants from the rest of polynomials and to give them a predominant role in the process of solving the system.

The precise definition of mutants is as follows.

Definition 3. *Let I be the ideal generated by the finite set of polynomials P. An element f in I can be written as*

$$f = \sum_{p \in P} f_p p \tag{2}$$

where $f_p \in K[\underline{x}]$. The maximum degree of $f_p p$, $p \in P$, is the level of this representation. The level of f is the minimum level of all of its representations. The polynomial f is called mutant with respect to P if $\deg(f)$ is less than its level.

The MutantXL algorithm [9] is a direct application of the mutant concepts to the XL algorithm. It was noted in [16] that there are two problems in the MutantXL algorithm that affect its performance. The first problem is, when the system generates a huge number of mutants. The second problem is, when the system generates an insufficient number of mutants to solve the system at a lower degree than XL. The MXL₂ algorithm handles the first problem by choosing the minimum number of mutants necessary to solve.

In [16], Mohamed et. al. also introduced a new technique for the space enlargement process to handle the second problem which is called the partial enlargement technique. In the process of space enlargement, MutantXL multiplies all the polynomials in P of degree D by all the terms of degree one such that each term is multiplied only once. In many cases, the last iteration of this process generates a very large number of dependent polynomials. These polynomials are reduced to zero. MXL₂ avoids this problem by using the partial enlargement technique. This means that, in the process of space enlargement MXL₂ multiplies only a subset of the polynomials of degree D in P and tries to solve. This step is repeated until the system is solved. The strategy for selecting a subset will be explained in the next section.

By these two improvements MXL_2 could outperform Magma's F_4 in terms of memory in all the cases of random systems and 57% of the cases of HFE systems that are considered in [16].

4   Description of the MXL_3 Algorithm

The main difference between MXL_2 and MXL_3 is that MXL_2 only works when the system of equations has a unique solution whereas MXL_3 can handle any system of equations with a finite number of solutions. Any XL-type algorithm eventually computes a Gröbner basis, however it is uncertain for which degree bound it occurs. Proposition 3 provides an easy to check condition that guarantees a Gröbner basis has been found. Experimental results show that in all the cases that we examined, using this alternative criterion reveals the Gröbner basis early. Another important difference is that MXL_3 multiplies only by some chosen monomials, while MXL_2 multiplies by all possible monomials. In addition to the notation of section 2, we also need the following notation.

4.1   Notation

Let $X := \{x_1, \ldots, x_n\}$ be a set of variables, upon which we impose the following order: $x_1 > x_2 > \ldots > x_n$. Let

$$R = \mathbb{F}_2[x_1, \ldots, x_n]/\langle x_1^2 - x_1, \ldots, x_n^2 - x_n \rangle$$

be the Boolean polynomial ring in X with the monomials of R ordered by the graded lexicographical order $<_{glex}$. We consider elements of R as polynomials over $\mathbb{F}_2$ where degree of each term w.r.t any variable is 0 or 1. Let $P = (p_1, \ldots, p_m) \in R^m$ be an m-tuple of polynomials in R.

Throughout the operation of the algorithm described in this paper, a degree bound D will be used. This degree bound denotes the maximum degree of the polynomials contained in P. Also, we use ED as a degree bound for the eliminated subset of P, ($P_{\leq ED}$). Note that the content of P is changed throughout the operation of the algorithm. We define the leading variable $\text{LV}(p)$ for $p \in P$ as the largest variable in $\text{HT}(p)$, according to the order defined on the variables set. Also, we define the subset $\text{LV}(P, x)$ as the set of all polynomials of P with leading variable x.

4.2 MXL_3 Algorithm

The algorithm performs the following steps:

- *Initialize*: Set $P = \{p_1, \ldots, p_m\}$, $D = \max\{\deg(p) : p \in P\}$, the elimination degree $ED = \min\{\deg(p) : p \in P\}$, the set of mutants $M = \emptyset$, the extension flag *newExtend* = *true*, and the partitioned variable $x = x_1$.

– *Repeat*

    Echelonize: Consider each term in $P_{\leq ED}$ as a new variable. Set $P_{\leq ED} = \widetilde{P}_{\leq ED}$, where $\widetilde{P}_{\leq ED}$ is the row echelon form of $P_{\leq ED}$.

    Here polynomials are identified with their coefficient vectors as explained in [11].

    ExtractMutants: Add all the new elements of $P_{<ED}$ to M.

    Gröbner: If $(ED < D$ or $newExtend = true)$, $M_{<ED} = \emptyset$ and $\left|P_{=(ED-1)}\right| = \left|T_{=(ED-1)}\right|$ then set $G = P_{\leq(ED-1)}$, return G and terminate.

    Enlarge: If $M \neq \emptyset$, then **Multiply**(P, M, ED), otherwise

      Extend$(P, D, x, ED, newExtend)$.

Multiply(P, M, ED)

– Set $k = \min\{\deg(p)\colon p \in M\}$.
– Set $y = \max\{\mathrm{LV}(p) : p \in M_{=k}\}$.
– Select a necessary number of mutants of $M_{=k}$, multiply the selected mutants by all variables $\leq y$, remove the selected mutants from M, add the new polynomials to P.

    (The necessary number of mutants is numerically computed as in [16].)

– Set $ED = k + 1$.

Extend$(P, D, x, ED, newExtend)$

– If $newExtend = true$, then increment D by 1, set $x = \min\{\mathrm{LV}(p) : p \in P_{=D-1}\}$, and set $newExtend = false$. Otherwise, set $x = \min\{\mathrm{LV}(p) : p \in P_{=D-1}$ and $\mathrm{LV}(p) > x\}$ (the next-smallest leading variable).
– multiply all the polynomials of $\mathrm{LV}(P, x)$ (the current partition) by all the variables $\leq x$ without redundancy and add the newly obtained polynomials to P.
– If $x = x_1$, then set $newExtend = true$.
– Set $ED = D$.

We now explain the selection strategy that we use to avoid the redundancy produced from the extend step. During the multiplication process we keep the multiplier variable that gave rise to every new produced polynomial and we keep one for the original polynomials. When we extend the system, we multiply the polynomial p by all variables smaller than its previous multiplier variable. In case of the previous multiplier of p is one, we multiply by all variables. The target of this selection method is to speed up the extension process of the system. Only we multiply by monomials of degree one (variables) without any trivial redundancy.

    Let for example $p \in P$, $x_i p$, $x_j p$ be two polynomials in the extended system, and $x_i > x_j$. Then $x_i p$ is extended by multiplying it with variables $< x_i$ one of them being $x_j x_i p$, while the redundant polynomial $x_i x_j p$ can not be produced by $x_j p$ since $x_i > x_j$ and $x_j p$ is multiplied only by variables $< x_j$.

    The multiplication of mutants process provides another important improvement to our algorithm. Let the system have mutants of degree $k < D$ and x is the greatest leading variable of the set of mutants. MXL$_3$ multiplies these mutants by all variables $\leq x$ instead of multiplying by all variables as in MXL_2. The target of this improvement is to solve with as small number of polynomials as we can.

Let for example M be a set of mutant polynomials of degree k and let x_i be the smallest leading variable of the elements in M. We multiply the elements of M by all variables $\leq x_i$. The resulting polynomials have smallest leading variable $\leq x_i$, then all the old polynomials of degree $k+1$ with leading variable $> x_i$ will not play any role during the Gaussian elimination process. This will decrease the dimension of the system.

The following theorem establishes the correctness of the algorithm.

Theorem 1. *The* MXL_3 *algorithm computes a Gröbner basis* G *of the ideal generated by the set* $\{p_1, \ldots, p_m\}$ *of* R.

Proof. Termination: MXL_3 terminates only when it enlarges all the polynomials of degree $< ED$ and when P contains all the terms of degree $ED - 1$ as leading terms, at a certain degree $ED \leq D$. The worst case is to satisfy these two conditions at $ED = D = n + 1$. Let the system is extended up to degree n without satisfying the termination conditions of the algorithm. In this case, MXL_3 extends the system to the next degree $D = n + 1$. P has only one polynomial of degree n. In the *Enlarge* step, this polynomial is extended, *newExtend* is set to *true*, and ED to $n + 1$. After the *Echelonize* step, P still contains only one polynomial of degree $n = ED - 1$ which is equal to the number of all terms in the Boolean ring R with degree n. If $M \neq \emptyset$, MXL_3 loops between *Eliminate* and *Enlarge* a finite number of times until the set M becomes empty. So all the conditions of *Gröbner* step are satisfied. Then MXL_3 returns $G = P$ with highest degree n and terminates.

Correctness: MXL_3 returns a set of polynomials G with elements of maximum degree $d = ED - 1$, where $ED \leq D$. The set G satisfies the first condition of Proposition 3 since It is in the row echelon form and It contains all the terms of degree d as leading terms. Also, the *Gröbner* step returns G only when *newExtend* = *true* and $M_{<ED} = \emptyset$ which means that all the polynomials of degree $\leq d$ are enlarged. Then G satisfies the second condition of Proposition 3. Therefore G is a Gröbner basis for the ideal generated by the input system $\{p_1, \ldots, p_m\}$.

5   Experimental Results

We built our experiments to compare the efficiency of MXL_3 to the efficiency of F_4 in solving some random systems generated by Courtois [7] as well as some HFE systems generated by the code of John Baena. We run all the experiments on a Sun X4440 server, with four "Quad-Core AMD Opteron^{TM} Processor 8356" CPUs and 128 GB of main memory. Each CPU is running at 2.3 GHz. We used only one out of the 16 cores.

Tables 1 and 2 show the results of dense random systems with many solutions and the results of HFE systems of univariate degree 288, respectively. In both

Table 1. Performance of MXL$_3$ versus F_4 for dense random system

		MXL$_3$				F_4		
n	D	max. matrix	Memory	Time	D	max. matrix	Memory	Time
25	6	66631×76414	698	704	6	248495×108746	5128	1341
26	6	88513×102246	1207	1429	6	298592×148804	8431	3325
27	6	123938×140344	2315	2853	6	354189×197902	13312	6431
28	6	201636×197051	4836	7982	6	420773×261160	20433	13810
29	6	279288×281192	9375	18796	6	499222×340254	30044	25631
30	6	332615×351537	15062	33331	6	1283869×374081	72258	92033
31	6	415654×436598	23078	94191	6	868614×489702	108738	162118

tables we denote the number of variables and equations by n and the highest degree of the iteration steps by D. The tables also show the maximum matrix size, the memory used in Megabytes, and the execution time in seconds. It is evident from Tables 1 and 2 that MXL$_3$ solves the random generated systems and HFE systems faster and consumes less memory than F_4.

Table 1 shows that both MXL$_3$ and F_4 solve random systems up to a system of 31 variables. The solutions of MXL$_3$ are consistent to the results of Magma. When MXL$_3$ and F_4 tried to solve a 32 variables system, both were able to enlarge the system up to degree 6. When the system was enlarged to degree 7, they ran out of memory. For the 30 variables system we get a strange matrix size from Magma. We created many 30 variables random system and we obtain approximately the same numbers.

Table 2. Performance of MXL$_3$ versus F_4 for HFE(288,n) systems

		MXL$_3$				F_4		
n	D	max. matrix	Memory	Time	D	max. matrix	Memory	Time
30	5	86795×130211	1389	3106	5	149532×136004	7105	3806
35	5	155914×296872	5737	10047	5	200302×321883	40480	11032
36	5	173439×344968	7310	14183	5	219438×382252	50846	15220
37	5	192805×399151	9288	20375	5	247387×444867	66623	20787
38	5	212271×459985	11351	27089	5	274985×512311	83445	27305
39	5	234111×528068	15070	36833	5	305528×588400	104135	38013
40	5	258029×604033	20881	63460≈17.6 hours		ran out of memory		
45	5	404940×1126819	55216	299355≈3.46 days		ran out of memory		
47	5	457691×1417468	77967	371088≈4.3 days		ran out of memory		
48	5	517642×1583807	98913	689235≈7.9 days		ran out of memory		
49	5	561972×1765465	120524	751965≈8.7 days		ran out of memory		

Table 2 shows that all the HFE systems of univariate degree 288 up to 49 variables are solved by using MXL$_3$, whereas F_4 could only solve HFE systems up to 39 variables with the same memory resources.

In Table 3 we compare the performance of the MXL$_3$ algorithm against the F_4 algorithm in computing a Gröbner basis of the random system $n = 30$. For

MXL_3, we give the elimination degree (D), the matrix size for each level, the rank of the matrix (Rank), the number of mutants found (NM), the number of used mutants (UM), and the lowest degree of mutants found (MD). For F_4, we give the step degree (D), the matrix size, and the step memory in MB.

Table 3. Results for the system Random-30

		MXL₃						F₄	
Step	D	Matrix Size	Rank	NM	UM	MD	D	Matrix Size	Memory
1	2	30×466	30	0	0	-	2	30×466	14.2
2	3	930×4526	930	0	0	-	3	937×4526	14.2
3	4	13980×31931	13515	0	0	-	4	13320×30551	207
4	5	131690×174437	121365	0	0	-	5	106603×143547	4318
5	6	**332615×351537**	329051	31060	665	5	6	588160×437262	42843
6	6	302981×309033	302981	3596,12340	0,191	5,4	6	**1283869×374081**	72258
7	5	172945×174437	172945	2480,3160,90	0,0,11	4,3,2	2	722×466	72258
8	3	4510×4526	4510	315,15	0,1	2,1	3	4864×3782	72258
9	2	480×466	465	15	0	1	4	22421×19736	72258
10							5	103919×62858	72258

Table 3 shows that by using the mutant strategy, MXL_3 can easily solve the 30 variables random system with a smaller matrix size compared to F_4. MXL_3 starts to generate mutants at step 5. In this step 31060 mutants of degree 5 are generated, out of which only 665 are multiplied. Due to the degree of the generated mutants, the elimination degree remains the same in the next step, i.e. , $D = 6$. Starting from step 7, D starts to decrease. In step 8, the system generates 315 quadratic mutants and 15 linear mutants. By using only one of the linear mutants, MXL_3 generates additional 15 linear mutants in the next step, which in turn leads to solving the system.

Also, Table 3 shows that the number of reductions to zero is less than 8% for each iteration step. This explains practically that our improved selection strategy has strictly increased the efficiency of the algorithm since it avoids the redundant computations.

In Appendix A Table 4 presents a comparison between the maximum matrix size constructed by MXL_3 and MXL_2 on some random systems that have only one solution. The results show that MXL_3 solves with smaller number of polynomial equations and smaller number of terms than MXL_2. This due to the selection strategy of the multiplied variables that used is by MXL_3. In Appendix B Table 5 presents another comparison between MXL_3 and Magma's F_4 when the HFE parameter is setting to true. In this case MXL_3 also solves with smaller number of polynomials than Magma's F_4. For example the HFE challenge 1 $n = 80$ that was first solved with maximum matrix size 307126×1667009 by Faugère and Joux [14] using F_5 /2 algorithm [12] in May 2002, can be solved by MXL_3 with maximum matrix size 268840×1666981, while Magma solves it with maximum matrix size 293287×1666981. In this case Magma is faster than our implementation since it uses a very fast linear algebra implementation.

For the comparison with Faugère's F$_4$ algorithm, we used Magma (version V2.13-10). We used the field equations $x_i^2 = x_i$ and using the polynomial ring type for Magma that is defined over $\mathbb{F}_2$ such that all the terms are reduced modulo the field equations. When we use the new version of Magma (V2.15) and the new Magma type BooleanPolynomialRing, we have worse results in terms of the matrix size and the memory, although we obtained better results in terms of the running times. For MXL$_3$, we also used the Boolean polynomial ring in our C++ implementation. For the *Echelonize* step, we used an adapted version of M4RI [1], a library for dense matrix linear algebra over $\mathbb{F}_2$. Our adaptation is in changing the strategy of selecting a pivot during Gaussian elimination to keep the old elements in the system intact.

We chose to compare MXL$_3$ only with Magma's implementation of F$_4$ because both Faugère's algorithm and Steel's implementation are widely recognized as benchmarks for efficient Gröbner basis computation. A comparison with Faugère's F$_5$ algorithm has been suggested by some researchers. We consider this infeasible due to the controversy about the algorithm and the lack of a well recognized implementation.

F$_5$ is primary intended for homogeneous regular sequences There is no detailed description of how to adapt it for non-homogeneous sequences and moreover, no analysis exist on the behavior for such sequences. In the non-homogeneous case the F$_5$ criteria can discover trivial syzygies of the leading forms but it says nothing about what to do with the non-trivial ones which in turn yield mutants. In [9,16,10] the importance of mutants in the computation of Gröbner Bases for non-homogeneous sequences has been shown. F$_5$ says nothing about how to take advantage of those. Therefore, in the absence of such algorithm one relies on Buchberger's or the F$_4$ algorithm to compute a Gröbner Basis once mutants appear.

6   Conclusion and Future Work

In this paper, the MXL$_3$ algorithm is introduced as a new and efficient method to compute Gröbner bases on the Boolean polynomial ring. The experiments showed that both in classical cryptographic challenges and random systems, this new algorithm performs better in terms of memory than the F$_4$ algorithm implemented in Magma, currently the best publicly available implementation of F$_4$. The growth of the complexity shown in the experiments suggests that the difference is not marginal.

These experimental results demonstrate the importance of mutants in the computation of Gröbner bases, which was explored in a different setting in [10]. In combination with the techniques derived from the concepts of necessary number of mutants and partial enlargement, this new strategy has shown to be very successful unfolding the underlying structure of systems of equations.

Also, the new criterion for determining the termination of the new algorithm, proved to be efficiently checkable and sharp to detect a Gröbner basis. The fact that the MXL$_3$ algorithm terminates at the same degree as the F$_4$ algorithm in all experiments, suggests a connection between this criterion and other criteria to establish a Gröbner basis, a very interesting new direction, we will study next.

This paper further demonstrates the great potential of the mutant strategy and much more is still needed to be done to realize its full potential. Comparison with PolyBoRi [3] are planed as well as some improvements in the enlargement technique.

Acknowledgments

We would like to thank partial support from NSF China (No.6073131) and Taft foundation. Also, we would like to thank John Baena for supporting us with his code of generating HFE systems.

References

1. Albrecht, M., Bard, G.: M4RI Linear Algebra over GF(2) (2008),
   http://m4ri.sagemath.org/index.html
2. Becker, T., Kredel, H., Weispfenning, V.: Gröbner bases: a computational approach to commutative algebra, April 1993. Springer, London (1993)
3. Brickenstein, M., Dreyer, A.: Polybori: A framework for gröbner-basis computations with boolean polynomials. Journal of Symbolic Computation 44(9), 1326–1345 (2009); Effective Methods in Algebraic Geometry
4. Buchberger, B.: Ein Algorithmus zum Auffinden der Basiselemente des Restklassenringes nach einem nulldimensionalen Polynomideal (An Algorithm for Finding the Basis Elements in the Residue Class Ring Modulo a Zero Dimensional Polynomial Ideal). PhD thesis, Mathematical Institute, University of Innsbruck, Austria, 1965 (English translation in Journal of Symbolic Computation (2004)
5. Buchberger, B.: A criterion for detecting unnecessary reductions in the construction of gröbner bases. Johannes Kepler University Linz, London, UK, vol. 72, pp. 3–21. Springer, Heidelberg (1979)
6. Courtois, N., Klimov, A., Patarin, J., Shamir, A.: Efficient algorithms for solving overdefined systems of multivariate polynomial equations. In: Preneel, B. (ed.) EUROCRYPT 2000. LNCS, vol. 1807, pp. 392–407. Springer, Heidelberg (2000)
7. Courtois, N.T.: Experimental Algebraic Cryptanalysis of Block Ciphers (2007),
   http://www.cryptosystem.net/aes/toyciphers.html
8. Ding, J.: Mutants and its impact on polynomial solving strategies and algorithms. Privately distributed research note, University of Cincinnati and Technical University of Darmstadt (2006)
9. Ding, J., Buchmann, J., Mohamed, M.S.E., Moahmed, W.S.A., Weinmann, R.-P.: MutantXL. In: Proceedings of the 1st international conference on Symbolic Computation and Cryptography (SCC 2008), Beijing, China, April 2008, pp. 16–22. LMIB (2008)
10. Ding, J., Carbarcas, D., Schmidt, D., Buchmann, J., Tohaneanu, S.: Mutant Gröbner Basis Algorithm. In: Proceedings of the 1st international conference on Symbolic Computation and Cryptography (SCC 2008), Beijing, China, April 2008, pp. 23–32. LMIB (2008)
11. Faugère, J.-C.: A new efficient algorithm for computing Gröbner bases (F4). Pure and Applied Algebra 139(1-3), 61–88 (1999)

12. Faugère, J.-C.: A new efficient algorithm for computing Gröbner bases without reduction to zero (F5). In: Proceedings of the 2002 international symposium on Symbolic and algebraic computation (ISSAC), Lille, France, July 2002, pp. 75–83. ACM, New York (2002)
13. Faugère, J.-C., Ars, G.: Comparison of XL and Gröbner basis algorithms over Finite Fields. Research Report RR-5251, Institut National de Recherche en Informatique et en Automatique, INRIA (2004)
14. Faugère, J.-C., Joux, A.: Algebraic Cryptanalysis of Hidden Field Equation (HFE) Cryptosystems Using Gröbner Bases. In: Boneh, D. (ed.) CRYPTO 2003. LNCS, vol. 2729, pp. 44–60. Springer, Heidelberg (2003)
15. Mohamed, M.S.E., Ding, J., Buchmann, J., Werner, F.: Algebraic Attack on the MQQ Public Key Cryptosystem. In: Proceedings of the 8th International Conference on Cryptology And Network Security (CANS 2009), Kanazawa, Ishikawa, Japan, December 2009. LNCS, Springer, Heidelberg (to appear, 2009)
16. Mohamed, M.S.E., Mohamed, W.S.A.E., Ding, J., Buchmann, J.: MXL2: Solving Polynomial Equations over GF(2) using an Improved Mutant Strategy. In: Buchmann, J., Ding, J. (eds.) PQCrypto 2008. LNCS, vol. 5299, pp. 203–215. Springer, Heidelberg (2008)
17. Sugita, M., Kawazoe, M., Imai, H.: Relation between the XL Algorithm and Gröbner Basis Algorithms. Transactions on Fundamentals of Electronics, Communications and Computer Sciences (IEICE) E89-A(1), 11–18 (2006)

Appendix A

Table 4. Performance of MXL_3 versus MXL_2 for dense random system

n	MXL_3 max. matrix	MXL_2 max. matrix
15	1422×1577	1946×1758
16	2295×2573	2840×2861
17	3211×3676	3740×4184
18	4477×5335	6508×7043
19	8150×8039	9185×11212
20	8494×10564	14302×12384
21	16128×16115	14365×20945
22	20332×20737	35463×25342
23	23415×26407	39263×36343
24	52215×57171	75825×69708

Appendix B

Table 5. Performance of MXL_3 versus F_4 for HFE(96,n) systems

n	MXL_3 max. matrix	F_4 max. matrix
20	5236×5227	7053×6196
25	9979×9941	12459×15276
30	22515×31931	20003×31931
35	33705×59536	30081×59536
40	37005×84516	43124×102091
50	67525×251176	79116×251176
60	144030×523686	130755×523686
70	181335×974121	201343×974121
80	268840×1666981	293287×1666981

Improved Linear Cryptanalysis of SOSEMANUK

Joo Yeon Cho and Miia Hermelin

Helsinki University of Technology,
Department of Information and Computer Science,
P.O. Box 5400, FI-02015 TKK, Finland
{joo.cho,miia.hermelin}@tkk.fi

Abstract. The SOSEMANUK stream cipher is one of the finalists of the eSTREAM project. In this paper, we improve the linear cryptanalysis of SOSEMANUK presented in Asiacrypt 2008. We apply the generalized linear masking technique to SOSEMANUK and derive many linear approximations holding with the correlations of up to $2^{-25.5}$. We show that the data complexity of the linear attack on SOSEMANUK can be reduced by a factor of 2^{10} if multiple linear approximations are used. Since SOSEMANUK claims 128-bit security, our attack would not be a real threat on the security of SOSEMANUK.

Keywords: Stream Ciphers, Linear Cryptanalysis, SOSEMANUK, SOBER-128.

1 Introduction

SOSEMANUK [3] is a synchronous software-oriented stream cipher proposed by Berbain et al. in 2005. The SOSEMANUK cipher was submitted to the eSTREAM competition [12] and was selected as one of the four finalists of Profile 1 (software category) in the eSTREAM Portfolio. The eSTREAM project concluded in the final report that SOSEMANUK offers a very considerable margin for security as well as very reasonable performance trade-offs [2].

After the eSTREAM project closed, a linear attack against SOSEMANUK was presented by Lee et al. in Asiacrypt 2008 [10]. In this attack, authors used the linear masking method [7] to derive the best linear approximation of the nonlinear function. Then, they mounted a state recovery attack which was originally developed to cryptanalyze the Grain stream cipher version 0 [4]. The main idea of this attack is to collect a number of linear approximations which depend on partial initial state bits and use them to distinguish the right value of partial initial states from the wrong ones. Authors claimed that the full initial states of SOSEMANUK can be recovered with the time complexity of $2^{147.9}$, the memory complexity of $2^{147.1}$ and the data complexity of $2^{145.5}$.

In this paper, we improve Lee et al.'s linear attack on SOSEMANUK. We derive the best linear approximation of SOSEMANUK by the generalized linear masking method which was applied to the distinguishing attack on SNOW 2.0

D. Lee and S. Hong (Eds.): ICISC 2009, LNCS 5984, pp. 101–116, 2010.

by Nyberg et al. [14]. Our results show that the best linear approximation of SOSEMANUK is not a single but multiple. Moreover, many linear approximations have the same order of magnitude of the correlations as the highest one. If Lee et al.'s attack uses such multiple linear approximations holding with strong correlations, the data complexity of the attack can be reduced significantly. On the other hand, the time complexity of the attack is not much affected since the total amount of linear approximations is determined by the correlation of the dominant linear approximations. We estimate that the best attack requires around $2^{135.7}$ keystream bits with the time complexity $2^{147.4}$ and memory complexity $2^{146.8}$.

We note that SOSEMANUK claims the security level of 2^{128} complexity so that our analysis would not threaten the security of SOSEMANUK. Rather, we focus on the security analysis of each component of SOSEMANUK and the effect of their combinations. As a result, we hope to evaluate the security margin of the whole cipher more accurately. We also show that our method can enhance the performance of the distinguishing attack against SOBER-128 which adapts similar nonlinear components to SOSEMANUK.

This paper is organized as follows. In Section 2, the structure of the SOSEMANUK stream cipher is briefly described and the previous linear attacks are discussed. In Section 3, the linear approximations are derived and its capacity is computed. In Section 4, the improved correlation attack against SOSEMANUK is presented. In Section 5, our attack is applied to SOBER-128. Section 6 concludes this paper.

2   Preliminaries

2.1   Brief Description of SOSEMANUK

SOSEMANUK inherits the design structure of the stream cipher SNOW 2.0 [8] which is known for both strong security and high performance. SOSEMANUK aims at improving SNOW 2.0 by reducing the internal state size of the linear feedback shift register (LFSR) for better performance and adding a multiplexing function for avoiding some structural properties. SOSEMANUK also adapts the transformation function from the block cipher SERPENT [1] which was one of the five finalists of AES competition [11]. The structure of SOSEMANUK is shown in Figure 1.

SOSEMANUK uses a single 320-bit (10-word) LFSR which is operated on $\mathbb{F}_{2^{32}}$ with the following recurrence function:

$$s_{t+10} = s_{t+9} \oplus \alpha^{-1} s_{t+3} \oplus \alpha s_t, \quad t \geq 1 \tag{1}$$

where α is a root of the primitive polynomial $P(X) = X^4 + \beta^{23} X^3 + \beta^{245} X^2 + \beta^{48} X + \beta^{239}$ on $\mathbb{F}_{2^8}[X]$ and β is a root of the primitive polynomial $Q(X) = X^8 + X^7 + X^5 + X^3 + 1$ on $\mathbb{F}_2[X]$. The nonlinear block of SNOW-like structure is called *the Finite State Machine* (FSM). The FSM of SOSEMANUK contains two 32-bit registers $R1$ and $R2$ with the following relations:

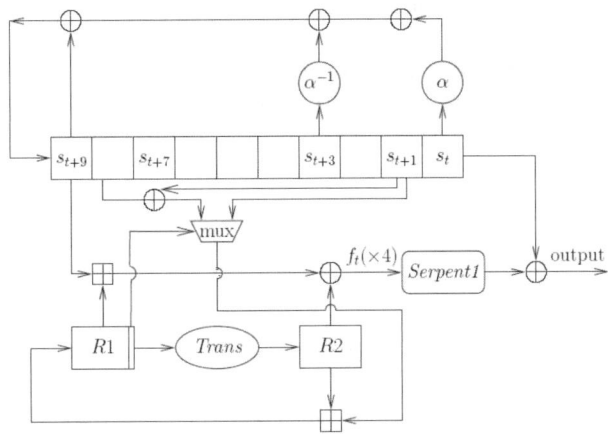

Fig. 1. Overview of SOSEMANUK

$$R1_{t+1} = R2_t \boxplus (r_t s_{t+9} \oplus s_{t+2})$$
$$R2_{t+1} = Trans(R1_t) \qquad\qquad (2)$$
$$f_t = (s_{t+9} \boxplus R1_t) \oplus R2_t$$

where r_t denotes the least significant bit of $R1_t$. The transition function Trans which is operated on $\mathbb{F}_{2^{32}}$ is defined as

$$\text{Trans}(R1_t) = (R1_t \times \text{0x54655307 mod } 2^{32})_{\lll 7}$$

where $x_{\lll 7}$ denotes x left-rotated by 7 bits and $\times$ denotes an arithmetic multiplication.

Four consecutive outputs of FSM become the input of the transformation function, which is called Serpent1, defined as

$$(z_{t+3}, z_{t+2}, z_{t+1}, z_t) = \text{Serpent1}(f_{t+3}, f_{t+2}, f_{t+1}, f_t) \oplus (s_{t+3}, s_{t+2}, s_{t+1}, s_t). \quad (3)$$

Serpent1 takes four 32-bit words as input and provides four 32-bit words as output in bitslice mode. Serpent1 uses an identical 4×4 transformation functions 32 times in parallel, each of which uses 4×4 S-box S_2 which is one of the eight distinct S-boxes used in SERPENT. For complete description of SOSEMANUK we refer to the paper [3].

2.2 Lee et al.'s Attack on SOSEMANUK in Asiacrypt 2008

Let n be a non-negative integer. Given two vectors $x = (x_0, \ldots, x_{n-1})$ and $y = (y_0, \ldots, y_{n-1})$ where $x, y \in \mathbb{F}_2^n$, let $x \cdot y$ denote a standard inner product defined as $x \cdot y = x_0 y_0 \oplus \ldots \oplus x_{n-1} y_{n-1}$. A linear mask is a constant vector that is used to compute an inner product of a n-bit string.

Let $f : \mathbb{F}_{2^n} \mapsto \mathbb{F}_{2^m}$ for some positive integers m and n. The correlation of f is $c(f) = c(f(x)) = 2^{-n} \left(\#\{x : f(x) = 0\} - \#\{x : f(x) = 1\} \right)$. Given a linear input mask $\Lambda \in \mathbb{F}_2^n$ and a linear output mask $\Gamma \in \mathbb{F}_2^m$, the correlation of the linear approximation $\Lambda \cdot x = \Gamma \cdot f(x)$ of f is $c_f(\Lambda; \Gamma) = c(\Lambda \cdot x \oplus \Gamma \cdot f(x))$.

In [10], the best linear approximations of FSM and Serpent1 were derived using a single linear mask Γ as follows:

$$\text{FSM}: \quad \Gamma \cdot f_t \oplus \Gamma \cdot f_{t+1} \oplus \Gamma \cdot s_{t+10} \oplus \Gamma \cdot s_{t+2} = 0 \tag{4}$$

$$\text{Serpent1}: \Gamma \cdot f_t \oplus \Gamma \cdot f_{t+1} \oplus \Gamma \cdot (s_t \oplus z_t) \oplus \Gamma \cdot (s_{t+3} \oplus z_{t+3}) = 0. \tag{5}$$

If (4) and (5) are linearly combined, f_t and f_{t+1} terms are canceled out and the linear approximation of SOSEMANUK is derived as

$$\Gamma \cdot s_{t+10} \oplus \Gamma \cdot s_{t+2} = \Gamma \cdot (s_t \oplus z_t) \oplus \Gamma \cdot (s_{t+3} \oplus z_{t+3}). \tag{6}$$

The highest correlation of (6) holds with the correlation of $2^{-21.4}$ [10]. The correlation attack presented in [10] reduced the data complexity of the attack by the so-called *Second LFSR derivative technique* that was developed by Berbain et al. in [4]. We will discuss this technique in Section 3. Finally, authors claimed that the attack requires around $2^{145.5}$ data, $2^{147.9}$ computing time and $2^{147.1}$ memory complexity.

3   Deriving Linear Approximations of SOSEMANUK

In this section, we derive the linear approximations of two nonlinear blocks: FSM and Serpent1. By combining them, we derive the linear approximation of SOSEMANUK which uses only the internal states of LFSR and the keystream bits as variables.

3.1   Linear Approximation of FSM

FSM uses the Trans-function and modular additions as the nonlinear components. If the linear masks of each nonlinear component are allowed to be different, a wider range of linear masks search is possible, which enables us to obtain multiple linear approximations with strong correlations. Our idea is depicted in Figure 2.

Firstly, we establish the linear approximations of each nonlinear components as follows:

$$\Gamma_2 \cdot R2_{t+1} = \Phi \cdot R1_t$$
$$\Lambda \cdot R1_{t+1} = \Gamma_1 \cdot R2_t \oplus \Gamma_4 \cdot (s_{t+2} \oplus r_t s_{t+9})$$
$$\Gamma_1 \cdot f_t = \Gamma_3 \cdot s_{t+9} \oplus \Phi \cdot R1_t \oplus \Gamma_1 \cdot R2_t$$
$$\Gamma_2 \cdot f_{t+1} = \Gamma_5 \cdot s_{t+10} \oplus \Lambda \cdot R1_{t+1} \oplus \Gamma_2 \cdot R2_{t+1}.$$

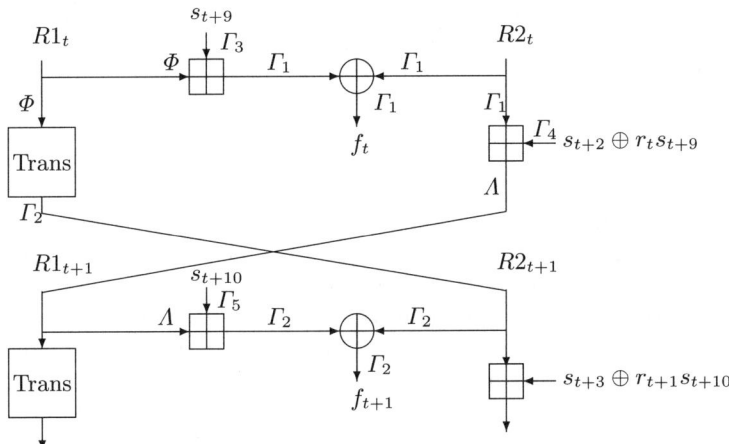

Fig. 2. Generalized linear masking of FSM

where $(\Gamma_1, \Gamma_2, \Gamma_3, \Gamma_4, \Gamma_5) \in \mathbb{F}_2^{32}$. If above approximations are linearly combined, the terms of $R1$ and $R2$ registers vanish. Then, we get the following approximation of FSM:

$$\Gamma_1 \cdot f_t \oplus \Gamma_2 \cdot f_{t+1} = \Gamma_3 \cdot s_{t+9} \oplus \Gamma_5 \cdot s_{t+10} \oplus \Gamma_4 \cdot (s_{t+2} \oplus r_t s_{t+9}). \qquad (7)$$

Since $r_t \in \{0, 1\}$, we get the following two approximations from (7):

$$(r_t = 0): \quad \Gamma_1 \cdot f_t \oplus \Gamma_2 \cdot f_{t+1} = \Gamma_3 \cdot s_{t+9} \oplus \Gamma_5 \cdot s_{t+10} \oplus \Gamma_4 \cdot s_{t+2} \qquad (8)$$
$$(r_t = 1): \quad \Gamma_1 \cdot f_t \oplus \Gamma_2 \cdot f_{t+1} = (\Gamma_3 \oplus \Gamma_4) \cdot s_{t+9} \oplus \Gamma_5 \cdot s_{t+10} \oplus \Gamma_4 \cdot s_{t+2}. \qquad (9)$$

Let us denote the correlations of modular addition and the Trans-function by

$$c_+(\Lambda_1, \Lambda_2; \Gamma) = 2 \Pr[\Lambda_1 \cdot x \oplus \Lambda_2 \cdot y = \Gamma \cdot (x \boxplus y)] - 1$$
$$c_{\text{Trans}}(\Lambda; \Gamma) = 2 \Pr[\Lambda \cdot x = \Gamma \cdot \text{Trans}(x)] - 1.$$

According to Correlation Theorem in [13], the correlations of both (8) and (9) are obtained by computing

$$c_{\text{FSM}}(\Gamma_1, \Gamma_2, \Gamma_3, \Gamma_4, \Gamma_5) = \frac{1}{2} \sum_{\Lambda=1}^{2^{32}-1} c_+(\Gamma_1, \Gamma_4; \Lambda) c_+(\Gamma_5, \Lambda; \Gamma_2) \sum_{\Phi=1}^{2^{32}-1} c_+(\Gamma_3, \Phi; \Gamma_1) c_{\text{Trans}}(\Phi; \Gamma_2) \quad (10)$$

where the constant $\frac{1}{2}$ comes from the assumption that $\Pr[r_t = 0] = \Pr[r_t = 1] = \frac{1}{2}$.

3.2 Linear Approximations of Serpent1

At every four clocks, Serpent1 substitutes 128-bit (4-word) inputs into 128-bit (4-word) outputs by 32 parallel S-boxes operated in the bitslice mode. For a fixed clock t, the inputs and outputs of Serpent1 are $(f_{t+i})_{i=0,1,2,3}$ and $(s_{t+i} \oplus z_{t+i})_{i=0,1,2,3}$, respectively. Hence, the general form of the linear approximation of Serpent1 is

$$\bigoplus_{i=0}^{3} A_i \cdot f_{t+i} = \bigoplus_{i=0}^{3} B_i \cdot (s_{t+i} \oplus z_{t+i}), \quad t \equiv 1 \pmod 4 \qquad (11)$$

where $A_i, B_i \in \mathbb{F}_2^{32}$ are the input and output linear masks, respectively.

In bitslice mode, the 4-bit input of the j-th S-box (out of 32 S-boxes) of Serpent1 is the concatenation of each j-th bit of $(f_{t+i})_{i=0,1,2,3}$. Let $a_j, b_j \in \mathbb{F}_{2^4}$ denote the input and output masks of the j-th S-box. The correlation of linear approximation using a_j and b_j is denoted by $c_S(a_j; b_j)$. Then, the correlation of (11) is equal to the multiplication of all the nonzero $c_S(a_j; b_j)$ where $0 \le j \le 31$ as

$$c_{\text{Serpent1}}(A_0, A_1, A_2, A_3, B_0, B_1, B_2, B_3) = \prod_{j \in J} c_S(a_j; b_j) \qquad (12)$$

where $J = \{j | \ c_S(a_j; b_j) \ne 0, \ 0 \le j \le 31\}$. Figure 3 shows an example of the linear approximation of Serpent1.

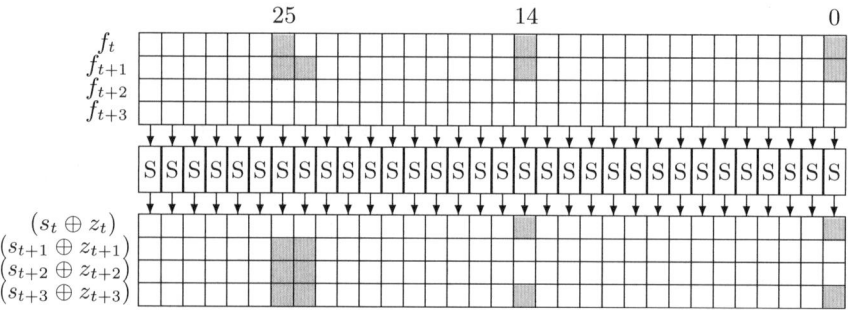

Fig. 3. An example of the linear approximation of Serpent1 with correlation of 2^{-4}

3.3   Approximations of SOSEMANUK

If we combine (7) and (11) in such a way that $(f_{t+i})_{i=0,1,2,3}$ terms vanish, we obtain the linear approximations of SOSEMANUK of which variables come from only the internal states of LFSR and the keystream. Obviously, such combination should satisfy the following condition:

$$(A_0, A_1, A_2, A_3) \in \{(\Gamma_1, \Gamma_2, 0, 0), (0, \Gamma_1, \Gamma_2, 0), (0, 0, \Gamma_1, \Gamma_2)\}.$$

Note that we can obtain (7) at clock $t, t+1$ and $t+2$. Hence, we derive the following form of the linear approximation for $t \equiv 1 \pmod 4$ as

$$\Gamma_3 \cdot s_{t+9+\tau} \oplus \Gamma_4 \cdot s_{t+2+\tau} \oplus \Gamma_5 \cdot s_{t+10+\tau} = \bigoplus_{i=0}^{3} B_i \cdot (s_{t+i} \oplus z_{t+i}), \quad \tau \in \{0, 1, 2\}. \ (13)$$

Let c_{sose} denote the correlation of (13). Then, $c_{sose} = \sum_{\Gamma_1, \Gamma_2} c_{\text{FSM}} \times c_{\text{Serpent1}}$ and due to the bitslice mode of Serpent1, c_{sose} is equal to $c_{\text{FSM}} \times c_{\text{Serpent1}}$ for some single pair (Γ_1, Γ_2).

Searching the Linear Masks. We searched the linear masks of (13) of which correlations are as strong as possible. Since the search space of the relevant linear masks $(\Gamma_i)_{i=1,\ldots,5}$ and $(B_j)_{j=0,\ldots,3}$ over $\mathbb{F}_2^{32}$ is too large, we allowed the linear masks that are of Hamming weights up to six. The reason for this decision is as follows. Due to the bitslice mode of Serpent1, c_{Serpent1} is determined by the Hamming weight of Γ_1 and Γ_2. Also, the correlation of FSM has three terms of c_+ which is limited by the Hamming weight of Γ_1 and Γ_2. Hence, the c_{sose} using the linear masks of the Hamming weight six is likely to be smaller than $2^{-6\cdot4} = 2^{-24}$ and it is much smaller than the highest correlation.

For efficient search, the following results help us to reduce the search space. For each $i = 0, \ldots, 31$, we denote the i-th bit of $X \in \mathbb{F}_{2^{32}}$ by X_i. Moreover, the vector of i least significant bits of X is denoted by $X_i' = (X_{i-1}, \ldots, X_0)$. Consider first the modular addition in $\mathbb{F}_{2^{32}}$, denoted by $\boxplus$. Lemma 4 given in [5] is stated as follows:

Lemma 1. *Let $X, Y \in \mathbb{F}_{2^{32}}$ and let $Z = X \boxplus Y$ be their sum modulo 2^{32}. Then $Z_0 = X_0 \oplus Y_0$, $Z_1 = X_1 \oplus Y_1 \oplus X_0 Y_0$ and for all $i = 2, \ldots, 31$, the bit $Z_i = X_i \oplus Y_i \oplus f_i(X_i', Y_i')$, where the function f_i is given by*

$$f_i(X_i', Y_i') = X_{i-1}Y_{i-1} \oplus \bigoplus_{j=0}^{i-2} X_j Y_j \left(\prod_{t=j+1}^{i-1} X_t \oplus Y_t \right).$$

We need the following concepts to formalize the next results. Let $p = \max\{i = 0, \ldots, 32 : X_i \neq 0\}$, that is, p is the largest index such that $X_p \neq 0$ and $X_i = 0$, if $i > p$. Then p is called the *most significant effective bit position* (MSEBP) of X. We denote $p = \text{MSP}(X)$.

Let $X = g(S) \in \mathbb{F}_{2^{32}}$ and $Y = h(S) \in \mathbb{F}_{2^{32}}$ be calculated from the n-bit internal state $S \in \mathbb{F}_{2^n}$ of the cipher using some functions g and h. We say that X and Y are statistically independent, if for all masks $\alpha, \beta \in \mathbb{F}_2^{32}$ and $(\alpha, \beta) \neq (0,0)$, the correlation $c(\alpha \cdot X \oplus \beta \cdot Y) = c(\alpha \cdot f(S) \oplus \beta \cdot g(S)) = 0$. Hence, if X and Y are statistically independent, each non-trivial linear combination of their bits has zero correlation. We have the following result about the possible input and output masks of the addition of statistically independent inputs:

Lemma 2. *Let $X, Y \in \mathbb{F}_{2^{32}}$ be statistically independent and let $Z = X \boxplus Y$. Let α, β and γ be 32-bit masks of the linear approximation $\alpha \cdot X \oplus \beta \cdot Y \oplus \gamma \cdot Z$ with correlation $c_+(\alpha, \beta; \gamma)$. If the correlation is non-zero, then $\text{MSP}(\alpha) = \text{MSP}(\beta) = \text{MSP}(\gamma)$.*

Proof. Let $p = \text{MSP}(\alpha), q = \text{MSP}(\beta)$ and $r = \text{MSP}(\gamma)$. Using Lemma 1, we have

$$\alpha \cdot X \oplus \beta \cdot Y \oplus \gamma \cdot Z = X_p \oplus Y_q \oplus Z_r \oplus L = X_p \oplus Y_q \oplus X_r \oplus Y_r \oplus f_r(X_r', Y_r') \oplus L,$$

where $L = L(X'_p, Y'_q, Z'_r)$ is a nonlinear function. But since X and Y are statistically independent, the correlation $c_+(\alpha, \beta; \gamma)$ can be non-zero only if $p = q = r$. $\square$

The previous lemma shows how to restrict the search space of the $\boxplus$-operation. We consider the Trans-function next. Let us denote $Z = R \times 0x54655307 \bmod 2^{32}$. The multiplication by $0x54655307$ is equal to the 14-consecutive modular additions as

$$Z = R \boxplus (R \ll 1) \boxplus (R \ll 2) \boxplus (R \ll 8) \boxplus (R \ll 9) \boxplus (R \ll 12) \boxplus (R \ll 14) \boxplus (R \ll 16)$$
$$\boxplus (R \ll 18) \boxplus (R \ll 21) \boxplus (R \ll 22) \boxplus (R \ll 26) \boxplus (R \ll 28) \boxplus (R \ll 30),$$

where $\ll$ denotes the left-shift operation. Similarly as for $\boxplus$-operation, the bit $Z_i = R_i \oplus g_i(R'_i)$, for all $i = 0, \ldots, 31$. The following corollary shows how the space of possible masks for Trans-function can be restricted.

Corollary 1. *Let $R \in \mathbb{F}_{2^{32}}$ be the input of the Trans-function. Let α and β be 32-bit input and output masks of the Trans-function, respectively. If the correlation c_{FSM} of the linear approximation of FSM is non-zero, then for some $q = 0, \ldots, 6$, we have $q + 25 = \mathrm{MSP}(\alpha) = \mathrm{MSP}(\beta)$. Moreover, $\beta_q = 1$ and $\beta_i = 0$ for all $i = q + 1, \ldots, 6$.*

Proof. Let us first show that $\mathrm{MSP}(\alpha) = \mathrm{MSP}(\beta)$. In all the $\boxplus$-additions in the FSM, the other input consists of some of the statistically independent LFSR state words $s_t, \ldots, s_{t+9}$. Hence, in all three $\boxplus$-additions, the two inputs are statistically independent of each other and by formula (10) and Lemma 2, the MSEBP of all the masks in the triples $(\Gamma_1, \Gamma_4, \Lambda)$, $(\Gamma_5, \Lambda, \Gamma_2)$ and $(\Gamma_3, \Phi, \Gamma_1)$ must be equal. Since $\alpha = \Phi$ and $\beta = \Gamma_2$, we have $\mathrm{MSP}(\alpha) = \mathrm{MSP}(\beta) = p$, for some $p = 0, \ldots, 31$.

Next we show that $p = q + 25$ for some $q = 0, \ldots, 6$ and $\beta_q = 1$. We divide the Trans-function to two steps: $Z = R \times 0x54655307 \bmod 2^{32}$ and $W = Z_{\lll 7}$, such that for each $i = 0, \ldots, 31$, we have $W_i = Z_{(i-7) \bmod 32}$. If the correlation $c_{\mathrm{Trans}}(\alpha; \beta)$ of the approximation is non-zero there must be no statistically independent linear terms in the approximation. Since $\alpha_p = 1$, the term R_p is included in the approximation. For all $i = 0, \ldots, 31$, the bit $Z_i = R_i \oplus g_i(R'_i)$. Hence, at least one of the bits $Z_p, \ldots, Z_{31}$, should be used in the approximation, otherwise R_p would be a statistically independent linear term and the correlation $c_{\mathrm{Trans}}(\alpha; \beta) = 0$. If $p = 31$, then bit $Z_{31} = W_6$ is used in the approximation, we have $\beta_6 = 1$ and the claim holds for $q = 6$.

Assume now $p < 31$. Since p is the MSEBP of α, we must have $\beta_6 = 0$. Otherwise, we would have the bit $Z_{31} = W_6 = R_{31} + g_{31}(R'_{31})$ in the approximation, but R_{31} would then be a lonely, statistically independent linear term giving zero correlation. Similarly we conclude that $\beta_i = 0$, for $i = (p + 8) \bmod 32, \ldots, 6$. Hence, we must have $\beta_{(p+7) \bmod 32} = 1$. Again, since p is MSEBP, we have $p > (p + 7) \bmod 32$. Hence, $p \geq 25$ such that $p = q + 25$, for some $q = 0, \ldots, 6$ and $\beta_{(p+7) \bmod 32} = \beta_q = 1$. $\square$

We note that part of Corollary 1 was heuristically used in [10] with the assumption that $\alpha = \beta$.

Our Results. We used Wallén's algorithm proposed in [15] by which the linear approximations of the modular addition of 2^n could be efficiently delivered. Unfortunately, we could not find the stronger approximation than the one reported in [10]. Instead, we found out there exist many linear approximations that have the same magnitude of correlations as the strongest one. The linear masks of the approximations with strong correlations are partially listed in Table 1. Note that $W_H(X)$ denotes the Hamming weight of X; that is, the number of nonzero bits of $X \in \mathbb{F}_2^{32}$. SOSEMANUK is composed of two nonlinear blocks that operate independently, which intends to remove the possibility of linear approximation that has strong correlation on both blocks simultaneously. On the other hand, the linear approximations of both blocks can be combined independently, which yields multiple linear approximations with equal correlations. Here is an example. Let us take the linear approximation of FSM which is located in the first line in Table 1: $(\Gamma_1, \Gamma_2, \Gamma_3, \Gamma_4, \Gamma_5) = (0x02004001, 0x03004001, 0x02004001, 0x02004001, 0x03004001)$ with the correlation of $2^{-17.4}$. The Γ_1 and Γ_2 are transformed into the input masks of Serpent1 that have four nonzero inputs of the S-boxes at the bit positions of $25, 24, 14, 0$, as shown in Figure 3. According to the S-box profile of Serpent1 displayed in Table 5, there exist multiple input and output masks of S-box that yield nonzero correlations. For instance, $c_S(3; 9) = c_S(3; 14) = 2^{-1}$ and $c_S(2; 7) = c_S(2; 14) =$

Table 1. Linear masks of FSM with $|c_{\text{FSM}}| \geq 2^{-18.5}$ where $\vee$ denotes a bitwise logical OR operation

Γ_1	Γ_2	Γ_3	Γ_4	Γ_5	c_{FSM}	$W_H(\Gamma_1 \vee \Gamma_2)$
02004001	03004001	02004001	02004001	03004001	$2^{-17.4}$	4
03004001	03004001	03004001	03004001	03004001	$2^{-17.4}$	4
02006001	03004001	02006001	02006001	03004001	$2^{-17.4}$	5
03006001	03004001	03006001	03006001	03004001	$2^{-17.4}$	5
02004001	03004001	02004001	02006001	03006001	$2^{-18.4}$	4
02004001	03004001	02004001	03004001	02004001	$2^{-18.4}$	4
03004001	03004001	03004001	03006001	03006001	$2^{-18.4}$	4
03004001	03004001	03004001	02004001	02004001	$2^{-18.4}$	4
02000201	02000301	03000301	02000201	02000301	$2^{-18.5}$	4
02000301	02000301	03000201	02000301	02000301	$2^{-18.5}$	4

Table 2. Evaluation of the number of linear approximations with respect to the correlations

source	$|c_{sose}|$	M	$M \times c_{sose}^2$
Lee et al.'s attack [10]	$2^{-21.4}$	8	$2^{-39.8}$
	$2^{-21.4}$	896	$2^{-33.0}$
	$2^{-22.5}$	7680	$2^{-32.1}$
this paper	$2^{-23.5}$	63104	$2^{-31.1}$
	$2^{-24.5}$	331776	$2^{-30.7}$
	$2^{-25.5}$	1391872	$2^{-30.6}$

2^{-1}. We obtain more linear approximations by taking (13) at clock $t, t+1$ and $t+2$. Also, both (8) and (9) have equal correlations. In total, there are $896 \approx 2^{9.8}$ linear approximations holding with the correlation of $2^{-21.4}$. Furthermore, we found that a large number of linear approximations have strong correlations slightly less than the strongest one. Table 2 summarizes the number of the linear approximations of (13) that have the correlations of up to $2^{-25.5}$.

4   Linear Cryptanalysis of SOSEMANUK

4.1   Generating Linear Approximations by Linear Recurrence

Given the linear approximation (13), a new linear approximation can be generated by applying the linear recurrence function of the LFSR to (13) at every clock. This technique was described in [4,10] and we give a simpler description using the matrix on this method.

Recall the linear recurrence function of SOSEMANUK. It is well known that the function (1) is equivalently expressed by the following transition matrix:

$$A = \begin{pmatrix} 0 & 1 & 0 & \cdots & 0 \\ 0 & 0 & 1 & \cdots & 0 \\ 0 & 0 & 0 & \cdots & 1 \\ a_0 & a_1 & a_2 & \cdots & a_9 \end{pmatrix}$$

where $(a_0, a_3, a_9) = (\alpha, \alpha^{-1}, 1)$ and the other $(a_i)_{i=1,2,4,5,6,7,8}$ are zeros over F_2^{32}. Let us denote the states of the LFSR at the clock t as $S_t = (s_t \; s_{t+1} \; \cdots \; s_{t+9})^T$ where $s_t \in F_2^{32}$ and the superscript T stands for the transpose of the matrix. The state update of LFSR is expressed as $S_{t+1} = A S_t$ for $t \geq 0$. By induction, the current state of LFSR is expressed as $S_t = A^t S_0$ and S_0 is called *the initial states* of the LFSR.

Suppose that $U = (u_0 \; u_1 \; \cdots \; u_9)$ and $W = (w_0 \; w_1 \; w_2 \; w_3)$ denotes linear mask matrices where $u_i, w_i \in F_2^{32}$, respectively. Then, the linear approximation of SOSEMANUK (13) is expressed as the following form:

$$U S_t \oplus W Z_t = 0 \iff U A^t S_0 \oplus W Z_t = 0, \quad t \equiv 1 \pmod 4 \tag{14}$$

where $Z_t = (z_t, z_{t+1}, z_{t+2}, z_{t+3})^T$.

4.2   Attack Method

Our attack algorithm is exactly same as [4,10] except that multiple linear approximations are derived at a fixed clock. Let us assume that N is the number of keystream words observation and M is the linear approximations of the form (14) derived at each clock. Then, we get totally $M \times N$ linear approximations for the attack and they are expressed as the following form:

$$\begin{pmatrix} U_0 \\ U_1 \\ \vdots \\ U_{M-1} \end{pmatrix} A^t S_0 \oplus \begin{pmatrix} W_0 \\ W_1 \\ \vdots \\ W_{M-1} \end{pmatrix} Z_t = 0, \quad t = 1, 2, \ldots, N. \tag{15}$$

Let l denote the length of the internal states of the LFSR over $\mathbb{F}_2$. Our attack aims at recovering m bits out of l state bits where $0 < m < l$. Let Ω_m denote a subspace of $\mathbb{F}_2^l$ such that $l - m$ coordinates at each U in Ω_m are always zeros. Without loss of generality, we assume that the vectors of the Ω_m have zero values from the first to the $(l - m)$-th coordinates. Hence, $|\Omega_m| = 2^m$.

The attack algorithm to recover the m state bits is described as follows;

1. Collect a sufficient number of linear approximations which satisfy $U_i A^t \in \Omega_m$ where $0 \le i \le M$ and $0 \le t \le N$.
2. For $K = 0$ to $K = 2^m - 1$,
    (a) Assign the values of m state bits by K;
    (b) Compute the correlation of the linear approximations using K;
3. Choose K whose correlation is maximal.

In Step 1, the expected number of linear approximations is $M \times N \times 2^{m-l}$. If we combine the $N \times M$ linear approximations pairwise, we can derive new linear approximations (holding with lower correlations) for the attack without increasing the number of the keystream observations. This technique is called *Second LFSR derivation* in [4]. From (15), a pairwise combined linear approximation is of the following form:

$$(U_i A^{\tau_1} \oplus U_j A^{\tau_2})S_0 \oplus (W_i Z_{\tau_1} \oplus W_j Z_{\tau_2}) = 0, \quad 1 \le i, j \le M, \ 1 \le \tau_1, \tau_2 \le N.$$

The amount of possible combinations are $N \times M \times 2$. Among those, we choose the linear approximations such that $(U_{i_1} A^{j_1} \oplus U_{i_2} A^{j_2}) \in \Omega_m$. Obviously, such approximations have the correlation of c_{sose}^2. The number of approximations that satisfy this condition is expected to be $N' = 2^{m-l}(N \times M)^2$.

Let us denote N' linear approximations by

$$U_i' S_0 \oplus W_i' Z_t = 0, \quad i = 0, \cdots, N' - 1. \tag{16}$$

where $U_i' \in \Omega_m$. In Step 2 and Step 3, the correlations of (16) are evaluated for all possible values of m state bits as follows:

$$\forall K \in \Omega_m, \quad D_K = (\#\{U_i' K \oplus W_i' Z_t = 0'\} - \#\{U_i' K \oplus W_i' Z_t = 1\})/N'.$$

For correctly guessed m state bits, D_K is close to c_{sose}^2. On the other hand, for incorrectly guessed state bits, D_K is close to zero.

Instead of evaluating (16) for all possible values of m state bits independently, we can reduce the computing complexity by the fast Walsh-Hadamard Transform. Let $f : \Omega_m \to \mathbb{R}$ be a real valued function. The Walsh-Hadamard Transform F of f is defined as

$$F(\nu) = \sum_{\eta \in \Omega_m} f(\eta)(-1)^{\eta \cdot \nu}, \quad \nu \in \Omega_m.$$

If the mapping f is defined as the frequencies of the vectors U_i' and W_i' for $i = 0, \cdots, N' - 1$, the fast Walsh-Hadamard Transform $F(K)$ for a fixed K indicates the D_K.

4.3   Attack Complexity

We estimate the complexity of the attack by the statistic method presented in [4,10]. Let l denote the length of the LFSR of SOSEMANUK in bits, i.e. $l = 320$. We target to recover m bits out of l bits by using the linear approximations whose correlations are larger than c_{sose}.

Data Complexity. Let Φ be the normal cumulative distribution function which is defined as

$$\Phi(x) = \frac{1}{\sqrt{2\pi}} \int_{-\infty}^{x} e^{-\frac{t^2}{2}} dt.$$

For the right value K_0 of the m state bits, the non-detection probability is

$$\Pr\left[D_{K_0} < \frac{3}{2}N'c_{sose}\right] = 1 - \Phi(3/\lambda)$$

and for the wrong value $K_i \neq K_0$ of the m state bits, the false-alarm probability is

$$\Pr\left[D_{K_i} < \frac{3}{2}N'c_{sose}\right] = 2^{-m}$$

where λ is determined by the condition $1 - \Phi(\lambda) = 2^{-m}$. Then, the number of approximation relations needed for the state recovery attack is $N' = (\frac{4\lambda}{3c_{sose}^2})^2$. Hence, the number of keystream observations N required for the attack is calculated as

$$N' = 2^{m-l-1}(N \times M)^2 = (\frac{4\lambda}{3c_{sose}^2})^2 \implies N = \frac{4\lambda 2^{(l-m+1)/2}}{3Mc_{sose}^2}. \qquad (17)$$

Since a 128-bit keystream is produced at each observation (every four clocks), the attack requires $128 \times N$ bits of data.

Time Complexity. Suppose that $M \times N$ linear approximations are obtained by observing the keystream and calculating the state recurrence matrix of LFSR. In order to perform the Second LFSR derivative technique, we need $(M \times N)^2$ operations in general. However, the operations can be reduced by applying sorting-and-combining technique used in [4,10]. First, $M \times N$ approximations are sorted out according to the value of $l - m$ state bits. Let the sorted approximations be represented by $X_1, X_2, \ldots, X_{M \times N}$. Then, two consecutive approximations X_i and X_{i+1} for $i = 1, \ldots, M \times N - 1$ are checked whether their $l - m$ state bits are same. If they are same, we know $X_i \oplus X_{i+1} \in \Omega_m$. It is known that the fast sorting algorithm requires around $(M \times N)\log(M \times N)$ operations. higher Let us assume that the N' linear approximations are generated by the Second LFSR derivative technique. As mentioned before, the evaluation of the N' linear approximations can be sped up by the fast Walsh-Hadamard Transform [4,10]. Since the space of the targeted state bits is 2^m, the evaluation by the fast Walsh-Hadamard Transform requires $2^m \log(2^m) = m \times 2^m$ operations. Hence, the time complexity of the attack for recovering the m state bits is approximately $m \times 2^m + (M \times N) \log(M \times N)$.

Let us assume $m \geq 138$ which is the parameter used in [10]. If the attack is performed on two non-overlapping sets of m state bits, we can recover $2m$ bits out of $320 + 64$ state bits. Then the remaining $384 - 2m$ bits can be searched exhaustively. Therefore, the time complexity required for the recovery of full internal state bits is around $T = 2 \times m \times 2^m + 2 \times M \times N \log(M \times N) + 2^{384 - 2 \times m}$.

Memory Complexity. In order to carry out the sorting-and-combining technique, we need to store $M \times N$ linear approximations, which needs around $l \times M \times N$ memory bits. The Fast Walsh transform needs around $2^m \times \lceil \log N' \rceil$ memory bits. Hence, the memory complexity is around $l \times M \times N + 2^m \times \lceil \log N' \rceil$.

Table 3 summarizes the best attack complexity achievable by using multiple linear approximations against SOSEMANUK.

Table 3. Comparison of the complexity with respect to the number of linear approximations

$|c_{sose}|$	M	m	λ	data (bits)	time	memory (bits)
$2^{-21.4}$	1	138	13.6	$2^{145.5}$	$2^{147.4}$	$2^{146.8}$
$2^{-21.4}$	896	138	13.6	$2^{135.7}$	$2^{147.4}$	$2^{146.8}$
$\geq 2^{-22.5}$	$896 + 7680$	139	13.6	$2^{134.1}$	$2^{148.8}$	$2^{148.5}$
$\geq 2^{-23.5}$	$896 + 7680 + 63104$	140	13.7	$2^{132.6}$	$2^{150.2}$	$2^{150.0}$
$\geq 2^{-24.5}$	$896 + 7680 + 63104 + 331776$	141	13.7	$2^{131.6}$	$2^{151.6}$	$2^{151.5}$
$\geq 2^{-25.5}$	$896 + 7680 + 63104 + 331776 + 1391872$	143	13.8	$2^{130.4}$	$2^{152.9}$	$2^{152.5}$

5   Improved Distinguishing Attack on SOBER-128

SOBER-128 is a software oriented stream cipher proposed in 2003 by Qualcomm Australia [9]. SOBER-128 consists of a 544-bit LFSR and a nonlinear filter (NLF). The length of supporting key size is 128-bit. The brief description of SOBER-128 algorithm is given in Appendix B.

The best attack against SOBER-128 is a distinguishing attack using a linear approximation with the correlation of $2^{-8.8}$ [6]. We discovered that there exist many linear approximations which hold with equal to or slightly less correlations than the highest one. The number of linear approximations with strong correlations is listed in Table 4. If these 96 linear approximations are used for the distinguishing attack, the data complexity of the attack is reduced to

$$N = 1 / \sum_{i=1}^{96} (2c_{sober,i}^{-6})^2 = (16 \cdot 2^{-103.6} + 24 \cdot 2^{-104.8} + 56 \cdot 2^{-106})^{-1} = 2^{98.4}.$$

For comparison, the distinguishing attack using a single linear approximation requires $2^{103.6}$ data complexity [6].

Table 4. The number of linear approximations of SOBER-128 and their correlations

source	$|c_{Sober}|$	# of linear approximations
[6]	$2^{-8.8}$	8
this paper	$2^{-8.8}$	16
	$2^{-8.9}$	24
	$2^{-9.0}$	56

6   Conclusion

SOSEMANUK adapts the core structures of two strong ciphering algorithms, aiming at reducing the possibility of attacks which are applicable to both ciphering blocks simultaneously. The existence of many linear approximations holding with strong correlations in both ciphering blocks seems to be an unexpected weakness of SOSEMANUK. We showed that the data complexity of the linear cryptanalysis presented in Asiacrypt 2008 can be reduced by a factor of 2^{10} if such multiple linear approximations are used. Even though we could not present any practical attack threatening the security of SOSEMANUK, we believe that our analysis techniques and results can be useful for analyzing SOSEMANUK-like ciphering algorithms.

Acknowledgment

We are grateful to anonymous reviewers of ICISC'09 for their very valuable comments that helped to improve the paper.

References

1. Anderson, R., Biham, E., Knudsen, L.: Serpent: A proposal for the advanced encryption standard. In: First Advanced Encryption Standard (AES) conference (1998)
2. Babbage, S., Canniere, C.: The eSTREAM portfolio (2008),
   http://www.ecrypt.eu.org/stream/portfolio.pdf
3. Berbain, C., Billet, O., Canteaut, A., Courtois, N., Gilbert, H., Goubin, L., Gouget, A., Granboulan, L., Lauradoux, C., Minier, M., Pornin, T., Sibert, H.: SOSE-MANUK: a fast software-oriented stream cipher, eSTREAM, ECRYPT Stream Cipher Project, Report 2005/027 (2005),
   http://www.ecrypt.eu.org/stream/sosemanukp3.html
4. Berbain, C., Gilbert, H., Maximov, A.: Cryptanalysis of grain. In: Robshaw, M.J.B. (ed.) FSE 2006. LNCS, vol. 4047, pp. 15–29. Springer, Heidelberg (2006)
5. Cho, J., Pieprzyk, J.: Algebraic attacks on SOBER-t32 and SOBER-t16 without stuttering. In: Roy, B., Meier, W. (eds.) FSE 2004. LNCS, vol. 3017, pp. 49–64. Springer, Heidelberg (2004)
6. Cho, J., Pieprzyk, J.: Distinguishing attack on SOBER-128 with linear masking. In: Batten, L.M., Safavi-Naini, R. (eds.) ACISP 2006. LNCS, vol. 4058, pp. 29–39. Springer, Heidelberg (2006)

7. Coppersmith, D., Halevi, S., Jutla, C.: Cryptanalysis of stream ciphers with linear masking. In: Yung, M. (ed.) CRYPTO 2002. LNCS, vol. 2442, pp. 515–532. Springer, Heidelberg (2002)
8. Ekdahl, P., Johansson, T.: A new version of the stream cipher SNOW. In: Nyberg, K., Heys, H.M. (eds.) SAC 2002. LNCS, vol. 2595, pp. 47–61. Springer, Heidelberg (2003)
9. Hawkes, P., Rose, G.: Primitive specification for SOBER-128, Cryptology ePrint Archive, Report 2003/081 (2003), http://eprint.iacr.org/
10. Lee, J., Lee, D., Park, S.: Cryptanalysis of SOSEMANUK and SNOW 2.0 using linear masks. In: Pieprzyk, J. (ed.) ASIACRYPT 2008. LNCS, vol. 5350, pp. 524–538. Springer, Heidelberg (2008)
11. NIST, Nist announces encryption standard finalists (1999), http://csrc.nist.gov/archive/aes/round2/r2report.pdf
12. ECRYPT NoE, eSTREAM - the ECRYPT stream cipher project (2005), http://www.ecrypt.eu.org/stream/
13. Nyberg, K.: Correlation theorems in cryptanalysis. Discrete Applied Mathematics 111, 177–188 (2001)
14. Nyberg, K., Wallen, J.: Improved linear distinguishers for SNOW 2.0. In: Robshaw, M.J.B. (ed.) FSE 2006. LNCS, vol. 4047, pp. 144–162. Springer, Heidelberg (2006)
15. Wallén, J.: Linear approximations of addition modulo 2^n. In: Johansson, T. (ed.) FSE 2003. LNCS, vol. 2887, pp. 261–273. Springer, Heidelberg (2003)

A   Correlation Table of S-Box of Serpent1

Given an input mask a and an output mask b where $a, b \in \mathbb{F}_2^4$, the correlation of the linear approximation $a \cdot x \oplus b \cdot S(x) = 0$ of the S-box is measured as follows:

$$c(a; b) = 2^{-4}(\#(a \cdot x \oplus b \cdot S(x) = 0) - \#(a \cdot x \oplus b \cdot S(x) = 1))$$

where the $\cdot$ notation stands for the standard inner product. The correlation table of the S-box is given in Table 5.

B   Brief Description of SOBER-128

SOBER-128 consists of an LFSR and a nonlinear filter (NLF). The LFSR consists of 17 words state registers which is denoted by the vector $(s_t, \cdots, s_{t+16})$. Since each s_i is a 32-bit integer, the size of LFSR is 544 bits. The new state of the LFSR is generated by the following connection polynomial

$$s_{t+17} = s_{t+15} \oplus s_{t+4} \oplus \gamma s_t,$$

where the constant $\gamma = 0\text{x}00000100$ (hexadecimal).

A Nonlinear Filter (NLF) produces an output word z_t by taking s_t, s_{t+1}, s_{t+6}, s_{t+13}, s_{t+16} from the LFSR states and the 32-bit constant K. The NLF consists of two substitution functions (S-box), one rotation, four adders modulo 2^{32} and three XOR additions.

Table 5. Correlation table of S-box used in Serpent1: $c(a; b)$

$a\backslash b$	1	2	3	4	5	6	7	8	9	a	b	c	d	e	f
1	0	0	0	0	2^{-1}	0	2^{-1}	0	-2^{-1}	0	2^{-1}	0	0	0	0
2	0	2^{-2}	2^{-2}	2^{-2}	-2^{-2}	0	2^{-1}	0	0	-2^{-2}	-2^{-2}	2^{-2}	-2^{-2}	2^{-1}	0
3	0	2^{-2}	2^{-2}	2^{-2}	2^{-2}	0	0	0	2^{-1}	-2^{-2}	2^{-2}	2^{-2}	-2^{-2}	-2^{-1}	0
4	0	2^{-2}	-2^{-2}	-2^{-2}	-2^{-2}	2^{-1}	0	0	0	-2^{-2}	2^{-2}	-2^{-2}	-2^{-2}	0	-2^{-1}
5	0	-2^{-2}	2^{-2}	-2^{-2}	2^{-2}	0	0	-2^{-1}	0	-2^{-2}	-2^{-2}	2^{-2}	2^{-2}	0	-2^{-1}
6	0	0	-2^{-1}	0	2^{-1}	0	0	0	0	-2^{-1}	0	-2^{-1}	0	0	0
7	0	2^{-1}	0	0	0	-2^{-1}	0	-2^{-1}	0	0	0	-2^{-1}	0	0	0
8	0	-2^{-2}	2^{-2}	0	0	2^{-2}	-2^{-2}	-2^{-2}	-2^{-2}	-2^{-1}	0	-2^{-2}	-2^{-2}	0	2^{-1}
9	0	-2^{-2}	2^{-2}	2^{-1}	0	-2^{-2}	-2^{-2}	2^{-2}	-2^{-2}	0	0	-2^{-2}	-2^{-2}	0	-2^{-1}
10	2^{-1}	0	0	-2^{-2}	-2^{-2}	-2^{-2}	2^{-2}	2^{-2}	-2^{-2}	-2^{-2}	-2^{-2}	0	0	-2^{-1}	0
11	-2^{-1}	0	0	2^{-2}	-2^{-2}	2^{-2}	2^{-2}	-2^{-2}	-2^{-2}	2^{-2}	-2^{-2}	0	0	-2^{-1}	0
12	0	0	0	2^{-2}	2^{-2}	2^{-2}	2^{-2}	2^{-2}	2^{-2}	-2^{-2}	-2^{-2}	-2^{-1}	2^{-1}	0	0
13	0	2^{-1}	2^{-1}	-2^{-2}	2^{-2}	2^{-2}	-2^{-2}	2^{-2}	-2^{-2}	2^{-2}	-2^{-2}	0	0	0	0
14	2^{-1}	-2^{-2}	2^{-2}	0	0	2^{-2}	2^{-2}	-2^{-2}	2^{-2}	2^{-1}	0	-2^{-2}	-2^{-2}	0	0
15	2^{-1}	2^{-2}	-2^{-2}	2^{-1}	0	2^{-2}	-2^{-2}	-2^{-2}	-2^{-2}	0	0	2^{-2}	2^{-2}	0	0

The function f is defined as $f(a) = \text{S-box}(a_H) \oplus a$, where the S-box takes 8-bit inputs and generates 32-bit outputs. Note that a_H is the most significant 8 bits of 32-bit word a. The output z_t of the nonlinear filter is described as follows

$$z_t = f((((f(s_t \boxplus s_{t+16}) \ggg 8) \boxplus s_{t+1}) \oplus K) \boxplus s_{t+6}) \boxplus s_{t+13},$$

where $\boxplus$ denotes an addition modulo 2^{32} and $\ggg 8$ denotes the right rotation by 8 bits.. The LFSR states and the constant K are initialized from the 128-bit secret key using the initialization procedure. More details can be found in the original paper describing SOBER-128 [9].

C Example of Linear Masks with the Strongest Correlations

Let us recall (13). If Γ_1 and Γ_2 is used in the bitslice mode and $\tau = 0$, the input of S-box can be 2 or 3. Since $c_S(2; 7) = c_S(2; 14) = 2^{-1}$ and $c_S(3; 9) = c_S(3; 14) = 2^{-1}$, there are 32 possible combinations. For $\tau = 1$, the input of S-box can be 4 or 6. Since $c_S(6; 3) = c_S(6; 5) = c_S(6; 11) = c_S(6; 13) = 2^{-1}$ and $c_S(4; 6) = c_S(4; 15) = 2^{-1}$, we get 384 possible combinations. For $\tau = 2$, the input of S-box can be 8 or 12. Since $c_S(8; 10) = c_S(8; 15) = 2^{-1}$ and $c_S(12; 12) = c_S(12; 13) = 2^{-1}$, there are 32 possible combinations. If we use both (8) and (9), we can get $2 \times (32 + 384 + 32) = 896$ linear approximations. Table 6 shows some linear masks with the strongest correlations for $\tau = 0$.

Table 6. Linear masks of approximations (13) with the correlation of $2^{-21.4}$ for $\tau = 0$

Γ_1	Γ_2	Γ_3	Γ_4	Γ_5	B_0	B_1	B_2	B_2	$|c_{sose}|$
02004001	03004001	02004001	02004001	03004001	03004001	01000000	01000000	02004001	$2^{-}21.4$
02004001	03004001	02004001	02004001	03004001	01004001	03000000	03000000	02004001	$2^{-}21.4$
02004001	03004001	02004001	02004001	03004001	02004001	01000000	01000000	03004001	$2^{-}21.4$
02004001	03004001	02004001	02004001	03004001	00004001	03000000	03000000	03004001	$2^{-}21.4$
02004001	03004001	02004001	02004001	03004001	03000001	01004000	01004000	02004001	$2^{-}21.4$
02004001	03004001	02004001	02004001	03004001	01000001	03004000	03004000	02004001	$2^{-}21.4$
02004001	03004001	02004001	02004001	03004001	02000001	01004000	01004000	03004001	$2^{-}21.4$
02004001	03004001	02004001	02004001	03004001	00000001	03004000	03004000	03004001	$2^{-}21.4$
02004001	03004001	02004001	02004001	03004001	03004000	01000001	01000001	02004001	$2^{-}21.4$
02004001	03004001	02004001	02004001	03004001	01004000	03000001	03000001	02004001	$2^{-}21.4$
02004001	03004001	02004001	02004001	03004001	02004000	01000001	01000001	03004001	$2^{-}21.4$
02004001	03004001	02004001	02004001	03004001	00004000	03000001	03000001	03004001	$2^{-}21.4$
02004001	03004001	02004001	02004001	03004001	03000000	01004001	01004001	02004001	$2^{-}21.4$
02004001	03004001	02004001	02004001	03004001	01000000	03004001	03004001	02004001	$2^{-}21.4$
02004001	03004001	02004001	02004001	03004001	02000000	01004001	01004001	03004001	$2^{-}21.4$
02004001	03004001	02004001	02004001	03004001	00000000	03004001	03004001	03004001	$2^{-}21.4$
03004001	03004001	03004001	03004001	03004001	03004001	00000000	00000000	03004001	$2^{-}21.4$
03004001	03004001	03004001	03004001	03004001	01004001	02000000	02000000	03004001	$2^{-}21.4$
03004001	03004001	03004001	03004001	03004001	02004001	01000000	01000000	03004001	$2^{-}21.4$
03004001	03004001	03004001	03004001	03004001	00004001	03000000	03000000	03004001	$2^{-}21.4$
03004001	03004001	03004001	03004001	03004001	03000001	00004000	00004000	03004001	$2^{-}21.4$
03004001	03004001	03004001	03004001	03004001	01000001	02004000	02004000	03004001	$2^{-}21.4$
03004001	03004001	03004001	03004001	03004001	02000001	01004000	01004000	03004001	$2^{-}21.4$
03004001	03004001	03004001	03004001	03004001	00000001	03004000	03004000	03004001	$2^{-}21.4$
03004001	03004001	03004001	03004001	03004001	03004000	00000001	00000001	03004001	$2^{-}21.4$
03004001	03004001	03004001	03004001	03004001	01004000	02000001	02000001	03004001	$2^{-}21.4$
03004001	03004001	03004001	03004001	03004001	02004000	01000001	01000001	03004001	$2^{-}21.4$
03004001	03004001	03004001	03004001	03004001	00004000	03000001	03000001	03004001	$2^{-}21.4$
03004001	03004001	03004001	03004001	03004001	03000000	00004001	00004001	03004001	$2^{-}21.4$
03004001	03004001	03004001	03004001	03004001	01000000	02004001	02004001	03004001	$2^{-}21.4$
03004001	03004001	03004001	03004001	03004001	02000000	01004001	01004001	03004001	$2^{-}21.4$
03004001	03004001	03004001	03004001	03004001	00000000	03004001	03004001	03004001	$2^{-}21.4$

Serial Model for Attack Tree Computations

Aivo Jürgenson[1,2] and Jan Willemson[3]

[1] Tallinn University of Technology, Raja 15, 12618 Tallinn, Estonia
aivo.jurgenson@eesti.ee
[2] Elion Enterprises Ltd, Endla 16, 15033 Tallinn, Estonia
[3] Cybernetica, Aleksandri 8a, Tartu 51004, Estonia
jan.willemson@gmail.com

Abstract. In this paper we extend the standard attack tree model by introducing temporal order to the attacker's decision making process. This will allow us to model the attacker's behaviour more accurately, since this way it is possible to study his actions related to dropping some of the elementary attacks due to them becoming obsolete based on the previous success/failure results. We propose an efficient algorithm for computing the attacker's expected outcome based on the given order of the elementary attacks and discuss the pros and cons of considering general rooted directed acyclic graphs instead of plain trees as the foundations for attack modelling.

1 Introduction

Attack tree (also called threat tree) approach to security evaluation is several decades old. It has been used for tasks like fault assessment of critical systems [1] or software vulnerability analysis [2,3]. The approach was first applied in the context of information systems (so-called *threat logic trees*) by Weiss [4] and later more widely adapted to information security by Bruce Schneier [5]. We refer to [6,7] for good overviews on the development and applications of the methodology.

Since their first introduction, attack trees have been used to describe attacks against various real-world applications like Border Gateway Protocol [8], SCADA protocols [9] and e-voting infrastructures [10]. Attack trees have found their place in computer science education [11] and several support tools like AttackTree+[1] and SecurITree[2] have been developed.

Early approaches to attack tree modelling were mostly concerned with just categorising the attacks [8] or modelling the attacker's behaviour by one specific parameter of the attacks like the cost, difficulty or severity [5,9,12]. A substantial step forward was taken by Buldas *et al.* [13] who introduced the idea of game-theoretic modelling of the attacker's decision making process based on several interconnected parameters like the cost, risks and penalties associated with different elementary attacks. This approach was later refined by Jürgenson and

---

[1] http://www.isograph-software.com/atpover.htm
[2] http://www.amenaza.com/

D. Lee and S. Hong (Eds.): ICISC 2009, LNCS 5984, pp. 118–128, 2010.

Willemson [14,15] and applied to the analysis of the security of several e-voting solutions by Buldas and Mägi [10].

So far, practically all the research in the field of attack trees has concentrated on what one could call a parallel model [4,5,3,8,9,16,12,13,14,10,15]. Essentially, the model assumes that all the elementary attacks take place simultaneously and hence the attacker's possible decisions based on success or failure of some of the elementary attacks are ignored. However, as noted already in [15], this model is unrealistic. In practice, the attacker is able to order his actions and try different alternative scenarios if some others fail or to stop trying altogether if some critical subset of elementary attacks has already failed or succeeded. Not risking with the hopeless or unnecessary attempts clearly reduces the amount of potential penalties and hence increases the attacker's expected outcome.

The main contribution of this paper is to surpass this shortcoming by introducing what one could call a serial model for attack trees. We extend the basic parallel model with temporal order of the elementary attacks and give the attacker some flexibility in skipping some of them or stopping the attack before all of the elementary attacks have been tried. The other contribution is a generalisation of the attack tree approach to accommodate arbitrary rooted directed acyclic graphs, which will enable us to conveniently ensure consistency of our computations in the general framework proposed by Mauw and Oostdijk [12].

The paper is organised as follows. In Section 2 we first briefly review the basic multi-parameter attack tree model. Sections 3 and 4 extend it by introducing attack descriptions based on general Boolean functions and temporal order of elementary attacks, respectively. Section 5 presents an efficient algorithm for computing the attacker's expected outcome of the attack tree with the predefined order of leaves. Finally, Section 6 draws some conclusions and sets directions for further work.

2   The Attack Tree Model

Basic idea of the attack tree approach is simple – the analysis begins by identifying one *primary threat* and continues by dividing the threat into subattacks, either all or some of them being necessary to materialise the primary threat. The subattacks can be divided further etc., until we reach the state where it does not make sense to divide the resulting attacks any more; these kinds of non-splittable attacks are called *elementary attacks* and the security analyst will have to evaluate them somehow. During the splitting process, a tree is formed having the primary threat in its root and elementary attacks in its leaves. Using the structure of the tree and the estimations of the leaves, it is then (hopefully) possible to give some estimations of the root node as well. In practice, it mostly turns out to be sufficient to consider only two kinds of splits in the internal nodes of the tree, giving rise to AND- and OR-nodes. As a result, an AND-OR-tree is obtained, forming the basis of the subsequent analysis.

The crucial contribution of Buldas *et al.* [13] was the introduction of four game-theoretically motivated parameters for each leaf node of the tree. This approach was later optimised in [15], where the authors concluded that only two parameters suffice. Following their approach, we consider the set of elementary attacks $\mathcal{X} = \{X_1, X_2, \ldots, X_n\}$ and give each one of them two parameters:

- p_i – success probability of the attack X_i,
- Expenses$_i$ – expected expenses (i.e. costs plus expected penalties) of the attack X_i.

Besides these parameters, there is a global value Gains expressing the benefit of the attacker if he is able to materialise the primary threat.

In the parallel model of [15], the expected outcome of the attacker is computed by maximising the expression

$$\text{Outcome}_S = p_S \cdot \text{Gains} - \sum_{X_i \in S} \text{Expenses}_i \tag{1}$$

over all the assignments $S \subseteq \mathcal{X}$ that make the Boolean formula $\mathcal{F}$, represented by the attack tree, true. (Here p_S denotes the success probability of the primary threat.) Like in the original model of Buldas *et al.* [13], we assume that the attacker behaves rationally, i.e. he attacks only if there is an attack scenario with a positive outcome. The defender's task is thus achieving a situation where all the attack scenarios would be non-beneficial for the attacker.

Our aim is to develop this model in two directions. In Section 3 we will generalise the attack tree model a bit to allow greater flexibility and expressive power of our model, and in Section 4 we will study the effects of introducing linear (temporal) order to the set of elementary attacks.

3   Attack Descriptions as Monotone Boolean Functions

Before proceeding, we briefly discuss a somewhat different perspective on attack tree construction. Contrary to the standard top-down ideology popularised by Schneier [5], a bottom-up approach is also possible. Say, our attacker has identified the set of elementary attacks $\mathcal{X}$ available to him and he needs to figure out, which subsets of $\mathcal{X}$ are sufficient to mount the root attack. In this paper we assume that the set of such subsets is monotone, i.e. if some set of elementary attacks suffices, then so does any of its supersets. This way it is very convenient to describe all the successful attacks by a monotone Boolean function $\mathcal{F}$ on the set of variables $\mathcal{X}$.

Of course, if we have constructed an attack tree then it naturally corresponds to a Boolean function. Unfortunately, considering only the formulae that have a tree structure is not always enough. Most notably, trees can not handle the situation, where the same lower-level attack is useful in several, otherwise independent higher-level attacks, and this is clearly a situation we can not ignore in practical security analysis.

Another shortcoming of the plain attack tree model follows from the general framework by Mauw and Oostdijk [12]. They argue that the semantics of an attack tree is inherently consistent if and only if the tree can be transformed into an equivalent form without changing the value of the expected outcome. When stating and proving their result, they essentially transform the underlying Boolean formula into a disjunctive normal form, but when doing so, they need to introduce several copies of some attacks, therefore breaking the tree structure in favour of a general rooted directed acyclic graph (RDAG). Since AND-OR-RDAGs are equivalent to monotone Boolean functions, there is no immediate need to take the generalisation any further.

Thus it would be more consistent and fruitful not to talk about *attack trees*, but rather *attack RDAGs*. On the other hand, as the structure of a tree is so much more convenient to analyse than a general RDAG, we should still try to stick to the trees whenever possible. We will see one specific example of a very efficient tree analysis algorithm in Section 5.

4   Ordering Elementary Attacks

After the attacker has selected the set of possible elementary attacks $\mathcal{X}$ and described the possible successful scenarios by means of a monotone Boolean function $\mathcal{F}$, he can start planning the attacks. Unlike the naïve parallel model of Schneier [5], the attacker has a lot of flexibility and choice. He may try some elementary attack first and based on its success or failure select the next elementary attack arbitrarily or even decide to stop attacking altogether (e.g. due to certain success or failure of the primary threat). Such a fully adaptive model is still too complicated to analyse with the current methods, thus we will limit the model to be semi-adaptive. I.e., we let the attacker to fix linear order of some elementary attacks in advance and assume that he tries them in succession, possibly skipping superfluous elementary attacks and stopping only if he knows that the Boolean value of $\mathcal{F}$ has been completely determined by the previous successes and failures of elementary attacks.

The full strategy of the attacker will be the following.

1. Create an attack RDAG with the set of leaf nodes $\mathcal{X} = \{X_1, X_2, \ldots, X_n\}$.
2. Select a subset $S \subseteq \mathcal{X}$ materialising the primary threat and consider the corresponding subtree.
3. Select a permutation α of S.
4. Based on the subtree and permutation α, compute the expected outcome.
5. Maximise the expected outcome over all the choices of S and α.

This paper is mostly concerned with item 4 in the above list, but doing so we must remember that when building a complete attack analysis tool, other items can not be disregarded either. Optimisations are possible, e.g. due to monotonicity there is no need to consider any subsets of attack suites that do not materialise the primary threat. Even more can be done along the lines of [15], Section 4.1, but these aspects remain outside of the scope of the current paper.

Since only one subset S and the corresponding subtree are relevant in the above step 4, we can w.l.o.g. assume that $S = \mathcal{X}$. The attacker's behaviour for permutation α will be modelled as shown in Algorithm 1.

Algorithm 1. Perform the attack

Require: The set of elementary attacks $\mathcal{X} = \{X_1, X_2, \ldots, X_n\}$, permutation $\alpha \in S_n$
and a monotone Boolean formula $\mathcal{F}$ describing the attack scenarios
1: **for** $i := 1$ to n **do**
2:     Consider $X_{\alpha(i)}$
3:     **if** success or failure of $X_{\alpha(i)}$ has no effect on the success or failure of the root
       node **then**
4:         Skip $X_{\alpha(i)}$
5:     **else**
6:         Try to perform $X_{\alpha(i)}$
7:         **if** the root node succeeds or fails **then**
8:             Stop
9:         **end if**
10:    **end if**
11: **end for**

Consider the example attack tree depicted in Figure 1, where we assume $\alpha = id$ for better readability.

The attacker starts off by trying the elementary attack X_1. Independent of whether it succeeds or fails, there are still other components needed to complete the root attack, so he tries X_2 as well. If it fails, we see that the whole tree fails, so it does not make sense to try X_3 and X_4. If both X_1 and X_2 have succeeded, we see that it is not necessary to try X_3, since X_1 and X_3 have a common OR-parent, so success or failure of X_4 determines the final outcome. If X_1 fails and X_2 succeeds, we need the success of both X_3 and X_4 to complete the task; if one of them fails, we stop and accept the failure.

The expected outcome of the attack based on permutation α will be defined as

$$\text{Outcome}_\alpha = p_\alpha \cdot \text{Gains} - \sum_{X_i \in \mathcal{X}} p_{\alpha,i} \cdot \text{Expenses}_i, \qquad (2)$$

where p_α is the success probability of the primary threat and $p_{\alpha,i}$ denotes the probability that the node X_i is encountered during Algorithm 1. Before proceeding, we will prove that the expected outcome of Algorithm 1 does not depend on the specific form of the formula $\mathcal{F}$. This essentially gives us the compliance of our attack tree model in the framework of Mauw and Oostdijk [12]. Formally, we will state and prove the following theorem, similar to Proposition 1 in [15].

Theorem 1. *Let $\mathcal{F}_1$ and $\mathcal{F}_2$ be two monotone Boolean formulae such that $\mathcal{F}_1 \equiv \mathcal{F}_2$, and let Outcome_α^1 and Outcome_α^2 be the expected outcomes obtained running Algorithm 1 on the corresponding formulae. Then*

$$\text{Outcome}_\alpha^1 = \text{Outcome}_\alpha^2.$$

Proof. We can observe that Algorithm 1 really does not depend on the attack description having a tree structure, all the decisions to skip or stop can be taken based on the Boolean function $\mathcal{F}$. Assume we have already fixed the results of the elementary attacks $X_{\alpha(1)}, \ldots, X_{\alpha(i-1)}$. Then we see that

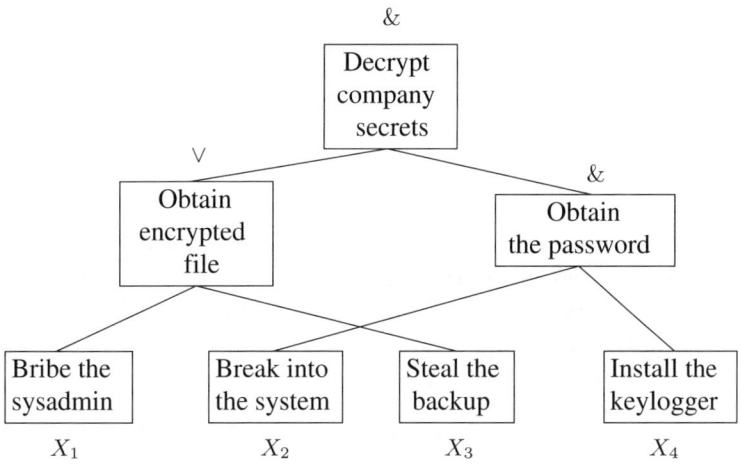

Fig. 1. An example attack tree. The left-to-right ordering of the leaf nodes in the tree represents the permutation $\alpha = id$ of the set $\mathcal{X} = \{X_1, X_2, X_3, X_4\}$.

- the node $X_{\alpha(i)}$ may be skipped if for all the values of $X_{\alpha(i+1)}, \ldots, X_{\alpha(n)}$ we have

$$\mathcal{F}\left(X_{\alpha(1)}, \ldots, X_{\alpha(i-1)}, t, X_{\alpha(i+1)}, \ldots, X_{\alpha(n)}\right) =$$
$$= \mathcal{F}\left(X_{\alpha(1)}, \ldots, X_{\alpha(i-1)}, f, X_{\alpha(i+1)}, \ldots, X_{\alpha(n)}\right),$$

- there is no need to proceed with Algorithm 1 after the node $X_{\alpha(i)}$ if for all the values of $X_{\alpha(i+1)}, \ldots, X_{\alpha(n)}$ we have

$$\mathcal{F}\left(X_{\alpha(1)}, \ldots, X_{\alpha(i-1)}, X_{\alpha(i)}, X_{\alpha(i+1)}, \ldots, X_{\alpha(n)}\right) = t$$

or

$$\mathcal{F}\left(X_{\alpha(1)}, \ldots, X_{\alpha(i-1)}, X_{\alpha(i)}, X_{\alpha(i+1)}, \ldots, X_{\alpha(n)}\right) = f. \qquad \square$$

Thus, our serial model for attack trees follows the guidelines given in Section 3 and it really is safe to talk about Boolean functions describing the attack scenarios.

Next we will show formally that introducing order to the elementary attacks really increases the attacker's expected outcome. Comparing (2) to (1) we get the following theorem.

Theorem 2. *Let $\mathcal{F}$ be a monotone Boolean function on $n \geq 2$ variables describing the attack scenarios. Let $\mathsf{Outcome}_\alpha$ be defined by (2) and let $\mathsf{Outcome}_\mathcal{X}$ be defined by (1) for $S = \mathcal{X}$. Then we have*

$$\mathsf{Outcome}_\alpha \geq \mathsf{Outcome}_\mathcal{X}. \tag{3}$$

If for all the elementary attacks X_i $(i = 1, \ldots, n)$ one also has $\mathsf{Expenses}_i > 0$, then strict inequality holds in (3).

Proof. First we note that by [15] we can compute the success probability of the attacker as follows:

$$p_{\mathcal{X}} = \sum_{\substack{S \subseteq \mathcal{X} \\ \mathcal{F}(S := \text{true}) = \text{true}}} \prod_{X_i \in S} p_i \prod_{X_j \in \mathcal{X} \setminus S} (1 - p_j),$$

where $\mathcal{F}(S := \text{true})$ denotes evaluation of the Boolean function $\mathcal{F}$, when all the variables of S are assigned the value true and all others the value false. This is exactly the total probability of all the successful branches of Algorithm 1 and thus $p_{\mathcal{X}} = p_\alpha$ (implying that p_α is actually independent of α). We also have that $\forall i \, p_{\alpha,i} \leq 1$ and hence the inequality (3) follows.

Assume now that for all X_i we have $\text{Expenses}_i > 0$. Then in order to prove that strict inequality holds in (3), we need to show that there exists such an index i that $p_{\alpha,i} < 1$. Consider the elementary attack $X_{\alpha(n)}$ that the attacker is supposed to try last. If there exists an evaluation of the Boolean variables $X_{\alpha(1)}, \ldots, X_{\alpha(n-1)}$ such that

$$\mathcal{F}\left(X_{\alpha(1)}, \ldots, X_{\alpha(n-1)}, t\right) = \mathcal{F}\left(X_{\alpha(1)}, \ldots, X_{\alpha(n-1)}, f\right),$$

then $X_{\alpha(n)}$ is superfluous in this scenario and hence $p_{\alpha,n} < 1$.

If on the other hand we have

$$\mathcal{F}\left(X_{\alpha(1)}, \ldots, X_{\alpha(n-1)}, t\right) \neq \mathcal{F}\left(X_{\alpha(1)}, \ldots, X_{\alpha(n-1)}, f\right)$$

for all evaluations of $X_{\alpha(1)}, \ldots, X_{\alpha(n-1)}$, then due to monotonicity of $\mathcal{F}$ we can only have that

$$\mathcal{F}\left(X_{\alpha(1)}, \ldots, X_{\alpha(n-1)}, f\right) = f$$

and

$$\mathcal{F}\left(X_{\alpha(1)}, \ldots, X_{\alpha(n-1)}, t\right) = t,$$

implying $\mathcal{F}(Y_1, \ldots, Y_n) \equiv Y_n$. But in this case all the elementary attacks before the last one get skipped, so $p_{\alpha,1} = \ldots = p_{\alpha,n-1} = 0$. $\square$

Thus, introducing ordering of the elementary attacks is guaranteed to give at least as good a result to the attacker as the routine described in [15]. In the interesting case, when all attack components have positive expenses, the attacker's expected outcome is strictly larger.

5   Computing the Expected Outcome

There are $n + 1$ parameters that need to be computed in order to find the expected outcome using the formula (2) – the total success probability p_α and the probabilities $p_{\alpha,i}$ that the node X_i is encountered during Algorithm 1. It turns out that there is an efficient algorithm for computing these quantities provided that the given monotone Boolean function can actually be described by a tree. In what follows we will also assume that the tree is binary, but this restriction is not a crucial one.

So let us have an attack tree with the leaf nodes $X_1, \ldots, X_n$ and the corresponding success probabilities p_i, $i = 1, \ldots, n$. We will assume that all these probabilities are independent and consider the permutation $\alpha \in S_n$. In order to explain the algorithm, we first introduce three extra parameters to each node Y, namely $Y.t$, $Y.f$ and $Y.u$ showing the probabilities that the node has been proven to be respectively true, false or yet undefined in the course of the analysis. Initially, we may set $Y.t = Y.f = 0$ and $Y.u = 1$ for all the nodes and the algorithm will work by incrementally adjusting these values, so that in the end of the process we will have $R.t = p_\alpha$ for the root node R. Throughout the computations we will of course retain the invariant $Y.t + Y.f + Y.u = 1$ for all the nodes Y, hence one of these parameters is actually superfluous. In the presentation version of the algorithm we will drop the parameter $Y.u$, even though it actually plays the central role.

Going back to the high-level description of Algorithm 1, we see that the most difficult step is step 3, where the attacker is supposed to find out whether the next elementary attack in his list may have any effect on the success or failure of the root node. Elementary attack does not have any effect iff there is a node on the path from that particular leaf to the root that has already been proven to be true or false. Thus the next elementary attack should be tried iff all the nodes on this path are undefined – and this is precisely the event that gives us the required probability $p_{\alpha,i}$.

Let the path from root R to the leaf X_i then be $(Y_0 = R, Y_1, \ldots, Y_m = X_i)$. Thus, we need to compute the probability

$$
\begin{aligned}
p_{\alpha,i} = \Pr[Y_0 = u\ \& \ Y_1 = u\ \& \ \ldots\ \& \ Y_m = u] = \\
= \Pr[Y_0 = u\,|\,Y_1 = u\,, \ldots\,,\, Y_m = u]\ \cdot \\
\cdot\Pr[Y_1 = u\,|\,Y_2 = u\,, \ldots\,,\, Y_m = u]\ \cdot\ldots \\
\ldots\cdot \Pr[Y_{m-1} = u\,|\,Y_m = u]\cdot\Pr[Y_m = u] = \\
= \Pr[Y_0 = u\,|\,Y_1 = u]\cdot\Pr[Y_1 = u\,|\,Y_2 = u]\cdot\ldots \\
\ldots\cdot \Pr[Y_{m-1} = u\,|\,Y_m = u]\cdot\Pr[Y_m = u]
\end{aligned}
\tag{4}
$$

The equations

$$
\Pr[Y_k = u\,|\,Y_{k+1} = u\,, \ldots\,,\, Y_m = u] = \Pr[Y_k = u\,|\,Y_{k+1} = u]
$$

hold due to the tree structure of our underlying RDAG and the independence assumption of the elementary attacks. In (4) we have $\Pr[Y_m = u] = \Pr[X_i = u] = 1$ and all the other probabilities are of the form $\Pr[Y_k = u\,|\,Y_{k+1} = u]$. Hence, we need to evaluate the probability that the parent node Y_k is undefined assuming that one of its children, Y_{k+1}, is undefined. This probability now depends on whether Y_k is an AND- or OR-node. If Y_k is an AND-node and Y_{k+1} is undefined, then so is Y_k, if its other child Z is either true or undefined, which is the case with probability $Z.t + Z.u = 1 - Z.f$. Similarly, if Y_k is an OR-node and Y_{k+1} is undefined, then so is Y_k, if its other child Z is either false or undefined, which is the case with probability $Z.f + Z.u = 1 - Z.t$.

This way, (4) gives an efficient way of computing $p_{\alpha,i}$ assuming that the current parameters of the internal nodes of the tree are known. Hence, we need the routines to update these as well. These routines are straightforward. If the elementary attack X_i is tried, only the parameters of the nodes on the path ($Y_m = X_i, \ldots, Y_1, Y_0 = R$) from that leaf to the root need to be changed. We do it by first setting $Y_m.t = p_i$, $Y_m.f = 1 - p_i$ and $Y_m.u = 0$ and then proceed towards the root. If the node we encounter is AND-node A with children B and C, we set

$$A.t = B.t \cdot C.t, \tag{5}$$
$$A.f = B.f + C.f - B.f \cdot C.f, \tag{6}$$

and if we encounter an OR-node A with children B and C, we set

$$A.t = B.t + C.t - B.t \cdot C.t, \tag{7}$$
$$A.f = B.f \cdot C.f. \tag{8}$$

As noted above, we see that the quantities $Y.u$ are actually never needed in the computations.

This way we get the full routine described as Algorithm 2.

Algorithm 2. Computing the probabilities $p_{\alpha,i}$

Require: An attack tree with leaf set $\mathcal{X} = \{X_1, X_2, \ldots, X_n\}$ and a permutation $\alpha \in S_n$
Ensure: The probabilities $p_{\alpha,i}$ for $i = 1, 2, \ldots, n$
 1: **for all** $Z \in \{X_1, \ldots, X_n\}$ **do**
 2:     $Z.t := 0$, $Z.f := 0$
 3: **end for**
 4: **for** $i := 1$ to n **do**
 5:     Find the path $(Y_0, Y_1, \ldots, Y_m)$ from the root $Y_0 = R$ to the leaf $Y_m = X_{\alpha(i)}$
 6:     $p_{\alpha,\alpha(i)} := \prod_{j=1}^{m}(1 - Z_j.a)$, where Z_j is the sibling node of Y_j and

$$a = \begin{cases} t, & \text{if } Y_{j-1} \text{ is an OR-node,} \\ f, & \text{if } Y_{j-1} \text{ is an AND-node} \end{cases}$$

 7:     $X_{\alpha(i)}.t = p_{\alpha(i)}$
 8:     $X_{\alpha(i)}.f = 1 - p_{\alpha(i)}$
 9:     Update the parameters of the nodes $Y_{m-1}, Y_{m-2}, \ldots, Y_0$ according to formulae (5)–(8)
10: **end for**

Algorithm 2 is very efficient. In order to compute the $n + 1$ necessary probabilities, it makes one run through all the leaves of the tree and at each run the path from the leaf to the root is traversed twice. Since the number of vertices on such a path in a (binary) tree can not be larger than the number of leaves n, we get that the worst-case time complexity of Algorithm 2 is $O(n^2)$. If the tree is roughly balanced, this estimate drops even to $O(n \log n)$. This is a huge performance increase compared to a naïve algorithm that one could design based on the complete attack scenario analysis described after Figure 1 in Section 4. We studied the naïve algorithm and it turns out that it is not only worst-case exponential, but also average-case exponential [17].

Of course, as noted in Section 4, Algorithm 2 is only one building block in the whole attack tree analysis. In order to find out the best attack strategy of the attacker, we should currently consider all the subsets of $\mathcal{X}$ and all their permutations. Optimisation results presented in [14] give a strong indication that a vast majority of the possible cases can actually be pruned out, but these methods remain outside of the scope of the current paper.

6   Conclusions and Further Work

In this paper we studied the effect of introducing a temporal order of elementary attacks into the attacker's decision making process together with some flexibility in retreating of some of them. It turns out that taking temporal dependencies into account allows the attacker to achieve better expected outcomes and as such, it brings the attack tree model one step closer to the reality. This reality comes for a price of immense increase in computational complexity, if we want to compute the attacker's exact outcome by considering all the possible scenarios in a naïve way.

Thus there are two main challenges for the future research. First, one may try to come up with optimisations to the computational process and in this paper we showed one possible optimisation which works well for attack trees. The second approach is approximation. In attack tree analysis we are usually not that much interested in the exact maximal outcome of the attacker, but we rather want to know whether it is positive or negative. This observation gives us huge potential for rough estimates, which still need to be studied, implemented and tried out in practice.

In this paper we limited ourselves to a semi-adaptive model, where the attacker is bound to the predefined order of elementary attacks and may only choose to drop some of them. Fully adaptive case where the attacker may choose the next elementary attack freely is of course even more realistic, but it is currently too complicated to analyse. Our model is also non-blocking in the sense that there are no elementary attacks, failure of which would block execution of the whole tree. However, in practice it happens that when failing some attack, the attacker might get jailed and is unable to carry on. Hence, future studies in the area of adaptive and possibly-blocking case are necessary.

As a little technical contribution we also discussed the somewhat inevitable generalisation of attack trees to RDAGs, but our results also show that whenever possible, we should still stick to the tree structure. Possible optimisations of RDAG-based algorithms remain the subject for future research as well.

Acknowledgments

This research was supported by Estonian Science Foundation grant no 7081. The authors are grateful to Margus Niitsoo for his discussions and helpful comments.

References

1. Vesely, W., Goldberg, F., Roberts, N., Haasl, D.: Fault Tree Handbook. US Government Printing Office, Systems and Reliability Research, Office of Nuclear Regulatory Research, U.S. Nuclear Regulatory Commission (January 1981)
2. Viega, J., McGraw, G.: Building Secure Software: How to Avoid Security Problems the Right Way. Addison Wesley Professional, Reading (2001)
3. Moore, A.P., Ellison, R.J., Linger, R.C.: Attack modeling for information security and survivability. Technical Report CMU/SEI-2001-TN-001, Software Engineering Institute (2001)
4. Weiss, J.D.: A system security engineering process. In: Proceedings of the 14th National Computer Security Conference, pp. 572–581 (1991)
5. Schneier, B.: Attack trees: Modeling security threats. Dr. Dobb's Journal 24(12), 21–29 (1999)
6. Edge, K.S.: A Framework for Analyzing and Mitigating the Vulnerabilities of Complex Systems via Attack and Protection Trees. PhD thesis, Air Force Institute of Technology, Ohio (2007)
7. Espedahlen, J.H.: Attack trees describing security in distributed internet-enabled metrology. Master's thesis, Department of Computer Science and Media Technology, Gjøvik University College (2007)
8. Convery, S., Cook, D., Franz, M.: An attack tree for the border gateway protocol. IETF Internet draft (2004),
   http://www.ietf.org/proceedings/04aug/I-D/
   draft-ietf-rpsec-bgpattack-00.txt
9. Byres, E., Franz, M., Miller, D.: The use of attack trees in assessing vulnerabilities in SCADA systems. In: International Infrastructure Survivability Workshop (IISW 2004), Lisbon, Portugal. IEEE, Los Alamitos (2004)
10. Buldas, A., Mägi, T.: Practical security analysis of e-voting systems. In: Miyaji, A., Kikuchi, H., Rannenberg, K. (eds.) IWSEC 2007. LNCS, vol. 4752, pp. 320–335. Springer, Heidelberg (2007)
11. Saini, V., Duan, Q., Paruchuri, V.: Threat modeling using attack trees. J. Comput. Small Coll. 23(4), 124–131 (2008)
12. Mauw, S., Oostdijk, M.: Foundations of attack trees. In: Won, D.H., Kim, S. (eds.) ICISC 2005. LNCS, vol. 3935, pp. 186–198. Springer, Heidelberg (2006)
13. Buldas, A., Laud, P., Priisalu, J., Saarepera, M., Willemson, J.: Rational Choice of Security Measures via Multi-Parameter Attack Trees. In: López, J. (ed.) CRITIS 2006. LNCS, vol. 4347, pp. 235–248. Springer, Heidelberg (2006)
14. Jürgenson, A., Willemson, J.: Processing multi-parameter attacktrees with estimated parameter values. In: Miyaji, A., Kikuchi, H., Rannenberg, K. (eds.) IWSEC 2007. LNCS, vol. 4752, pp. 308–319. Springer, Heidelberg (2007)
15. Jürgenson, A., Willemson, J.: Computing exact outcomes of multi-parameter attack trees. In: Meersman, R., Tari, Z. (eds.) OTM 2008, Part II. LNCS, vol. 5332, pp. 1036–1051. Springer, Heidelberg (2008)
16. Opel, A.: Design and implementation of a support tool for attack trees. Technical report, Otto-von-Guericke University, Internship Thesis (March 2005)
17. Jürgenson, A., Willemson, J.: Ründepuud: pooladaptiivne mudel ja ligikaudsed arvutused (in Estonian). Technical Report T-4-4, Cybernetica, Institute of Information Security (2009), http://research.cyber.ee/

Lightweight Cryptography and RFID: Tackling the Hidden Overheads

Axel Poschmann[1], Matt Robshaw[2], Frank Vater[3], and Christof Paar[4]

[1] Division of Mathematical Sciences, Nanyang Technological University, Singapore
aposchmann@ntu.edu.sg
[2] Orange Labs, 38-40 rue du Général Leclerc, Issy les Moulineaux, France
matt.robshaw@orange-ftgroup.com
[3] Innovations for High Performance Microelectronics, Frankfurt/Oder, Germany
vater@ihp-microelectronics.com
[4] Horst Görtz Institute for IT Security, Ruhr-University Bochum, Germany
christof.paar@rub.de

Abstract. The field of lightweight cryptography has developed significantly over recent years and many impressive implementation results have been published. However these results are often concerned with a core computation and when it comes to a real implementation there can be significant hidden overheads. In this paper we consider the case of CRYPTOGPS and we outline a full implementation that has been fabricated in ASIC. Interestingly, the implementation requirements still remain within the typically-cited limits for on-the-tag cryptography.

1 Introduction

Radio-frequency identification (RFID) tags are becoming a part of our everyday life and a wide range of applications from the supply chain to the intelligent home are often described in the literature. Yet, at the same time, security and privacy issues remain a major issue, not least in the battle against counterfeit goods, pharmaceutical products, and even engine components in the automotive and aeronautic industries [16].

It has long been recognised that cryptographic techniques might be used to help alleviate these problems. However they have all too often been considered as too expensive to implement, or too unsuited to the enviroment of use. Over recent years this view has begun to change and there have been substantial advances in cryptographic design, for instance in new block ciphers such as PRESENT [3]. And as well as the advances we might have expected in symmetric cryptography—which is typically viewed as the lightweight choice—there has been a growing understanding of which asymmetric techniques are available and how they might best be implemented. Indeed, given the essential nature of an RFID-based deployment with many (potentially unknown) players being involved—*i.e.* we have an *open* rather than a *closed* system—lightweight public-key cryptography should be viewed as a particularly attractive technology.

D. Lee and S. Hong (Eds.): ICISC 2009, LNCS 5984, pp. 129–145, 2010.
© Springer-Verlag Berlin Heidelberg 2010

Some of the more recent implementation results in the literature have been very impressive. The oft-cited opinion is that there are around 2 000-3 000 gate equivalents (GE) available for on-tag security features,[1] and despite this representing a formidable challenge several algorithms claim to achieve this.

In this paper we highlight a problem with many of these estimates and we observe that figures are often given for the cryptographic core of a computation. For instance, estimates for the feasibility of elliptic curve cryptography might consider just the elliptic curve operation while implementation results for CRYPTOGPS [21,22] are focused on the protocol computations. This means that when it comes to a real implementation there can be significant hidden overheads.

The main purpose of this paper is to highlight this issue, but also to re-examine the case of one particular proposal in particular, that of CRYPTOGPS. To do this we will describe a full implementation of CRYPTOGPS which includes all the additional functionality that would be required in a real deployment. Further, noting that implementation results for lightweight cryptography are often derived from an FPGA implementation or ASIC synthesis tools, we have gone one step further and we report on the results of the full ASIC fabrication of a fully-supported version of CRYPTOGPS.

1.1   Related Work

Over recent years a lot of work on public key cryptography for RFID tags has centered around elliptic curves. A comparison between different ECC implementations is not always easy because the choice of the underlying curve determines both efficiency and security of the algorithm. However no implementation has been published so far that comes under 5 000 GE which would, even then, be too great for passive RFID-tags. Instead several elliptic curve implementations with a significantly lower security level than 80-bit exist, but their size lies in the range of 10 000 GE or above [2,6,8].

Gaubatz et al. [9] have investigated the hardware efficiency of the NTRUencrypt algorithm [18,26] with the following parameter set $(N, p, q) = (167, 3, 128)$ that offers a security level of around 57 bits. Though their implementation requires only 2 850 GE, it takes 29 225 clock cycles, which translates to 292 ms for the response to be computed at the typical clocking frequency of 100 KHz. Further, it is noteworthy that more than 80% of the area is occupied with storage elements and that already a bit serial datapath is used. This implies that the opportunities for future improvement are very limited. Oren et al. propose a public key identification scheme called WIPR [27]. Their ASIC implementation requires 5 705 GE and 66 048 clock cycles, though a proposed optimisation [32] suggests a reduced area requirement of around 4 700 GE.

In this paper, however, we will concentrate on the CRYPTOGPS scheme. The name GPS is derived from the inventors Girault, Poupard, and Stern, but the term CRYPTOGPS is increasingly used to avoid confusion with the geographical

---

[1] The gate equivalent (GE) is a unit of area and is equivalent to the physical space occupied by a logical NAND gate for the given manufacturing process.

positioning system. A description of the scheme and numerous variants can be found in [10,14,29]. It is standardised within ISO/IEC 9798-5 [19] and listed in the final NESSIE portfolio [20]. Some initial analysis of the ASIC implementation requirements for the elliptic-curve based variant of the CRYPTOGPS identification scheme are available [21,22]. There implementation estimates range between 300–900 GE, but they are only concerned with the core on-tag operation in CRYPTOGPS. A more complete implementation in the form of a fully-functioning FPGA prototype is described in [12]. But in moving from an FPGA implementation to a dedicated RFID-tag implementation there are many differences and complications to consider and this is one of the goals behind this paper.

1.2   This Paper

This paper is organized as follows. First we introduce the CRYPTOGPS identification scheme and we provide a summary of some of the optimisations that are available. Then we turn to the question of how an implementation would look in reality and what additional functionality—over and above the core CRYPTOGPS computations—would be required. In Section 3 we describe the engineering and design challenges that needed to be overcome in designing an ASIC that incorporates three different (two round-based and one serialised) variants of the CRYPTOGPS scheme. In Section 4.2 we discuss our results before we draw our conclusions in Section 5.

2   The CRYPTOGPS Identification Scheme

A public key identification scheme [23] allows the possessor of a secret key to prove possession of that secret by means of an interactive protocol. Thus, in the case of an RFID deployment, the tag would "prove" to a reader that it contains a tag-specific secret and the reader is thereby assured that the tag is genuine. Only a device possessing the key could provide the necessary responses. While at first sight this might appear to be quite a specialised functionality, for instance we don't have the conventional public key services of encryption or digital signatures[2], interactive identification schemes have been deployed widely. In particular the CRYPTOGPS scheme seems to allow a particularly compact implementation on the tag. This allows us to consider RFID tags with public key capability which can open up previously unavailable application areas.

2.1   Overview of CRYPTOGPS

There are many variants and optimisations of CRYPTOGPS. One variant uses RSA-like moduli but here, and in Figure 1, we illustrate the essential elements of CRYPTOGPS using elliptic curve operations. For the system as a whole there are

---

[2] Identification schemes can be converted to signature schemes in a standard way [23] though some computational advantages can be lost.

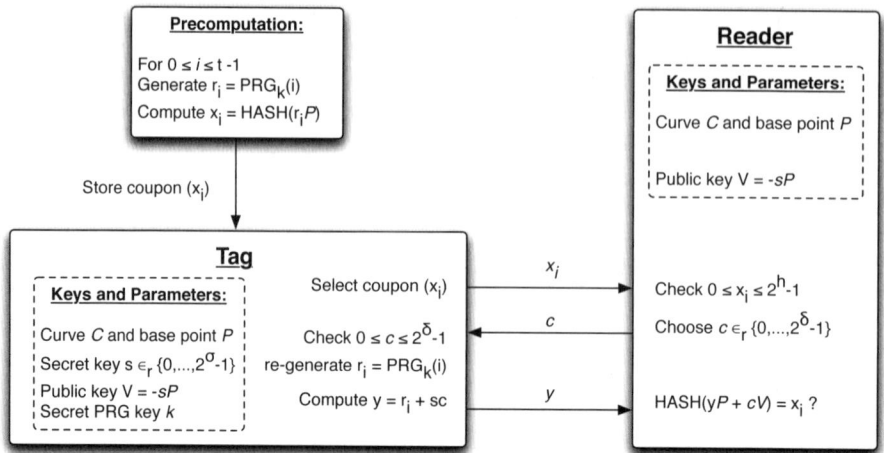

Fig. 1. An overview of the elliptic curve-based variant of CRYPTOGPS with most available optimisations implemented. Note that the elliptic curve parameters are not required on the tag and the only computations that are required are those of the PRG$_k$ to generate r_i and computation of the response y.

the shared parameters of the elliptic curve $\mathcal{C}$ and a base point P on that curve. These are not required on the tag and so they do not impact our implementation. The CRYPTOGPS secret key s is stored on the tag and is assumed to be σ bits in length. The public key $V = -sP$ is an elliptic curve point and we assume that this is available to the reader by some mechanism. To take full advantage of the optimisations described in Section 2.2 the tag is required to support a *pseudo-random generator* (PRG) that uses a tag-specific secret key k. Note that k is required at initialisation to perform some pre-computation, but afterwards k is never needed outside the tag.

Several parameter sizes need to be set and the appropriate choices will depend on the application and the security level. We have already mentioned σ which for a security level of 80 bits is set to $\sigma = 160$. The length of the challenge c from the reader to the tag will be denoted δ and the particular value will depend on different optimisations. The length of the pseudo-random numbers r_i will be denoted ρ and it is a requirement of CRYPTOGPS that we set $\rho = \sigma + \delta + 80$.

2.2   Implementing CRYPTOGPS in Theory

Of particular practical interest are a series of optimisations designed to ease the computation and storage costs of CRYPTOGPS implementation.

- One important optimisation is the use of *coupons*. In [11] Girault describes a storage/computation trade-off for CRYPTOGPS that uses t coupons, each consisting of a pair (r_i, x_i) for $1 \leq i \leq t$. These coupons are stored on the tag before deployment. Figure 1 shows a general overview of the elliptic curve-based variant of CRYPTOGPS where both pre-computation and reader verification use a hash function HASH giving h-bit outputs. However when coupons are used neither the elliptic curve operation nor the hash function are needed on the tag.

- As a further improvement to the storage costs of coupons, we can generate the r_i using a keyed *pseudo-random generator* PRG$_k$ as described in [15,19]. This is done at the time of tag manufacture, and then the necessary r_i can be re-computed on the tag at the time of verification.
- The on-tag computation $y = r_i + sc$ can be optimised by using what is termed a *Low Hamming Weight (LHW) challenge* [13]. This effectively turns the integer multiplication into a few simple integer additions.

The combination of coupons and the LHW challenge lends CRYPTOGPS its advantageous performance. While coupons carry a storage cost and they are not to everyone's tastes, this approach encapsulates today's typical environment of use; we want aggressive and cheap performance on the tag and in most applications RFID tags will only be verified a moderate number of times, perhaps over several hops in the supply chain. After this the tag would be thrown away or deactivated as is currently recommended in a variety of policy statements on privacy.

2.3 Implementing CRYPTOGPS in Practice

In abstract terms, Section 2.2 gave an outline of how we would implement CRYPTOGPS. But these optimisations carry their own problems and it is a task of some difficulty to arrive at a good solution in practice.

Implementing the LHW challenge. In order to avoid the rather demanding $(\sigma \times \delta)$-bit multiplication that is required, it is possible to use a series of simple additions [13]. For this purpose it is required to turn the challenge c into a *Low Hamming Weight (LHW) challenge* [13] such that at least $\sigma - 1$ zero bits lie between two subsequent 1 bits. When using binary representations of the multiplicands it is easy to see that multiplications can be performed using the basic `Shift-And-Add` multiplication algorithm [28]. When a bit of the input challenge c is 0, the multiplicand s is shifted to the left by one position. When the input challenge c is 1, the multiplicand s is shifted to the left and the result is added (with carry) to the multiplicand s. This way a complete multiplication can be reduced to simple shiftings and additions. Since in our case we use a low Hamming weight challenge that has all 1 bits at least $\sigma - 1$ zero bits apart, it is ensured that there is no overlap in subsequent additions of s. In other words s is never added more than once at the same time.

In our implementation the secret is of size $\sigma = |s| = 160$ and the challenge c is of length $\delta = |c| = 848$ with a Hamming weight of 5. The specifications of CRYPTOGPS state that the parameters are typically set to $\rho = |r| = \sigma + \delta + 80$ and so for our chosen values, achieving a probability of impersonation of 2^{-32} requires $\delta = 848$ bits [13] and this leads to $\rho = |r| = 160 + 848 + 80 = 1088$ bits.

However 848 bits is quite a long challenge to transmit from the reader to the tag, and so work in [12,22] has considered this issue. In particular two encoding schemes have been proposed that require that we use only 40 bits to encode the complete 848-bit challenge c. We build on this work and in our implementation we will use a modified variant of the encoding scheme that was proposed for the 8-bit architecture in [22]. In particular it assumes that the challenge c is represented as five 8-bit chunks n_i so that $c = n_4\|n_3\|n_2\|n_1\|n_0$. Then, each n_i consists of the 5-bit number $c_{i,1}$ and the 3-bit number $c_{i,2}$, and so $n_i = c_{i,2}\|c_{i,1}$, and these are used to encode the exact position of one of the five non-zero bits of the 848-bit low Hamming weight challenge. In particular, the positions p_0, ..., p_4 of the non-zero bits of the challenge c can be calculated using the following equations:

$$p_i = \begin{cases} 8 \cdot c_{0,1} + c_{0,2} & \text{for } i = 0 \\ 160 + 8 \cdot c_{i,1} + c_{i,2} & \text{for } 1 \leq i \leq 4 \end{cases}$$

Two examples of the encoding can be found in Appendix I.

Using a PRG. Storing coupons cost memory and in both hardware and software implementations for embedded devices this can be a significant cost factor. Hence, the size of the coupons limits the number of available coupons for a given amount of memory or increases the cost. One approach uses a hash function to reduce the size of the x_i that need to be stored [15]. A second improvement is to observe that, above a certain threshold, it can be cheaper to implement a way of re-generating the r_i than to store them. The ISO standard 9798 [19] suggests using a tag-specific keyed PRG for doing this. While there are a variety of lightweight algorithms available [4,17] we decided to use the lightweight block cipher PRESENT in an appropriate mode to regenerate the r_i. The most efficient choice was to use the output feedback mode (OFB) [25] for our CRYPTOGPS implementations. Clearly care needs to be taken to manage the state of the cipher between calls to the tag to ensure that no repetitions in r_i are generated.

Summary. The following optimisations have been considered for this prototype:

1. Coupons are used to avoid hash and elliptic curve operations on the tag.
2. LHW challenges are used to reduce the on-tag $(\sigma \times \delta)$-bit multiplication to simple additions.
3. Compact encodings of the LHW challenge are used to reduce the transmission time.
4. A PRG is used to eliminate the need to store the r_i.

The implementations to be described in Sections 3.1 and 3.2 take the complete compact challenge c and a 64-bit initialization vector IV at the beginning of the computation. Though the secret s will be fixed in practical applications we also implemented a version with variable s. This gave us the flexibility for additional testing. The 64-bit IV was used to initialize a PRESENT-80 core in OFB mode. At the end of one run, *i.e.* after 17 complete iterations of PRESENT (since $17 \times 64 = 1088$), the ASIC outputs the internal state of the PRESENT core, allowing the state to be managed for the next run. In total, we implemented three different architectures.

1. One variant with a round-based PRESENT-80 core, an internal datapath of 8 bits and a fixed secret s. We refer to this variant as GPS-64/8-F and describe the implementation in Section 3.1.
2. A second variant uses a serialised PRESENT-80 core instead of a round-based one. For this variant it is advantageous to use an internal datapath of 4 bits. Again this was implemented with a fixed secret s. Details for the variant GPS-4/4-F are provided in Section 3.2.
3. A third variant returned to the round-based approach but allowed the secret s to be updated. This covers the few applications where one might envisage changing the key and it allows for some additional testing. This third variant, referred to as GPS-64/8-V, uses a round-based PRESENT-80 core, an internal datapath of 8 bits and a variable secret s, see Sections 3.1.

3 Hardware Architectures of CRYPTOGPS

In the next section we provide more details on the two round-based implementations, denoted CRYPTOGPS-64/8-F and CRYPTOGPS-64/8-V, before we describe the serialised implementation CRYPTOGPS-4/4-F. During our work the design of the prototype board posed several challenging limitations and these are discussed in Section 4.1. As we will see, one issue is that the fabricated chips were mounted on a board and a microcontroller used to simulate the remaining parts of an RFID tag. These components needed to be synchronized and a handshake protocol was implemented. This is referred to in the sections that follow since we need to identify where this created a moderate performance overhead.

3.1 Round-Based Implementations

The architecture of CRYPTOGPS-64/8-F is depicted in Figure 2(a). We use a round-based implementation of PRESENT, a `Controller` component, a full-adder component `Addwc` for the CRYPTOGPS computation, and `S_Storage` for holding the tag secret s. The variant CRYPTOGPS-64/8-V uses essentially the same architecture although the storage of s is handled differently. Here we describe these different components in detail and the relative space they occupy within the manufactured ASIC is nicely illustrated in Figure 3.

The controller consists of four separate but interacting FSMs each one for the central control, I/O, `S_Storage`, and PRESENT. It requires 64 clock cycles to initialize the ASIC and to load the values IV, c_{in}, and s. In the round-based version it requires 32 cycles to create 64 pseudo-random bits using PRESENT and to add it with the appropriate chunk of the secret s. Due to the handshaking protocol, it then requires 64 cycles to output the result in 8-bit chunks. Since we have to compute 1088 bits, we have to repeat this procedure another 16 times. Finally, the internal state of PRESENT needs to be stored outside the ASIC so

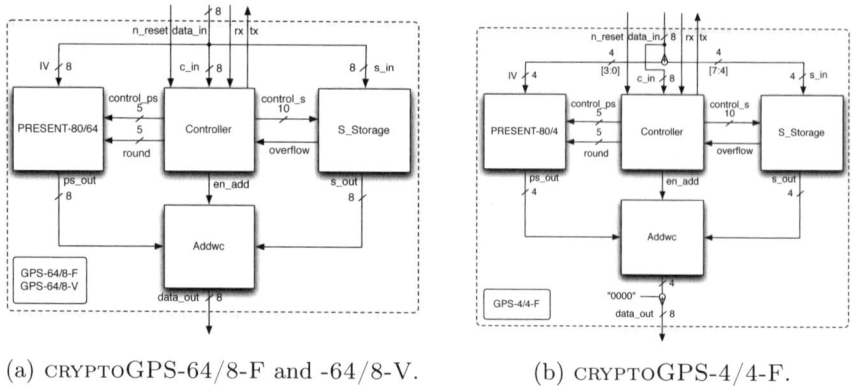

(a) CRYPTOGPS-64/8-F and -64/8-V.   (b) CRYPTOGPS-4/4-F.

Fig. 2. Top-level architectures of the CRYPTOGPS-core

that it can be used as the new IV for the next iteration of CRYPTOGPS. In total, including I/O overhead, it takes $(17 \times (32 + 32)) + 32 = 1120$ clock cycles for one complete run of CRYPTOGPS. If we assume a more realistic scenario where the CRYPTOGPS module is part of an integrated circuit, *i.e.* on an RFID tag, then there is no need for a handshaking protocol and only 724 cycles are required.

The ADDWC component consists of a flip-flop to store the carry bit and a ripple carry adder in order to keep the area requirements to a minimum. For the round-based variants GPS-64/8-F and GPS-64/8-V it has a datapath width of 8 bits, *i.e.* two 8-bit input values are added.

The architecture of the S_Storage component for a fixed secret s consists of an 8-bit AND gate, an 8-bit OR gate, a gated register with 8-bit input, and an 8-bit 20-to-1 MUX. These require 11, 11, 48, and 249 GE respectively, in total 319 GE. The appropriate 8-bit chunk of s is chosen by MUX and it is combined using AND with an 8-bit signal denoted n_zero. In fact n_zero is an eight-fold replication of a single bit and so n_zero can either be set to 00000000 or 11111111. This way the resulting value a is either set to 8-bits of s or 00000000 before being processed by the shifting component. To start, the input value a is appended to the string 00000000 to yield the intermediate state b and this is rotated by c2 positions to the left. Since c2 has three bits the shifting offset varies between 0 and 7. Finally it outputs two 8-bit values c and d, which consist of the eight most significant (c) and the eight least significant (d) bits of b, the internal state. The value c is stored in an 8-bit gated register and d is combined using OR with the output of the gated register.

Varying the secret s. To allow for additional testing we implemented one version of CRYPTOGPS with a key s that can be changed. This would not be the typical implementation in practice since the key for an RFID tag is normally set at the time of manufacture and cannot be changed. Adding this feature clearly imposes an additional cost: in our prototype the area overhead is 54%, mainly due to the additional storage for the secret, but also due to a more complex finite state machine (see Table 1).

The S_Storage component that supports variable secrets s consists of an 8-bit 4-to-1 input MUX, an 8-bit 3-to-1 output MUX, an 8-bit AND, an 8-bit OR and 22 gated shifting registers that each store 8 bits. Twenty of these shifting registers are required to store the complete secret s while the remaining two are required to temporarily store the shifted values for the next addition cycle.

3.2   Serialised Implementations

To reduce the space demands we explored a serialised version of PRESENT-80 implementation (see Figure 2(b)). While the general form of the PRESENT and the Addwc components are relatively unchanged, the Controller and the S_Storage components are different and we describe them in more detail. Further, since the internal datapath of this variant is 4 bits, and since the outputs of the PRESENT, S_Storage, and Addwc components are 4-bits wide, the 4-bit output signal data_out is padded with 0000 to fit the 8-bit I/O interface.

Three out of four FSMs of the Controller module are similar to those used for the round-based variants. However the FSM of the serialised PRESENT-80 component is significantly more complex than a round-based implementation. It requires 64 clock cycles to initialize the ASIC and load the values IV, c_{in} and s. In the serialised version it requires 563 cycles to create 64 pseudo-random bits by the PRESENT component and to add it to the appropriate chunk of the secret s. Here we encounter an artificial delay since, due to the design of the board (see Section 4.1), it requires 64 cycles to output the result in 4-bit chunks. Since we have to compute 1088 bits, we have to repeat this procedure another 16 times. Finally the internal state of the PRESENT component has to be stored outside the ASIC as the new IV for the next iteration of CRYPTOGPS. So in total, including the I/O overhead, it takes $17 \cdot (527 + 64) + 64 = 10,111$ clock cycles for one complete run of CRYPTOGPS. Without the overhead this drops to $9,319$ cycles.

4   Implementation of CRYPTOGPS

ASIC fabrication is notoriously expensive and poses a formidable barrier. For our ASIC implementation of CRYPTOGPS we took advantage of the facilities provided by IHP Microelectronics[3] which offer so-called *multi-design ASICs*. Here different designs from different customers are bundled on the same wafer, and this permits significant cost savings for the production of the lithographic mask, which in turn allows us to fabricate designs for a very limited budget.

4.1   The CRYPTOGPS Proof-of-Concept Prototype Board

While the work in this paper demonstrates that a full implementation of CRYPTOGPS on an RFID tag is both feasible and, in terms of silicon, economically

---

[3] *Innovations for High Performance Microelectronics*, Frankfurt/Oder, Germany.

viable, our implementations still fall short of a fully functioning RFID tag. There is no radio/communication interface. This shortfall has no impact on the conclusions that can be drawn; indeed it serves to illustrate just how close to a prototype RFID tag we are. Nevertheless this communication with the outside world needs to be provided for testing and evaluation purposes.

To achieve this the fabricated chips were mounted on a board and an `ATMEL ATmega32a` [1] microcontroller, denoted μC, was used to simulate the remaining parts of an RFID tag. As such it provides the ASIC with the challenge c_{in} (and the secret s for the variant that allowed a variable secret) and receives the output of the ASIC. Since the microcontroller is clocked independently of the ASIC, these two components have to be synchronized when they are communicating. For this reason a handshake protocol was implemented, given in Appendix II, and this lead to an increase of around 150 GE in the area requirements for the implementation. For the proof-of-concept prototype it was important to demonstrate the different functionalities of the CRYPTOGPS variants. Therefore an external adapter provided a serial-to-USB interface for easy communication with a PC. The microcontroller converts the bit serial data stream from the serial interface to the 8-bit parallel I/O of the ASIC, and vice versa.

The `ATMEL ATmega32a` has a single power supply of 3.3 volts and the ASIC uses two different power supplies; one for the core (2.5 V) and one for the pads (3.3 V). This allows us to consider the power consumption of the cryptographic core without any influence of the pads. This is important since the cryptographic core would be integrated into a full custom design and directly connected to a main component. The ASIC design is in fact limited by the pads which means that the core itself occupies more space than is strictly required. The size of the die is $1,372 \times 1,179$ μm^2 yet the core itself requires only 445×645 μm^2. After fabrication the die was put in a relatively large QFP-80 package, so as to be compatible with the test equipment at IHP.

4.2   Results and Discussion

For functional and post-synthesis simulation we used *Mentor Graphics Modelsim SE PLUS 6.3a* [24] while *Synopsys DesignCompiler* version *Z-2007.12-SP1* [30] was used to synthesize the designs to the *IHP* standard cell library *SESAME-LP2-IHP0.25UM*, which is compatible with the *IHP 0.25 μm SGB25V* process and has a typical voltage of 2.5 Volt [5].

Table 1 details the post-layout area requirements of every component of the three different architectures of CRYPTOGPS while Table 2 provides area figures for comparison reasons for two different design steps: post-synthesis (*syn.*) and post-layout (*lay.*). As we can see flexibility comes at a high price; while the fixed secret variants of CRYPTOGPS can hardwire *s* and select the appropriate chunk with MUXes, a variant that allows *s* to change requires 160 additional

Table 1. Breakdown of the post-layout implementation results of three different architectures of CRYPTOGPS

Component	PRESENT		Addwc		Controller		S_Storage		Sum
	[GE]	%	[GE]	%	[GE]	%	[GE]	%	[GE]
GPS-64/8-V	1,751	39.5	67	1.5	1,127	25.5	1,483	33.5	4,428
GPS-64/8-F	1,751	60.9	60	2.1	905	31.5	159	5.5	2,876
GPS-4/4-F	1,200	50.0	35	1.5	905	37.7	263	11.9	2,403

Table 2. Post-synthesis and manufactured implementation results of three different architectures of CRYPTOGPS. We provide area figures for the two different design steps of post-synthesis (*syn.*) and post-layout (*lay.*). We also include figures for other low-cost asymmetric cryptographic implementations.

	Security level [bits]	Data path size	Cycles per block	Logic process	Design step	Area [GE]
GPS-64/8-V	80	8	724	0.25 IHP	*syn.*	3,861
					lay.	4,428
GPS-64/8-F	80	8	724	0.25 IHP	*syn.*	2,433
					lay.	2,876
GPS-4/4-F	80	4	9,319	0.25 IHP	*syn.*	2,143
					lay.	2,403
WIPR [27]	80	8	66,048	0.35 AMS	*syn.*	5,705
ECC-$(2^{67})^2$ [2]	67	1	418,250	0.25	*syn.*	12,944
ECC-112 [8]	56	1	195,264	0.35 AMI	*syn.*	10,113
NTRUencrypt [9]	57	1	29,225	0.13 TSMC	*syn.*	2,850

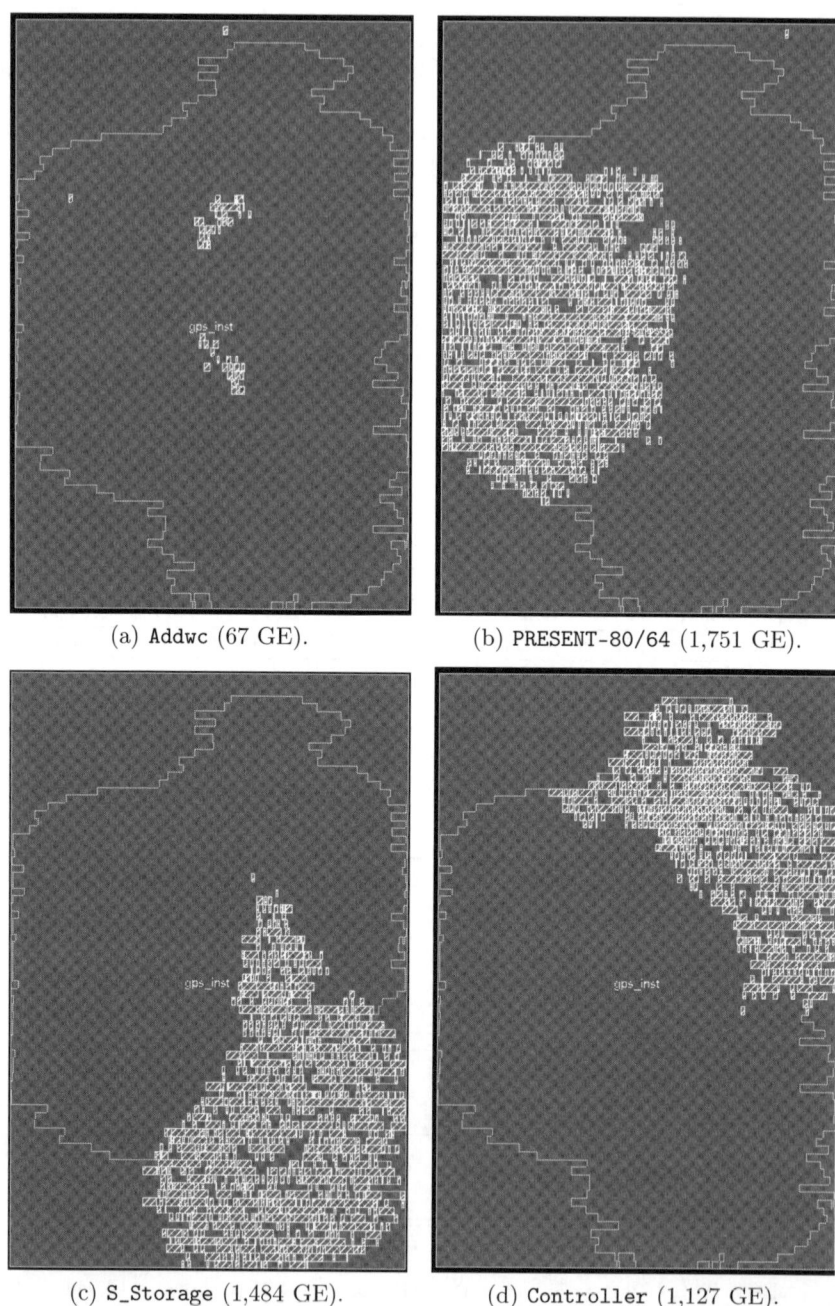

(a) Addwc (67 GE).   (b) PRESENT-80/64 (1,751 GE).

(c) S_Storage (1,484 GE).   (d) Controller (1,127 GE).

Fig. 3. Area shares of single components within the GPS-64/8-V ASIC

flip-flops and a more complex finite state machine. Together this constitutes a significant overhead of $1,550$ GE (see Table 1). The area occupied by the different components of the CRYPTOGPS implementation are illustrated in Figure 3.

We can also see from Table 2 that, for a single challenge, the round-based variants CRYPTOGPS-64/8-F and CRYPTOGPS-64/8-V require 724 clock cycles while the serialised variant CRYPTOGPS-4/4-F requires $9,319$ clock cycles. This is as one would expect, and at a frequency of 100 KHz this translates to 7.24 ms and 93.19 ms, both of which are well below the typical target of 200 ms. Since we omitted the timing overhead introduced by the handshaking protocol, these figures offer a realistic view of the timing demands of an embedded CRYPTOGPS core. Given that the processing time for serialised PRESENT is nearly 13 *times* longer than the round-based version it offers only a marginal benefit.

Interestingly we observe that the post-synthesis area requirements are $3,861$, $2,433$, and $2,143$ GE depending on the variant. However filler cells, clock tree insertion and other layout overheads introduce a 12 to 18 % area increment and after manufacturing, these figures increase to $4,428$, $2,876$ and $2,405$ GE, respectively. Such an overhead is common and has been remarked on in other work [7]. Post-synthesis and post-layout current figures were simulated with *Synopsys DesignCompiler* version *Z-2007.12-SP1* and *Synopsys PrimePower* respectively. The results, ranging from 1.6 μA to 2.7 μA depending on the variant, indicate that CRYPTOGPS is well-suited for passive RFID-tags.

5   Conclusions

In the field of lightweight cryptography hidden overheads are crucial. So while much attention is often focused on the headline implementation of the cryptographic core, additional mechanisms required to make the solution functional can be overlooked. In this paper we have made two contributions. The first is to highlight and quantify the unseen overheads for CRYPTOGPS. We have undertaken the design of a full version of the scheme yet the total costs still remain surprisingly modest; a fully-functioning version of CRYPTOGPS can be envisaged for 2000-3000 GE depending on the variant. The second contribution of the paper is to go through the full fabrication process and to produce a final functioning ASIC. This allows us to give increasingly accurate performance measurements, moving us one additional step closer to putting cryptography, indeed asymmetric cryptography, onto RFID tags.

Acknowledgements

We would like to thank Loïc Juniot, Marc Girault, Henri Gilbert, and Peter Langendörfer for their help and contributions. The research was supported in part by the Singapore National Research Foundation under Research Grant NRF-CRP2-2007-03.

References

1. Atmel Corporation. Datasheet of ATMega32a, an 8-bit AVR Microcontroller with 32K Bytes In-System Programmable Flash (2003), http://atmel.com/dyn/resources/prod_documents/doc8155.pdf
2. Batina, L., Guajardo, J., Kerins, T., Mentens, N., Tuyls, P., Verbauwhede, I.: An elliptic curve processor suitable for RFID-tags. Cryptology ePrint Archive, Report 2006/227 (2006), http://eprint.iacr.org/
3. Bogdanov, A., Leander, G., Knudsen, L.R., Paar, C., Poschmann, A., Robshaw, M.J.B., Seurin, Y., Vikkelsoe, C.: PRESENT: An Ultra-Lightweight Block Cipher. In: Paillier, P., Verbauwhede, I. (eds.) CHES 2007. LNCS, vol. 4727, pp. 450–466. Springer, Heidelberg (2007)
4. De Cannière, C., Preneel, B.: TRIVIUM. In: Robshaw, M.J.B., Billet, O. (eds.) New Stream Cipher Designs. LNCS, vol. 4986, pp. 244–266. Springer, Heidelberg (2008)
5. Dolphin Integration. Sesame-lp2 – description of the standard cells for the process ihp 0.25 μm – vic specifications (December 2005)
6. Eisenbarth, T., Kumar, S., Paar, C., Poschmann, A., Uhsadel, L.: A Survey of Lightweight Cryptography Implementations. IEEE Design & Test of Computers – Special Issue on Secure ICs for Secure Embedded Computing 24(6), 522–533 (2007)
7. Feldhofer, M., Wolkerstorfer, J., Rijmen, V.: AES Implementation on a Grain of Sand. In: IEE Proceedings Information Security, vol. 152(1), pp. 13–20 (2005)
8. Fürbass, F., Wolkerstorfer, J.: ECC Processor with Low Die Size for RFID Applications. In: Proceedings of The IEEE International Symposium on Circuits and Systems 2007 – ISCAS 2007, pp. 1835–1838 (2007)
9. Gaubatz, G., Kaps, J.-P., Sunar, B.: Public key cryptography in sensor networks—revisited. In: Castelluccia, C., Hartenstein, H., Paar, C., Westhoff, D. (eds.) ESAS 2004. LNCS, vol. 3313, pp. 2–18. Springer, Heidelberg (2005)
10. Girault, M.: Self-certified public keys. In: Davies, D.W. (ed.) EUROCRYPT 1991. LNCS, vol. 547, pp. 490–497. Springer, Heidelberg (1991)
11. Girault, M.: Low-Size Coupons for Low-Cost IC Cards. In: Domingo-Ferrer, J., Chan, D., Watson, A. (eds.) Proceedings of the fourth working conference on Smart card research and advanced applications, Norwell, MA, USA, pp. 39–50. Kluwer Academic Publishers, Dordrecht (2001)
12. Girault, M., Juniot, L., Robshaw, M.: The Feasibility of On-the-Tag Public Key Cryptography. In: Conference on RFID Security 2007 – Workshop Record (2007), http://rfidsec07.etsit.uma.es/slides/papers/paper-32.pdf
13. Girault, M., Lefranc, D.: Public Key Authentication with One (Online) Single Addition. In: Joye, M., Quisquater, J.-J. (eds.) CHES 2004. LNCS, vol. 3156, pp. 413–427. Springer, Heidelberg (2004)
14. Girault, M., Poupard, G., Stern, J.: On the Fly Authentication and Signature Schemes Based on Groups of Unknown Order. Journal of Cryptology 19, 463–487 (2006)
15. Girault, M., Stern, J.: On the Length of Cryptographic Hash-Values Used in Identification Schemes. In: Desmedt, Y.G. (ed.) CRYPTO 1994. LNCS, vol. 839, pp. 202–215. Springer, Heidelberg (1994)
16. Handfield, R.B., Nichols, E.L.: Introduction to Supply Chain Management. Prentice-Hall, Upper Saddle River (1999)
17. Hell, M., Johansson, T., Meier, W.: The Grain Family of Stream Ciphers. In: Robshaw, M.J.B., Billet, O. (eds.) New Stream Cipher Designs. LNCS, vol. 4986, pp. 179–190. Springer, Heidelberg (2008)

18. Hoffstein, J., Pipher, J., Silverman, J.: NTRU: A Ring-based Public Key Cryptosystem. In: Buhler, J.P. (ed.) ANTS 1998. LNCS, vol. 1423, pp. 267–288. Springer, Heidelberg (1998)
19. ISO/IEC. International Standard ISO/IEC 9798 Information technology – Security techniques – Entity authentication – Part 5: Mechanisms using Zero-Knowledge Techniques,
    http://www.iso.org/iso/iso_catalogue/catalogue_tc/
    catalogue_detail.htm?csnumber=39720
20. IST-1999-12324. Final Report of European Project IST-1999-12324: New European Schemes for Signatures, Integrity, and Encryption (NESSIE) (April 2004),
    https://www.cosic.esat.kuleuven.be/nessie/
21. McLoone, M., Robshaw, M.J.B.: Public Key Cryptography and RFID. In: Abe, M. (ed.) CT-RSA 2007. LNCS, vol. 4377, pp. 372–384. Springer, Heidelberg (2006)
22. McLoone, M., Robshaw, M.J.B.: New Architectures for Low-Cost Public Key Cryptography on RFID Tags. In: Proceedings of IEEE International Conference on Security and Privacy of Emerging Areas in Communication Networks (SecureComm 2005), pp. 1827–1830. IEEE, Los Alamitos (2007)
23. Menezes, A.J., van Oorschot, P.C., Vanstone, S.A.: Handbook of Applied Cryptography, 1st edn. CRC Press, Boca Raton (1996)
24. Mentor Graphics Corporation. ModelSim SE User's Manual,
    http://www.model.com/resources/resources_manuals.asp
25. National Institute of Standards and Technology. SP800-38A: Recommendation for Block Cipher Modes of Operation (December 2001)
26. NTRU Corporation, NTRUencrypt, http://www.ntru.com
27. Oren, Y., Feldhofer, M.: WIPR – public-key identification on two grains of sand. Technical report (July 2008), http://iss.oy.ne.ro/WIPR
28. Parhami, B.: Computer Arithmetic: Algorithms and Hardware Designs, September 1999. Oxford University Press, Oxford (1999)
29. Poupard, G., Stern, J.: Security Analysis of a Practical "on the fly" Authentication and Signature Generation. In: Nyberg, K. (ed.) EUROCRYPT 1998, vol. 1403, pp. 422–436. Springer, Heidelberg (1998)
30. Synopsys. Design compiler user guide - version a-2007.12 (December 2007),
    https://solvnet.synopsys.com/dow_retrieve/A-2007.12/dcug/dcug.html
31. Virtual Silicon Inc. 0.18um VIP Standard Cell Library Tape Out Ready, Part Number: UMCL18G212T3, Process: UMC Logic 0.18um Generic II Technology: 0.18μm (July 2004)
32. Wu, J., Stinson, D.: How to Improve Security and Reduce Hardware Demands of the WIPR RFID Protocol. In: Proceedings of IEEE International Conference on RFID, Orlando, Florida, USA (April 2009)

Appendix I: Challenge Encoding

Consider two example challenges $C_{comp,1}$ and $C_{comp,2}$. The all-zero compact transmitted challenge $C_{comp,1}$ gives the following $c_{i,1}$ and $c_{i,2}$, from which it is easy to compute $P(i)$ using Section 2.3.

$$C_{comp,1} = \frac{n_4}{00}\bigg|\frac{n_3}{00}\bigg|\frac{n_2}{00}\bigg|\frac{n_1}{00}\bigg|\frac{n_0}{00}$$

i	n_i	$c_{i,2}$	$c_{i,1}$	$P(i)$
0	0x00	000	00000	0
1	0x00	000	00000	160
2	0x00	000	00000	320
3	0x00	000	00000	480
4	0x00	000	00000	640

We can then recover the whole 848-bit challenge c as:[4]

	864	832	800	768	736	704	672
$C_{comp,1} =$	00000000	00000000	00000000	00000000	00000000	00000000	00000000

	640	608	576	544	512	480	448
	00000001	00000000	00000000	00000000	00000000	00000001	00000000

	416	384	352	320	288	256	224
	00000000	00000000	00000000	00000001	00000000	00000000	00000000

	192	160	128	96	64	32	0
	00000000	00000001	00000000	00000000	00000000	00000000	00000001

For the second example, set $C_{comp,2}$ as shown below, which leads to the associate values of $P(i)$:

$$C_{comp,2} = \frac{n_4}{44}\bigg|\frac{n_3}{E3}\bigg|\frac{n_2}{A2}\bigg|\frac{n_1}{C1}\bigg|\frac{n_0}{20}$$

i	n_i	$c_{i,2}$	$c_{i,1}$	$P(i)$
0	0x20	001	00000	$8 \cdot 0 + 1 = 1$
1	0xC1	110	00001	$1 + 160 + 8 \cdot 1 + 6 = 175$
2	0xA2	101	00010	$175 + 160 + 8 \cdot 2 + 5 = 356$
3	0xE3	111	00011	$356 + 160 + 8 \cdot 3 + 7 = 547$
4	0x44	010	00100	$547 + 160 + 8 \cdot 4 + 2 = 741$

The associated challenge, in hexadecimal notation, is then given as:

	864	832	800	768	736	704	672
$C_{comp,2} =$	00000000	00000000	00000000	00000000	00000020	00000000	00000000

	640	608	576	544	512	480	448
	00000000	00000000	00000000	00000000	00000008	00000000	00000000

	416	384	352	320	288	256	224
	00000000	00000000	00000010	00000000	00000000	00000000	00000000

	192	160	128	96	64	32	0
	00000000	00008000	00000000	00000000	00000000	00000000	00000002

---

[4] Note that throughout this example we padded the challenge with 48 zeros to the left in order to gain a multiple of 64 ($848 + 48 = 896 = 14 \times 64$).

Appendix II: Communication between ASIC and Board

One requirement of the shared design ASIC was that all variants have the same I/O pins. In order to have the possibility of using a small packaging we tried to use as few pins as possible. Beside the mandatory pins for power supply we decided to use the following 20 I/O pins: clk, n_reset, rx as the input channel and tx as the output channel of the ASIC for the I/O handshake protocol, data_in is used to load values in 8-bit chunks into the ASIC and data_out is used to output the result in 8-bit chunks.

Since the microcontroller (μC) is clocked independently from the ASIC, both components have to be synchronized when they are communicating. Therefore a handshake protocol with the following steps was implemented (see Figure 4):

1. μC sets input data
2. wait until input data valid
3. μC sets tx to '0' indicating that input data are valid
4. wait until ASIC notices that input is valid (IO_READ_WAIT)
5. ASIC sets rx to '0' indicating that input is being read (IO_READ_INPUT)
6. ASIC reads input (IO_READ_INPUT)
7. ASIC sets rx to '1' indicating the successful read of input (IO_READ_ACK)
8. wait until μC notices that rx was set to '1'
9. μC sets tx to '1' thus finishing the input procedure
10. ASIC computes the response
11. ASIC sets rx to '0' indicating that output data are valid (IO_WRITE_WAIT)
12. wait until μC notices that output is valid (IO_WRITE_WAIT)
13. μC sets tx to '0' indicating that output is being read
14. μC reads output (IO_WROTE_OUTPUT)
15. μC sets tx to '1' indicating that the output was successfully read
16. wait until ASIC notices that tx was set to '1'
17. ASIC sets rx to '1' thus finishing the output procedure.

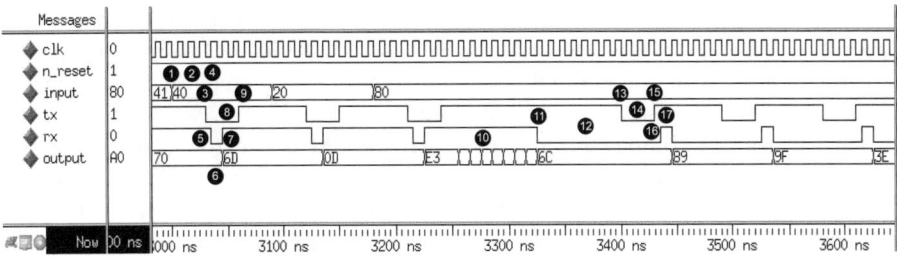

Fig. 4. Signal flow of the handshake protocol for communication between board and CRYPTOGPS ASIC

Power Analysis of Single-Rail Storage Elements as Used in MDPL[*]

Amir Moradi[1], Thomas Eisenbarth[1], Axel Poschmann[2], and Christof Paar[1]

[1] Horst Görtz Institute for IT Security, Ruhr University Bochum, Germany
{moradi,eisenbarth,cpaar}@crypto.rub.de
[2] Division of Mathematical Sciences, Nanyang Technological University, Singapore
aposchmann@ntu.edu.sg

Abstract. Several dual-rail logic styles make use of single-rail flip-flops for storing intermediate states. We show that single mask bits, as applied by various side-channel resistant logic styles such as MDPL and iMDPL, are not sufficient to obfuscate the remaining leakage of single-rail flip-flops.

By applying simple models for the leakage of masked flip-flops, we design a new attack on circuits implemented using masked single-rail flip-flops. Contrary to previous attacks on masked logic styles, our attack does not predict the mask bit and does not need detailed knowledge about the attacked device, e.g., the circuit layout. Moreover, our attack works even if all the load capacitances of the complementary signals are perfectly balanced and even if the PRNG is ideally unbiased. Finally, after performing the attack on DRSL, MDPL, and iMDPL circuits we show that single-bit masks do not influence the exploitability of the revealed leakage of the masked flip-flops.

1   Introduction

Since Differential Power Analysis (DPA) was introduced by Kocher *et al.* [5] to physically attack cryptographic devices, several countermeasures have been proposed to improve the resistance of implementations. Sense Amplifier Based Logic (SABL), which is a Dual-Rail Precharge (DRP) logic, has been proposed by Tiri *et al.* [17] as the first DPA countermeasure at the cell level. In fact, in theory using a full-custom design tool enables to equalize the load capacitances of each couple of complementary logic signals and hence to make the power consumption independent of the processed data. Afterwards, Wave Dynamic Differential Logic (WDDL) [19] has been introduced in order to avoid the usage of full-custom design tools especially for the routing process. Since some place and route methods such as [4,20] were proposed to diminish the load imbalances of complementary signals, the data-dependent time of evaluation and the memory effect of WDDL cells make it vulnerable to DPA attacks [6,15].

---

[*] The work described in this paper has been supported in part by the European Commission through the ICT programme under contract ICT-2007-216676 ECRYPT II.

D. Lee and S. Hong (Eds.): ICISC 2009, LNCS 5984, pp. 146–160, 2010.

Although it has been shown that masking at cell level can not prevent the information leakage because of the presence of glitches [7], its combination with precharge logics led to Random Switching Logic (RSL) [16] in order to equalize the circuit transition probability. However, Tiri and Schaumont [18] showed that the single mask-bit in RSL just adds one bit of entropy. On the other hand, in order to use semi-custom design tools without routing constraints, Masked Dual-Rail Precharge Logic (MDPL) [12] was introduced. It works similar to WDDL and employs a single mask-bit to nullify the effect of load imbalances. Moreover, Dual-Rail Random Switching Logic (DRSL) [2] was proposed as the dual-rail version of RSL and to avoid the need of a central module to control the precharge signals.

Suzuki *et al.* showed that MDPL is susceptible to the early propagation effect [14]. The practical evaluation of the MDPL microprocessor of the SCARD prototype chip[1] proved that the early propagation effect which resulted in a vulnerability of CMOS circuits also exists for MDPL cells [11]. In order to cope with early propagation issues, the designers of MDPL introduced a so called Evaluation-Precharge Detection Unit (EPDU), which consists of three (CMOS) AND gates and two (CMOS) OR gates. The EPDU is applied to all improved MDPL (iMDPL) gates, hence it is not surprising that the area requirements for iMDPL gates increased significantly compared to MDPL.

Concurrently, Gierlichs [3] presented an attack on MDPL that exploits a deviation in the mask bit distribution and unbalanced dual-rails in the target cell. In order to mount this attack an adversary requires detailed knowledge on the layout-level of the target device. However, in practice this information is not publicly available or requires insider knowledge or expensive equipment and time-consuming efforts, such as reverse-engineering.

At that time, Schaumont and Tiri [13] showed that already slightly unbalanced complementary wires can be exploited to mount classical DPA attacks after only a simple filtering operation. Contrary to Gierlichs they did not exploit the unbalanced wires of the mask bit signal, but rather use only the unbalanced dual-rail wires of the logical signals.

Note that the attacks of Gierlichs and of Schaumont/Tiri can also be mounted on circuits built in iMDPL, but again require unbalanced wires and detailed knowledge of the device under attack. Therefore both attacks assume a rather strong attacker model. Furthermore, both attacks and also the attacks by Suzuki *et al.* [14] and Popp *et al.* [11] exploit leakage of the combinatorial part of a circuit. Contrary to this, a key recovery attack on special circuits built in MDPL and DRSL that exploits the leakage of the underlying flip-flops has been presented in [9]. The authors gain the Hamming distance (HD) of the mask bit with a Simple Power Analysis (SPA) and subsequently attack the circuit with a Correlation Power Analysis (CPA) [1]. Note that the success rate of any SPA

---

[1] During the SCARD (Side-Channel Analysis Resistant Design Flow, www.scard-project.eu) project a prototype chip was built, that contains amongst other components three MC 8051s and three AES co-processors built in CMOS, a DRP logic, and MDPL.

strongly depends on the architecture of the attacked device. However, this attack is focused on a special type of flip-flops and a special architecture of the circuit that might not lead to a successful result in practice.

Moreover, practical attacks on the MDPL AES co-processor of the SCARD chip presented in [10] show that not only the early propagation effect of MDPL cells does not break the masked hardware but also the attack proposed by Schaumont/Tiri is not capable of revealing the secrets in this case. Further, it has been shown that a bias of the mask bit in the SCARD chip does not threaten the resistance of the device.

In this work first we analyze the information leakage of CMOS flip-flops as well as the flip-flops of some known DPA-resistant logic styles. Using the introduced leakage models, we present an attack on certain types of flip-flops in masked logic styles that does not require any knowledge of the layout of the device nor unbalanced wires. Our attack works even if a masked dual-rail ASIC has perfectly balanced wires. Yet, perfectly balanced loads can never be achieved in practice because electrical effects will always cause different wire capacitances, even when the routing is done manually in a full-custom design process. This however underlines the strength of our attack. Indeed, our attack is based on the fact that although combinational parts of the masked logic styles, e.g., iMDPL, are in dual-rail mode and decrease the leakage significantly, their sequential parts are built in single-rail leading to a serious vulnerability.

The remainder of this work is organized as follows: in Sect. 2 we recall the design of standard CMOS flip-flops which are used in many proposed side-channel resistant logic styles, e.g., WDDL and MDPL. We also develop leakage models for CMOS, DRP, and masked flip-flops. Based on these leakage models we propose a new attack in Sect. 3. Subsequently, we present our results of a simulated attack on implementations of a reduced round AES in Sect. 4. Further, we discuss on practical issues in Sect. 5, and finally Sect. 6 concludes the paper.

2   Information Leakage of Flip-Flops

In this section we describe leakage models of flip-flops. Starting with CMOS flip-flops in Sect. 2.1, we continue with DRP flip-flops in Sect. 2.2, and finally end with masked flip-flops in Sect. 2.3.

2.1   CMOS Flip-Flops

The information leakage of CMOS flip-flops was already modeled by the first DPA attacks. It is well-known that the dynamic power consumption is higher when the content of a single-bit flip-flop is changed than if the content remains unchanged. Therefore, HD of the registers is applied to partially model the power consumption of a circuit. We generally review the structure of an edge-sensitive flip-flop to figure out its information leakage.

Typically, edge-sensitive flip-flops are built using two consecutive latches. The block diagram of a positive-edge flip-flop is shown in Fig. 6. Note that the negative-edge one can be constructed by swapping the CLK and CLKN signals. In fact, each manufacturer has its own design to build edge-sensitive CMOS flip-flops, but the fundamental architecture corresponds to that shown in Fig. 6. We define two operation phases for a flip-flop: sampling phase and hold phase. In a positive-edge flip-flop, the first latch samples the input during the sampling phase while the CLK signal is stable at 0. When the CLK signal switches to 1, i.e., beginning of the hold phase, the connection of the two latches is established and the content of the flip-flop is updated. Obviously, at this point in time the power consumption is influenced by the change of the content of the second latch (i.e., flip-flop content). As mentioned, this leakage is widely used as HD model. However, during the sampling phase, changing the input signal (i.e., d) results in a change of the content of the first latch, and it also affects the power consumption.

Suppose a circuit with k synchronous flip-flops where all of the flip-flops are controlled and are triggered by a clock signal. As mentioned before, toggling the input signal at the sampling phase directly affects the power consumption. Our simulation results show that the difference between the effect of the rising and the falling toggles in the input signal is negligible. Thus, the toggle count model is an appropriate choice to model the leakage of the flip-flops at the sampling phase as follows:

$$\begin{aligned} Leak_{\circledS} &= \textstyle\sum_{i=1}^{k} \text{ number of toggles at the input signal d of the } i\text{th FF} \\ &= \text{ToggleCount} \left(D = [d_k, \ldots, d_2, d_1] \right) \end{aligned} \tag{1}$$

Also, the well known HD model describes the power consumption at the hold phase.

$$\begin{aligned} Leak_{\circledH} &= \textstyle\sum_{i=1}^{k} \text{ number of toggles at the output signal q of the } i\text{th FF} \\ &= \text{HD} \left(Q^{(t)} = \left[q_k^{(t)}, \ldots, q_2^{(t)}, q_1^{(t)} \right], Q^{(t+1)} \right) \end{aligned} \tag{2}$$

2.2 DRP Flip-Flops

Amongst DRP logic styles, we focus on SABL [17] and WDDL [19], because with regards to side-channel resistance they are the best investigated logic styles. Since SABL is a full-custom logic style, its flip-flop was specifically designed to have a constant internal power consumption independently of the logic values. As shown in Fig. 7, an SABL flip-flop similarly to the CMOS flip-flop consists of two stages. The first stage stores the complementary input values d and $\overline{d}$ at the negative edge of the CLK, while the second stage is precharged. At the next positive clock edge, the second stage stores the data values from the first stage. Then, the first stage is precharged and the second one provides the output values q and $\overline{q}$ [6]. Assuming fully balanced capacitances, the power consumption of an SABL flip-flop is constant in every clock cycle independently of the input and output values. Therefore, leakage models similar to those presented in Sect. 2.1 can not be introduced for SABL flip-flops.

Two ways to launch the precharge wave in WDDL have been proposed, hence, there are two types of WDDL flip-flops:

(*i*) Single Dynamic Differential Logic (SDDL) flip-flop which uses two CMOS flip-flops as shown in Fig. 8(a)
(*ii*) Master-Slave Dynamic Differential Logic (M-S DDL) flip-flop which employs four CMOS flip-flops as shown in Fig. 8(b).

In fact, in comparison with SDDL FF's (with the same clock frequency) using M-S DDL FF's causes the operation frequency of the circuit to be divided by 2.

In order to model the power consumption of an SDDL FF, we first consider the power consumption of one of the internal CMOS flip-flops. The input signal, d, is 0 at the precharge phase (when CLK is 1). It may switch to 1 once at the evaluation phase (when CLK is 0). Therefore, if there are k synchronous SDDL flip-flops, the leakage is defined as follows.

$$Leak_{\text{\textcircled{S}}}\,[\text{SDDL1}] = \sum_{i=1}^{k} \text{number of toggles at signal d of the } i\text{th FF} \\ = \text{HW}\,(D = [d_k, \ldots, d_2, d_1]) \tag{3}$$

Also, the HD of the output signals is clearly leaking at the hold phase.

$$Leak_{\text{\textcircled{H}}}\,[\text{SDDL1}] = \text{HD}\left(Q^{(t)} = \left[q_k^{(t)}, \ldots, q_2^{(t)}, q_1^{(t)}\right], Q^{(t+1)}\right) \tag{4}$$

Similarly, the leakages of the second internal CMOS flip-flops are defined as follows.

$$Leak_{\text{\textcircled{S}}}\,[\text{SDDL0}] = \text{HW}\left(\overline{D} = \left[\overline{d}_k, \ldots, \overline{d}_2, \overline{d}_1\right]\right) \tag{5}$$

$$Leak_{\text{\textcircled{H}}}\,[\text{SDDL0}] = \text{HD}\left(\overline{Q}^{(t)} = \left[\overline{q}_k^{(t)}, \ldots, \overline{q}_2^{(t)}, \overline{q}_1^{(t)}\right], \overline{Q}^{(t+1)}\right) \tag{6}$$

Now, the whole leakage for each phase can be easily computed by adding two leakages.

$$Leak_{\text{\textcircled{S}}}\,[\text{SDDL}] = Leak_{\text{\textcircled{S}}}\,[\text{SDDL1}] + Leak_{\text{\textcircled{S}}}\,[\text{SDDL0}] \\ = \text{HW}\,(D) + \text{HW}\,(\overline{D}) = k \tag{7}$$

$$Leak_{\text{\textcircled{H}}}\,[\text{SDDL}] = Leak_{\text{\textcircled{H}}}\,[\text{SDDL1}] + Leak_{\text{\textcircled{H}}}\,[\text{SDDL0}] \\ = \text{HD}\,(Q^{(t)}, Q^{(t+1)}) + \text{HD}\left(\overline{Q}^{(t)}, \overline{Q}^{(t+1)}\right) \\ = 2 \cdot \text{HD}\,(Q^{(t)}, Q^{(t+1)}) \tag{8}$$

Therefore, SDDL flip-flops do not leak any information during the sampling phase, but their leakage is twice of the CMOS flip-flops in the hold phase (again note that we do not consider the unbalanced capacitances of the complementary wires in this article). Thus, successful power analysis attacks can be mounted on hardware where SDDL flip-flops are used.

As shown in Fig. 8(b), there are two sampling and two hold phases in each precharge-evaluation phase in the case of M-S DDL FF's. In each clock cycle every dual-rail flip-flops contain precharge value, i.e., $(0,0)$, and are replaced by a differential value, $(1,0)$ or $(0,1)$, or vice versa. Thus, both leakage models in sampling and hold phases are similar to that defined in Eq. 7, hence they are data-independent. As a result, it is not possible to perform a power analysis attack using our leakage model and our assumptions on M-S DDL FF's.

2.3   Masked Flip-Flops

In the case of DRSL, MDPL, and iMDPL flip-flops, each of the logic styles has a special circuit to mask the input signal using the mask bit of the next clock cycle. However, all have in common that they use a CMOS flip-flop. Although the early propagation problem of the MDPL gates is solved in the improved version, i.e., iMDPL, the structure of the flip-flops is the same for both versions. Cell schematic of the original MDPL and iMDPL flip-flops are shown in Fig. 9. The structure of the DRSL flip-flop is the same as MDPL; a DRSL XOR gate is used instead of the MDPL XOR [2]. The input signal of the internal CMOS flip-flop, i.e., d_{m_n}, is 0 at the precharge phase (when CLK is 1). It switches to 1 once at the evaluation phase (when CLK is 0) depending on d and the next mask bit, m_n. Therefore, if there are k synchronous masked flip-flops, the leakage during the sampling phase can be modeled as follows:

$$
\begin{aligned}
Leak_{\circledS}\,[\text{Masked}] &= \textstyle\sum_{i=1}^{k} \text{ number of toggles at } d_{m_n} \text{ of the } i\text{th FF} \\
&= \mathrm{HW}\left(D_{m_n} = \left[d_{k_{m_n}}, \ldots, d_{2_{m_n}}, d_{1_{m_n}}\right]\right) \\
&= \mathrm{HW}\left(\left[d_k, \ldots, d_2, d_1\right]_{m_n}\right) = \mathrm{HW}\left(D \oplus [m_n, \ldots, m_n]\right)
\end{aligned}
\tag{9}
$$

In other words, what is leaked at the sampling phase is the HW of the masked input values. Moreover, the HD of the output signals is leaking at the hold phase.

$$
\begin{aligned}
Leak_{\oplus}\,[\text{Masked}] &= \textstyle\sum_{i=1}^{k} \text{ number of toggles at } q_m \text{ of the } i\text{th FF} \\
&= \mathrm{HD}\left(Q_m^{(t)} = \left[q_{k_m}^{(t)}, \ldots, q_{2_m}^{(t)}, q_{1_m}^{(t)}\right], Q_{m_n}^{(t+1)}\right) \\
&= \mathrm{HW}\left(Q_m^{(t)} \oplus Q_{m_n}^{(t+1)}\right) \\
&= \mathrm{HW}\left(\left(Q^{(t)} \oplus [m, \ldots, m]\right) \oplus \left(Q^{(t+1)} \oplus [m_n, \ldots, m_n]\right)\right) \\
&= \mathrm{HW}\left(\left(Q^{(t)} \oplus Q^{(t+1)}\right) \oplus \left([m, \ldots, m] \oplus [m_n, \ldots, m_n]\right)\right) \\
&= \mathrm{HW}\left(\left(Q^{(t)} \oplus Q^{(t+1)}\right) \oplus [m', \ldots, m']\right) \;;\; m' = m \oplus m_n \\
&= \mathrm{HD}\left(Q^{(t)}, Q^{(t+1)} \oplus [m', \ldots, m']\right)
\end{aligned}
\tag{10}
$$

Clearly, it is not possible to mount a classical DPA or CPA using the leakages described above, because the mask bit (m_n or m') which contributes to the leakages is refreshed every clock cycle, e.g., by a PRNG. In the next section we illustrate a new attack strategy to reveal the secrets using the presented leakage models.

MDPL has a timing constraint for the flip-flops. The constraint requires creating the clock tree in a specific manner [12]. An alternative design (similar to the M-S DDL flip-flop) which uses four CMOS flip-flops has been proposed for cases where the timing constraint can not be met [12]. As mentioned for the M-S DDL, this kind of flip-flop requires four times the area and the clock rate must be doubled in order to keep the data rate of the circuit constant. Of course this results in a significant increase of the power consumption. However, a design employing this type of flip-flop does not leak any information under our assumptions. This design has not been proposed for DRSL and iMDPL, but it is applicable for them with all its disadvantages. However, it was not considered in the literature and in implementations, e.g., the SCARD chip.

Also, a modification on the structure of MDPL and DRSL flip-flops has been proposed in [9], i.e., make use of two CMOS flip-flops in each masked flip-flop in order to prevent the leakage. The leakage models of the new masked flip-flops are as follows:

$$Leak_\circledS [\text{Masked}^*] = \text{HW} \left(D \oplus [m_n, \dots, m_n]\right) + \text{HW} \left(\overline{D} \oplus [m_n, \dots, m_n]\right)$$
$$= k \tag{11}$$

$$Leak_\oplus [\text{Masked}^*] = \text{HD} \left(Q^{(t)}, Q^{(t+1)} \oplus [m', \dots, m']\right) + $$
$$\text{HD} \left(\overline{Q}^{(t)}, \overline{Q}^{(t+1)} \oplus [m', \dots, m']\right) \tag{12}$$
$$= 2 \cdot \text{HD} \left(Q^{(t)}, Q^{(t+1)} \oplus [m', \dots, m']\right)$$

The proposed modification prevents sampling-phase leakage, but it increases the leakage of the hold phase compared to the original design.

3   Our Proposed Attack

For simplicity, we assume an 8-bit masked flip-flop as the target of the attack. As illustrated in the previous section, during the sampling phase HW of the masked input signals, $Leak_\circledS = \text{HW}(D_{m_n})$, is leaking. In fact, we are looking for a technique to discover a relation between the unmasked values D and HW of the masked values. Table 1 shows all possible values of HW of an 8-bit masked input, D_{m_n}. As shown in the fourth column, the average of HWs, $\mu(\text{HW} (D_{m_n}))$, is always 4. In other words, the mask bit switches the flip-flop's content between two complementary states where sum of HWs is always 8. However, the difference between HWs when the mask bit is 0 or 1, $|\text{HW} (D_0) - \text{HW} (D_1)|$, takes certain values depending on HW of D. Indeed, there is a relation between the unmasked value, D, and the difference between HWs. This difference is given in the last column of Table 1. We call it *Difference of Hamming Weights* $(\text{DHW} (D) = |\#\text{ofBits} - 2 \cdot \text{HW} (D)|)$ and later will use it to mount an attack without prediction or estimation of the mask bit.

One can also conclude from Table 1 that the distance of one individual leakage $\text{HW}(D_{m_n})$ for an unknown mask bit m_n to the average of HWs $\mu(\text{HW}(D_{m_n}))$ is the same independent of the mask bit m_n. Hence,

$$|\mu(\text{HW}(D_{m_n})) - \text{HW}(D_0)| = |\mu(\text{HW}(D_{m_n})) - \text{HW}(D_1)| = \frac{1}{2}\text{DHW}(D)$$

We can not directly predict the leakage of a masked flip-flop, but by subtracting the average power consumption and taking the absolute value $\mu(Leak_\circledS) = \mu(\text{HW}(D_{m_n}))$ from the individual power consumption

$$|Leak_\circledS - \mu(Leak_\circledS)| = |\text{HW}(D_{m_n}) - \mu(\text{HW}(D_{m_n}))| = \frac{1}{2}\text{DHW}(D)$$

we can predict this distance using the Difference of Hamming Weights. We now use the DHW(D) as a hypothetical power model and perform a CPA attack on

Table 1. HW of an 8-bit data masked by a single mask bit

HW (D)	HW (D_{m_n})		μ(HW (D_{m_n}))	DHW (D) = | HW (D_0) − HW (D_1) | = | 8 − 2 · HW (D) |
	$m_n = 0$	$m_n = 1$		
0	0	8	4	8
1	1	7	4	6
2	2	6	4	4
3	3	5	4	2
4	4	4	4	0
5	5	3	4	2
6	6	2	4	4
7	7	1	4	6
8	8	0	4	8

Algorithm 1. The attack algorithm (for a single point of measurements)

1: $\mu = \frac{\sum_{i=1}^{z} p_i}{z}$; $p_i : i^{\text{th}}$ measured power value, z: # of measurements
2: **for all** measured power values $p_i, 1 \leq i \leq z$ **do**
3:     $\widehat{p_i} = |p_i - \mu|$
4: **end for**
5: **Perform** a **CPA** on $\widehat{P} = \{\widehat{p_i}; 1 \leq i \leq z\}$ **using leakage model** DHW $(\cdot)$

---

the preprocessed power traces. For clarity, a pseudocode overview of the attack is given in Algorithm 1.

The illustrated leakage model, DHW $(\cdot)$, fits the sampling phase leakage of the masked flip-flops, $Leak_{\circledS}$. Also, it can be applied to the hold phase leakage, $Leak_{\circledH}$, by replacing HW with HD in Table 1. In fact, the table is the same for HD, just the notation will be changed, i.e., *Difference of Hamming Distances* is

$$\text{DHD}\left(Q^{(t)}, Q^{(t+1)}\right) = \left|\#\text{ofBits} - 2 \cdot \text{HD}\left(Q^{(t)}, Q^{(t+1)}\right)\right|.$$

In comparison with Zero-Offset second order DPA [21], which similarly does a preprocessing step on power traces before running straight DPA, the preprocessing of our attack shows a similar time complexity of $O(z \cdot t)$, where each power trace consists of t points. On the other hand, since in masked precharged logic styles the mask bit is represented by two precharged complementary signals, the information of the mask bit, which is essentially required to perform a second-order DPA attack, is not leaking (without considering the difference between the unbalanced capacitances). Consequently, not only a classical DPA is not possible, but also a Zero-Offset 2DPA could not recover the secrets without knowing the layout details, i.e., knowledge about the loading imbalances. Our simulation results (which are not presented here) confirmed these issues. In fact, the preprocessing step of our proposed attack tries to remove the effect of single mask bit by folding the power values from an estimated mean value. Thus, from this point of view, our proposed attack can be considered as a second-order DPA attack.

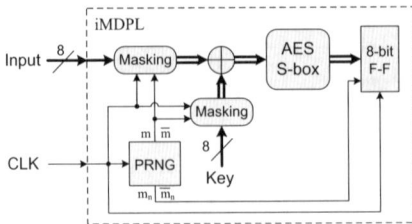

Fig. 1. Block diagram of the attacked device

However, the preprocessing step is similar to the one suggested in [13], i.e., estimation of and folding around the empirical mean value per sampled time instant. Note that in their attack the preprocessing step takes place to classify the power values based on the estimated mask bit due to the leakage caused by the loading imbalances of a combinational circuit, then a CPA (or even DPA) attack using a normal HW model is performed. However, in our proposed attack after the same preprocessing step the newly proposed DHW or DHD model is used in a CPA attack to defeat the effect of the single-bit mask. Moreover, since their attack has been verified using weighted toggle count model to simulate the power consumption of a post placed-and-routed combinational circuit, they did not consider the power consumption and the leakage of the flips-flops. As a result, the principles of the attack presented in [13] and our proposed one are not the same. Further, the applicability of their attack in practice has been discussed in [10].

In fact, our leakage models, DHW and DHD, are adapted to the fact that although the masked circuits are DRP circuits, the flip-flops are only single-rail. In the next section the simulation results of attacks performed using our leakage models are presented.

4   Simulation Results

In order to evaluate the efficiency of the proposed attack, we analyzed the circuit shown in Fig. 1. It consists of an 8-bit key addition and an AES S-box followed by an 8-bit flip-flop. The circuit is implemented using iMDPL cells. We simulated the HSPICE description files for thousands of random inputs using *Synopsys Nanosim* version *A-2007.12* in 0.18μm technology and 1.8V supply voltage to obtain the power supply current traces. As mentioned earlier, we do not consider the difference between the capacitances of complementary wires arising from different routings. Thus, we did not put any capacitances manually at the gate outputs.

First, we take a look at the leakage of the sampling phase $Leak_{\text{S}}$. As described in Sect. 2.3, this leakage is caused by the toggling of inputs of the flip-flops that are the outputs of a combinational circuit. Since the depth (and consequently the delay time) of all output signals of a combinational circuit are not the same, the sampling phase leakage does not appear at specific points of the power traces.

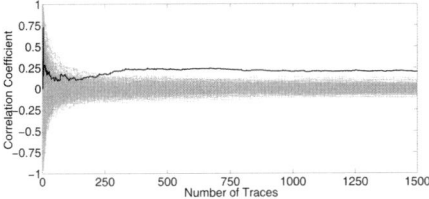

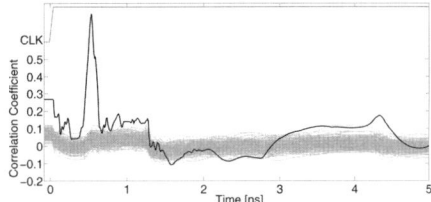

Fig. 2. Correlation coefficient of the key hypotheses vs. the number of traces using the sampling phase leakage model

Fig. 3. Correlation coefficient of the key hypotheses using the hold phase leakage model

Moreover, in MDPL circuits, where the time-of-evaluation depends on the processed data (and on the mask bit), the leakage is caused at different time instances of the sampling phase. Therefore, the integral (or the average) of the power values during a specific period of time is used to mount the attack on the sampling phase[2]. Finally, we performed the attack which is described in Algorithm 1 using the leakage model presented in Eq. 9. The correlation coefficient of the correct key hypothesis (solid black line) and the wrong hypotheses (gray lines) plotted over the number of measurements is shown in Fig. 2.

Contrary to the sampling phase leakage it is expected that the leakage of the hold phase appears at specific point(s) of the power traces, because the hold phase leakage $Leak_{\oplus}$ coincides with the positive clock edge (beginning of the precharge phase), and all the synchronous flip-flops are triggered at the same time. The previous attack was repeated using the leakage model presented in Eq. 10. As a result Fig. 3 shows the correlation coefficient of the key hypotheses for the different points of power traces using 1 500 measurements. Obviously, the maximum correlation for the correct key guess appears directly after the rising edge of the clock signal.

We limited the attack results to the iMDPL circuits since the structure (and, hence, our leakage models) of MDPL and DRSL flip-flops are identical to iMDPL. Indeed, we repeated the attack on corresponding MDPL and DRSL circuits as well as the modified structure proposed in [9] (just using hold-phase leakage). All attacks led to the same results as shown for the iMDPL.

5   Practical Issues

Since our proposed leakage model and hence our attack is a second-order attack, we compare the sensitivity to noise of our proposed attack to that of a corresponding first-order attack.

We consider a set of $1,000,000$ random bytes assuming a HW leakage with additive white Gaussian noise featuring zero mean and a specified standard deviation. To model the effect of noise to the attack, we determine the correlation

---

[2] This step needs to be performed because of the high accuracy of the simulations. In power traces measured from a real chip these leakages appear as a single peak [8].

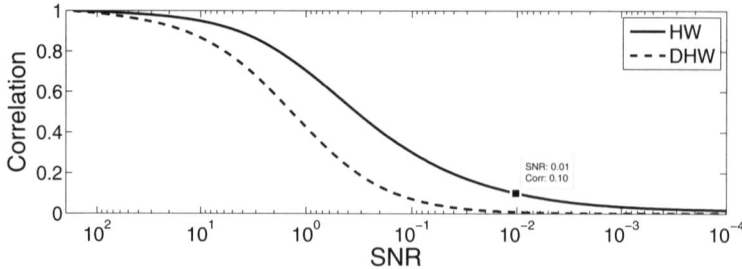

Fig. 4. Comparison of DHW model (of a single-bit masked ciruit) and HW model (of the corresponding unmasked circuit), correlation of the predictions and measurements over SNR

between HWs and noisy HWs (i.e., HW+noise as the simulated noisy measurement) for different noise standard deviations (and hence different SNRs). As usual for a hamming weight model, each bit has an equal contribution to the power consumption.

It should be noted that in order to make simulation and calculations closer to real measurements, noisy HW values are rounded to decimal values restricted to a byte since most of the measurement tools (i.e., digital oscilloscopes) use 8-bit analogue to digital converters and hence real measured power values are stepwise to 256 steps. In order to compare the noise effect on our proposed DHW-based attack, the same scenario is repeated for the masked circuit by masking the input bytes (by a random mask bit for each byte) before extracting the HW and adding noise. When analyzing the generated data, the new preprocessing step is performed according to the scheme presented by Algorithm 1. A comparison between these two experiments over their signal to noise ratio, SNR = var(signal)/var(noise), is depicted in Fig. 4. As expected, correlation between the predictions and measurements is decreased for low SNRs. However, the correlation for the DHW model (single-bit masked circuit) decreases more rapidly than that of HW model (unprotected circuit). It means, our proposed attack is more sensitive to noise than a straightforward CPA.

To investigate the applicability of our proposed attack in the presence of noise, we performed another experiment where additionally to the previous case an 8-bit key XOR followed by an AES Sbox is taken into account (similar to the circuit in Fig. 1). First, a first-order CPA attack using HW model of an unmasked circuit is performed for all possible values of the secret key (256 cases). The success rate of this attack is obtained for different signal to noise ratios[3]. Then, the same scenario is repeated for the single-bit masked circuit. This means, our proposed attack using DHW model (Algorithm 1) is performed for all possible secret keys, and success rates are computed for different signal to noise ratios. Fig. 5 depicts a comparison of success rates over SNR, threshold of SNR for a

---

[3] Success rate is computed as a ratio of the number of successful attacks over the number of all cases.

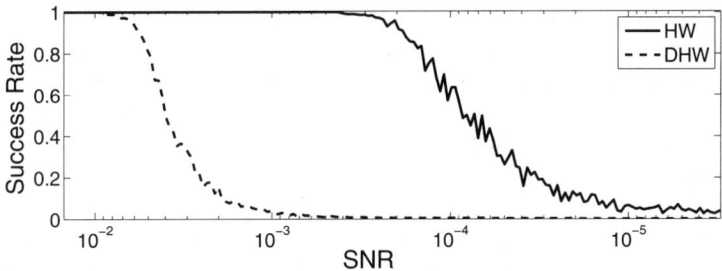

Fig. 5. Comparison of HW and DHW attacks, success rate over SNR

100% success rate in our proposed attack is higher than that of a straightforward CPA. In other words, our proposed attack on a single-bit masked circuit stops succeeding earlier than a first-order CPA on a corresponding unprotected circuit with an increasig SNR. Mapping the SNR threshold of DHW attack, i.e., 0.01, to the diagrams of Fig. 4 clarifies maximum correlation, i.e., 0.01, which can be achieved by a successful DHW attack at the threshold point. At the same SNR, maximum correlation for a successful first order CPA attack is around 0.1. It means, DHW attack works on a single-bit masked circuit if correlation between predictions and measurements of the same unprotected circuit (i.e., when mask bit generator is off and mask bit is always 0) is greater than 0.1.

Note that these observations are for $1,000,000$ measurements. The SNR threshold for a successful DHW attack and hence minimum required correlation value for the unprotected circuit are increased by deducting the number of measurements, e.g., we got 0.1 and 0.3 as SNR threshold and minimum required correlation respectively using $10,000$ measurements. Also, it should be noted that in our simulations we have supposed that the leakages are linearly related to predictions (HW), which does not hold precisely in practice. Moreover, in our proposed attack (and in our simulation as well) we have taken all of single-bit masked registers into account. In other words, all the masked registers in the architecture which are triggered at the same time must be considered in the attack. Otherwise, the DHW/DHD model does not fit to the folded measurements.

6   Conclusion

In this work we discussed the leakage for a wide range of side-channel resistant logic styles. Unlike most of the previous contributions, we did not focus our analysis on combinational parts of the logic. Instead we analyzed the leakage of flip-flop designs for various side-channel resistant logic styles. Our results show that logic masking where more than one flip-flop shares a single-bit mask does not prevent information leakage of those flip-flops. In other words, using the leakage we found in the masked flip-flops, a single-bit mask can not improve the security.

We furthermore presented a new attacking scheme that exploits the leakage of masked flip-flops. The attack does neither rely on unbalanced loads for the two parts of a differential signal, nor does the attacker need a detailed knowledge of the target layout or implementation. Instead it uses the newly proposed *Difference of Hamming Weight* (DHW) and *Difference of Hamming Distance* (DHD) model for predicting the data-dependent power consumption of the masked flip-flops. Using DHW and DHD as power model for a classical CPA attack on pre-processed power traces simply renders the single bit masks of a flip-flop useless. Hence the attack neither needs a biased PRNG nor is a mask bit detection step needed as in [13]. We proved the feasibility of our attack on two different ciphers and most of the masked DRP logic styles proposed so far.

Since most of the prior analysis of side-channel resistant logic styles focused on the combinational logic, so did the research to improve those logic styles. We think it is time to switch the focus of research to find methods for designing side-channel resistant flip-flops with a decent area and power consumption and a low impact on the operation frequency. One possible approach could be combining semi-custom design for combinational logic with full-custom flip-flop design.

References

1. Brier, E., Clavier, C., Olivier, F.: Correlation Power Analysis with a Leakage Model. In: Joye, M., Quisquater, J.-J. (eds.) CHES 2004. LNCS, vol. 3156, pp. 16–29. Springer, Heidelberg (2004)
2. Chen, Z., Zhou, Y.: Dual-Rail Random Switching Logic: A Countermeasure to Reduce Side Channel Leakage. In: Goubin, L., Matsui, M. (eds.) CHES 2006. LNCS, vol. 4249, pp. 242–254. Springer, Heidelberg (2006)
3. Gierlichs, B.: DPA-Resistance Without Routing Constraints? In: Paillier, P., Verbauwhede, I. (eds.) CHES 2007. LNCS, vol. 4727, pp. 107–120. Springer, Heidelberg (2007)
4. Guilley, S., Hoogvorst, P., Mathieu, Y., Pacalet, R.: The Backend Duplication Method. In: Rao, J.R., Sunar, B. (eds.) CHES 2005. LNCS, vol. 3659, pp. 383–397. Springer, Heidelberg (2005)
5. Kocher, P.C., Jaffe, J., Jun, B.: Differential Power Analysis. In: Wiener, M. (ed.) CRYPTO 1999. LNCS, vol. 1666, pp. 388–397. Springer, Heidelberg (1999)
6. Mangard, S., Oswald, E., Popp, T.: Power Analysis Attacks: Revealing the Secrets of Smart Cards. Springer, Heidelberg (2007)
7. Mangard, S., Popp, T., Gammel, B.M.: Side-Channel Leakage of Masked CMOS Gates. In: Menezes, A. (ed.) CT-RSA 2005. LNCS, vol. 3376, pp. 351–365. Springer, Heidelberg (2005)
8. Mangard, S., Pramstaller, N., Oswald, E.: Successfully Attacking Masked AES Hardware Implementations. In: Rao, J.R., Sunar, B. (eds.) CHES 2005. LNCS, vol. 3659, pp. 157–171. Springer, Heidelberg (2005)
9. Moradi, A., Salmasizadeh, M., Shalmani, M.T.M.: Power Analysis Attacks on MDPL and DRSL Implementations. In: Nam, K.-H., Rhee, G. (eds.) ICISC 2007. LNCS, vol. 4817, pp. 259–272. Springer, Heidelberg (2007)
10. Popp, T., Kirschbaum, M., Mangard, S.: Practical Attacks on Masked Hardware. In: Fischlin, M. (ed.) RSA Conference 2009. LNCS, vol. 5473. Springer, Heidelberg (2009)

11. Popp, T., Kirschbaum, M., Zefferer, T., Mangard, S.: Evaluation of the Masked Logic Style MDPL on a Prototype Chip. In: Paillier, P., Verbauwhede, I. (eds.) CHES 2007. LNCS, vol. 4727, pp. 81–94. Springer, Heidelberg (2007)

12. Popp, T., Mangard, S.: Masked Dual-Rail Pre-charge Logic: DPA-Resistance without Routing Constraints. In: Rao, J.R., Sunar, B. (eds.) CHES 2005. LNCS, vol. 3659, pp. 172–186. Springer, Heidelberg (2005)

13. Schaumont, P., Tiri, K.: Masking and Dual-Rail Logic Don't Add Up. In: Paillier, P., Verbauwhede, I. (eds.) CHES 2007. LNCS, vol. 4727, pp. 95–106. Springer, Heidelberg (2007)

14. Suzuki, D., Saeki, M.: Security Evaluation of DPA Countermeasures Using Dual-Rail Pre-charge Logic Style. In: Goubin, L., Matsui, M. (eds.) CHES 2006. LNCS, vol. 4249, pp. 255–269. Springer, Heidelberg (2006)

15. Suzuki, D., Saeki, M., Ichikawa, T.: DPA Leakage Models for CMOS Logic Circuits. In: Rao, J.R., Sunar, B. (eds.) CHES 2005. LNCS, vol. 3659, pp. 366–382. Springer, Heidelberg (2005)

16. Suzuki, D., Saeki, M., Ichikawa, T.: Random Switching Logic: A New Countermeasure against DPA and Second-Order DPA at the Logic Level. IEICE Trans. Fundam. Electron. Commun. Comput. Sci. E90-A(1), 160–168 (2007), http://eprint.iacr.org/2004/346

17. Tiri, K., Akmal, M., Verbauwhede, I.: A Dynamic and Differential CMOS Logic with Signal Independent Power Consumption to Withstand Differential Power Analysis on Smart Cards. In: European Solid-State Circuits Conference - ESS-CIRC 2002, pp. 403–406 (2002)

18. Tiri, K., Schaumont, P.: Changing the Odds Against Masked Logic. In: Biham, E., Youssef, A.M. (eds.) SAC 2006. LNCS, vol. 4356, pp. 134–146. Springer, Heidelberg (2007)

19. Tiri, K., Verbauwhede, I.: A Logic Level Design Methodology for a Secure DPA Resistant ASIC or FPGA Implementation. In: Design, Automation and Test in Europe Coneference - DATE 2004, pp. 246–251 (2004)

20. Tiri, K., Verbauwhede, I.: Place and Route for Secure Standard Cell Design. In: Conference on Smart Card Research and Advanced Applications - CARDIS 2004, pp. 143–158. Kluwer Academic Publishers, Dordrecht (2004)

21. Waddle, J., Wagner, D.: Towards Efficient Second-Order Power Analysis. In: Joye, M., Quisquater, J.-J. (eds.) CHES 2004. LNCS, vol. 3156, pp. 1–15. Springer, Heidelberg (2004)

Appendix I - Schematics of Flip-Flops

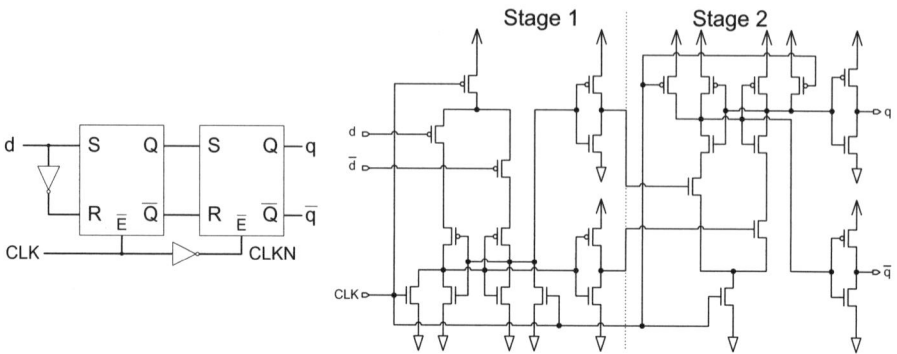

Fig. 6. Typical block diagram of an edge-sensitive flip-flop

Fig. 7. SABL-DFF

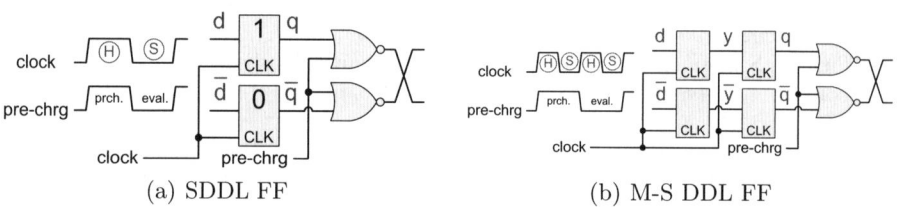

(a) SDDL FF

(b) M-S DDL FF

Fig. 8. WDDL flip-flops

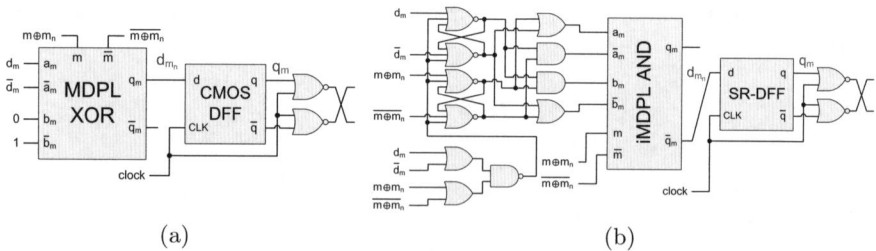

(a)

(b)

Fig. 9. (a) MDPL-DFF and (b) iMDPL-DFF

A Timing Attack against Patterson Algorithm in the McEliece PKC

Abdulhadi Shoufan[1], Falko Strenzke[2], H. Gregor Molter[3], and Marc Stöttinger[3]

[1] Center for Advanced Security Research Darmstadt CASED, Germany[*]
abdul.shoufan@cased.de
[2] FlexSecure GmbH, Germany[**]
strenzke@flexsecure.de
[3] Technische Universität Darmstadt, Germany
Integrated Circuits and Systems Lab, Department of Computer Science,
Technische Universität Darmstadt, Germany
{molter,stoettinger}@iss.tu-darmstadt.de

Abstract. The security of McEliece public-key cryptosystem is based on the difficulty of the decoding problem which is NP-hard. In this paper we propose a timing attack on the Patterson Algorithm, which is used for efficient decoding in Goppa codes. The attack is based on the relation between the error vector weight and the iteration number of the extended Euclidean algorithm used in Patterson Algorithm. This attack enables the extraction of the secret error vector with minimal overhead. A countermeasure is proposed and verified for a FPGA implementation.

Keywords: Side channel attack, timing attack, post quantum cryptography, code-based cryptography.

1 Introduction

The security of applied public-key cryptography relies on the incapability of modern computing systems to solve some mathematical problems in acceptable times. The factorization of large integers and the determination of discrete logarithms belong to this class of problem [1,2,3,4]. It is assumed, however, that these cryptosystems will be threatened, if a quantum computer with sufficient qubits emerges [5,6,7]. To avoid this risk before maturity, several cryptosystems were proposed in the literature such as hash-based, code-based, lattice-based, and multivariate-quadratic-equation-based cryptosystems, see [8,9,10,11]. All these systems are assumed to be resistant against quantum computers. Additionally, hardware solutions were proposed to address the performance question of these systems, see [12,13,14,15].

The McEliece public-key cryptosystem (McEliece-PKC) belongs to the class of code-based cryptography. The security of this system relies on the NP-hardness

---

[*] This work was supported by CASED.
[**] A part of the work of F. Strenzke was done at Cryptography and Computeralgebra Lab, TU-Darmstadt, Germany.

D. Lee and S. Hong (Eds.): ICISC 2009, LNCS 5984, pp. 161–175, 2010.
© Springer-Verlag Berlin Heidelberg 2010

of the decoding problem [16]. As no quantum algorithm has been proposed to solve this problem efficiently, so far, McEliece-PKC is regarded as secure against quantum computers. The security level of McEliece-PKC depends on the size of the underlying code. This has two effects: The public key and the private key are large and the decoding process is highly time-consuming. McEliece, therefore, employed Goppa codes for this cryptosystem, since an efficient decoding algorithm is available for this code, which is the Patterson Algorithm [17].

Nowadays, however, it is well-understood that algorithmic strength of a cryptosystem is only one condition for its security. The implementation of cryptographic systems must be secured against side channel attacks [18,19,20,21]. Especially for systems such as the McEliece-PKC, which is, due to its quantum computer resistance, designated to be used in high security contexts, side channel security becomes a very important issue.

In [22] a timing attack on the McEliece cryptosystem was proposed. This attack is based on the fact that the degree of the error locator polynomial equals the hamming weight of the error vector which is embedded in the ciphertext. During decryption, the error locator polynomial is evaluated n times, where n is the code length. Thus, the degree of this polynomial has a measurable influence on the decryption time. An attacker tries to change the decryption time by changing the hamming weight of the error vector of a chosen ciphertext. The proposed countermeasure in [22] relies on correcting the degree of the error locator polynomial: If this degree is detected to be less than the designated error weight, it is increased artificially to close the described timing side channel.

Our contribution: An in-depth investigation of the Patterson Algorithm, however, discloses another side channel which can not be closed by the countermeasure proposed in [22]. Specifically, the time behavior of the extended Euclidean Algorithm (XGCD), which is employed for determining the error locator polynomial, depends on the error weight. In this paper we provide a detailed analysis of this side channel, describe the attack procedure based upon, propose a countermeasure to close this channel, and provide an implementation outline of the attack and a corresponding countermeasure for an FPGA implementation.

Paper Structure: Section 2 provides a brief introduction into the McEliece-PKC and outlines the related timing attack. Section 3 details the attack proposed in this work including the side channel analysis, the attack procedure, the countermeasure and an implementation outline. Section 4 concludes the paper.

2   Preliminaries

2.1   McEliece Cryptosystem

This section provides a brief algorithmic description of McEliece-PKC. For details, interested readers are referred to special literature on coding theory, e.g., [23], and cryptography, e.g., [24]. Similarly to other cryptosystems, a plain implementation of McEliece-PKC is attackable by adaptive chosen-ciphertext attacks

(CCA2). For simplicity, the following description of the cryptosystem does not take into consideration any CCA2 conversion such as Pointcheval's [25] or Kobara and Imai's [26]. It can be shown, that the presence of a CCA2 conversion does not prevent our attack [22].

Key Generation: As this process is irrelevant for our purpose, a detailed description is given in Appendix A. In the following, only the private and the public keys are specified which are generated based on the domain parameters m and t, the code length n, and the code dimension k.

The private key consists of two parts: Firstly, a monic irreducible *Goppa polynomial* $g(x) = x^t + g_{t-1}x^{t-1} + \ldots + g_1 x + g_0$, where g_i's are random elements of the field $\mathbb{GF}(2^m)$. Secondly, a $n \times n$ permutation matrix P. Besides the parameters t and m, the public key consists of an $(mt \times k)$ matrix $\mathbf{R}^T$. The control matrix $\mathbf{H}$, which is created based on $g(x)$ is also secret. After generating the public key, $\mathbf{H}$ can either be stored for decryption or destroyed. In the latter case, $\mathbf{H}$ must be regenerated during decryption.

Encryption: Algorithm 1 depicts the encryption procedure in McEliece-PKC, which is self-explanatory.

Algorithm 1. McEliece-PKC Encryption

Require: k-bit plaintext m; public key $\mathbf{R}^T$.
Ensure: n-bit ciphertext z.
  1: Expand the public key $\mathbf{R}^T$ to $\mathbf{G} = \left[\mathbf{R}^T | \mathbb{I}_k\right]$.
  2: Generate a random n-bit error vector e with a hamming weight $w_e = t$.
  3: Encode the message $z := m\mathbf{G}$.
  4: Imprint t errors $z := z \oplus e$.
  5: **return** z.

Decryption: Algorithm 2 presents the decryption process in McEliece-PKC, which is clearly more complex than the encryption. For efficient error correction, the *Patterson Algorithm* [17] is employed to determine the error locator polynomial $\sigma(x)$, which will be abbreviated as ELP in the following. Patterson Algorithm is included in Algorithm 2 from step 2 to 7. By evaluating the ELP for all elements of $\mathbb{GF}(2^m)$, all error bits are revealed: An error at the i-th position of z causes $\sigma(\alpha_i)$ to be zero.

Notation: To facilitate referring to a certain step in a certain algorithm, we use the notation (A.x, S.y) to refer to step y of algorithm x. For instance, (A.2, S.6) refers to the determination of the error locator polynomial during decryption.

2.2   Side Channel of ELP Evaluation

In this section we briefly describe the timing attack proposed in [22] and discuss its countermeasure.

Algorithm 2. McEliece-PKC Decryption

Require: n-bit ciphertext z; private key $(\mathbf{P}, g(x))$.
Ensure: k-bit plaintext m.

1: Permute z: $z' = z\mathbf{P}$.
2: Determine the syndrome polynomial
   $S_{z'}(x) = z'\mathbf{H}^T(x^{t-1}, \ldots, x, 1)^T$. // the multiplication by the coefficient vector is used to transform the vector into a polynomial
3: Invert $S_{z'}^{-1}(x)$.
4: Let $\tau(x) = \sqrt{S_{z'}^{-1}(x) + x}$.
5: Find two polynomials $a(x)$ and $b(x)$, so that
   $b(x)\tau(x) = a(x) \bmod (g(x))$, and $\deg(a) \le \lfloor \frac{t}{2} \rfloor$ hold.
6: Determine the error locator polynomial
   $\sigma(x) = a^2(x) + xb(x)^2$,
   where $\deg(\sigma) \le t$
7: Reconstruct the error vector
   $e' = (\sigma(\alpha_0), \sigma(\alpha_1), \ldots, \sigma(\alpha_{n-1})) \oplus (1, \ldots, 1)$.
8: Permute the error vector $e = e'\mathbf{P}^T$.
9: Reconstruct the plaintext $m = z \oplus e$.
10: **return** m

Side Channel Analysis: According to (A.2, S.7), the ELP is evaluated for each element of $\mathbb{GF}(2^m)$ to reconstruct the error vector. By definition $\sigma(\alpha)$ is given by the following equation, where $\mathcal{T}_e = \{i|e_i = 1\}$ and e is the error vector.

$$\sigma(x) = \prod_{j \in \mathcal{T}_e} (x - \alpha_j) \in \mathbb{F}_{2^m}[x] \ . \tag{1}$$

If $e = e_7e_6e_5e_4e_3e_2e_1e_0 = 01100001$, for instance, then $\sigma(x) = (x - \alpha_6)(x - \alpha_5)(x - \alpha_0)$. Obviously, the time required to evaluate the ELP in (A.2, S.7) strongly depends on the weight of the error vector, as the latter determines the degree of this polynomial.

Concept of the Attack: The attacker exploits this behavior in order to find a plaintext to a certain ciphertext. Particularly, he flips a single bit at position i in the ciphertext and uses the timing side channel in order to determine whether e_i used during encryption was 0 or 1. He does this for all bit positions. Once he has reconstructed the error vector, he can easily recover the message.

Countermeasure: To avoid the differences in the decryption time arising from the different degrees of $\sigma(x)$, the countermeasure proposed in [22] relies on artificially raising of the degree of $\sigma(x)$ if it is found to be lower than t.

3   Side Channel of ELP Determination

A deeper insight into Algorithm 2, however, reveals another timing side channel, which cannot be closed by the countermeasure proposed in [22]. Specifically, the time needed to determine the ELP in (A.2, S.5) and (A.2, S.6) depends on the error weight. This side channel is available irrespective of the countermeasure proposed in [22]. Fig. 1 illustrates this aspect. In a naïve implementation, McEliece-PKC decryption leaks two side channels in both the determination and the evaluation of ELP. The work in [22] detected the second side channel and proposes a corresponding countermeasure. In our work we detect the first side channel and propose a countermeasure which closes both channels.

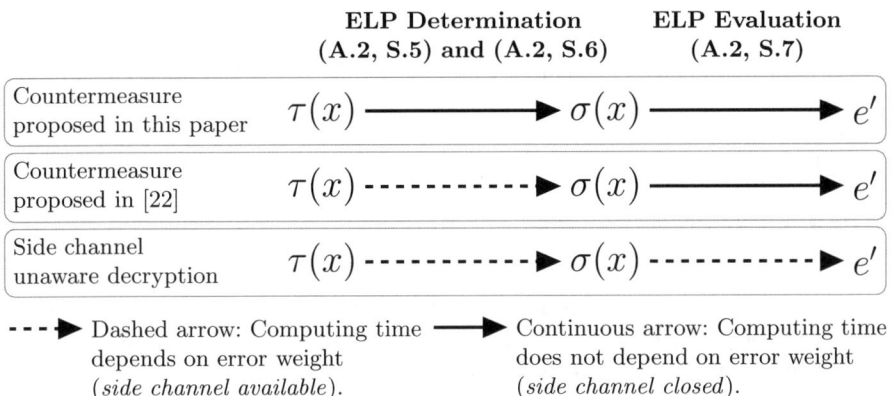

	ELP Determination (A.2, S.5) and (A.2, S.6)	ELP Evaluation (A.2, S.7)
Countermeasure proposed in this paper	$\tau(x) \longrightarrow \sigma(x)$	$\longrightarrow e'$
Countermeasure proposed in [22]	$\tau(x) \dashrightarrow \sigma(x)$	$\longrightarrow e'$
Side channel unaware decryption	$\tau(x) \dashrightarrow \sigma(x)$	$\dashrightarrow e'$

$\dashrightarrow$ Dashed arrow: Computing time depends on error weight (*side channel available*). $\longrightarrow$ Continuous arrow: Computing time does not depend on error weight (*side channel closed*).

Fig. 1. Illustration of Timing Side Channels in McEliece-PKC

3.1   Side Channel Analysis

The error locator polynomial is established in (A.2, S.6). For $\sigma(x)$ to be of degree t the degrees of $a(x)$ and $b(x)$ must fulfill the following conditions:

1. If t is odd, then the degree of $b(x)$ must be equal to $\frac{t-1}{2}$ to determine the leading term of $\sigma(x)$. The degree of $a(x)$ must be equal or less than $\frac{t-1}{2}$.
2. If t is even, then the degree of $a(x)$ must be equal to $\frac{t}{2}$ to determine the leading term of $\sigma(x)$. The degree of $b(x)$ must be equal or less than $\frac{t}{2} - 1$.

These conditions lead to the following inequalities:

$$\deg(a) \leq \left\lfloor \frac{t}{2} \right\rfloor \text{ and} \tag{2}$$

$$\deg(b) \leq \left\lfloor \frac{t-1}{2} \right\rfloor . \tag{3}$$

Usually, the determination of $a(x)$ and $b(x)$ in (A.2, S.5) is performed using the extended Euclidean algorithm (XGCD) with $\tau(x)$ and $g(x)$ as input polynomials, see Algorithm 3. The iterative processing is stopped when the degree of the

---

Algorithm 3. XGCD with break condition

Require: $\tau(x)$, $g(x)$
Ensure: $a(x)$ and $b(x)$, with $b(x)\tau(x) = a(x) \bmod (g(x))$ and $\deg(a) \leq d_{\text{break}}$
  1: $r_{-1}(x) = g(x)$
  2: $r_0(x) = \tau(x)$
  3: $b_{-1}(x) = 0$
  4: $b_0(x) = 1$
  5: i=0
  6: **while** $\deg(r_i(x)) > d_{\text{break}}$ **do**
  7:     $i = i + 1$
  8:     $q_i(x) = r_{i-2}(x)/r_{i-1}(x)$
  9:     $r_i(x) = r_{i-2}(x) \bmod r_{i-1}(x)$
10:     $b_i(x) = b_{i-2}(x) + q_i(x) \cdot b_{i-1}(x)$
11: **end while**
12: $a(x) = r_i(x)$
13: $b(x) = b_i(x)$
14: **return** $a(x)$ and $b(x)$

---

remainder polynomial $r(x)$ becomes equal to or less than $\lfloor \frac{t}{2} \rfloor$. We denote Equation (2) as the *break condition* and denote $\lfloor \frac{t}{2} \rfloor = d_{\text{break}}$. Furthermore, N refers to the number of iterations in Algorithm 3.

In McEliece-PKC, the error vector always has a weight $w_e = t$. In this case, we get equality either in (2) or in (3)[1]. Furthermore, due to Equation (1) recall that any error vector with a weight $w_e < t$ results in an ELP of a degree w_e. In consideration of Algorithm 3, this effect is caused by returning two polynomials $a(x)$ and $b(x)$, where neither (2) nor (3) becomes an equation. The purpose of the following analysis is to show how this aspect is associated with a reduction of the iteration number N in Algorithm 3. This, on its part, affects the execution time of XGCD and offers a side channel for attacking the McEliece-PKC. Recall that this timing side channel is available independently of the countermeasure detailed in Section 2.2.

Table 1 depicts the dependency of the iteration number N on the error weight w_e for different values of w_e and t. Based on w_e the degree of the ELP, i.e., $\deg(\sigma)$, is given. Also, the possible values of $\deg(a)$ and $\deg(b)$ are determined based on the following equation, given in (A.2, S.6):

$$\sigma(x) = a^2(x) + x \cdot b^2(x) . \qquad (4)$$

From Algorithm 3, however, $\deg(b)$ can be determined as:

$$\deg(b) = \sum_{i=1}^{N} \deg(q_i) . \qquad (5)$$

In Table 1, the iteration number N is set to be equal to $\deg(b)$. This is based on the assumption that the degree of the quotient polynomial $q_i(x)$ in each iteration

---

[1] For even t, we get equality in (2), for odd t, we get equality in (3).

Table 1. Relation of iteration count N to the error weight w_e. Assumption: degree of the quotient polynomial $q_i(x)$ equals one in each XGCD iteration.

	t	20	19	even t	odd t
$w_e = t$	$\deg(\sigma)$	20	19		
	$\deg(a)$	$= 10$	≤ 9		
	$\deg(b)$	≤ 9	$= 9$		
	N	≤ 9	$= 9$	$\leq \frac{t}{2} - 1$	$= \frac{t-1}{2}$
$w_e = t - 1$	$\deg(\sigma)$	19	18		
	$\deg(a)$	≤ 9	$= 9$		
	$\deg(b)$	$= 9$	≤ 8		
	N	$= 9$	≤ 8	$= \frac{t}{2} - 1$	$\leq \frac{t-1}{2} - 1$
$w_e = t - 2$	$\deg(\sigma)$	18	17		
	$\deg(a)$	$= 9$	≤ 8		
	$\deg(b)$	≤ 8	$= 8$		
	N	≤ 8	$= 8$	$\leq \frac{t}{2} - 2$	$= \frac{t-1}{2} - 1$
$w_e = t - 3$	$\deg(\sigma)$	17	16		
	$\deg(a)$	≤ 8	$= 8$		
	$\deg(b)$	$= 8$	≤ 7		
	N	$= 8$	≤ 7	$= \frac{t}{2} - 2$	$\leq \frac{t-1}{2} - 2$

equals one. In the following, we show that this is not strictly true, but is fulfilled with a very high probability for realistic values of the McEliece parameters m and t.

If $\deg(q_i) = 1$ for all $i \in \{1, 2, \ldots N\}$, then according to (5) the interation number equals $\deg(b)$, as

$$\deg(b) = \sum_{i=1}^{N} 1 = N = \left\lfloor \frac{t-1}{2} \right\rfloor . \tag{6}$$

However, if $\deg(q_i) = Q > 1$ for any $i \in \{1, 2, \ldots N\}$, then the iteration number N is reduced by $Q - 1$ compared to the case where $\deg(q_i) = 1$ for all i's. Note that this does not affect the degree of $b(x)$ due to Equation (5).

From Algorithm 3, the degree of $q_i(x)$ can be written as:

$$\deg(q_i) = \deg(r_{i-2}) - \deg(r_{i-1}) . \tag{7}$$

For $\deg(q_i)$ to be one, the degree of the remainder r_{i-1} must have decreased exactly by one compared to r_{i-2}. This happens with a probability of $1 - 2^{-m}$. For $m = 11$, for instance, the above assumption is true in 99.95% of the cases[2].

Thus, the probability for all $q_i(x)$ with $i \in \{1, 2, \ldots N\}$ having degree one becomes

$$p_1 = \left(1 - 2^{-m} \right)^N , \tag{8}$$

---

[2] This corresponds to the probability, that an 11-bit vector with uniformly distributed bits is different from zero.

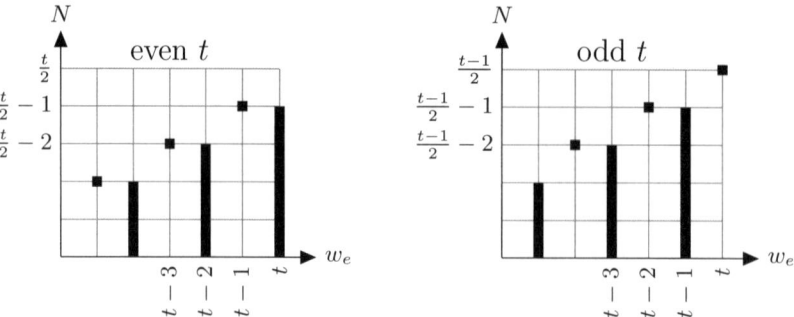

Fig. 2. Possible XGCD iteration counts as a function of the error vector weight

where N is given by Equation (6). For $m = 11$ and $t = 50$, p_1 becomes 98.83% which is still high. Thus, in the majority of the cases we will encounter the maximal number of iteration $N = \deg(b)$. Fig. 2 illustrates the results of Table 1 graphically, where the dots and bars in this figure represent exact values or value ranges of N, respectively. From this figure and based on the previous analysis, the following important conclusions can be drawn:

1. **If t is odd**, then reducing the number of errors w_e in a ciphertext from t to $t-1$, leads to reducing the iteration number N, see right part of Fig. 2.
2. **If t is even**, then reducing w_e to $t-1$ is not sufficient to reduce the iteration number. At least two bits must be flipped by the attacker in this case, in order to potentially reach $w_e = t - 2$, see left part of Fig. 2.
3. The lower w_e, the lower N, however, the more difficult is the attack. This is because the probability to correctly guess l positions of the error vector that have the value 1 is given as follows:

$$p_2 = \prod_{i=0}^{l-1} \frac{t - i}{2^m - i} \ . \tag{9}$$

Table 2 shows some examples for this probability. Obviously l may be used as a trade-off parameter to control the attack. Lower l values, on the one hand, demand less computation to find the right bits. On the other hand, a lower l value causes less reduction of N and the time measurement must be more accurate to eliminate noise. Therefore, lower l values may be more appropriate for attacking devices with low computation power and low noise such as smart cards. For attacking a server, in contrast, higher values of l may be more helpfull. In general, a server may offer the computation power needed to rule the exponential relation between the number of guessed bit positions l and the probability for a right guess according to (9).

Note: We analyzed the side channel of ELP determination with respect to XGCD applied in (A.2, S.5), so far. In this note we address the squaring of $a(x)$

Table 2. Probability to create manipulated ciphertexts with a given w_e

w_e	Probability	Example: $t = 50$ and $m = 11$
$t - 1$	$\frac{t}{2^m}$	2.44%
$t - 2$	$\frac{t}{2^m} \frac{t-1}{2^m-1}$	0.06%
$t - 3$	$\frac{t}{2^m} \frac{t-1}{2^m-1} \frac{t-2}{2^m-2}$	0.0026%

and $b(x)$ in (A.2, S.6). Considering Table 1 it can be seen that manipulated ciphertexts, i.e. ciphertexts with $w_e < t$, result in polynomials $a(x)$ and $b(x)$ with degrees, which are most likely equal to or less than the case of $w_e = t$. Consequently, the squaring in (A.2, S.6) will be faster and the decryption time will again be smaller. Thus, the effect of this manipulation on the squaring time enhances the side channel of XGCD discussed above. As this effect, however, will be removed by the same countermeasure proposed in Section 3.3, it is not analyzed here, for brevity.

3.2   Attack Procedure

Note: Encrypting a message in McEliece-PKC includes imprinting t errors into the encoded message, see (A.1, S.4). In the following we use the concept of *correct bit*, which should be considered from the attackers' point of view. This concept refers to a bit of the error vector which has a value of one. Thus, the purpose of the attack is to find all the t correct bits imprinted in the $n-$bit ciphertext z.

In this section we first describe the attack procedure for an odd t, where flipping only one correct bit is sufficient. Then, we remark how the procedure can be modified to attack systems with an even t. In the following, we assume an implementation with the countermeasure presented in [22] to eliminate the effect of the ELP evaluation channel and to highlight only the ELP determination channel.

The proposed attack relies on flipping a bit z_i of the ciphertext z and measuring the decryption time. We distinguish two cases:

1. If the corresponding bit of the error vector is not a correct bit $(e_i = 0)$, then the bit flipping causes adding an additional error, so that $w_e > t$. It can be shown that the ELP will have a degree of t and the XGCD iteration number will be equal to $\frac{t-1}{2}$ in this case, see [22].
2. If the corresponding bit of the error vector is a correct bit $(e_i = 1)$, then the bit flipping causes the removal of this error, so that $w_e = t - 1$. Thus, the XGCD iteration number will be equal to or less than $\frac{t-1}{2} - 1$ and the decryption time will be shorter than in the previous case.

This procedure is repeated for all bits of z as depicted in Algorithm 4. The function OneHot(n, i) delivers an $n-$bit vector where only the $i-$th bit is one. To improve results, a measurement may be repeated several times, which is adjusted using the parameter M.

Algorithm 4. Timing attack based on the ELP evaluation for odd t

---

Require: Ciphertext z, McEliece parameters $(t, n = 2^m)$, attack precision parameter M.

Ensure: Error vector e shrouded in z.

1: $e := 0$
2: **for** $i = 0$ to $n - 1$ **do**
3:    $c = z \oplus \text{OneHot}(n, i)$.
4:    **for** $j = 1$ to M **do**
5:        Provoke decrypting c and measure the decryption time $T_{i,j}$
6:    **end for**
7:    Determine T_i as the mean value of all $T_{i,j}$'s and insert it into a list L.
8: **end for**
9: Sort L according to increasing T_i values.
10: **for** $k = 0$ to $t - 1$ **do**
11:    Get the the index i of the k-th element of L.
12:    $e_i := 1$
13: **end for**
14: **return** e.

For the case of even t, Algorithm 4 must be modified to support flipping of at least two bits of the ciphertext. For this purpose, the first for-loop may be replaced by two nested loops. The extern loop flips one bit, say z_i. The inner loop flips all the other bits from z_{i+1} to z_{n-1} one-by-one and proceeds as the first for-loop of Algorithm 4. This implements a maximum-likelihood strategy concerning the error positions.

3.3   Countermeasure

The idea of the countermeasure is to detect the conditions for an untimely termination of XGCD and, if this is the case, to enforce the continuation of XGCD execution until proper degrees of $a(x)$ and $b(x)$ are reached, which would result from a ciphertext with $w_e = t$, see Algorithm 5.

Referring to previous analysis and Table 1 the break condition of XGCD in consideration of the presented attack can be rewritten as follows:

– **If t is even,** then the degree of $a(x)$ can be used to detect a ciphertext with $w_e < t$. Specifically, $\deg(a)$ must be equal to d_{break} to make sure that $w_e \geq t$. For instance, if $t = 20$ then $\deg(a)$ must be equal to 10 in the last iteration, see the condition in (A.5, S.12).

– **If t is odd,** then a ciphertext with $w_e < t$ can be detected by examining the degree of $b(x)$, which also must be equal to d_{break} in the last iteration, provided that z was not corrupted, see the condition in (A.5, S.16).

In both cases the timing side channel arising in the event of $w_e < t$ are closed. Enforcing the continuation of XGCD execution is achieved by manipulating the remainder polynomials $r_i(x)$ to have a degree which is equal to $\deg(r_{i-1}) - 1$, see steps 13 and 17 of Algorithm 5. This manipulation is performed using predefined

Algorithm 5. XGCD with countermeasure

Require: $\tau(x)$, $g(x)$
Ensure: $a(x)$ and $b(x)$, with $b(x)\tau(x) = a(x) \bmod (g(x))$ and $\deg(a) \leq d_{\text{break}}$
1: $r_{-1}(x) = g(x)$
2: $r_0(x) = \tau(x)$
3: $b_{-1}(x) = 0$
4: $b_0(x) = 1$
5: $i = 0$
6: **while** $\deg(r_i(x)) > d_{\text{break}}$ **do**
7:     $i = i + 1$
8:     $q_i(x) = r_{i-2}(x)/r_{i-1}(x)$
9:     $r_i(x) = r_{i-2}(x) \bmod r_{i-1}(x)$
10:     $b_i(x) = b_{i-2}(x) + q_i(x) \cdot b_{i-1}(x)$
11:     **if** t even **then**
12:         **if** $\deg(r_i) < d_{\text{break}}$ **then**
13:             Manipulate $r_i(x)$, so that $\deg(r_i) = \deg(r_{i-1}) - 1$
14:         **end if**
15:     **else**
16:         **if** $\deg(r_i) \leq d_{\text{break}}$ AND $\deg(b_i) < d_{\text{break}}$ **then**
17:             Manipulate $r_i(x)$, so that $\deg(r_i) = \deg(r_{i-1}) - 1$
18:         **end if**
19:     **end if**
20: **end while**
21: $a(x) = r_i(x)$
22: $b(x) = b_i(x)$
23: **return** $a(x)$ and $b(x)$

coefficients or pseudo random coefficients which are derived *deterministically* from the ciphertext. Note that it is not advisable to use random data to implement this countermeasure. Otherwise an attacker may gather information by detecting that the decryption of a manipulated ciphertext is not deterministic. He could observe this by repeatedly letting the device decrypt the respective manipulated ciphertext, and determine the variance of quantities like the timing or power consumption at a certain point in time. Note that this countermeasure leads to falsifying the result, however, only in the case of manipulated ciphertexts. Understandably, this falsification is not critical in this case.

3.4 Implementation

Attack Execution: To prove the proposed attack and its countermeasure we simulated it for a proprietary FPGA implementation using Virtex-5 from Xilinx. The McEliece-PKC parameters are $t = 50$ and $m = 11$. We decrypted three ciphertexts z_1, z_2, and z_3, where z_1 is an incorrupted ciphertext, z_2 is z_1 after flipping one correct bit, and z_3 is z_1 after flipping two correct bits. Table 3 summarizes the number of clock cycles needed to decrypt the three ciphertexts. These results prove the feasibility of the timing attack and confirm the analysis given in Section 3.1. Apparently, flipping one bit is not sufficient in the case of even t. At least two bits must be flipped to reduce the iteration number and obtain a considerable difference in the decryption time. Table 3 additionally includes the decryption clock cycles for the same ciphertexts after implementing the countermeasure described in the following.

Table 3. Timing Attack Procedure Example

z	w_e	No. cycles without countermeasure	No. cycles with countermeasure
z_1	t	189,138	189,138
z_2	$t-1$	189,138	189,138
z_3	$t-2$	188,836	189,138

Countermeasure Implementation: The goal of the countermeasure is to defeat the described attack without increasing the clock cycles necessary for the computation of the XGCD compared to the original implementation. As our McEliece-PKC implementation has an even t ($t = 50$), the proposed countermeasure relates to steps 12 and 13 in Algorithm 5. If we find out that $\deg(r_i) < d_{\mathrm{break}}$ in any iteration i, then the corresponding ciphertext is manipulated. In this case we alter $r_i(x)$ to $r_i'(x)$ so that $\deg(r_i') = \deg(r_{i-1}) - 1$. This means, not only the highest coefficient of $r_i(x)$ is set to a non-zero value, but also all other potential leading zero coefficients. The results in Table 3 show that the described countermeasure closes the obvious timing side channel completely.

4   Conclusion

In this paper we have shown that the McEliece-PKC like most known public key cryptosystems, bears a high risk of leaking secret information through side channels if the implementation does not feature appropriate countermeasures. We have detailed a timing attack, which was also implemented and executed on an existing FPGA implementation of the cryptosystem. Our results show the high vulnerability of an implementation without countermeasures. Clearly, other parts of the cryptosystem require to be inspected with the same accuracy. This is especially true for the decryption phase, where the secret Goppa polynomial is employed in different operations. The McEliece-PKC, though existing for 30 years, has not experienced wide uses so far. But since it is one of the candidates for post quantum public key cryptosystems, it might become practically relevant in the near future.

References

1. Diffie, W., Hellman, M.: New Directions in Cryptography. IEEE Transactions on Information Theory 22(6), 644–654 (1976)
2. Rivest, R., Shamir, A., Adleman, L.: A Method for Obtaining Digital Signatures and Public-Key Cryptosystems. Communications of the ACM 21(2), 120–126 (1978)

3. Miller, V.: Use of Elliptic Curves in Cryptography. In: Williams, H.C. (ed.) CRYPTO 1985. LNCS, vol. 218, pp. 417–426. Springer, Heidelberg (1986)
4. ElGamal, T.: A Public Key Cryptosystem and A Signature Based on Discrete Logarims. IEEE Transactions on Information Theory (1985)
5. Shor, P.W.: Algorithms For Quantum Computation: Discrete Logarithms and Factoring. In: Proceedings, 35th Annual Symposium on Foundation of Computer Science (1994)
6. Shor, P.W.: Polynomial Time Algorithms for Prime Factorization and Discrete Logarithms on a Quantum Computer. SIAM Journal on Computing 26(5), 1484–1509 (1997)
7. Proos, J., Zalka, C.: Shor's Discrete Logarithm Quantum Algorithm for Elliptic Curves (2003)
8. Merkle, R.: A Certified Digital Signature. In: Brassard, G. (ed.) CRYPTO 1989. LNCS, vol. 435, pp. 218–238. Springer, Heidelberg (1990)
9. McEliece, R.J.: A Public Key Cryptosystem Based on Algebraic Coding Theory. DSN Progress Report 42-44 , 114–116
10. Lenstra, A.K., Lovasz, J.L.: Factoring Polynomials with Rational Coefficients. Math., 515–534 (1982)
11. Fell, H., Diffie, W.: Analysis of a Public Key Approach Based on Polynomial Substitution. In: Williams, H.C. (ed.) CRYPTO 1985. LNCS, vol. 218, pp. 340–349. Springer, Heidelberg (1986)
12. Balasubramanian, S., et al.: Fast Multivariate Signature Generation in Hardware: The Case of Rainbow. In: 19th IEEE Int. Conf. on Application-specific Systems, Architectures and Processors ASAP (2008)
13. El-Hadedy, M., Gligoroski, D., Knapskog, S.J.: High Performance Implementation of a Public Key Block Cipher - MQQ, for FPGA Platforms. In: International Conference on ReConFigurable Computing and FPGAs, ReConFig 2008 (2008)
14. Beuchat, J.C., Sendrier, N., Tisserand, A., Villard, G.: FPGA Implementation of a Recently Published Signature Scheme. Rapport de recherche RR LIP 2004-14 (2004)
15. Shoufan, A., Wink, T., Molter, G., Huss, S., Strenzke, F.: A Novel Processor Architecture for McEliece Cryptosystem and FPGA Platforms. In: 20th IEEE Int. Conf. on Application-specific Systems, Architectures and Processors ASAP 2009 (2009)
16. Menezes, A., van Oorschot, P., Vanstone, S.: Handbook of Applied Cryptography. CRC Press, Boca Raton (1996)
17. Patterson, N.: Algebraic Decoding of Goppa Codes. IEEE Transactions Information Theory 21, 203–207 (1975)
18. Kocher, P.: Timing Attacks on Implementations of Diffie-Hellman, RSA, DSS, and Other Systems. In: Proceedings of the 16th Annual International Cryptology Conference on Advances in Cryptology, pp. 104–113 (1996)
19. Kocher, P.: Differential power analysis. In: Wiener, M. (ed.) CRYPTO 1999. LNCS, vol. 1666, pp. 388–397. Springer, Heidelberg (1999)
20. Tsunoo, Y., Tsujihara, E., Minematsu, K., Miyauchi, H.: Cryptanalysis of Block Ciphers Implemented on Computers with Cache. In: International Symposium on Information Theory and Applications, pp. 803–806 (2002)
21. Schindler, W., Lemke, K., Paar, C.: A stochastic model for differential side channel cryptanalysis. In: Rao, J.R., Sunar, B. (eds.) CHES 2005. LNCS, vol. 3659, pp. 30–46. Springer, Heidelberg (2005)

22. Strenzke, F., Tews, E., Molter, H.G., Overbeck, R., Shoufan, A.: Side Channels in the McEliece PKC. In: Buchmann, J., Ding, J. (eds.) PQCrypto 2008. LNCS, vol. 5299, pp. 30–46. Springer, Heidelberg (2008)

23. Lin, S.: Error Control Coding: Fundamentals and Applications. Prentice-Hall, Englewood Cliffs (1983)

24. Rodriguez-Henriques, F., Saqib, N., Perez, A., Koc, C.: Cryptographic Algorithms on Reconfigurable Hardware. Springer, Heidelberg (2006)

25. Pointcheval, D.: Chosen-ciphertext security for any one-way cryptosystem. In: Imai, H., Zheng, Y. (eds.) PKC 2000. LNCS, vol. 1751, pp. 129–146. Springer, Heidelberg (2000)

26. Kobara, K., Imai, H.: Semantically Secure McEliece Public-Key Cryptosystems - Conversions for McEliece PKC. In: Practice and Theory in Public Key Cryptography - PKC '01 Proceedings (2001)

A   Key Generation in McEliece-PKC

Algorithm 6. McEliece-PKC Key Generation

Require: McEliece domain parameters m and t.
    Let $n = 2^m$ and $k = n - mt$.
Ensure: The public key $\mathbf{R}^T$ and the private key $(\mathbf{P}, g(x))$.
 1: Construct $\mathbb{GF}(2^m) = \{\alpha_0, \alpha_1, \ldots, \alpha_{n-1}\}$.
 2: Create a random monic, irreducible polynomial $g(x)$ with $\deg(g) = t$, having coefficients in $\mathbb{GF}(2^m)$ and $x \in \mathbb{GF}(2^m)$.
 3: Create the auxiliary matrices $\mathbf{X}$, $\mathbf{Y}$, and $\mathbf{Z}$.
 4: Calculate the $t \times n$ control matrix $\mathbf{H} = \mathbf{XYZ}$.
 5: Create a random $n \times n$ permutation matrix $\mathbf{P}$.
 6: Calculate the permutated control matrix $\widetilde{\mathbf{H}} = \mathbf{HP}^T$.
 7: Transform the $t \times n$ matrix $\widetilde{\mathbf{H}}$ over $\mathbb{GF}(2^m)$ into a $mt \times n$ matrix $\mathbf{H}_2$ over $\mathbb{GF}(2)$.
 8: Bring $\mathbf{H}_2$ into the systematic form $\widetilde{\mathbf{G}} = [\mathbb{I}_{mt}|\mathbf{R}]$.
 9: The expanded public key is the $k \times n$ matrix over $\mathbb{GF}(2)$, denoted as $\mathbf{G} = [\mathbf{R}^T|\mathbb{I}_k]$.

10: **return** $\mathbf{R}^T$ and $(\mathbf{P}, g(x))$

Key Generation. Algorithm 6 depicts the key generation in McEliece-PKC. Based on the domain parameters m and t, the code length n and its dimension k are determined. The first step in the key generation is to construct the basic finite field $\mathbb{GF}(2^m)$. With $m = 11$, for instance, this field contains 2048 elements $\alpha_0, \alpha_1, \ldots, \alpha_{2047}$, which are all 11-bit vectors. The next step is to generate a monic, irreducible polynomial $g(x) = x^t + g_{t-1}x^{t-1} + \ldots + g_1 x + g_0$, which is denoted as *Goppa polynomial*. All coefficients of $g(x)$ are elements of $\mathbb{GF}(2^m)$. This polynomial is part of the private key which is kept secret.

Based on $g(x)$ and the field $\mathbb{GF}(2^m)$ the control matrix $\mathbf{H}$ is created. This step is performed using three auxiliary matrices $\mathbf{X}$, $\mathbf{Y}$, and $\mathbf{Z}$, as given in Appendix A. Note that $g(\alpha_i)^{-1}$ indicates the multiplicative inverse of $g(\alpha_i)$ in $\mathbb{GF}(2^m)$, where $g(\alpha_i)$ results from the evaluation of $g(x)$ for the element α_i.

$$\mathbf{X} = \underbrace{\begin{bmatrix} g_t & 0 & 0 & \cdots & 0 \\ g_{t-1} & g_t & 0 & \cdots & 0 \\ \vdots & \vdots & \vdots & \ddots & \vdots \\ g_1 & g_2 & g_3 & \cdots & g_t \end{bmatrix}}_{t \times t \text{ matrix}}, \quad \mathbf{Y} = \underbrace{\begin{bmatrix} 1 & 1 & \cdots & 1 \\ \alpha_0 & \alpha_1 & \cdots & \alpha_{n-1} \\ \vdots & \vdots & \ddots & \vdots \\ \alpha_0^{t-1} & \alpha_1^{t-1} & \cdots & \alpha_{n-1}^{t-1} \end{bmatrix}}_{t \times n \text{ matrix}},$$

$$\mathbf{Z} = \underbrace{\begin{bmatrix} g(\alpha_0)^{-1} & 0 & \cdots & 0 \\ 0 & g(\alpha_1)^{-1} & \cdots & 0 \\ \vdots & \vdots & \ddots & \vdots \\ 0 & 0 & \cdots & g(\alpha_{n-1})^{-1} \end{bmatrix}}_{n \times n \text{ matrix}}$$

Fig. 3. Auxiliary Matrices for the Control Matrix $\mathbf{H}$

Subsequently, the control matrix is permuted using a random matrix P, which is also kept secret as a part of the private key. Although the resulting matrix $\widetilde{\mathbf{H}}$ can now be used as a public key, this is inefficient because of the huge length of this key. The next steps, therefore, aim at producing a shorter public key. First $\widetilde{\mathbf{H}}$ is expanded to the binary form $\mathbf{H}_2$, which is converted into a systematic form $\widetilde{\mathbf{G}}$, where $\mathbb{I}$ is the identity matrix. Lastly, $\widetilde{\mathbf{G}}$ is transposed into $\mathbf{G}$ and $\mathbf{G}$'s left submatrix $\mathbf{R}^T$ is returned as the public key.

Side-Channel Analysis of Cryptographic Software via Early-Terminating Multiplications

Johann Großschädl[1,2], Elisabeth Oswald[2], Dan Page[2], and Michael Tunstall[2]

[1] University of Luxembourg,
Laboratory of Algorithmics, Cryptology and Security (LACS),
6, rue Richard Coudenhove-Kalergi, L–1359 Luxembourg, Luxembourg
johann.groszschaedl@uni.lu
[2] University of Bristol,
Department of Computer Science,
Merchant Venturers Building, Woodland Road, Bristol, BS8 1UB, U.K.
{johann,eoswald,page,tunstall}@cs.bris.ac.uk

Abstract. The design of embedded processors demands a careful trade-off between many conflicting objectives such as performance, silicon area and power consumption. Finding such a trade-off often ignores the issue of security, which can cause, otherwise secure, cryptographic software to leak information through so-called micro-architectural side channels. In this paper we show that early-terminating integer multipliers found in various embedded processors (e.g., ARM7TDMI) represent an instance of this problem. The early-termination mechanism causes differences in the time taken to execute a multiply instruction depending on the magnitude of the operands (e.g., up to three clock cycles on an ARM7TDMI processor), which are observable via variations in execution time and power consumption. Exploiting the early-termination mechanism makes Simple Power Analysis (SPA) attacks relatively straightforward to conduct, and may even allow one to attack implementations with integrated countermeasures that would not leak any information when executed on a processor with a constant-latency multiplier. We describe several case studies, including both secret-key (RC6, AES) and public-key algorithms (RSA, ECIES) to demonstrate the threat posed by embedded processors with early-terminating multipliers.

Keywords: Side-channel attack, power analysis, computer arithmetic, general-purpose processor, micro-architectural cryptanalysis.

1 Introduction

Within the context of embedded system design, factors such as silicon area and power consumption need to be carefully balanced against performance. This is particularly important when a single component acts as a bottleneck to performance, or is particularly large or power hungry; examples include the dedicated multiplier circuits that exist within embedded processor cores. Approaches to the realisation of such circuits form a large design space. Ignoring issues such as

D. Lee and S. Hong (Eds.): ICISC 2009, LNCS 5984, pp. 176–192, 2010.
© Springer-Verlag Berlin Heidelberg 2010

pipelining, at one extreme are fully parallel designs built entirely from combinatorial logic, for example those based on Wallace or Dadda trees [13]. Such designs represent a low-latency solution since they produce a result in a single clock cycle, but do so at the expense of area and power consumption.

At the other end of the design space are multipliers that are iterative in the sense that they make iterative use of modest combinatorial logic (e.g., based on a bit-serial approach). Bit-serial multipliers essentially allow the opposite trade-off by increasing latency but reducing area and power. Of course, intermediate points in the design space exist; these represent approaches which try to reduce the area requirements of low-latency designs or reduce the latency of low-area or low-power designs. Well-known ways to arrive at such a compromise include the implementation of a digit-serial multiplier [20], the recoding of one of the operands into a radix-4 representation [10], or a combination of both [15].

Numerous 32-bit processors intended for the embedded market are equipped with digit-serial integer multipliers. For example, ARM7 processors such as the ARM7TDMI [5] contain a (32×8)-bit multiplier; other embedded processors feature (32×12)-bit multipliers (Intel StrongARM SA-1100 [22]) or (32×16)-bit multipliers (e.g., MIPS32 4Km [26], PowerPC 440x6 [21], as well as certain ARM9 models). These processors execute a (32×32)-bit multiplication in an iterative fashion by making several passes through the datapath; each iteration processes an 8, 12, or 16-bit digit of the multiplier-operand, starting with the least-significant digit. The result of the first iteration is fed back into the multiplier and combined with the intermediate products of the following iterations to eventually yield the full result [15]. Generally speaking, a w-bit processor core comprising of a digit-serial multiplier with a digit-size of $k < w$ bits requires $\lceil w/k \rceil$ cycles to calculate the $2w$-bit product of a $(w \times w)$-bit multiplication (an extra clock cycle may be necessary if the full product is to be written back to general-purpose registers).

One of the reasons why digit-serial multipliers are attractive is the proliferation of Digital Signal Processing (DSP) and multimedia applications in mobile and embedded devices, e.g. cell phones or PDAs. These application domains are multiplication-intensive, which means that the latency of multiply instructions impacts heavily on overall performance. In order to better support DSP/multimedia kernels, many processors with digit-serial multipliers employ a technique commonly referred to as *early termination* [15]. That is, after each iteration the multiplier checks whether the remaining digits are all zero; if this is the case the multiplication is terminated early and the result is immediately returned. The early-termination mechanism can reduce the latency of multiply instructions if the operands are small, which is generally the case in DSP and multimedia applications. For example, a processor with an early-terminating (32×8)-bit multiplier can multiply two 8-bit pixel colour values in a single cycle, or two 16-bit audio samples in two clock cycles (instead of four cycles as would be the case without early termination).

Both Kocher et al. [25] and Ravi et al. [33] stress the importance of considering security as an additional dimension in the embedded system design space that demands the same attention as more traditional metrics of interest such as cost, performance, and power. Within this setting, the threat of side-channel analysis against embedded systems poses a particularly hard problem. By passively profiling or actively influencing execution of cryptographic software, it is possible that an attacker can recover otherwise secret information stored in an embedded device. Focusing on power analysis attacks, Simple Power Analysis (SPA) refers to a scenario where an attacker typically collects only one, or very few, power traces and attempts to recover secret information by focusing on differences between patterns within each trace. In contrast, Differential Power Analysis (DPA) typically uses several or many traces and analyses differences between the traces [24].

The problem of side-channel leakage becomes especially pronounced if a processor itself causes otherwise secure cryptographic software to leak information through a *micro-architectural side channel* [4]. Put simply, micro-architectural attacks exploit certain features or effects of "standard" processor components (e.g., cache systems, branch prediction units) to induce or amplify side-channel leakage. In recent years, micro-architectural cryptanalysis based on cache hits or misses [32,9,1] as well as branch (mis-)predictions [2,3] has been studied extensively, and several successful attacks are reported in the recent literature [7,31]. These approaches allow an attacker to extract secret keys from cryptographic software, even if it features sophisticated side-channel countermeasures that would completely prevent leakage on processors without cache sub-system or branch prediction unit.

In this paper we show that early-terminating integer multipliers are a prime example of a micro-architectural side channel and that they can leak significant information about the secret keys used in cryptographic software. As described previously, the early-termination mechanism causes differences in the latency of multiply instructions, which are observable via variations in execution time and power consumption. For example, the latency of a (32×32)-bit multiply instruction producing a 64-bit result can vary by up to three clock cycles on a processor with an early-terminating (32×8)-bit multiplier (e.g., ARM7TDMI and ARM920T), or up to two cycles if the multiplier has a digit-size of 12 bits (e.g., StrongARM SA-1100), or one cycle in the case of an early-terminating (32×16)-bit multiplier (e.g., MIPS32 4Km, certain PowerPC models).

Side-channel attacks exploiting the early-termination mechanism belong to the category of micro-architectural attacks since the level of susceptibility depends mainly on the micro-architectural design of a processor. However, micro-architectural cryptanalysis based on early-terminating multiplication differs in some aspects from cache attacks and branch-prediction attacks. Firstly, some variants of cache attacks (e.g., those described in [31,1]), as well as the Simple Branch Prediction Analysis (SBPA) attack [2], rely on other processes (e.g., a so-called "spy" process running in parallel on the same processor) to evict cache lines or to reveal the branch predictor state. An early-termination attack, on the other hand, is completely passive in the sense that it does not require a spy process running on the target processor: instead, our attacks work by feeding cryptographic software carefully chosen input content (plaintexts) that provoke the early-termination mechanism. Often, very few such inputs, and hence very few executions of the implementation under attack, suffice to extract the entire secret key. A second difference is the type of processors for which said attacks are relevant. While cache memory and branch prediction units can be found in almost any high-performance processor, they are less common in the embedded market, especially in the low-power segment. Early-terminating multipliers, on the other hand, are widely deployed in embedded processors and, as such, early-termination attacks expand the scope of micro-architectural cryptanalysis into the embedded domain.

Our contribution in this paper is threefold. First, we describe in detail how early-terminating multipliers work and what information they can leak through power and timing side channels. Even though side-channel leakage due to data-dependent instruction timing has been investigated within other contexts, the threat posed by the early-termination effect is still widely unknown. Our second contribution is to survey vulnerable cryptographic algorithms, and to explain how such vulnerabilities can be practically used to mount attacks. We conducted numerous experiments with software implementations of AES, RC6, RSA, and ECC on an ARM7 processor. In all our experiments we succeeded in extracting the entire key with just a few power traces; in some cases a single trace was sufficient. The third and final contribution is an analysis of potential hardware and software-based countermeasures.

2   Background

In this section, we describe the early-termination mechanism in detail, using the ARM7TDMI [5,15] as a concrete example. We focus on this specific platform because it has a dominant role in the 32-bit embedded processor market. However, we point out that the attacks described in this paper can be mounted on any embedded processor with an early-terminating integer multiplier, including (but not limited to) the StrongARM SA-1100, the MIPS32 4Km, and certain PowerPC models.

We use the following notation: w refers to the processor's word size; in our case $w = 32$ since we are dealing with an ARM7 processor. Let x_i with $0 \leq i < w$ denote the i-th bit of some w-bit word x. Furthermore, let $x_{(y)}$ denote x written in base-y. For example, $F0_{(16)}$ is the decimal value 240 written in base-16, $X = (X_0, X_1, \ldots X_{n-1})_{(256)}$ is a vector of n elements where each element is written in base-256 (i.e., each element is a byte).

2.1   Multiplication on an ARM7TDMI

The ARM instruction set provides several (32×32)-bit multiplication instructions which pass two 32-bit inputs x and y to the multiplier circuit. For example, the umull and mul instructions produce 64-bit and 32-bit unsigned outputs

---

Algorithm 1. A functional description of ARM7TDMI multiplication

---

Input: The 32-bit integers x and y.
Output: The 64-bit result $r = x \cdot y$.

1 $t_0 \leftarrow 0$
2 **for** $i = 0$ **up to** 3 **step** 1 **do**
3      $t_1 \leftarrow x \cdot y_{7...0}$
4      $t_0 \leftarrow t_0 + (t_1 \ll 8i)$
5      $y \leftarrow y \gg 8$
6   **if** $y = 0$ **then return** t_0
7 **end**

---

respectively [6]. Signed alternatives are provided that function in a similar manner; however, we exclusively consider unsigned instructions because they are more commonly used in cryptographic algorithms. We term x the multiplicand and y the multiplier. In principle, one can imagine the multiplication hardware operating as described in Algorithm 1.

The (32×8)-bit multiplier processes one 8-bit digit of y in each step, working from the least-significant to the most-significant. After the i-th step, if $y = 0$ then the algorithm terminates early and immediately returns the accumulated result in t_0. Since y is right-shifted at each step, this essentially means each j-th digit of the original y, with $j > i$, is checked: if all digits are set to zero then early termination occurs. On the other hand, if $y \neq 0$, then at least one such j-th digit is non-zero, and hence a (32×8)-bit multiplication is used to form a partial product t_1, which is scaled and added to t_0. The early-termination mechanism means one can consider the algorithm taking between 1 and 4 steps.

Due to this early termination, a (32×32)-bit multiplication is executed in a single clock cycle if bits y_8 to y_{31} of the multiplier y are all set to zero, in two clock cycles if y_{16} to y_{31} are all set to zero (but y_8 to y_{15} are not), in three clock cycles if bits y_{24} to y_{31} are all zero (but y_8 to y_{23} are not), and in four cycles otherwise. The so-called "long" multiply instructions that return a 64-bit result (e.g., umull) need an additional clock cycle since they have to write-back two 32-bit words into general-purpose registers via a single write port [15]. Putting everything together, the umull instruction occupies the Execute stage[1] of the pipeline for between two and five clock cycles, depending on the magnitude of the multiplier-operand y.

2.2 Recovering Multiplication Latency Using SPA

"Long" multiply instructions, such as umull [6], allow one to specify two source registers (Rm, Rs) from which the operands to be multiplied are read, and two destination registers (RdLo, RdHi) into which the lower (resp. upper) part of the 64-bit product $Rm \times Rs$ is placed. The ARM7TDMI supports early termination

---

[1] The ARM7TDMI processor has a simple three-stage pipeline comprising of Fetch, Decode, and Execute stages [5].

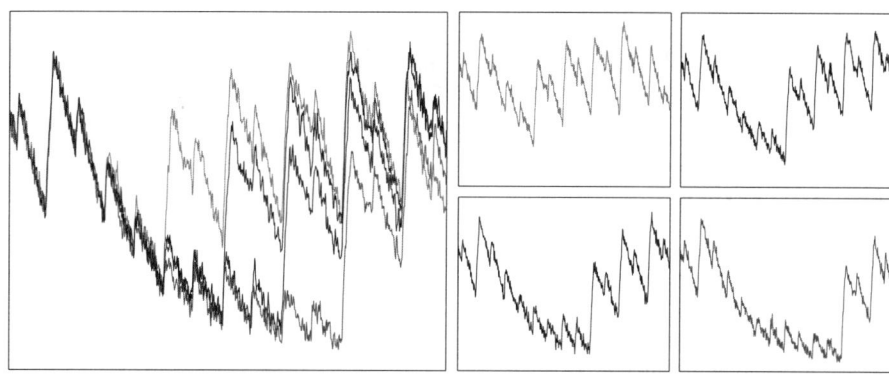

Fig. 1. Overlaid (left) and individual (right) power consumption traces showing ARM7 multiplications that take 2, 3, 4 and 5 clock cycles (top left to bottom right)

on Rs, which means that the latency of the umull instruction can vary by up to three clock cycles depending on the magnitude of the operand in Rs [5]. In what follows, we assume that the multiplicand x is stored in Rm and the multiplier y in Rs. Consequently, the value of y provokes early termination; where an operand within some pseudo-code algorithm or source code is fed to the multiplier circuit as y, we term it an *early-terminating operand.*

As mentioned above, the umull instruction occupies the Execute stage of the ARM7TDMI pipeline for between two and five clock cycles, depending on the magnitude of y. As a result, the number of clock cycles required to execute the umull instruction leaks information about the multiplier y. The exact information returned is the number of most-significant 8-bit digits of y that are set to zero, excluding the least-significant digit, which is always processed (see Algorithm 1). This observation can be made in a "course-grained" way by noting timing differences over an entire execution, or in a "fine-grained" way by monitoring the power consumption of the processor while it executes a particular umull instruction. Figure 1 shows exemplar power consumption traces from an ARM7TDMI core clocked at 7.37 MHz to demonstrate this side channel. These traces have been captured using a Tektronix DPO 7104 digital oscilloscope with a differential probe connected to a 1 Ω shunt in the power supply line.

The umull instruction terminates early on the operand read from register Rs, i.e. the multiplier y according to our definition from above. On the other hand, the second operand read from register Rm has no impact as to whether or not early termination occurs. If one of the two operands to be multiplied is small and known *a priori*, then the programmer can reduce the latency of the umull instruction by assigning registers in such a way that this operand provokes the early-termination mechanism. Optimising compilers also try to increase the probability of early termination through appropriate assignment of small operands (e.g. loop counters, array indices). However, there is no guarantee that a given compiler performs optimisations so that early termination occurs (or does not

---

Algorithm 2. The AES-128 encryption function

Input: The 128-bit plaintext block P, and 128-bit key K.
Output: The 128-bit ciphertext block C.

1 $X \leftarrow \texttt{AddRoundKey}(P, K)$
2 **for** $i \leftarrow 1$ **to** 10 **do**
3      $X \leftarrow \texttt{ShiftRows}(X)$
4      $X \leftarrow \texttt{SubBytes}(X)$
5   **if** $i \neq 10$ **then**
6          $X \leftarrow \texttt{MixColumns}(X)$
7   **end**
8      $K \leftarrow \texttt{KeySchedule}(K)$
9      $X \leftarrow \texttt{AddRoundKey}(X, K)$
10 **end**
11 $C \leftarrow X$
12 **return** C

---

occur) on certain input data *or* that an optimisation decision will be safe if the same program is executed on a different, but compatible, processor (e.g., with a different multiplier type). Furthermore, there exist a number of scenarios where a programmer has little or no control over the early-termination mechanism; one may think of Java applets executed in a virtual machine running on a processor. In this case it depends primarily on the virtual machine whether or not the multiplication of a given pair of operands terminates early.

3   Early-Termination Attacks

In the following we demonstrate that the early-termination mechanism facilitates SPA attacks on both secret-key and public-key cryptosystems.

3.1   AES

The basic structure of the Advanced Encryption Standard (AES) [30], as used to perform encryption, is illustrated in Algorithm 2. Note that we restrict ourselves to considering AES-128 and that the description omits a permutation typically used to convert the 128-bit plaintext $P = (P_0, P_1, \ldots, P_{15})_{(256)}$ and key $K = (K_0, K_1, \ldots, K_{15})_{(256)}$ into a matrix form as described in [30]. The encryption itself is realised through iterated use of a number of round functions on a state matrix X:

- The $\texttt{AddRoundKey}$ function mixes a round key with the state using an XOR operation.
- The $\texttt{ShiftRows}$ function is a byte-wise permutation of the state.
- The $\texttt{SubBytes}$ function applies a substitution table (i.e., an S-box) to each byte of the state; formally, this table is an inversion over $\mathbb{F}_{2^8}$ followed by an affine transformation.

Algorithm 3. The AES `MixColumns` function

Input: $X = (X_0, X_1, \ldots, X_{15})_{(256)}$
Output: $Y = (Y_0, Y_1, \ldots, Y_{15})_{(256)}$

1 **for** $i \leftarrow 0$ **to** 15 **do**
2      $Y_i = 2 \bullet X_i \oplus 3 \bullet X_{(i+4) \bmod 16} \oplus X_{(i+8) \bmod 16} \oplus X_{(i+12) \bmod 16}$
3 **end**
4 **return** Y

Algorithm 4. An implementation of the `xtime` function on a 32-bit platform

Input: $A = (a_0, a_1, a_2, a_3)_{(256)}$
Output: $B = (\texttt{xtime}(a_0), \texttt{xtime}(a_1), \texttt{xtime}(a_2), \texttt{xtime}(a_3))_{(256)}$

1 $R_1 \leftarrow A \wedge 80808080_{(16)}$
2 $R_1 \leftarrow R_1 \gg 7$
3 $R_2 \leftarrow R_1 \cdot 1B_{(16)}$
4 $R_1 \leftarrow A \ll 1$
5 $R_1 \leftarrow R_1 \wedge \text{FEFEFEFE}_{(16)}$
6 $R_1 \leftarrow R_1 \oplus R_2$
7 **return** R_1

- The `MixColumns` function is shown in Algorithm 3, where $\bullet$ represents polynomial multiplication over the field $\mathbb{F}_{2^8}$ modulo the irreducible polynomial $x^8 + x^4 + x^3 + x + 1$. That is, polynomial multiplication by 2 and 3 denotes multiplication with x and $x + 1$, respectively.
- The `KeySchedule` function generates the next round key from the previous one. The first round key is the input key with no changes, subsequent round keys are generated using the `SubBytes` function and XOR operations.

An 8-bit implementation typically represents the state as an array of 16 bytes and implements each step of the round function in a direct manner. Within such an implementation, the `xtime` function [14] (a polynomial multiplication by 2) used by `MixColumns` (and within the S-box used in `SubBytes`) can be implemented as a look-up table, or careful use of data-independent control-flow, to prevent side-channel attacks. More specifically, using a look-up table avoids the data-dependent XOR needed to perform reduction by the irreducible polynomial $x^8 + x^4 + x^3 + x + 1$.

On a 32-bit platform it can be attractive to compute (rather than look-up) the results of `xtime` as described in Algorithm 4. Intuitively, this approach, due to Bertoni *et al.* [8], appears more time-consuming than a single look-up; however, it allows four applications of `xtime` to be computed in parallel. Compared to the traditional T-tables approach to implementing AES on 32-bit platforms [14], this realisation of `xtime` allows a trade-off toward performance over memory footprint (which is crucial for various embedded applications) and also guards against cache-based side-channel attacks.

Algorithm 5. The RC6 encryption function

Input: A 4-tuple of 32-bit plaintext values (A, B, C, D).
Output: A 4-tuple of 32-bit ciphertext values (A, B, C, D).

1 $B \leftarrow B + S[0]$
2 $D \leftarrow D + S[1]$
3 **for** $i = 0$ **up to** r **do**
4      $t \leftarrow (B \cdot (2B + 1)) \ll 5$
5      $u \leftarrow (D \cdot (2D + 1)) \ll 5$
6      $A \leftarrow ((A \oplus t) \ll u) + S[2i]$
7      $C \leftarrow ((C \oplus u) \ll t) + S[2i + 1]$
8      $(A, B, C, D) \leftarrow (B, C, D, A)$
9 **end**
10 $A \leftarrow A + S[2r + 2]$
11 $C \leftarrow C + S[2r + 3]$
12 **return** (A, B, C, D)

Assuming that R_1 holds the early-terminating operand[2], the danger of this approach is clear: if an attacker can recover how many clock cycles it takes to compute the multiplication in step 3, he can determine how many of the most-significant bytes of R_1 are set to zero. The full version of this paper [18] presents some concrete attacks applied to AES as implemented on an ARM7TDMI processor [5]. In one of these attacks we were able to extract the entire 128-bit key using just eight power consumption traces.

3.2   RC6

Consider encryption using the block cipher RC6 [34] as described in Algorithm 5 for the specific case of $w = 32$; this description assumes that the round keys represented by S are an auxiliary input. Focusing on the plaintext input B, the pertinent feature with regard to early termination occurs in step 4 which, crucially, is after the initial whitening step. In the first round (i.e. when $i = 0$), this step represents a (32×32)-bit unsigned multiplication where both operands are derived from the input B and $S[0]$.

Assume the early-terminating operand for this multiplication is $B + S[0]$. An attacker can recover the number of cycles taken by this multiplication. Using adaptive choices of input B, the attacker can perform trial encryptions until the whitening step computes a result $B + S[0]$ in which the most-significant byte is zero. Since this intermediate value is used as the early-terminating operand in

---

[2] An optimising C compiler would rather use the constant $1B_{(16)}$ as early-terminating operand (even though there is no guarantee for this). However, the attack on xtime is nonetheless practically relevant if we consider a Java implementation of Algorithm 4. In this case the programmer has no control over the early-termination mechanism since it depends primarily on the virtual machine whether R_1 or $1B_{(16)}$ is the early-terminating operand.

Algorithm 6. The left-to-right binary exponentiation algorithm

---

Input: The integers x, y and N.
Output: The integer $r = x^y \pmod{N}$.

1 $t \leftarrow x$
2 **for** $i = |y| - 2$ **downto** 0 **do**
3      $t \leftarrow t^2 \pmod{N}$
4   **if** $y_i = 1$ **then**
5          $t \leftarrow t \cdot x \pmod{N}$
6   **end**
7 **end**
8 **return** t

---

step 4, the fact that the most significant byte is zero causes early termination. In an ideal setting, this would mean one could search for a B such that $B + S[0] = 0$ (i.e. $S[0] = -B$), and hence recover $S[0]$. However, as detailed in Subsection 2.1 and 2.2, one can not recover information about the least-significant byte of the early-terminating operand. This means that instead of getting $S[0]$ directly, one narrows the possible range of values: one finds that $B + S[0] \in \{0 \dots 255\}$. Even so, one can view this as leaking 24 bits of the 32-bit round key $S[0]$; the same approach also yields $S[1]$ via observation of the second multiplication involving D (within the same set of acquisitions).

3.3   Exponentiation in $\mathbb{Z}_N$ (e.g., RSA)

A central operation in the RSA algorithm [35] is exponentiation in $\mathbb{Z}_N$ where $N = p \cdot q$ for secret, large primes p and q. In "textbook" RSA, this operation takes plaintext (resp. ciphertext) x and exponentiates it by a key y to compute ciphertext (resp. plaintext) $r = x^y \bmod N$. Let y_i denote the i-th bit in the binary expansion of y, and S and M represent modular squaring operations and multiplications in $\mathbb{Z}_N$.

Typically, x is controllable by an attacker while y is fixed: either it represents the public or private RSA exponent. The classic square-and-multiply technique (left-to-right binary exponentiation) described in Algorithm 6 provides a simple method to compute r. Within the i-th iteration of the algorithm a multiplication is executed if, and only if, $y_i = 1$. This leaks the value of y if an attacker can distinguish squaring operations (i.e., step 3) from multiplications (i.e., step 5): if the attacker observes the sequence SM during iteration i (i.e., a squaring operation then a multiplication is executed) then $y_i = 1$, whereas if he observes S alone then $y_i = 0$.

Since all inputs and the output r of Algorithm 6 are multi-precision integers (e.g. 1024 bits held in 32-bit words), a method such as Montgomery multiplication [28] is typically used to perform the modular arithmetic. Step 3 uses t as both operands to the modular multiplication; since t is essentially random as the algorithm progresses, both operands are random. However, the multiplication in step 5 uses x as one operand. If the digits of x form early-terminating operands to (32×32)-bit multiply instructions within the Montgomery multiplication, the early-termination mechanism can be invoked. Specifically, if an attacker controls x, he can select a value that is "special" in the sense it has a low weight (i.e. a number of 32-bit digits are zero). Such an x permits the attacker to distinguish between modular squaring operations and multiplications based on how often the early-termination mechanism is invoked; following the reasoning above this leaks y which, depending on the context, is potentially the private key.

Interestingly, this approach not only works for "textbook RSA" as outlined above, but also when the plaintext (resp. the ciphertext) is padded according to PKCS #1 [36]. The PKCS #1 standard provides recommendations for the implementation of public-key cryptography based on the RSA algorithm, covering both encryption and the generation/verification of digital signatures. Version 2.1 of PKCS #1 specifies two padding schemes for encryption, namely the Optimal Asymmetric Encryption Padding (OAEP) and an older padding scheme from PKCS #1 version 1.5, which is not recommended for new applications. In both cases the message is first encoded before the encryption (i.e., modular exponentiation) is performed. Conversely, the decryption of the ciphertext starts with a modular exponentiation to recover the plaintext, which is then decoded into the original message.

Assume an attacker wishes to extract the secret key used in an RSA decryption operation by exploiting the early-termination mechanism: to achieve this he manipulates the ciphertext such that it has a low weight (e.g., by injecting a number of 32-bit words that are set to zero). As mentioned previously, the decryption process starts with a modular exponentiation of the ciphertext using the secret exponent, followed by the decoding of the obtained plaintext to retrieve the original message. Consequently, a manipulation of the ciphertext can only be detected *after* the exponentiation has finished. Any multiply instruction using one of the low-weight words as operand will terminate early, thereby enabling an attacker to distinguish modular multiplications from modular squarings when the exponentiation is performed as described in Algorithm 6. Extracting the secret key from a PKCS #1-compliant implementation of RSA decryption is, in essence, no harder than attacking textbook RSA, provided that the attacker has the possibility to manipulate a ciphertext or to inject chosen ciphertexts.

Attacking SPA-Resistant m-ary Exponentiation. The early-termination mechanism amplifies side-channel leakage, but an SPA attack is, of course, also possible without exploiting this mechanism. In order to thwart SPA attacks on RSA, a number of regular exponentiation techniques have been proposed; these range from the square-and-multiply-always algorithm to m-ary exponentiation with a recoded exponent [23]. The aim of all these algorithms is to perform the exponentiation in such a way that always the same sequence of basic operations (modular multiplications, modular squarings) is executed, irrespective of the exponent. The m-ary exponentiation method uses the m-ary expansion of the exponent y, whereby m is usually a power of two, i.e. $m = 2^k$. It uses a table of $m - 2$ pre-computed powers of the base x, i.e. x^i for $i \in \{1, \ldots, m - 1\}$, and processes a k-bit digit of the exponent y at a time, which reduces the number of modular multiplications compared to the binary method. Möller proposed in [27] a recoding scheme for m-ary exponentiation where each k-bit digit that is equal to zero is substituted with $-m$, and the next most significant digit gets incremented by one. This leads to an exponent recoded with k-bit digits in the set $\{1, 2, \ldots, m-1\} \cup \{-m\}$. An overview of other exponent recoding schemes yielding regular m-ary exponentiation can be found in [23].

Unfortunately, these regular m-ary exponentiation techniques succumb to a SPA attack when exploiting the early-termination effect. The attacker just needs to select the base x in such a way that exactly one of the pre-computed powers of x contains bytes that are equal to zero at the "right" positions. Whenever a multiplication with this power of x is performed, the early-termination mechanism is invoked, which leaks the value of the corresponding k-bit digit from the private exponent [27]. Repeating this attack with other values of x such that a different power of x contains a number of bytes equal to zero will eventually allow the attacker to fully recover the private exponent. The early-termination effect makes attacking these regular m-ary exponentiation methods—which are designed to provide SPA resistance—almost as easy as attacking a completely unprotected implementation such as the square-and-multiply technique shown in Algorithm 6.

3.4   Point Multiplication on $E(\mathbb{F}_p)$ (e.g., ECIES)

Consider an elliptic curve $E(\mathbb{F}_p)$. A central operation to cryptographic schemes based on such a curve is scalar multiplication [19] of some point $P \in E$ by a secret integer d, i.e., $Q = d \cdot P$. Let d_i denote the i-th bit in the binary expansion of d, and A and D represent point addition and point doubling operations on E, respectively. Depending on the exact setting P might be fixed or unknown; consider instead a setting where P is supplied as input and hence is controllable by an attacker.

The double-and-add algorithm [19] provides a simple method to compute Q; since this is the additive analogue to the square-and-multiply algorithm, it is vulnerable to similar side-channel attacks [12]. One way to harden the algorithm is to split the point addition operation into parts each of which is identical, in terms of the field operations it performs, to a point doubling. Put simply, instead of a sequence such as DA the attacker now observes the sequence XXX where each X represents an atomic, indistinguishable operation which could either be a point doubling operation or a step in a point addition.

Point doubling and addition sequences introduced by Gebotys and Gebotys [16] was the first example of this; multiplication by small constants is performed using shifts. Several "dummy" operations are included to pad the sequences so the same operation occurs at each index. Gebotys and Gebotys are careful to note in [16, Section 2] that on their experimental platform (a StarCore SC140 DSP), "the only field operations which had variable clock cycle counts were the modular reductions which may or may not be required after additions, subtractions, or shifts." Of course, where an early-terminating multiplier is used to perform (32×32)-bit multiply instructions within the field multiplication and squaring operations, this ceases to be true.

In order to overcome this countermeasure, an attacker can select a P whose x or y coordinates are "special" in the sense they have a low weight (i.e. a number of 32-bit digits are set to zero). In such a setting, *even though* a high-level SPA countermeasure is implemented, an attacker can still distinguish between a point doubling operation and a point addition by observing when this low-weight coordinate is used and hence the early-termination mechanism is invoked more often than usual. This may be viewed as related to the attack of Goubin [17] where an attacker attempts to provoke computation by using "special" points (e.g., one where the x or y coordinate is set to zero).

The elliptic curve (EC) point multiplication operation is a central operation of all EC-based cryptosystems: given an EC point P and a scalar value d, the operation $Q = d \cdot P$ outputs another point Q on the curve. There exist various implementation strategies for this including the simple binary algorithm (aka double-and-add method [19]). In this algorithm, a sequence of point additions and point doublings are performed. More precisely, a point doubling operation is carried out in every iteration, whereas a point addition operation is executed if, and only if, the i-th bit of d equals one. It has been observed in [12] that naïve implementations of EC point multiplication are vulnerable to SPA attacks. To thwart such attacks, a number of SPA-resistant implementations were proposed using, for instance, indistinguishable operations [11] (see e.g. [16] for a concrete implementation). The goal of indistinguishable operations is to make addition and doubling operations "look alike" in terms of their power profiles.

By exploiting the early termination feature of a multiplier, we can break the binary algorithm even if the point addition and point doubling are implemented using indistinguishable operations. In the i-th step of the binary algorithm, the base point P is added if (and only if) $d_i = 1$. Now, if we set P to be a special point, i.e., a point which has either one or both coordinates with leading bytes of zeroes, then the early termination will always occur when P is added to the current intermediate point. Assuming that the intermediate points which occur during the execution of the binary algorithm have random coordinates (i.e. do not lead to early termination in the same way as P does), the point addition is identifiable because of the early-termination effect. Identifying the point addition operation allows identifying the bits of d which are equal to one.

The remaining problem is to identify EC-based cryptosystems in which the attacker can control (i.e., choose) the base point. Typically, EC cryptosystems supply a base point G as part of their domain parameters; since this point is fixed it can not be chosen by an attacker. This rules out schemes such as ECDSA [29] where point multiplication within the signature generation function uses G as the base point. However, KEM-DEM based encryption schemes such as ECIES [37] use a Diffie-Hellman (DH)-style key exchange mechanism within their KEM component. In the decryption step of such a KEM, the private key is used to multiply a point derived from the ciphertext (i.e., the point can be chosen by an attacker). Consequently, this point multiplication leaks the private key if it is

---

Algorithm 7. A constant time algorithm to replace ARM7 multiplication

---

Input: The 32-bit integers x and y.
Output: The 64-bit result $r = x \cdot y$.

1 $\gamma \leftarrow (y \wedge \mathtt{00FFFFFF}_{(16)}) + \mathtt{01000000}_{(16)}$
2 $\tau \leftarrow (y \wedge \mathtt{FF000000}_{(16)}) \gg 24$
3 $r \leftarrow x \cdot \gamma$
4 $r \leftarrow r + ((x \cdot \tau) \ll 24)$
5 $r \leftarrow r - (x \ll 24)$
6 **return** r

---

executed on an early-terming multiplier and the attacker chooses the base point appropriately. Using the same observation, other DH-based protocols including ephemeral and static versions of ECDH, as well as ECMQV, are vulnerable.

4   Countermeasures

Given the simplicity and broad applicability of the attacks described in Section 3, it is clearly attractive to examine potential countermeasures. The most invasive countermeasure would be to alter the processor itself. For example, one can easily imagine including a dedicated instruction (or a processor mode) that disables the early-termination mechanism during execution of security-critical regions of a program. However, this is disadvantageous in the sense that such an approach is potentially costly and can not be retrospectively applied to existing processors. As such, one can also consider software-only countermeasures. The simplest approach of this type is to ensure that secret information is never used as an early-terminating operand. In the context of AES-128, this means placing the constant value $\mathtt{1B}_{(16)}$ in the register that governs how long a multiplication takes, i.e., $\mathtt{Rs}$ rather than R_1.

Where this is not possible (e.g., both operand leak secret information, or the programmer does not directly control instructions being executed as could be the case in interpreter-based platforms such as Java), one can imagine replacing each use of an insecure multiply instruction with a more heavy-weight function that executes a (32×32)-bit multiplication in constant time. Algorithm 7 shows an example: it forces the number of cycles required to perform a multiplication to be data-independent. Essentially, this works by masking the multiplier y so that the most-significant byte in one multiplication is always non-zero, and the other is always a multiplication with one byte. The two invocations of the real multiply instruction in steps 3 and 4 therefore leak no information.

Using Algorithm 7 within our software implementation of AES-128 increases the execution time from 1.24 msec to 1.56 msec. However, this is still a massive improvement over implementing the MixColumns transformation in a byte-wise manner; our implementation requires 2.53 msec in this case. The impact on an implementation of modular exponentiation is larger; for example, the execution time of a 1024-bit modular exponentiation on the ARM7TDMI was increased from 1.6 to 3.135 seconds (at 7.37 MHz).

5   Conclusions

In this paper we described and analysed security issues that arise when crypto-graphic software is executed on a processor equipped with an early-terminating multiplier. Even though the early-termination mechanism provides advantages for some application domains (most notably digital signal and multimedia pro-cessing), it poses a serious challenge for security-critical applications that need to resist side-channel attacks. We explained why, and demonstrated how, the early-termination mechanism causes differences in the latency of multiply in-structions; in turn, this results in easily observable variations in execution time and power consumption. Such data-dependent variations make power analysis fairly straightforward, and may even allow an attacker to extract the secret key from implementations with integrated high-level countermeasures.

While the side-channel leakage caused by the early-termination mechanism is obvious for public-key cryptosystems performing multi-precision multiplications (e.g., RSA, ECIES), we also demonstrated that block ciphers, such as RC6, are vulnerable to SPA attacks when executed on an ARM7TDMI processor. Conse-quently, careful attention must be paid to the implementation of cryptographic software at a low level so that the early-termination effect does not produce side-channel leakage; this can be costly and difficult to achieve via software-only countermeasures, especially in the case of RSA. Another conclusion that can be drawn from the discovery of security issues caused by early-terminating multi-pliers (and all other micro-architectural side channels) is that processor vendors need to reassess their objectives in micro-architectural design: security aspects require—and deserve—the same attention as other metrics of interest such as performance, silicon area, and power consumption.

Acknowledgements

The authors are grateful to Çetin Koç, Marcel Medwed, Stefan Tillich, and the anonymous reviewers for their valuable comments and suggestions on a previous version of this paper.

The work described in this paper has been supported by the EPSRC under grants EP/E001556/1 and EP/F039638/1, and, in part, by the European Com-mission through the ICT Programme under contract ICT-2007-216676 ECRYPT II. The information in this paper reflects only the authors' views, is provided as is, and no guarantee or warranty is given that the information is fit for any particular purpose. The user thereof uses the information at its sole risk and liability.

References

1. Acıiçmez, O.: Yet another microarchitectural attack: Exploiting I-cache. In: Pro-ceedings of the 1st ACM Workshop on Computer Security Architecture (CSAW 2007), pp. 11–18. ACM Press, New York (2007)

2. Acıiçmez, O., Koç, Ç.K., Seifert, J.-P.: On the power of simple branch prediction analysis. In: Proceedings of the 2nd ACM Symposium on Information, Computer and Communications Security (ASIACCS 2007), pp. 312–320. ACM Press, New York (2007)

3. Acıiçmez, O., Koç, Ç.K., Seifert, J.-P.: Predicting secret keys via branch prediction. In: Abe, M. (ed.) CT-RSA 2007. LNCS, vol. 4377, pp. 225–242. Springer, Heidelberg (2006)

4. Acıiçmez, O., Seifert, J.-P., Koç, Ç.K.: Micro-architectural cryptanalysis. IEEE Security & Privacy 5(4), 62–64 (2007)

5. ARM Limited. ARM7TDMI Technical Reference Manual (Revision r4p1). ARM Doc No. DDI 0210, Issue C (November 2004)

6. ARM Limited. ARM Architecture Reference Manual. ARM Doc No. DDI 0100, Issue I (July 2005)

7. Bernstein, D.J.: Cache-timing attacks on AES. Preprint (2005), http://cr.yp.to/papers.html#cachetiming

8. Bertoni, G., Breveglieri, L., Fragneto, P., Macchetti, M., Marchesin, S.: Efficient software implementation of AES on 32-bit platforms. In: Kaliski Jr., B.S., Koç, Ç.K., Paar, C. (eds.) CHES 2002. LNCS, vol. 2523, pp. 159–171. Springer, Heidelberg (2003)

9. Bertoni, G., Zaccaria, V., Breveglieri, L., Monchiero, M., Palermo, G.: AES power attack based on induced cache miss and countermeasure. In: Proceedings of the 6th International Conference on Information Technology: Coding and Computing (ITCC 2005), vol. 1, pp. 586–591. IEEE Computer Society Press, Los Alamitos (2005)

10. Booth, A.D.: A signed binary multiplication technique. Quarterly Journal of Mechanics and Applied Mathematics 4(2), 236–240 (1951)

11. Brier, E., Joye, M.: Weierstraß elliptic curves and side-channel attacks. In: Naccache, D., Paillier, P. (eds.) PKC 2002. LNCS, vol. 2274, pp. 335–345. Springer, Heidelberg (2002)

12. Coron, J.-S.: Resistance against differential power analysis for elliptic curve cryptosystems. In: Koç, Ç.K., Paar, C. (eds.) CHES 1999. LNCS, vol. 1717, pp. 292–302. Springer, Heidelberg (1999)

13. Dadda, L.: Some schemes for parallel multipliers. Alta Frequenza 34(5), 349–356 (1965)

14. Daemen, J., Rijmen, V.: The Design of Rijndael: AES – The Advanced Encryption Standard. Springer, Heidelberg (2002)

15. Furber, S.B.: ARM System-on-Chip Architecture, 2nd edn. Addison-Wesley, Reading (2000)

16. Gebotys, C.H., Gebotys, R.J.: Secure elliptic curve implementations: An analysis of resistance to power-attacks in a DSP processor. In: Kaliski Jr., B.S., Koç, Ç.K., Paar, C. (eds.) CHES 2002. LNCS, vol. 2523, pp. 114–128. Springer, Heidelberg (2003)

17. Goubin, L.: A refined power-analysis attack on elliptic curve cryptosystems. In: Desmedt, Y.G. (ed.) PKC 2003. LNCS, vol. 2567, pp. 199–210. Springer, Heidelberg (2002)

18. Großschädl, J., Oswald, E., Page, D., Tunstall, M.: Side-channel analysis of cryptographic software via early-terminating multiplications. Cryptology ePrint Archive, Report 2009/538 (2009), http://eprint.iacr.org/

19. Hankerson, D.R., Menezes, A.J., Vanstone, S.A.: Guide to Elliptic Curve Cryptography. Springer, Heidelberg (2004)

20. Hartley, R., Corbett, P.: Digit-serial processing techniques. IEEE Transactions on Circuits and Systems 37(6), 707–719 (1990)
21. IBM Corporation: PowerPC 440x6 Embedded Processor Core User's Manual (Version 07) (July 2008),
    http://www.ibm.com/chips/techlib/techlib.nsf/products/
    PowerPC_440_Embedded_Core
22. Intel Corporation. Intel® StrongARM® SA-1100 Microprocessor for Embedded Applications. Brief datasheet, order number 278092-005 (June 1999)
23. Joye, M., Tunstall, M.: Exponent recoding and regular exponentiation algorithms. In: Preneel, B. (ed.) AFRICACRYPT 2009. LNCS, vol. 5580, pp. 334–349. Springer, Heidelberg (2009)
24. Kocher, P.C., Jaffe, J., Jun, B.: Differential power analysis. In: Wiener, M. (ed.) CRYPTO 1999. LNCS, vol. 1666, pp. 388–397. Springer, Heidelberg (1999)
25. Kocher, P.C., Lee, R.B., McGraw, G.E., Raghunathan, A., Ravi, S.: Security as a new dimension in embedded system design. In: Proceedings of the 41st Design Automation Conference (DAC 2004), pp. 753–760. ACM Press, New York (2004)
26. MIPS Technologies, Inc. MIPS32 4Km™ Processor Core Datasheet (November 2004),
    http://www.mips.com/products/processors/32-64-bit-cores/mips32-m4k/
27. Möller, B.: Securing elliptic curve point multiplication against side-channel attacks. In: Davida, G.I., Frankel, Y. (eds.) ISC 2001. LNCS, vol. 2200, pp. 324–334. Springer, Heidelberg (2001)
28. Montgomery, P.L.: Modular multiplication without trial division. Mathematics of Computation 44(170), 519–521 (1985)
29. National Institute of Standards and Technology (NIST). Digital Signature Standard (DSS). FIPS Publication 186-2 (February 2000)
30. National Institute of Standards and Technology (NIST). Advanced Encryption Standard (AES). FIPS Publication 197 (November 2001)
31. Osvik, D.A., Shamir, A., Tromer, E.: Cache attacks and countermeasures: The case of AES. In: Pointcheval, D. (ed.) CT-RSA 2006. LNCS, vol. 3860, pp. 1–20. Springer, Heidelberg (2006)
32. Page, D.: Theoretical use of cache memory as a cryptanalytic side-channel. Technical Report CSTR-02-003, Department of Computer Science, University of Bristol, Bristol, U.K. (June 2002)
33. Ravi, S., Raghunathan, A., Kocher, P.C., Hattangady, S.: Security in embedded systems: Design challenges. ACM Transactions on Embedded Computing Systems 3(3), 461–491 (2004)
34. Rivest, R.L., Robshaw, M.J., Sidney, R., Yin, Y.L.: The RC6™ block cipher. Technical report, RSA Laboratories, Bedford, MA, USA (August 1998),
    ftp://ftp.rsasecurity.com/pub/rsalabs/rc6/rc6v11.pdf
35. Rivest, R.L., Shamir, A., Adleman, L.M.: A method for obtaining digital signatures and public key cryptosystems. Communications of the ACM 21(2), 120–126 (1978)
36. RSA Security, Inc. PKCS #1 v2.1: RSA Cryptography Standard (June 2002),
    ftp://ftp.rsasecurity.com/pub/pkcs/pkcs-1/pkcs-1v2-1.pdf
37. Standards for Efficient Cryptography Group (SECG). SEC 1: Elliptic Curve Cryptography (September 2000),
    http://www.secg.org/download/aid-385/sec1_final.pdf

First CPIR Protocol with Data-Dependent Computation

Helger Lipmaa[1,2]

[1] Cybernetica AS, Estonia
[2] Tallinn University, Estonia

Abstract. We design a new $(n, 1)$-CPIR protocol BddCpir for ℓ-bit strings as a combination of a noncryptographic (BDD-based) data structure and a more basic cryptographic primitive (communication-efficient $(2, 1)$-CPIR). BddCpir is the first CPIR protocol where server's online computation depends substantially on the concrete database. We then show that (a) for reasonably small values of ℓ, BddCpir is guaranteed to have simultaneously log-squared communication and sublinear online computation, and (b) BddCpir can handle huge but sparse matrices, common in data-mining applications, significantly more efficiently compared to all previous protocols. The security of BddCpir can be based on the well-known Decisional Composite Residuosity assumption.

Keywords: Binary decision diagram, computationally-private information retrieval, privacy-preserving data mining, sublinear communication.

1 Introduction

(Single-database) computationally-private information retrieval (CPIR) is one of the most basic cryptographic protocols in the client-server setting. More precisely, in an $(n, 1)$-CPIR protocol, the client retrieves an element chosen by him from server's n-element database of ℓ-bit strings, so that the server obtains no knowledge about which element was transfered. It is always required that the total communication of the CPIR protocol be less than $n\ell$ bits. CPIR protocols constructed in [18,12] are almost optimally communication-efficient. Unfortunately, in all prior nontrivial CPIR protocols, the server's online computational complexity is $\Omega(n)$ public-key operations. Thus, in most of the applications, one is restricted to databases of size say $n = 2^{10}$, which makes computation-efficiency the main bottleneck in deploying CPIR protocols in practice.

In the case of multiple servers, [3] constructed several sublinear-computation information-theoretically private information retrieval protocols. They posed as an open problem to design a sublinear-computation single-server CPIR protocol. This goal has remained so elusive that many researchers have claimed linear computation to be lower-bound for any CPIR, see for example [5, Sect. 1.2], [6, Sect. 2.3] and [12, Sect. 3] for just a few examples. Based on empirical research, Carbunar and Sion [6] argued that in the foreseeable future all linear-communication CPIR protocols will be at least one order of magnitude slower than the trivial CPIR protocol, where the server just transfers the whole database to the client.

D. Lee and S. Hong (Eds.): ICISC 2009, LNCS 5984, pp. 193–210, 2010.
© Springer-Verlag Berlin Heidelberg 2010

Our Contributions. Up to now, one has considered CPIR to be a basic primitive where the server does a fixed amount of work that does not depend on her concrete database. We show that one can efficiently combine noncryptographic data preprocessing with the cryptographic protocol, such that the combination is still secure and at the same time more efficient than the prior work. (In fact it is clear that without preprocessing, the server has to do some online work with every database element.) This in particular shows that $(n, 1)$-CPIR is not a monolithic cryptographic primitive *per se* but can be seen as a combination of a "noncryptographic" data structure (in our case, based on binary decision diagrams) and a more basic cryptographic primitive (in our case, a communication-efficient $(2, 1)$-CPIR). In our opinion, this presents a significant paradigm shift.

Now, let x be the client's index, let $f = (f_0, \ldots, f_{n-1})$ be the server's database. In the new $(n, 1)$-CPIR protocol BddCpir, we write down an optimized BDD for the function f, $f(x) := f_x$, and then use the PrivateBDD protocol [14] to cryptocompute f. We describe an optimized version of it in Sect. 3 in full detail. In particular, [14] assumed that a strong oblivious transfer protocol is used in every node. We show that a $(2, 1)$-CPIR protocol can be used instead. Our variant of the PrivateBDD protocol also has communication that is linear in the length $\text{len}(\mathcal{F})$ of the constructed BDD. More precisely, when using Lipmaa's $(2, 1)$-CPIR protocol from [18], the communication complexity of BddCpir is proportional to $|x| \cdot (|f(x)| + \text{len}(\mathcal{F}))$; see Sect. 3. Server's online computation in BddCpir is dominated by $\text{size}(f)$ public-key operations, where $\text{size}(f)$ is the size of the BDD that corresponds to server's *fixed* input f. This should be contrasted to more general two-party computation protocols where the computation is dominated by the size of the (say) circuit where server's input f is a variable.

After that, we present two different applications. First, for $\ell = 1$, we show that in BddCpir, server's online computational complexity is upperbounded by $(1+o(1))n/\log_2 n$ public-key operations, while the communication complexity is $\Theta(k \cdot \log^2 n)$, where k is the security parameter. The offline computational complexity of this variant of BddCpir is $O(n)$ *non-cryptographic* operations, while setting up the data structure, and $\tilde{O}(t)$, when t elements are updated. Alternatively, this result shows that one can implement secure function evaluation of any $f : \{0, 1\}^m \to \{0, 1\}$ with communication complexity $O(m^2 \cdot k)$ and server's online computation $O(2^m/m)$. This means that say for databases of size 2^{14}, about 7 times less public-key operations *in the worst case* are needed than in Lipmaa's $(n, 1)$-CPIR from [18]. Importantly, the new protocol has exactly the same communication complexity as Lipmaa's CPIR. In general (and again in the worst case), about 4 to 8 times larger databases can be handled than with Lipmaa's $(n, 1)$-CPIR in the same time, which brings us closer to the practical deployment of $(n, 1)$-CPIR protocols. Moreover, for any ℓ, one can construct a CPIR protocol with communication complexity $\Theta(\ell \cdot \log n + k \cdot \log^2 n)$ and online computation of $\Theta(n\ell/(\log n + \log \ell))$ public-key operations. Thus, if $\ell = o(\log n)$, then BddCpir has still guaranteed sublinear online computation.

However, clearly, the BDD depends on the concrete database. If the databases are well-structured, then one can decrease the computation much more. We show that if the database is sparse, with $c \ll n$ non-zero elements, the BddCpir protocol has the same communication complexity as before, but its online computational complexity is reduced to $\approx c \cdot \log_2 n$. This version of BddCpir can be used in any of the innumerable privacy-preserving data-mining applications that deal with huge (say, $10\,000$ times $10\,000$) but very sparse Boolean matrices. Here, linear-time CPIR protocols are clearly not applicable. However, if the matrix is very sparse, then one can efficiently present the matrix as a BDD, and then apply BddCpir. As an example, the BddCpir protocol can handle $20\,000 \times 20\,000$ permutation matrices about 700 times faster than linear-time CPIR protocols. Moreover, representation as a BDD does not necessarily carry with itself additional cost, since many common data-mining subroutines can be efficiently performed on BDDs [9]. We emphasize that this example is important: the main reason why cryptography-based privacy-preserving data mining has not taken off is the utter inefficiency of existing cryptographic methods in handling huge but structured data. Instead, one uses insecure but severely more efficient methods, see e.g. [1], when processing such data.

In addition, in many existing cryptographic protocols where the server has to cryptocompute some value and then return it to the client, because of the lack of more efficient methods, the server precomputes a database of possible answers and then the client and the server execute an $(n, 1)$-CPIR protocol. In such cases, the database has a clear structure, and thus the BddCpir protocol can be applied.

As a separate contribution, we show how to optimize the PrivateBDD protocol even further. In particular, we present three versions of Lipmaa's $(n, 1)$-CPIR protocol from [18] that have the communication complexity of $2\ell + (2 + o(1)) \log^2 n \cdot k$, $(1 + o(1))\ell + (1 + o(1)) \log^2 n \cdot \log \log n \cdot k$ and $\Theta(\ell \cdot \log n / \log \log n + k \cdot \log^2 n / \log \log n)$, respectively. The balancing techniques are applicable also in the case of the new BddCpir protocol. In particular, the second of those results shows that the new CPIR protocol achieves optimal rate $1 + o(1)$ in the case of a large ℓ, while simultaneously achieving sublinear computation in the case of a large n.

In Sect. 4 we also discuss how to modify BddCpir so that it will also protect server's privacy, that is, to an oblivious transfer (OT) protocol in a virtually costless way.

2 Preliminaries

Client's input is $x \in \{0, 1\}^m$, server's input is a function $f : \{0, 1\}^m \to \{0, 1\}^{\sigma\ell}$ for suitably chosen σ and ℓ. (See the next paragraph for the precise meaning of σ and ℓ, in a concrete application they are chosen so as to minimize the cost of the BddCpir protocol.) We also denote $f(x)$ by f_x, that is, we think of f as of the characteristic function of the vector $f = (f_0, \ldots, f_{2^m-1})$. Also, n denotes the server's database size, and k denotes the security parameter. If A is either a set or a (randomized) algorithm, then $a \leftarrow A$ denotes assignment of a according to the implicit random distribution. All logarithms have base 2.

(Integer-Valued) Binary Decision Diagrams. A *binary decision diagram* (BDD, or a branching program, [24]) is a fanout-2 directed acyclic graph (V, E), where the non-terminal (that is, non-sink) nodes are labeled by variables from some variable set $\{x_0, \ldots, x_{m-1}\}$, the sinks are labeled by ℓ-bit strings and the two outgoing edges of every internal node are respectively labeled by 0 and 1. Usually, it is assumed that a BDD has 1-bit sink labels, then it can be assumed to have two terminal nodes. A BDD with longer sink labels is thus sometimes called *multi-terminal*. A BDD that has σ sources computes some function $f : \{0,1\}^m \to \{0,1\}^{\sigma\ell}$. Every source and every assignment of the variables selects one path from this source to some sink as follows. The path starts from the source. If the current version of path does not end at a sink, test the variable at the endpoint of the path. Select one of the outgoing edges depending on the value of this variable, and append this edge and its endpoint to the path. If the path ends at a sink, return the label of this sink as the value of the corresponding source. The BDD's value is then equal to the concatenation of its source values.

In an *ordered binary decision diagram* (OBDD), an order π of the labels is chosen, and for any edge $(u, v) \in E$ it must hold that $\pi(u) < \pi(v)$. A BDD is a *decision tree* if the underlying graph is a tree. A BDD is *layered* if its set of nodes can be divided into disjoint sets V_j such that every edge from a node in set V_j ends in a node in set V_{j+1}. For a BDD P, let $\mathsf{len}(P)$ be its length (that is, the length of its longest path), $\mathsf{size}(P)$ be its size (that is, the number of non-terminal nodes). Let $\mathsf{BDD}(f)/\mathsf{OBDD}(f)$ be the minimal size of any BDD/OBDD computing f. It is known that any Boolean function $f : \{0,1\}^m \to \{0,1\}$ has $\mathsf{BDD}(f) \leq (1+o(1))2^m/m$ [4, Thm. 1] and $\mathsf{OBDD}(f) \leq (2+o(1))2^m/m$ [17,13,4].

Public-Key Cryptosystems. Let $\Pi = (\mathsf{G}, \mathsf{E}, \mathsf{D})$ be a length-flexible additively-homomorphic public-key cryptosystem [7], where G is a randomized key generation algorithm, E is a randomized encryption algorithm and D is a decryption algorithm. in a length-flexible cryptosystem, both E and D receive an additional length parameter ℓ, so that $\mathsf{E}_{\mathsf{pk}}(\ell, \cdot)$ encrypts plaintexts from some set $\{0,1\}^{\leq \ell}$. In the case of the DJ01 cryptosystem from [7], for every integer $\ell > 0$, $\mathsf{E}_{\mathsf{pk}}(\ell, \cdot) \in \{0,1\}^{\lceil \ell/k \rceil \cdot k + k}$. (In some other length-flexible cryptosystems like [8], the resulting ciphertext is longer.) In practice, $2^\ell < N$ where N is the public key of the DJ01 cryptosystem.

Thus, in the case of the DJ01 cryptosystem, $\mathsf{E}_{\mathsf{pk}}(\ell, M)$ is a valid plaintext of $\mathsf{E}_{\mathsf{pk}}(\lceil \ell/k \rceil \cdot k + k, \cdot)$, and therefore one can multiple-encrypt messages as say in

$$C \leftarrow \mathsf{E}_{\mathsf{pk}}(\ell + 2k, \mathsf{E}_{\mathsf{pk}}(\ell + k, \mathsf{E}_{\mathsf{pk}}(\ell, M))),$$

and then recover M by multiple-decrypting,

$$M \leftarrow \mathsf{D}_{\mathsf{sk}}(\ell + 2k, \mathsf{D}_{\mathsf{sk}}(\ell + k, \mathsf{D}_{\mathsf{sk}}(\ell, C))).$$

Note that the length of j-times encrypted M is $\lceil \ell/k \rceil \cdot k + jk \leq \ell + (j+1) \cdot k$ bits. Additionally, in any length-flexible additively-homomorphic cryptosystem, $\mathsf{E}_{\mathsf{pk}}(\ell, M_1) \cdot \mathsf{E}_{\mathsf{pk}}(\ell, M_2) = \mathsf{E}_{\mathsf{pk}}(\ell, M_1 + M_2)$, where the addition is modulo the public key N. We will also need the existence of a compression function C that, given pk, ℓ' and ℓ for $\ell' \geq \ell$, and $\mathsf{E}_{\mathsf{pk}}(\ell', M)$ for $M \in \{0,1\}^\ell$, returns $\mathsf{E}_{\mathsf{pk}}(\ell, M) \in \{0,1\}^{\lceil \ell/k \rceil \cdot k + k}$. As shown in [18] and later in [14], DJ01 has a very simple compress function that just reduces $\mathsf{E}_{\mathsf{pk}}(\ell', M)$ modulo some power of N.

In the CPA (*chosen-plaintext attack*) game, the challenger first generates a random key pair $(\mathsf{sk}, \mathsf{pk}) \leftarrow \mathsf{G}(1^k)$, and sends pk to the attacker. The attacker chooses two messages M_0, M_1 and a length parameter ℓ, and sends them to the challenger. The challenger picks a random bit b, and sends a ciphertext $\mathsf{E}_{\mathsf{pk}}(\ell, M_b)$ to the attacker. The attacker outputs a bit b', and wins if $b = b'$. A cryptosystem is *CPA-secure* if the probability that any nonuniform probabilistic polynomial-time attacker wins in the CPA-game is negligibly different from $1/2$.

Clearly, because of the existence of the compress function, a CPA-secure length-flexible cryptosystem remains CPA-secure even if the adversary sends many message pairs (M_{j0}, M_{j1}) and length parameters ℓ_j, and has to guess b after seeing encryptions of all M_{jb} under the corresponding length parameters ℓ_j. This so-called LFCPA-security [18] of the cryptosystem is crucial for the security of the efficient PrivateBDD protocol as defined in the next section. The DJ01 cryptosystem [7] is CPA-secure under the Decisional Composite Residuosity Assumption [22].

CPIR. In a 1-out-of-n computationally-private information retrieval protocol, $(n, 1)$-CPIR, for ℓ-bit strings, the client has an index $x \in \{0, \ldots, n-1\}$ and the server has a database $f = (f_0, \ldots, f_{n-1})$ with $f_i \in \{0,1\}^\ell$. The client obtains f_x. The new $(n, 1)$-CPIR protocol BddCpir, proposed in this paper, is based on an $(2, 1)$-CPIR protocol that satisfies some very specific requirements. Namely, we say that an $(n, 1)$-CPIR protocol $\Gamma = (\mathsf{Q}, \mathsf{R}, \mathsf{A}, \mathsf{C})$ is *BDD-friendly* if it satisfies the next four assumptions:

1. Γ has two messages, a query $\mathsf{Q}(\ell, x)$ from the client and a reply $\mathsf{R}(\ell, f, \mathsf{Q})$ from the server, such that the stateful client can recover f_x by computing $\mathsf{A}(\ell, x, \mathsf{R}(\ell, f, \mathsf{Q}))$.
2. Γ is uniform in ℓ, that is, it can be easily modified to work on other values of ℓ.
3. $|\mathsf{Q}(\ell, \cdot)|, |\mathsf{R}(\ell, \cdot, \cdot)| \leq \ell + \Theta(k)$.
4. The compress function C maps $\mathsf{Q}(\ell', x)$ to $\mathsf{Q}(\ell, x)$ for any $\ell' \geq \ell$ and x.

That is, $\Gamma = (\mathsf{Q}, \mathsf{R}, \mathsf{A}, \mathsf{C})$ is a quadruple of probabilistic polynomial-time algorithms, with $\mathsf{A}(\ell, x, \mathsf{R}(\ell, f, \mathsf{Q}(\ell, x))) = f_x$, and $\mathsf{C}(\ell', \ell, \mathsf{Q}(\ell', x)) = \mathsf{Q}(\ell, x)$ for any $\ell' \geq \ell$, x and f. For related work on computation-efficient CPIR protocols, see for example [10,2].

Let $\Pi = (\mathsf{G}, \mathsf{E}, \mathsf{D})$ be a length-flexible additively homomorphic public-key cryptosystem. Client's private input is $x \in \{0, 1\}$, server's private input is $f = (f_0, f_1)$ for $f_0, f_1 \in \{0, 1\}^\ell$. In [18], Lipmaa proposed a $(2, 1)$-CPIR protocol that consists of the next three steps:

---

1. The client sets $(\mathsf{sk}, \mathsf{pk}) \leftarrow \mathsf{G}(1^k)$, $c \leftarrow \mathsf{E}_{\mathsf{pk}}(\ell, x)$, and sends $\mathsf{Q}(\ell, x) \leftarrow (\mathsf{pk}, c)$ to the server.
2. The server replies with $\mathsf{R} = \mathsf{R}(\ell, f, (\mathsf{pk}, c)) \leftarrow \mathsf{E}_{\mathsf{pk}}(\ell, f_0) \cdot c^{f_1 - f_0}$.
3. The client outputs $\mathsf{A}(\ell, x, \mathsf{R}) := \mathsf{D}_{\mathsf{sk}}(\ell, \mathsf{R})$.

If $x \in \{0, 1\}$, then clearly

$$\mathsf{R}(\ell, f, (\mathsf{pk}, \mathsf{E}_{\mathsf{pk}}(\ell, x))) = \mathsf{E}_{\mathsf{pk}}(\ell, f_0) \cdot c^{f_1 - f_0} = \mathsf{E}_{\mathsf{pk}}(\ell, f_0) \cdot \mathsf{E}_{\mathsf{pk}}(\ell, x)^{f_1 - f_0}$$
$$= \mathsf{E}_{\mathsf{pk}}(\ell, f_0 + (f_1 - f_0) \cdot x) = \mathsf{E}_{\mathsf{pk}}(\ell, f_x).$$

If Π has a compress function, then Lipmaa's $(2, 1)$-CPIR protocol has also a compress function C that just compresses both involved ciphertexts. Importantly, $|\mathsf{Q}(\ell, \cdot)|, |\mathsf{R}(\ell, \cdot, \cdot)| \leq \ell + 2k$ and thus, this $(2, 1)$-CPIR protocol is BDD-friendly.

Semisimulatable Privacy. Let $\Gamma = (\mathsf{Q}, \mathsf{R}, \mathsf{A}, \mathsf{C})$ be a 2-message $(n, 1)$-CPIR protocol. As many previous papers [21,18,14], we only require (semisimulatable) privacy in the malicious model. More precisely, client's privacy is guaranteed in the sense of indistinguishability (CPA-security), while server's privacy is guaranteed (if at all) in the sense of simulatability. This assumption makes it possible to design 2-message $(n, 1)$-CPIR protocols that are both communication and computation-efficient. We now give an informal definition of privacy.

For the *CPA-security* (that is, the privacy) *of the client*, no malicious nonuniform probabilistic polynomial-time server should be able to distinguish, with non-negligible probability, between the distributions $\mathsf{Q}(\ell, x_0)$ and $\mathsf{Q}(\ell, x_1)$ that correspond to any two of client's inputs x_0 and x_1 that are chosen by herself. For *server-privacy*, we require the existence of an unbounded simulator that, given client's message Q^* and client's legitimate output corresponding to this message, generates server's message that is statistically indistinguishable from server's message R in the real protocol; here Q^* does not have to be correctly computed. A protocol is *private* if it is both client-private and server-private.

Any $(n, 1)$-CPIR protocol Γ must be client-private, that is, CPA-secure. Lipmaa's $(2, 1)$-CPIR protocol [18], when based on the DJ01 cryptosystem [7], is CPA-secure under the DCR Assumption [22]. Because of the existence of the compression function, if Γ is CPA-secure then it is also difficult to distinguish between any two polynomially large sets $\{\mathsf{Q}(\ell_i, x_{i0})\}$ and $\{\mathsf{Q}(\ell_i, x_{i1}))\}$, even if the same public key pk is used in all of them. A private $(n, 1)$-CPIR protocol is also known as an $(n, 1)$-*oblivious transfer protocol*.

3   The PrivateBDD Protocol

Next, we describe the PrivateBDD cryptocomputing protocol from [14]. It generalizes the cryptocomputing process, done in several previous $(n, 1)$-CPIR protocols [15,23,18]. Our exposition is simpler than the more general exposition of [14]. The concrete protocol has also some small differences compared to the protocol of [14]. More precisely, while the description given by us can be inferred from the description in [14], we have opted to describe explicitly the most efficient known implementation of the PrivateBDD. Moreover, Ishai and Paskin [14] used a strong oblivious transfer protocol at every node of the underlying BDD, while we just use an efficient $(2,1)$-CPIR protocol. There are also other minor differences.

In the PrivateBDD protocol for some set $\mathcal{F}$ of functions, the client has private input $x \in \{0,1\}^m$, the server has private input $f : \{0,1\}^m \to \{0,1\}^{\sigma\ell}$ with $f \in \mathcal{F}$, and the client will receive private output $f(x)$. Here, $\mathcal{F} = \{f : \{0,1\}^m \to \{0,1\}^{\sigma\ell}\}$ is a set of functions, where every $f \in \mathcal{F}$ can be computed by some polynomial-size BDD P_f that has σ sources and ℓ-bit sink labels. Define $\mathsf{len}(\mathcal{F}) := \max_{f \in \mathcal{F}} \mathsf{len}(P_f)$. Let $\Gamma' = (\mathsf{Q}', \mathsf{R}', \mathsf{A}', \mathsf{C}')$ be a BDD-friendly $(2,1)$-CPIR protocol. Since we are going to recursively apply Γ' on databases that consist of the R' values of some other runs of Γ', we need to define the next few values. Namely, let

$$|\mathsf{Q}^{(1)}(\ell)| := |\mathsf{Q}'(\ell, x)|,$$
$$|\mathsf{R}^{(j)}(\ell)| := |\mathsf{R}'(|\mathsf{Q}^{(j)}(\ell)|, f, \mathsf{Q}')|,$$
$$|\mathsf{Q}^{(j+1)}(\ell)| := |\mathsf{Q}'(|\mathsf{R}^{(j)}(\ell)|, x)|.$$

We will assume that those values are well-defined, that is, that they do not depend on the concrete values of x and f. Because Γ' has to be private, this assumption is reasonable. If Γ' is BDD-friendly, then $|\mathsf{Q}^{(j)}(\ell)| = |\mathsf{R}^{(j)}(\ell)| \le \ell + j \cdot \Theta(k)$.

Now, BDDs are usually evaluated in a top-down manner by following the σ paths that are consistent with the assignment of the input variables x_j. It is unlikely that one can evaluate BDDs like this in a private manner. Instead, following [14], we use a bottom-up way of evaluating a BDD. In the non-private version of this process, the sinks' output values are equal to their labels. At every non-terminal node v that is labeled by some x_j and for which the output values R_{v_0} and R_{v_1} of both children are known, one sets the output value R_v of v to be equal to $\mathsf{R}_{v_{x_j}}$. The value of the BDD is equal to the concatenation of the output values of the sources.

In the private version, the server also executes the BDD P_f bottom-up, that is, starting from the sinks. The output values R_v of the sinks are equal to their ℓ-bit labels. Initially, R_v is undefined for all other nodes. At every node v of the BDD with label x_j and children v_0/v_1 such that the output values $\mathsf{R}_{v_0}/\mathsf{R}_{v_1}$ of v_0/v_1 are known but the output value R_v of v is not yet defined, the server uses Γ to obliviously propagate the value $\mathsf{R}_{v_{x_j}}$ upwards as R_v. The server does this for all nodes in some ordering, and then sends the output values of the σ sources to the client. (Ishai and Paskin [14] only considered the depth-first ordering, while sometimes some other ordering may be more efficient.) For every source, the client applies the decoding procedure A' repeatedly to obtain the label of the sink that is uniquely determined by this source and by client's input x. Complete description of the PrivateBDD protocol for $\mathcal{F}$ is given by Protocol 1.

---

1. **Common inputs:** $m, \sigma, \ell, \mathcal{F}, \mathsf{len}(\mathcal{F})$.
2. **Private inputs:** the server has a function $f : \{0,1\}^m \to \{0,1\}^{\sigma\ell}$ from $\mathcal{F}$, and the client has bitstring $x \in \{0,1\}^m$.
3. **Offline phase:** server computes an efficient BDD P_f for f that has σ sources and ℓ-bit sink labels, and where $\mathsf{len}(P_f) \leq \mathsf{len}(\mathcal{F})$. Let $\ell_{\max} := |\mathsf{Q}^{(\mathsf{len}(\mathcal{F})-1)}(\ell)|$.
4. **Online phase:**
   (a) **Client does:** For $j \in \{0, \ldots, m-1\}$, set $\mathsf{Q}_j \leftarrow \mathsf{Q}'(\ell_{\max}, x_j)$. Send $\mathsf{Q}(\ell, x) \leftarrow (\mathsf{Q}_0, \ldots, \mathsf{Q}_{m-1})$ to the server.
   (b) **Server does:**
      i. For all sinks v of P_f, set R_v to be their label. For non-terminal nodes v, set $\mathsf{R}_v \leftarrow \bot$.
      ii. Do by following some ordering of the nodes:
         A. Let v be some node with $\mathsf{R}_v = \bot$, with children v_0 and v_1 that have $\mathsf{R}_{v_0}, \mathsf{R}_{v_1} \neq \bot$; if no such node exists then exit the loop.
         B. Assume that v is labeled by x_i and edges from v to v_0/v_1 are labeled by $0/1$.
         C. Compute and store $\mathsf{R}_v \leftarrow \mathsf{R}(\ell^*, (\mathsf{R}_{v_0}, \mathsf{R}_{v_1}), \mathsf{C}(\ell_{\max}, \ell^*, \mathsf{Q}_i))$, where $\ell^* \leftarrow \max(|\mathsf{R}_{v_0}|, |\mathsf{R}_{v_1}|)$. // If BDD is layered then $|\mathsf{R}_{v_0}| = |\mathsf{R}_{v_1}|$.
      iii. For all σ sources v, send R_v to the client.
   (c) **Client does:** For any source v, compute private output from R_v by applying A' recursively up to $\mathsf{len}(\mathcal{F})$ times.

Protocol 1. The PrivateBDD protocol

Theorem 1. *Let $\Gamma' = (\mathsf{Q}', \mathsf{R}', \mathsf{A}', \mathsf{C}')$ be a CPA-secure BDD-friendly $(2, 1)$-CPIR protocol. Let $\mathcal{F}$ be a set of functions from $\{0,1\}^m$ to $\{0,1\}^{\sigma\ell}$ where every $f \in \mathcal{F}$ can be computed by a polynomial-size BDD P_f. Then $\mathcal{F}$ has a CPA-secure cryptocomputing protocol with the communication complexity $m \cdot |\mathsf{Q}^{(\mathsf{len}(\mathcal{F}))}(\ell)| + \sigma \cdot |\mathsf{R}^{(\mathsf{len}(\mathcal{F}))}(\ell)| = (m + \sigma)(\ell + \mathsf{len}(\mathcal{F}) \cdot k)$. Server's online computation is dominated by $\mathsf{size}(P_f)$ public-key operations. Additionally, if P_f is layered, then the PrivateBDD protocol is server-private in the semihonest model.*

Proof. CPA-security follows by a standard hybrid argument from the LFCPA-security of Γ', and thus from the CPA-security of Γ' and from the existence of C'. If P_f is layered, then the client is completely oblivious to the shape of the BDD, except the length of it: he just forms queries corresponding to his input bits by using his knowledge of the length of the BDD (and on the output length ℓ), and then receives multiple-"encryptions" of the outputs. The communication complexity part is straightforward. Server has to compute R at every node of P_f. □

Alternatively, this theorem shows that if any $f : \{0,1\} \to \{0,1\}^{\sigma\ell}$ has an "efficient" cryptocomputing protocol, then any $F : \{0,1\}^m \to \{0,1\}^{\sigma\ell}$ has an "efficient" cryptocomputing protocol.

If the compress function C does not exist, then the client has to submit up to $\mathsf{len}(P)$ different queries $\mathsf{Q}(\ell', x_j)$ for every x_j and every $\ell' = |\mathsf{Q}^{(i)}(\ell)|$ for

$i \leq \text{len}(P) - 1$. This can increase the communication by a factor of $\text{len}(P)$. The existence of C makes it possible to compute $\mathsf{Q}(|\mathsf{Q}^{(i)}(\ell)|, x_j)$ from $\mathsf{Q}(\ell_{\max}, x_j)$.

We assume throughout this paper that we are working with Lipmaa's $(2, 1)$-CPIR from [18], which is currently the only known $(2, 1)$-CPIR protocol that allows the PrivateBDD protocol to achieve the communication complexity that is polynomial in $\text{len}(\mathcal{F})$ (thus the name "BDD-friendly"). A precise result follows:

Corollary 1. *Assume that the DCR Assumption [22] is true. Let $\mathcal{F}$ be a set of functions $f : \{0,1\}^m \rightarrow \{0,1\}^{\sigma\ell}$, and for any $f \in \mathcal{F}$ let P_f be some σ-source polynomial-size BDD with ℓ-bit sink labels that computes f. Then $\mathcal{F}$ has a CPA-secure cryptocomputing protocol with the communication upperbounded by $k + (m + \sigma) \cdot (\ell + (\text{len}(\mathcal{F}) + 2) \cdot k)$, and server's online computation dominated by $\text{size}(\mathcal{F})$ public-key operations.*

Proof. Let $\Pi = (\mathsf{G}, \mathsf{E}, \mathsf{D})$ be the DJ01 length-flexible cryptosystem [7]. This version of the PrivateBDD protocol generates one single $(\mathsf{sk}, \mathsf{pk}) \leftarrow \mathsf{G}(1^k)$ and uses the same pk to construct all m queries Q_j. Because Lipmaa's $(2, 1)$-CPIR is BDD-friendly and CPA-secure, the CPA-security of PrivateBDD follows from a standard hybrid argument. Computation-efficiency is straightforward. To calculate the communication efficiency, note that $\mathsf{Q}_j = \mathsf{Q}'(\ell_{\max}, x_j) = \mathsf{E}_{\mathsf{pk}}(\ell + \text{len}(\mathcal{F}) \cdot k, x_j)$. Thus,

$$|\mathsf{Q}_j| = |\mathsf{E}_{\mathsf{pk}}(\ell + \text{len}(\mathcal{F}) \cdot k, x_j)| = (\lceil \ell/k \rceil + \text{len}(\mathcal{F}) + 1) \cdot k \leq \ell + (\text{len}(\mathcal{F}) + 2) \cdot k.$$

Therefore, the client sends a public key (of length say k) and at most $m \cdot (\ell + (\text{len}(\mathcal{F}) + 2) \cdot k)$ additional bits. The output of the BDD is equal to σ ($\leq \text{len}(\mathcal{F})$)-times encryptions of sink values, where the sinks are selected by the encrypted client inputs x_j. Server's communication consists of σ ($\leq \text{len}(\mathcal{F})$)-times encrypted messages of length $\leq \ell + (\text{len}(\mathcal{F}) + 2) \cdot k$. $\square$

All CPIR protocols that follow the Kushilevitz-Ostrovsky recursion technique [15,23,18] can be seen as using PrivateBDD to cryptocompute an ordered n'-ary decision tree, with $\sigma = 1$, $m = \lceil \log_{n'} n \rceil$ and varying values of n'. However, in the case of [15,23], the underlying $(n', 1)$-CPIR protocol is not very efficient and thus the communication-complexity of the resulting $(n, 1)$-CPIR protocols of [15,23] is not polylogarithmic. On the other hand, Lipmaa's $(n, 1)$-CPIR protocol from [18] uses his $(2, 1)$-CPIR protocol in combination with an ordered binary decision tree, to achieve the communication complexity $\Theta(m \cdot (\ell + \text{len}(P_f) \cdot k)) = \Theta(\ell \cdot \log n + k \cdot \log^2 n)$, agreeing with Cor. 1. Note that such CPIR protocols do not explicitly need the C function, because they cryptocompute an ordered binary decision tree where every x_i is only tested on the ith level of the tree. More generally, the C function is not necessary if the underlying BDD is ordered.

4   New Computation-Efficient $(n, 1)$-CPIR Protocol

Assume that $\sigma = 1$ and that the database size is $n = 2^m$, that is, that the server's database consists of $n = 2^m$ bits. (If n is not a power of 2 then one can round up the database size by using additional dummy elements.) In this case, we can restate the goals of an $(n, 1)$-CPIR protocol as follows.

Assume that the client has an input $x \in \{0, 1\}^m$, and that the server's input is a Boolean function $f : \{0, 1\}^m \to \{0, 1\}^\ell$, such that $f(x) = f_x$. The client needs to retrieve $f(x)$. Thus in this case, $\mathcal{F}$ is the set of all functions, $\mathcal{F} = \{f : \{0, 1\}^m \to \{0, 1\}^\ell\}$. In the new $(n, 1)$-CPIR protocol, the client and the server run PrivateBDD for this $\mathcal{F}$. That is:

- In the offline phase of BddCpir, the server computes and stores an efficient BDD P_f for the concrete f.
- In the online phase of BddCpir, the client and the server follow PrivateBDD as specified in Protocol 1. Here, the server uses P_f.

In BddCpir, server's online computational complexity is proportional to $\mathsf{size}(P_f)$ while the communication complexity is proportional to $\mathsf{len}(\mathcal{F})$. We emphasize once more that P_f is computed after server's input f has been fixed.

The size (and to a lesser extent, also the length) of P_f will depend heavily on f (and $\mathcal{F}$), and not much can be said about it unless we know the concrete database or at least some of its properties. In what follows, we will consider two different database classes. First, we look at the case of arbitrary databases. We show that for any possible database f, as long as $\ell = o(\log n)$, the new $(n, 1)$-CPIR protocol has server's computation upperbounded by $o(n)$ public-key operations. Second, we look at the case where it is known that f is a very sparse database (like in many privacy-preserving data mining applications). We show than in the case, BddCpir is computationally significantly more efficient than any other existing CPIR protocol.

4.1 Class 1: Arbitrary Databases

In [4], it was shown that any Boolean function f can be computed by a BDD P_f of size $(1 + o(1))2^m/m$ and length $(1 + o(1))m$. However, this construction is reasonably efficient only when $m \geq 25$. Instead, we will describe an OBDD $\mathsf{WP}(f)$ from [17,13,4] that meets the upperbound $\mathsf{OBDD}(P_f) \leq (2 + o(1))2^m/m$. This OBDD also has the benefit of having optimal length m. Based on this result, even if f is an arbitrary Boolean database, the BddCpir protocol has communication complexity $\Theta(k \cdot \log^2 n)$ and server's online computational complexity $\Theta(n/\log n)$.

Let $f : \{0, 1\}^m \to \{0, 1\}$ be a Boolean function. (See Fig. 1 for the concrete case $m = 6$ of the next general construction.) Prot. 2 describes the corresponding OBDD $\mathsf{WP}(f)$, as found in say [24]. Briefly, the idea of $\mathsf{WP}(f)$ is to first branch according to first d variables. After that, the number of possible subfunctions on the last $m - d$ variables will be sufficiently small, so that one can branch according to corresponding subfunctions.

Clearly, this OBDD computes f and has length m. The size of $\mathsf{WP}(f)$ depends on d. There are two different recommendations for d. In [4], it was recommend to fix

$$d := m - \lfloor \log_2(m - 2\log_2 m) \rfloor. \tag{1}$$

- The BDD starts out as a depth-d, where d is fixed later, ordered binary decision tree where one branches on variables $x_0, \ldots, x_{d-1}$. This part of the BDD has $2^d - 1$ nodes.
- The BDD has $2^{2^{m-d}}$ more nodes that correspond to all subfunctions g of f on its last $m - d$ variables. These extra nodes are layered in $m - d$ more levels. The node for a subfunction that first essentially depends on the jth variable out of these $m - d$ variables (but not on earlier ones) is on level $d + j$; nodes that correspond to constant subfunctions are on level m. The extra nodes are labeled by corresponding subfunctions g. Note that the $m - d$ lowest levels have 2, $2^2 - 2^1 = 2$, $2^4 - 2^2 = 12$, $\ldots$, $2^{2^{m-d}} - 2^{2^{m-d-1}}$ nodes respectively.
- Let v_g be an extra (non-terminal) node. Assume that $g(y_1, \ldots, y_{m-d})$ first essentially depends on y_j. For $i \in \{0, 1\}$, let $g_{|y_j = i}$ be the function that we get from g when we set $y_j \leftarrow i$. Add an i-edge from v_g to $v_{g_{|y_j = i}}$.
- The above part of the construction only depends on the value of $n = 2^m$ and not on the concrete database. The next part depends on the database: The 2^{d-1} nodes on level d are labeled by subsequent $2^{m-d+1} = 2 \cdot 2^{m-d}$ values of the 2^m-bit database f. For a fixed level d node v', consider the first 2^{m-d} bits of this label to be the truth table of some subfunction g_0, and the last 2^{m-d} bits to be a truth table of some subfunction g_1. Add a 0-edge from v' to v_{g_0} and a 1-edge from v' to v_{g_1}.

Protocol 2. The description of $\mathsf{WP}(f)$

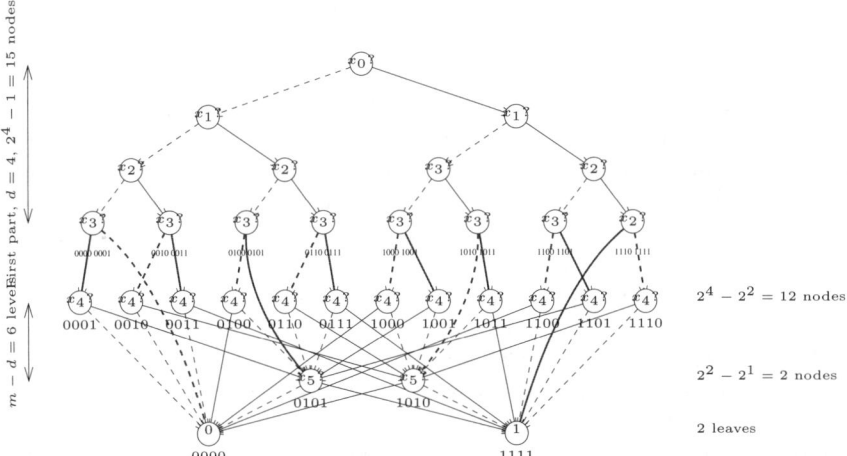

Fig. 1. Pictorial representation of OBDD corresponding to the presented upper-bound $(2 + o(1))2^m/m$ for $n = 2^m = 64$ and $d = 4$ computed according to Eq. (2). Only blue values and edges depend on the concrete database, which is equal to a sequence of binary presentations of all 4-bit integers. Everything else depends just on the value of m. For the sake of simplicity, we use the truth tables of corresponding subfunctions to label the extra nodes. The concrete database is $f = (0, 0, 0, 0; 0, 0, 0, 1; 0, 0, 1, 0; 0, 0, 1, 1; 0, 1, 0, 0, \ldots)$.

For such d, as it is shown in [4], $\mathsf{WP}(f)$ has size upperbounded by $(2+o(1))2^m/m$. However, for this choice of d to work, one has to assume that $m \geq 7$. Therefore, if m is small, we follow the recommendation of [24] to take

$$d := m - \lfloor \log_2(m + 1 - \log_2 m) \rfloor. \tag{2}$$

It is known [24] that with this choice of d, the size of $\mathsf{WP}(f)$ is $(3 + o(1))2^m/m$.

Example 1. If $m = 6$, then $d = 4$ according to Eq. (2). The complete ordered decision tree (which corresponds to the use of Lipmaa's CPIR protocol from [18]) has $2^m - 1 = 63$ non-terminal nodes. The OBDD $\mathsf{WP}(f)$ has $2^d - 1 + 2^{2^{m-d}} - 2 = 15 + 16 - 2 = 29$ non-terminal nodes. Thus even in this pet case, the BddCpir protocol requires $63/29 \approx 2$ times less public-key operations than Lipmaa's CPIR protocol. See Tbl. 1 for $2^m - 1$ and the size of $\mathsf{WP}(f)$ for other values of m, where an optimal d has been numerically optimized. (Note that this usually agrees with d computed according to Eq. (2).) There we see that for $m = 20$, the BddCpir protocol requires 8 times less public-key operations than Lipmaa's CPIR protocol.

We emphasize that it is natural to compare the efficiency of the new BddCpir protocol and Lipmaa's CPIR from [18] in the number of public-key operations since in both cases, one uses the same underlying public-key primitive on the plaintexts of the same length. Thus, one can expect that the actual running time of the BddCpir protocol (measured in seconds) is also about 4 to 8 smaller than the actual running time of Lipmaa's CPIR protocol, while having exactly the same communication complexity.

Now, let us proceed to compute the efficiency of this variation of the BddCpir protocol. *Offline* computation of the BddCpir protocol (the construction of the OBDD that corresponds to the upperbound) takes $O(2^m)$ *non-cryptographic* operations. This value is not so important because the offline computation has to be only done once per database, and not once per query. As evident from the construction of $\mathsf{WP}(f)$, only the location of $2^d \approx 2^m/(m + 1 - \log_2 m) = (1 + o(1)) \cdot 2^m/m$ edges depends on the database. Thus even when the database is completely changed, one has to change $O(2^d) = O(2^m/m)$ edges. This takes $O(2^m/m)$ time in the RAM model, and can be compared to the 2^m work that is necessary to update the database itself. In the case t elements of the database are updated, exactly the location of t edges is changed.

Online evaluation of the BDD $\mathsf{WP}(f)$ on concrete input x takes $(3+o(1))2^m/m$ public-key operations. As depicted by Tbl. 1, this is smaller than the trivial $n = 2^m$ for any $m \geq 3$. To the best of our knowledge, this is the first $(n, 1)$-CPIR with this property. Note that the upperbound $\Theta(2^m/m)$ is also tight because there exist functions f with $\mathsf{BDD}(f) = (1 - o(1))2^m/m$ [4].

Theorem 2. *Assume that the DCR Assumption holds. Then there exists a CPA-secure $(n, 1)$-CPIR protocol for 1-bit strings with the communication complexity $\Theta(\log^2 n) \cdot k$ and server's online computation of $O(n/\log n)$ public-key operations.*

Table 1. The comparison of the size of the binary decision tree and $\mathsf{WP}(f)$

m	$2^m - 1$	$\mathsf{WP}(f)$	Opt. d	Imprv.	m	$2^m - 1$	$\mathsf{WP}(f)$	Opt. d	Imprv.
1	1	1	1	1.0	13	8 191	1 277	10	6.41425
2	3	3	1	1.0	14	16 383	2 301	11	7.11995
3	7	5	2	1.4	15	32 767	4 349	12	7.53438
4	15	9	3	1.66667	16	65 535	8 445	13	7.76021
5	31	17	4	1.82353	17	131 071	16 637	14	7.87828
6	63	29	4	2.17241	18	262 143	33 021	15	7.93868
7	127	45	5	2.82222	19	524 287	65 789	16	7.96922
8	255	77	6	3.31169	20	1 048 575	131 069	16	8.00018
9	511	141	7	3.62411	21	2 097 151	196 605	17	10.6668
10	1 023	269	8	3.80297	22	4 194 303	327 677	18	12.8001
11	2 047	509	8	4.02161	23	8 388 607	589 821	19	14.2223
12	4 095	765	9	5.35294	24	16 777 215	1 114 109	20	15.0589

Proof. Follows from Cor. 1 and the upperbound of [17,13,4], by letting $\mathcal{F}$ to be the set of all Boolean functions $f : \{0,1\}^{\lceil \log_2 n \rceil} \to \{0,1\}$, and using the OBDD $\mathsf{WP}(f)$.   □

Now, let $f : \{0,1\}^m \to \{0,1\}^\ell$ for some $\ell \geq 1$. By the already mentioned upperbound of [17,13,4], clearly $\mathsf{BDD}(f) \leq \ell \cdot (2 + o(1))2^m/m$ by just evaluating ℓ BDDs in parallel. Thus, there exists a sublinear-computation CPIR protocol for say any $\ell \leq m/3$. However, we can prove the next more precise result.

Theorem 3. *(1) Let* $f : \{0,1\}^m \to \{0,1\}^\ell$ *for some* $\ell \geq 1$. *For* $\ell \geq 1$, $\mathsf{OBDD}(f) \leq (2 + o(1)) \cdot 2^m \cdot \ell/(m + \log_2 \ell)$. *(2) Assume that the DCR Assumption holds. There exists a CPA-secure* $(n, 1)$-*CPIR protocol for* ℓ-*bit strings with the communication complexity* $\Theta(\ell \cdot \log n + k \cdot \log^2 n)$ *and online computation of* $O(\ell \cdot n/(\log n + \log \ell))$ *public-key operations.*

Proof (Of Thm. 3). We follow the same ideas as in constructing $\mathsf{WP}(f)$. The new OBDD starts with a complete binary tree of depth d and then has $2^{\ell \cdot 2^{m-d}}$ extra nodes that correspond to all possible subfunctions $f' : \{0,1\}^{m-d} \to \{0,1\}^\ell$, with 2^ℓ of those extra nodes being the sinks. The edges are added in the natural way. Thus, this BDD has $2^d - 1 + 2^{\ell 2^{m-d}} - 2^\ell$ non-terminal nodes. This value is (almost) minimized when $d = \ell \cdot 2^{m-d}$, that is, when $d = W(2^m \ell \ln 2)/\ln 2$. Here $W(x)$ is the Lambert's W-function, that is the inverse function of $f(w) = w \cdot \exp(w)$. Using this value of d, we get that the constructed OBDD has then

$$2 \cdot \exp(W(2^m \ell \cdot \ln 2)) - 2^\ell - 1$$

non-terminal nodes. Next, we use the first two elements of the series expansion of $W(z) = \ln z - \ln \ln z + \dots$, to find that the constructed OBDD has approximately

$$2 \cdot \exp(\ln(2^m \ell \ln 2) - \ln \ln(2^m \ell \ln 2)) - 2^\ell - 1 = \frac{2^{m+1}\ell}{m + \log_2 \ell + \log_2 \ln 2} - 2^\ell - 1$$

$$\leq 2 \cdot \frac{2^m \ell}{m + \log_2 \ell}$$

non-terminal nodes. Because d has to be integral, the computations are not precise, and there will be a small additional multiplicative constant $1 + o(1)$ that this expression will be multiplied with. Note that the size of this OBDD is smaller than the trivial $2^m - 1$ if say $\ell \leq (m + \log_2 \ell)/3$ or say $\ell \leq (m + \log m)/3$. $\qquad\qquad\qquad\qquad\qquad\qquad\qquad\qquad\qquad\qquad\qquad\qquad\qquad\qquad\qquad\quad\Box$

4.2 Case 2: CPIR for Sparse Matrices

In almost all real life data, there is a lot of redundancy. Otherwise, most of the existing data-mining and machine learning algorithms would not be useful in practice. As a concrete application area of the BddCpir protocol, consider privacy-preserving data mining scenarios that often deal with huge (say, 20 000 times 20 000) but very sparse Boolean matrices. For example, in such applications every row of this matrix could be a transaction (say in a supermarket) and every column would correspond to some item sold in this supermarket. An element m_{ij} of this matrix would be 1 exactly when during the ith transaction the jth item was actually bought.

One of the most basic operations in such applications is private retrieval of a single matrix element. Clearly, linear-time CPIR protocols are not applicable in this case due to the raw size of the matrices. However, if the matrix is very sparse, then one can efficiently present the matrix as a BDD (as was recommended say in [9]), and then apply the BddCpir protocol. As noted in [9], BDD is a good data structure for representing sparse matrices. In particular, if the matrix is very sparse, then the next straightforward OBDD representation is already good enough. Namely, assume that the Boolean matrix has dimension $n_1 \times n_2$ and contains $c \ll n_1 n_2$ ones. We can then represent the matrix as a join of c paths of length $\lceil \log_2 n_1 + \log_2 n_2 \rceil$, where every sink (and thus every path) corresponds to exactly one 1 entry in the matrix. Thus, the size of this OBDD representation is upperbounded by $c \cdot \lceil \log_2 n_1 + \log_2 n_2 \rceil$ [9] while its length is upperbounded by $\lceil \log_2 n_1 + \log_2 n_2 \rceil$. This is an upperbound, since all paths share at least one (and usually more) nodes. Thus, in the case of sparse but huge matrices, we can use this trivial representation and then just apply BddCpir to this. Note that, as shown in [9], many matrix algorithms can be performed efficiently on the OBDD representation of sparse matrices, which makes the OBDD representation of sparse matrices reasonable in many data-mining applications and thus one could apply more complex privacy-preserving operations on the top of CPIR.

As a concrete example, assume that we have a $20\,000 \times 20\,000$ matrix. If this matrix has exactly one 1 in every row (like the permutation matrices), then BddCpir has server's online computation dominated by $\leq 20\,000{\cdot}2 \log_2(20\,000) \approx 2^{19.1}$ public-key operations, while all previous CPIR protocols need $20\,000^2 \approx 2^{28.6}$ public-key operations. If the matrix has say 20 ones in every row in average (this is typical in shopping-basket applications), then BddCpir is still about 35 times faster than CPIR protocols with linear computation.

More generally, we have the next result.

Theorem 4. *Assume that the DCR Assumption holds. Assume that* $f = (f_0, \ldots, f_{n-1})$ *is a sparse (not necessary Boolean) database that has* $c \ll n$ *non-zero entries. Then there exists a CPA-secure* $(n, 1)$-*CPIR protocol for* ℓ-*bit strings with the communication complexity* $\Theta(\ell \cdot \log n + k \cdot \log^2 n)$ *and server's online computation of* $\approx c \cdot \log_2 n$ *public-key operations.*

Proof (Sketch.). Similarly to the sparse matrix case, one can construct a trivial BDD with c sinks and paths that has length $\approx \log_2 n$ and size $\approx c \cdot \log_2 n$. According to Cor. 1, in this case BddCpir has communication complexity $\Theta(\ell \cdot \log n + k \cdot \log^2 n)$, and server's online computation is dominated by $\approx c \cdot \log_2 n$ public-key operations.   □

In particular, if $c = \Theta(\sqrt{n})$ as in the sparse matrix case, then server's online computation is dominated by $O(\sqrt{n} \cdot \log_2 n)$ public-key operations. Moreover, if $c = n$, then we actually have a complete binary decision tree, which corresponds to the CPIR of [18], and therefore this solution is never less efficient than [18].

5   Discussions

Server-Privacy. Recall that an $(n, 1)$-CPIR protocol that also achieves server-privacy is usually called an $(n, 1)$-OT protocol. As said earlier, as the minimum, the underlying BDD has to be layered or otherwise the protocol will not preserve server's privacy. Most of the BDDs that appear in practice can be easily made layered, and in fact layering makes the BDD at most quadratically larger [14]. Quadratic increase in computation time is not desirable in the case of CPIR. We will now show that one can make WP(f) layered in a virtually costless way. For this, first one has to add $m - d - j$ dummy nodes per each node on bottom d levels, or

$$\sum_{j=1}^{m-d} (m - d - j)(2^{2^j} - 2^{2^{j-1}}) = \sum_{j=1}^{m-d-1} 2^{2^j} + 2 = \Theta(2^{2^{m-d-1}})$$

nodes in total. Now, if d is chosen according to Eq. (1), this will be $(2 + o(1))2^{m/2}/m$ nodes. If d is chosen according to Eq. (2), this will be $(\sqrt{2} + o(1))2^{m/2}/\sqrt{m}$ nodes. Both values are negligible compared to the total number of nodes $\Theta(2^m/m)$ in the BDD. In addition, for every node on the level d—and there are $(1 + o(1))2^m/m^2$ such nodes if d is chosen according to Eq. (1) and $(1 + o(1))2^m/m$ if according to Eq. (2)—there are database-dependent edges to nodes in bottom layers. Because the number of bottom layers is $m - d$, if d is chosen according to Eq. (2), at most $(1 + o(1))2^m \log m/m^2$ new edges will be added.

After making the BDD layered, we must add privacy against a malicious server. There are many existing CPIR-to-OT transformations. In particular, the transformation from [16] takes $m = \log_2 n$ public-key operations, and modifies the CPIR protocol to a server-private protocol. (With the caveat that the public key has to be rough.) See [16,14] for more discussions.

Balancing. Let $f : \{0,1\}^m \to \{0,1\}^{\sigma\ell}$. In PrivateBDD, the client sends m messages and the server sends σ messages. If $m \gg \sigma$ and $\sigma\ell \gg m$, then one can improve the communication complexity by balancing, as follows. Without loss of generality, assume that $\sigma \mid m$. Denote $b := m/\sigma$. Then, for $j \in \{0,\ldots,b-1\}$, let $f_j : \{0,1\}^m \to \{0,1\}^{\sigma\ell/b}$. Here, f_0 computes the first ℓ/b bits of every source (that is, computes f restricted on the first ℓ/b bits of the sink values), f_1 computes the next ℓ/b bits of every source, etc. We then execute the PrivateBDD protocol (by reusing client's first message) in parallel for every f_j, and concatenate the private outputs. Thus, in this balanced version, the client sends m messages of length $\leq (\ell/b + (\text{len}(\mathcal{F}) + 2) \cdot k)$. The server returns $b\sigma$ messages of the same length. Thus, the total communication complexity of the balanced protocol is $\leq (m + b\sigma)(\ell/b + (\text{len}(\mathcal{F}) + 2) \cdot k) = 2m(\sigma\ell/m + (\text{len}(\mathcal{F}) + 2) \cdot k) = 2\sigma\ell + 2m(\text{len}(\mathcal{F}) + 2) \cdot k$. Thus, if $\ell \gg m \cdot \text{len}(\mathcal{F}) \cdot k$, then this version of the PrivateBDD protocol has information rate $1/2$.

If ℓ is even longer, then one can define $b := \alpha m/\sigma$ for some $\alpha > 1$, then the balanced protocol has communication complexity $(1+1/\alpha)\sigma\ell + (\alpha+1)m(\text{len}(\mathcal{F}) + 2)k$, or—for large values of ℓ and α—information rate $1 + o(1)$. For example, one can take $\alpha = \log_2 m$, then the communication complexity is $(1 + o(1))\sigma\ell + (\log_2 m + 1) \cdot m \cdot (\text{len}(\mathcal{F}) + 2)k$.

In another variant of balancing, we define $\ell_{\max} \approx (\ell + \text{len}(\mathcal{F})k)/b$. Then, after every b levels of the BDD, the length of the intermediate output values grows longer than $\ell_{\max}$, which requires us to double the remaining of the BDD like say in [23]. Here, the total communication complexity is $(m + 2^b\sigma)/b \cdot (\ell + \text{len}(\mathcal{F}) \cdot k)$. Defining $b := \log_2(m/\sigma)$, this will become $(m+2)/(\log_2 m - \log_2 \sigma) \cdot (\ell + \text{len}(\mathcal{F}) \cdot k)$. For integer b, the communication complexity is $(1 + o(1)) \cdot m/(\log_2 m - \log_2 \sigma) \cdot (\ell + \text{len}(\mathcal{F}) \cdot k)$.

By using the first balancing technique, the communication complexity of Lipmaa's $(n, 1)$-CPIR protocol from [18] can be improved to $2\ell + (1+o(1)) \cdot \log_2^2 n \cdot k$. By using the second balancing technique, the communication complexity of Lipmaa's $(n, 1)$-CPIR protocol can be improved to $\Theta((\ell \cdot \log n + k \cdot \log^2 n)/\log\log n)$. Balancing can also be used on some variations of the BddCpir protocol, especially when ℓ is large.

More Optimizations. Note that in the case of Lipmaa's $(n, 1)$-CPIR protocol, the client knows in advance in what depth every of the BDD input variable x_j is used. Thus, he does not have to send values $\mathsf{Q}(\ell_{\max}, x_j)$, but can send values $\mathsf{Q}(\ell + (j - 1) \cdot k, x_j)$ for every j. This optimization was used in [18] but it is also valid in other similar contexts, including both presented variations of the BddCpir protocol.

Further Work. The first (though somewhat sketchy) version of BddCpir was presented in an earlier preprint [20] in Spring of 2008, and it is based on a very standard security assumption. In the meantime, several fully-homomorphic public-key cryptosystems have been proposed, starting with [11]. Given a fully-homomorphic cryptosystem where on can encrypt integers modulo a large N, it is easy to construct a CPIR protocol with communication complexity $\Theta(\log n + k)$, see e.g. [19] or an earlier eprint version of [18] (as available from the author's homepage), though there might be earlier works. We are currently working on a paper that shows that based on a fully-homomorphic cryptosystem, one can construct a CPIR protocol with communication complexity $\Theta(\log n + k)$ (note that all trivial approaches result in communication complexity $\Theta(k \cdot \log n)$, since Gentry's cryptosystem makes it only possible to encrypt Boolean values) and sublinear computation. Nevertheless, it is important to achieve sublinear computation under a well-known assumption, as done in the current paper.

Acknowledgments. The author was supported by Estonian Science Foundation, grant #8058, European Union through the European Regional Development Fund and the 6th Framework Programme project AEOLUS (FP6-IST-15964).

References

1. Agrawal, R., Srikant, R.: Privacy-Preserving Data Mining. In: Proceedings of the 2000 ACM SIGMOD Conference on Management of Data, Dallas, TX, USA, May 2000, pp. 439–450 (2000)
2. Aguilar-Melchor, C., Gaborit, P.: A Lattice-Based Computationally-Efficient Private Information Retrieval Protocol. In: Lucks, S., Sadeghi, A.-R., Wolf, C. (eds.) WEWORC 2007. LNCS, vol. 4945, pp. 50–54. Springer, Heidelberg (2008), http://eprint.iacr.org/2007/446
3. Beimel, A., Ishai, Y., Malkin, T.: Reducing the Servers Computation in Private Information Retrieval: PIR with Preprocessing. In: Bellare, M. (ed.) CRYPTO 2000. LNCS, vol. 1880, pp. 55–73. Springer, Heidelberg (2000)
4. Breitbart, Y., Hunt III, H.B., Rosenkrantz, D.J.: On The Size of Binary Decision Diagrams Representing Boolean Functions. Theoretical Computer Science 145(1&2), 45–69 (1995)
5. Canetti, R., Ishai, Y., Kumar, R., Reiter, M.K., Rubinfeld, R., Wright, R.N.: Selective Private Function Evaluation with Applications to Private Statistics. In: PODC 2001, Rhode Island, USA, August 26–29, pp. 293–304. ACM Press, Newport (2001)
6. Carbunar, B., Sion, R.: On the Computational Practicality of Private Information Retrieval. In: NDSS 2007, San Diego, California, USA, February 27–March 2 (2007)
7. Damgård, I., Jurik, M.: A Generalisation, a Simplification and Some Applications of Paillier's Probabilistic Public-Key System. In: Kim, K.-c. (ed.) PKC 2001. LNCS, vol. 1992, pp. 119–136. Springer, Heidelberg (2001)
8. Damgård, I., Jurik, M.: A Length-Flexible Threshold Cryptosystem with Applications. In: Safavi-Naini, R., Seberry, J. (eds.) ACISP 2003. LNCS, vol. 2727, pp. 350–364. Springer, Heidelberg (2003)
9. Fujita, M., McGeer, P.C., Yang, J.C.Y.: Multi-Terminal Binary Decision Diagrams: An Efficient Data Structure for Matrix Representation. Formal Methods in System Design 10(2/3), 149–169 (1997)

10. Gasarch, W., Yerukhimovich, A.: Computationally Inexpensive cPIR (2007), Work in progress (January 2009), http://www.cs.umd.edu/~arkady/
11. Gentry, C.: Fully Homomorphic Encryption Using Ideal Lattices. In: Mitzenmacher, M. (ed.) STOC 2009, May 31–Jun 2, 2009, pp. 169–178. ACM Press, Bethesda (2009)
12. Gentry, C., Ramzan, Z.: Single-Database Private Information Retrieval with Constant Communication Rate. In: Caires, L., Italiano, G.F., Monteiro, L., Palamidessi, C., Yung, M. (eds.) ICALP 2005. LNCS, vol. 3580, pp. 803–815. Springer, Heidelberg (2005)
13. Heap, M.A., Mercer, M.R.: Least Upper Bounds on OBDD Sizes. IEEE Transactions on Computers 43(6), 764–767 (1994)
14. Ishai, Y., Paskin, A.: Evaluating Branching Programs on Encrypted Data. In: Vadhan, S.P. (ed.) TCC 2007. LNCS, vol. 4392, pp. 575–594. Springer, Heidelberg (2007)
15. Kushilevitz, E., Ostrovsky, R.: Replication is Not Needed: Single Database, Computationally-Private Information Retrieval. In: FOCS 1997, October 20–22, pp. 364–373. IEEE Computer Society, Los Alamitos (1997)
16. Laur, S., Lipmaa, H.: A New Protocol for Conditional Disclosure of Secrets And Its Applications. In: Katz, J., Yung, M. (eds.) ACNS 2007. LNCS, vol. 4521, pp. 207–225. Springer, Heidelberg (2007)
17. Liaw, H.T., Lin, C.S.: On the OBDD-Representation of General Boolean Functions. IEEE Transactions on Computers 41(6), 661–664 (1992)
18. Lipmaa, H.: An Oblivious Transfer Protocol with Log-Squared Communication. In: Zhou, J., López, J., Deng, R.H., Bao, F. (eds.) ISC 2005. LNCS, vol. 3650, pp. 314–328. Springer, Heidelberg (2005)
19. Lipmaa, H.: New Communication-Efficient Oblivious Transfer Protocols Based on Pairings. In: Wu, T.-C., Lei, C.-L., Rijmen, V., Lee, D.-T. (eds.) ISC 2008. LNCS, vol. 5222, pp. 441–454. Springer, Heidelberg (2008)
20. Lipmaa, H.: Private Branching Programs: On Communication-Efficient Cryptocomputing. Tech. Rep. 2008/107, International Association for Cryptologic Research (2008), http://eprint.iacr.org/2008/107
21. Naor, M., Pinkas, B.: Oblivious Transfer And Polynomial Evaluation. In: STOC 1999, May 1-4, 1999, pp. 245–254. ACM Press, Atlanta (1999)
22. Paillier, P.: Public-Key Cryptosystems Based on Composite Degree Residuosity Classes. In: Stern, J. (ed.) EUROCRYPT 1999. LNCS, vol. 1592, pp. 223–238. Springer, Heidelberg (1999)
23. Stern, J.P.: A New And Efficient All Or Nothing Disclosure of Secrets Protocol. In: Ohta, K., Pei, D. (eds.) ASIACRYPT 1998. LNCS, vol. 1514, pp. 357–371. Springer, Heidelberg (1998)
24. Wegener, I.: Branching Programs and Binary Decision Diagrams: Theory and Applications. Monographs on Discrete Mathematics and Applications, Society for Industrial Mathematics (2000)

Efficient Fuzzy Matching and Intersection on Private Datasets

Qingsong Ye[1], Ron Steinfeld[1], Josef Pieprzyk[1], and Huaxiong Wang[1,2]

[1] Centre for Advanced Computing – Algorithms and Cryptography
Department of Computing, Macquarie University, NSW 2109, Australia
{qingsong,rons,josef}@ics.mq.edu.au
[2] Division of Mathematical Sciences
School of Physical and Mathematical Sciences
Nanyang Technological University, Singapore
hxwang@ntu.edu.sg

Abstract. At Eurocrypt'04, Freedman, Nissim and Pinkas introduced a fuzzy private matching problem. The problem is defined as follows. Given two parties, each of them having a set of vectors where each vector has T integer components, the fuzzy private matching is to securely test if each vector of one set matches any vector of another set for at least t components where $t < T$. In the conclusion of their paper, they asked whether it was possible to design a fuzzy private matching protocol without incurring a communication complexity with the factor $\binom{T}{t}$. We answer their question in the affirmative by presenting a protocol based on homomorphic encryption, combined with the novel notion of a *share-hiding error-correcting secret sharing scheme*, which we show how to implement with efficient decoding using interleaved Reed-Solomon codes. This scheme may be of independent interest. Our protocol is provably secure against passive adversaries, and has better efficiency than previous protocols for certain parameter values.

Keywords: Private matching, private set intersection, fuzzy private matching, homomorphic encryption, error correction, secret sharing.

1 Introduction

In Eurocrypt'04, Freedman, Nissim and Pinkas (FNP) [4] introduced the private fuzzy matching problem. The problem is defined for two parties. Each party holds a set of vectors, where each vector has its length equal to T. The number of vectors in the two sets are m and n, respectively. The fuzzy private matching of the two sets computes the intersection of two sets by considering a match if any pair of vectors from both sets has at least t out of T common components ($t < T$). The computation must preserve the privacy of the sets, i.e. the other party learns no more than the result of the operation.

This error-tolerance property is useful in many applications. For example, database entries are not always accurate or full (e.g. due to errors, omissions, or inconsistent spellings), for example, in the case of biometric pattern matching. Due to the human error and error-prone biometric systems, it would be useful to have an algorithm still reporting a match if two datasets are similar within a threshold.

D. Lee and S. Hong (Eds.): ICISC 2009, LNCS 5984, pp. 211–228, 2010.

In [4], Freedman, Nissim and Pinkas gave a simple 2-out-of-3 fuzzy private matching protocol. However, this protocol is not efficient as it requires $O\left(m\binom{T}{t}\right)$ communication complexity and $O\left(mn\binom{T}{t}\right)$ computation complexity. As an open problem, they posed the question of how to construct the private fuzzy matching without incurring a communication complexity with the exponential $\binom{T}{t}$ factor.

Recently, Chmielewski and Hoepman [3] proposed two fuzzy matching protocols with polynomial communication complexity, but at the expense of an exponential $\binom{T}{t}$ factor in the *computation* complexity. We show how to further improve one of these protocols (to be called CH1), making *both* communication and computation polynomial in T. We also show that the second protocol in [3], to be called CH2 (which is claimed to have even better communication complexity) is insecure.

Our solution is based on polynomial encoding and a *share-hiding random error-correcting threshold secret sharing scheme* based on interleaved Reed-Solomon codes.

We first explain the notion of an error-correcting secret sharing scheme. In an ordinary t-of-T secret sharing scheme, the secret can be efficiently recovered from any t shares. However, if one is given a 'noisy' vector of T shares, out of which only t shares are correct and the rest are random values, one may have to try all $\binom{T}{t}$ subsets of t shares until the correct subset is found and the secret is recovered (assuming that the correct secret can be identified). The idea of an error-correcting threshold t-of-T secret sharing scheme is to add additional redundancy to the shares of the secret, such that the correct secret can be efficiently recovered (in time polynomial in T) even in the 'noisy' setting above, where an unknown subset of t of T given shares are correct and the rest are random. At the same time, we also require a *share hiding* privacy property: when there are $< t$ correct shares the above 'noisy' vector of T shares gives no information on the position of the correct shares. This problem naturally leads to consider error correcting codes to perform this decoding. As we explain, although the Shamir t-of-T secret sharing scheme can also be viewed as a Reed Solomon error correcting code, it does *not* quite achieve the goal (since it requires at least $\sqrt{Tt}$ correct shares for efficient decoding, which may be much larger than t). We show how to modify the Shamir scheme into an error-correcting secret sharing scheme by using the concept of interleaved Reed Solomon codes.

Given our share hiding error-correcting secret sharing scheme, the idea of our protocol (based on the CH1 protocol) is to let one party, Alice, send to the other party Bob encryptions of her database elements using a homomorphic encryption scheme. Using the homomorphic property, Bob can compute the ciphertext of the *difference vector* between each pair of Alice's and Bob's database words. Bob then homomorphically adds this difference vector to the shares vector of an encryption key, created using the error-correcting secret sharing scheme, and sends the resulting ciphertexts to Alice. As a result, Alice's decryption consists of share vectors having correct shares of Bob's key in the positions where Alice's word matched Bob's word, and, if there are at least t matches, Alice can use the error-correcting property to recover Bob's key (which is then used by Alice to decrypt a ciphertext of Bob's matching word). In order to hide the non-matching elements of Bob, we utilize the randomization technique used in the original FNP private matching protocol (if the element of the Alice dataset is different from the element of the Bob dataset, then this element will be multiplied by a random number). Moreover the share hiding property also hides the location of the matching elements when there are less than t matches. We remark that the original CH1 protocol in [3] did not make use of an error correcting secret sharing scheme, which forced an exponential search by Alice in decoding.

We prove the security of our protocol against passive attacks and explain its efficiency advantages relative to previous protocols.

1.1   Private Matching and Set Intersection in FNP

We briefly review the (not fuzzy) private matching and set intersection in [4], since it is the basis and the extension of the private fuzzy matching discussed in the same paper.

Polynomial Representation of Datasets and Private Matching. Let $(\mathcal{K}, \mathcal{E}, \mathcal{D})$ be a semantically-secure public-key cryptosystem with additive homomorphic properties, such as Paillier's [9]. Recall that, given $\mathcal{E}(a)$, $\mathcal{E}(b)$ and a constant c, one can compute $\mathcal{E}(a + b) = \mathcal{E}(a) \odot \mathcal{E}(b)$ and $\mathcal{E}(a \cdot c) = \mathcal{E}(a)^c$.

There are two parties in the protocol, namely, Alice and Bob. Bob owns a value b, while Alice possesses a dataset $A' = \{a_1, \ldots, a_m\}$ and wants to test if $b \in A'$ or not. Alice does not want to reveal A to Bob, and Bob is unwilling to disclose b to Alice.

The protocol runs as follows.

- Alice first presents her dataset A' in the form of a polynomial

$$\mathcal{P}(y) = \prod_{a_i \in A'} (y - a_i) = \sum_{i=0}^{m} \alpha_i y^i, \text{ where } \alpha_m = 1$$

- Applied in the homomorphic encryption. Alice encrypts her polynomial $\mathcal{P}$ with her public-key. Note that the encrypted polynomial $\mathcal{E}(\mathcal{P})$ contains the encryptions of all coefficients α_i except α_m. Next she sends $\mathcal{E}(\mathcal{P})$ to Bob.
- Using the homomorphic properties, Bob evaluates the polynomial for his input b according to the following formula

$$\mathcal{E}(\mathcal{P}(b)) = \mathcal{E}(\alpha_0) \odot \mathcal{E}(\alpha_1)^b \odot \mathcal{E}(\alpha_2)^{b^2} \odot \ldots \odot \mathcal{E}(\alpha_{m-1})^{b^{m-1}} \odot \mathcal{E}(1)^{b^m},$$

and sends the result $\mathcal{E}(\gamma \mathcal{P}(b) + b)$ to Alice, where γ is a random non-zero integer. Note that $b \in A'$ if and only if $\mathcal{P}(b) = 0$.
- When Alice receives the cryptogram, she decrypts it and checks if the decrypted message belongs to the set A'. If it does she knows the value b, otherwise she knows a random value.

Private Computation of Set Intersection. Suppose Alice and Bob, each has a dataset $A' = \{a_1, \ldots, a_m\}$ and $B' = \{b_1, \ldots, b_n\}$ respectively, where the set cardinalities m and n are publicly known. Alice wishes to learn the intersection of two sets $A \cap B$. To compute the set intersection, we simply run the above private matching protocol m times in parallel for each of $b_j \in B$. In the end, Alice decrypts all the cryptograms and checks if each one is in A, and then establishes $A \cap B$.

1.2 Related Work on Fuzzy Private Matching

A simple 2-out-of-3 fuzzy matching protocol is given in [4]. We are going to call it the FNP protocol. Although it is flawed (for a detailed analysis refer to [3]), the approach seems to be sound. Alice has m 3-tuples $A_1, \ldots, A_m$, where $A_i = (a_{i1}, a_{i2}, a_{i3})$ for $i = 1, \ldots, m$. Let P_1, P_2, P_3 be polynomials, such that P_ℓ is used to encode the ℓ-th elements $(a_{1\ell}, \ldots, a_{m\ell})$ of the 3-tuples. For each $i = 1, \ldots, m$, Alice chooses a random value $\gamma_i = P_1(a_{i1}) = P_2(a_{i2}) = P_3(a_{i3})$. Note that for each polynomial P_ℓ; $\ell = 1, 2, 3$, there are m equations so the degree of the polynomials P_ℓ is at most $m - 1$.

Next Alice sends $(\mathcal{E}(P_1), \mathcal{E}(P_2), \mathcal{E}(P_3))$ to Bob in the form of encrypted coefficients as in Section 1.1.

For every 3-tuple B_j in his dataset of size n, Bob responds to Alice in a manner similar to the protocol in Section 1.1. He computes the encrypted values $\mathcal{E}(r \cdot (P_1(b_{j1}) - P_2(b_{j2})) + B_j)$, $\mathcal{E}(r' \cdot (P_2(b_{j2}) - P_3(b_{j3})) + B_j)$ and $\mathcal{E}(r'' \cdot (P_1(b_{j1}) - P_3(b_{j3})) + B_j)$ by encoding B_j as $b_{j1}||b_{j2}||b_{j3}$, where r, r' and r'' are random values. If two elements in A_i are the same as those in B_j, Alice obtains B_j in one of the entries after decrypting received ciphertexts.

The generalization of this approach for matching t our of T positions is possible but the resulting protocol is not going to be efficient. Clearly, for each B_j; $j = 1, \ldots, n$, Alice has to check all the combinations $\binom{T}{t}$ so both communication and computation complexities of the protocol have the factor $\binom{T}{t}$.

Chmielewski and Hoepman [3] extend the FNP protocol and propose two modified protocols that we call CH1 and CH2, both avoiding the $\binom{T}{t}$ factor in the communication complexity, but at the expense of a $\binom{T}{t}$ factor in computation. The protocol CH1 has quadratic complexity, while CH2 has linear complexity. Unfortunately, the protocol CH2 is insecure, as we explain below. Our work shows how to improve CH1 by further removing the $\binom{T}{t}$ factor from the computation. Both protocols CH1 and CH2, are achieved by combining secret sharing [12] and homomorphic encryption. The idea of the CH1 protocol (which forms the basis for our protocol) was already explained in the Introduction. Here we explain the CH2 protocol and why it is insecure.

CH2 Protocol. For each secret vector $B_j \in B$, Bob constructs t-out-of-T secret sharing that defines a collection of shares $(s_{j1}, \ldots, s_{jT})$. Note that, B_j is encoded as $b_{j1}||b_{j2}|| \ldots ||b_{jT}$ for a convenience. If $b_{j\ell} = b_{j'\ell}$, then $s_{j\ell} = s_{j'\ell}$ where $j \neq j'$. Bob also constructs T polynomials of degree n, $P_1, \ldots, P_T$ such that

$$((P_\ell(b_{1\ell}) = s_{1\ell}) \text{ and } (P_\ell(b_{2\ell}) = s_{2\ell}) \text{ and }, \ldots, \text{ and } (P_\ell(b_{n\ell}) = s_{n\ell})).$$

Bob sends all $\mathcal{E}(P_\ell)$ to Alice for $\ell = 1, \ldots, T$.

For $i = 1, \ldots, m$ and $\ell = 1, \ldots, T$, Alice computes $\mathcal{E}(P_\ell(a_{i\ell}))$ using homomorphic properties. Note that $P_\ell(a_{i\ell}) = s_{j\ell}$ if $a_{i\ell} = b_{j\ell}$. To hide the information about $a_{i\ell}$, Alice random selects a integer $r_{i\ell}$ and sends $\mathcal{E}(P_\ell(a_{i\ell}) + r_{i\ell})$ to Bob for $i \in \{1, \ldots, m\}$.

Assume that Bob does not want to reveal any information about $s_{j\ell}$. Bob decrypts $\mathcal{E}(P_\ell(a_{i\ell}) + r_{i\ell})$, and prepares t-out-of-T shares $(\hat{s}_{i1}, \ldots, \hat{s}_{iT})$ of a value 0 for $i = 1, \ldots, m$. Bob sends $P_\ell(a_{i\ell}) + r_{i\ell} + \hat{s}_{i\ell}$ to Alice. Note that $P_\ell(a_{i\ell}) + r_{i\ell} + \hat{s}_{i\ell} = s_{j\ell} + r_{i\ell} + \hat{s}_{i\ell}$ if $a_{i\ell} = b_{j\ell}$ for some j.

After receiving all the values from Bob, Alice computes $v_{i\ell} = (P_\ell(a_{i\ell}) + r_{i\ell} + \hat{s}_{i\ell}) - r_{i\ell}$ for all i and ℓ. For each $i = 1, \ldots, m$, Alice tries to computes A_i' from all $\binom{T}{t}$

combinations of $(v_{i1}, \ldots, v_{iT})$ by using t-out-of-T secret sharing scheme. If $A_i' \in_f A$, then Alice adds A_i' to her output set.

Attack on CH2 Protocol. We show that CH2 is insecure. Suppose that A_1 and A_2 are two words in Alice's dataset and B_1, B_2, B_3 are three words in Bob's dataset. Suppose that A_1 matches B_1 on $t-1$ letters in positions $1, \ldots, (t-1)$, matches B_2 on $t-1$ letters in positions $t, \ldots, 2t-2$, and matches B_3 on $t-1$ letters in positions $2t-1, \ldots, 3t-3$. Suppose further that A_2 matches B_2 on $t-1$ letters in positions $1, \ldots, (t-1)$, matches B_3 on $t-1$ letters in positions $t, \ldots, 2t-2$, and matches B_1 on $t-1$ letters in positions $2t-1, \ldots, 3t-3$.

The above condition implies that the shares $v_{i\ell}$ obtained by Alice in CH2, are related to Bob's shares $s_{j\ell}$ and $\hat{s}_{j\ell}$ as follows: $v_{1\ell} = s_{1\ell} + \hat{s}_{1\ell}$ for $\ell = 1, \ldots, t-1$, $v_{1\ell} = s_{2\ell} + \hat{s}_{1\ell}$ for $\ell = t, \ldots, 2t-2$, $v_{1\ell} = s_{3\ell} + \hat{s}_{1\ell}$ for $\ell = 2t-1, \ldots, 3t-3$, $v_{2\ell} = s_{2\ell} + \hat{s}_{2\ell}$ for $\ell = 1, \ldots, t-1$, $v_{2\ell} = s_{3\ell} + \hat{s}_{2\ell}$ for $\ell = t, \ldots, 2t-2$, $v_{2\ell} = s_{1\ell} + \hat{s}_{2\ell}$ for $\ell = 2t-1, \ldots, 3t-3$. Assume we are using t-of-T Shamir sharing for the 5 secret sharing vectors $\{s_{j\ell}\}_\ell, \{\hat{s}_{i\ell}\}_\ell$ for $j \in \{1,2,3\}$ and $i \in \{1,2\}$. Each sharing has a polynomial of degree $\leq t-1$ associated with it, so we have $5t$ random variables (coefficients) involved. On the other hand, the above relations give us overall $6(t-1)$ known linear equations in these random variables. For sufficiently large t, we have $6(t-1) > 5t$, which means we can find a linear dependency among the equations. The corresponding non-trivial linear combination of the $v_{i\ell}$'s will be zero, and this can be detected by Alice. On the other hand, for example, if the A_1 and A_2 don't match the $B_1, \ldots B_3$ in any position, the $v_{i\ell}$'s will be independent and uniformly random, so the tested non-trivial linear combination of them will be zero with negligible probability $1/p$. Hence the attack allows Alice to tell when the prescribed condition holds, which is a privacy leak (since the condition involves only $t-1 < t$ matches between any A_i and B_j).

2 Preliminaries

2.1 Additively Homomorphic Encryption

We will utilize an additive homomorphic public key cryptosystem, such as Paillier [9]. Following Adida and Wikstrom [1], we use the following definition.

Definition 1 ([1]). *A cryptosystem* $(\mathcal{K}, \mathcal{E}, \mathcal{D})$ *defined by the key generator, encryption and decryption algorithms, respectively, is said to be homomorphic if for every key pair* $(pk, sk) \in \mathcal{K}(1^l)$, *the following conditions hold.*

1. *The message space* $\mathcal{M}$ *is a subset of an additive abelian group* $\mathcal{G}(\mathcal{M})$.
2. *The randomizer space* $\mathcal{R}$ *is an additive abelian group.*
3. *The ciphertext space is an multiplicative abelian group.*
4. *Given a public key* pk, *the group operations can be computed in polynomial time. For every* $m, m' \in \mathcal{M}$ *and* $r, r' \in \mathcal{R}$, *the following relation holds*

$$\mathcal{E}(m, r) \odot \mathcal{E}(m', r') = \mathcal{E}(m + m', r + r').$$

5. *The cryptosystem is said to be additive if the message space* $\mathcal{M}$ *is the additive modular group* $\mathbb{Z}_n$ *for some integer* $n > 1$.

When such operations are performed, we require that the resulting ciphertexts be re-randomized for security reasons. During such a process, the ciphertext e of the plaintext m is transformed into e' such that e' is still a valid cryptogram for the same message m but created with a different random string.

For simplicity, we use $\mathcal{E}(m)$ to represent $\mathcal{E}(r, m)$ in the rest of the presentation as we assume that there is always a corresponding random string r.

2.2 Definitions

We use the usual asymptotic notation O, o, Ω, ω. We say that a function $f(s)$ is *negligible*, denoted $f(s) = \text{neg}(s)$, if $f(s) = 1/s^{\omega(1)}$. For two probability distributions D_1, D_2 parameterized by a security parameter s, we say that D_1 and D_2 are *computationally indistinguishable*, denoted $D_1 =_c D_2$, if any distinguisher A with run-time $O(\text{poly}(s))$ has negligible distinguishing advantage $|\Pr_{x \leftarrow D_1}[A(x) = 1] - \Pr_{x \leftarrow D_2}[A(x) = 1]| = \text{neg}(s)$. We say that D_1 and D_2 are *statistically indistinguishable*, denoted $D_1 =_s D_2$, if any distinguisher A with unbounded run-time has negligible distinguishing advantage.

Throughout this chapter, the computations are carried out over an arbitrary finite field $\mathcal{F}$. There are two parties Alice $\mathcal{I}_C$ and Bob $\mathcal{I}_S$. Let $A = \{A_1, \ldots, A_m\}$ and $B = \{B_1, \ldots, B_n\}$ be Alice's and Bob's datasets respectively. We call the dataset elements *words*, and assume that each word consists of an ordered list of T *letters* from $\mathcal{F}$, i.e. $A_i = (a_{i1}, \ldots, a_{iT}) \in \mathcal{F}^T$, $B_j = (b_{j1}, \ldots, b_{jT}) \in \mathcal{F}^T$.

Definition 2. *Given two words A_i and B_j defined as above and integer $t \leq T$, we say that A_i and B_j are t-fuzzy equal, written as $A_i \approx_t B_j$, if the words A_i and B_j agree on at least t letters, i.e. if*

$$|\{\ell : a_{i\ell} = b_{j\ell}\}| \geq t.$$

Definition 3. *Given two datasets A and B as defined above and integer $t \leq T$, the t-fuzzy set intersection of datasets A and B, denoted $A \cap_t B$ is defined as*

$$A \cap_t B = \{(A_i, B_j)|A_i \in A, B_j \in B, A_i \approx_t B_j\}.$$

Now we formally define the private fuzzy matching protocol. Let client Alice $\mathcal{I}_C$ and server Bob $\mathcal{I}_S$ be two probabilistic polynomial time interactive Turing machines. The interaction of $\mathcal{I}_C$ and $\mathcal{I}_S$ yields a result to Alice $\mathcal{I}_C$ only (server Bob outputs nothing).

We use the standard definitions for passive security of two-party computation, adapted to the private fuzzy matching setting.

Definition 4. (Private Fuzzy Matching) *A protocol Π for two probabilistic polynomial time interactive Turing machines, Client $\mathcal{I}_C$ and Server $\mathcal{I}_S$, is said to be a passive-secure t-fuzzy matching protocol if it satisfies the following properties. The common input to both $\mathcal{I}_C$ and $\mathcal{I}_S$ is a security parameter s (implicit below). The private input of $\mathcal{I}_C$ is dataset A and the private input of $\mathcal{I}_S$ is dataset B.*

Completeness. *If both parties follow the protocol, then at the end of the protocol, with probability $\geq 1 - \text{neg}(s)$ (over the random coins of $\mathcal{I}_C$ and $\mathcal{I}_S$), $\mathcal{I}_C$ learns the t-fuzzy set intersection $A \cap_t B$.*

<u>Security Against Passive Attacks.</u> Let $\text{View}_{C,\Pi}(A, B)$ and $\text{View}_{S,\Pi}(A, B)$ denote the protocol view of Client and Server, respectively, after a run of protocol Π with private inputs (A, B) in which both parties follow the protocol. Then there exist simulator algorithms $\mathcal{S}_C$ and $\mathcal{S}_S$ respectively, with run-time $O(\text{poly}(s))$, that, for all A, B, can simulate the view of Client and Server, respectively, given only their own private input and output, i.e.:

$$\mathcal{S}_C(A, A \cap_t B) =_c \text{View}_{C,\Pi}(A, B) \text{ and } \mathcal{S}_S(B) =_c \text{View}_{S,\Pi}(A, B).$$

3   Share-Hiding Error-Correcting Secret Sharing from Interleaved Reed-Solomon Codes

For our protocol we introduce a primitive that we call a *Share-Hiding Error-Correcting Threshold Secret Sharing Scheme* (SHEC-TSS). In this section, we give the relevant coding background and our SHEC-TSS construction from Interleaved Reed-Solomon codes. We start by formulating abstractly the properties we require from a SHEC-TSS scheme.

Our first requirement is *random error correction*: the secret can be recovered with high probability from a 'noisy' n share vector, in which a subset I of $|I| \geq t$ shares are correct (the rest being uniformly random), even without knowing the positions of the correct shares. It can be viewed as a strengthening of the usual *correctness* requirement on a t-of-n threshold scheme, i.e. that any t shares can be used to recover the secret. The formal definition follows.

Definition 5. *Let $\delta > 0$. A t-of-n secret sharing scheme SS with share space S is called δ-random error correcting if it has the following property. Let $C = (c_1, \ldots, c_n) \in S^n$ be the share vector for some secret s using scheme SS, and let $I \subseteq [n]$ be a subset of size $|I| \geq t$. Let $D_{C,I}$ denote the the probability distribution of 'noisy share vectors' $\bar{C} = (\bar{c}_1, \ldots, \bar{c}_n)$ generated as follows: For $i \in I$, we set $\bar{c}_i = c_i$ (i.e. $\bar{C}$ agrees with C on shares with indices in I), and for $i \in [n] - I$, we choose $\bar{c}_i$ independently and uniformly at random from share space S. Then there exists an efficient (probabilistic poly-time) decoding algorithm D that, given n, t and $\bar{C}$ sampled from distribution $D_{C,I}$, returns C with probability at least $1 - \delta$ over the random choice of $\bar{c}_i$ for $i \in [n] - I$ and the random coins of D (note that D must succeed with probability $\geq 1 - \delta$ for every valid share vector C and every $I \subseteq [n]$ with $|I| \geq t$).*

Our second requirement is *share hiding*: for any fixed secret, any collection I of $|I| < t$ shares is a uniformly random $(t - 1)$-tuple of elements from the share space. It can be viewed as a strengthening of the usual *security* requirement for a t-of-n threshold scheme, i.e. that any subset of $< t$ shares gives no information on the secret. The formal definition follows.

Definition 6. *A t-of-n secret sharing scheme SS with share space S is called* share hiding *if it has the following property. Fix a secret s and let $C = (c_1, \ldots, c_n) \in S^n$ be the share vector for s generated with randomness ω. Then, for each s and subset $I \subseteq [n]$ of size $|I| < t$, the $|I|$-tuple of shares $(s_i)_{i \in I}$ is uniformly random in $S^{|I|}$ (over the choice of randomness ω).*

Remark 1. The name 'share hiding' comes from the following useful implication that is used in our protocol: let $I \subseteq [n]$ be a share subset and let $D_{C,I}$ denote the distribution of noisy n-share vectors generated as in Def. 5, in which the $|I|$ shares indexed by I are correct, and the rest chosen uniformly at random. Then the share hiding property implies that when $|I| < t$, $D_{C,I}$ is the uniform distribution of n-tuples on the share space, independent of the subset I – hence the correct share subset I is 'hidden'.

Remark 2. The share hiding requirement implies the standard perfect security for t-of-n secret sharing, but the converse is not true in general (see next remark).

Remark 3. It is easy to satisfy the random error correcting property while violating the share hiding property, e.g. share s with a standard t-of-n secret sharing scheme and define the ith share for the new scheme to be the ith share s_i for the old scheme concatanated with some redundancy information on s_i.

Finally, our third technical requirement is *sparsity*.

Definition 7. *Let $\delta > 0$. A t-of-n secret sharing scheme SS with share space S is called δ-sparse if a uniformly random n-tuple from S^n has probability at most δ to agree with a valid share vector of some secret s on $\geq t$ positions.*

We can now formally define the notion of a SHEC-TSS.

Definition 8. *A t-of-n secret sharing scheme SS is called Share-Hiding Error-Correcting (SHEC-TSS) with error δ, if it is δ-random error correcting, share hiding, and δ-sparse.*

Reed and Solomon [10] discovered the Reed-Solomon code, an important class of error-correcting code. The key idea behind a Reed-Solomon code is that the original data are encoded as a polynomial. The polynomial is then encoded by its evaluation at various points, and these values are what is actually sent. During transmission, some of these values may become corrupted. The Reed-Solomon decoding algorithm can reconstruct the original polynomial as long as sufficient values are received correctly, and hence decode the original data.

Definition 9. *Let p be a prime number and let $t \leq n \leq p$ and let $z = (z_1, \dots, z_n) \in \mathbb{Z}_p^n$ be a vector of n distinct elements in $\mathbb{Z}_p$. The Reed-Solomon code $RS_{n,t,p,z}$ over the field $\mathbb{Z}_p$ with t message symbols and n code symbols is defined as follows. Given a message vector $m = [m_0, m_2, \dots, m_{t-1}] \in \mathbb{Z}_p^t$, let $P(x)$ be the polynomial*

$$P(x) = m_{t-1}x^{t-1} + \dots + m_1 x + m_0.$$

Then the codeword $C(m) \in \mathbb{Z}_p^n$ for this message vector is the list of the first n values of the polynomial $P(x)$:

$$C(m) = [P(z_1), P(z_2), \dots, P(z_n)].$$

Since any two distinct polynomials of degree $t - 1$ agree on at most $t - 1$ points, the minimum Hamming distance between any two distinct codewords in the code $RS_{n,t,p,z}$ is $n - t + 1$. This allows deterministic unique error-correction of a noisy codeword if at most $(n-t+1)/2$ coordinates are incorrect, i.e. at least $t' = t + (n-t-1)/2$ coordinates are correct. However, in our application, we wish to be able to recover the codeword when t' is as close to t as possible, where t defines a security threshold (so that $t-1$ correct coordinates give no information on the codeword), and the incorrect coordinates are uniformly random and independent in $\mathbb{Z}_p$. The celebrated Reed-Solomon list-decoding algorithm of Guruswami-Sudan [5] gives a unique solution with high probability in our setting, when the number of correct coordinates $t' \geq \sqrt{tn}$, but this is still not sufficiently close to t for our application. To reduce t' closer to t, we use the *Interleaved Reed-Solomon Code* defined as follows.

Definition 10. *Let p be a prime number, $r \geq 1$ an integer, $t \leq n \leq p$, and let $z = (z_1, \ldots, z_n) \in \mathbb{Z}_p^n$ be a vector of n distinct elements in $\mathbb{Z}_p$. The* Interleaved Reed-Solomon code *$IRS_{n,t,p,r,z}$ over the field $\mathbb{Z}_p$ with $r \cdot t$ message symbols and $r \cdot n$ code symbols is defined as follows. Given a message vector $m = (m_1, \ldots, m_r)$ with $m_\ell = [m_{\ell,0}, \ldots, m_{\ell,t-1}] \in \mathbb{Z}_p^t$ for $\ell \in [r]$, let $P_\ell(x)$ be the polynomial*

$$P_\ell(x) = m_{\ell,t-1}x^{t-1} + \ldots + m_{\ell,0}.$$

Then the codeword $C(m) \in (\mathbb{Z}_p^r)^n$ for this message is the vector

$$C(m) = [(P_1(z_1), \ldots, P_r(z_1)), \ldots, (P_1(z_n), \ldots, P_r(z_n))].$$

For $i \in [n]$, we refer to $(P_1(z_i), \ldots, P_r(z_i)) \in \mathbb{Z}_p^r$ as the ith coordinate of the codeword $C(m)$.

Bleichenbacher, Kiayias and Yung [2] showed the following.

Theorem 1 ([2]). *Fix integer parameters $t \leq n \leq p$ with p prime and $r \geq n - t + 1$, and a vector $z = (z_1, \ldots, z_n) \in \mathbb{Z}_p^n$ with $z_i \neq z_j$ for $i \neq j$. There exists an efficient (run-time $O(\text{poly}(n, \log p))$) decoding algorithm D for code $IRS_{n,t,p,r,z}$ that, given n, t, p, r, z and a noisy codeword $Y = C + E \in (\mathbb{Z}_p^r)^n$ with $C \in IRS_{n,t,p,r,z}$ and $E \in (\mathbb{Z}_p^r)^n$ a noise vector with some subset I of $t' \geq t + 1$ coordinates fixed to 0^r and the remaining $n - t'$ coordinates chosen independently and uniformly at random in $\mathbb{Z}_p^r$, returns C with probability at least $1 - (n - t')/q$ over the choice of E and the random coins of D.*

The above algorithm works when the number of correct coordinates in Y is $t' \geq t + 1$, but not for $t' = t$: in that case it is easy to see that C cannot be uniquely decoded from Y if we allow C to be an arbitrary codeword in code $IRS_{n,t,p,r,z}$. To deal with this problem, our secret sharing scheme introduces additional redundancy by restricting C to a subset of codewords whose r polynomials all share the *same* constant coefficient (the secret), i.e. we are using a modified interleaved Reed Solomon code $IRS'_{n,t,p,r,z}$ in which the codewords satisfy $P_\ell(0) = P_1(0)$ for all $\ell \in [r]$. We also make sure that $z_i \neq 0$ for $i \in [r]$. Below, we show that a natural adaptation of the decoding algorithm from Theorem 1 to the code $IRS'_{n,t,p,r,z}$ provides a unique solution with high probability even for $t' = t$, as required.

We formalize our construction of a random-error correcting secret sharing scheme as follows.

Definition 11. *Let p be a prime number, $r \geq 1$ an integer, $t < n < p$, and let $z = (z_1, \ldots, z_n) \in \mathbb{Z}_p$ be a vector of n distinct non-zero elements in $\mathbb{Z}_p$. The t-of-n threshold secret sharing scheme $IRS'_{n,t,p,z,r}$ over the field $\mathbb{Z}_p$ with threshold t and n shares is defined as follows. Given a secret $s \in \mathbb{Z}_p$, the dealer chooses r random polynomials $P_\ell(x)$ of degree $\leq t - 1$ with $P_\ell(0) = s$ for $\ell \in [r]$. The share vector $C(s)$ for secret s is*

$$C(s) = [(P_1(z_1), \ldots, P_r(z_1)), \ldots, (P_1(z_n), \ldots, P_r(z_n))],$$

where for $i \in [n]$, the ith share is $(P_1(z_i), \ldots, P_r(z_i)) \in \mathbb{Z}_p^r$.

We now present our main result.

Theorem 2. *Let $IRS'_{n,t,p,z,r}$ be the t-of-n secret sharing scheme defined above. If $r \geq n - t + 1$, the scheme is a SHEC-TSS with error $\delta \leq n/p$.*

Proof. The share hiding property follows from the fact that the collection of $t' < t$ valid shares $c_{i,\ell}$ plus the secret s imposes $t' + 1 \leq t$ constraints of the form $P_\ell(0) = s$ and $P_\ell(z_i) = c_{i,\ell}$ for t' distinct non-zero z_i, on the degree $\leq t - 1$ polynomials P_ℓ. Since there is a unique solution for P_ℓ passing through any t given points, there are exactly $p^{t-t'-1} \geq 1$ possible choices for each polynomial P_ℓ satisfying the given constraints, regardless of the values of the $c_{i,\ell}$; the result follows by the uniformly random choice of the P_ℓ.

We now establish the δ-sparse property. Fix a subset $I \subseteq [n]$ with $|I| = t$. The probability that a uniformly random vector $Y \in (\mathbb{Z}_p^r)^n$ matches any valid share vector C of $IRS'_{n,t,p,r,z}$ on the shares with indices in I is $1/p^{r-1}$. This is because there is a unique polynomial P_1 of degree $\leq t - 1$ satisfying $P_1(z_i) = y_{i,1}$ for $i \in I$, and unique polynomials $P_2, \ldots, P_r$ of degree $\leq t - 1$ satisfying $P_\ell(0) = P_1(0)$ and $P_\ell(z_i) = c_{i,\ell}$ for $i \in I - \{i^*\}$, where i^* is one element of I. Hence, the random vector Y will match the valid codeword C also on the i^*th share if and only if $P_\ell(z_{i^*}) = c_{i^*,\ell}$ for $\ell \geq 2$, which holds with probability $1/p^{r-1}$. By taking a union bound over all subsets I of size t we conclude that δ-sparsity holds with $\delta \leq \binom{n}{t}/p^{r-1} = \binom{n}{n-t}/p^{r-1} \leq (n/p)^{n-t} \leq n/p$, using $r \geq n - t + 1$ and $\binom{n}{n-t} \leq n^{n-t}$.

Now we prove the random error-correcting property by explaining the appropriate modifications to the algorithm of Theorem 1 and its analysis in [2]. The decoding algorithm accepts as input n, t, p, z, r and a noisy share vector $Y = (y_1, \ldots, y_n)$ with $y_i = (y_{i,1}, \ldots, y_{i,r}) \in \mathbb{Z}_p^r$ for $i \in [n]$ sampled from the distribution $D_{C,I}$ as in Definition 5, where $C = (c_1, \ldots, c_n)$ is the share vector for some secret s using scheme $IRS'_{n,t,p,z,r}$, and I is a subset of $[n]$ with $|I| \geq t$. The decoding algorithm does not know $|I|$, and therefore tries to decode using a guess t' for $|I|$, until it succeeds. The algorithm works as follows.

- Repeat the following for $t' = t, t+1, \ldots, n$:
  - Randomize: Select r random polynomials $Q_1(x), \ldots, Q_r(x)$ of degree $\leq t-1$ with $Q_\ell(0) = Q_1(0) = s'$ for $\ell \in [r]$, and set $y_{i,\ell} := y_{i,\ell} + Q_\ell(z_i)$ for $i \in [n]$ and $\ell \in [r]$.

- Solve: Find a polynomial $E(x)$ of degree $\leq n - t'$ with constant term 1, and r polynomials $m_\ell(x)$ for $\ell \in [r]$ of degree $\leq n - t' + t - 1$ such that the following linear system of equations is satisfied:

$$m_\ell(z_i) = y_{i,\ell} E(z_i), m_\ell(0) = m_1(0), E(0) = 1, \text{ for } i \in [n], \ell \in [r]. \quad (1)$$

- If the solution $m_1, \ldots, m_r, E$ to (1) is unique and $m_\ell(x)$ is divisible by $E(x)$ for $\ell \in [r]$, then compute polynomials $P_\ell(x) = m_\ell(x)/E(x) - Q_\ell(x)$ for $\ell \in [r]$, and return share vector C determined by those polynomials (with $P_1(0) = m_1(0) - s'$ being the corresponding secret), and terminate.
- If no solution is found for any $t' \in \{t, \ldots, n\}$, terminate and return *failure*.

We note that the algorithm in [2] works in essentially the same way, except that it does not impose the constraints $m_\ell(0) = m_1(0)$ for $\ell \in [r]$. The run-time of each iteration of the algorithm is dominated by the Gaussian elimination procedure for solving the linear system of equations over $\mathbb{Z}_p$ of dimension $\leq r \cdot n$, which can be done in time $O((rn)^3 \log^2 p)$. Thus the overall run-time is $O(n \cdot (rn)^3 \log^2 p)$, which is polynomial in the input length, as required.

The randomization step randomizes the r solution polynomials $P_1, \ldots, P_r$ corresponding to the vector Y, i.e. after this step, we know that there exists a subset $I \subseteq [n]$ of size $|I| \geq t$ and r random polynomials $P_1', \ldots, P_r'$ of degree $\leq t - 1$ such that $y_{i,\ell} = P_\ell'(z_i)$ for $i \in I$ and $\ell \in [r]$, and $y_{i,\ell}$ uniformly random for $i \in [n] - I$ and $\ell \in [r]$, and $P_\ell'(0) = P_1'(0) = s + s'$ for $\ell \in [r]$. When $t' \leq |I|$, the polynomials P_ℓ' give rise to the following desired solution $m_1^*, \ldots, m_r^*, E^*$ to system (1):

$$E^*(x) = (-1)^{n-|I|} \prod_{i \in [n]-I} (x/z_i - 1), m_\ell^*(x) = P_\ell'(x) \cdot E^*(x), \ell \in [r].$$

However, note that when $t' < |I|$, the system (1) will not have a unique solution, so the algorithm will increment t' until it reaches $t' = |I|$ (indeed, when $t' < |I|$, one can take any subset I' of I of size $|I'| = t'$ and construct a distinct solution to (1) associated with I' by replacing I with I' in the above definition of E^*).

Our goal is to show that when $t' = |I|$, the above desired solution is indeed the unique one. We note that (1) is a linear system with $r \cdot n$ equations and $r \cdot (n - t' + t) + (n - t') - (r - 1)$ variables. A necessary condition for the system to have a unique solution is that it is not under determined; that is, the number of equations is at least equal to the number of variables. It is easy to see that if $r \geq n - t' + 1$, the system (1) is not under determined when $t' \geq t$ (whereas the system in [2] has $r - 1$ additional variables, and is not under determined only for $t' \geq t + 1$).

We now explain how to modify the argument in [2] to show that when the system (1) is not under determined, it has a unique solution with probability at least $1 - (n - t)/p$ over the random choice of the P_ℓ for $\ell \in [r]$ and $y_{i,\ell}$ for $i \in [n] - I$ and $\ell \in [r]$ - we call those the *random variables*.

The argument works in three steps as follows. Starting from the matrix A of the system (1), the first step removes some rows from A to obtain a square matrix $\hat{A}$. The second step is a rearrangement of the rows of $\hat{A}$ to give a matrix $\hat{A}^*$. The final step is to show that the determinant of $\hat{A}^*$ is a *non-zero* polynomial of degree $\leq n - t$ in the random variables, by showing that the determinant is non-zero for *some* choice of values for the random variables. It then follows by the Schwartz Lemma [11] that the determinant of $\hat{A}^*$ is non-zero (and hence the original system has a unique solution) with probability at least $1 - (n - t)/p$ over the uniform choice of the random variables.

First Step. The matrix A for our system (1) has the following form (where we arrange the variables with the $n - t' + t$ coefficients of m_1 first, followed by the $n - t' + t - 1$ non-constant coefficients of m_ℓ for $\ell = 2, \ldots, r$, and finally the non-constant coefficients of E):

$$A = \begin{bmatrix} M & 0 & 0 & \cdots & 0 & -M_1 \\ K & \bar{M} & 0 & \cdots & 0 & -M_2 \\ K & 0 & \bar{M} & \cdots & 0 & -M_3 \\ \vdots & \vdots & \vdots & \cdots & \vdots & \vdots \\ K & \cdots & \cdots & \cdots & \bar{M} & -M_r \end{bmatrix},$$

where

$$M = \begin{bmatrix} 1 & z_1 & z_1^2 & \cdots & z_1^{n-t'+t-1} \\ 1 & z_2 & z_2^2 & \cdots & z_2^{n-t'+t-1} \\ \vdots & \vdots & \cdots & \cdots & \vdots \\ 1 & z_n & z_n^2 & \cdots & z_n^{n-t'+t-1} \end{bmatrix},$$

$\bar{M}$ is the $n \times n - t' + t - 1$ submatrix of M with the first of column of M (all ones) removed, K is a $n \times (n - t' + t)$ matrix whose elements are all zero except for the leftmost column whose entries are all 1, and for $\ell \in [r]$, M_ℓ is a $n \times (n - t')$ matrix whose (i, j)th element $M_\ell[i, j]$ is related to the (i, j)th element of $\bar{M}$ as follows:

$$M_\ell[i, j] = y_{i,\ell} \cdot \bar{M}[i, j], i \in [n], j \in [n - t']. \tag{2}$$

Since the number of rows of A exceeds the number of columns by $N = r \cdot (t' - t + 1) - (n - t' + 1)$, we need to remove N rows from A to make it square. The rows of A are naturally divided into r blocks of n rows each, indexed from 1 to r from top to bottom. Similarly to [2], we remove from A the bottom $t' - t + 1 \geq 1$ rows of the last $c < r$ blocks of A (note that this makes the c diagonal block matrices in the corresponding blocks, square matrices of dimension $n - t' + t - 1$), where $c = \lfloor N/(t' - t + 1) \rfloor$. This leaves $N \bmod (t' - t + 1)$ remaining rows to remove – they are removed from the bottom of block $r - c \geq 1$. This gives the square matrix $\hat{A}$.

Second Step. In this step, we make the diagonal block matrices of the top $r - c$ blocks square (and hence all block matrices along the diagonal square, thanks to Step 1) by swapping some rows from those blocks to the bottom of the matrix. As in [2], we assume, without loss of generality, that $I = \{n - t' + 1, \ldots, n\}$, and we define the *surplus* s_ℓ of block $\ell \in [r - c]$ of $\hat{A}$ as the number of rows that should be swapped from the ℓth block to the bottom of the matrix, in order to make the the corresponding diagonal block matrix square, i.e. $s_1 = t' - t - x_1$ and $s_\ell = t' - t + 1 - x_\ell$ for $\ell \geq 2$, where x_ℓ is the number of rows removed from block ℓ in Step 1. We observe that, since matrix $\hat{A}$ is square and the number of columns of the M_ℓ matrices on the right is $n - t'$, we have $\sum_{\ell \in [r-c]} s_\ell = n - t'$. We swap rows $1, \ldots, s_1$ of block 1 to the bottom, then rows $s_1 + 1, \ldots, s_1 + s_2$ of block 2 to the bottom, and so on until rows

$\sum_{\ell < r-c} s_\ell + 1, \ldots, \sum_{\ell \leq r-c} s_\ell = n - t$ of block $r - c$. The resulting matrix $\hat{A}^*$ has the form:

$$\hat{A}^* = \begin{bmatrix} N_1 & 0 & 0 & \cdots & 0 & -M_1' \\ K & \bar{N}_2 & 0 & \cdots & 0 & -M_2' \\ K & 0 & \bar{N}_3 & \cdots & 0 & -M_3' \\ \vdots & \vdots & \vdots & \cdots & \vdots & \vdots \\ K & \cdots & \cdots & \cdots & \bar{N}_r & -M_r' \\ V_1 & V_2 & \cdots & \cdots & V_r & -\hat{M} \end{bmatrix},$$

where N_1 is a Vandermonde matrix relative to a subset of the z_i's, and for $\ell \geq 2$, N_r' is a scaled Vandermonde matrix relative to a subset of the z_i's (we recall that a Vandermonde matrix of dimension k relative to $(z_1, \ldots, z_k)$ has $(1, z_i, z_i^2, \ldots, z_i^{k-1})$ as its ith row for $i = 1, \ldots, k$. If the ith row is of the form $(z_i, z_i^2, \ldots, z_i^k)$ for $i = 1, \ldots, k$, we call the matrix a *scaled* Vandermonde matrix). Similarly, for $\ell \geq 1$, M_ℓ' is M_ℓ with some rows removed. The matrices $V_1, \ldots, V_r$ and $\hat{M}$ consist of the rows of M, $\bar{M}$, and $M_1, \ldots, M_r$ swapped to the bottom in this step.

Step 3. We show that $\det(\hat{A}^*)$ is non-zero polynomial D in the random variables of degree $n - t'$. The degree follows from the fact that only the last $n - t'$ columns of $\hat{A}^*$ depend on the random variables, and each element in those columns is linear in the random variables. To show that D is a non-zero polynomial, we show that it evaluates to a non-zero value for certain values of the random variables. Namely, we set the polynomials $P_\ell = 1$ for $\ell \in [r]$ (note that this satisfies the constraint that all P_ℓ have the same constant coefficient). This implies $y_{i,\ell} = 1$ for all $i \in \{n - t' + 1, \ldots, n\}$ (since $I = \{n - t' + t, \ldots, b\}$) and $\ell \in [r]$. We also set $y_{i,\ell} = 1$ for all rows i, ℓ which have not been moved to the bottom of the matrix in Step 2. On the other hand, we set $y_{i,\ell} = 0$ for all rows i, ℓ which have been moved to the bottom in Step 2 (note that these rows have $i \leq n - t'$ by construction, therefore the corresponding random variables $y_{i,\ell}$ can take on arbitrary values, independent of the P_ℓ's). For this setting of the random variables, we have that M_1' is equal to the submatrix of N_1 consisting of columns 2 to $n - t + 1$, and for $\ell \geq 2$, M_ℓ' is equal to the submatrix of N_ℓ consisting of the first $n - t$ columns. We also have that $\hat{M}$ is the zero matrix.

We now perform elementary row operations on $\hat{A}^*$ (with the above setting of the random variables) to zero out all elements below the square block matrices $N_1, \ldots, N_r$ along the diagonal. Since N_ℓ for $\ell \in [r]$ is a Vandermonde (or scaled Vandermonde) matrix, and the z_i's are distinct and non-zero, then N_ℓ is full rank and has non-zero determinant (it is well known that a Vandermonde matrix relative to $z_1, \ldots, z_k$ has a non-zero determinant when the z_i are distinct; the scaled Vandermonde matrix can be obtained by multiplying each row of a Vandermonde matrix by the corresponding z_i, so the scaled Vandermonde matrix has a non-zero determinant when the z_i are all *non-zero* and distinct). First, we eliminate all 1 elements in the first column of $\hat{A}^*$. Since N_1 is full rank, we can express each row $(1, 0, \ldots, 0)$ of K as a linear combination of the rows of N_1. Subtracting this linear combination of the first $n - t$ rows of $\hat{A}^*$ from the rows below, we eliminate the 1 elements in the first column of these rows. Furthermore, since M_1' consists of the submatrix of N_1 *except the first column*, this operation has no effect on the elements of M_ℓ' for $\ell \geq 2$. Next, we similarly eliminate the elements in V_1 by expressing each row of V_1 as a linear combination of the rows of N_1 and subtracting this combination of rows of $\hat{A}^*$ from the non-zero first s_1 rows of V_1. Due to the relation of M_1' and N_1 explained above and the fact that $\hat{M} = 0$, the first s_1 rows of $\hat{M}$ after this operation are the first s_1 rows of V_1 before this operation (without the first column). Similarly, we eliminate the s_ℓ non-zero rows of V_ℓ using N_ℓ for $\ell = 2, \ldots, r$. At the end, we get all zero elements below the diagonal square block matrices $N_1, \ldots, N_r$, and the matrix $\hat{M}$ has the form of a scaled Vandermonde matrix relative to a subset of the z_i's, and therefore has a non-zero determinant. It follows that $\det(\hat{A}^*)$ is the product of the non-zero determinants of the N_ℓ for $\ell \in [r]$ and $\hat{M}$, so $\det(\hat{A}^*)$ is non-zero for the above setting of the random variables, as claimed. □

4   Private Fuzzy Matching Protocol

We show how to combine our our error correcting secret sharing scheme with homomorphic encryption to get a simple protocol secure in the passive case, which has quadratic communication complexity in the size of the datasets. Our protocol is similar to a fuzzy matching protocol of [3]. However, the protocol of [3] requires computation *exponential* in the size of the datasets. In contrast, our protocol makes use of error correction techniques to improve computation complexity to be *polynomial* in the size of the datasets.

Our simple protocol is shown in Fig. 1.

Theorem 3. *The protocol Γ_1 is a passive-secure t-fuzzy matching protocol, assuming that the underlying homomorphic cryptosystem $\mathcal{E}$ and one-time symmetric cryptosystem E are semantically secure.*

Proof. We first show completeness. For each $i \in [m]$, $j \in [n]$, let $I_{ij} = \{k \in [T] : a_{ik} = b_{jk}\}$. Note that if $k \in I_{ij}$, i.e. A_i matches B_j on the kth letter, then the share $\bar{C}_{ijk}$ decrypted by Alice matches the corresponding share C_{ijk} for secret B_j created by Bob, whereas if $k \notin I_{ij}$ the share $\bar{C}_{ijk}$ is independent and uniformly random in $(\mathbb{Z}_p)^r$, thanks to the uniform independent choice of γ_{ijk}^ℓ for $\ell \in [r]$. There are two cases to consider.

The first case is that $A_i \approx_t B_j$, so that $|I_{ij}| \geq t$. In this case, $\bar{C}_{ij}$ is sampled from the noisy share vector distribution $D_{C_{ij}, I_{ij}}$ defined in Def. 5. Since $|I_{ij}| \geq t$ and $r \geq T - t + 1$, we conclude from the δ-random error correcting property of $IRS'_{T,t,p,r,z}$ that in this case, except with probability $\delta \leq (T-t)/p \leq T/p$, Alice recovers secret key $s = k_j^{sym}$ so that $\bar{B}_j = D(k_j^{sym}, \rho_j) = B_j$ and Alice correctly adds (A_i, B_j) to the output set S.

The second case is that A_i is not t-fuzzy equal to B_j so that $|I_{ij}| < t$. In this case, we claim that Alice correctly concludes that $(A_i, B_j) \notin A \cap_t B$, except with probability at most T/p. This is because, in order for Alice to make a mistake, $\bar{C}_{ij}$ would have to match *some* valid share vector $\hat{C}$ of scheme $IRS'_{T,t,p,r,z}$ on at least t shares. To bound the probability of this bad event B, we first observe that $|I_{ij}| < t$ implies, by the share-hiding property of $IRS'_{T,t,p,r,z}$, that the probability distribution of $\bar{C}_{ij}$ is uniform on $(\mathbb{Z}_p^r)^T$, independent of the secret k_j^{sym}. It follows from the δ-sparse property of $IRS'_{T,t,p,r,z}$ that event B occurs with probability $\leq \delta \leq T/p$. We conclude that, for each i, j, Alice makes a mistake with probability at most T/p, hence the overall protocol

Input: Security parameter k, Alice has a dataset $A = \{A_1, \ldots, A_m\}$ and Bob owns a dataset $B = \{B_1, \ldots, B_n\}$, where $A_i = (a_{i1}, \ldots, a_{iT}) \in \mathbb{Z}_p^T$ and $B_j = (b_{j1}, \ldots, b_{jT}) \in \mathbb{Z}_p^T$, for some prime $p \geq 2^k mnT$.

Output: Alice learns $A \cap_t B$.

  0. **Setup.** Alice and Bob agree on T distinct points $z = (z_1, \ldots, z_T) \in (\mathbb{Z}_p \setminus \{0\})^n$ and parameter $r \geq T - t + 2$ for the t-of-T secret sharing scheme $IRS'_{T,t,p,r,z}$ over $\mathbb{Z}_p$, a homomorphic public key cryptosystem $(\mathcal{K}, \mathcal{E}, \mathcal{D})$ with plaintext space $\mathbb{Z}_p$, a one-time symmetric cryptosystem (E, D) with key space K^{sym} and plaintext space $\mathbb{Z}_p^T$. All arithmetic below is defined over $\mathbb{Z}_p$.

  1. Bob
    (a) for $j \in [n]$ generates random symmetric key $k_j^{sym} \in K^{sym}$ and computes ciphertext $\rho_j = E(k_j^{sym}, B_j)$.
    (b) sends $(\rho_1, \ldots, \rho_n)$ to Alice (the B_j's are indexed in a random order).

  2. Alice
    (a) generates a homomorphic cryptosystem key pair (k_p, k_s) using $\mathcal{K}(1^l)$,
    (b) sends public key k_p and ciphertexts $c_{ik} = \mathcal{E}(a_{ik})$ to Bob for $i \in [m]$ and $k \in [T]$.

  3. Bob, for $i \in [m]$, $j \in [n]$:
    (a) computes a random share vector $C_{ij} = (C_{ij1}, \ldots, C_{ijT}) \in (\mathbb{Z}_p^r)^T$ for secret k_j^{sym} using the t-of-T secret sharing scheme $IRS'_{T,t,p,z,r}$, i.e. $C_{ijk} = (C_{ijk}^1, \ldots, C_{ijk}^r)$ with $C_{ijk}^\ell = P_{ij}^\ell(z_k) \in \mathbb{Z}_p$ and $P_{ij}^1(x), \ldots, P_{ij}^r(x)$ are random polynomials over $\mathbb{Z}_p$ of degree $\leq t - 1$ with $P_{ij}^\ell(0) = k_j^{sym}$ for $\ell \in [r]$.
    (b) using c_{ik}, and the homomorphic properties of $\mathcal{E}$, computes ciphertext $\eta_{ijk}^\ell = \mathcal{E}(\bar{C}_{ijk}^\ell)$ for $\bar{C}_{ijk}^\ell = C_{ijk}^\ell + \gamma_{ijk}^\ell \cdot (a_{ik} - b_{jk})$, where γ_{ijk}^ℓ is chosen uniformly and independently from $\mathbb{Z}_p$.
    (c) sends all η_{ijk}^ℓ's to Alice.

  4. Alice
    (a) initializes output set S to empty.
    (b) decrypts η_{ijk}^ℓ's to $\bar{C}_{ijk}^\ell = \mathcal{D}(\eta_{ijk}^\ell)$ for $i \in [m]$, $j \in [n]$, $k \in [T]$ and $\ell \in [r]$.
    (c) for $i \in [m]$ and $j \in [n]$,
      i. runs the decoding algorithm from Theorem 2 for secret sharing scheme $IRS'_{T,t,p,r,z}$ on noisy share vector $\bar{C}_{ij} = (\bar{C}_{ij1}, \ldots, \bar{C}_{ijT})$, where $\bar{C}_{ijk} = (\bar{C}_{ijk}^1, \ldots, \bar{C}_{ijk}^r) \in (\mathbb{Z}_p)^r$ for $k \in [T]$. If the decoding algorithm succeeds to recover share vector C_{ij} matching $\bar{C}_{ij}$ on $\geq t$ shares, conclude $A_i \cap_t B_j$ and add $(A_i, \bar{B}_j)$ to output set S, where $\bar{B}_j = D(s, \rho_j)$ and s is the secret corresponding to share vector C_{ij}.
      ii. otherwise, conclude $(A_i, B_j) \notin A \cap_t B$.
    (d) return $S = A \cap_t B$.

Fig. 1. Protocol Γ_1: Computation-Efficient Fuzzy Private Matching Protocol

success probability is at least $1 - mnT/p \geq 1 - 2^{-k}$ using $p \geq 2^k \cdot mnT$. This completes the completeness proof.

The security against passive attacks is shown as follows.

Bob's protocol view consists of just the public key k_p and ciphertexts c_{ik} for Alice's dataset. Accordingly, Bob's view simulator S_B simply generates a key pair (k_p, k_s) for $\mathcal{E}$ to get public key k_p, and simulates ciphertexts $c_{ik} = \mathcal{E}(0)$ (i.e. by encrypting 0 messages). By a standard hybrid argument, the semantic security of the encryption scheme $\mathcal{E}$ implies that this simulation is computationally indistinguishable from the view of Bob in the real protocol (in which $c_{ik} = \mathcal{E}(a_{ik})$).

Alice's protocol view consists of the symmetric key ciphertexts ρ_j and the public key ciphertexts η^ℓ_{ijk}. On input $(A, A \cap_t B)$, Alice's view simulator S_A works as follows. First, S_A generates random keys $k^{sym}_j \in K^{sym}$ for $j \in [n]$. Then, S_A determines from $A \cap_t B$ the number N of distinct words B_j such that $(A_i, B_j) \in A \cap_t B$ for some $i \in [m]$, and chooses a random subset V of N indices $j \in [n]$ to assign to those N words B_j. Now for each $j \in V$, S_A computes ciphertexts $\rho_j = E(k^{sym}_j, B_j)$, and C^ℓ_{ijk} for $\ell \in [r]$ and $k \in [T]$ in exactly the same way as Bob computes them in the real protocol (this is possible since Bob knows the corresponding A_is and B_js). Finally, for each $j \in [n] - V$, S_A computes $\rho_j = E(k^{sym}_j, 0)$ (where $0 \in (\mathbb{Z}^r_p)^T$) and $\eta^\ell_{ijk} = \mathcal{E}(\bar{C}^\ell_{ijk})$ for independent uniformly random $\bar{C}^\ell_{ijk} \in \mathbb{Z}_p$. To analyse this simulation, note that for (i, j) with $j \in V$ the simulation of the ρ_j and C^ℓ_{ijk} is perfect since the simulation exactly follows the protocol. For all other (i, j), we know that A_i is not fuzzy t-equal to B_j, and in this case in the real protocol, as shown in the correctness proof above, the noisy share vector $\bar{C}_{ij}$ is uniformly random in $(\mathbb{Z}^r_p)^T$, independent of the secret k^{sym}_j, perfectly matching the simulation of the η^ℓ_{ijk} for $j \in [n] - V$. Finally, a standard hybrid argument shows that the semantic security of the one-time symmetric encryption scheme E implies that the simulation of the ρ_j (as encryption of zero under a random key) for $j \in [n] - V$ is computationally indistinguishable from the real protocol (encryption of B_j under a random key). This completes the security proof. $\square$

Implementation Remarks. For simplicity, we assumed in the version of the protocol presented above that we use a homomorphic encryption scheme with plaintext space $\mathbb{Z}_p$ for p prime (the Okamoto-Uchiyama [8] cryptosystem is one such example). Our protocol can also directly work with the Paillier cryptosystem [9], in which the plaintext space is $\mathbb{Z}_N$, where $N = pq$ and p, q are distinct primes. The correctness and security analysis of our protocol naturally extend to this case, as long as the $z_i, z_i - z_j$ and $a_{i,\ell} - b_{j,\ell}$ are non-zero mod p and mod q; this can be easily ensured by restricting $z_i, a_{i,\ell}, b_{j,\ell} < \min(p, q)$ (or just relying on the hardness of factoring n). With the same assumptions on the z_i's, the proof of Theorem 2 also extends (by analysing the linear system of equations mod n separately mod p and mod q), except that unique decoding may fail with probability at most $\delta \le (n - t) \cdot (1/p + 1/q)$. This leads to the correctness condition $N/(p + q) > 2^k mnT$.

In practice, there are actually three separate parameters in our protocol which were assumed to be equal above: the size of the dataset letter space p_d, the encryption scheme plaintext space N, and the secret sharing modulus p. Our protocol correctness only requires $p > 2^k mnT$ for security parameter k, which may typically be much smaller than N for the same security parameter (e.g. for security parameter $k = 80$, $m, n < 2^{20}$ and $T < 2^{10}$ we have $2^k mnT < 2^{130}$ while $N \approx 2^{1024}$). In this case we may improve the efficiency of the protocol by taking $p \approx 2^k mnT$ much smaller than N (assuming that $p_d < p$), which reduces the complexity of error correction. To maintain security of our protocol in this case, Step 3(b) would have to be modified so that η^ℓ_{ijk} are computed as ciphertexts of $\bar{C}^\ell_{ijk} = C^\ell_{ijk} + \gamma^\ell_{ijk} \cdot (a_{ik} - b_{jk}) + w^\ell_{ijk} \cdot p$, where γ^ℓ_{ijk} is chosen uniformly and independently in $\mathbb{Z}_N$, and w^ℓ_{ijk} is chosen uniformly and independently in $\mathbb{Z}_s$ where

$s = \lfloor N/p \rfloor$. In step 4(c), the decrypted plaintexts in $\mathbb{Z}_N$ would be reduced modulo p before proceeding with the decoding in $\mathbb{Z}_p$. With this modification, for the case when A_i is not fuzzy t-equal to B_j in the simulation proof of Theorem 3, the noisy share vectors $\bar{C}_{ij}$ decrypted by Alice in Step 4 of the real protocol have coordinates uniformly random in $\mathbb{Z}_N$ for unmatching positions and coordinates uniformly random in $\mathbb{Z}_{k \cdot p}$ for matching positions. The latter are statistically indistinguishable from uniform on $\mathbb{Z}_N$ if N/p is sufficiently large (namely the statistical distance is $\leq mnTp/N$); thus ensuring that $N > 2^k mnTp$, maintains statistical security of the protocol (the simulation consists of choosing the coordinates of $\bar{C}_{ij}$ uniformly and independently at random from $\mathbb{Z}_N$). If the condition $p_d < p$ does not hold, a possible solution is to hash the letters from $\mathbb{Z}_{p_d}$ to $\mathbb{Z}_p$ using a collision-resistant hash function, and then apply the previous protocol.

Efficiency. The communication and computation complexity of our scheme are summarised in Table 1, which also includes the values for previous protocols.

Table 1. Comparison of protocol efficiency with previous protocols, with $m = n$, ℓ_{pk} and ℓ_{sym} are the ciphertext lengths of the homomorphic encryption scheme $\mathcal{E}$ and symmetric encryption E, respectively, k is the security parameter. Also, $T_{\mathcal{E}}, T_{\mathcal{D}}, T_{\mathcal{H}}, T_{\mathcal{A}}$ denote the encryption/decryption time and time for a homomorphic scalar multiplication/homomorphic addition for $\mathcal{E}$, $T'_{\mathcal{E}} = T_{\mathcal{E}} + T_{\mathcal{D}} + T_{\mathcal{H}}$, and T_{sym} denotes the encryption time for E. Only dominant terms (proportional to n^2) are shown.

Scheme	Communication	Computation
Ours	$O(n^2 T^2 \ell_{pk})$	$O(n^2(\mathrm{poly}(T) + T^2 T'_{\mathcal{E}}))$
CH1 [3]	$O(n^2 T \ell_{pk})$	$O(n^2(\binom{T}{t}\mathrm{poly}(T) + T T'_{\mathcal{E}}))$
Yao [13]	$O(n^2 T(\log p + \log T) \ell_{sym})$	$O(n^2 T T_{sym})$
IW [6]	$O(n^2 k T_{\mathcal{D}} \ell_{sym})$	$O(n^2 k(T^2 T_{\mathcal{A}} + T_{\mathcal{D}} T_{sym}))$

Compared to the CH1 protocol [3], our protocol dramatically improves computation by a factor $O(\binom{T}{t}/\mathrm{poly}(T))$ but has larger communication by a linear factor $O(T)$ (due to our use of error correcting secret sharing). We also compare our protocol to two other protocols based on the generic Yao 'garbled circuit' protocol for two-party computation. Since one can choose $\ell_{pk} \approx \log p$, we see that compared to the generic Yao protocol [13], our protocol's communication is roughly a factor $O(T/\ell_{sym})$ times that of the Yao protocol, hence we expect an improvement in the case $T = O(\ell_{sym})$. Although this may not be a huge improvement, we believe it is still a useful, simpler and more natural alternative to the Yao protocol for this application. Note that Yao's protocol is generic and applies to any Boolean ciruit; to apply it to our problem, we represent the fuzzy matching function as a boolean circuit having the n^2 database words as input. Such a circuit can be implemented with $O(n^2 T(\log p + \log T))$ 2-input gates, giving the complexity estimate in Table 1 (in practice, one could use the Fairplay compiler [7] to generate the circuit). The last row in Table 1 corresponds to the fuzzy matching protocol of Indyk and Woodruff [6]. The latter protocol has a dominant communication complexity term (the n^2 term) independent of T, but uses (as a subprotocol) the Yao protocol applied to the decryption circuit $\mathcal{D}$ of a homomorphic encryption scheme, which typically has complexity $T_{\mathcal{D}} = O(\ell_{pk}^3)$, where ℓ_{pk} is the length of the public key. Thus we expect our protocol to be more efficient in the case $T^2 = O(k \ell_{pk}^2)$.

5   Conclusion

We presented a novel share hiding random error-correcting secret sharing scheme based on interleaved Reed-Solomon codes, and showed how to apply it to construct a simple protocol for private fuzzy matching. We believe our secret sharing scheme may find further cryptographic applications in future. The size of shares in our t-of-n scheme is $O((n - t)k)$, where k is the length of the secret. An interesting open problem is to find alternative constructions with smaller shares, as this will improve our protocol's communication efficiency further.

Acknowledgements. The work of Q. Ye, R. Steinfeld and J. Pieprzyk was supported in part by Australian Research Council grant DP0987734. The work of R. Steinfeld was also supported in part by a Macquarie University Research Fellowship (MQRF). The work of H. Wang is supported in part by the Australian Research Council under ARC Discovery Project DP0665035 the Singapore National Research Foundation under Research Grant NRF-CRP2-2007-03.

References

[1] Adida, B., Wikstrom, D.: How to shuffle in public. In: Vadhan, S.P. (ed.) TCC 2007. LNCS, vol. 4392, pp. 555–574. Springer, Heidelberg (2007)

[2] Bleichenbacher, D., Kiayias, A., Yung, M.: Decoding interleaved reed-solomon codes over noisy channels. Theoretical Computer Science 379, 348–360 (2007)

[3] Chmielewski, L., Hoepman, J.-H.: Fuzzy private matching (extended abstract). In: The 3rd International Conference on Availability, Security and Reliability, pp. 327–334. IEEE CS Press, Los Alamitos (2008)

[4] Freedman, M.J., Nissim, K., Pinkas, B.: Efficient private matching and set intersection. In: Cachin, C., Camenisch, J.L. (eds.) EUROCRYPT 2004. LNCS, vol. 3027, pp. 1–19. Springer, Heidelberg (2004)

[5] Guruswami, V., Sudan, M.: Improved decoding of reed-solomon and algebraic-geometric codes. IEEE Transactions on Information Theory 45, 1757–1767 (1999)

[6] Indyk, P., Woodruff, D.: Polylogarithmic private approximations and efficient matching. In: Halevi, S., Rabin, T. (eds.) TCC 2006. LNCS, vol. 3876, pp. 245–264. Springer, Heidelberg (2006); See also ECCC, Report No. 117 (2005)

[7] Malkhi, D., Nisan, N., Pinkas, B., Sella, Y.: Fairplay – a secure two-party computation system. In: Proceedings of the 13th USENIX Security Symposium. USENIX Association (2004)

[8] Okamoto, T., Uchiyama, S.: A new public-key cryptosystem as secure as factoring. In: Nyberg, K. (ed.) EUROCRYPT 1998. LNCS, vol. 1403, pp. 308–318. Springer, Heidelberg (1998)

[9] Paillier, P.: Public-key cryptosystems based on composite degree residuosity classes. In: Stern, J. (ed.) EUROCRYPT 1999. LNCS, vol. 1592, pp. 223–238. Springer, Heidelberg (1999)

[10] Reed, I.S., Solomon, G.: Polynomial codes over certain finite fields. Journal of Society for Industrial and Applied Mathematics 8(2), 300–304 (1960)

[11] Schwartz, J.: Fast probabilistic algorithms for verification of polynomial identities. Journal of the ACM 27, 701–717 (1980)

[12] Shamir, A.: How to share a secret. Communications of the ACM 22, 612–613 (1979)

[13] Yao, A.: How to generate and exchange secrets. In: Proceedings of the 27th FOCS, pp. 162–167 (1986)

Efficient Privacy-Preserving Face Recognition

Ahmad-Reza Sadeghi, Thomas Schneider, and Immo Wehrenberg

Horst Görtz Institute for IT-Security, Ruhr-University Bochum, Germany
{ahmad.sadeghi,thomas.schneider}@trust.rub.de* , immo.wehrenberg@rub.de

Abstract. Automatic recognition of human faces is becoming increasingly popular in civilian and law enforcement applications that require reliable recognition of humans. However, the rapid improvement and widespread deployment of this technology raises strong concerns regarding the violation of individuals' privacy. A typical application scenario for privacy-preserving face recognition concerns a client who privately searches for a specific face image in the face image database of a server.

In this paper we present a privacy-preserving face recognition scheme that substantially improves over previous work in terms of communication- and computation efficiency: the most recent proposal of Erkin et al. (PETS'09) requires $\mathcal{O}(\log M)$ rounds and computationally expensive operations on homomorphically encrypted data to recognize a face in a database of M faces. Our improved scheme requires only $\mathcal{O}(1)$ rounds and has a substantially smaller online communication complexity (by a factor of 15 for each database entry) and less computation complexity.

Our solution is based on known cryptographic building blocks combining homomorphic encryption with garbled circuits. Our implementation results show the practicality of our scheme also for large databases (e.g., for $M = 1000$ we need less than 13 seconds and less than 4 MByte online communication on two 2.4GHz PCs connected via Gigabit Ethernet).

Keywords: Secure Two-Party Computation, Face Recognition, Privacy.

1 Introduction

In the last decade biometric identification and authentication have increasingly gained importance for a variety of enterprise, civilian and law enforcement applications. Examples vary from fingerprinting and iris scanning systems, to voice and face recognition systems, etc. Many governments have already rolled out electronic passports [18] and IDs [27] that contain biometric information (e.g., image, fingerprints, and iris scan) of their legitimate holders.

In particular it seems that facial recognition systems have become popular aimed to be installed in surveillance of public places [17], and access and border control at airports [8] to name some. For some of these use cases one requires online search with short response times and low amount of online communication.

Moreover, face recognition is ubiquitously used also in online photo albums such as Google Picasa and social networking platforms such as Facebook which

---

* Supported by EU FP6 project SPEED, EU FP7 project CACE and ECRYPT II.

D. Lee and S. Hong (Eds.): ICISC 2009, LNCS 5984, pp. 229–244, 2010.
© Springer-Verlag Berlin Heidelberg 2010

have become popular to share photos with family and friends. These platforms support automatic detection and tagging of faces in uploaded images.[1] Additionally, images can be tagged with the place they were taken.[2]

The widespread use of such face recognition systems, however, raises also privacy risks since biometric information can be collected and misused to profile and track individuals against their will. These issues raise the desire to construct privacy-preserving face recognition systems [12].

In this paper we concentrate on efficient privacy-preserving face recognition systems. The typical scenario here is a client-server application where the client needs to know whether a specific face image is contained in the database of a server with the following requirements: the client trusts the server to correctly perform the matching algorithm for the face recognition but without revealing any useful information to the server about the requested image as well as about the outcome of the matching algorithm. The server requires privacy of its database beyond the outcome of the matching algorithm to the client.

In the most recent proposal for privacy-preserving face recognition [12] the authors use the standard and popular Eigenface [34,33] recognition algorithm and design a protocol that performs operations on encrypted images by means of homomorphic encryption schemes, more concretely, Pailler [29,11] as well as a cryptographic protocol for comparing two Pailler-encrypted values based on the Damgård, Geisler and Krøigård [9,10] cryptosystem). They demonstrate that privacy-preserving face recognition is possible in principle and give required choices of parameter sizes to achieve a good classification rate. However, the proposed protocol requires $\mathcal{O}(\log N)$ rounds of online communication as well as computationally expensive operations on homomorphically encrypted data to recognize a face in the database of N faces. Due to these restrictions, the proposed protocol cannot be deployed in practical large-scale applications. In this paper we address this aspect and show that one can do better w.r.t. efficiency.

Basically one can identify two approaches for secure computation: the first approach is to perform the required operations on encrypted data by means of homomorphic encryption (see, e.g., [29,11]). The other approach is based on Garbled Circuit (GC) à la Yao [35,22]: the function to be computed is represented by a garbled circuit i.e., the inputs and the function are encrypted ("garbled"). Then the client obliviously obtains the keys corresponding to his inputs and decrypts the garbled function. Homomorphic Encryption requires low communication complexity but huge round and computation complexity whereas GC has low online complexity (rounds, communication and computation) but large offline communication complexity. We present a protocol for privacy-preserving face recognition based on a hybrid protocol which combines the advantages of both approaches. A protocol based on GC only is given in the full version [32].

---

[1] http://picasa.google.com/features-nametags.html; http://face.com
[2] Geotagging can be done either manually or automatically on iPhones using GPS http://www.saltpepper.net/geotag

Contribution. We give an efficient and secure privacy-preserving face recognition protocol based on the Eigenfaces recognition algorithm [34,33] and a combination of known cryptographic techniques, in particular Homomorphic Encryption and Garbled Circuits. Our protocol substantially improves over previous work [12] as it has only a constant number of $\mathcal{O}(1)$ rounds and allows to shift most of the computation and communication into a pre-computation phase. The remaining online phase is highly efficient and allows for a quick response time which is especially important in applications such as biometric access control.

Related Work. *Privacy-Preserving Face Recognition* allows a client to obliviously detect if the image of a face is contained in a database of faces held by server. We give a detailed summary of previous work on privacy-preserving face recognition [12] in §3.1. Our protocol has a substantially improved efficiency.

The related problem of *Privacy-Preserving Face Detection* [3] allows a client to detect faces on his image using a private classifier held by server without revealing the face or the classifier to the other party.

In order to preserve privacy, faces can be de-identified such that face recognition software cannot reliably recognize de-identified faces, even though many facial details are preserved as described in [28].

2 Preliminaries

In this section we summarize our conventions and setting in §2.1 and cryptographic tools used in our constructions in §2.2 (additively homomorphic encryption (HE), oblivious transfer (OT), and garbled circuits (GC) with free XOR). A summary of the face recognition algorithm using Eigenfaces is given in §2.3. Readers familiar with the prerequisites may safely skip to §3.

2.1 Parameters, Notation and Model

We denote symmetric security parameter by t and the asymmetric security parameter, i.e., bitlength of RSA moduli, by T. Recommended parameters for short-term security (until 2010) are for example $t = 80$ and $T = 1024$, whereas for long-term security $t = 128$ and $T = 3072$ are recommended [16]. The statistical correctness parameter is denoted with κ [3] and the statistical security parameter with σ. In practice, one can choose $\kappa = 40$ and $\sigma = 80$.

We work in the semi-honest model where participants are assumed to be honest-but-curious (details later in §3). Our improved protocols can be proven in this model based on existing proofs for the basic building blocks from which they are composed. We further note that efficient garbled circuits of [21] (and thus our work) requires the use of random oracles. We could also use correlation-robust hash functions [19], resulting in slightly more expensive computation of garbled circuits [31] (see below).

---

[3] The probability that the protocol computes a wrong result (e.g., caused by an overflow) is bounded by $2^{-\kappa}$.

2.2   Cryptographic Tools

Homomorphic Encryption (HE). We use a semantically secure additively homomorphic public-key encryption scheme. In an additively homomorphic cryptosystem, given encryptions $[\![a]\!]$ and $[\![b]\!]$, an encryption $[\![a+b]\!]$ can be computed as $[\![a + b]\!] = [\![a]\!][\![b]\!]$, where all operations are performed in the corresponding plaintext or ciphertext structure. From this property follows, that multiplication of an encryption $[\![a]\!]$ with a constant c can be computed efficiently as $[\![c \cdot a]\!] = [\![a]\!]^c$ (e.g., with the square-and-multiply method).

As instantiation we use the Paillier cryptosystem [29,11] which has plaintext space $\mathbb{Z}_N$ and ciphertext space $\mathbb{Z}_{N^2}^*$, where N is a T-bit RSA modulus. This scheme is semantically secure under the decisional composite residuosity assumption (DCRA). For details on the encryption and decryption function we refer to [11]. The protocol for privacy-preserving face recognition proposed in [12] additionally uses the additively homomorphic cryptosystem of Damgård, Geisler and Krøigård (DGK) which reduces the ciphertext space to $\mathbb{Z}_N^*$ [9,10].

Oblivious Transfer (OT). For our construction we use parallel 1-out-of-2 Oblivious Transfer for m bitstrings of bitlength ℓ, denoted as OT_ℓ^m. It is a two-party protocol where the server $\mathcal{S}$ inputs m pairs of ℓ-bit strings $S_i = \langle s_i^0, s_i^1 \rangle$ for $i = 1, .., m$ with $s_i^0, s_i^1 \in \{0,1\}^\ell$. Client $\mathcal{C}$ inputs m choice bits $b_i \in \{0,1\}$. At the end of the protocol, $\mathcal{C}$ learns $s_i^{b_i}$, but nothing about $s_i^{1-b_i}$ whereas $\mathcal{S}$ learns nothing about b_i. We use OT_ℓ^m as a black-box primitive in our constructions. It can be instantiated efficiently with different protocols [25,1,23,19]. It is possible to pre-compute all OTs in a setup phase while the online phase consists of 2 messages with $\Theta(2mt)$ bits. Additionally, the number of public-key operations in the setup phase can be reduced to be constant with the extensions of [19].

Garbled Circuit (GC). Yao's Garbled Circuit approach [35,22], is the most efficient method for secure evaluation of a boolean circuit C. We summarize its ideas in the following. First, server $\mathcal{S}$ creates a *garbled circuit* $\widetilde{C}$ with algorithm CreateGC: for each wire W_i of the circuit, he randomly chooses a *complementary garbled value* $\widehat{w}_i = \langle \widetilde{w}_i^0, \widetilde{w}_i^1 \rangle$ consisting of two secrets, $\widetilde{w}_i^0$ and $\widetilde{w}_i^1$, where $\widetilde{w}_i^j$ is the *garbled value* of W_i's value j. (Note: $\widetilde{w}_i^j$ does not reveal j.) Further, for each gate G_i, $\mathcal{S}$ creates and sends to client $\mathcal{C}$ a *garbled table* $\widetilde{T}_i$ with the following property: given a set of garbled values of G_i's inputs, $\widetilde{T}_i$ allows to recover the garbled value of the corresponding G_i's output, and nothing else. Then garbled values corresponding to $\mathcal{C}$'s inputs x_j are (obliviously) transferred to $\mathcal{C}$ with a parallel oblivious transfer protocol OT (see below): $\mathcal{S}$ inputs complementary garbled values $\widetilde{W}_j$ into the protocol; $\mathcal{C}$ inputs x_j and obtains $\widetilde{w}_j^{x_j}$ as outputs.

Now, $\mathcal{C}$ can evaluate the garbled circuit $\widetilde{C}$ with algorithm EvalGC to obtain the garbled output simply by evaluating the garbled circuit gate by gate, using the garbled tables $\widetilde{T}_i$. Finally, $\mathcal{C}$ determines the plain values corresponding to the obtained garbled output values using an output translation table received by $\mathcal{S}$. Correctness of GC follows from method of construction of garbled tables $\widetilde{T}_i$.

Implementation Details. For most efficient implementation of the garbled circuit we use several extensions of Yao's garbled circuit methodology as summarized in [31]: the *"free XOR"* trick of [21] allows "free" evaluation of XOR gates (no communication and negligible computation); for each non-XOR gate (e.g., AND, OR, ...) we use *garbled row reduction* [26,31] which allows to omit the first entry of the garbled tables, i.e., for each non-XOR gate with 2 inputs a garbled table of $\Theta(3t)$ bits is transferred; *point-and-permute* [24] allows fast GC evaluation, i.e., evaluation of a 2 input non-XOR gate requires in the random oracle model one invocation of a suitably chosen cryptographic hash function such as SHA-256. In the standard model, two invocations are needed [31].

Efficient Circuit Constructions. We use the following efficient circuit building blocks from [20] operating on ℓ-bit numbers: Subtraction SUB_ℓ, Comparison CMP_ℓ, and Multiplexer MUX_ℓ circuits of size ℓ non-XOR gates. Circuits can be automatically generated from a high-level description with the compiler of [30].

2.3   Face Recognition Using Eigenfaces

A well-known algorithms for face recognition is the so-called *Eigenfaces* algorithm introduced in [34,33]. This algorithm achieves reasonable classification rates of approximately 96% [12] and is simple enough to be implemented as privacy-preserving protocol (cf. §3). The Eigenfaces algorithm transforms face images into their characteristic feature vectors in a low-dimensional vector space (face space), whose basis consists of *Eigenfaces*. The Eigenfaces are determined through Principal Component Analysis (PCA) from a set of training images; every face is represented as a vector in the face space by projecting the face image onto the subspace spanned by the Eigenfaces. Recognition is done by first projecting the face image into the face space and afterwards locating the closest feature vector. For details on the enrollment process we refer to [12] and original papers on Eigenfaces [34,33]. In the following we briefly summarize the recognition process of the Eigenfaces algorithm. A pseudocode description and the naming conventions and sizes of parameters are given in Appendix §A.

Inputs and Outputs: The algorithm obtains as input the query face image Γ represented as a pixel image with N pixels. Additionally, the algorithm obtains the parameters determined in the enrollment phase as inputs: the average face Ψ which is the mean of all training images, the Eigenfaces $u_1, .., u_K$ which span the K-dimensional face space, the projected faces $\Omega_1, .., \Omega_M$ being the projections of the M faces in the database into the face space, and the threshold value τ. The output r of the recognition algorithm is the index of that face in the database which is closest to the query face Γ or the special symbol $\bot$ if no match was found, i.e., all faces have a larger distance than the threshold τ.

Recognition Algorithm: The recognition algorithm consists of three phases:

1. Projection: First, the average face Ψ is subtracted from the face Γ and the result is projected into the K-dimensional face space using the Eigenfaces $u_1, .., u_K$. The result is the projected K-dimensional face $\bar{\Omega}$.

2. **Distance:** Now, the square of the Euclidean distance D_i between the projected K-dimensional face $\bar{\Omega}$ and all projected K-dimensional faces in the database Ω_i, $i = 1, .., M$, is computed.
3. **Minimum:** Finally, the minimum distance D_{min} is selected. If D_{min} is smaller than threshold τ, the index of the minimum value, i.e., the identifier i_{min} of the match found, is returned to $\mathcal{C}$ as result $r = i_{min}$. Otherwise, the image was not found and the special symbol $r = \bot$ is returned.

3   Privacy-Preserving Face Recognition

Privacy-Preserving Face Recognition allows a client to obliviously detect if the image of a face is contained in a database of faces held by a server. This can be achieved by securely evaluating a face recognition algorithm within a cryptographic protocol. In the following we concentrate on the Eigenface algorithm described in §2.3 which was also used in [12]. Our techniques can be extended to implement different recognition algorithms as discussed in the full version [32].

3.1   Privacy-Preserving Face Recognition Using Eigenfaces

The inputs and outputs of the Eigenfaces algorithm are distributed between client $\mathcal{C}$ and server $\mathcal{S}$ as shown in Fig. 1(a). Both parties want to hide their inputs from the other party during the protocol run, i.e., $\mathcal{C}$ does not want to reveal for which face she is searching while $\mathcal{S}$ does not want to reveal the faces in his database or the details of the applied transformation into the face space (including Eigenfaces which might reveal critical information about faces in DB).

In the semi-honest model we are working in, parties are assumed to follow the protocol but try to learn additional information from the protocol trace beyond what can be derived from the inputs and outputs of the algorithm when used as a black-box. In particular this requires that all internal results of the Eigenfaces algorithm, including the values passed between the different phases $\bar{\Omega}$ and $D_1, .., D_M$, are "hidden" from both parties. For practical applications it is sufficient to assume that both parties are computationally bounded, i.e., no polynomial-time adversary can derive information from "hidden" values.

For implementing the privacy-preserving Eigenfaces algorithm and "hiding" the intermediate values, different techniques can be used as listed in Fig. 1(b).

To the best of our knowledge, the only previous work on privacy-preserving face recognition [12] uses homomorphic encryption (HE) to implement the Eigenfaces algorithm in a privacy-preserving way, i.e., computations are performed on homomorphically encrypted data and the intermediate values are homomorphically encrypted (denoted as $[\![\cdot]\!]$). We summarize this protocol in §3.2.

Our Hybrid protocol presented in §4.1 substantially improves the efficiency of this protocol by implementing the Projection and Distance phase using homomorphic encryption and the Minimum phase with a garbled circuit. An alternative protocol which is entirely based on garbled circuits and hides intermediate values as garbled values (denoted as $\tilde{\cdot}$) is presented in the full version [32]. Our improvements over previous work are summarized in §5.

Client $\mathcal{C}$ Server $\mathcal{S}$

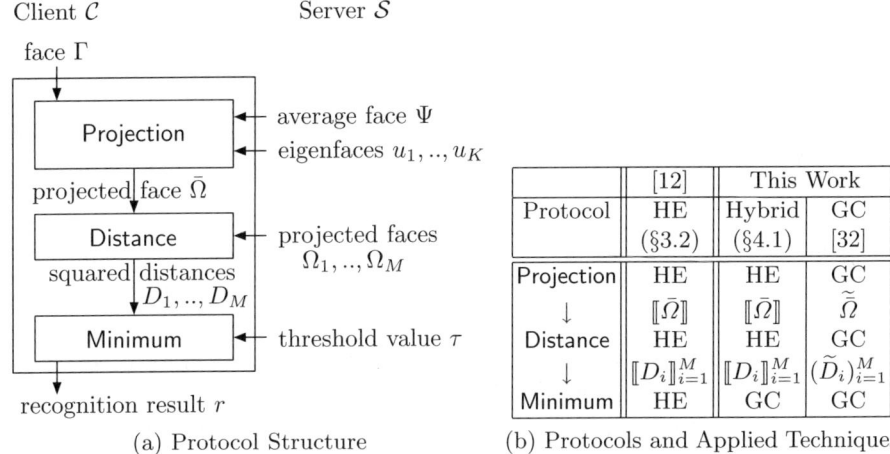

(a) Protocol Structure   (b) Protocols and Applied Techniques

Fig. 1. Privacy-Preserving Face Recognition using Eigenfaces

3.2   Previous Work: Privacy-Preserving Face Recognition Using HE

In [12], the authors describe describe a protocol for privacy-preserving face recognition which implements the Eigenfaces recognition algorithm of §2.3 on homomorphically encrypted data. Their protocol is secure in the semi-honest model, i.e., players are honest-but-curious [12, Appendix A].

Projection. First, $\mathcal{C}$ and $\mathcal{S}$ jointly compute the projection of the face image Γ into the eigenspace spanned by the Eigenfaces $u_1, .., u_K$ as follows: $\mathcal{C}$ generates a secret/public key pair of a homomorphic encryption scheme (cf. §2.2) and encrypts the face Γ as $[\![\Gamma]\!] = ([\![\Gamma_1]\!], .., [\![\Gamma_N]\!])$. $\mathcal{C}$ sends the encrypted face $[\![\Gamma]\!]$ along with the public key to $\mathcal{S}$. Using the homomorphic properties, $\mathcal{S}$ projects the encrypted face into the low-dimensional face space and obtains the encryption of the projected face $[\![\bar{\Omega}]\!] = ([\![\bar{\omega}_1]\!], .., [\![\bar{\omega}_K]\!])$ by computing for $i = 1, .., K$: $[\![\bar{\omega}_i]\!] = [\![-\sum_{j=1}^{N} u_{i,j}\Psi_j]\!] \cdot \prod_{j=1}^{N}[\![\Gamma_j]\!]^{u_{i,j}}$. The first factor can already be computed in the pre-computation phase.

Distance. After Projection, $\mathcal{C}$ and $\mathcal{S}$ jointly compute the encryption of the Euclidean distances between the projected face $[\![\bar{\Omega}]\!]$ and all projected faces $\Omega_1, .., \Omega_M$ in the database held by $\mathcal{S}$. This is done by computing for $i = 1, .., M$: $[\![D_i]\!] = [\![||\Omega_i - \bar{\Omega}||^2]\!] = [\![S_{1,i}]\!] \cdot [\![S_{2,i}]\!] \cdot [\![S_3]\!]$, where $[\![S_{1,i}]\!] = [\![\sum_{j=1}^{K} \omega_{i,j}^2]\!] = \prod_{j=1}^{K}[\![\omega_{i,j}^2]\!]$ and $[\![S_{2,i}]\!] = [\![\sum_{j=1}^{K}(-2\omega_{i,j}\bar{\omega}_j)]\!] = \prod_{j=1}^{K}[\![\bar{\omega}_j]\!]^{-2\omega_{i,j}}$ can be computed by $\mathcal{S}$ from $[\![\bar{\Omega}]\!]$ without interaction with $\mathcal{C}$. To obtain $[\![S_3]\!] = [\![\sum_{j=1}^{K}\bar{\omega}_j^2]\!]$ from $[\![\bar{\Omega}]\!]$, the following protocol is suggested in [12]: For $j = 1, .., K$: $\mathcal{S}$ chooses $r_j \in_R \mathbb{Z}_n$, computes $[\![x_j]\!] = [\![\bar{\omega}_j + r_j]\!] = [\![\bar{\omega}_j]\!] \cdot [\![r_j]\!]$ and sends $[\![x_j]\!]$ to $\mathcal{C}$. $\mathcal{C}$ decrypts $[\![x_j]\!]$, computes $[\![S_3']\!] = [\![\sum_{j=1}^{K} x_j^2]\!]$, and sends $[\![S_3']\!]$ to $\mathcal{S}$. $\mathcal{S}$ finally computes $[\![S_3]\!] = [\![S_3']\!] \cdot [\![-\sum_{j=1}^{K} r_j^2]\!] \cdot \prod_{j=1}^{K}[\![\bar{\omega}_j]\!]^{-2r_j}$.

Minimum. As last step, $\mathcal{C}$ and $\mathcal{S}$ jointly compute the minimum value D from $[\![D_1]\!], .., [\![D_M]\!]$ and its index Id. If the minimum value D is smaller than the threshold value τ known by $\mathcal{S}$, then $\mathcal{C}$ obtains the result Id. To achieve this, [12] suggests the following protocol: Choose the minimum value and index from the list of encrypted value and id pairs $([\![D_0 = \tau]\!], [\![\mathsf{Id}_0 = \bot]\!]), ([\![D_i]\!], [\![\mathsf{Id}_i]\!])_{i=1}^{M}$. For this, they apply a straight-forward recursive algorithm for minimum selection based on a sub-protocol which compares two encrypted distances and returns a re-randomized encryption of the minimum and its index to $\mathcal{S}$. For this sub-protocol, an optimized version of the homomorphic encryption-based comparison protocol of Damgård, Geisler and Krøigaard (DGK) [9,10] is used.

Complexity of Minimum *protocol (cf. Table 1).* The Minimum protocol of [12] requires a logarithmic number of $6\lceil \log_2(M+1) \rceil + 1$ moves. Overall, $8M$ Paillier ciphertexts and $2\ell'M$ DGK ciphertexts are sent in the online phase, where $\ell' = 50$ is the length of the squared distances $D_1, .., D_M$ among which the minimum is selected (cf. Table 3 in Appendix §A). This results in a communication complexity of $(16 + 2\ell')MT$ bits. The asymptotic online computation complexity is dominated by approximately $2M$ Paillier decryptions and $\ell'M$ DGK decryptions for $\mathcal{C}$ and the same number of exponentiations for $\mathcal{S}$.

4   Our Protocols for Privacy-Preserving Face Recognition

In the following we present our Hybrid protocol which improves over the protocol of [12] (cf. §3.2) and is better suited for larger database sizes. An alternative protocol based on garbled circuits only is given in the full version [32].

4.1   Privacy-Preserving Face Recognition Using Hybrid of HE + GC

Our hybrid protocol for privacy-preserving face recognition improves over the protocol in [12] by replacing the Minimum protocol with a more efficient protocol based on garbled circuits. Additionally, the Distance protocol proposed in [12] can be slightly improved by packing together the messages sent from server $\mathcal{S}$ to client $\mathcal{C}$ into a single ciphertext as detailed in the full version [32]. We concentrate on the core improvements of the Minimum protocol in the following.

Hybrid Minimum Protocol

The most efficient protocols for secure comparison in the setting with two computationally bounded parties is still based on Yao's garbled circuit (GC) approach [35,26,20] as briefly explained in §2.2. This also includes the natural generalization to selecting the minimum value and index of multiple values. As shown in [20], these GC based protocols clearly outperform comparison protocols based on homomorphic encryption [13,6,14,9,10]. In the following we show how the protocols of [20] can be adopted to yield a highly efficient, constant round Minimum protocol for our Hybrid privacy-preserving face recognition protocol.

Overview. The high-level structure of our improved Minimum protocol is shown in Fig. 3(a) in Appendix §B and consists of several building-blocks: the sub-protocol ParallelConvert converts the homomorphically encrypted distances held by server $\mathcal{S}$, $[\![D_1]\!], .., [\![D_M]\!]$, into their corresponding garbled values $\widetilde{D}_1, .., \widetilde{D}_M$ output to client $\mathcal{C}$ (details below). These garbled values are used to evaluate a garbled circuit $\widetilde{C}_{\text{Minimum}}$ which computes the Minimum phase of Algorithm 1 in Appendix §A (details on how the underlying circuit C_{Minimum} is constructed below). The garbled circuit $\widetilde{C}_{\text{Minimum}}$ can be created already in the setup phase using algorithm CreateGC and sent to $\mathcal{C}$ before the online phase starts. The garbled values $\widetilde{\tau}$ which correspond to server's threshold value τ are selected by $\mathcal{S}$ (Select) and transferred to $\mathcal{C}$ as well (either in the setup phase or in the online phase depending on how often the database changes). Finally, $\mathcal{C}$ evaluates $\widetilde{C}_{\text{Minimum}}$ on the garbled values $\widetilde{\tau}, \widetilde{D}_1, .., \widetilde{D}_M$ and obtains the correct output r.

ParallelConvert *protocol.* An efficient ParallelConvert protocol is given in [20] which we summarize in the following (see [20] and [4] for a detailed description): $\mathcal{S}$ blinds the homomorphically encrypted ℓ'-bit values $[\![D_i]\!]$, $i = 1, .., M$ with a randomly chosen additive T-bit mask $R_i \in_R \mathbb{Z}_n$ and sends the blinded values $[\![D_i + R_i]\!]$ to $\mathcal{C}$ who can decrypt. Then, $\mathcal{C}$ and $\mathcal{S}$ jointly run a garbled circuit protocol in order to obliviously take off the mask R_i with a subtraction circuit. For improved efficiency, multiple values $[\![D_i]\!]$ can be packed together into a single ciphertext before blinding. To avoid an overflow when adding the T-bit random mask, the most significant κ bits are left as correctness margin, where κ is a statistical correctness parameter (e.g., $\kappa = 40$). This allows to pack $M' = \lfloor \frac{T-\kappa}{\ell'} \rfloor$ values into one ciphertext resulting in $m = \lceil \frac{M}{M'} \rceil$ packed Paillier ciphertexts for the M values. The ParallelConvert protocol consists of 3 moves.

Circuit C_{Minimum} which computes the required functionality of the Minimum protocol is shown in Fig. 3(b) in Appendix §B: First, the minimum value $D_{\text{min}} = min(D_1, .., D_M)$ and the corresponding index $i_{\text{min}} \in \{1, .., M\}$ are computed with the MIN circuit. The MIN circuit is similar to the circuit evaluated in a first-price auction where the highest bid and the index of the highest bidder is selected [26]. An efficient construction of this circuit has size $|\text{MIN}| \sim 2\ell'M$ non-XOR gates [20]. Afterwards, the minimum value D_{min} is compared with the threshold value τ using a comparison circuit CMP. The output c of the CMP circuit is 1 if $D_{\text{min}} \leq \tau$ and 0 otherwise. Depending on c, the multiplexer MUX chooses either the minimum index i_{min} if $c = 1$ as output or the special symbol $\bot$ otherwise (e.g., $\bot = 0$). The circuit has size $|C_{\text{Minimum}}| \sim 2\ell'M$ non-XOR gates.

Complexity. The complexity of our improved Minimum protocol and the one proposed in [12] is given in Table 1. For the computation complexity the table contains only the dominant costs: the number of Paillier and Damgård-Geisler-Krøigård (DGK) decryptions (Dec) and exponentiations (Exp) as well as the number of evaluations of a cryptographic hash function (Hash).

Table 1. Complexity of Minimum Protocols with Parameters M: # faces in database, ℓ': bitlength of values $D_1, .., D_M$, t: symmetric security parameter, T: asymmetric security parameter, κ: statistical correctness parameter, $m \sim \frac{\ell'}{T-\kappa}M$

	HE §3.2 [12]	Hybrid §4.1
Round Complexity	$6\lceil\log(M+1)\rceil + 1$ moves	3 moves
Asymptotic Communication Complexity [bits]		
online	$(2\ell' + 16)MT$	$2\ell'Mt + 2mT$
offline		$\text{OT}_t^{\ell'M} + 9\ell'Mt$
Asymptotic Computation Complexity		
$\mathcal{C}$ online	$\approx 2M\ \text{Dec}_{\text{Paillier}} + \ell'M\ \text{Dec}_{\text{DGK}}$	$m\ \text{Dec}_{\text{Paillier}} + 3\ell'M\ \text{Hash}$
$\mathcal{S}$ online	$\approx 2M\ \text{Exp}_{\text{Paillier}} + \ell'M\ \text{Exp}_{\text{DGK}}$	$m\ \text{Exp}_{\text{Paillier}}$

Our improved Minimum protocol requires a constant number of 3 moves for the ParallelConvert protocol ($\tilde{\tau}$ can be sent with the last message). The online communication complexity is determined by the ParallelConvert protocol for converting M values of bitlength ℓ', i.e., m Paillier ciphertexts and the online part of the $\text{OT}_t^{\ell'M}$ protocol which is asymptotically $2\ell'Mt + 2mT$ bits (cf. §2.2). The online computation complexity requires $\mathcal{S}$ to pack the m ciphertexts (corresponds to m exponentiations) and $\mathcal{C}$ to decrypt them. After the OT protocol, $\mathcal{C}$ needs to evaluate a garbled circuit consisting of approximately $3\ell'M$ non-XOR gates ($\ell'M$ to subtract the random masks in the ParallelConvert protocol and $2\ell'M$ for C_{Minimum}) which requires to invoke a cryptographic hash function (e.g., SHA-256) the same number of times. The offline communication consists of the $\text{OT}_t^{\ell'M}$ protocol and transferring the GC ($3t$ bits per non-XOR gate, cf. §2.2).

Improvements (cf. Table 1). Most notably, the *round complexity* of our improved Minimum protocol is independent of the size M of the database.

The *online communication complexity* of our protocol is smaller by a factor of approximately T/t, e.g., $1024/80 \approx 13$ for short-term security and 38 for long-term security (see §5.1 for details).

The *online computation complexity* of our protocol is substantially lower, as the number of Paillier operations is reduced by a factor of approximately $2M/m = 2M' = \frac{2(T-\kappa)}{\ell'}$, e.g., $\frac{2(1024-40)}{50} \approx 40$ for short-term security and 121 for long-term security. GC evaluation (which requires one invocation of SHA-256 per gate) is computationally less expensive than the modular arithmetics needed for the DGK public-key cryptosystem used in [12] (see §5.2 for details).

5   Complexity Improvements

In the following we compare our improved protocol with the protocol of [12]: communication- and round complexity in §5.1 and computation complexity in §5.2. We consider different recommended sizes of security parameters for short-, medium-, and long-term security [16] (cf. Appendix §C for parameter sizes).

5.1   Round Complexity and Asymptotic Communication Complexity

HE vs. Hybrid (Table 2). Our Hybrid protocol substantially improves the performance of the HE protocol proposed in [12]: the round complexity is reduced from logarithmic in the size of the database M down to a small constant of 6 moves. The online communication complexity of the Minimum protocol (§4.1) is reduced to only 6.6% of the previous solution for short-term security. For medium- and long-term security the savings are even better. Our improvements of the Distance protocol (in full version [32]) down to 23% for short-term security are negligible w.r.t. the overall communication complexity as it has small communication complexity (few KBytes) independent of the database size M.

Table 2. Round- and Communication Complexity – HE vs. Hybrid. M: size of DB

Protocol	HE §3.2 [12]			Hybrid §4.1 (Improvement)		
Round Complexity [moves]	$6\lceil \log(M+1)\rceil + 4$			6 ($\mathcal{O}(\log M) \rightarrow \mathcal{O}(1)$)		
Security Level	Short	Medium	Long	Short	Medium	Long
Asymptotic Communication Complexity (online)						
Projection [MB]	2.5	5.0	7.5	2.5	5.0	7.5
Distance [kB]	3.2	6.5	9.8	0.75 (23%)	1.0 (15%)	1.5 (15%)
Minimum [kB per face in DB]	15	29	44	0.99 (6.6%)	1.4 (4.8%)	1.6 (3.6%)

5.2   Online Computation Complexity

Hybrid protocol (§4.1). We have implemented the Hybrid protocol for privacy-preserving recognition described in §4.1 in Python to quantify its online computation complexity. Although interpreted Python code runs substantially slower than compiled code we chose it for platform independence. We perform performance measurements on two standard PCs (AMD Athlon64 X2 5000+ (2.6GHz), 2 Cores, 4 GB Memory running on Gentoo Linux x86_64) communicating via TCP/IP6 over a Gigabit Ethernet connection. Both machines were clocked to 2.4GHz via CPU frequency scaling to make the performance comparable to [12]. The implementation is running in the cPython-2.6 interpreter and uses gmpy module (version 1.04) to access GNU GMP library (version 4.3.1).

In comparison, the protocol in [12] was implemented in C++ using the GNU GMP library (version 4.2.4) and executed on a single PC (2.4 GHz AMD Opteron with dual-core processor and 4 GB RAM under Linux) as two threads. This implementation neglects latencies of communication stack and network which could result in non-negligible slow-downs due to their logarithmic round complexity.

Although our implementation is closer to a real-world setting and uses a substantially slower programming language, it still outperforms that of [12] especially for larger database sizes due to our algorithmic protocol improvements of the Minimum protocol as shown in Fig. 2(a). Surprisingly, our implementation is about 30% faster than the C++ implementation of [12] even in the homomorphic encryption-based parts of the protocol (Projection and Distance). Presumably this is due to faster multiplication in GMP version 4.3.

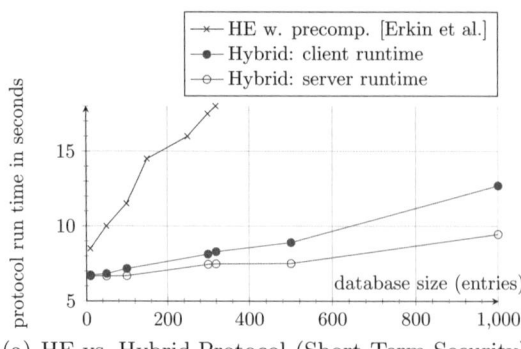

	Security Level		
Client	Short	Medium	Long
Projection	0.49	0.60	0.72
Distance	6.08	16.87	31.73
Minimum	1.86	2.71	4.49
Sum	8.43	20.18	36.95
Server	Short	Medium	Long
Projection	6.58	17.43	32.37
Distance	0.47	1.52	3.03
Minimum	0.06	0.21	0.54
Sum	7.11	19.15	35.94

(a) HE vs. Hybrid Protocol (Short-Term Security)   (b) Hybrid Protocol for $M = 320$

Fig. 2. Comparison of Timing Complexity in [s]

In contrast to the HE-based protocol of [12], our protocol scales well with increasing security level as shown in Fig. 2(b), as symmetric security parameter t increases much slower than its asymmetric equivalent T (cf. Appendix §C).

Overall, the implementation results confirm that our Hybrid protocol allows privacy-preserving face recognition even for large databases.

5.3   Conclusion and Future Work

The methods for constructing efficient protocols for privacy-preserving face recognition presented in this paper can be further improved into various directions.

Algorithmic Improvements for better classification accuracy might be achieved by using different face recognition algorithms. Fisherfaces [5], which determine the projection matrix with Linear Discriminant Analysis (LDA), can be used instead of Eigenfaces. A different distance metric than Euclidean distance could be used, e.g., Hamming distance or Manhattan distance. The Minimum phase could be based on meaning or scoring instead of minimum selection.

Further Protocol Improvements could be achieved with a different homomorphic encryption scheme that allows both, additions and multiplications [7,2,15] to avoid the additional communication round for computing Euclidean Distance.

Further Implementation Improvements can be achieved by exploiting parallelism on multi-core architectures or graphics processing units (GPUs).

Acknowledgements. We thank Wilko Henecka for extending the compiler of [30] to generate the underlying circuits, authors of [12] for detailed information on their protocol, and anonymous reviewers of ICISC 2009 for helpful comments.

References

1. Aiello, W., Ishai, Y., Reingold, O.: Priced oblivious transfer: How to sell digital goods. In: Pfitzmann, B. (ed.) EUROCRYPT 2001. LNCS, vol. 2045, pp. 119–135. Springer, Heidelberg (2001)

2. Armknecht, F., Sadeghi, A.-R.: A new approach for algebraically homomorphic encryption. Cryptology ePrint Archive, Report 2008/422 (2008), http://eprint.iacr.org/2008/422
3. Avidan, S., Butman, M.: Efficient methods for privacy preserving face detection. In: Advances in Neural Information Processing Systems (NIPS'06), pp. 57–64. MIT Press, Cambridge (2006)
4. Barni, M., Failla, P., Kolesnikov, V., Lazzeretti, R., Sadeghi, A.-R., Schneider, T.: Secure evaluation of private linear branching programs with medical applications. In: Backes, M., Ning, P. (eds.) ESORICS 2009. LNCS, vol. 5789, pp. 424–439. Springer, Heidelberg (2009)
5. Belhumeur, P.N., Hespanha, J.P., Kriegman, D.J.: Eigenfaces vs. Fisherfaces: Recognition using class specific linear projection. IEEE Transactions on Pattern Analysis and Machine Intelligence 19(7), 711–720 (1997)
6. Blake, I.F., Kolesnikov, V.: Strong conditional oblivious transfer and computing on intervals. In: Lee, P.J. (ed.) ASIACRYPT 2004. LNCS, vol. 3329, pp. 515–529. Springer, Heidelberg (2004)
7. Boneh, D., Goh, E.-J., Nissim, K.: Evaluating 2-DNF formulas on ciphertexts. In: Kilian, J. (ed.) TCC 2005. LNCS, vol. 3378, pp. 325–341. Springer, Heidelberg (2005)
8. Bowcott, O.: Interpol wants facial recognition database to catch suspects. Guardian (October 20, 2008), http://www.guardian.co.uk/world/2008/oct/20/interpol-facial-recognition
9. Damgård, I.B., Geisler, M., Krøigård, M.: Efficient and secure comparison for on-line auctions. In: Pieprzyk, J., Ghodosi, H., Dawson, E. (eds.) ACISP 2007. LNCS, vol. 4586, pp. 416–430. Springer, Heidelberg (2007)
10. Damgård, I., Geisler, M., Krøigård, M.: A correction to efficient and secure comparison for on-line auctions. Cryptology ePrint Archive, Report 2008/321 (2008), http://eprint.iacr.org/2008/321
11. Damgård, I., Jurik, M.: A generalisation, a simplification and some applications of Paillier's probabilistic public-key system. In: Kim, K.-c. (ed.) PKC 2001. LNCS, vol. 1992, pp. 119–136. Springer, Heidelberg (2001)
12. Erkin, Z., Franz, M., Guajardo, J., Katzenbeisser, S., Lagendijk, I., Toft, T.: Privacy-preserving face recognition. In: Goldberg, I., Atallah, M.J. (eds.) Privacy Enhancing Technologies. LNCS, vol. 5672, pp. 235–253. Springer, Heidelberg (2009)
13. Fischlin, M.: A cost-effective pay-per-multiplication comparison method for millionaires. In: Naccache, D. (ed.) CT-RSA 2001. LNCS, vol. 2020, pp. 457–472. Springer, Heidelberg (2001)
14. Garay, J.A., Schoenmakers, B., Villegas, J.: Practical and secure solutions for integer comparison. In: Okamoto, T., Wang, X. (eds.) PKC 2007. LNCS, vol. 4450, pp. 330–342. Springer, Heidelberg (2007)
15. Gentry, C.: Fully homomorphic encryption using ideal lattices. In: ACM Symposium on Theory of Computing (STOC'09), pp. 169–178. ACM, New York (2009)
16. Giry, D., Quisquater, J.-J.: Cryptographic key length recommendation (March 2009), http://keylength.com
17. Grose, T.: When surveillance cameras talk. Time Magazine (February 11, 2008), http://www.time.com/time/world/article/0,8599,1711972,00.html
18. Interational Civil Aviation Organization (ICAO). Machine Readable Travel Documents (MRTD), Doc 9303, Part 1, 5th (edn.) (2003)
19. Ishai, Y., Kilian, J., Nissim, K., Petrank, E.: Extending oblivious transfers efficiently. In: Boneh, D. (ed.) CRYPTO 2003. LNCS, vol. 2729, pp. 145–161. Springer, Heidelberg (2003)

20. Kolesnikov, V., Sadeghi, A.-R., Schneider, T.: Improved garbled circuit building blocks and applications to auctions and computing minima. In: Cryptology and Network Security (CANS '09). LNCS. Springer, Heidelberg (2009), http://www.springerlink.com/content/175204h13h038581

21. Kolesnikov, V., Schneider, T.: Improved garbled circuit: Free XOR gates and applications. In: Aceto, L., Damgård, I., Goldberg, L.A., Halldórsson, M.M., Ingólfsdóttir, A., Walukiewicz, I. (eds.) ICALP 2008, Part II. LNCS, vol. 5126, pp. 486–498. Springer, Heidelberg (2008)

22. Lindell, Y., Pinkas, B.: A proof of Yao's protocol for secure two-party computation. ECCC Report TR04-063, Electronic Colloquium on Computational Complexity, ECCC (2004)

23. Lipmaa, H.: Verifiable homomorphic oblivious transfer and private equality test. In: Laih, C.-S. (ed.) ASIACRYPT 2003. LNCS, vol. 2894, pp. 416–433. Springer, Heidelberg (2003)

24. Malkhi, D., Nisan, N., Pinkas, B., Sella, Y.: Fairplay a secure two-party computation system. In: USENIX (2004), http://fairplayproject.net

25. Naor, M., Pinkas, B.: Efficient oblivious transfer protocols. In: ACM-SIAM Symposium On Discrete Algorithms (SODA'01), pp. 448–457. Society for Industrial and Applied Mathematics (2001)

26. Naor, M., Pinkas, B., Sumner, R.: Privacy preserving auctions and mechanism design. In: ACM Conference on Electronic Commerce, pp. 129–139 (1999)

27. Naumann, I., Hogben, G.: Privacy features of European eID card specifications. Network Security 2008(8), 9–13 (2008); European Network and Information Security Agency (ENISA)

28. Newton, E.M., Sweeney, L., Malin, B.: Preserving privacy by de-identifying face images. IEEE Transactions on Knowledge and Data Engineering 17(2), 232–243 (2005)

29. Paillier, P.: Public-key cryptosystems based on composite degree residuosity classes. In: Stern, J. (ed.) EUROCRYPT 1999. LNCS, vol. 1592, pp. 223–238. Springer, Heidelberg (1999)

30. Paus, A., Sadeghi, A.-R., Schneider, T.: Practical secure evaluation of semiprivate functions. In: Abdalla, M., Pointcheval, D., Fouque, P.-A., Vergnaud, D. (eds.) ACNS 2009. LNCS, vol. 5536, pp. 89–106. Springer, Heidelberg (2009), http://www.trust.rub.de/FairplaySPF

31. Pinkas, B., Schneider, T., Smart, N.P., Williams, S.C.: Secure two-party computation is practical. In: Advances in Cryptology ASIACRYPT 2009. LNCS, Springer, Heidelberg (2009), http://www.springerlink.com/content/3p52033869154003

32. Sadeghi, A.-R., Schneider, T., Wehrenberg, I.: Efficient privacy-preserving face recognition. Cryptology ePrint Archive, Report 2009/507 (2009), http://eprint.iacr.org/2009/507

33. Turk, M., Pentland, A.: Eigenfaces for recognition. Journal of Cognitive Neuro-science 3(1), 71–86 (1991)

34. Turk, M., Pentland, A.: Face recognition using eigenfaces. In: IEEE Computer Vision and Pattern Recognition (CVPR'91), pp. 586–591. IEEE, Los Alamitos (1991)

35. Yao, A.C.: How to generate and exchange secrets. In: IEEE Symposium on Foundations of Computer Science (FOCS'86), pp. 162–167. IEEE, Los Alamitos (1986)

A   Face Recognition Using Eigenfaces: Details

Algorithm 1 shows the pseudocode description of the Eigenfaces algorithm and Table 3 the naming conventions and sizes of the parameters.

Algorithm 1. Face recognition using Eigenfaces [34,33].

Input face Γ, average face Ψ; Eigenfaces $u_1, .., u_K$; projected faces $\Omega_1, .., \Omega_M$; threshold value τ

Output recognition result $r \in \{1, .., M\} \cup \bot$

    {Phase 1: Projection}
1: **for** $i = 1$ to K **do**
2:    $\bar{\omega}_i = u_i^T (\Gamma - \Psi)$
3: **end for**
4: projected face $\bar{\Omega} := (\bar{\omega}_1, .., \bar{\omega}_K)$

    {Phase 2: Distance}
5: **for** $i = 1$ to M **do**
6:    compute squared distance $D_i = ||\bar{\Omega} - \Omega_i||^2 = \sum_{j=1}^{K} (\bar{\omega}_j - \omega_{i,j})^2$
7: **end for**

    {Phase 3: Minimum}
8: compute minimum value $D_{\min} = \min\{D_1, .., D_M\}$ and index $i_{\min}$: $D_{\min} = D_{i_{\min}}$
9: **if** $D_{\min} \leq \tau$ **then**
10:    Return $r = i_{\min}$
11: **else**
12:    Return $r = \bot$
13: **end if**

Table 3. Parameters and Sizes for Privacy-Preserving Face Recognition

Parameter	Size [12]	Description
M		number of faces in database
	$N = 10304$	size of a face in pixels
	$K = 12$	number of Eigenfaces
$\Gamma, \Psi \in [0, 2^8 - 1]^N$		face, average face
$u_1, .., u_K \in [-2^7, 2^7 - 1]^N$		Eigenfaces
$\bar{\Omega}, \Omega_1, .., \Omega_M \in [-2^{31}, 2^{31} - 1]^K$		projected face, projected faces in database
$D_1, .., D_M \in [0, 2^{50} - 1]$		squared distances between projected images
$\tau \in [0, 2^{50} - 1]$		threshold value

B   Improved **Minimum** Protocol: Details

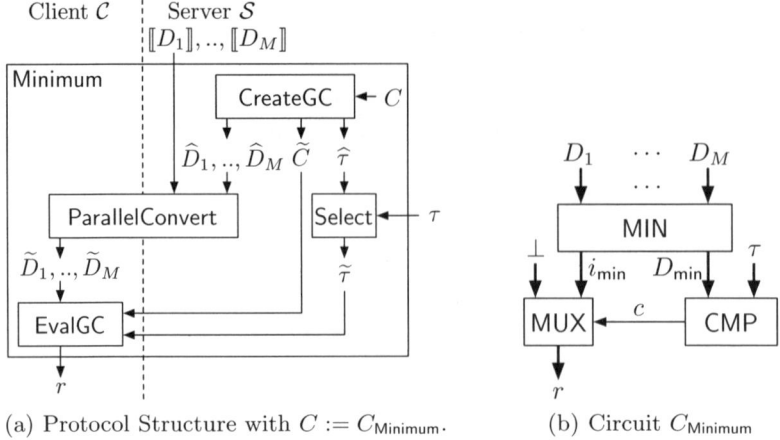

(a) Protocol Structure with $C := C_{\text{Minimum}}$.   (b) Circuit C_{Minimum}

Fig. 3. Improved Minimum Protocol

C   Parameter Sizes

We compare the complexity for different recommended sizes of security parameters – short-term (recommended use up to 2010), medium-term (up to 2030) and long-term security [16]. The sizes for the security parameters and corresponding parameter sizes for our Hybrid protocol are summarized in Table 4: we use statistical security parameter $\sigma = 80$ and statistical correctness parameter $\kappa = 40$. According to Table 3, the input length for the Distance protocol is $\ell = 32$ and for the Minimum protocol (§4.1) is $\ell' = 50$.

Table 4. Size of Security Parameters (t: symmetric security parameter, T: asymmetric security parameter) and Corresponding Parameters for Hybrid Protocol (M': # values packed into one ciphertext before blinding)

Security Level	Security Parameters		Minimum (§4.1)
	t	T	M'
Short-Term	80	1024	19
Medium-Term	112	2048	40
Long -Term	128	3072	60

Linear, Constant-Rounds Bit-Decomposition

Tord Reistad[1] and Tomas Toft[2,*]

[1] NTNU
Trondheim, Norway
tordr@item.ntnu.no
[2] Dept. of CS Aarhus University
IT-parken, Aabogade 34
DK-8200 Aarhus N, Denmark
ttoft@cs.au.dk

Abstract. When performing secure multiparty computation, tasks may often be simple or difficult depending on the representation chosen. Hence, being able to switch representation efficiently may allow more efficient protocols.

We present a new protocol for bit-decomposition: converting a ring element $x \in \mathbb{Z}_M$ to its binary representation, $x_{(\log M)-1}, \ldots, x_0$. The protocol can be based on arbitrary secure arithmetic in $\mathbb{Z}_M$; this is achievable for Shamir shared values as well as (threshold) Paillier encrypted ones, implying solutions for both these popular MPC primitives. For additively homomorphic primitives (which is typical, and the case for both examples) the solution is constant-rounds and requires only $O(\log M)$ secure ring multiplications.

The solution is secure against active adversaries assuming the existence of additional primitives. These exist for both the Shamir sharing based approach as well as the Paillier based one.

Keywords: Constant-rounds secure multiparty computation, bit-decomposition.

1 Introduction

Since Yao introduced the concept of secure multiparty computation (MPC) [Yao82] – evaluate a function on distributed, private inputs without revealing additional information on those inputs – it has been rigorously studied. Different approaches have been suggested, including garbled circuits [Yao86], secret sharing based approaches [BGW88, CCD88], and techniques relying on homomorphic, public-key cryptography, e.g. [CDN01].

It has been demonstrated that any function can be evaluated by describing it as a Boolean circuit and providing the inputs in binary, e.g. stored as 0 and 1 in some field or ring over which the secure computation is performed. However, alternative representations may provide greater efficiency. If, for example, the

---

* Work partially performed while at CWI Amsterdam and TU Eindhoven.

D. Lee and S. Hong (Eds.): ICISC 2009, LNCS 5984, pp. 245–257, 2010.

the function consists entirely of integer addition and multiplication, this can be simulated with arithmetic over $\mathbb{Z}_M$, where M is chosen larger than the maximal result possible. With primitives providing secure computation in $\mathbb{Z}_M$ – e.g. based on Shamir sharing if M is chosen prime [Sha79, BGW88] – this is much simpler than using ring arithmetic to emulate the Boolean gates needed to "simulate" the integer computation.

Unfortunately, other operations become difficult when integers are stored as ring elements, e.g. division, modulo reduction, and exponentiation. To get the best of both worlds, a way of changing representation is needed. To go from binary to ring element is easy: it is a linear combination in the ring. The other direction is more difficult, in particular when adding the requirement that the solution must be constant-rounds, i.e. that only a constant number of messages may be sent overall.

Related work. The problem of constant-rounds bit-decomposition was first solved by Damgård *et al.* in the context of secret shared inputs, [DFK+06]; this was later improved by a constant factor by Nishide and Ohta [NO07]. Both solutions require $O(\ell \log \ell)$ secure multiplications, where ℓ is the bit-length of the modulus defining the field. These solutions provided the same security guarantees as the primitives, i.e. to ensure active or adaptive security, it was sufficient to utilize secure arithmetic providing this.

Independently, Schoenmakers and Tuyls considered *practical* bit-decomposition of Paillier encrypted values, i.e. the cryptographic setting, where they obtained linear – *but non-constant-rounds* – solutions [ST06, Pai99]. (They also noted the applicability of [DFK+06] for the Paillier based setting.) The solution of [ST06] was also secure against active adversaries, however, this needed additional "proofs of correctness" added to the basic protocol – in difference to the above solutions, secure arithmetic was not sufficient by itself.

A constant-rounds, *almost* linear solution was proposed by Toft [Tof09]. The problem of bit-decomposition was first reduced to that of postfix comparison (PFC) (using $O(\ell)$ secure multiplications), which was then solved using $O(\ell \cdot \log^{*(c)} \ell)$ multiplications. Similarly to [DFK+06] and [NO07], security was inherited from the primitives implying security against both active and adaptive adversaries immediately, both based on secret sharing as well on (threshold) Paillier encryption.

Contribution. We present a novel, constant-rounds, linear solution to the PFC problem, and hence also to that of bit-decomposition. The solution is applicable for arbitrary secure arithmetic in $\mathbb{Z}_M$,[1] i.e. it is applicable for both secret sharing as well as Paillier based primitives. The protocol not only improves the theoretic complexity, it is also practical in the sense that the constants involved are similar to previous constant-rounds solutions.

---

[1] Our only restrictions are that M is odd and that it is possible to generate random, invertible elements efficiently. Further, the transformation to the PFC problem must also be constant-rounds. Focus will be on the cases where M is either prime (Shamir sharing) or an RSA modulus (Paillier encryption) were all requirements are satisfied.

In difference to [DFK$^+$06, NO07, Tof09], perfect security cannot be provided, even if this is guaranteed by the primitives. Security is at most statistical, which still allows it to be unconditional. This further implies that we require M to be sufficiently large – $M > 2^{2(\kappa + \log n)}$ where κ is the security parameter and n the number of parties.

Similarly to [ST06], active security is *not* directly obtained from active security of the primitives. As there, active security is achievable when the parties can demonstrate that a provided input is less than some public bound. For both the Shamir based setting and the Paillier based setting, a constant-complexity protocol exists implying actively secure, constant-rounds, $O(\ell)$ bit-decomposition protocols in these settings, where $\ell = \log M$.

An overview of this paper. Section 2 presents the model of secure computation used along with additional high-level constructs. Then in Sect. 3 the postfix comparison problem is introduced. The basic solution is presented in Sect. 4. Finally, the steps needed to achieve security against active adversaries are then discussed in Sect. 5, while Sect. 6 contains concluding remarks.

2 Secure Arithmetic – Notation and Primitives

We present our result based on abstract protocols. The model of secure computation is simply the arithmetic black-box (ABB) of Damgård and Nielsen [DN03]. It is described as an ideal functionality in the UC framework of Canetti, [Can00], and the present work can be used together with any realizing protocols. Naturally, the Paillier based protocols of [DN03] realize this functionality, but it can equally well be realized with perfect, active, and adaptive security with Shamir sharing over primes field $\mathbb{F}_M$ [Sha79] and the protocols of Ben-Or *et al.* [BGW88].

2.1 The Arithmetic Black-Box

The arithmetic black-box allows a number of parties to securely store and reveal secret values of a ring, $\mathbb{Z}_M$, as well as perform arithmetic operations. Borrowing notation from secret sharing, a value, v, stored within the functionality will be written in square brackets, $[v]$. The notation, $[v]_B$ will be used to refer to a bit-decomposed value, i.e. it is shorthand for $[v_{\hat{\ell}-1}], \ldots, [v_0]$ of some bit-length $\hat{\ell}$. The ABB provides the following operations; we assume that it is realized using additively homomorphic primitives.

- **Input:** Party P may input a value $v \in \mathbb{Z}_M$. Depending on the primitives, this can mean secret share, encrypt and broadcast, etc.
- **Output:** The parties may output a stored $[v]$; following this, all parties know the now public v. This refers to reconstruction, decryption, etc.
- **Linear combination:** The parties may decide to compute a linear combination of stored values, $[\sum_i \alpha_i v_i] \leftarrow \sum_i \alpha_i [v_i]$. This follows immediately from the homomorphic property assumed above.
- **Multiplication:** The parties may compute products, $[v \cdot u] \leftarrow [v] \cdot [u]$ – this requires interaction, at least for the examples considered.

Note that secure computation is written using infix notation. Moreover, linear combinations and multiplications may be written together in larger expressions. Though further from the primitives, it improves readability as it emphasizes the intuition behind the secure computations performed.

Regarding complexity, we will only consider rounds and communication size. Note that this implies that linear combinations are considered costless. For rounds, it is assumed that the other primitives all require $O(1)$ rounds, and that an arbitrary amount may be performed in parallel. Note that with abstract primitives, we can only count the number of sequential executions, not the actual number of rounds of a concrete realization. Under big-O, the two are equivalent, though.

For communication complexity, the number of invocations of the primitives are simply counted. Moreover, rather than counting them individually, similarly to previous work they will simply be referred to collectively as *secure multiplications*. (An input from every party will be considered equivalent to a single multiplication – multiplication protocols typically require each party to provide at least one input).

We stress that security is only shown in the ABB model of computation, i.e. we are only concerned with primitives that securely realizes this ideal functionality. This reduces security to a question of ensuring that inputs are proper, e.g. taken from some subset of $\mathbb{Z}_M$, as well as ensuring that no information leaks when values are output.

2.2 Complex Primitives

The protocols proposed will not be presented directly in the ABB model. A number of high-level primitives are simply sketched – these are obtained from previous work. We assume five rounds of preprocessing, where all random values needed are generated and prepared in parallel. Hence, round complexity of the primitives below are "online only." The number of multiplications is still the overall count.

Random, unknown elements. The parties can generate uniformly random, unknown elements. Each party inputs a random value, the sum of these is uniformly random and unknown assuming even a single honest party. This is considered equivalent to one multiplication. Random, invertible elements can be generated by verifying that the element indeed is invertible: generate two elements and publish the product. If this is invertible, then so was the first element, while the second acts as a one-time-pad masking it within the group. This consists of three multiplications.

Element inversion, constant-rounds multiplication, and prefix-products. Element inversion is possible using four secure multiplications with one round online: generate a random, multiplicative mask; mask and reveal the input; invert the (public) masked value; and securely unmask. This may be further used to obtain constant-rounds, unbounded fan-in multiplication of invertible elements in one round using five multiplications per input. Both are due to Bar-Ilan and Beaver [BB89]. This may then be used to compute prefix-products: given an array of invertible values, $([v_0], \ldots, [v_{m-1}])$, compute $([p_0], \ldots, [p_{m-1}])$, where $[p_i] = \prod_{j=0}^{i} [v_j]$. Complexity is $5m$ multiplications in one round; see [DFK+06, Tof09] for details.

Random bit generation. We require a protocol for generating a uniformly random bit which is unknown to all parties. If M is prime, this is achievable with two secure multiplications, [DFK+06]. For non-prime M it can be achieved by letting each party share a uniformly random value in $\{1, -1\}$, computing the product of these, and mapping the result (which is still ± 1) to $\{0, 1\}$.

Note that when M is not prime, complexity is $O(n)$ multiplications, where n is the number of parties. For simplicity, we consider M prime in the analysis. In general, by assuming only a constant number of parties this factor disappears under big-O. This problem is not exclusive to our work; the factor n occurs in *all* comparable solutions known to the authors.

Comparison. A protocol for comparing bit-decomposed values is required, i.e. we allow expressions of the form

$$[a > b] \leftarrow [a]_B \overset{?}{>} [b]_B .$$

The comparison protocol of Reistad [Rei09] solves this problem using $7\hat{\ell} + 3$ multiplications in three rounds, where $\hat{\ell}$ is the bit-length. See Sections 4.1 and 4.3 for more information.

Random, bit-decomposed element generation. Another requirement is the ability to generate a uniformly random, unknown element along with its bit-decomposition. This can be achieved by generating ℓ random bits and viewing these as the binary representation. Computing the value itself is a simple linear combination, while a comparison is used to verify that the value is indeed less than M. Overall, this requires $6\ell + 3$ multiplications; the comparison is slightly cheaper than above as one input is public. In the event of failure, the protocol must be rerun; as in previous work on bit-decomposition, we generate multiple candidates in parallel and assume a factor of four efficiency loss, i.e. $24\ell + 12$ multiplications. If *expected constant-rounds* suffices, then only a factor of two is required, i.e. $12\ell + 6$ multiplications. See [DFK+06] for justification.

This primitive is the most expensive with regard to preprocessing, i.e. this is where the five rounds originate. Note that the failure probability depends on M. If this can be chosen freely – e.g. as a Mersenne prime – then the issue can be eliminated and complexity essentially reduced to 2ℓ multiplications.

Least significant bit (LSB) gate. Finally, the ability to extract the least significant bit of an $\hat{\ell}$-bit value, $[x]$, of bounded size will be needed. [ST06] describes a way to do this for Paillier encrypted values when there is sufficient "headroom" in the ring, $2^{\hat{\ell}+\kappa+\log n} < M$, where κ is a security parameter and n is the number of parties. The result is not limited to the case of Paillier encryption, but can be utilized with arbitrary realizing protocols.

The idea is that the parties initially generate a random, unknown bit m_0, and that each party P_k inputs a uniformly random $(\kappa + \hat{\ell} - 1)$-bit value, $\left[m^{(k)}\right]$ from which a random mask is computed,

$$[m] \leftarrow 2(\sum_{k=1}^{n} m^{(k)}) + [m_0].$$

Then $d = [x] + [m]$ is computed and output. By the assumption on the size of M, we have $d_0 = x_0 \oplus m_0$, where d_0 and x_0 are the least significant bits of d and x respectively. Thus, $[x_0]$ is easily obtained, $[x_0] \leftarrow d_0 + [m_0] - 2d_0[m_0]$. Overall, this is considered equivalent to three multiplications.

As the ABB is secure by definition, only one potential leak exists: d. However, m_0 is unknown and uniformly random, so for any honest party, P_k, $2 \cdot \left[m^{(k)}\right] + [m_0]$ statistically hides any information, and no adversary can learn anything, even when all but one parties are corrupt. Note that this is where perfect security is lost – the LSB gate is only statistically secure.

3   The Postfix Comparison Problem

The postfix comparison problem was introduced by Toft in [Tof09].

Problem 1 (Postfix Comparison [Tof09]). *Given two secret, $\hat{\ell}$-bit values* $[a]_B = \left(\left[a_{\hat{\ell}-1}\right], \left[a_{\hat{\ell}-2}\right], \dots, [a_0]\right)$ *and* $[b]_B = \left(\left[b_{\hat{\ell}-1}\right], \left[b_{\hat{\ell}-2}\right], \dots, [b_0]\right)$, *compute*

$$[c_i] = \left[a \bmod 2^i\right]_B \overset{?}{>} \left[b \bmod 2^i\right]_B$$

for all $i \in \{1, 2, \dots, \hat{\ell}\}$.

¿From that paper, we get the following lemma, which states that a protocol for solving the problem of bit-decomposition can be obtained from any protocol solving the PFC problem.

Lemma 1 ([Tof09]). *Given a constant-rounds solution to Problem 1 using* $O(f(\ell))$ *secure multiplications, constant-rounds bit-decomposition is achievable using* $O(\ell + f(\ell))$ *secure multiplications.*

The proof is by construction, which we sketch, see [Tof09] for the full explanation.

To bit-decompose $[x]$, first compute $\left[x \bmod 2^i\right]$ for all i. Now, a bit, $[x_i]$, of $[x]$ can be computed using only arithmetic, $2^{-i}(\left[x \bmod 2^{i+1}\right] - \left[x \bmod 2^i\right])$. To reduce $[x]$ modulo all powers of 2, first add a random, bit-decomposed mask, $[r]_B$, *over the integers*:

$$[c]_B = [x] + [r]_B.$$

Then reduce both c and r modulo 2^i (easy, as they are already decomposed) and simulate computation modulo 2^i using secure $\mathbb{Z}_M$ arithmetic:

$$\left[x \bmod 2^i\right] \leftarrow \left[c \bmod 2^i\right] - \left[r \bmod 2^i\right] + 2^i \cdot \left(\left[r \bmod 2^i\right]_B \overset{?}{>} \left[c \bmod 2^i\right]_B\right).$$

The integer addition of $[x]$ and $[r]_B$ is achieved by computing and revealing $\tilde{c} = [x] + [r] \bmod M$ using ring arithmetic. This reveals no information, as $\tilde{c}$ is uniformly random. We now have $c \in \{\tilde{c}, \tilde{c} + M\}$; both values are known, so it is merely a matter of securely choosing the bits of the relevant candidate: compare $[r]_B$ and $\tilde{c}$ to determine if an overflow has occurred, and use the outcome to select the right candidate using arithmetic. The comparisons of $r \bmod 2^i$ and $c \bmod 2^i$ for all i is a postfix comparison problem. This transformation requires $24\ell + 12 + 6\ell + 3 = 30\ell + 15$ multiplications and two online rounds (the public $\tilde{c}$ improves efficiency slightly).

4   The New Constant-Rounds Solution

The proposed solution is based on (a variation of) a comparison protocol due to Reistad, [Rei09]. The parts relevant for this paper – including the minor alterations – are presented in Sect. 4.1. The improved postfix comparison protocol is then presented and analyzed in Sect. 4.2. The solution has a restriction, which must be eliminated in order to obtain the final bit-decomposition protocol, this is described in Sect. 4.3. For the purpose of this section, assume that the parties are honest-but-curious.

4.1   The Comparison of [Rei09]

Let $[r]_B$ and $[c]_B$ be two $\hat{\ell}$-bit, bit-decomposed numbers to be compared. Further, let κ be a security parameter, let n be the number of parties, and assume that $2^{\hat{\ell}+\kappa+\log n} < M$. The overall idea for computing $[r > c]$ is to first compute a value, $[e_i]$, for each bit-position, i. The expression is written with intuition in mind; details on how to perform the actual computation follow below.

$$[e_i] \leftarrow [r_i]\,(1 - [c_i])2^{\sum_{j=i+1}^{\hat{\ell}-1}[r_j]\oplus[c_j]}. \tag{1}$$

Note that $[e_i]$ is either 0 (when $[r_i]$ is not set, or when both $[r_i]$ and $[c_i]$ are set) or a distinct power of two strictly less than $2^{\hat{\ell}} - 2^{\hat{\ell}} < M$ by assumption so the computation can be viewed as occurring over the integers. Note also that $[e_i] = 1$ can only occur when i is the most significant differing bit-position. Thus, all values except at most one are even. And an odd value, 1, occurs only if r_i is set at the most significant differing bit-position, i.e. if $[r]_B$ is bigger than $[c]_B$.

Since at most one value is odd and this exists exactly when $[r]_B > [c]_B$, computing the least significant bit, $[E_0]$, of

$$[E] \leftarrow \sum_{i=0}^{\hat{\ell}-1}[e_i]$$

provides the desired result. This bit is determined with a LSB gate.

Security of this protocol is trivial: the arithmetic black-box can only leak information when something is deliberately output, and this only occurs in subprotocols, which have already been considered.

For the computation of the $[e_i]$ above, $2^{\sum_{j=i+1}^{\hat{\ell}}[r_j]\oplus[c_j]}$ must be computed for every bit-position, i. This is done by first computing $[r_j \oplus c_j] \leftarrow [r_j] + [c_j] - 2[r_j][c_j]$ for each bit-position, j. Rewriting the exponentiation of Eq. (1) as

$$\prod_{j=i+1}^{\hat{\ell}-1} (1 + [r_j \oplus c_j]),$$

illustrates not only how to compute it for a single bit-position, it also allows it to be computed efficiently for *every* such position: it is simply a prefix-product with terms $1 + [r_j \oplus c_j]$ and the most significant bit-position first. This is computable in $O(1)$ rounds since all terms are invertible – they are either 1 or 2, and M is odd.

Analyzing the protocol in more detail, it can be seen that $7\hat{\ell}+3$ multiplications are needed, and these can be performed in three rounds (plus preprocessing). First $[c_i r_i]$ is computed for every position. Then $5\hat{\ell}$ multiplications are needed for the prefix-product for the exponentiations, while an additional multiplication is needed for each of the $\hat{\ell}$ instantiations of Eq. (1). (Note that the multiplications from the $\oplus$ operations may be reused.) The LSB gate is then applied to conclude the computation.

4.2   Solving the PFCP with [Rei09]

Recall the PFC problem: we are given two $\hat{\ell}$-bit values, $[r]_B$ and $[c]_B$, and must compare all postfixes, i.e. all reduction modulo 2-powers. The above comparison cannot be applied naively at every bit-position, that would be too costly. Our goal is therefore to compute a value, $[E^{(k)}]$, for every bit-length, $k \in \{1, \ldots, \hat{\ell}\}$, equivalent to $[E]$ above. This suffices as the goal are the least significant bits of these values, and the LSB-gate requires only constant work.

Values similar to the $[e_i]$ above cannot be computed; there is a quadratic number of them. Instead the $[e_i]$ are computed as before. These are equivalent to the desired $\left[e_i^{(\hat{\ell}-1)}\right]$, and will be used in *all* the ensuing computation,

$$\left[\tilde{E}^{(k)}\right] \leftarrow \sum_{i=0}^{k-1} [e_i].$$

The computed values quite likely differ from the desired $\left[E^{(k)}\right]$. However, $[e_i]$ is only off from $\left[e_i^{(k)}\right]$ – which should have been used – by a factor of some two-power, $2^{\sum_{j=k}^{\hat{\ell}-1}[r_j]\oplus[c_j]}$. For any fixed k, this value is also fixed. Therefore $\left[\tilde{E}^{(k)}\right]$ is also simply "wrong" by a factor of this.

To "correct" $\left[\tilde{E}^{(k)}\right]$, first note that $\left[2^{\sum_{j=k}^{\hat{\ell}-1} r_j \oplus c_j}\right]$ has already been computed by the prefix-product. Further, the factor can be eliminated as it is invertible. I.e. the desired $\left[E^{(k)}\right]$ is securely computable.

$$\left[E^{(k)}\right] \leftarrow \left[\tilde{E}^{(k)}\right] \cdot \left[2^{\sum_{j=k}^{\hat{\ell}-1} r_j \oplus c_j}\right]^{-1}$$

At this point, invoking an LSB-gate on every $\left[E^{(k)}\right]$ provides the final result.

Correctness follows from the above discussion along with that of Sect. 4.1. Regarding security, the protocol clearly does not leak information. More values are output from the ABB, but this still occurs only in sub-protocols. Thus, no information is leaked.

We conclude with a complexity analysis of the protocol. Securely computing both the factors, $\left[2^{\sum_{j=k}^{\hat{\ell}-1} [r_j] \oplus [c_j]}\right]$, and the $[e_i]$ for all bit-positions, i, and bit-lengths, k, requires only $7\hat{\ell}$ secure multiplications in 3 rounds. All that was required was the computation of $[r_j \oplus c_j]$ for every bit-position, the prefix-product, and the concluding computation for each $[e_i]$.

Computing the $\left[\tilde{E}^{(k)}\right]$ is costless at this point, while correcting them – computing the $\left[E^{(k)}\right]$ – requires $\hat{\ell}$ additional multiplications. The element inversions are costless as they can reuse the masking from the prefix-product. Thus, only one multiplication is needed per bit-length, and these may all be processed in parallel. Similarly, the concluding LSB-gates are are equivalent to three multiplications each and may also be executed concurrently.

Combining all of the above, the requirement is $(7+1+3)\hat{\ell} = 11\hat{\ell}$ multiplications in four rounds plus preprocessing. Thus, the following theorem is obtained.

Theorem 1. *There exists a protocol which solves postfix comparison problems of size $\hat{\ell}$ in $O(1)$ rounds using $O(\hat{\ell})$ secure multiplications of elements of $\mathbb{Z}_M$, for $M > 2^{\hat{\ell}+\kappa+\log n}$.*

4.3   Performing Bit-Decomposition

It remains to apply Lemma 1 and Theorem 1 to obtain the main result of this paper. There is, however, still one problem to be solved. The PFC problem to solve is of size $\ell = \lceil \log M \rceil$, but to apply Theorem 1 we must have $M > 2^{\ell+\kappa+\log n}$; this is of course contradictory.

Assuming that $M > 2^{2(\kappa+\log n)}$, then the following variation of the above solution fixes the problem. The trick, taken from [Rei09], consists of considering pairs of bit-positions rather than single bit-positions when computing the $[e_i]$. This results in half as many $[e_i]$, thereby halving the bit-length needed. I.e. the resulting modified $\left[E^{(k)}\right]$ have at least $\kappa + \log n$ bits of headroom in $\mathbb{Z}_M$, allowing the LSB-gate to be applied. This was the sole reason for the restriction on M. For simplicity it is assumed that ℓ is even in the following, where Eq. (1) is replaced by Eq. (2) which is computed only for the *odd* bit-positions, i.

First values, $[u_i]$, are computed,

$$[u_i] \leftarrow [r_i] \wedge (\neg [c_i]) \vee (\neg([r_i] \oplus [c_i])) \wedge [r_{i-1}] \wedge (\neg [c_{i-1}]).$$

Note that this is simply a comparison circuit for 2-bit numbers. Though somewhat complex, the expression translates readily to arithmetic.

$$[r_i] (1 - [c_i]) + (1 + 2 [r_i] \cdot [c_i] - [r_i] - [c_i]) [r_{i-1}] (1 - [c_{i-1}])$$

The $[u_i]$ are then used in the computation replacing Eq. (1). $[e'_i]$ is set to a 2-power exactly when the 2-bit position of $[r]_B$ is greater than that position of $[c]_B$, and the powers are smaller, as only the number of differing 2-bit blocks are "counted."

$$[e'_i] \leftarrow [u_i] \cdot 2^{\sum_{j=((i-1)/2)+1}^{\ell/2-1} ([r_{2j}]\oplus[c_{2j}])\vee([r_{2j+1}]\oplus[c_{2j+1}])} \tag{2}$$

Again, the expression is slightly more involved than before, but it can also be translated to a prefix-product,

$$\prod_{j=i+1}^{\hat{\ell}-1} (1 + ([r_{2j} \oplus c_{2j}] + [r_{2j+1} \oplus c_{2j+1}] - [r_{2j} \oplus c_{2j}] \cdot [r_{2j+1} \oplus c_{2j+1}])),$$

where the $\oplus$ is computed as above. Overall, Eq. (2) requires only $10\ell/2$ multiplications in four rounds.

The smaller $\left[\tilde{E}^{(k)} \right]$ can now be computed, however, there are two cases, as values $[e'_i]$ are also needed for the even bit-positions.

$$[e'_i] \leftarrow [r_i] (1 - [c_i]) \cdot 2^{\sum_{j=(i/2)+1}^{\ell/2-1} ([r_{2j}]\oplus[c_{2j}])\vee([r_{2j+1}]\oplus[c_{2j+1}])}$$

At this point we may compute

$$\left[\tilde{E}^{(k)} \right] \leftarrow \begin{cases} \sum_{i=0}^{k/2-1} \left[e'_{2i+1} \right] & \text{when } k \text{ is even} \\ \left[e'_{k-1} \right] + \sum_{i=0}^{(k-1)/2-1} \left[e'_{2i+1} \right] & \text{when } k \text{ is odd} \end{cases}$$

after which the incorrect powers of 2 can be eliminated and the LSB-gates applied as above. This solves the PFC problem such that $[x]_B$ can be determined. The final complexity is $(10/2 + 1/2 + 1 + 3)\ell = 9.5\ell$ multiplications in 5 rounds plus preprocessing and the conversion to the PFC problem, i.e. $9.5\ell + 30\ell + 15 = 39.5\ell + 15$ secure multiplications in $5 + 2 + 5 = 12$ rounds overall (including preprocessing). The result is summarized in the following theorem.

Theorem 2. *There exists a protocol which bit-decomposes a secret value, $[x]$ of $\mathbb{Z}_M$, to $[x]_B$ using $O(\ell)$ secure multiplications in $O(1)$ rounds. The protocol is statistically secure against passive adversaries when the arithmetic primitives are this. When they only provide computational security, then so does the present protocol.*

5   Active Security

As noted in the introduction, active security is not immediate. Even when actively secure protocols are used for the computation, problems occur when the parties are asked to share a random value from a domain different from $\mathbb{Z}_M$. For example, when M is not a prime, the parties must verify that inputs are really ± 1 during the bit-generation protocol. This is easily achieved with a zero-knowledge proof in the case of Paillier values, [DJ01]. The problem does not affect the solution based on Shamir sharing. There $\mathbb{Z}_M$ must be a field which implies that M is a prime. A second problem occurs in the LSB gates. It must be verified that the masks, $[m^{(k)}]$, are indeed of the specified bit-length. But these are the only problems.

By the definition of the arithmetic black-box, no adversary can do other harm. Thus, given a *constant-work* means of proving that a value is of bounded size (an interval proof), the solution can be made secure against active adversaries. There exists such proofs for both our examples.

As noted in [ST06], it is possible to demonstrate that a Paillier encryption contains a value within a specified range using the results of [Bou00, Lip03, DJ02]. The solution reveals no other information than the fact that indeed the value was from the desired range. Hence, active security is quite easily obtained in a Paillier based setting.

Regarding protocols based on Shamir sharing, such a proof is not immediate. It is, however, possible to obtain efficient range proofs by taking a detour through linear integer secret sharing (LISS). The solution follows directly from LISS, hence we only sketch it; see [Tho09] for a full explanation.

First off, LISS not only provides secret sharing of integer values, it can also form the basis for unconditionally and actively secure MPC. Further, it is possible convert a linear integer secret sharing to a Shamir sharing over $\mathbb{Z}_M$ simply by reducing the individual share modulo M. The solution is therefore to first share the $m^{(k)}$ using LISS, and for each of them demonstrate that it is in the desired range using constant work, [Tho09]. Secondly, those secret sharings are then converted to Shamir sharings over $\mathbb{Z}_M$. This ensures that the Shamir shared value is of bounded size as required.

6   Conclusion

We have proposed a novel protocol for constant-rounds bit-decomposition based on secure arithmetic with improved theoretic complexity compared to previous solutions. The complexity reached – $O(\ell)$ – appears optimal, as this is also the number of outputs, however, that this is the case is not immediately clear. Proving that $\Omega(\ell)$ secure multiplications is indeed a lower bound is left as an open problem.

Unfortunately, the present solution also has some minor "defects" compared to the previous ones. Firstly, "only" statistical security is guaranteed (at most), rather than perfect. This still allows linear, constant-rounds, unconditionally secure bit-decomposition, though. That security cannot be perfect also implies that the underlying ring must be sufficiently large to accommodate the large, random elements needed for statistical security. I.e. the protocol is only applicable for large moduli.

A second, worse "defect" is that – similarly to [ST06] – the basic solution does not provide out-of-the-box active security. This must be obtained through additional protocols, which of course increases complexity of the operations where these are needed. However as demonstrated, efficient, active security can be achieved quite readily for both Paillier based and Shamir sharing based settings.

We conclude by comparing the explicit complexity of our solution to that of previous ones, Table 1 taken from [Tof09]. Counting the exact number of secure multiplications provides a direct comparison for the case of passive security. It is noted that the proposed protocol not only improves theoretic complexity, it is also highly competitive with regard to the constants involved. In particular, if M can be chosen as a Mersenne prime, the overall number of secure multiplications can be reduced to essentially 17.5ℓ.

Table 1. Complexity of constant-rounds bit-decomposition

	Rounds	Multiplications
[DFK+06]	38	$94\ell \log \ell + 63\ell + 30\sqrt{\ell}$
[NO07]	25	$47\ell \log \ell + 63\ell + 30\sqrt{\ell}$
[Tof09]	$23 + c$	$(31 + 26c)\ell \cdot \log^{*(c)}\ell + 71\ell + 14c\sqrt{\ell}\log^{*(c)}(\ell) + 30\sqrt{\ell}$
This paper	12	$39.5\ell + 15$

With regard to active security, the comparison is not fair. The present solution must of course also take into account the proofs that the masks shared by parties are well-formed. Their complexity depends on the realizing primitives, which are outside the arithmetic black-box; they are therefore not included in the overview. Complexity is reasonable, though. The main trick is that any positive integer can be written as the sum of four squares, thus only eight multiplications (over the integer scheme) are needed to show that an input is both upper and lower bounded. In addition to this, there is the cost of transferring the input to the scheme of the ABB.

Acknowledgements. The authors would like to thank Ivan Damgård for comments and suggestions.

References

[BB89]   Bar-Ilan, J., Beaver, D.: Non-cryptographic fault-tolerant computing in a constant number of rounds of interaction. In: Rudnicki, P. (ed.) Proceedings of the eighth annual ACM Symposium on Principles of distributed computing, pp. 201–209. ACM Press, New York (1989)

[BGW88]   Ben-Or, M., Goldwasser, S., Wigderson, A.: Completeness theorems for noncryptographic fault-tolerant distributed computations. In: 20th Annual ACM Symposium on Theory of Computing, pp. 1–10. ACM Press, New York (1988)

[Bou00]   Boudot, F.: Efficient proofs that a committed number lies in an interval. In: Preneel, B. (ed.) EUROCRYPT 2000. LNCS, vol. 1807, pp. 431–444. Springer, Heidelberg (2000)

[Can00]   Canetti, R.: Universally composable security: A new paradigm for cryptographic protocols. Cryptology ePrint Archive, Report 2000/067 (2000), http://eprint.iacr.org/

[CCD88]   Chaum, D., Crépeau, C., Damgård, I.: Multiparty unconditionally secure protocols. In: 20th Annual ACM Symposium on Theory of Computing, pp. 11–19. ACM Press, New York (1988)

[CDN01]   Cramer, R., Damgård, I., Nielsen, J.: Multiparty computation from threshold homomorphic encryption. In: Pfitzmann, B. (ed.) EUROCRYPT 2001. LNCS, vol. 2045, pp. 280–300. Springer, Heidelberg (2001)

[DFK+06]   Damgård, I., Fitzi, M., Kiltz, E., Nielsen, J., Toft, T.: Unconditionally secure constant-rounds multi-party computation for equality, comparison, bits and exponentiation. In: Halevi, S., Rabin, T. (eds.) TCC 2006. LNCS, vol. 3876, pp. 285–304. Springer, Heidelberg (2006)

[DJ01]   Damgård, I., Jurik, M.: A generalisation, a simplification and some applications of paillier's probabilistic public-key system. In: Kim, K.-c. (ed.) PKC 2001. LNCS, vol. 1992, pp. 119–136. Springer, Heidelberg (2001)

[DJ02]   Damgård, I.B., Jurik, M.: Client/Server tradeoffs for online elections. In: Naccache, D., Paillier, P. (eds.) PKC 2002. LNCS, vol. 2274, pp. 125–140. Springer, Heidelberg (2002)

[DN03]   Damgård, I., Nielsen, J.: Universally composable efficient multiparty computation from threshold homomorphic encryption. In: Boneh, D. (ed.) CRYPTO 2003. LNCS, vol. 2729, pp. 247–264. Springer, Heidelberg (2003)

[Lip03]   Lipmaa, H.: On diophantine complexity and statistical zero-knowledge arguments. In: Laih, C.-S. (ed.) ASIACRYPT 2003. LNCS, vol. 2894, pp. 398–415. Springer, Heidelberg (2003)

[NO07]   Nishide, T., Ohta, K.: Multiparty computation for interval, equality, and comparison without bit-decomposition protocol. In: Okamoto, T., Wang, X. (eds.) PKC 2007. LNCS, vol. 4450, pp. 343–360. Springer, Heidelberg (2007)

[Pai99]   Paillier, P.: Public-key cryptosystems based on composite degree residuosity classes. In: Stern, J. (ed.) EUROCRYPT 1999. LNCS, vol. 1592, pp. 223–238. Springer, Heidelberg (1999)

[Rei09]   Reistad, T.: Multiparty comparison - an improved multiparty protocol for comparison of secret-shared values. In: Proceedings of SECRYPT 2009, pp. 325–330 (2009)

[Sha79]   Shamir, A.: How to share a secret. Communications of the ACM 22(11), 612–613 (1979)

[ST06]   Schoenmakers, B., Tuyls, P.: Efficient binary conversion for paillier encrypted values. In: Vaudenay, S. (ed.) EUROCRYPT 2006. LNCS, vol. 4004, pp. 522–537. Springer, Heidelberg (2006)

[Tho09]   Thorbek, R.: Linear Integer Secret Sharing. PhD thesis, Aarhus University (2009)

[Tof09]   Toft, T.: Constant-rounds, almost-linear bit-decomposition of secret shared values. In: Fischlin, M. (ed.) RSA Conference 2009. LNCS, vol. 5473, pp. 357–371. Springer, Heidelberg (2009)

[Yao82]   Yao, A.: Protocols for secure computations (extended abstract). In: 23th Annual Symposium on Foundations of Computer Science (FOCS 1982), pp. 160–164. IEEE Computer Society Press, Los Alamitos (1982)

[Yao86]   Yao, A.: How to generate and exchange secrets (extended abstract). In: 27th Annual Symposium on Foundations of Computer Science, pp. 162–167. IEEE Computer Society Press, Los Alamitos (1986)

Attacking and Repairing the Improved ModOnions Protocol*

Nikita Borisov[1], Marek Klonowski[2],
Mirosław Kutyłowski[2], and Anna Lauks-Dutka[2]

[1] Department of Electrical and Computer Engineering,
University of Illinois at Urbana-Champaign
nikita@uiuc.edu
[2] Institute of Mathematics and Computer Science, Wrocław University of Technology
{Marek.Klonowski,Miroslaw.Kutylowski,Anna.Lauks}@pwr.wroc.pl

Abstract. In this paper, we present a new class of attacks against an
anonymous communication protocol, originally presented in ACNS 2008.
The protocol itself was proposed as an improved version of ModOnions,
which uses universal re-encryption in order to avoid replay attacks. However, ModOnions allowed the *detour attack*, introduced by Danezis to
re-route ModOnions to attackers in such a way that the entire path is
revealed. The ACNS 2008 proposal addressed this by using a more complicated key management scheme. The revised protocol is immune to
detour attacks. We show, however, that the ModOnion construction is
highly malleable and this property can be exploited in order to redirect
ModOnions. Our attacks require detailed probing and are less efficient
than the detour attack, but they can nevertheless recover the full onion
path while avoiding detection and investigation. Motivated by this, we
present a new modification to the ModOnion protocol that dramatically
reduces the malleability of the encryption primitive. It addresses the class
of attacks we present and it makes other attacks difficult to formulate.

1   Introduction

Mix networks have been a popular scheme for anonymous communication since
they were first introduced by Chaum [2]. The basics of the design are that
messages are protected by a layered ("onion") encryption, with each mix in the
path removing a layer of encryption and shuffling a batch of incoming messages
before forwarding them onwards. This way, each mix only knows its predecessor
and successor in the forwarding path of a message transmitted through the mix,
and an outside observer cannot link inputs of the mix to the outputs due to
encryption.

The idea of mixes is very appealing and became the basic component of major
anonymous communication protocols. However, despite of the importance of
the problem, we are still far away from providing an ultimate solution that

---

* Partially supported by Polish Ministry of Science and Higher Education, grant N
N206 2701 33.

D. Lee and S. Hong (Eds.): ICISC 2009, LNCS 5984, pp. 258–273, 2010.

would provide a satisfactory resilience to attempts of breaking anonymity. The main reason is that in a practical setting an adversary has many other attack possibilities than merely observing the incoming and outcoming messages of a mix. This includes issues such as traffic analysis (static and dynamic) as well as active attacks where an adversary may inject messages or modify them. So far, research on anonymous communication protocols is a step-by-step advance, where protocol proposals (dealing with certain classes of problems) are followed by new attack methods.

Replay attack, ModOnions and detour attacks. Two rogue mixes can carry out a *replay* attack, where one mix will re-send one or more copy of a message, and the other look for duplicate incoming messages. This way the two mixes can detect that they are on the same forwarding paths even if they are separated by many honest mixes. The traditional defense to this attack is to have each mix look for and discard message duplicates [5], requiring the mixes to maintain state. Note that most of anonymous routing protocols are not immune against replay attack. Even the most popular TOR protocol (introduced in [6]) can be affected by elaborated forms of reply attack as reported in [13]. TOR is quite different from the regular Onion Routing and to protect integrity of a message it uses enumerating packages and labeling streams. Such an approach protects to some extent from reply attacks, however makes TOR vulnerable to different statistical attacks. The fact remains, however that TOR is the most secure implemented solution. ModOnions [9] take an alternate approach, using Universal Re-Encryption (URE) [8] to re-randomize the messages ("onions"), such that duplicate copies of an onion cannot be linked. Re-encryption of such onions is possible, since instead of a single onion with a message hidden at each "layer" of the onion, there is a group of onions to be processed together, each encoding a different routing information for a path. When processed properly, each node on the path gets information from one of these onions and re-randomizes the rest. Last not least, ModOnions can be signed by some intermediate servers (for instance in order to prevent spam) and the signatures can be re-encrypted while processing [10].

ModOnions addressed the replay attacks, but it turned out that they are susceptible to the *detour attack* [4], where a ModOnion is redirected to go back to the attacker after each routing step, and a mix is used as a decryption oracle. Klonowski et al. presented a defense against the detour attacks by modifying the key management scheme and using different keys for the final decryption [11].

1.1   Results

New attacks. We show that the improved scheme presented in [11] is still vulnerable to redirection attacks that allow the recovery of the forwarding path. Our first attack uses the fact that a form of oracle decryption is still possible even in the modified scheme. It is no longer possible for an attacker to learn the next hop in a path, but he can verify a guess of a forwarding path if he controls both the first and last node. The number of guesses depends on the size of the network and the length of the forwarding paths; the attack is feasible for a medium-sized network of 50 nodes using paths of length 5, but quickly becomes impractical for larger parameters.

Our second attack relies on *malleability* of the URE scheme, which makes it possible for an attacker to modify the encrypted plaintext of a message without knowing the key under which it is encrypted. This makes it possible to selectively modify an onion and use probes to recover its structure and learn the next hop, all while avoiding detection. This attack requires many fewer probes and is practical for most network sizes.

Patches. Using previous observations we propose a new extension to Mod-Onions that drastically limits the malleability of the scheme such that any modification to the plaintext will be detected with high probability. This makes the odds of success of our attacks negligible, as a large number of probes must all be modified in such a way as to escape detection. By introducing this integrity check into the ModOnion protocol, our extension should make the design of new attacks more difficult as well.

2   ModOnions Protocol from [11]

In this section we recall the improved version of the ModOnions protocol (Onion Routing with Universal Re-Encryption) from [11]. This protocol uses as a building block an extension of Universal Re-Encryption recalled below. At first let us recall details and properties of Universal Re-Encryption (from [8]).

2.1   Universal Re–encryption

Universal Re-Encryption is based on the ElGamal encryption scheme. Construction of this encryption scheme is based on a cyclic group G, where discrete logarithm, DDH problems are hard. Namely, let p, q be prime numbers such that $p = 2q + 1$ and let g be the generator of G, which is the subgroup of $\mathbb{Z}_p^*$ of order q. A private key is a non-zero $x < q$ chosen uniformly at random, the corresponding public key is y, where $y = g^x \bmod p$. For a message $m < p$, a ciphertext of m is a pair (s, r), where $r := g^k \bmod p$ and $s := m \cdot y^k \bmod p$ and $0 < k < q$ is chosen at random.

The ElGamal scheme is a probabilistic one: the same message encrypted for the second time yields a different ciphertext with overwhelming probability. Moreover, given two ciphertexts, it seems to be infeasible in practice to say whether they have been encrypted under the same key (unless, of course, the decryption key is given). This property is called *key-privacy* (see [8]). ElGamal cryptosystem has yet another important property. Everyone can re-encrypt a ciphertext (α, β) and get (α', β') where $\alpha' := \alpha \cdot y^{k'} \bmod p$, $\beta' := \beta \cdot g^{k'} \bmod p$ for $k' < q$ chosen at random and the public key y. Moreover, without the decryption key it is infeasible to find that (α, β) and (α', β') correspond to the same plaintext.

In [8] Golle et al. proposed a slightly modified version of this scheme that is called universal re-encryption scheme or *URE* for short. It consists of the following procedures:

Setup: A generator g of a cyclic group G of prime order is chosen, where discrete logarithm problem and DDH assumption is hard. Then G and g are published.

Key generation: Alice chooses a private key x at random; then the corresponding public key y is computed as $y = g^x$.

Encryption: To encrypt a message m for Alice, Bob generates uniformly at random values k_0 and k_1 ($k_0, k_1 < p$). Then, the ciphertext of m is a quadruple: $(\alpha_0, \beta_0; \alpha_1, \beta_1) := \left(m \cdot y^{k_0}, g^{k_0}; y^{k_1}, g^{k_1} \right)$. Let us note that this is a pair of two ElGamal ciphertexts with plaintext messages m and 1 (neutral element of G), respectively.

Decryption: Alice computes $m_0 := \frac{\alpha_0}{\beta_0^x}$ and $m_1 := \frac{\alpha_1}{\beta_1^x}$. Message m_0 is accepted if and only if $m_1 = 1$.

Re-encryption: Two random values k_0' and k_1' are chosen. Then we compute: $\left(\alpha_0 \cdot \alpha_1^{k_0'}, \beta_0 \cdot \beta_1^{k_0'}; \alpha_1^{k_1'}, \beta_1^{k_1'} \right)$, which is a ciphertext of the same plaintext.

From now on we assume that $E_x(m)$ denotes an URE ciphertext of a message m for a secret decryption key x. Note that there are many possible values for $E_x(m)$, since URE is a probabilistic encryption scheme.

2.2 Extension of Universal Re–encryption

Let us assume that there are λ distinct servers on each routing path, each server s_i has a private key x_i and the corresponding public key $y_i = g^{x_i}$. To encrypt a message m, which should go through the nodes $s_1, \ldots, s_\lambda$, first values k_0 and k_1 are generated at random. Then the ciphertext has the following form:

$$E_{x_1+x_2+\cdots+x_\lambda}(m) = (\alpha_0, \beta_0; \alpha_1, \beta_1) := \left(m \cdot (y_1 y_2 \ldots y_\lambda)^{k_0}, g^{k_0}; (y_1 y_2 \ldots y_\lambda)^{k_1}, g^{k_1} \right).$$

Obviously, $y_1 y_2 \ldots y_\lambda$ is a kind of *cumulative* public key, since

$$E_{x_1+x_2+\cdots+x_\lambda}(m) = \left(m \cdot g^{k_0 \sum_{i=1}^{\lambda} x_i}, g^{k_0}; g^{k_1 \sum_{i=1}^{\lambda} x_i}, g^{k_1} \right).$$

Moreover, $E_{x_1+\cdots+x_\lambda}(m)$ is a ciphertext of m with the decryption key equal to $\sum_{i=1}^{\lambda} x_i$. Hence it can be re-encrypted in a regular way. Moreover, such a ciphertext can be *partially decrypted*, for instance, by the first server s_1. Namely, it computes $E_{x_2+\cdots+x_\lambda}(m)$ as the following quadruple:

$$(\alpha_0', \beta_0'; \alpha_1', \beta_1') := \left(\frac{\alpha_0}{\beta_0^{x_1}}, \beta_0; \frac{\alpha_1}{\beta_1^{x_1}}, \beta_1 \right).$$

It is obvious that it still is a correct URE ciphertext for the "reduced" decryption key $\sum_{i=2}^{\lambda} x_i$, and therefore it also can be re-encrypted as it was described above.

2.3 Description of ModOnions Protocol from [11]

The core idea of protocol introduced in [11] is that each server s has two different pairs of keys:

- transport keys: a private key x_s and a public key $y_s := g^{x_s}$,
- destination keys: a private key $x_s^\star$ and a public key $y_s^\star := g^{x_s^\star}$.

Now the blocks encoding intermediate nodes on the routing path $s_1, s_2, \ldots, s_\lambda$ are constructed as follows:

$$E_{x_{s_1}^\star} (\text{send to } s_2),$$

$$E_{x_{s_1} + \cdots + x_{s_{i-1}} + x_{s_i}^\star} (\text{send to } s_{i+1}) \quad \text{for all } 2 \leq i \leq \lambda - 1,$$

$$E_{x_{s_1} + \cdots + x_{s_{\lambda-1}} + x_{s_\lambda}^\star} (m, t), \quad \text{where } t \text{ is a current time.}$$

Note that:

- λ is a static parameter of the protocol,
- E denotes encryption scheme with properties as in [9, 11],
- for each block one of destination keys $x_i^\star$ is used and only once; moreover, it is the destination key of the final recipient of the information stored in the block.

Routing. When a server s gets Modified ModOnion the following steps of the protocol are executed:

1. Server s copies all blocks of a ModOnion. Then it decrypts all blocks with its private destination key.
2. If every previous server on the path is honest, then after decryption exactly one of the blocks should contain a correct message.
   Case 1: one of the decryptions yields a correct name of the next server s'. Then:
   (a) All blocks (as obtained from the previous server), except for the one containing s', are decrypted with the private transport key of s. The blocks obtained are then re-encrypted in the regular way.
   (b) A random block replaces the block containing s'.
   (c) The resulting blocks are permuted at random.
   (d) The ModOnion obtained in this way is sent to s'.
   Note that the number of blocks in a ModOnion remains unchanged.
   Case 2: after decryption s obtains one meaningful message with destination s. Then the message is delivered.
   Case 3: the result of decryption for all blocks is meaningless. Then the investigation procedure is launched.

Investigation procedure. Investigation procedure is a part of the protocol launched by the node detecting dishonest behavior of other nodes. In this procedure consecutive nodes from the path proves correct processing of the ModOnion. It is assumed that malicious node, once caught is permanently excluded from the protocol. Detailed description can be found in [9].

3   Attacks on the ModOnions Protocol from [11]

In this section we present two attacks on the improved ModOnions Protocol described in the previous section.

3.1   Attack 1: Guessing the Path

The modification to the ModOnions ensured that a router no longer acts as a decryption oracle for the destination key, thus making it impossible to carry out the detour attack. However, the router still acts as a decryption oracle for the transport key. This lets the attacker verify a guess for the path the onion will take. Suppose that an onion is sent to s_6 along a path s_1, s_2, s_3, s_4, s_5, with s_1 and s_5 being malicious. The onion that arrives at node s_1 will have the following form (we skip the permutation of blocks for clarity of presentation):

$$E_{x_{s_1}^\star} (\text{send to } s_2),$$
$$E_{x_{s_1} + x_{s_2}^\star} (\text{send to } s_3),$$
$$E_{x_{s_1} + x_{s_2} + x_{s_3}^\star} (\text{send to } s_4),$$
$$E_{x_{s_1} + x_{s_2} + x_{s_3} + x_{s_4}^\star} (\text{send to } s_5),$$
$$E_{x_{s_1} + x_{s_2} + x_{s_3} + x_{s_4} + x_{s_5}^\star} (\text{send to } s_6),$$
$$E_{x_{s_1} + x_{s_2} + x_{s_3} + x_{s_4} + x_{s_5} + x_{s_6}^\star} (m, t).$$

s_1 can no longer use s_2 to reveal the next router in the path. However, it can use it as a decryption oracle to partially decrypt the message using the transport key x_{s_2}. If s_1 then guesses that s_3 and s_4 are the next routers on the path, it can use them as decryption oracles as well. After this, the onion will include the block $E_{x_{s_5}^\star}$ (send to s_6). By performing a trial decryption with key $x_{s_5}^\star$ (which is available to the attacker since s_5 is compromised), the attacker can learn both that the guess of s_3 and s_4 is correct and that s_6 is the ultimate destination of the message.

We next describe the attack in more detail.

1. After receiving the onion, s_1 partially decrypts it with $x_{s_1}^\star$ to learn the destination s_2.
2. Then s_1 uses x_{s_1} to partially decrypt the remaining blocks and gets:

$$E_{x_{s_2}^\star} (\text{send to } s_3),$$
$$E_{x_{s_2} + x_{s_3}^\star} (\text{send to } s_4),$$
$$E_{x_{s_2} + x_{s_3} + x_{s_4}^\star} (\text{send to } s_5),$$
$$E_{x_{s_2} + x_{s_3} + x_{s_4} + x_{s_5}^\star} (\text{send to } s_6),$$
$$E_{x_{s_2} + x_{s_3} + x_{s_4} + x_{s_5} + x_{s_6}^\star} (m, t).$$

Let us call this onion O_1.

3. URE has the property that given a ciphertext encrypted with key x, $E_x(m)$, it is possible to produce a new ciphertext encrypted under the key $x + x'$, as long as x' is known. (One can think about this as a partial decryption under the key $-x'$.) This allows s_1 to wrap the blocks of O_1 in an extra layer of encryption so that these blocks are blindly partially decrypted and passed along by s_2. The new onion includes the original blocks of O_1 (after blinding them) as well as a new destination block:

$$E_{x_{s_2}^\star} (\text{send to } s_1),$$

$$E_{x'+x_{s_2}^\star} (\text{send to } s_3),$$

$$E_{x'+x_{s_2}+x_{s_3}^\star} (\text{send to } s_4),$$

$$E_{x'+x_{s_2}+x_{s_3}+x_{s_4}^\star} (\text{send to } s_5),$$

$$E_{x'+x_{s_2}+x_{s_3}+x_{s_4}+x_{s_5}^\star} (\text{send to } s_6),$$

$$E_{x'+x_{s_2}+x_{s_3}+x_{s_4}+x_{s_5}+x_{s_6}^\star} (m, t).$$

4. This onion is then sent to s_2. Node s_2 partially decrypts with $x_{s_2}^\star$ to learn that s_1 is the next hop.[1] Note that the second block will remain encrypted under x' and so s_2 will only find one plaintext block, therefore no investigation will be started.

5. s_2 partially decrypts the onion with x_{s_2} and forwards the following blocks to s_1:

$$\text{random},$$

$$E_{x'+x_{s_2}^\star - x_{s_2}} (\text{send to } s_3),$$

$$E_{x'+x_{s_3}^\star} (\text{send to } s_4),$$

$$E_{x'+x_{s_3}+x_{s_4}^\star} (\text{send to } s_5),$$

$$E_{x'+x_{s_3}+x_{s_4}+x_{s_5}^\star} (\text{send to } s_6),$$

$$E_{x'+x_{s_3}+x_{s_4}+x_{s_5}+x_{s_6}^\star} (m, t).$$

6. s_1 partially decrypts the onion with x', obtaining a new onion O_2:

$$\text{random},$$

$$E_{x_{s_2}^\star - x_{s_2}} (\text{send to } s_3),$$

$$E_{x_{s_3}^\star} (\text{send to } s_4),$$

$$E_{x_{s_3}+x_{s_4}^\star} (\text{send to } s_5),$$

$$E_{x_{s_3}+x_{s_4}+x_{s_5}^\star} (\text{send to } s_6),$$

$$E_{x_{s_3}+x_{s_4}+x_{s_5}+x_{s_6}^\star} (m, t).$$

Note that O_2 contains all the blocks of O_1, partially decrypted with the key x_{s_2}. We will call the steps 3–6 an oracle decryption, writing $O_2 = D_{x_{s_2}}(O_1)$.[2]

7. Now the attacker can proceed with guessing the path. For each (honest) router s_i, with $i \neq 2$, the attacker performs an oracle decryption to obtain $O_{s_i} = D_{x_{s_i}}(O_2)$.[3]

---

[1] s_2 may get suspicious about forwarding an onion back to s_1, but technically, s_5 or any other malicious node can act as the next hop to avoid this problem.

[2] This process is very similar to the oracle decryption proposed by Danezis [4].

[3] A minor caveat is that O_2 is one block longer than O_1: s_1 cannot distinguish the random block from the others and discard it. For the sake of simplicity of description we assume that ModOnions may have variable length. However, if we assume that the ModOnions always contain the same number of blocks, then s_1 will need to split O_2 into two onions and obtain oracle decryption of both.

8. For each pair (i, j), with $j \neq i$ and $j \neq 2$, the attacker performs another oracle decryption to obtain $O_{s_i, s_j} = D_{x_{s_j}}(O_{s_i})$.
9. For a correct guess of s_3, s_4, the onion O_{s_3, s_4} will have the form:

$$
\begin{aligned}
&\text{random,} \\
&\text{random,} \\
&\text{random,} \\
&E_{x_{s_2}^* - x_{s_2} - x_{s_3} - x_{s_4}} (\text{send to } s_3), \\
&E_{x_{s_3}^* - x_{s_3} - x_{s_4}} (\text{send to } s_4), \\
&E_{x_{s_4}^* - x_{s_4}} (\text{send to } s_5), \\
&E_{x_{s_5}^*} (\text{send to } s_6), \\
&E_{x_{s_5} + x_{s_6}^*} (m, t).
\end{aligned}
$$

By performing a trial decryption of all blocks with $x_{s_5}^*$, the attacker can learn s_6, which is the final destination of the message in this example.

This attack will work whenever s_1 and s_5 are at the beginning and end of the path. If the attacker has compromised more nodes, he can trial decrypt with the destination key of every compromised node to detect whether they lie on the path. (A trial decryption should also be performed on the intermediate onions O_{s_i} to detect cases where a compromised node is in the fourth position on the path.)

Note that there is another easy way to test a guess for a path: s_1 can follow the protocol, but insert $E_{x_{s_2} + x_{s_3} + x_{s_4} + x_{s_5}^*} (tag)$ instead of a random block into the onion forwarded to s_2. However, to test multiple guesses, onions would need to be replayed and the destination would get multiple copies of the same message, launching an investigation. Using the decryption oracles, no investigation will be started.

Complexity. The adversary needs to perform at most $(N - 1) + \binom{N-1}{2}$ oracle decryptions, where N is the number of honest routers in the network. For a network with 50 routers, this is a little over $1\,000$ oracle decryptions, making the attack expensive, but feasible. (To speed up the attack, decryptions at multiple routers can be carried out in parallel.) However, with larger networks the attack becomes infeasible; similarly, by increasing the path length from 5 to k, the complexity of the attack grows to $\Omega(N^{k-3})$.

3.2   Attack 2: The Two-hop Attack

Our second attack exploits the fact that URE allows an attacker to replace the plaintext of a message without knowing the encryption key as well as the plaintext removed. So, for example, given a block $E_{x_{s_i}} (\text{send to } s_j)$, an attacker can change it to $E_{x_{s_i}} (\text{send to } s_1)$. Using this technique, an attacker s_1 could change the received blocks

$$E_{x_{s_2}^\star}(\text{send to } s_3),$$
$$E_{x_{s_2}+x_{s_3}^\star}(\text{send to } s_4),$$
$$E_{x_{s_2}+x_{s_3}+x_{s_4}^\star}(\text{send to } s_5),$$
$$E_{x_{s_2}+x_{s_3}+x_{s_4}+x_{s_5}^\star}(\text{send to } s_6),$$
$$E_{x_{s_2}+x_{s_3}+x_{s_4}+x_{s_5}+x_{s_6}^\star}(m,t)$$

to the following form:

$$E_{x_{s_2}^\star}(\text{send to } s_3),$$
$$E_{x_{s_2}+x_{s_3}^\star}(\textbf{send to } \textbf{s}_\textbf{1}),$$
$$E_{x_{s_2}+x_{s_3}+x_{s_4}^\star}(\text{send to } s_5),$$
$$E_{x_{s_2}+x_{s_3}+x_{s_4}+x_{s_5}^\star}(\text{send to } s_6),$$
$$E_{x_{s_2}+x_{s_3}+x_{s_4}+x_{s_5}+x_{s_6}^\star}(m,t).$$

If s_1 sent these blocks to s_2, they would travel two hops, over to s_3 and back to s_1 (in a transformed form). s_1 would then learn that s_3 follows s_2 in the path of the onion. However, to adjust the onion properly, s_1 would need to know the order of the blocks. Since this is unknown, s_1 recovers the order by probing, as explained below in detail:

1. s_1 receives an onion to be forwarded. After picking out the destination and partial decryption, the onion has the following form:

$$E_{x_{s_2}^\star}(\text{send to } s_3),$$
$$E_{x_{s_2}+x_{s_3}^\star}(\text{send to } s_4),$$
$$E_{x_{s_2}+x_{s_3}+x_{s_4}^\star}(\text{send to } s_5),$$
$$E_{x_{s_2}+x_{s_3}+x_{s_4}+x_{s_5}^\star}(\text{send to } s_6),$$
$$E_{x_{s_2}+x_{s_3}+x_{s_4}+x_{s_5}+x_{s_6}^\star}(m,t).$$

2. s_1 replaces the plaintext of all but one of the blocks with the directive "send to s_1," obtaining an onion like the following:

$$E_{x_{s_2}^\star}(\textbf{send to } \textbf{s}_\textbf{1}),$$
$$E_{x_{s_2}+x_{s_3}^\star}(\textbf{send to } \textbf{s}_\textbf{1}),$$
$$E_{x_{s_2}+x_{s_3}+x_{s_4}^\star}(\text{send to } s_5),$$
$$E_{x_{s_2}+x_{s_3}+x_{s_4}+x_{s_5}^\star}(\textbf{send to } \textbf{s}_\textbf{1}),$$
$$E_{x_{s_2}+x_{s_3}+x_{s_4}+x_{s_5}+x_{s_6}^\star}(\textbf{send to } \textbf{s}_\textbf{1}).$$

In this case, the third block is left unmodified.

3. This new onion is sent to s_2, along with a tag block inserted as the random block:

$$E_{x_{s_2}+x'}(tag),$$
$$E_{x_{s_2}^\star}(\text{send to } s_1),$$
$$E_{x_{s_2}+x_{s_3}^\star}(\text{send to } s_1),$$
$$E_{x_{s_2}+x_{s_3}+x_{s_4}^\star}(\text{send to } s_5),$$
$$E_{x_{s_2}+x_{s_3}+x_{s_4}+x_{s_5}^\star}(\text{send to } s_1),$$
$$E_{x_{s_2}+x_{s_3}+x_{s_4}+x_{s_5}+x_{s_6}^\star}(\text{send to } s_1).$$

for some random key x'.

4. The onion received back from s_2 has the following form:

$$E_{x'}(tag),$$
$$\text{random},$$
$$E_{x_{s_3}^\star}(\text{send to } s_1),$$
$$E_{x_{s_3}+x_{s_4}^\star}(\text{send to } s_5),$$
$$E_{x_{s_3}+x_{s_4}+x_{s_5}^\star}(\text{send to } s_1),$$
$$E_{x_{s_3}+x_{s_4}+x_{s_5}+x_{s_6}^\star}(\text{send to } s_1).$$

s_1 notices the tag and declares this probe to be a failure.

5. s_1 starts with the original onion and once again replaces all but one of the blocks with "send to s_1", this time leaving a different block unmodified:

$$E_{x_{s_2}+x'}(tag),$$
$$E_{x_{s_2}^\star}(\textbf{send to } \textbf{s}_3),$$
$$E_{x_{s_2}+x_{s_3}^\star}(\textbf{send to } \textbf{s}_1),$$
$$E_{x_{s_2}+x_{s_3}+x_{s_4}^\star}(\textbf{send to } \textbf{s}_1),$$
$$E_{x_{s_2}+x_{s_3}+x_{s_4}+x_{s_5}^\star}(\textbf{send to } \textbf{s}_1),$$
$$E_{x_{s_2}+x_{s_3}+x_{s_4}+x_{s_5}+x_{s_6}^\star}(\textbf{send to } \textbf{s}_1).$$

6. s_1 once again sends the onion to s_2, along with a tag. s_2 now finds s_3 to be the destination of the onion, and forwards it there. s_3 then forwards the onion back to s_1, after all partial decryptions and inserting random blocks it has the form:

$$E_{x'-x_{s_3}}(tag),$$
$$\text{random},$$
$$\text{random},$$
$$E_{x_{s_4}^\star}(\textbf{send to } \textbf{s}_1),$$
$$E_{x_{s_4}+x_{s_5}^\star}(\textbf{send to } \textbf{s}_1),$$
$$E_{x_{s_4}+x_{s_5}+x_{s_6}^\star}(\textbf{send to } \textbf{s}_1).$$

7. Note that s_1 cannot decrypt any of the blocks of the onion, so it suspects that s_3 is the hop following s_2 in the onion path. To double check, it can resend the onion with a tag of $E_{x_{s_2}+x_{s_3}+x'}(tag)$. This time, the onion will come back with $E_{x'}(tag)$ as one of its blocks.

After these steps, s_1 learns the identity of the next hop in the path. It can now use s_2 as a decryption oracle to obtain a copy of an onion that would have been sent by s_2 to s_3 during normal forwarding. Thus it can assume the role of s_2 and repeat this attack with s_3 to learn the identity of s_4, and so on.

4   Defense: Context-Sensitive Encryption

A core problem that is exploited by all the attacks on ModOnions is that the onion construction is highly malleable: an attacker can make extensive modifications to the encrypted onion and still produce a valid result. To defend against them, we must reduce or eliminate this ability.

A non-malleable encryption scheme [7], such as Cramer–Shoup [3], would ensure that any modification to the ciphertext will result in a "random looking" plaintext upon decryption. However, a non-malleable scheme will, by definition, prevent the re-randomization used in re-encryption. Canetti et al. defined a relaxed version of non-malleability, called Re-randomizable Chosen Ciphertext Adversary security (RCCA) [1]. Prabhakaran and Rosulek later produced an RCCA-secure scheme, based on Cramer–Shoup and the "double strand" construction used in the Frikken–Golle universal re-encryption scheme we use in this paper [12]. However, this scheme cannot be used with ModOnions since it does not support key privacy, which is a requirement for anonymous message forwarding.

Instead, we propose a new modification to the ModOnions protocol that dramatically reduces the malleability of the scheme. Since all attacks on ModOnions rely on redirecting the onion to follow a different path, our modification centers around making such redirection impossible. It entangles the encryption construction with the onion path, such that if the path is modified, the decryption produces an invalid result and thus an attack is detected. Our main approach is to use a *context-sensitive* encryption/decryption key. Each router will have a collection of n distinct transport and n distinct destination keys, $x_{s_i,1}, \ldots, x_{s_i,n}$ and $x^*_{s_i,1}, \ldots, x^*_{s_i,n}$. Whenever a router needs to use a transport or a destination key, it picks the key based on context by selecting $x_{s_i,H(s_{i-1}||s_i||s_{i+1})}$, where $H : \{0,1\}^* \to \mathbb{Z}_n$ is a hash function and s_{i-1} and s_{i+1} are the identifiers preceding and following s_i in the onion path. (In fact, n need not to be large. Even $n = 2$ yields probability of 0.5 of detection of a malicious node in most cases, so it prevents systematic attacks).

4.1   Context-Sensitive Onion Construction

We now describe our construction in more detail. Suppose a node s_0 wishes to send a message to s_6, following a path s_1, s_2, s_3, s_4, s_5. We assume that it has the public keys for all routers, i.e., $y_{s_i,j} = g^{x_{s_i,j}}$. s_0 creates a ModOnion as before, but using context-sensitive keys. The first block of the onion would be:

$$E_{x^*_{s_1},H(s_0||s_1||s_2)}(\text{send to } s_2).$$

The next block would be:

$$E_{x_{s_1},H(s_0||s_1||s_2)+x^*_{s_2},H(s_1||s_2||s_3)}(\text{send to } s_3)$$

Notice that the transport key for s_1 is made context-sensitive as well. For s_2's destination key, the context used is the part of the path known to s_2. Proceeding in this manner, the complete onion has the following form:

$$E_{x^*_{s_1},H(s_0||s_1||s_2)}(\text{send to } s_2)$$
$$E_{x_{s_1},H(s_0||s_1||s_2)+x^*_{s_2},H(s_1||s_2||s_3)}(\text{send to } s_3)$$
$$E_{x_{s_1},H(s_0||s_1||s_2)+x_{s_2},H(s_1||s_2||s_3)+x^*_{s_3},H(s_2||s_3||s_4)}(\text{send to } s_4)$$
$$E_{x_{s_1},H(s_0||s_1||s_2)+x_{s_2},H(s_1||s_2||s_3)+x_{s_3},H(s_2||s_3||s_4)+x^*_{s_4},H(s_3||s_4|s_5)}(\text{send to } s_5)$$
$$E_{x_{s_1},H(s_0||s_1||s_2)+x_{s_2},H(s_1||s_2||s_3)+x_{s_3},H(s_2||s_3||s_4)+x_{s_4},H(s_3||s_4||s_5)+x^*_{s_5},H(s_4||s_5||s_6)}(\text{send to } s_6)$$
$$E_{x_{s_1},H(s_0||s_1||s_2)+x_{s_2},H(s_1||s_2||s_3)+x_{s_3},H(s_2||s_3||s_4)+x_{s_4},H(s_3||s_4||s_5)+x_{s_5},H(s_4||s_5||s_6)+x^*_{s_6},H(s_5||s_6)}(m,t)$$

Forwarding of the onions proceeds in a similar fashion as before, except that context-sensitive keys are used. Notice that when s_1 receives the onion, it does not yet know what the next hop in the path will be. We nevertheless want to use context-sensitive encryption here to reduce the possibility of attack. To resolve this problem, s_1 uses a brute-force search for all possible destination keys. That is, it performs a trial decryption of each block with the keys $x^*_{s_1,1}, x^*_{s_1,2}, \cdots, x^*_{s_1,n}$. This search will certainly slow down the decryption process, but even for $n = 100$, the trial decryptions should take less than a second on a modern PC, and of course, n is a tunable parameter.

After a trial decryption succeeds with key $x^*_{s_1,j}$ for some j, s_1 verifies that the contents of the decrypted message ("send to s_2") matches the recovered context $s_0||s_1||s_i$, i.e., that $H(s_0||s_1||s_2) = j$. If there is a discrepancy, the onion is discarded and an investigation is started. Otherwise, it replaces the destination block with a random one, partially decrypts the rest of the onion with the key $x_{s_1,H(s_0||s_1||s_2)}$, re-randomizes and shuffles the blocks, and forwards the new onion to s_2.

If the decrypted plaintext contains a message, rather than a redirection directive, the router once again verifies that the correct context is used, i.e., that $H(s_0||s_1) = m$ and discards a message otherwise.

5   Security Analysis of the Modified ModOnion Scheme

Defending against the Two-Hop Attack.   As the two-hop attack makes extensive use of modifying the onion contents, it is severely impacted by the use of context-sensitive encryption. In the case of an unsuccessful probe, s_2 will receive an onion with the block:

$$E_{x^*_{s_2,H(s_1||s_2||s_3)}}(\text{send to } s_1).$$

After a brute-force search, the decryption will succeed using a key $x^*_{s_2,i}$ for some i, but the odds that $i = H(s_1||s_2||s_1)$ are only $1/n$. Therefore, s_2 will launch an investigation with probability $\frac{n-1}{n}$ Similarly, for a successful probe, s_3 will receive an onion with:

$$E_{x^*_{s_3,H(s_2||s_3||s_4)}}(\text{send to } s_1)$$

and launch an investigation whenever $H(s_2||s_3||s_4) \neq H(s_2||s_3||s_1)$.

The context-sensitive encryption acts as an integrity check on the message contents, effectively preventing any modifications of the onion. For the two-hop attack to succeed without detection, it must be the case that:

$$H(s_1||s_2||s_3) = H(s_1||s_2||s_1),\ H(s_2||s_3||s_4){=}H(s_2||s_3||s_1),\ H(s_3||s_4||s_5){=}H(s_3||s_4||s_1),$$
$$H(s_4||s_5||s_6) = H(s_4||s_5||s_1),\ H(s_5||s_6) = H(s_5||s_6||s_1)$$

otherwise one of the nodes will notice the attack and start an investigation. The odds of this are $\frac{1}{n^5}$, so even very small values of n provide an effective defense.

Defending against the Path-Guessing Attack. The path guessing attack does not modify any onion plaintext and thus is not immediately thwarted by context-sensitive encryption. However, using a router as a decryption oracle becomes significantly more complicated. Consider, for example, using s_3 as a decryption oracle in the path-guessing attack. If s_1 were to follow the same steps as in Section 3.1 for oracle decryption (but using $E_{x^*_{s_3,H(s_1||s_3||s_1)}}$ as the new destination block), it would receive an onion where all blocks have been decrypted with the key $x_{s_3,H(s_1||s_3||s_1)}$. However, the blocks in the real path would have in fact been encrypted with $x_{s_3,H(s_2||s_3||s_4)}$, and thus the oracle decryption would be useless (unless the hashes happen to match).

However, s_1 can perform a trial to verify a guess of an entire path. It would start by creating the following destination fields:

$$E_{x^*_{s_2,H(s_1||s_2||s_3)}}(\text{send to } s_3)$$
$$E_{x_{s_2,H(s_1||s_2||s_3)}+x^*_{s_3,H(s_2||s_3||s_4)}}(\text{send to } s_4)$$
$$E_{x_{s_2,H(s_1||s_2||s_3)}+x_{s_3,H(s_2||s_3||s_4)}+x^*_{s_4,H(s_3||s_4||s_5)}}(\text{send to } s_5)$$

Then it would wrap all the existing blocks of the original onion (O_1 in Section 3.1) in a layer of encryption with random key x':

$$E_x(m) \rightarrow E_{x+x'}(m).$$

When the onion is sent to s_2, it will be forwarded along the path s_2, s_3, s_4, s_5, with the corresponding context-sensitive decryptions happening along the way.

In other words, s_5 will receive blocks that has been partially decrypted with the key $x_{s_2,H(s_1||s_2||s_3)} + x_{s_3,H(s_2||s_3||s_4)} + x_{s_4,H(s_3||s_4||s_5)}$. If the path guess is correct, s_5 will receive an onion that will contain a block $E_{x'+x^*_{s_5,H(s_4||s_5||s_6)}}$ (send to s_6), which it could locate by trial decryption. If the path guess is incorrect, s_5 would receive an onion with blocks that it cannot decrypt.

This attack is slower than the (already slow) path guessing attack. In our particular case (s_3, s_4 honest, s_5 corrupted) it requires $(N-1)(N-2)C$ path guesses, where N is the number of honest nodes in the network and C is the number of nodes collaborating with s_1. Possibility to parallelize this process is limited due to the fact that every probe must pass through s_2 first, limiting the rate that can be used without arousing suspicion. If the size of the network is such that the attack is still practical, increasing the path length can easily eliminate it.

Possibility of Tagging Attacks. The modified construction of onions and the context-sensitive encryption still potentially allow the adversary to replace the plaintext (the address of the next server or the message) in a single block or put something in the place of the random block. To some extent, this can be useful for a tagging attack. Let us consider the following scenario: an onion gets to some corrupted node s_i. This node wants to add a special tag, so that if this onion arrives at another node controlled by the adversary, then he will be able to recognize this event.

There are two ways in which the adversary may try to achieve that goal. According to the first method, s_i can copy some block of the onion, change the original plaintext there into some "tag" message, blind the ciphertext with some additional key x' and use it as the random block created himself. The adversary will be able to recognize the tag if and only if the block used is a block addressed to a node under control of the adversary. This occurs with probability f, where f is the fraction of nodes controlled by the adversary in the network. If the adversary replaces some other blocks with the blocks constructed as above, then the chance to detect a tag may increase at most λ times, where λ is the number of blocks. So, the probability remains small for the case when f is reasonable. However, if the tag is not recognized by some adversary node, then it will be detected that some block is missing and an investigation will be started.

According to the second method, the adversary creates a ciphertext that encodes some "tag" by using the public keys of arbitrarily chosen nodes and some blinding factor x' and replaces some original block with this ciphertext. In this case tagging remains undetected by honest nodes as long as the tag is inserted in the random block created by s_i. The tag can be read by an adversary node only if the path for the tag is guessed correctly. If this path has length k, then this probability equals $\frac{f}{(N-1)^{k-1}}$, where f is the fraction of nodes controlled by the adversary and N is the overall number of nodes. The adversary may increase this probability by replacing more blocks by the blocks with tags. However, in most cases the tags are undetected, but the block removed will be found missing leading to an investigation.

Countermeasures against Tagging Attacks. Since only the first method of tagging attacks presented above is a serious threat is a real threat, we concentrate on preventing a node to put some extra information in the random block. For this purpose we need a public key P. Peculiarity of this public key is that it has no owner holding the corresponding private key. We also assume that each message contains sending time information and that each message will be delivered in time T - otherwise we talk about an irregularity that has to be investigated. The protocol may look as follows:

- instead of a random block the node should construct a ciphertext of 1 using public key P,
- when a ModOnion is transmitted from node n_i to n_j, the node n_j starts a checking procedure with a probability p, independently of other events (in particular, whether checking has been already initiated for another copy of the same message). The checking procedure consists of the following steps:
  1. the message is stored by S_j,
  2. s_i is asked to resend the same message (re-encryption applies),
  3. s_j waits time T and afterwards demands a proof from s_i that one of the blocks of the ModOnion is a ciphertext 1 created as described above. The proof can be given by presenting the random exponent used for creating the ciphertext.

Alternatively, instead of revealing the encryption exponent, s_i may provide a zero-knowledge proof that one of the ciphertexts of the onion is a ciphertext of 1 under key P (without revealing which). In this case we do not have to wait with the proof, but the proof might be too intensive computationally.

Note that no proof should reveal which block is random, unless the message cannot be sent anymore without starting an investigation. Indeed, otherwise s_j would know two random blocks and could insert a tag in one of them without possibility to be caught.

6   Conclusions

We presented two new types of attacks on the ModOnions protocol showing that, despite modifications in [11], the protocol is still insecure. However, we introduce a patch that successfully defends against these new attacks without providing any new information to intermediate nodes. The main remaining threat seems to be the tagging attack.

Acknowledgment

We thank the anonymous reviewers for the comments, especially for the remarks concerning the tagging attack.

References

1. Canetti, R., Krawczyk, H., Nielsen, J.B.: Relaxing chosen-ciphertext security. In: Boneh, D. (ed.) CRYPTO 2003. LNCS, vol. 2729, pp. 565–582. Springer, Heidelberg (2003)
2. Chaum, D.: Untraceable Electronic Mail, Return Addresses, and Digital Pseudonyms. Communications of the ACM 24(2), 84–88 (1981)
3. Cramer, R., Shoup, V.: A Practical Public Key Cryptosystem Provably Secure Against Adaptive Chosen Ciphertext Attack. In: Krawczyk, H. (ed.) CRYPTO 1998. LNCS, vol. 1462, pp. 13–25. Springer, Heidelberg (1998)
4. Danezis, G.: Breaking Four Mix-Related Schemes Based on Universal Re-encryption. In: Katsikas, S.K., López, J., Backes, M., Gritzalis, S., Preneel, B. (eds.) ISC 2006. LNCS, vol. 4176, pp. 46–59. Springer, Heidelberg (2006)
5. Danezis, G., Dingledine, R., Mathewson, N.: Mixminion: design of a type III anonymous remailer protocol. In: IEEE Symposium on Security and Privacy, pp. 2–15 (2003)
6. Dingledine, R., Mathewson, N., Syverson, P.F.: Tor: The Second-Generation Onion Router. In: USENIX Security Symposium 2004, pp. 303–320 (2004)
7. Dolev, D., Naor, M.: Non-malleable cryptography. In: ACM Symposium on Theory of Computing, pp. 542–552 (1991)
8. Golle, P., Jakobsson, M., Juels, A., Syverson, P.F.: Universal Re-encryption for Mixnets. In: Okamoto, T. (ed.) CT-RSA 2004. LNCS, vol. 2964, pp. 163–178. Springer, Heidelberg (2004)
9. Gomułkiewicz, M., Klonowski, M., Kutyłowski, M.: Onions Based on Universal Re-encryption — Anonymous Communication Immune Against Repetitive Attack. In: Lim, C.H., Yung, M. (eds.) WISA 2004. LNCS, vol. 3325, pp. 400–410. Springer, Heidelberg (2005)
10. Klonowski, M., Kutyłowski, M., Lauks, A., Zagórski, F.: Universal Re-encryption of Signatures and Controlling Anonymous Information Flow. In: WARTACRYPT 2004 Conference on Cryptology, vol. 33, pp. 179–188. Tatra Mountains Mathematical Publications (2006)
11. Klonowski, M., Kutyłowski, M., Lauks, A.: Repelling Detour Attack against Onions with Re-Encryption. In: Bellovin, S.M., Gennaro, R., Keromytis, A.D., Yung, M. (eds.) ACNS 2008. LNCS, vol. 5037, pp. 296–308. Springer, Heidelberg (2008)
12. Prabhakaran, M., Rosulek, M.: Rerandomizable RCCA encryption. In: Menezes, A. (ed.) CRYPTO 2007. LNCS, vol. 4622, pp. 517–534. Springer, Heidelberg (2007)
13. Pries, R., Yu, W., Fu, X., Wei Zhao, W.: A New Replay Attack Against Anonymous Communication Networks. In: Proceedings of IEEE International Conference on Communication, pp. 1578–1582 (2008)
14. Tsiounis, Y., Yung, M.: On the Security of ElGamal Based Encryption. In: Imai, H., Zheng, Y. (eds.) PKC 1998. LNCS, vol. 1431, pp. 117–134. Springer, Heidelberg (1998)

Secret Handshakes with Revocation Support

Alessandro Sorniotti[1,2] and Refik Molva[2]

[1] SAP Research,
805, Docteur Maurice Donat,
06250 Mougins, France
[2] Institut Eurécom
2229, Route des Crêtes
06560 Valbonne, France
first.last@eurecom.fr

Abstract. Revocation of credentials in Secret Handshakes is a difficult challenge, as it mixes the conflicting requirements of tracing revoked users and of the untraceability and unlinkability of legitimate protocol players. The schemes proposed in the literature are either limited versions of secret handshake supporting revocation, or they support more complete versions of secret handshake with no possibility of introducing revocation. In this paper we present a simple protocol that allows a user to prove to a verifier possession of a credential. Credentials can be revoked simply by publishing a value in a revocation list. This protocol is extremely flexible, as with it, we can achieve revocation for each of the different nuances of Secret Handshakes known in the literature. We prove the security of the new scheme without random oracles.

1 Introduction

The topic of secret handshakes is gaining momentum in research, as evidenced by the number of recent publications on the subject [1,21,10,23,12]. The concept has been introduced by Balfanz and colleagues in [5] as protocols that can be used by two parties to share a key only if they both belong to a common secret group. The protocol makes sure that an outsider, or an illegitimate group member does not learn anything by interacting with a legitimate user or eavesdropping on protocol exchanges.

The original protocol by Balfanz et al. [5] suffers from a number of shortcomings, namely it only allows users to prove membership to the same group, and it requires multiple credentials, as exchanged credentials are traceable over multiple executions. These shortcomings have been fixed by subsequent schemes that support the reuse of credentials and allow to match properties different from a user's own [10,25,15,14,21].

In spite of these enhancements, Secret Handshakes still suffer from significant limitations due to the inherent difficulty of supporting revocation of credentials. Revocation represents indeed an interesting challenge: on the one hand, protocol messages need to be untraceable; on the other, revocation requires means of tagging credentials in order to single out the revoked ones and refuse to interact with users bearing them.

D. Lee and S. Hong (Eds.): ICISC 2009, LNCS 5984, pp. 274–299, 2010.

So far this problem has still not been solved: among the schemes presented in the literature, there are either limited versions of secret handshake schemes that support revocation [27,5,10], or other schemes that support more complete versions of secret handshake with no possibility of introducing revocation, at least not without radical changes to the protocol [1,23].

The contributions of this paper are manifold: (i) we present a novel scheme called RevocationMatching, a building block for addressing in a comprehensive way all Secret Handshake scenarios known in the literature, with the additional feature of revocation; (ii) with RevocationMatching we can build each of the different "flavors" of secret handshake, own-group membership secret handshakes [5,10,18,25,27], secret handshakes with dynamic matching [1] or secret handshake with dynamic controlled matching [23], adding revocation support to each. In addition, (iii) our scheme supports the existence of multiple CAs, which also represent an interesting advancement to the state of the art of Secret Handshakes.

In all the different schemes that we propose, credentials can be efficiently revoked. After their revocation, credentials naturally lose their untraceability; however, as we shall see, only users authorized to match a given credential will be able to trace the revoked credential; for other users, the credential will still be unlinkable and untraceable. We analyze the security of RevocationMatching and of the derived Secret Handshake schemes *without* random oracles, by reduction to intractable problems.

2 Related Work and Contribution

The goal of this Section is to walk the reader through the related work carried out in the field of secret handshakes, highlighting the different existing protocols and positioning the contribution of this paper.

Secret Handshakes have been introduced by Balfanz et al. [5] as a mechanism devised for two users to simultaneously prove to each other possession of a property, for instance membership to a certain group. The ability to prove and verify is strictly controlled by a certification authority, that issues property credentials and matching references respectively allowing to prove to another user, and to verify another user's, possession of a property. Balfanz' original scheme, as many other schemes in the literature, only supports proving and verifying membership to the same group: for this reason, we shall call this family of schemes *own-group membership secret handshakes*. The proposed scheme supports revocation, but has a number of drawbacks, for instance the fact that it relies on one-time credentials to achieve untraceability. After this seminal work, many papers have further investigated the subject of secret handshake, considerably advancing the state of the art. The work by Castelluccia et al. [10] has shown how, under some specific requirements (namely CA-obliviousness), secret handshakes can be obtained from PKI-enabled encryption schemes. Other schemes have followed this approach [25,15] offering similar results, albeit with different nuances of unlinkability. Almost all the schemes in this family support revocation of credentials; however the functionalities offered are limited to proving and verifying membership to a common group.

[14,21] show how leveraging on authenticated key exchanges, we can build Secret Handshakes. Shin and Gligor [21] use password-authenticated key exchanges to establish a common key, provided that there is a match of one common interest or "wish". This protocol is very similar to the family of *Secure Matchmaking* protocols [4,28]. Protocols in this family support revocation but suffer from a drawback: the CA cannot exercise any control over who has the right to match which property. While this is a good feature in matchmaking-like scenarios, it is an undesirable feature in more sensitive scenarios (see [23]). In addition, schemes in this family are again limited to proof and verification of membership to a common group.

An advancement on this front has recently been put forward by Ateniese et al. [1], who have introduced *dynamic matching* and Sorniotti et al. [23] who have proposed the similar concept of *dynamic controlled matching*. Both schemes allow more flexible types of handshakes: members of different groups, or more generally, users holding credentials for different properties, can conduct a successful secret handshake if credentials match the other user's matching references. The difference between the two schemes is the control that the CA retains over the matching ability. Both schemes are extremely flexible, covering the functionalities of own-group membership secret handshakes and adding dynamic matching; however, neither of them support revocation of credentials.

A related topic is represented by oblivious signature-based envelopes (OS-BEs), introduced by Li et al. in [16]; using OSBE, a sender can send an envelope to a receiver, with the assurance that the receiver will only be able to open it if he holds the signature on an agreed-upon message. Nasserian and Tsudik in [19] argue – with no proofs – that two symmetric instances of OSBE may yield a Secret Handshake: however OSBE does not consider unlinkability and untraceability, as it requires the explicit agreement on a signature beforehand. Camenisch et al. have shown in [9] how dynamic accumulators [20,6] can be used to achieve efficient revocation for anonymous credentials. However dynamic accumulators, quoting Balfanz [5], are ill-suited for secret handshakes, mainly due to the fact that when a verifier has checked that a prover's witness belongs to the accumulator, he has already disclosed the prover's affiliation and can then selfishly refuse to reveal his own witness, or can reveal a fake one. Turning accumulator based asymmetric membership verification into symmetric handshakes is indeed an interesting open challenge. In addition, it is not possible to control who can verify what, dynamic matching cannot be supported, and finally, tracing traitors is not feasible.

The scheme that we present in this paper can reproduce the functionalities of the different families of secret handshakes that we have discussed in this Section, with the built-in revocation support. In addition, our scheme supports as well the existence of multiple CAs, which represent an interesting advancement to the state of the art of Secret Handshakes.

3   An Overview of the Solution

In this Section we give the reader an insight on the reasons and choices behind the actual design of the scheme.

At first, let us describe the notation used in the sequel of the paper. Given a security parameter k, let $\mathbb{G}_1$, $\mathbb{G}_2$ and $\mathbb{G}_T$ be groups of order q for some large prime q, where the bit-size of q is determined by the security parameter k. Our scheme uses a computable, non-degenerate bilinear map $\hat{e} : \mathbb{G}_1 \times \mathbb{G}_2 \to \mathbb{G}_T$ for which the *Symmetric External Diffie-Hellman (SXDH)* problem is assumed to be hard. The SXDH assumption in short allows for the existence of a bilinear pairing, but assumes that the Decisional Diffie-Hellman problem is hard in both $\mathbb{G}_1$ and $\mathbb{G}_2$ (see [1] for more details).

We then describe how we represent strings into group elements. Following [7,26], let $\tilde{g} \xleftarrow{R} \mathbb{G}_2$; let us also choose $n + 1$ random values $\{y_i\}_{i=0}^n \xleftarrow{R} \mathbb{Z}_q^*$; we assign $\tilde{g}_0 = \tilde{g}^{y_0}, \tilde{g}_1 = \tilde{g}^{y_1}, \ldots, \tilde{g}_n = \tilde{g}^{y_n}$. If $v \in \{0,1\}^n$ is an n-bit string, let us define $h(v) = y_0 + \sum_{i \in V(v)} y_i \in \mathbb{Z}_q^*$, where $V(v)$ represents the set of indexes i for which the ith bit of v is equal to 1. We also define $\tilde{H}(v) = \tilde{g}_0 \prod_{i \in V(v)} \tilde{g}_i = \tilde{g}^{h(v)} \in \mathbb{G}_2$.

Our starting objective is to design a scheme that helps a prover convince a verifier that she owns the credential for a property; however, the verification will be successful only for entitled verifiers. The exchange must satisfy the standard security requirements for Secret Handshakes, detector and impersonator resistance and untraceability of properties and identities. On top of this, we also want to support revocation of credentials. To this end, we need some means of secretly "labeling" each credential, so that we can later on reveal the label and use it as a handle to refuse handshake instances embedding it. In this section we try to walk the reader through the design of the solution.

Let us assume that g and $\tilde{g}$ are generators of $\mathbb{G}_1$ and $\mathbb{G}_2$ respectively. Also, $t \in \mathbb{Z}_q^*$ is a master secret. Then, given a property p, matching references can be formed as $\tilde{g}^{h(p)t} \in \mathbb{G}_2$ and given to verifiers; in order to successfully authenticate as a possessor of property p, a prover must then prove knowledge of $g^{h(p)t} \in \mathbb{G}_1$. However, instead of simply giving that value to the prover, we pick a random value $x \in \mathbb{Z}_q^*$, different for every credential, and give x and $g^{(x+h(p)t)}$ to the prover. $g^{(x+h(p)t)}$ is the credential and x is the aforementioned tag, called *identification handle* in the rest of this paper, used to identify credentials that need to be revoked.

Then, a prover can be authenticated by a verifier as follows: the verifier sends a challenge $\hat{e}(g, \tilde{g})^m$ and receives $\langle g^{r(x+h(p)t)}, g^r \rangle$ from the prover, where r is a random number, used by the prover to salt the handshake message. The prover can compute $K = (\hat{e}(g, \tilde{g})^m)^{rx}$ and the verifier can compute $K' = \left(\hat{e}\left(g^{r(x+h(p)t)}, \tilde{g}\right) / \hat{e}\left(g^r, \tilde{g}^{h(p)t}\right) \right)^m$; if the authentication is successful, K and K' are the same.

If the credential is to be revoked at some point, all we need to do is reveal $\tilde{g}^x$, called *revocation handle* in the rest of the paper. This way, the verifier can verify if the credential used by the prover has been revoked, by checking if $\hat{e}\left(g^{r(x+h(p)t)}, \tilde{g}\right) = \hat{e}\left(g^r, \tilde{g}^{h(p)t} \cdot \tilde{g}^x\right)$ holds.

Two challenges arise: first, it should be impossible to use the value x in order to trace credentials before they have been revoked; and second, a user should be forced to send credentials unmodified. The solution presented above respects the privacy of users: prior to the revocation of a given credential, an attacker cannot use the identification handle to link two different instances of the handshake to the same user: it is easy to show that linking the same x through subsequent instances of the protocol, is equivalent to solving DDH in $\mathbb{G}_1$.

However this solution still does not force the attacker to send his credentials unmodified, which would imply that an attacker can circumvent revocation. In order to prevent this attack, we also introduce another public parameter $W = g^w$, where $w \xleftarrow{R} \mathbb{Z}_q^*$ is kept secret. Each credential is multiplied by a different random number, for instance $g^{z(x+h(p)t)}$; in addition, the prover also receives $\tilde{g}^{z^{-1}}$ and $\tilde{g}^{(zw)^{-1}}$. The verifier then computes $K = \left(\hat{e} \left(g^{rz(x+h(p)t)}, \tilde{g}^{z^{-1}} \right) / \hat{e} \left(g^r, \tilde{g}^{h(p)t} \right) \right)^m$. In addition we require verifier to also verify that $\hat{e} \left(g, \tilde{g}^{z^{-1}} \right) = \hat{e} \left(W, \tilde{g}^{(zw)^{-1}} \right)$.

The protocol introduced in the next Section is not very different from the simple one that we proposed here. Among the modifications, we include an additional random number used to also salt the terms $\tilde{g}^{z^{-1}}$ and $\tilde{g}^{(zw)^{-1}}$, which would otherwise not be randomized and open up to tracing attacks.

4   RevocationMatching: A Prover-Verifier Scheme with Revocation Capabilities

RevocationMatching is a protocol wherein a prover can convince a verifier that she owns a property. The active parties are essentially users, that can behave as provers and verifiers, and a trusted entity that we will call certification authority (CA). Provers receive from the CA credentials for a given property, allowing them to convince a verifier that they possess that property. Verifiers in turn receive from the CA credentials matching references for a given property, which allow them to verify the possession of that property. In case of compromised credentials, the CA adds a value called revocation handle to a publicly available revocation list: this way, verifiers may refuse to interact with users bearing revoked credentials.

RevocationMatching consists of the following algorithms and protocols:

- Setup: according to the security parameter k, the CA chooses $g, \tilde{g}$, where g is a random generator of $\mathbb{G}_1$ and $\tilde{g}$ of $\mathbb{G}_2$. The CA sets $e = \hat{e}(g, \tilde{g})$. The CA also picks $w, t \xleftarrow{R} \mathbb{Z}_q^*$ and sets $W \leftarrow g^w$ and $T \leftarrow \tilde{g}^t$. Finally the CA picks $\{y_i\}_{i=0}^n \xleftarrow{R} \mathbb{Z}_q^*$ and assigns $g_0 \leftarrow g^{y_0}, g_1 \leftarrow g^{y_1}, \ldots, g_n \leftarrow g^{y_n}$ and $\tilde{g}_0 \leftarrow \tilde{g}^{y_0}, \tilde{g}_1 \leftarrow \tilde{g}^{y_1}, \ldots, \tilde{g}_n \leftarrow \tilde{g}^{y_n}$; this way, given a string v, $H(v) = g^{h(v)}$ and $\tilde{H}(v) = \tilde{g}^{h(v)}$. The system's public parameters are $\{q, \mathbb{G}_1, \mathbb{G}_2, g, \tilde{g}, W, T, g_0, \ldots, g_n, \tilde{g}_0, \ldots, \tilde{g}_n, \hat{e}, e\}$. The values $w, t, y_0, \ldots, y_n$ are instead kept secret by the CA;

- Certify: upon user request, the CA verifies that the supplicant user $u \in \mathcal{U}$ possesses the property $p \in \mathcal{P}$ she will later claim to have during the protocol execution; after a successful check, the CA issues to u the appropriate credential, which is made of two separate components: an identification handle, later used for revocation, and the actual credential. To hand out the identification handle for a given pair (u, p), the CA picks the identification handle $x_{u,p} \xleftarrow{R} \mathbb{Z}_q^*$, randomly drawn upon each query, and gives it to the supplicant user. The CA then forms the credential as a tuple $cred_{u,p} = \langle C_{u,p,1}, C_{u,p,2}, C_{u,p,3} \rangle$ where $C_{u,p,1} = g^{z(x_{u,p}+h(p)(t+h(p)))}$, $C_{u,p,2} = \tilde{g}^{z^{-1}}$ and $C_{u,p,3} = \tilde{g}^{(zw)^{-1}}$, where $z \in \mathbb{Z}_q^*$ is randomly drawn upon each query. The user can verify the validity of the credential by checking that $\hat{e}(C_{u,p,1}, C_{u,p,2}) = \hat{e}(g^{x_{u,p}}, \tilde{g}) \cdot \hat{e}(H(p), T \cdot \tilde{H}(p))$;
- Grant: upon a user's request, the CA verifies that – according to the policies of the system – user u is entitled to verify that another user possesses property $p \in \mathcal{P}$. If the checking is successful, the CA issues the appropriate matching reference $match_p = \left(T \cdot \tilde{H}(p)\right)^{h(p)}$; the user verifies that $\hat{e}(g, match_p) = \hat{e}(H(p), T \cdot \tilde{H}(p))$;
- Authenticate: let A be a prover and B a verifier. A has $cred_{A,p_1}$ and x_{A,p_1} to prove possession of property p_1; B holds $match_{p_2}$ to detect property p_2. The protocol proceeds as follows:
  1. B picks $m \xleftarrow{R} \mathbb{Z}_q^*$ and sends e^m to A
  2. A picks $r, s \xleftarrow{R} \mathbb{Z}_q^*$ and sends B the tuple $\left\langle g^r, (C_{A,p_1,1})^{rs}, (C_{A,p_1,2})^{s^{-1}}, (C_{A,p_1,3})^{s^{-1}} \right\rangle$. A locally computes $K = (e^m)^{rx_{A,p_1}}$
  3. B checks whether

$$\hat{e}\left(W, (C_{A,p_1,3})^{s^{-1}}\right) = \hat{e}\left(g, (C_{A,p_1,2})^{s^{-1}}\right) \tag{1}$$

  and locally computes

$$K = \left(\frac{\hat{e}\left((C_{A,p_1,1})^{rs}, (C_{A,p_1,2})^{s^{-1}}\right)}{\hat{e}(g^r, match_{p_2})}\right)^m \tag{2}$$

At the end of the protocol, A and B share the same key K if $p_1 = p_2$.
- Revoke: if the credential for property p of user $u \in \mathcal{U}$ is to be revoked, the CA adds the so-called *revocation handle* $rev_{u,p} = \tilde{g}^{x_{u,p}}$ to a publicly available revocation list L_{rev}. Notice the tight relationship between the identification handle $x_{u,p}$ and the corresponding revocation handle $rev_{u,p} = \tilde{g}^{x_{u,p}}$.

  Let us assume that a given user A is using the protocol to convince user B she owns a property; B receives $\left\langle g^r, (C_{A,p,1})^{rs}, (C_{A,p,2})^{s^{-1}}, (C_{A,p,3})^{s^{-1}} \right\rangle$ from A. B behaves as follows: first, she performs the check of Equation 1; then, before computing the key K, she verifies whether A is using a revoked credential by checking if the following identity

$$\hat{e}\left((C_{A,p,1})^{rs}, (C_{A,p,2})^{s^{-1}}\right) = \hat{e}(g^r, match_p \cdot rev) \tag{3}$$

is verified with any of the revocation handles rev in the list L_{rev}. If the check is successful, B discards the current handshake instance. Notice that if B does not have the correct matching reference for the received credential, Revoke would fail altogether; however, so would Authenticate, in which case, the receiving user would discard the handshake instance anyway. It is clear that after revocation, credentials can be traced *only* by users that possess the matching reference for the property object of that credential; these users were already potentially able to match the given credential. For other users, past and future transcripts of handshake instances produced from that credentials are still untraceable and unlinkable.

Alice :	pick $r, s, m \xleftarrow{R} \mathbb{Z}_q^*$
Alice $\longrightarrow$ Bob :	$\left\langle g^r, (C_{A,p_1,1})^{rs}, (C_{A,p_1,2})^{s^{-1}}, (C_{A,p_1,3})^{s^{-1}}, e^m \right\rangle$
Bob :	pick $r', s', m' \xleftarrow{R} \mathbb{Z}_q^*$
Bob $\longrightarrow$ Alice :	$\left\langle g^{r'}, (C_{B,p_2,1})^{r's'}, (C_{B,p_2,2})^{s'^{-1}}, (C_{B,p_2,3})^{s'^{-1}}, e^{m'} \right\rangle$
Alice :	check that Equation 1 holds, otherwise abort
Alice :	check that Equation 3 is not satisfied with any $rev \in L_{rev}$, otherwise abort
Alice :	compute $K_1 = \left(e^{m'}\right)^{rx_{A,p_1}}$
Alice :	compute $K_2 = \left(\dfrac{\hat{e}\left((C_{B,p_2,1})^{r's'}, (C_{B,p_2,2})^{s'^{-1}}\right)}{\hat{e}(g^{r'}, match_{p_2})} \right)^m$
Bob :	check that Equation 1 holds, otherwise abort
Bob :	check that Equation 3 is not satisfied with any $rev \in L_{rev}$, otherwise abort
Bob :	compute $K_1 = \left(\dfrac{\hat{e}\left((C_{A,p_1,1})^{rs}, (C_{A,p_1,2})^{s^{-1}}\right)}{\hat{e}(g^r, match_{p_1})} \right)^{m'}$
Bob :	compute $K_2 = (e^m)^{r'x_{A,p_1}}$
Alice $\longleftrightarrow$ Bob:	mutual proof of knowledge of K_1 and K_2

Fig. 1. Secret Handshake with Dynamic Controlled Matching

5   Building Secret Handshakes

In this section, we show how RevocationMatching can be used to build a two-party Handshake scheme. This scheme helps two users share a key in case of simultaneous successful matching of properties, and gives no clue about one another's properties otherwise. The resulting scheme, contrary to many secret handshake schemes in the state of the art, does not only allow users to verify if they possess the same property (e.g. if they belong to the same secret group). Our scheme also supports dynamic matching, as introduced by Ateniese et al. in [1]: with dynamic matching, users can match properties different from the ones they possess. For instance, a member of CIA and a member of MI5 can successfully authenticate with a secret handshake. Additional use-cases are described in [23].

We actually consider two different flavors of dynamic matching, thus proposing a total of three different schemes (four considering the multiple CA scenario): in the first scheme, credentials and matching references are issued by the certification authority; this way, the CA retains the control over who can prove what and who can verify what. In the second scheme instead, while credentials are still issued by the certification authority, matching references can be computed by users without any required intervention by the CA. We will refer to the first scheme as Secret Handshake with Dynamic Controlled Matching, and to the second one as Secret Handshake with Dynamic Matching.

5.1   Secret Handshake with Dynamic Controlled Matching

In this scheme, users receive credentials and matching references from the certification authority. Matching references can only be computed by the CA. Notice that they do not necessarily refer to the same property as credentials; this way we effectively achieve Secret Handshake with dynamic controlled matching [23]. However, notice that the CA may enforce the policy by which only users owning a given property will receive the matching reference for it, thus achieving own-group membership secret handshakes too [5,10,18,25,27].

The secret handshake is achieved by running two symmetric instances of RevocationMatching, wherein each of the two users plays in turn the role of prover and verifier. Each user will then end up with two keys, one computed in the role of prover and the other one computed in the role of verifier. We borrow the idea of computing two separate keys at each user's side from Ateniese et al. [1]. To seal the handshake, the two users have to prove one another knowledge of both keys simultaneously, for instance trying to establish a secure channel with a key resulting from the hash of the concatenation of both keys.

Let us assume that two users, Alice and Bob, want to perform a Secret Handshake and share a key if the Handshake is successful. Alice owns the tuple $\langle cred_{A,p_1}, match_{p_2},\ x_{A,p_1}\rangle$ and Bob owns $\langle cred_{B,p_2}, match_{p_1},\ x_{B,p_2}\rangle$. Figure 1 shows how the handshake is carried out.

At the completion of the protocol, Alice and Bob share the same keypair if and only if each user's credential matches the other user's matching reference. If not, one of the two keys, or both, will be different. By requiring them to prove to one another knowledge of both keys simultaneously, either both users learn of a mutual matching, or they do not learn anything at all. In particular, they do not learn – in case of a failed handshake – if just one of the two matchings have failed, and if so which one, or if both did fail.

5.2   Multiple CA Support

The scheme also supports the existence of multiple CAs. Multiple CAs may be a requirement when the properties at stake are – for example – membership to different secret agencies that do not want to delegate the execution of Certify,

Grant and Revoke for security reasons. In a multiple CA scenario, a handshake can be successful even in hybrid situations in which Alice has a credential for property p_1 issued from CA_1 and a matching reference for property p_2 issued from CA_2 and Bob has a credential for property p_2 issued from CA_2 and a matching reference for property p_1 issued from CA_1.

A multiple CA scenario can be supported as follows: one of the CAs picks $\{q, \mathbb{G}_1, \mathbb{G}_2, g, \tilde{g}, T, g_0, \ldots, g_n, \tilde{g}_0, \ldots, \tilde{g}_n, \hat{e}, e\}$; the values $\{y_i\}_{i=0}^n \xleftarrow{R} \mathbb{Z}_q^*$ and t are shared among all the CAs. Then the CAs jointly generate $W = g^w$ and $\tilde{g}^{w^{-1}}$, such that w is unknown: the CAs can achieve this either by using a trusted dealer or by performing the following joint computation: they organize themselves in a chain; the first node A picks $a \xleftarrow{R} \mathbb{Z}_q^*$ and sends to B, the next node, g^a and $\tilde{g}^{a^{-1}}$; B in turn picks $b \xleftarrow{R} \mathbb{Z}_q^*$ and sends to the next node g^{ab} and $\tilde{g}^{(ab)^{-1}}$ and so forth until the last node is reached.

Finally, each CA picks a secret value $t_{CA} \xleftarrow{R} \mathbb{Z}_q^*$ and publishes $T_{CA} \leftarrow g^{t_{CA}}$; the public parameters are $\{q, \mathbb{G}_1, \mathbb{G}_2, g, \tilde{g}, W, T, T_{CA_1}, \ldots, T_{CA_n}, g_0, \ldots, g_n, \tilde{g}_0, \ldots, \tilde{g}_n, \hat{e}, e\}$; each CA keeps the values $\{y_i\}_{i=0}^n \xleftarrow{R} \mathbb{Z}_q^*$, t, t_{CA} and $\tilde{g}^{w^{-1}}$ secret.

A given CA forms credentials as $cred_{u,p} = \langle C_{u,p,1}, C_{u,p,2}, C_{u,p,3} \rangle$ where $C_{u,p,1} = W^{z(x_{u,p} + h(p)t_{CA}(t+h(p)))}$, $C_{u,p,2} = \left(\tilde{g}^{w^{-1}}\right)^{z^{-1}}$ and $C_{u,p,3} = \tilde{g}^{z^{-1}}$; the matching reference is formed as $match_p = \left(T \cdot \tilde{H}(p)\right)^{h(p)t_{CA}}$. The check of Equation 1 becomes $\hat{e}\left(W, (C_{u,p,2})^{s^{-1}}\right) = \hat{e}\left(g, (C_{u,p,3})^{s^{-1}}\right)$. Users cannot any longer verify the correctness of credentials and matching reference; for this reason, the issuing CA also gives the value $H(p)^{t_{CA}}$ to the supplicant user; the user can verify that $\hat{e}(H(p)^{t_{CA}}, \tilde{g}) = \hat{e}\left(T_{CA}, \tilde{H}(p)\right)$ and then use $H(p)^{t_{CA}}$ instead of $H(p)$ in the verification equations.

Revocation handles must be published in a common revocation list, where all CAs publish revocation handles. The list is common, public, and there is nothing that gives away which CA is behind which revocation value. For the rest, the scheme behaves as before.

5.3 Secret Handshake with Dynamic Matching

In the scheme described in this Section, each user can freely compute matching references of his choice: this way we effectively achieve dynamic matching, in the sense first defined by Ateniese et al. [1]. The secret handshake with dynamic matching is essentially equal to the scheme introduced in Section 5.1, with a substantial difference: the parameter T is now equal to $\tilde{g}$, and consequently, $t = 1$; as a consequence, we simplify $C_{u,p,1} = g^{z(x_{u,p} + h(p))}$ and $match_p = \tilde{H}(p) = \tilde{g}^{h(p)}$. Notice that now users are able to create matching references at their will.

With this scheme, two users with valid credentials can interact expressing *wishes* on the property certified by the other user's credential; wishes are represented by self-generated matching references. Both users at the end of the protocol share a common key pair if they both own credentials for the property expected by the other user. Notice that this change makes it impossible to support multiple CAs, as specified in Section 5.2.

Revocation handles are also formed differently, as $rev_{u,p} = \tilde{g}^{x_{u,p}+h(p)}$. Consequently when a user B receives from user A $\left\langle g^r, (C_{A,p,1})^{rs}, (C_{A,p,2})^{s^{-1}}, \right.$ $\left. (C_{A,p,3})^{s^{-1}} \right\rangle$, B verifies whether A is using a revoked credential by checking if $\hat{e}\left((C_{A,p,1})^{rs}, (C_{A,p,2})^{s^{-1}}\right) = \hat{e}(g^r, rev)$ is verified with any of the revocation handles rev in the list L_{rev}. If the check is successful, B discards the current handshake instance and declines any further interaction.

The change in how the revocation handle is constructed can be explained through the fact that in this case every user has the right to match any property. A revoked credential therefore loses its untraceability to every other user. However, the revocation handle still does not reveal anything about the nature of the certified property.

6   Security Analysis

Before proceeding further, we state two well-known hard problems:

Definition 1 (*Decisional Diffie-Hellman* Problem). *We say that the Decisional Diffie-Hellman Problem (DDH) is hard if, for all probabilistic, polynomial-time algorithms $\mathcal{B}$,*

$$\mathsf{AdvDDH}_B := Pr[\mathcal{B}(g, g^a, g^b, g^x) = \textit{true if } x = ab] - \tfrac{1}{2}$$

is negligible in the security parameter. We assume a random choice of $g \in \mathbb{G}_1$, $a, b \in \mathbb{Z}_q^*$; x is equal to ab with probability $\tfrac{1}{2}$ and is otherwise equal to a random value in $\mathbb{Z}_q^*/\{ab\}$ with the same probability.

Definition 2 (*Bilinear Decisional Diffie-Hellman* Problem). *We say that the Bilinear Decisional Diffie-Hellman Problem (BDDH) is hard if, for all probabilistic, polynomial-time algorithms $\mathcal{B}$,*

$$\mathsf{AdvBDDH}_B := Pr[\mathcal{B}(g, g^a, g^b, g^c, \tilde{g}, \tilde{g}^a, \tilde{g}^b, \tilde{g}^x) = \textit{true if } x = abc] - \tfrac{1}{2}$$

is negligible in the security parameter. We assume a random choice of $g \in \mathbb{G}_1$, $\tilde{g} \in \mathbb{G}_2$ and $a, b, c \in \mathbb{Z}_q^*$; x is equal to abc with probability $\tfrac{1}{2}$ and is otherwise equal to a random value in $\mathbb{Z}_q^*/\{abc\}$ with the same probability.

We also introduce the following new intractability assumption; we will give evidence of its hardness in Appendix A. In demonstrating the complexity assumption, we follow the approach presented by Victor Shoup in [22] and extensively used by the research community [2,8,17]. As an example, the well known SDH assumption was thus proved by Boneh and Boyen in [8].

Definition 3. *[SM Problem] Let $w, y, m \in \mathbb{Z}_q^*$, let g be a generator of $\mathbb{G}_1$ and $\tilde{g}$ be a generator of $\mathbb{G}_2$. Let oracle $O_{w,y}(\cdot)$ take input $x \in \mathbb{Z}_q^*$ and produce output $g^{z(x+y)}, \tilde{g}^{z^{-1}}$ and $\tilde{g}^{(zw)^{-1}}$ where z is randomly drawn from $\mathbb{Z}_q^*$ upon each oracle query. We say that the SM Problem is hard if, for all probabilistic, polynomial-time algorithms $\mathcal{A}$,*

$$\mathsf{AdvSM}_{\mathcal{A}} := Pr[\mathcal{A}(g, g^w, \tilde{g}, \tilde{g}^y, \tilde{g}^m, O_{w,y}) =$$
$$a, a^{s(x_* + y)}, \tilde{g}^{(sw)^{-1}}, \tilde{g}^{(s)^{-1}}, \hat{e}\,(a, \tilde{g})^{mx_*}]$$

such that $(x_*) \notin \mathcal{O}$, *is negligible in the security parameter;* $a \in \mathbb{G}_1$. $\mathcal{O}$ *is the set of queries* $\mathcal{A}$ *makes to oracle* $O_{w,y}$. *This probability is taken over random choice of* $g \in \mathbb{G}_1$, $\tilde{g} \in \mathbb{G}_2$, *and* $w, y, m \in \mathbb{Z}_q^*$. $a \in \mathbb{G}_1$ *can be chosen freely by the adversary.*

Intuitively, the assumption tells that it is unfeasible to compute a tuple $\left\langle g^{s(x_* + y)}, \tilde{g}^{s^{-1}}, \tilde{g}^{(sw)^{-1}} \right\rangle$ for a new value x_* and prove knowledge of it, yet having an oracle that can do so for any query. The new assumption is generic enough to be of independent interest, for instance to realize signature protocols or oblivious signature-based envelopes. Our assumption could have had a simpler formulation had we chosen not to embed the proof of knowledge of x_* in it.

6.1   Security Analysis of RevocationMatching

In this section we analyze the security requirements of RevocationMatching. We base our security analysis on the security definitions and attacker model presented by Balfanz and colleagues in [5] and Ateniese and colleagues in [1].

At first, we briefly recapitulate some preliminary definitions: a complete description of the security definition and attacker model can be found in [5,1]. A *protocol instance* is the interaction of two users according to the rules of the protocol. We say that during a protocol instance a prover sends a *handshake tuple*. The handshake tuple *contains* a property, in that it is formed out of a credential certifying possession of a property, which is then the *object* of the protocol instance. At the end of the Authenticate algorithm, users are asked to prove to one another knowledge of a locally computed key. It is a necessary prerequisite that the proof of knowledge does not – in any way – leak the actual value of the key. If the computed key is the same for both user, we say that the prover has *proved* to or *convinced* a verifier that she owns the property object of the handshake; and that the verifier has *verified* or *detected* the presence of a property within a handshake tuple during a protocol instance.

To analyze the security of RevocationMatching, we identify four different objectives that an attacker might have. An attacker may:

- **detection:** try as a verifier to detect a prover's property without the appropriate matching reference;
- **impersonation:** try as a prover to convince a verifier that she possesses a given property without the appropriate property credential;
- **linking:** try to link different protocol executions to a given user;
- **tracing:** try to link different protocol executions to a given property;

The sequel of this Section analyzes RevocationMatching with respect to these four requirements. Appendix B presents proofs of the claims made in this Section. Notice that the proofs do not rely on random oracles.

Untraceability. Consider an adversary $\mathcal{A}$ whose goal is to check if two handshake tuples contain the same property, without owning the legitimate matching reference; an adversary with this ability can link together the different users that own credentials for a given property. In order to be general enough we consider an active adversary that engages in protocol executions; this adversary clearly also includes a passive one who just eavesdrops protocol instances.

To capture the attacker we define a game called TraceProperty. TraceProperty develops as follows:

- **Setup:** during the setup phase, the challenger generates the parameters of the system;
- **Query:** during the query phase, $\mathcal{A}$ can receive valid credentials, matching references and revocation handles, and can engage in RevocationMatching protocol execution with legitimate users;
- **Challenge:** then the challenger randomly chooses two properties p_1 and p_2 and sends $\mathcal{A}$ two handshake tuples, one for property p_1 and the other for property p_2; both properties have not been object of a query in the previous phase; $\mathcal{A}$ is then challenged to return true if $p_1 = p_2$;

Lemma 1. *Suppose that there is a probabilistic, polynomial time adversary $\mathcal{A}$ with an advantage*

$$\mathsf{AdvTraceProperty}_A := Pr[\mathcal{A} \ wins \ the \ game \ \mathsf{TraceProperty}] - \tfrac{1}{2}$$

in the TraceProperty game. Then a probabilistic, polynomial time algorithm $\mathcal{B}$ solves the Decisional Diffie-Hellman problem (DDH) with the same advantage.

A proof of Lemma 1 can be found in Appendix B.1.

Unlinkability. Consider an adversary $\mathcal{A}$ whose goal is to check if two handshake tuples come from the same user; an adversary with this ability can link together the same user over multiple protocol execution. In order to be general enough we consider an active adversary that engages in protocol executions; this adversary clearly also includes a passive one who just eavesdrops protocol instance.

Let us first of all notice that there are two values that can be linked to a user, the identification handle $x_{u,p}$, and z, the random number drawn at each call to Certify and used to salt the credentials. Between the two, $x_{u,p}$ is the only one that can be traced over two different handshake tuples. Indeed, tracing the value z is impossible, since over successive handshake tuples, it always appears multiplied by a different random value s chosen at random by the user himself. To capture the attacker we define a game called TraceUser. TraceUser develops as follows:

- **Setup:** during the setup phase, the challenger generates the parameters of the system;
- **Query:** during the query phase, $\mathcal{A}$ can receive valid credentials, matching references and revocation handles, and can engage in RevocationMatching protocol execution with legitimate users;

– **Challenge:** eventually $\mathcal{A}$ receives from the challenger two handshake tuples containing the same property from users u_1 and u_2, u_1 and u_2 being chosen randomly by the challenger; $\mathcal{A}$ is challenged to return true if $u_1 = u_2$;

Lemma 2. *Suppose that there is a probabilistic, polynomial time adversary $\mathcal{A}$ with an advantage*

$$\mathsf{AdvTraceUser}_A := Pr[\mathcal{A} \text{ wins the game } \mathsf{TraceUser}] - \tfrac{1}{2}$$

in the TraceUser *game. Then a probabilistic, polynomial time algorithm $\mathcal{B}$ solves the Decisional Diffie-Hellman problem (DDH) with the same advantage.*

A proof of Lemma 2 can be found in Appendix B.2.

Detector Resistance. Let $\mathcal{A}$ be an adversary whose goal is to engage in RevocationMatching protocol instances and – acting as a verifier – to detect the prover's property, without owning the appropriate matching reference. We call detector resistance the resilience to such kind of an attacker.

To capture this kind of attack, we define a game called Detect; Detect develops as follows:

– **Setup:** during the setup phase, the challenger generates the parameters of the system;
– **Query:** the adversary $\mathcal{A}$ queries the system for an arbitrary number of tuples $\langle cred_{u_i,p_i}, match_{p_i}, \; x_{u_i,p_i}, rev_{u_i,p_i} \rangle$ for any given pairs $(u_i, p_i) \in \mathcal{U} \times \mathcal{P}$. She is then free to engage in RevocationMatching protocol execution with legitimate users;
– **Challenge:** $\mathcal{A}$ chooses a property p_* for which she does not own the matching reference. Also the challenger chooses a property p_o, among the ones for which the adversary does not have a matching reference. Then, challenger and adversary engage in a protocol execution; the challenger – acting as a prover – presents a credential for property p_o and the adversary – acting as a verifier – wins the game if she can correctly whether or not $p_o = p_*$;

This game is very similar to TraceProperty, and the reduction to prove it is a straightforward adaptation of the one used to prove Lemma 1. Indeed an adversary $\mathcal{A}$ who has an advantage on the detection of a property without the appropriate matching reference (Detect game) can clearly link together properties over multiple handshake instances (TraceProperty game) by repetedly detecting the property in each of them and linking after the detection.

Impersonation Resistance. Let $\mathcal{A}$'s goal be the impersonation of a user owning a non-revoked credential for a given property. To capture this attacker's goal we define the a game called Impersonate, which develops as follows:

– **Setup:** during the setup phase, the challenger generates the parameters of the system;

– **Query:** the adversary $\mathcal{A}$ queries the system for an arbitrary number of tuples $\langle cred_{u_i,p_i}, match_{p_i},\ x_{u_i,p_i}, rev_{u_i,p_i} \rangle$ for any given pairs $(u_i, p_i) \in \mathcal{U} \times \mathcal{P}$. She is then free to engage in RevocationMatching protocol execution with legitimate users; $\mathcal{A}$ eventually decides that this phase of the game is over. The challenger then issues revocation handles for each credential handed out to the attacker in the previous phase, thus revoking them;

– **Challenge:** $\mathcal{A}$ then declares $p_* \in \mathcal{P}$ which will be the object of the challenge; $\mathcal{A}$ is then required to engage in a RevocationMatching instance with the challenger, and wins the game if she can output the correct key computed acting as a prover (notice that the same is required in [1,5]); in order to successfully win the game, it must not be possible for the challenger to abort the handshake due to the fact that the credentials used by the attacker have been revoked;

Notice that the game covers a wide range of attacks. Recall that the attacker receives a number of credentials during the query phase. The attacker can win the game in two ways: (i) forge a brand new credential or (ii) use an old credential yet circumventing revocation. Let us set $X_{u,p} = x_{u,p} + h(p)(t + h(p))$. When the attacker is challenged, she produces the tuple $\left\langle g^r, g^{rsX_{u_*,p_*}}, \tilde{g}^{s^{-1}}, \tilde{g}^{(sw)^{-1}} \right\rangle$. If we define the set

$$Q_{\mathcal{A}} = \{ X_{u,p} \in \mathbb{Z}_q^* : \mathcal{A} \text{ has received } g^{zX_{u,p}}, \tilde{g}^{z^{-1}}, \tilde{g}^{(zw)^{-1}} \text{ during the query phase} \}$$

then (i) implies $X_{u_*,p_*} \notin Q_{\mathcal{A}}$ and (ii) implies $X_{u_*,p_*} \in Q_{\mathcal{A}}$. We then define two different games: Impersonate1 is the aforementioned Impersonate game when $X_{u_*,p_*} \notin Q_{\mathcal{A}}$, and Impersonate2 when $X_{u_*,p_*} \in Q_{\mathcal{A}}$.

Lemma 3. *Suppose that there is a probabilistic, polynomial time adversary $\mathcal{A}$ with an advantage*

$$\textsf{AdvImpersonate1}_A := Pr[\mathcal{A} \text{ wins the game Impersonate1}]$$

in the Impersonate1 *game. Then a probabilistic, polynomial time algorithm $\mathcal{B}$ solves the SM Problem with the same advantage.*

Lemma 4. *Suppose that there is a probabilistic, polynomial time adversary $\mathcal{A}$ with an advantage*

$$\textsf{AdvImpersonate2}_A := Pr[\mathcal{A} \text{ wins the game Impersonate2}]$$

in the Impersonate2 *game. Then a probabilistic, polynomial time algorithm $\mathcal{B}$ solves the Bilinear Decisional Diffie-Hellman Problem (BDDH) with the same advantage.*

Appendixes B.3 and B.4 present the proofs of Lemmas 3 and 4, respectively. The presence of two different games to prove the same security requirement is justified by the fact that the two games cover all possible scenarios, with no possibility of hidden attacks. Indeed, either the credential produced by the attacker belongs to a set or it does not, and both cases are covered.

6.2   Security Analysis of Secret Handshake with Dynamic Controlled Matching

In Section 5.1 we showed how to construct a protocol for Secret Handshake with dynamic controlled matching. The security requirements that have been identified for RevocationMatching in the previous Section must still hold unmodified for Secret Handshake. In the analysis of the security of secret handshake we require, as in Section 6.1, that the proof of knowledge of the keys does not – in any way – leak their actual value. In addition, we require that users prove to each other knowledge of both keys simultaneously. The same is required by other protocols in the state of the art, for instance in [1]. Examples of how this can be achieved can be found in [13].

Under these assumptions, it is straightforward how the security games and proofs devised for the latter can be adapted for Secret Handshakes: indeed untraceability and unlinkability games stay the same. As for detector and impersonation resistance, the proofs of Section 6.1 tell us that an adversary is not able to run a successful single instance of RevocationMatching acting as a rogue prover or verifier; as a consequence, given that a successful Secret Handshake requires two successful symmetric instances of RevocationMatching, an attacker acting as a rogue prover, verifier or both cannot have success in either of these two games.

6.3   Security Analysis of Secret Handshake with Dynamic Matching

In Section 5.3 we presented a scheme that achieves secret handshake with dynamic matching, wherein users can freely compute matching references, thus being able to match any property they want from another user. As in the previous Section, we require users to prove knowledge of both keys simultaneously, without leaking any information about them.

Let us first of all make some general considerations about the nature of the protocol. User A has the right to engage in an arbitrary number of protocol executions with any user B. If A has a legitimate credential for the wish of B (the matching reference generated by B), and guesses correctly the property object of the B's credential, then she has legitimately disclosed the challenger's property. If she is successful twice, we might say that she has been able to trace the property over two different protocol instances. Both situations are acceptable as they do not mean that a user, by simply performing secret handshake repeatedly, trying all possible matching references, will eventually discover another user's credential. Indeed, by requiring users to prove to one another knowledge of both keys, the protocol assures that if A does not have a valid credential for B's matching reference, A has no point in trying exhaustively all possible matching references to discover B's credential: one of the two instances of RevocationMatching would always fail and so would the handshake.

Among the security requirements sketched in Section 6.2, the ones related to the untraceability of identities and untraceability of properties are still the same, and the games and proofs provided in Section 6.1 still hold unchanged. As for impersonation resistance, Impersonate2 does not apply any longer, since revocation handles are now formed as $\tilde{g}^{x_{u,p}+h(p)}$; it is therefore impossible for an attacker to reuse already received credentials, yet circumventing revocation. Impersonate1 instead remains unchanged and so does its proof.

Finally, the requirement of detector resistance vanishes, since users are explicitly allowed to freely match any property by computing matching references at their will. However, as we pointed out before, a successful detection requires the user to own a credential for the other user's wish.

6.4   Security Analysis of a Multiple CA Scenario

Due to space restrictions we do not include the proofs of security of a multiple-CA scenario, but leave them for an extended version of the paper; nonetheless, we give here a sketch of the security analysis.

The handshake tuples produced in a multiple CA scenario are the same as in the normal case, therefore the security proofs can be easily adapted from the ones presented in the Appendixes. It remains to demonstrate that colluding CAs cannot forge credentials and matching references from a target CA_*. Forging $C_{u,p,1} = g^{zw(x_{u,p}+h(p)t_{CA_*}(t+h(p)))}$ from g^w and and $g^{t_{CA_*}}$ intuitively breaks the computational Diffie-Hellman problem; forging $match_p = (T \cdot \tilde{H}(p))^{h(p)t_{CA_*}}$ from $g^{t_{CA_*}}$ intuitively breaks the SXDH assumption, since there is no isomorphism between $\mathbb{G}_1$ and $\mathbb{G}_2$.

In addition, notice that upon a failed handshake, the information about the CA who generated the credential is not leaked; moreover, an adversary cannot trace credentials based on the CA who generated them; a similar game to TraceUser or TraceProperty can be created to show this: tracing the value t_{CA} in $g^{zwrs(x_{u,p}+h(p)t_{CA_*}(t+h(p)))}$ from g^r and $g^{t_{CA}}$ intuitively breaks the decisional Diffie-Hellman problem.

7   Conclusion and Future Work

In this paper we have presented a novel protocol called RevocationMatching, and showed how with it, we can support revocation in each of the different versions of Secret Handshake known in literature, own-group membership, dynamic matching and dynamic controlled matching. In the study of the security of the protocol, we have discovered an interesting new complexity assumption; we plan to analyze in more details its relationship with other complexity assumptions as well as its possible use in signature schemes and OSBE schemes. Moreover, we intend to study more closely dynamic accumulators: although they appear not to be perfectly suited for symmetric handshakes, they represent an interesting alternative when revocation requirements clash with untraceable credentials.

References

1. Ateniese, G., Blanton, M., Kirsch, J.: Secret handshakes with dynamic and fuzzy matching. In: Network and Distributed System Security Symposuim, February, pp. 159–177. The Internet Society (2007); CERIAS TR 2007-24

2. Ateniese, G., Camenisch, J., Hohenberger, S., de Medeiros, B.: Practical group signatures without random oracles (2005)
3. Bagherzandi, A., Cheon, J.-H., Jarecki, S.: Multisignatures secure under the discrete logarithm assumption and a generalized forking lemma. In: CCS 2008: Proceedings of the 15th ACM conference on Computer and communications security, pp. 449–458. ACM, New York (2008)
4. Baldwin, R.W., Gramlich, W.C.: Cryptographic protocol for trustable match making. In: IEEE Symposium on Security and Privacy (1985)
5. Balfanz, D., Durfee, G., Shankar, N., Smetters, D.K., Staddon, J., Wong, H.-C.: Secret handshakes from pairing-based key agreements. In: IEEE Symposium on Security and Privacy, pp. 180–196 (2003)
6. Benaloh, J., Automation, G.: One-way accumulators: A decentralized alternative to digital signatures, pp. 274–285. Springer, Heidelberg (1993)
7. Boneh, D., Boyen, X.: Efficient selective-id secure identity-based encryption without random oracles. In: Cachin, C., Camenisch, J.L. (eds.) EUROCRYPT 2004. LNCS, vol. 3027, pp. 223–238. Springer, Heidelberg (2004)
8. Boneh, D., Boyen, X.: Short signatures without random oracles and the sdh assumption in bilinear groups. J. Cryptology 21(2), 149–177 (2008)
9. Camenisch, J., Lysyanskaya, A.: Dynamic accumulators and application to efficient revocation of anonymous credentials. In: Yung, M. (ed.) CRYPTO 2002. LNCS, vol. 2442, pp. 61–76. Springer, Heidelberg (2002)
10. Castelluccia, C., Jarecki, S., Tsudik, G.: Secret handshakes from ca-oblivious encryption. In: Lee, P.J. (ed.) ASIACRYPT 2004. LNCS, vol. 3329, pp. 293–307. Springer, Heidelberg (2004)
11. Changshe Ma, J.W., Zheng, D.: Fast digital signature schemes as secure as diffie-hellman assumptions. Cryptology ePrint Archive, Report 2007/019 (2007)
12. Hoepman, J.-H.: Private handshakes. In: Stajano, F., Meadows, C., Capkun, S., Moore, T. (eds.) ESAS 2007. LNCS, vol. 4572, pp. 31–42. Springer, Heidelberg (2007)
13. Jain, G.: Zero knowledge proofs: A survey (2008)
14. Jarecki, S., Kim, J., Tsudik, G.: Beyond secret handshakes: Affiliation-hiding authenticated key exchange. In: Malkin, T.G. (ed.) CT-RSA 2008. LNCS, vol. 4964, pp. 352–369. Springer, Heidelberg (2008)
15. Jarecki, S., Liu, X.: Unlinkable secret handshakes and key-private group key management schemes. In: Katz, J., Yung, M. (eds.) ACNS 2007. LNCS, vol. 4521, pp. 270–287. Springer, Heidelberg (2007)
16. Li, N., Du, W., Boneh, D.: Oblivious signature-based envelope. Distrib. Comput. 17(4), 293–302 (2005)
17. Lysyanskaya, A., Rivest, R.L., Sahai, A., Wolf, S.: Pseudonym systems. In: Heys, H.M., Adams, C.M. (eds.) SAC 1999. LNCS, vol. 1758, pp. 184–199. Springer, Heidelberg (2000)
18. Meadows, C.: A more efficient cryptographic matchmaking protocol for use in the absence of a continuously available third party. sp, 134 (1986)
19. Nasserian, S., Tsudik, G.: Revisiting oblivious signaturebased envelopes: New constructs and properties. In: Di Crescenzo, G., Rubin, A. (eds.) FC 2006. LNCS, vol. 4107, pp. 221–235. Springer, Heidelberg (2006)
20. Pfitzmann, B.: Collision-free accumulators and fail-stop signature schemes without trees, pp. 480–494. Springer, Heidelberg (1997)
21. Shin, J.S., Gligor, V.D.: A new privacy-enhanced matchmaking protocol. In: Network and Distributed System Security Symposuim, February 2007. The Internet Society (2007)

22. Shoup, V.: Lower bounds for discrete logarithms and related problems. In: Fumy, W. (ed.) EUROCRYPT 1997. LNCS, vol. 1233, pp. 256–266. Springer, Heidelberg (1997)
23. Sorniotti, A., Molva, R.: A provably secure secret handshake with dynamic controlled matching. In: Proceedings of The 24th International Information IFIP SEC 2009, Paphos, Cyprus, May 18-20 (2009)
24. Tso, R., Gu, C., Okamoto, T., Okamoto, E.: Efficient id-based digital signatures with message recovery. In: Bao, F., Ling, S., Okamoto, T., Wang, H., Xing, C. (eds.) CANS 2007. LNCS, vol. 4856, pp. 47–59. Springer, Heidelberg (2007)
25. Vergnaud, D.: Rsa-based secret handshakes. In: Ytrehus, Ø. (ed.) WCC 2005. LNCS, vol. 3969, pp. 252–274. Springer, Heidelberg (2006)
26. Waters, B.: Efficient identity-based encryption without random oracles. In: Cramer, R. (ed.) EUROCRYPT 2005. LNCS, vol. 3494, pp. 114–127. Springer, Heidelberg (2005)
27. Xu, S., Yung, M.: k-anonymous secret handshakes with reusable credentials. In: CCS 2004: Proceedings of the 11th ACM conference on Computer and communications security (2004)
28. Zhang, K., Needham, R.: A private matchmaking protocol (2001)

A   Security of the New Assumption in Generic Groups

In what follows we will provide evidence as to the hardness of the problem introduced in Definitions 3, by proving a lower bound on the computational complexity under the generic group model. The generic group model is a theoretical framework for the analysis of the success of algorithms in groups where the representation of the elements reveals no information to the attacker. The most popular is the one presented by Victor Shoup [22]. The model has been used to provide evidence as to the hardness of several computational problems [2,8,17].

Internally, the simulator represents the elements of $\mathbb{G}_1$ as their discrete logarithms relative to a chosen generator. To represent the images of the elements of $\mathbb{G}_1$ for the attacker, we use a random one-to-one mapping $\xi_1 : \mathbb{Z}_q^* \to \{0,1\}^{\lceil log_2 q \rceil}$, where q is the group order. For instance, the group element g^a is represented internally as a, whereas the attacker is given the external string representation $\xi_1(a) \in \{0,1\}^{\lceil log_2 q \rceil}$. We similarly define a second mapping $\xi_2 : \mathbb{Z}_q^* \to \{0,1\}^{\lceil log_2 q \rceil}$ to represent $\mathbb{G}_2$, and a third mapping $\xi_T :\to \{0,1\}^{\lceil log_2 q \rceil}$ to represent $\mathbb{G}_T$. The adversary communicates with the oracles using the string representation of the group elements exclusively. Notice that the adversary is given $q = |\mathbb{G}_1| = |\mathbb{G}_2| = |\mathbb{G}_T|$.

The following theorem establishes the unconditional hardness of the SM problem in the generic bilinear group model. Our proof uses a technique similar to the one adopted by Ateniese et al. in [2].

Theorem 1. *Suppose $\mathcal{A}$ is an algorithm that is able to solve the SMproblem in generic bilinear groups of order q, making at most q_G oracle queries for the group operations in $\mathbb{G}_1$, $\mathbb{G}_2$, and $\mathbb{G}_T$, the oracle $O_{w,y}(\cdot)$ and the bilinear pairing $\hat{e}$, all counted together. Suppose also that the integers $w, y, m \in \mathbb{Z}_q^*$ and the encoding functions ξ_1, ξ_2, ξ_T are chosen at random. Then, the probability ϵ that $\mathcal{A}$ on* input $(q, \xi_1(1), \xi_1(w), \xi_2(1), \xi_2(y), \xi_2(m))$ produces in output $(\xi_1(r), \xi_1(rs(x_* + y)), \xi_2((sw)^{-1}), \xi_2((s)^{-1}), \xi_T(rx_*m))$ with x_* not previously queried to $O_{w,y}$, is bounded by $\epsilon \leq \dfrac{(q_G + 5)^2}{q} = O(q_G^2/q)$.

Proof. Consider an algorithm $\mathcal{B}$ that plays the following game with $\mathcal{A}$.

$\mathcal{B}$ maintains three lists of pairs $L_1 = \{(F_{1,i}, \xi_{1,i}) : i = 1, \ldots, \tau_1\}$, $L_2 = \{(F_{2,i}, \xi_{2,i}) : i = 1, \ldots, \tau_2\}$ and $L_T = \{(F_{T,i}, \xi_{T,i}) : i = 1, \ldots, \tau_T\}$, such that, at step τ in the game, $\tau_1 + \tau_2 + \tau_T = \tau + 5$. The entries $F_{1,i}$, $F_{2,i}$ and $F_{T,i}$ are polynomials with coefficients in $\mathbb{Z}_q^*$. The entries $\xi_{1,i}$, $\xi_{2,i}$, $\xi_{T,i}$ will be all the strings given out to the adversary.

The lists are initialized at step $\tau = 0$ by setting $\tau_1 = 2$, $\tau_2 = 3$, $\tau_T = 0$ and assigning $F_{1,1} = 1$, $F_{1,2} = W$, $F_{2,1} = 1$, $F_{2,2} = Y$ and $F_{2,3} = M$ where W, Y and M are indeterminants. The corresponding $\xi_{1,\cdot}$ and $\xi_{2,\cdot}$ are set to random distinct strings. In what follows we describe how $\mathcal{B}$ answers $\mathcal{A}$'s query:

Group operations: $\mathcal{A}$ may request a group operation in $\mathbb{G}_1$ as a multiplication or as a division. Before answering a $\mathbb{G}_1$ query, the simulator $\mathcal{B}$ starts by incrementing the τ_1 counter by one. $\mathcal{A}$ gives $\mathcal{B}$ two operands $\xi_{1,i}$, $\xi_{1,j}$ with $1 \leq i, j < \tau_1$, and a multiply/divide selection bit. To respond, $\mathcal{B}$ creates a polynomial $F_{1,\tau_1} \leftarrow F_{1,i} \pm F_{1,j}$. If the result is identical to an earlier polynomial $F_{1,l}$ for some $l < \tau_1$, the simulator $\mathcal{B}$ duplicates its string representation $\xi_{1,\tau_1} \leftarrow \xi_{1,l}$; otherwise, it lets ξ_{1,τ_1} be a fresh random string in $\{0,1\}^{\lceil log_2 q \rceil}$, distinct from $\xi_{1,1}, \ldots, \xi_{1,\tau_1 - 1}$. The simulator appends the pair $(F_{1,\tau_1}, \xi_{1,\tau_1})$ to the list $L-1$ and gives the string ξ_{1,τ_1} back to $\mathcal{A}$. Group operation queries in $\mathbb{G}_2$ and $\mathbb{G}_T$ are answered in a similar way, based on the lists L_2 and L_T respectively.

Pairing: A pairing query consists of two operands $\xi_{1,i}$ and $\xi_{2,j}$ with $1 \leq i \leq \tau_1$ and $1 \leq j \leq \tau_2$ for the current values of τ_1 and τ_2. Upon receipt of such a query from $\mathcal{A}$, the counter τ_T is incremented. The simulator then computes the product of polynomials $F_{T,\tau_T} \leftarrow F_{1,i} \cdot F_{2,j}$. If the same polynomial was already present in L_T, i.e., if $F_{T,\tau_T} = F_{T,l}$ for some $l < \tau_T$, then $\mathcal{B}$ simply clones the associated string $\xi_{T,\tau_T} \leftarrow \xi_{T,l}$, otherwise it sets ξ_{T,τ_T} to a new random string in $\{0,1\}^{\lceil log_2 q \rceil}$, distinct from $\xi_{T,1}, \ldots, \xi_{1,\tau_T - 1}$. The simulator then adds the pair $(F_{T,\tau_T}, \xi_{T,\tau_T})$ to the list L_T, and gives the string ξ_{T,τ_T} to $\mathcal{A}$.

Oracle O: Let τ_O be a counter initialized to 0 and $\mathcal{O}$ an empty set. At the beginning of any oracle query, $\mathcal{A}$ inputs $x \in \mathbb{Z}_q^*$; to start, $\mathcal{B}$ adds x to the set $\mathcal{O}$ and increments the counter τ_1 and τ_O by one, and the counter τ_2 by two, choosing a *new* indeterminant Z_{τ_O}; it then sets $F_{1,\tau_1} \leftarrow Z_{\tau_O}(x + Y)$; it also sets $F_{2,\tau_2 - 1} \leftarrow Z_{\tau_O}^{-1}$ and $F_{2,\tau_O} \leftarrow (Z_{\tau_O} W)^{-1}$. If the same polynomials were already present in L_1 or L_2, i.e., if $F_{1,\tau_1} = F_{1,l}$ for some $l < \tau_1$, or, for $j \in \{0,1\}$, $F_{2,\tau_2 - j} = F_{2,l'}$ for some $l' < \tau_2$, then $\mathcal{B}$ simply clones the associated string $\xi_{1,\tau_1} \leftarrow \xi_{T,l}$, $\xi_{2,\tau_2 - j} \leftarrow \xi_{2,l'}$; otherwise it sets the strings ξ_{1,τ_1} and $\xi_{2,\tau_2 - j}$ to distinct random values in $\{0,1\}^{\lceil log_2 q \rceil}$, different from the other strings already contained in the lists. The simulator then adds the pairs $(F_{1,\tau_1}, \xi_{1,\tau_1})$ to the list L_1 and $(F_{2,\tau_2-j}, \xi_{2,\tau_2-j})$ to the list L_2, giving the strings ξ_{1,τ_1} and ξ_{2,τ_2-j} to $\mathcal{A}$.

We assume that the SXDH assumption holds, therefore we do not create any isomorphism between $\mathbb{G}_1$ and $\mathbb{G}_2$ or vice versa.

When $\mathcal{A}$ terminates, it returns the tuple $\langle \xi_{1,\alpha}, \xi_{1,\beta}, \xi_{2,\gamma}, \xi_{2,\delta}, \xi_{T,k} \rangle$ where $1 \leq \alpha, \beta, \leq \tau_1$, $1 \leq \gamma, \delta \leq \tau_2$ and $1 \leq k \leq \tau_T$. Let $F_{1,\alpha}$, $F_{1,\beta}$, $F_{2,\gamma}$, $F_{2,\delta}$ and $F_{T,k}$ be the corresponding polynomials in the lists L_1, L_2 and L_T, and g^α, g^β, $\tilde{g}^\gamma$, $\tilde{g}^\delta$, $\hat{e}(g, \tilde{g})^k$ the corresponding elements in $\mathbb{G}_1^2 \times \mathbb{G}_2^2 \times \mathbb{G}_T$.

In order to exhibit the correctness of $\mathcal{A}$'s answer, $\mathcal{B}$ should check that the system of equation

$$\begin{cases} \left(\dfrac{\hat{e}(g^\beta, \tilde{g}^\gamma)}{\hat{e}(g^\alpha, \tilde{g}^y)} \right)^m = \hat{e}(g, \tilde{g})^k & (4) \\[4mm] \dfrac{\hat{e}(g, \tilde{g}^\gamma)}{\hat{e}(g^w, \tilde{g}^\delta)} = 1 & (5) \end{cases}$$

is verified. Let us set $\alpha = r$, $k = rx_*m$ and $\gamma = s^{-1}$, for some integers $r, x_*, s \in \mathbb{Z}_q^*$. If the above system is verified, we can rewrite $g^\alpha = g^r$, $g^\beta = g^{rs(x_*+y)}$, $\tilde{g}^\gamma = \tilde{g}^{(s)^{-1}}$, $\tilde{g}^\delta = \tilde{g}^{(ws)^{-1}}$, $\hat{e}(g, \tilde{g})^k = \hat{e}(g, \tilde{g})^{rx_*m}$; if $x_* \notin \mathcal{O}$ the attacker has produced a valid answer, according to Definition 3.

In order to verify the system above within the simulation framework, $\mathcal{B}$ computes

$$\begin{cases} F_{T,*} = (F_{1,\beta} \cdot F_{2,\gamma} - F_{1,\alpha} \cdot Y) M - F_{T,K} & (6) \\[2mm] F_{T,\circ} = F_{2,\gamma} - F_{2,\delta} \cdot W & (7) \end{cases}$$

To proceed with our demonstration, first of all we show that it is not possible that $F_{T,*} = F_{T,\circ} = 0$ for every value of W, Y, M and $Z_i, 1 \leq i \leq \tau_O$. This result implies that the success of $\mathcal{A}$ in the game must depend on the particular values assigned to W, Y, M and Z_i.

Let us first observe that the polynomials $F_{1,\alpha}$, $F_{1,\beta}$ are by construction formed as

$$F_{1,\alpha} = \alpha_0 + \alpha_1 W + \sum_{i=1}^{\tau_O} (\alpha_{2,i} Z_i (x_i + Y))$$

$$F_{1,\beta} = \beta_0 + \beta_1 W + \sum_{i=1}^{\tau_O} (\beta_{2,i} Z_i (x_i + Y))$$

where x_i is the element of $\mathbb{Z}_q^*$ queried upon the i-th query to the oracle O. The polynomials $F_{2,\gamma}$ and $F_{2,\delta}$ instead are formed as

$$F_{2,\gamma} = \gamma_0 + \gamma_1 Y + \gamma_2 M + \sum_{i=1}^{\tau_O} (\gamma_{3,i} Z_i^{-1} + \gamma_{4,i} (Z_i W)^{-1})$$

$$F_{2,\delta} = \delta_0 + \delta_1 Y + \delta_2 M + \sum_{i=1}^{\tau_O} (\delta_{3,i} Z_i^{-1} + \delta_{4,i} (Z_i W)^{-1})$$

Plugging these equations back in Equation 7, gives us

$$\gamma_0 + \gamma_1 Y + \gamma_2 M + \sum_{i=1}^{\tau_O} (\gamma_{3,i} Z_i^{-1} + \gamma_{4,i}(Z_i W)^{-1}) =$$

$$\delta_0 W + \delta_1 WY + \delta_2 WM + \sum_{i=1}^{\tau_O} (\delta_{3,i} Z_i^{-1} W + \delta_{4,i} Z_i^{-1}) \tag{8}$$

If the attacker wins the game, Equation 8 must be symbolically equal to zero; simplifying all the unique terms, we are left with

$$\sum_{i=1}^{\tau_O} (\gamma_{3,i} Z_i^{-1}) = W \sum_{i=1}^{\tau_O} (\delta_{4,i}(Z_i W)^{-1}) \tag{9}$$

from which we conclude that $F_{2,\gamma} = \sum_{i=1}^{\tau_O} (\gamma_{3,i} Z_i^{-1})$.

Let us now consider Equation 6, which can be rewritten as

$$\left(\left(\sum_{i=1}^{\tau_O} (\beta_0 \gamma_{3,i} Z_i^{-1} + \beta_1 \gamma_{3,i} Z_i^{-1} W + \sum_{j=1}^{\tau_O} (\beta_{2,j} \gamma_{3,i} Z_i^{-1} Z_j (x_j + Y))) \right) - \right.$$

$$\left. \left(\alpha_0 Y + \alpha_1 WY + \sum_{i=1}^{\tau_O} (\alpha_{2,i} Z_i Y (x_i + Y)) \right) \right) M = F_{T,K} \tag{10}$$

If the attacker wins the game, Equation 10 must be symbolically equal to zero. First of all, we notice that each term of the left hand of the equation contains M. Therefore, from $F_{T,K}$ we delete all the terms that do not contain M. Then, we simplify M on both sides. Further more, we simplify all the unique terms, ending up with $\beta_{2,j} \gamma_{3,i} (x_j + Y) - \alpha_0 Y = K_0$.

Now, $\alpha_0 = \beta_{2,j} \gamma_{3,i}$ since they are the only coefficients of Y. Then $K_0 = \beta_{2,j} \gamma_{3,i} x_j$. However this is not a valid solution, x_j is the j-th value queried to oracle O, and thus belongs to $\mathcal{O}$. We therefore conclude that it is impossible for the attacker to win the game for every value of W, Y, M and Z_i; instead this depends on a lucky instantiation of such variables.

The simulator $\mathcal{B}$ therefore chooses random values $\bar{w}, \bar{y}, \bar{m}, \bar{z}_1, \ldots, \bar{z}_{\tau_O}$ for each of the variables W, Y, M and Z_i. Let us analyze the probability that the attacker has won the game given the chosen assignment of the variables: this happens if (i) no two non-identical polynomials in the lists L_1, L_2 and L_T assume the same value and (ii) if the assignment satisfies $F_{T,*} = F_{T,\circ} = 0$. If (i) is true, $\mathcal{B}$'s simulation was flawed because two group elements – that were equal – have been presented as distinct to the attacker.

Summing up, the probability of success of the attacker is bounded by the probability that any of the following equations holds:

$$F_{1,i}(\bar{w}, \bar{y}, \bar{m}, \bar{z}_1, \ldots, \bar{z}_{\tau_O}) - F_{1,j}(\bar{w}, \bar{y}, \bar{m}, \bar{z}_1, \ldots, \bar{z}_{\tau_O}) = 0, \quad i,j \text{ s.t. } F_{1,i} \neq F_{1,j} \tag{11}$$

$$F_{2,i}(\bar{w}, \bar{y}, \bar{m}, \bar{z}_1, \ldots, \bar{z}_{\tau_O}) - F_{2,j}(\bar{w}, \bar{y}, \bar{m}, \bar{z}_1, \ldots, \bar{z}_{\tau_O}) = 0, \quad i,j \text{ s.t. } F_{2,i} \neq F_{2,j} \tag{12}$$

$$F_{T,i}(\bar{w}, \bar{y}, \bar{m}, \bar{z}_1, \ldots, \bar{z}_{\tau_O}) - F_{T,j}(\bar{w}, \bar{y}, \bar{m}, \bar{z}_1, \ldots, \bar{z}_{\tau_O}) = 0, \quad i,j \text{ s.t. } F_{T,i} \neq F_{T,j} \tag{13}$$

$$F_{T,*}(\bar{w}, \bar{y}, \bar{m}, \bar{z}_1, \ldots, \bar{z}_{\tau_O}) - 1 = 0 \tag{14}$$

$$F_{T,\circ}(\bar{w}, \bar{y}, \bar{m}, \ldots, \bar{z}_{\tau_O}) - 1 = 0 \tag{15}$$

For fixed i, j each non-trivial polynomial 11, 12, 13 has degree at most 1 and it vanishes with probability $\leq 1/q$. Polynomials 14 and 15 have too degree at most 1 and vanish with probability $\leq 1/q$. We sum over all the (i, j) to bound the overall success probability ϵ of the attacker $\mathcal{A}$ as $\epsilon \leq \binom{\tau_1}{2}\frac{1}{q} + \binom{\tau_2}{2}\frac{1}{q} + \binom{\tau_T}{2}\frac{1}{q} + \frac{2}{q}$. Since $\tau_1 + \tau_2 + \tau_T \leq q_G + 5$, we end up with $\epsilon \leq \dfrac{(q_G + 5)^2}{q} = O(q_G^2/q)$ $\qquad\square$

B   Proofs of Security of **RevocationMatching**

In this section we present proofs of the security claims presented in Section 6.1.

B.1   Proof of Lemma 1

Proof. We define $\mathcal{B}$ as follows. $\mathcal{B}$ is given an instance $\langle g, g^a, g^b, g^\sigma \rangle$ of the DDH problem in $\mathbb{G}_1$ and wishes to use $\mathcal{A}$ to decide if $\sigma = ab$. The algorithm $\mathcal{B}$ simulates an environment in which $\mathcal{A}$ operates, using $\mathcal{A}$'s advantage in the game TraceProperty to help compute the solution to the DDH problem.

Setup. Here is a high-level description of how the algorithm $\mathcal{B}$ will work. $\mathcal{B}$ uses g as the one received from the DDH challenge, picks and publishes the public parameters according to the rules of the protocol.

Queries. At first, $\mathcal{A}$ queries $\mathcal{B}$ for an arbitrary number of tuples $\langle cred_{u_i,p_i}, match_{p_i}, x_{u_i,p_i}, rev_{u_i,p_i} \rangle$ for any given pairs $(u_i, p_i) \in \mathcal{U} \times \mathcal{P}$. The queries can be adaptive. $\mathcal{B}$ answers truthfully abiding by the rules of the protocol.

Challenge. At the end of this phase $\mathcal{A}$ initiates two handshake instances by sending e^{m_1} and e^{m_2}; $\mathcal{B}$ picks $x_1, x_2, s_1, s_2, r \xleftarrow{R} \mathbb{Z}_q^*$ and $p \xleftarrow{R} \mathcal{P}$ and generates two handshake tuples as follows:

$$\left\langle g^r, g^{rs_1(x_1+h(p)(bt+h(p)))}, \tilde{g}^{(s_1)^{-1}}, \tilde{g}^{(s_1 w)^{-1}} \right\rangle$$

$$\left\langle g^a, g^{as_2(x_2+h^2(p))}g^{\sigma s_2 h(p)t}, \tilde{g}^{(s_2)^{-1}}, \tilde{g}^{(s_2 w)^{-1}} \right\rangle$$

Analysis of $\mathcal{A}$'s response. It is straightforward to verify that, if $\mathcal{A}$ wins the game, $\mathcal{B}$ can give the same answer to solve the DDH problem. Indeed, if $\mathcal{A}$ wins the game, she is able to decide if $\exists \alpha \in \mathbb{Z}_q^*$ such that

$$\begin{cases} (r(x_1 + h(p)(bt + h(p))) - r\alpha)m_1 = rm_1x_1 \\ (a(x_2 + h^2(p)) + \sigma h(p)t - a\alpha)m_2 = am_2x_2 \end{cases} \tag{16}$$

If $\mathcal{A}$'s answer is positive, it means that the system of equations is verified. Then we can solve the first equation as $\alpha = h(p)bt + h^2(p)$, and plugging in the second equation $\mathcal{B}$ can verify that $\sigma = ab$, which is the positive answer to the DDH problem. If not, $\mathcal{B}$ can give the negative answer to DDH. □

B.2   Proof of Lemma 2

Proof. We define $\mathcal{B}$ as follows. $\mathcal{B}$ is given an instance $\langle g, g^a, g^b, g^\sigma \rangle$ of the DDH problem in $\mathbb{G}_1$ and wishes to use $\mathcal{A}$ to decide if $\sigma = ab$. The algorithm $\mathcal{B}$ simulates an environment in which $\mathcal{A}$ operates, using $\mathcal{A}$'s advantage in the game TraceCredential to help compute the solution to the DDH problem.

Setup. Here is a high-level description of how the algorithm $\mathcal{B}$ will work. $\mathcal{B}$ uses g as the one received from the DDH challenge, picks and publishes the public parameters according to the rules of the protocol.

Queries. $\mathcal{A}$ can query $\mathcal{B}$ for an arbitrary number of tuples $\langle cred_{u_i,p_i}, match_{p_i}, x_{u_i,p_i}, rev_{u_i,p_i} \rangle$ for any given pairs $(u_i, p_i) \in \mathcal{U} \times \mathcal{P}$. The queries can be adaptive. $\mathcal{B}$ answers truthfully abiding by the rules of the protocol.

Challenge. At the end of this phase, $\mathcal{A}$ chooses a property p_*; $\mathcal{B}$ picks $r, s_1, s_2 \xleftarrow{R} \mathbb{Z}_q^*$ and prepares two handshake tuples as follows:

$$\left\langle g^r, g^{rs_1(b+h(p)(t+h(p)))}, \tilde{g}^{(s_1)^{-1}}, \tilde{g}^{(s_1w)^{-1}} \right\rangle$$

$$\left\langle g^a, g^{s_2\sigma} g^{as_2(h(p)(t+h(p)))}, \tilde{g}^{(s_2)^{-1}}, \tilde{g}^{(s_2w)^{-1}} \right\rangle$$

Analysis of $\mathcal{A}$'s response. It is straightforward to verify that, if $\mathcal{A}$ wins the game, $\mathcal{B}$ can give the same answer to solve the DDH problem. Indeed, if $\mathcal{A}$ wins the game, she is able to tell if both handshake messages contain the same identification handle x_*. Let us assume this is the case. Then, the same revocation handle $rev_* = \tilde{g}^{x_*}$ can be used to revoke both credentials. Then, performing a check as described in Equation 3, the following system

$$\begin{cases} r(b + h(p)(t + h(p))) - rh(p)(t + h(p)) = rx_* \\ \sigma + a(h(p)(t + h(p))) - ah(p)(t + h(p)) = ax_* \end{cases} \tag{17}$$

should hold.

Then we can solve the first equation as $x_* = b$, and plugging in the second equation $\mathcal{B}$ can verify that $\sigma = ab$, which is the positive answer to the DDH problem. If not, $\mathcal{B}$ can give the negative answer to DDH. □

B.3   Proof of Lemma 3

Proof. We define $\mathcal{B}$ as follows. $\mathcal{B}$ is given an instance $\langle g, g^w, \tilde{g}, \tilde{g}^y, \tilde{g}^m, O_{w,y} \rangle$ of the SM problem and wishes to use $\mathcal{A}$ to produce the tuple $\langle g^r, g^{rs(x_*+y)}, \tilde{g}^{s^{-1}}, \tilde{g}^{(ws)^{-1}}, \hat{e}(g,\tilde{g})^{rx_*m} \rangle$, such that x_* has not been queried to O. The algorithm $\mathcal{B}$ simulates an environment in which $\mathcal{A}$ operates.

Setup. Here is a high-level description of how the algorithm $\mathcal{B}$ will work. $\mathcal{B}$ sets public parameters $g, \tilde{g}$ as the ones received from the challenge. It then sets $W \leftarrow g^w$, $T \leftarrow \tilde{g}^y$; the other public parameters are set according to the rules of the protocol.

Queries. $\mathcal{A}$ queries $\mathcal{B}$ for an arbitrary number of tuples $\langle cred_{u_i,p_i}, match_{p_i}, x_{u_i,p_i}, rev_{u_i,p_i} \rangle$ for any given pairs $(u_i, p_i) \in \mathcal{U} \times \mathcal{P}$. The queries can be adaptive. Upon a query for (u_i, p_i), $\mathcal{B}$ answers picking $x_{u_i,p_i} \xleftarrow{R} \mathbb{Z}_q^*$; $\mathcal{B}$ then queries the oracle $O_{w,y}$ providing $\frac{x_{u_i,p_i}+h^2(p)}{h(p)}$ as input, adding the value $\frac{x_{u_i,p_i}+h^2(p)}{h(p)}$ to the set $\mathcal{O}$ of queries to oracle O. The output of the oracle is $(g^{z(\frac{x_{u_i,p_i}+h^2(p)}{h(p)}+y)}, \tilde{g}^{z^{-1}}, \tilde{g}^{(zw)^{-1}})$. $\mathcal{B}$ then assigns $C_{u_i,p_i,1} \leftarrow \left(g^{z(\frac{x_{u_i,p_i}+h^2(p)}{h(p)}+y)} \right)^{h(p)}$, $C_{u_i,p_i,2} \leftarrow \tilde{g}^{z^{-1}}$, $C_{u_i,p_i,3} \leftarrow \tilde{g}^{(zw)^{-1}}$, $match_{p_i} = \left(T\tilde{H}(p) \right)^{h(p)}$, $rev_{u_i,p_i} = \tilde{g}^{x_{u_i,p_i}}$ and gives the requested parameters to $\mathcal{A}$. The attacker can successfully perform all the checks mandated by the protocol; his view is therefore undistinguishable from a standard protocol instantiation.

Challenge. $\mathcal{A}$ then declares that this phase of the game is over. $\mathcal{B}$ therefore revokes each of the credentials $\mathcal{A}$ requested in the previous phase. $\mathcal{A}$ then chooses a property $p_* \in \mathcal{P}$. $\mathcal{A}$ receives from $\mathcal{B}$ the matching reference $\left(T\tilde{H}(p) \right)^{h(p)}$ of property p_*. $\mathcal{B}$ challenges $\mathcal{A}$ by sending $\hat{e}(g, \tilde{g}^m)$ and $\mathcal{A}$ answers the challenge with the tuple $\langle g^\alpha, g^\beta, \tilde{g}^\gamma, \tilde{g}^\delta, e^k \rangle$.

Analysis of $\mathcal{A}$'s response. If $\mathcal{A}$ wins the game, $\mathcal{B}$ can check that $\hat{e}(g^w, \tilde{g}^\delta) = \hat{e}(g, \tilde{g}^\gamma)$ and that $\left(\frac{\hat{e}(g^\beta, \tilde{g}^\gamma)}{\hat{e}(g^\alpha, match_{p_*})} \right)^m = \left(\frac{\hat{e}(g^\beta, \tilde{g}^\gamma)}{\hat{e}\left(g^\alpha, \tilde{g}^{h(p_*)(y+h(p_*))} \right)} \right)^m = e^k$ as mandated by the Authenticate step of RevocationMatching described in Section 4.

Let us set $\alpha = r$, $k = rx_*m$ and $\gamma = s^{-1}$, for some integers $r, x_*, s \in \mathbb{Z}_q^*$ unknown to $\mathcal{B}$. Then, from the first Equation we derive that $\delta = (ws)^{-1}$ and from the second Equation we derive that $\beta = rs(x_* + h(p_*)(y + h(p_*)))$. Notice that by the definition of the game, the attacker has not received a credential containing $x_* + h(p_*)(y + h(p_*))$; factoring $h(p_*)$ we derive that $\frac{x_*+h^2(p_*)}{h(p_*)}$ cannot belong to the set $\mathcal{O}$. Therefore we conclude that, if $\mathcal{A}$ wins the game, $\mathcal{B}$ can provide $\left\langle (g^\alpha)^{h(p_*)}, g^\beta, \tilde{g}^\gamma, \tilde{g}^\delta, \hat{e}(g,\tilde{g})^k \cdot \hat{e}(g^\alpha, \tilde{g}^m)^{h^2(p_*)} \right\rangle$ as an answer to the SM problem. $\qquad \square$

B.4   Proof of Lemma 4

Proof. We define $\mathcal{B}$ as follows. $\mathcal{B}$ is given an instance $\langle g, g^a, g^b, g^c, \tilde{g}, \tilde{g}^a, \tilde{g}^b, \tilde{g}^\sigma \rangle$ of the BDDH problem and wishes to use $\mathcal{A}$ to decide if $\sigma = abc$. The algorithm $\mathcal{B}$ simulates an environment in which $\mathcal{A}$ operates.

Setup. Here is a high-level description of how the algorithm $\mathcal{B}$ will work. $\mathcal{B}$ sets $g, \tilde{g}$ as the ones received from the BDDH instance; T is set to be equal to $\tilde{g}^{at}$. It then sets all the remaining parameters as mandated in the rules of the protocol.

Queries. $\mathcal{A}$ queries $\mathcal{B}$ for an arbitrary number of $\langle cred_{u_i,p_i}, match_{p_i}, x_{u_i,p_i}, rev_{u_i,p_i} \rangle$ for any given pairs $(u_i, p_i) \in \mathcal{U} \times \mathcal{P}$. The queries can be adaptive. $\mathcal{B}$ answers by picking for each query $x_{u_i,p_i}, z \xleftarrow{R} \mathbb{Z}_q^*$, and giving $C_{u_i,p_i,1} \leftarrow g^{z(x_{u_i,p_i}+h(p_i)(at+h(p_i)))}$, $C_{u_i,p_i,2} = \tilde{g}^{z^{-1}}$, $C_{u_i,p_i,3} = \tilde{g}^{(zw)^{-1}}$, $match_{p_i} = \tilde{g}^{h(p_i)(at+h(p_i))}$, $rev_{u_i,p_i} = \tilde{g}^{x_{u_i,p_i}}$ to the attacker. The attacker can successfully perform all the checks mandated by the protocol; his view is therefore undistinguishable from a standard protocol instantiation. $\mathcal{B}$ adds to a list V the tuple $(\tilde{g}^{x_{u_i,p_i}+h(p_i)(at+h(p_i))}, u_i, p_i, x_{u_i,p_i})$ for each query of $\mathcal{A}$ and keeps it for later use.

Challenge. $\mathcal{A}$ then declares that this phase of the game is over. $\mathcal{B}$ therefore revokes each credential requested by $\mathcal{A}$ in the previous phase. $\mathcal{A}$ then declares property $p_* \in \mathcal{P}$. $\mathcal{B}$ challenges $\mathcal{A}$ by sending $\hat{e}(g, \tilde{g})^{bc}$ and $\mathcal{A}$ answers the challenge with the tuple $\langle g^\alpha, g^\beta, \tilde{g}^\gamma, \tilde{g}^\delta, \hat{e}(g, \tilde{g})^k \rangle$.

Analysis of $\mathcal{A}$'s response. If $\mathcal{A}$ wins the game, $\mathcal{B}$ can check that
$$\left(\frac{\hat{e}(g^\beta, \tilde{g}^\gamma)}{\hat{e}(g^\alpha, match_{p_*})} \right)^{bc} = \hat{e}(g, \tilde{g})^k \text{ and that } \hat{e}(g^w, \tilde{g}^\delta) = \hat{e}(g, \tilde{g}^\gamma) \text{ as mandated by}$$
the Authenticate step of RevocationMatching described in Section 4.

Let us set $\alpha = r$, $k = rx_*bc$, $\gamma = s^{-1}$ and $\beta = rsv_*$ for some integers $r, x_*, s, v_* \in \mathbb{Z}_q^*$ unknown to $\mathcal{B}$. Then, from the first Equation we derive that $\delta = (ws)^{-1}$.

We know by definition that the attacker has already received $C_{u_o,p_o,1} = g^{zv_*} = g^{z(x_{u_o,p_o}+h(p_o)(at+h(p_o)))}$ during the previous query phase. Consequently, the revocation handle $rev_{u_o,p_o} = \tilde{g}^{x_{u_o,p_o}}$ has also been published. $\mathcal{B}$ can easily recover u_o and p_o, since she can check for which $\tilde{g}^{x_{u_o,p_o}+h(p_o)(at+h(p_o))}$ in the list V, $\hat{e}(g^\beta, \tilde{g}^\gamma) = \hat{e}(g^\alpha, \tilde{g}^{x_{u_o,p_o}+h(p_o)(at+h(p_o))})$ holds and look up the respective $h(p_o)$ and x_{u_o,p_o}.

If $p_o = p_*$, then $\mathcal{A}$ has lost the game, since a successful answer of the attacker cannot be revoked by any of the issued revocation handles, whereas if $p_o = p_*$, the credential can be revoked with rev_{u_o,p_o}. Then it must be that $p_o \neq p_*$; in this case $x_* = x_{u_o,p_o} + h(p_o)(at + h(p_o)) - h(p_*)(at + h(p_*))$.

Then $k = rbc(x_{u_o,p_o} + h^2(p_o) - h^2(p_*)) + rabct(h(p_o) - h(p_*))$. However $\mathcal{B}$ is still not able to use $\mathcal{A}$'s answer to solve the BDDH problem since $\mathcal{B}$ cannot compute $\hat{e}(g, \tilde{g})^{rbc(x_{u_o,p_o}+h^2(p_o)-h^2(p_*))}$. Using the generalized forking lemma [3] presented by Bagherzandi et al. and used to a similar end in [24,11], we know that $\mathcal{A}$ can be executed twice with the same random tape that produced r but with different parameters. In particular, in the forked instance $\mathcal{B}$ can replace $T = \tilde{g}^{at}$ by $\tilde{g}^{t}$. Therefore from the forked instance, $\mathcal{B}$ recovers

$$\hat{e}\left(g,\tilde{g}\right)^{rbc} = \left(\hat{e}\left(g,\tilde{g}\right)^{k'}\right)^{\left(x_{u_o,p_o}+h(p_o)(t+h(p_o))-h(p_*)(t+h(p_*))\right)^{-1}}$$

and is finally able to decide if $\sigma = abc$ by checking if

$$\hat{e}\left(g^{\alpha},\tilde{g}^{\sigma}\right) = \left(\frac{\hat{e}\left(g,\tilde{g}\right)^{k}}{\left(\hat{e}\left(g,\tilde{g}\right)^{rbc}\right)^{\left(x_{u_o,p_o}+h^2(p_o)-h^2(p_*)\right)}}\right)^{\left((h(p_o)-h(p_*))t\right)^{-1}}$$
□

Practical Rebound Attack on 12-Round Cheetah-256

Shuang Wu, Dengguo Feng, and Wenling Wu

State Key Lab of Information Security, Institute of Software
Chinese Academy of Sciences
Beijing 100190, China
{wushuang,feng,wwl}@is.iscas.ac.cn

Abstract. In this paper, we propose cryptanalysis of the hash function Cheetah-256. Cheetah is accepted as a first round candidate of SHA-3 competition hosted by NIST [1], but it is not in the second round.

First, we discuss relation between degrees of freedom injected from round message blocks and round number of a pseudo-collision attack on hash functions with S boxes and MDS diffusion. A pseudo-collision attack on 8-round Cheetah-256 can be derived by trivially applying original rebound techniques.

Then, we propose a rebound differential path for semi-free start collision attack on 12-round Cheetah-256 and an observation of the neutral bytes' influence on state values. Based on this observation, algebraic message modifications are designed using the neutral bytes and total complexity is reduced to 2^{24}. This is a practical rebound attack.

Keywords: Hash function, collision attack, rebound attack, message modification, Cheetah-256, SHA-3 candidates.

1 Introduction

The SHA-3 competition hosted by NIST aims to find a new cryptographic hash standard as a replacement of SHA-2. The Cheetah hash function [3] is selected as a first round candidate of the SHA-3 competition [1], but it didn't pass to the second round.

In FSE 2009, Florian Mendel et al. proposed a powerful tool "rebound attack" [4] for cryptanalysis of hash functions with AES-like [2] SPN designs. In this paper, we improved rebound attack and applied it to Cheetah-256. When there are degrees of freedom injected from round message blocks, we can extend round number and reduce complexity of the inbound steps. Then we analyzed the algebraic relation between neutral bytes and the state values and found a solution of message modification. Complexity of the semi-free start collision attack was significantly reduced to 2^{24}. Semi-free start collision pairs can be found in a few minutes. The practical result is given in Appendix A.

Another method to improved rebound techniques is proposed by Florian Mendel et al. in SAC 2009 [6]. In SAC 2009, we also proposed a rebound attack on another first round candidate of SHA-3 competition, the LANE hash function [7].

D. Lee and S. Hong (Eds.): ICISC 2009, LNCS 5984, pp. 300–314, 2010.

This paper is organized as follows. Compression function of Cheetah-256 is briefly described in section 2. In section 3, we discussed the relation between degrees of freedom and the round number of the attack. In section 4, we described all details of the semi-free start collision attack on 12-round Cheetah-256. Section 5 is the conclusion.

2   Specification of Cheetah-256 Compression Function

The Cheetah-256 hash function uses iterative structure with block counters and a last block permutation. We will not describe padding rules and last block permutation here since they do not influence this attack. In this section, we will briefly describe compression function of Cheetah-256.

Compression function of Cheetah-256 uses a 16-round 256-bit block cipher in Davies-Meyer Mode. The 1024-bit message block is used as the key of this block cipher. Message Schedule follows an AES-like procedure. Message block is treated as a byte array of size 8×16 and the round message blocks $K_0, K_1, ..., K_{15}$ for each round are generated as in Figure 1.

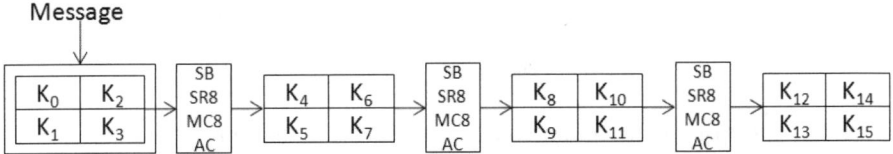

Fig. 1. Message Schedule of Cheetah-256

Figure 2 shows how these blocks are used in the iteration. In this paper, BlockCounter is not considered, since we only deal with the first block and BlockCounter=0 for the first block.

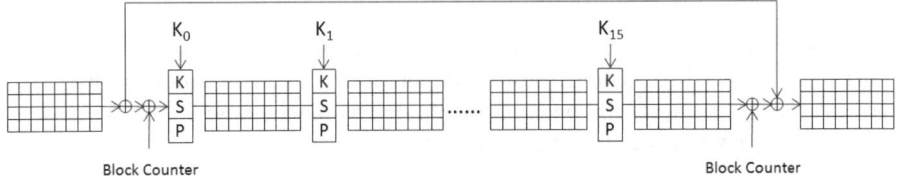

Fig. 2. Compression Function of Cheetah-256

Here we define all operations used in Cheetah-256.

- **SB,S.** The non-linear operation SB(S) applies S-Box to each byte of the state. The S-box is the same as the one used in AES.
- **SR4,SR8.** The permutation SR4 and SR8 rotates bytes of the 4×8 and 8×16 state leftwards cyclically. Shift vector defines offset amount of the rotation for each row. Shift vector is (0,1,3,4) for SR4 and (0,1,2,3,5,6,7,8) for SR8.

- **MC4,MC8.** The diffusion layer MC4 and MC8 multiplies the 4×8 and 8×16 state by a MDS matrix over $GF(2^8)$. Matrices A_4 and A_8 are also defined here.

$$MC4(s) = A_4 \cdot s, A_4 = \begin{pmatrix} 02\ 03\ 01\ 01 \\ 01\ 02\ 03\ 01 \\ 01\ 01\ 02\ 03 \\ 03\ 01\ 01\ 02 \end{pmatrix}$$

$$MC8(s) = A_8 \cdot s, A_8 = \begin{pmatrix} 02\ 0c\ 06\ 08\ 01\ 04\ 01\ 01 \\ 01\ 02\ 0c\ 06\ 08\ 01\ 04\ 01 \\ 01\ 01\ 02\ 0c\ 06\ 08\ 01\ 04 \\ 04\ 01\ 01\ 02\ 0c\ 06\ 08\ 01 \\ 01\ 04\ 01\ 01\ 02\ 0c\ 06\ 08 \\ 08\ 01\ 04\ 01\ 01\ 02\ 0c\ 06 \\ 06\ 08\ 01\ 04\ 01\ 01\ 02\ 0c \\ 0c\ 06\ 08\ 01\ 04\ 01\ 01\ 02 \end{pmatrix}$$

- **P.** Combination of SR4 and MC4.

$$P(\cdot) = MC4 \cdot SR4(\cdot)$$

- **AC.** Addition of the round constant to the first column.

$$m_{i,0}+ = S[4 * r + i], 0 \le i \le 3$$

where S stands for the S-box and r is the round index in message expansion.
- **K.** Addition of the round message block to the internal state.

3   Rebound Attack and Round Message Blocks

In this section, we discuss how degrees of freedom injected from round message blocks can be used to extend round number of a standard rebound differential path. A rebound differential path of pseudo-collision attack on 8-round Cheetah-256 cab be derived using this technique.

3.1   Rebound Attack on 5-Round Whirlpool

In FSE 2009, Florian Mendel et al. proposed the original 4-round rebound differential path for Whirlpool [4]. In this path, degrees of freedom from round message blocks are not used. According to message expansion used in Whirlpool, input chain value of the compression function can be determined from any one of the expanded message block. So only one round message block is free to use. Once a block is used, this rebound differential path can be extended to 5 rounds. In the following figure, feedback operations are omitted.

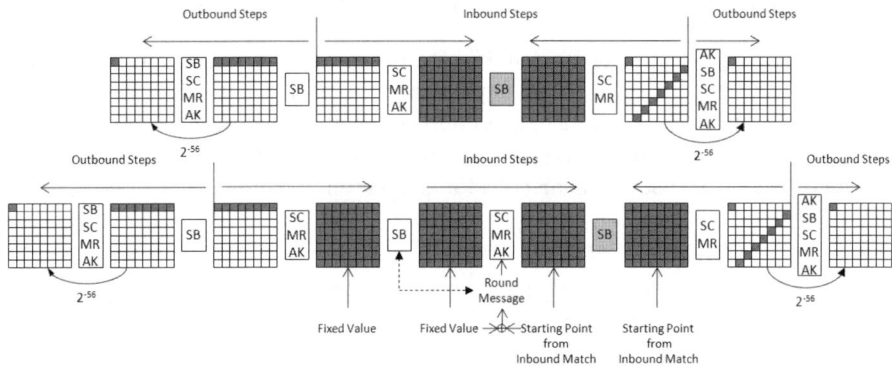

Fig. 3. 4-round and 5-round Rebound Differential Paths for Whirlpool

As shown in Figure 3, inbound steps of a rebound differential path, one SB operation is chosen as the matching point. Note if no degrees of freedom are available, there would be only one SB in the inbound steps. In Figure 3, the rightmost SB in the inbound steps is chosen. Dark background color is used to indicate the chosen SB. Any SB in the inbound steps can be chosen as the matching point.

A principle of the inbound steps is that internal state differences must propagate with probability of 1 on both sides of the chosen SB. All linear operations are perfect for difference propagation. The only problem is S-Box. Degrees of freedom from round message blocks are used to make sure difference can pass through SB operations. The method is to fix state value before and after the SB operation. Fixed value and difference can make this S-box behaves linear.

In Figure 3, difference from left side of the inbound steps propagates to the right direction. When it comes to the first SB, the state value are randomly chosen and fixed. So the state after SB is fixed too, both in difference and value. Then the difference continues to the chosen SB, where it matches with the difference from right side. There are 64 active S-boxes in the matching point, so differences from both sides can match with probability of 2^{-64}.

When a match is found, at least two values can be selected for each S-box. So there will be at least 2^{64} values for the matching states, which are called the starting points. Then we calculated the state values backwards. In Figure 3, starting point and our previously fixed state value meet at an AK operation. State differences on both sides of AK are the same. State values can be connected by setting round message block to XOR value of both sides of AK.

Dotted lines are used to indicate the connections between S-boxes and round message blocks. One message block can extend the inbound steps for one round. Since only one message block is available in Whirlpool, we can attack $4 + 1 = 5$ rounds, which could be extended to semi-free start near-collision attack on 7 rounds.

3.2   Pseudo-Collision Attack on 8-Round Cheetah-256

From the message expansion used in Cheetah-256, we know round message blocks $K_{4i}, K_{4i+1}, K_{4i+2}$ and K_{4i+3} are independent from each other. By trivially applying original rebound techniques, a pseudo-collision attack on 8-round Cheetah-256 can be derived using degrees of freedom in K_4, K_5, K_6 and K_7. This attack can be extended to pseudo-near-collision attack on 10 rounds.

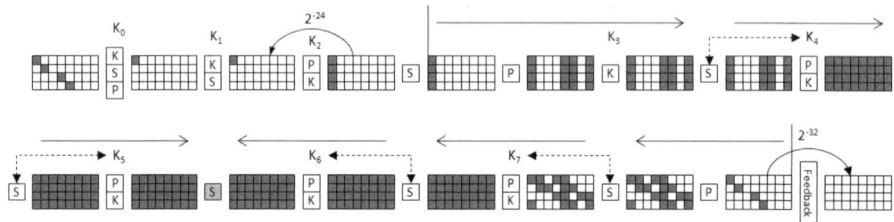

Fig. 4. 8-round Rebound Differential Path for Cheetah-256

A pseudo-collision attack on 6-round Cheetah-512 can be derived in a similar way, and extended to pseudo-near-collision attack on 8(.5) rounds. The attack on 8.5-round Cheetah-512 is mentioned in the report slides of Florian Mendel et al. at the FSE 2009 conference.

Mario Lamberger et al. have proposed an improved way to use degrees of freedom in the round message block [8]. With their techniques, the inbound steps can be extended for three rounds using only one message block. In this paper, we use different techniques.

4   Semi-Free Start Collision Attack on 12-Round Cheetah-256

In a semi-free start collision attack, differences are injected from message blocks. It is quite different from the original rebound attack on Whirlpool. Here we propose a differential path for 12-round Cheetah-256 in Figure 5.

Before we describe details about the attack, notations that will be used in this section are given below.

- $S[\cdot] : GF(2^8) \to GF(2^8)$. The S-box.
- $D(a,b) = \{x \in GF(2^8) | S[x] + S[x+a] = b\}$.
- $R(a,b) = \{y \in GF(2^8) | S^{-1}[y] + S^{-1}[y+b] = a\} = \{S[x] | x \in D(a,b)\}$.
- $a \triangleright b \Leftrightarrow D(a,b) \neq \emptyset$. $a \not\triangleright b \Leftrightarrow D(a,b) = \emptyset$.
- $d^*(a,b)$ Random element in $D(a,b)$, which is defined iff $a \triangleright b$.
- $r^*(a,b)$ Random element in $R(a,b)$, which is defined iff $a \triangleright b$.
- $s_i \xrightarrow{K} s_i' \xrightarrow{S} s_i'' \xrightarrow{SR4} s_i''' \xrightarrow{MC4} s_{i+1}$. State values.
- $s_i(m,n)$. The byte at m-th row and n-th column in s_i.
- $\triangle s_i, \triangle s_i', \triangle s_i''$. State differences.

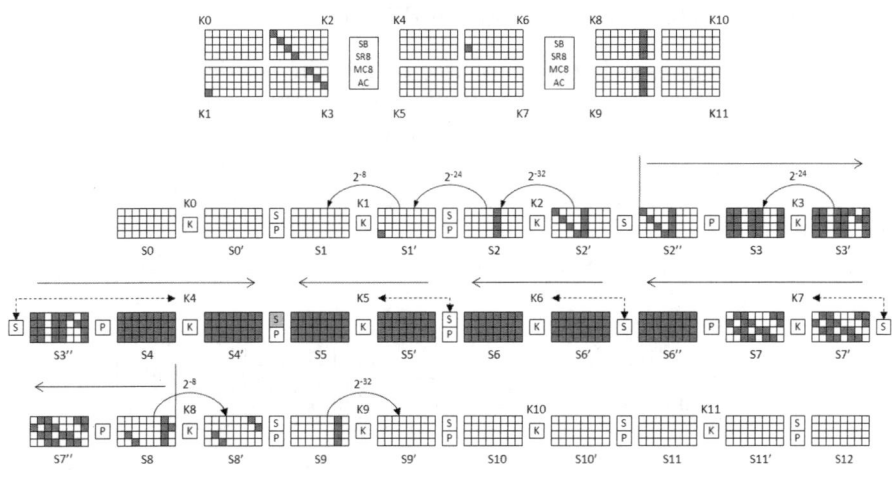

Fig. 5. 12-round Rebound Differential Path for Cheetah-256

- $\triangle s_i \rhd \triangle s_j$ iff for all $0 \le m \le 3$ and $0 \le n \le 7$, $\triangle s_i(m,n) \rhd \triangle s_j(m,n)$.
- (i,j) The j-th neutral byte of the column indexed by i of neutral bytes in K_4'' and K_7 as indexed in Figure 6.
- $d_{i,j}$ Difference for modification in neutral byte (i,j).
- δ_i Difference for modification required in the i-th active byte as indexed in Figure 8.

4.1 Detailed Steps of the Attack

This attack can be described in the following steps:

Step 1: We start from randomly choosing non-zero values for $\triangle K_6$ and $\triangle K_3$.

Step 2: Choose random differences in $\triangle s_2''$ and $\triangle s_8$, the left and right ends of the inbound steps. According to message expansion, $\triangle K_8$ always follows the pattern of $d \cdot (06, 0c, 02, 01)^T$ for certain d. We choose difference $\triangle s_8(1,6) = 0c \cdot D$, $\triangle s_8(2,6) = 02 \cdot D$ and $\triangle s_8(3,6) = D$ for random D in order to increase the probability of difference propagation $\triangle s_8 \to \triangle s_8'$ from 2^{-24} to 2^{-8}.

Step 3: Propagate differences from both sides and meet at the chosen S-box in the 5-th round. The fixing value techniques are used to make S-boxes behave linear. This is similar to original rebound attack.

Step 4: Once differences from both sides matches, which means $\triangle s_4' \rhd \triangle s_4''$. Select a starting point, then K_4, K_5, K_6 and K_7 can be calculated.

Step 5: Calculate $\triangle K_3$ from $\triangle K_6$ and the values in the first column of K_6 and K_7. If $\triangle K_3$ equals our previously chosen one in step 1, we have succeeded in finding a correct inbound differential path. The probability is 2^{-24}.

Step 6: For each value fulfilling the correct inbound path, difference propagations are calculated backwards and forwards in the outbound steps. Probability for every outbound steps are given in Figure 5.

4.2   Neutral Bytes and Message Modifications

In K_4 and K_7, degrees of freedom are used only in the positions of active bytes. Let $K_4' = P^{-1}(K_4)$, we have $s_4' = P(s_3'') + K_4 = P(s_3'' + K_4')$. There are 10 neutral bytes in K_4' and 16 neutral bytes in K_7. Figure 6 shows positions of the neutral bytes and the bytes in other round message blocks influenced by them. Let $K_4'' = MC4^{-1}(K_4)$ and we denote neutral bytes by order of column in K_4'' and K_7 from 1 to d.

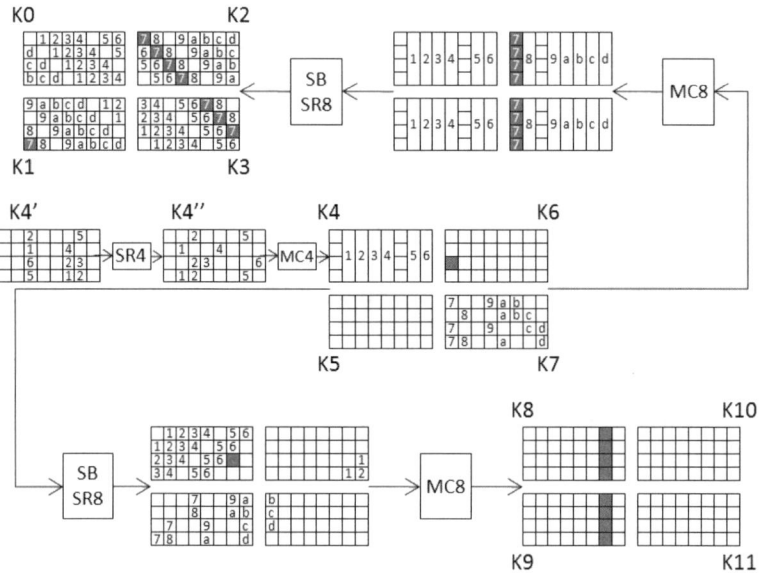

Fig. 6. Neutral Bytes in K_4, K_7 and the Influence on Round Message Blocks

Neutral bytes can be modified to increase probability of the outbound steps shown in Figure 5. Modifications on the neutral bytes in K_4 and K_7 will affect the state value in two ways as shown in Figure 7.

First, modifications in K_4 and K_7 will directly change state values in s_3'' and s_7', but only in the non-active bytes which will not affect active bytes in s_2'' and s_8'. Second, K_3 and K_8 are changed due to message expansion and they will affect the active bytes in s_2'' and s_8'. So the active bytes in s_2'' and s_8' will be affected only once. This simple algebraic relation between neutral bytes and state values allows us to modify certain bytes of the state values as we want.

Message modifications can be described in three phases. After each phase, the state values will be updated due to the modifications on message blocks.

Phase I: modify $\triangle K_3$. $\triangle K_3$ are affected by neutral bytes $(7,1),(7,2)$ and $(7,3)$. In order to make sure the modification succeed, we need to change steps of the attack described in Section 4.1.

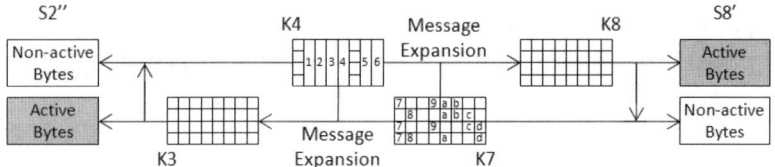

Fig. 7. Influence of Neutral Bytes on Active State Bytes

In Step 1, we choose a possible $\triangle K_3$ instead of a random one. Since $\triangle K_1, \triangle K_2$ and $\triangle K_3$ are calculated from $\triangle K_6$ and the values in the first column of K_6 and K_7. Now we can calculate the difference in the state $SB(K_3)$.

$$
A_8^{-1} \cdot \begin{pmatrix} 0 \\ 0 \\ \triangle K_6(2,0) \\ 0 \\ 0 \\ 0 \\ 0 \\ 0 \end{pmatrix} = \begin{pmatrix} 3a \\ ab \\ 78 \\ 54 \\ c2 \\ 81 \\ 66 \\ ca \end{pmatrix} \cdot \triangle K_6(2,0)
$$

Choose random $\triangle K_3'$ such that

$$
\triangle K_3'(0,5) \triangleright c2 \cdot \triangle K_6(2,0)
$$
$$
\triangle K_3'(1,6) \triangleright 81 \cdot \triangle K_6(2,0)
$$
$$
\triangle K_3'(2,7) \triangleright 66 \cdot \triangle K_6(2,0)
$$

When a match is found, we calculate values of all the message blocks and states from s_2'' to s_8'. In order to modify $\triangle K_3$ to $\triangle K_3'$, we need to introduce three differences on the active bytes of $SB(K_3)$ by $d_{7,1}, d_{7,2}$ and $d_{7,3}$ as in the following equation.

$$
\begin{pmatrix} ? \\ ? \\ ? \\ ? \\ S[K_3(0,5)] + r^*(\triangle K_3'(0,5), c2 \cdot \triangle K_6(2,0)) \\ S[K_3(1,6)] + r^*(\triangle K_3'(1,6), 81 \cdot \triangle K_6(2,0)) \\ S[K_3(2,7)] + r^*(\triangle K_3'(2,7), 66 \cdot \triangle K_6(2,0)) \\ ? \end{pmatrix} = A_8^{-1} \cdot \begin{pmatrix} 0 \\ 0 \\ 0 \\ 0 \\ d_{7,1} \\ 0 \\ d_{7,2} \\ d_{7,3} \end{pmatrix}
$$

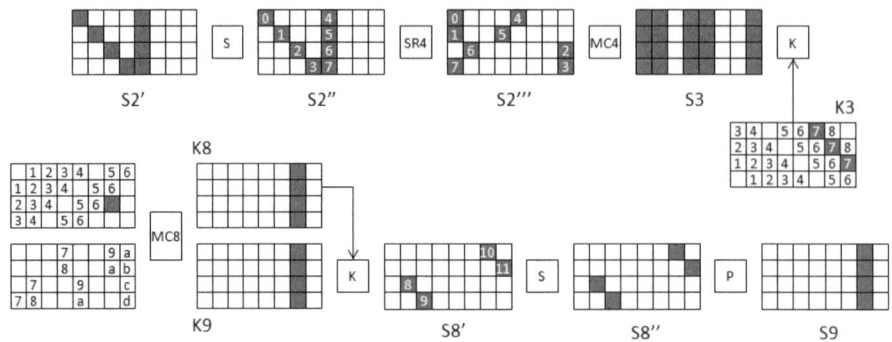

Fig. 8. Indexes of Active Bytes in s_2'' and s_8'

which can be simplified to

$$
\begin{pmatrix} d_{7,1} \\ d_{7,2} \\ d_{7,3} \end{pmatrix} = \begin{pmatrix} 78\ 3a\ ca \\ 54\ ab\ 3a \\ c2\ 78\ ab \end{pmatrix}^{-1} \cdot \begin{pmatrix} S[K_3(0,5)] + r^*(\triangle K_3'(0,5), c2 \cdot \triangle K_6(2,0)) \\ S[K_3(1,6)] + r^*(\triangle K_3'(1,6), 81 \cdot \triangle K_6(2,0)) \\ S[K_3(2,7)] + r^*(\triangle K_3'(2,7), 66 \cdot \triangle K_6(2,0)) \end{pmatrix}
$$

Modify the 7-th column of neutral bytes with $d_{7,1}, d_{7,2}$ and $d_{7,3}$ will change $\triangle K_3$ to $\triangle K_3'$ with probability of 1.

Now all degrees of freedom in column 7 of neutral bytes are used, therefore all difference in message blocks are fixed. We have to modify state difference instead of message difference in the following phases.

Phase II: modify s_2'' and s_8'. In this section, we describe how to modify s_2'' and s_8' in order to get our desired difference of s_2' and s_9 in the backward and forward directions simultaneously. We use δ to denote the difference from message modifications. Active bytes in s_2'' and s_8' are indexed from 0 to 11 as shown in Figure 8.

The same as in phase I, we need to change certain steps in the attack for message modifications. In Step 2, we first choose a random byte of difference in $\triangle s_1''$ and calculate $\triangle s_2 = P(\triangle s_1'')$. Let $\triangle s_2' = \triangle s_2$ and choose random differences in positions $(0,0), (1,1), (2,2), (3,3)$ of $\triangle s_2'$. Then $\triangle s_2''$ is chosen such that $\triangle s_2' \triangleright \triangle s_2''$. Now we can always modify s_2'' and change $\triangle s_2'$ to what we have chosen in the 5-th column.

We can't always modify s_2' and s_9 to cancel $\triangle K_2$ and $\triangle K_8$ since differences in the message blocks are dynamic during the attack and can't be pre-computed. They have to be satisfied by chance. We will talk about this Section 4.3.

We have found a solution of message modifications without using neutral bytes in column $9, b, c, d$. Degrees of freedom in neutral byte columns we use are listed in Table 1.

From now on, we use δ to denote the difference for modification. δ_i stands for the difference we need in the i-th active byte shown in Figure 7. Determining all $\{d_{i,j}\}$ in the neutral bytes from $\{\delta_i\}$ is like solving an non-linear equation group.

Table 1. Degrees of Freedom in the Neutral Byte Columns of Index

Index of neutral byte column	1 2 3 4 5 6 8 a
Degrees of freedom	2 3 1 1 2 1 2 3

Table 2. The Order of Solving Equations in Phase II

Step	Active bytes	Index of neutral byte columns used	Index of fixed column	Degrees of freedom left in each column		
				1 2 3 4 5 6 8 a		
				2 3 1 1 2 1 2 3		
1	0 1 7	1 2 3	3	1 2 0 1 2 1 2 3		
2	2 3	6 8	6	1 2 0 1 2 0 1 3		
3	4	4 5 [6]	4	1 2 0 0 1 0 1 3		
4	5	[3 4] 5	5	1 2 0 0 0 0 1 3		
5	6	1 2 [3 4]	1	0 1 0 0 0 0 1 3		
6	9	2 [3 4]	2	0 1 0 0 0 0 0 3		
7	8	[1 2 3 4] 8	8	0 0 0 0 0 0 0 3		
8	10	[5 6] a	-	0 0 0 0 0 0 0 2		
9	11	[6] a	-	0 0 0 0 0 0 0 1		

The order we solve these equations is shown in Table 2. In this table, the first column is the set of active bytes. The neutral byte columns that influence these active bytes are listed in the second column. The third column shows the column of neutral bytes that will be fixed after we solve the equation of each row. Numbers in "[·]" stands for indexes of the fixed neutral byte columns. When degrees of freedom in a column of neutral bytes are all used, differences for modification in this column can be fixed. Underlined numbers stand for used neutral byte columns in this step.

First, δ_0, δ_1 and δ_7 requires degree of freedom of three bytes from column 1,2,3. Since there is only one byte in column 3, d_3 can be determined. Second, δ_2 and δ_3 require degree of freedom of two bytes from column 6,8. Since there is only one byte in column 6, d_6 is determined. Similar techniques are used for the rest of the equations.

Following this order, we used 14 neutral bytes to introduce our desired differences in 12 active bytes. The byte $(a, 3)$ is left unused, which will be used to modify s_1 in phase III. We leave details of solving the equation group described in the Appendix B.

Once we have solved all equations and get $\{d_{i,j}\}$ for $i \in \{1, 2, 3, 4, 5, 6, 8, a\}$, all values of round message blocks and states from s_1' to s_9' will be updated once more. Now, we have $\triangle s_9' = 0$ and there will be only one byte of difference in s_1.

Phase III: modify s_1. By observing the influence of neutral bytes given in Figure 6, we found an interesting property of $(a,3) = K_7(3,4)$. Modifying $(a,3)$ won't change K_3 and the active bytes in both s_2' and s_8'. So the difference propagations satisfied by phase II will not be destroyed. But $(a,3)$ will affect $K_2(0,4)$, which allows us to control the value in $SB(s_1')$ and change the value of $\triangle s_1'$ to cancel $\triangle K_1$.

After all three phases of message modifications, a semi-free start collision of 12-round Cheetah-256 compression function is found.

4.3   Complexity of This Attack

In the inbound steps, there are 32 active S-boxes at the matching point. So, the probability is 2^{-32} and complexity is 2^{32}. We have found a way to reduce the complexity of inbound match when there is degree of freedom injected.

In Figure 5, $\triangle s_5'$ is calculated from $\triangle s_6$. So, we can match the $\triangle s_4'$ and $P^{-1}(\triangle s_5)$ column by column. If a column is not matched, we go back to the related bytes in $\triangle s_5'$ and change them. Each column can be matched with complexity 2^4 and there are 8 columns. So total complexity of our improved inbound steps is $8 \cdot 2^4 = 2^7$. The same technique has been used in the cryptanalysis of Twister [5].

Now for the outbound steps. If the message modification is possible, probability of the outbound steps can be increased to 2^{-8}. We have to cancel $\triangle K_8$ by chance, according to the way we choose $\triangle s_8$ described in Section 4.1. Now we only need to find the probability that the message modification is possible.

As we have shown in Section 4.2, phase I is always possible because of the way we choose $\triangle K_3'$. In phase II and phase III, differences in round message blocks are dynamic. Message modification is possible iff:

$$\triangle K_2(0,0) \rhd \triangle s_2'(0,0), \triangle K_2(1,1) \rhd \triangle s_2'(1,1), \triangle K_2(2,2) \rhd \triangle s_2'(2,2),$$
$$\triangle K_2(3,3) \rhd \triangle s_2'(3,3), \triangle s_8'(2,1) \rhd \triangle s_8''(2,1), \triangle s_8'(3,2) \rhd \triangle s_8''(3,2),$$
$$\triangle s_8'(0,6) \rhd \triangle s_8''(0,6), \triangle s_8'(1,7) \rhd \triangle s_8''(0,7), \triangle K_1(3,0) \rhd \triangle s_1''$$

where $\triangle s_8'' = P^{-1}(\triangle K_9)$. Since there are 9 conditions, the probability is 2^{-9}.

So the total complexity of this attack is $2^7 \cdot 2^8 \cdot 2^9 = 2^{24}$.

5   Conclusion

In this paper, we proposed a rebound differential path of 12-round Cheetah-256 compression function for semi-free start collision attack. We also designed the algebraic message modifications using degrees of freedom in the neutral bytes and reduced the total complexity of the attack to 2^{24}. The attack is implemented and collision pairs can be found in a few minutes.

A generated collision pair is shown in Table 3 of Appendix A. Byte order in this table is the same as in the internal round state and the first expanded message block.

The positions of different bytes in message pairs are underlined. The last block permutation is not applied. Our results do not hurt collision resistance of the full Cheetah-256.

Since degrees of freedom in the inbound steps and 6 neutral bytes are not used, it's possible to improve this attack or attack more rounds. This will be the future work.

Acknowledgments. The authors would like to thank the anonymous referees for their valuable comments. Furthermore, this work is supported by the National High-Tech Research and Development 863 Plan of China (No. 2007AA01Z470), the National Natural Science Foundation of China (No. 60873259), the National Grand Fundamental Research 973 Program of China (No. 2004CB318004) and the Knowledge Innovation Project of The Chinese Academy of Sciences.

References

1. National Institute of Standards and Technology: Announcing Request for Candidate Algorithm Nominations for a New Cryptographic Hash Algorithm (SHA-3) Family. Federal Register 27(212), 62212–62220 (November 2007), http://csrc.nist.gov/groups/ST/hash/documents/FR_Notice_Nov07.pdf
2. National Institute of Standards and Technology: FIPS PUB 197, Advanced Encryption Standard (AES). Federal Information Processing Standards Publication 197, U.S. Department of Commerce (November 2001)
3. Khovratovich, D., Biryukov, A., Nikolić, I.: The Hash Function Cheetah: Speciffication and Supporting Documentation, http://csrc.nist.gov/groups/ST/hash/sha-3/Round1/documents/Cheetah.zip
4. Mendel, F., Rechberger, C., Schläffer, M., Thomsen, S.S.: The Rebound Attack: Cryptanalysis of Reduced Whirlpool and Grøstl. In: Dunkelman, O. (ed.) Fast Software Encryption. LNCS, vol. 5665, pp. 260–276. Springer, Heidelberg (2009)
5. Mendel, F., Rechberger, C., Schläffer, M.: Cryptanalysis of Twister. In: Abdalla, M., Pointcheval, D., Fouque, P.-A., Vergnaud, D. (eds.) ACNS 2009. LNCS, vol. 5536, pp. 342–353. Springer, Heidelberg (2009)
6. Mendel, F., Peyrin, T., Rechberger, C., Schläffer, M.: Improved Cryptanalysis of the Reduced Grøstl Compression Function, ECHO Permutation and AES Block Cipher. In: Jacobson Jr., M.J., Rijmen, V., Safavi-Naini, R. (eds.) SAC 2009. LNCS, vol. 5867, pp. 16–35. Springer, Heidelberg (to appear 2009)
7. Wu, S., Feng, D., Wu, W.: Cryptanalysis of the LANE hash function. In: Jacobson Jr., M.J., Rijmen, V., Safavi-Naini, R. (eds.) SAC 2009. LNCS, vol. 5867, pp. 126–140. Springer, Heidelberg (to appear 2009)
8. Lamberger, M., Mendel, F., Rechberger, C., Schläffer, M.: Rebound Distinguishers: Results on the Full Whirlpool Compression Function. In: Matsui, M. (ed.) ASIACRYPT 2009. LNCS, Springer, Heidelberg (to appear 2009)

Appendix A

Table 3. Semi-free Start Collision for 12-round Cheetah-256

Initial Value	FB 58 EB B5 88 7C 31 DE
	4A 94 CE 32 CF 13 64 81
	EE 21 A9 0E 0D 70 3D EC
	C7 E0 08 6D F2 89 45 AD
M_1	7E 34 45 79 84 42 4F 78 <u>FB</u> DB 14 15 31 9C CF 0C
	CA 6D 45 3C 0A CE 4B 5D 83 <u>07</u> A2 DB 02 FE 83 20
	51 AE 1A DF 6D A0 C4 CE F9 E0 <u>03</u> AD 10 A8 D6 A2
	80 B2 22 AC 28 B0 CA 48 7B 02 25 <u>45</u> D0 52 11 69
	E9 52 01 BA 60 97 4F EA 0B 2D 8A FD A1 <u>51</u> 48 CB
	E4 7A 14 E5 52 5D E4 FE 51 76 56 0C 29 F3 <u>9D</u> 19
	79 61 C1 49 9E 22 5C 7B AB F5 25 55 97 5F BC <u>13</u>
	<u>31</u> AA 32 03 20 1A 09 8E 13 4E 7D 13 F4 52 A5 49
M_2	7E 34 45 79 84 42 4F 78 <u>0E</u> DB 14 15 31 9C CF 0C
	CA 6D 45 3C 0A CE 4B 5D 83 <u>7A</u> A2 DB 02 FE 83 20
	51 AE 1A DF 6D A0 C4 CE F9 E0 <u>7B</u> AD 10 A8 D6 A2
	80 B2 22 AC 28 B0 CA 48 7B 02 25 <u>36</u> D0 52 11 69
	E9 52 01 BA 60 97 4F EA 0B 2D 8A FD A1 <u>5F</u> 48 CB
	E4 7A 14 E5 52 5D E4 FE 51 76 56 0C 29 F3 <u>69</u> 19
	79 61 C1 49 9E 22 5C 7B AB F5 25 55 97 5F BC <u>78</u>
	<u>0D</u> AA 32 03 20 1A 09 8E 13 4E 7D 13 F4 52 A5 49
Hash Value	9E 51 1F 09 6D FC 7D 00
	6F 03 57 EF CD 05 22 F8
	CF 4E 81 CB FD A6 21 6C
	38 33 45 C8 A5 20 A3 CA

Appendix B

Here, we explain details of solving the equations in Phase II of the message modification. First, calculate all desired differences δ_i in the active bytes of s_2'' and s_8':

$$\delta_0 = s_2''(0,0) + r^*(\triangle K_2(0,0), \triangle s_2''(0,0))$$
$$\delta_1 = s_2''(1,1) + r^*(\triangle K_2(1,1), \triangle s_2''(1,1))$$
$$\delta_2 = s_2''(2,2) + r^*(\triangle K_2(2,2), \triangle s_2''(2,2))$$
$$\delta_3 = s_2''(3,3) + r^*(\triangle K_2(3,3), \triangle s_2''(3,3))$$
$$\delta_4 = s_2''(0,4) + r^*(\triangle s_2'(0,4), \triangle s_2''(0,4))$$
$$\delta_5 = s_2''(1,4) + r^*(\triangle s_2'(1,4), \triangle s_2''(1,4))$$
$$\delta_6 = s_2''(2,4) + r^*(\triangle s_2'(2,4), \triangle s_2''(2,4))$$
$$\delta_7 = s_2''(3,4) + r^*(\triangle s_2'(3,4), \triangle s_2''(3,4))$$

Let $\triangle s_8'' = P^{-1}(\triangle K_9)$,

$$\delta_8 = s_8'(2,1) + d^*(\triangle s_8'(2,1), \triangle s_8''(2,1))$$
$$\delta_9 = s_8'(3,2) + d^*(\triangle s_8'(3,2), \triangle s_8''(3,2))$$
$$\delta_{10} = s_8'(0,6) + d^*(\triangle s_8'(0,6), \triangle s_8''(0,6))$$
$$\delta_{11} = s_8'(1,7) + d^*(\triangle s_8'(1,7), \triangle s_8''(1,7))$$

First, for the backward direction of outbound steps, we calculate all differences in $SB(K_3)$ from differences in neutral bytes. The results are shown in Table 4, where "*" stands for the values we don't use.

Table 4. Values of $\delta SB(K_3)$

35 d_3	25 d_4		73 $d_{5,1}$ +12 $d_{5,2}$	35 d_6			
35 $d_{2,1}$ + bb $d_{2,2}$ + ab $d_{2,3}$	bb d3	*		35 $d_{5,1}$ +ab $d_{5,2}$	*		78 $d_{8,1}$ +3a $d_{8,2}$
26 $d_{1,1}$ +43 $d_{1,2}$	40 $d_{2,1}$ +32 $d_{2,2}$ +43 $d_{2,3}$	*	26 d_4		*	*	
	3e $d_{1,1}$ +18 $d_{1,2}$	*	0c d_3	3e d_4		*	0c d_6

Now check the first column of s_2'''.

$$\begin{pmatrix} \delta_0 \\ \delta_1 \\ ? \\ \delta_7 \end{pmatrix} = A_4^{-1} \cdot \begin{pmatrix} \delta K_3(0,0) \\ \delta K_3(1,0) \\ \delta K_3(2,0) \\ 0 \end{pmatrix} \Rightarrow \begin{pmatrix} \delta K_3(0,0) \\ \delta K_3(1,0) \\ \delta K_3(2,0) \end{pmatrix} = \begin{pmatrix} 0e & 0b & 0d \\ 09 & 0e & 0b \\ 0b & 0d & 09 \end{pmatrix}^{-1} \cdot \begin{pmatrix} \delta_0 \\ \delta_1 \\ \delta_7 \end{pmatrix}$$

which implies,

$$S[K_3(0,0)] + S[K_3(0,0) + \delta K_3(0,0)] = 35 \cdot d_3$$
$$S[K_3(1,0)] + S[K_3(1,0) + \delta K_3(1,0)] = 35 \cdot d_{2,1} + bb \cdot d_{2,2} + ab \cdot d_{2,3}$$
$$S[K_3(2,0)] + S[K_3(2,0) + \delta K_3(2,0)] = 26 \cdot d_{1,1} + 43 \cdot d_{1,2}$$

So, value of d_3 can be determined and we have got two equations for columns 1 and 2. We can derive linear equations for the rest columns of s_2''' with a similar technique.

Second, for the forward direction to modify s_8', it is a little different. Use active byte 9 as an example. According to Table 2, before we modify byte 9, columns

1, 3, 4, 5, 6 of neutral bytes are fixed. The only byte of freedom in column 2 will be used for active byte 9 which is in the third column of s'_8,

$$
A_8 \cdot \begin{pmatrix} S[K_4(0,2)] + S[K_4(0,2) + 02 \cdot d_{2,1} + d_{2,2} + d_{2,3}] \\ S[K_4(1,3)] + S[K_4(1,3) + 03 \cdot d_3] \\ S[K_4(2,4)] + S[K_4(2,4) + d_4] \\ 0 \\ 0 \\ 0 \\ 0 \\ 0 \end{pmatrix} = \begin{pmatrix} ? \\ ? \\ ? \\ \delta K_8(3,2) \\ ? \\ ? \\ ? \\ ? \end{pmatrix}
$$

since $\delta_9 = \delta K_8(3,2)$, we have,

$$
04 \cdot (S[K_4(0,2)] + S[K_4(0,2) + 02 \cdot d_{2,1} + d_{2,2} + d_{2,3}]) + S[K_4(2,4)]
$$
$$
+ S[K_4(2,4) + d_4] + S[K_4(1,3)] + S[K_4(1,3) + 03 \cdot d_3] = \delta_9
$$
$$
\Rightarrow 02 \cdot d_{2,1} + d_{2,2} + d_{2,3} = K_4(0,2) + S^{-1}[S[K_4(0,2)] +
$$
$$
04^{-1} \cdot (S[K_4(2,4)] + S[K_4(2,4) + d_4] + S[K_4(1,3)] + S[K_4(1,3) + 03 \cdot d_3] + \delta_9)]
$$

This is also an linear equation of $d_{2,1}, d_{2,2}$ and $d_{2,3}$.

From Table 2, we know two more linear equations of them can be derived from steps 1 and 5. After applying the same techniques for other neutral columns, we turned the non-linear equation group into a linear one. All differences $d_{i,j}$ can be calculated by solving the linear equation group.

Preimage Attacks on Reduced Steps of ARIRANG and PKC98-Hash

Deukjo Hong, Bonwook Koo, Woo-Hwan Kim, and Daesung Kwon

The Attached Institute of ETRI, P.O.Box 1, Yuseong, Daejeon, 305-600, Korea
{hongdj,whkim5,bwkoo,ds_kwon}@ensec.re.kr

Abstract. In this paper, we present the preimage attacks on step-reduced ARIRANG and PKC98-Hash. Our attacks find the preimages of 35 steps out of 40 steps of ARIRANG and 80 steps out of 96 steps of PKC98-Hash, faster than the brute force attack. We applied recently developed techniques of preimage attack. Our attack for ARIRANG is the improvement of the previous attack, and our attack for PKC98-hash is the first analysis result of its preimage resistance.

Keywords: SHA-3 candidate, ARIRANG, PKC98-hash, Preimage Attack, Hash Function, Meet-in-the-middle.

1   Introduction

A cryptographic hash function is a function which generates a fixed-length output for an arbitrary-length message and should satisfy some security notions such as preimage resistance, 2nd-preimage resistance and collision resistance. Recently widely trusted and used hash functions such as MD5[12] and SHA-1[2] have been partially or totally broken. For this reason, NIST is developing one or more additional hash functions through a public competition, called SHA-3 project [3], similar to the development process of the Advanced Encryption Standard (AES)[1].

ARIRANG [6] is one of the 1st round SHA-3 candidates submitted by Chang et al. but fails to be in the 2nd round. It uses a MD-like domain extender with a counter and there are 4 versions ARIRANG-224, ARIRANG-256, ARIRANG-384, and ARIRANG-512 of ARIRANG by their output length. The output of ARIRANG-224 is just a 32-bit truncation of the output of ARIRANG-256, and the output of ARIRANG-384 is just a 128-bit truncation of the output of ARIRANG-512 and the number of steps of each compression function of them is all 40 steps. Guo et al. published the collision attack for ARIRANG-256, 512 with compression function reduced to 26 steps, and pseudo-collision attack for full step ARIRANG-224, 384 [8]. And a preimage attack for 33-step reduced ARIRANG-256, 512 is known [9].

At PKC'98, Shin et al. published a new hash function [17] which uses the MD(Merkle-Damgård) domain extender and a compression function of 96 steps for 160-bit hash value. This hash function does not have a name, so we give

D. Lee and S. Hong (Eds.): ICISC 2009, LNCS 5984, pp. 315–331, 2010.

a temporary name PKC98-hash for this hash function. PKC98-hash has been broken by Chang et al. in collision resistance point of view. They gave a collision attack of the full step PKC98-hash faster than the birthday attack at SAC 2002 [7]. But there is no result regarding preimage resistance yet.

Both hash functions use the MD-like domain extender and compression function of Davies-Meyer construction with a sequence of step functions and the linear message schedule. So the recently developed techniques for the preimage attack could be applied to them.

Our attacks are based on the framework and techniques of the meet-in-the-middle preimage attacks on MD4-based hash functions, which have been recently developed [4,5,13,14,15,16]. The *chunk-pair-searching technique* proposed for SHA-0 and SHA-1 is applicable to the MD4-like hash functions with linear message expansion. The *initial-structure technique* and the *partial-fixing technique for unknown carry behavior* were proposed for MD5 [16] and used for SHA-0 and SHA-1 [5]. In particular, the partial-fixing technique works very efficiently for SHA-0 and SHA-1.

Our Results

We improve the preimage attack on ARIRANG. Our attack finds the preimages of 35 steps out of 40 steps of ARIRANG, while the previous attack works for 33 steps. It requires the computational complexity of $2^{240.94}$ and the memory of $2^{32} \times 9$ words for ARIRANG-256, and the computational complexity of $2^{480.94}$ and the memory of $2^{64} \times 9$ words for ARIRANG-512. We also present the first preimage attack on PKC98-hash. Our attack finds the preimage of 80 steps out of 96 steps PKC98-hash. It requires the computational complexity of 2^{152} and the memory of $2^{16} \times 7$ words.

Table 1. Preimage attack results on ARIRANG and PKC98-hash

Algorithm	Reference	Steps	Complexity	
			Computation	Memory
ARIRANG-256	[9]	33	2^{241}	$2^{32} \times 9$ words
ARIRANG-256	This paper	35	$2^{240.94}$	$2^{32} \times 9$ words
ARIRANG-512	[9]	33	2^{481}	$2^{64} \times 9$ words
ARIRANG-512	This paper	35	$2^{480.94}$	$2^{64} \times 9$ words
PKC98-hash	This paper	80	2^{152}	$2^{16} \times 7$ words

2   Descriptions of Hash Functions

We briefly describe the specifications of the ARIRANG and PKC98-hash.

2.1   Hash Function ARIRANG

ARIRANG uses an MD-like domain extender with a counter XOR and the length of chaining variables and hash values are 256-bit for ARIRANG-256 and 512-bit for ARIRANG-512.

Let n be 256 or 512 for ARIRANG-256 and ARIRANG-512 respectively. Then, for an input message M, a single bit 1 is appended followed by 0s until the length becomes $7n/4$ modulo $2n$, and $n/4$-bit representation of the length of M is appended to produce the padded message M^*.

The padded message M^* is partitioned into $2n$-bit message blocks $(M_1, M_2, ..., M_N)$. Let compress : $\{0,1\}^n \times \{0,1\}^{2n} \to \{0,1\}^n$ be the compression function of ARIRANG. Then, the hash value H^N for the input message M as follows.

1. $H_{i-1} \leftarrow H_{i-1} \oplus \mathsf{ctr}^i$
2. $H_i \leftarrow \mathsf{compress}(H_{i-1}, M_i)$

for $i = 1, ..., N - 1$, where ctr^i's are n-bit counters, and ctr^N is set to a constant P. The H_0 is the initial values defined in the specification.

Compression Function. The compression function of ARIRANG consists of 40 iterations of a step function $\mathsf{step}(\cdot, \cdot, \cdot)$, Feedforward$_1$, Feedforward$_2$ and a message schedule. If (H_{i-1}, M_i) is the input of the compression function, then n-bit state is updated as follows.

1. $\mathsf{state}_0 \leftarrow H^{i-1}$;
2. $\mathsf{state}_{j+1} \leftarrow \mathsf{step}(\mathsf{state}_j, w_{2j}, w_{2j+1})$ for $j = 0, ..., 19$;
3. $\mathsf{state}_{20} \leftarrow \mathsf{state}_{20} \oplus \mathsf{state}_0$;
4. $\mathsf{state}_{j+1} \leftarrow \mathsf{step}(\mathsf{state}_j, w_{2j}, w_{2j+1})$ for $j = 20, ..., 39$;
5. $H_i \leftarrow \mathsf{state}_{40} \oplus \mathsf{state}_0$;

Message Schedule. The message schedule partition the $2n$-bit input message block M_i into 16 $n/8$-bit message words $m_0, ..., m_{15}$ and additionally generate 16 $n/8$-bit message words $m_{16}, ..., m_{32}$ from $m_0, ..., m_{15}$. The pair of message words w_{2j}, w_{2j+1} used in the j-th step, $j = 0, ..., 39$, is defined by $w_{2j} = m_{\sigma(2j)}$ and $w_{2j+1} = m_{\sigma(2j+1)}$.

$m_{16}, ..., m_{32}$ are generated by the following equations.

$$m_{\sigma(20t)} = \left(\bigoplus_{k=0}^{3} m_{\sigma(20t+2k+13)} \oplus K_{4t} \right)^{\lll 5}, \tag{1}$$

$$m_{\sigma(20t+1)} = \left(\bigoplus_{k=0}^{3} m_{\sigma(20t+2k+12)} \oplus K_{4t+1} \right)^{\lll 11}, \tag{2}$$

$$m_{\sigma(20t+2)} = \left(\bigoplus_{k=0}^{3} m_{\sigma(20t+2k+3)} \oplus K_{4t+2} \right)^{\lll 19}, \tag{3}$$

$$m_{\sigma(20t+3)} = \left(\bigoplus_{k=0}^{3} m_{\sigma(20t+2k+2)} \oplus K_{4t+3} \right)^{\lll 31}, \tag{4}$$

where $t = 0, 1, 2, 3$ and $K_0, ..., K_{15}$ are $n/8$-bit constants defined in the specifications.

The index function σ is defined in the Table 2.

Table 2. The index function σ

α	$\sigma(2\alpha)$	$\sigma(2\alpha+1)$	$\sigma(2\alpha+20)$	$\sigma(2\alpha+21)$	$\sigma(2\alpha+40)$	$\sigma(2\alpha+41)$	$\sigma(2\alpha+60)$	$\sigma(2\alpha+61)$
0	16	17	20	21	24	25	28	29
1	0	1	3	6	12	5	7	2
2	2	3	9	12	14	7	13	8
3	4	5	15	2	0	9	3	14
4	6	7	5	8	2	11	9	4
5	18	19	22	23	26	27	30	31
6	8	9	11	14	4	13	15	10
7	10	11	1	4	6	15	5	0
8	12	13	7	10	8	1	11	6
9	14	15	13	0	10	3	1	12

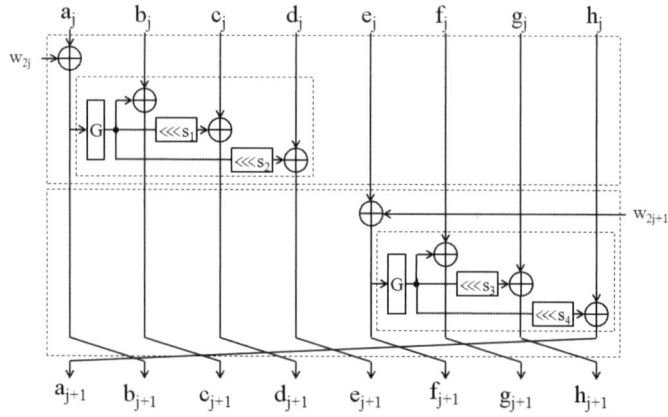

Fig. 1. The j-th step function of the compression function of ARIRANG. (The rotation number are $(s_1, s_2, s_3, s_4) = (13, 23, 29, 7)$ for ARIRANG-256, and $(s_1, s_2, s_3, s_4) = (29, 41, 53, 13)$ for ARIRANG-512).

Step Function. The step function $\text{step}(\cdot, \cdot, \cdot)$ has three inputs state_j, w_{2j} and $_{2j+1}$ for $j=0, 1, ..., 39$. In the step function, each state_j is partitioned into $\text{state}_j = a_j \| b_j \| c_j \| d_j \| e_j \| f_j \| g_j \| h_j$, where $a_j, ..., h_j$ are $n/8$ bits. On the inputs state_j, w_{2j} and w_{2j+1}, the step function outputs state_{j+1} via the procedure of Fig. 1.

In the attack procedure, we consider step function $\text{step}(\cdot, \cdot, \cdot)$ as composition of two sequential half step functions $\text{step}_L(\cdot, \cdot)$ and $\text{step}_R(\cdot, \cdot)$ by function G and its corresponding operations. $\text{step}_L(\cdot, \cdot)$ has two inputs state_j, w_{2j} and outputs intermediate state state_j^*. And $\text{step}_R(\cdot, \cdot)$ generates the output of the $\text{step}(\cdot, \cdot, \cdot)$, state_{j+1} from state_j^* and w_{2j+1}.

In the step function, the function G is the nonlinear function consisting of 8-bit S-boxes and an MDS matrix. We do not give any specific description of the G function because our attack does not exploit it. For the more detailed explanation, see [6].

2.2 PKC98-Hash

PKC98-hash uses the MD domain extender and the length of chaining variables and hash values are 160-bit.

The input message M is padded and partitioned into 512-bit message blocks $(M_1, ..., M_N)$. Let compress : $\{0, 1\}^{160} \times \{0, 1\}^{512} \to \{0, 1\}^{160}$ be the compression function of PKC98-hash. Then, the hash value H_N for the input message M as follows: $H_i \leftarrow$ compress(H_{i-1}, M_i) for $i = 1, ..., N$, where the H_0 is the initial values defined in the specification.

Compression Function. The compression function of PKC98-hash consists of 96 iterations of step function step$(\cdot, \cdot)$, Feedforward, and a message schedule. If (H^{i-1}, M_i) is the input of the compression function, then 160-bit state is updated as follows. Note that the addition "$+$" is 32-bit-wise modulo addition for Feedforward. Similarly, we use "$-$" to denote 32-bit-wise subtraction.

1. state$_0 \leftarrow H_{i-1}$;
2. state$_{j+1} \leftarrow$ step(state$_j$, w_j) for $j = 0, ..., 95$;
3. $H_i \leftarrow$ state$_0 +$ state$_{96}$;
4. return H_i;

Message Schedule. The message schedule partition the 512-bit input message block M_i into 16 32-bit message words $m_0, ..., m_{15}$ and using these message words, generate 8 more 32-bit message words $m_{16}, ..., m_{23}$ by the following equation.

$$m_{15+t} = (m_t \oplus m_{(2+t)} \oplus m_{(7+t)} \oplus m_{(12+t)})^{\lll 1}, \tag{5}$$

where $t = 0, 1, ..., 15$. And each message word w_j used in the j-th step is defined by the following relations.

$$w_j = m_{\rho^r(j-24r)}, \tag{6}$$

where $r = \lfloor j/24 \rfloor$. The index function ρ is defined in the Table 3. Note that ρ^0 means the identity function.

Table 3. The message word schedule ρ

j	0	1	2	3	4	5	6	7	8	9	10	11	12	13	14	15	16	17	18	19	20	21	22	23
$\rho(j)$	4	21	17	1	23	18	12	10	5	16	8	0	20	3	22	6	11	19	15	2	7	14	9	13

Step Function. In the step function, each state$_j$ is partitioned into state$_j = a_j\|b_j\|c_j\|d_j\|e_j$, where $a_j, ..., e_j$ are 32-bit words. For $0 \leq r < 4$, $0 \leq k < 24$, let $j = 24r + k$, then the j-th step function has two inputs state$_j$ and w_j and outputs state$_{j+1}$ according to the following procedure.

1. $a_{j+1} = e_j$;
2. $c_{j+1} = b_j^{\lll 10}$;
3. $d_{j+1} = c_j$;
4. $e_{j+1} = d_j$;
5. $b_{j+1} = (f_r(a_j, b_j, c_j, d_j, e_j) + w_j + K_r)^{\lll s(j)}$;

The rotation number $s(j)$ is dependent on message words. It is determined as $s(j) = w_{\rho^3 - r(k)} \mod 32$. For $0 \leq r < 4$, K_r is a constant and f_r is a nonlinear boolean function. f_1 is equal to f_3. Essentially, our attack does not use any properties of K_r and f_r, so we omit the description of them.

3   Techniques for Preimage Attack

In this section, we introduce the techniques used in our preimage attacks.

3.1   Converting a Pseudo-preimage Attack to a Preimage Attack

For a given hash value y, a pair of (x, M) is called a pseudo-preimage if $y = \text{compress}(x, M)$ and x is not equal to the initial value H_0.

In Fact 9.99 of [11], an algorithm is given for converting a pseudo-preimage attack to a preimage attack for the Merkle-Damgård construction. We assume the computational complexity of the pseudo-preimage attack is 2^t and the length of the chaining variable is n bits. For simplicity, we also assume that each preimage generated the preimage attack guarantees one block message is prepended. Then, the conversion is as follows.

1. For a given hash value H, make a table of $2^{(n-t)/2}$ pseudo-preimages (x, M_2).
2. Repeat the following procedure at most $2^{(n+t)/2}$ times.
   (a) Choose a 1-block message M_1 randomly, and compute its hash value $x' = \text{CF}(H_0, M_1)$.
   (b) Check whether there exists an entry such that $x' = x$.
   (c) If a match is found, then halt and output $M = M_1 \| M_2$ as a preimage for H.

This conversion requires the computational complexity of $2^{(n+t)/2+1}$ (and the memory of $2^{(n-t)/2}$ (x, M_2)'s), and so it is meaningful only if $t < n - 2$.

3.2   Splice-and-Cut and Auxiliary Techniques

Sasaki and Aoki have developed several techniques for finding a preimage by using a meet-in-the-middle attack.

The *splice-and-cut* technique was proposed a basic technique for applying a meet-in-the-middle attack. Regarding the first and the last steps as consecutive, it consists of dividing the targeted compression function into two chunks of steps such that each chunk include at least one message word independent to the opposite chunk, and using a meet-in-the-middle attack to find a pseudo-preimage. The *partial-matching* and *partial-fixing* techniques are used to skip several steps between chunks. Recently, the *initial-structure* and *partial-fixing for unknown carry behavior* techniques were developed and proposed for attacking HAS-160[15], MD5[4], and SHA-0/1[5].

3.3 Computing Kernels of Each Independent Chunk

Since ARIRANG and PKC98-hash have linear message expansions, we can efficiently search for a chunk separation and neutral words by applying the kernel computing approach proposed for SHA-0 and SHA-1[5].

Let w_j be the message word used in the j-th step for $j = 0, ..., l$, expanded from a message block $M = [m_0 \ \cdots \ m_{15}]$. For simplicity, we assume that $w_0, w_1, ..., w_{t-1}$ are used in the first chunk and $w_t, w_{t+1}, ..., w_{s-1}$ are used in the second chunk. We can regard it as a $l \times 16$ binary matrix W satisfying $[w_0 \ \cdots \ w_l]^T = WM^T$, and have two sub-matrices W_1 and W_2 satisfying $[w_0 \ w_1 \cdots \ w_{t-1}]^T = W_1 M^T$ and $[w_t \ w_{t+1} \cdots \ w_{s-1}]^T = W_2 M^T$, respectively. We assume that rank $W_1 = \kappa_1 < 16$ and rank $W_2 = \kappa_2 < 16$. Then, W_1 and W_2 have non-trivial kernels ker W_1 and ker W_2, respectively. If we find a pair of binary vectors in ker$W_1 \times$ kerW_2 which do not share any nonzero bit position, we can set neutral words according to the vectors. Consider the example explained in [5]. Assume that we are given u and v as follows.

$$\begin{cases} u = [1\ 0\ 1\ 1\ 0\ 0\ 0\ 0\ 0\ 0\ 0\ 0\ 0\ 0\ 0\ 0]^T \in \text{ker } W_1, \\ v = [0\ 1\ 0\ 0\ 1\ 0\ 0\ 0\ 0\ 0\ 0\ 0\ 0\ 0\ 0\ 0]^T \in \text{ker } W_2. \end{cases}$$

Then, $W_1 u = 0$ and $W_2 v = 0$ holds. It implies that m_0 can be used as a neutral word for the second chunk if we set $m_0 = m_2 = m_3$, and that m_1 can be used as a neutral word for the first chunk if we set $m_1 = m_4$. If both W_1 and W_2 do not have full rank but there exists no such pair of $(u, v) \in$ ker$W_1 \times$ kerW_2, we can easily construct an invertible matrix R such that $R^{-1}u$ and $R^{-1}v$ do not share any nonzero bit position for a $(u, v) \in$ ker $W_1 \times$ ker W_2. If such a matrix is constructed, we have $WM^T = (WR)(R^{-1}M^T)$, and we use $W' = WR$ and $M'^T = [m'_0 \ \cdots \ m'_{15}]^T = R^{-1}M^T$ as the message expansion and the message block converted by R.

4 Preimage Attack on ARIRANG

This section describes the attack on ARIRANG reduced to 35 steps. We give the detailed description of the attack on ARIRANG-256, because the attack on ARIRANG-512 is similar to that on ARIRANG-256.

4.1 Chunk Separation for 35-Step ARIRANG

We divide a step function into two functions as explained in Section 2.1, and we omit the rotations and the constant XORs in the message schedule. Then, we can regard the message schedule as a 80×16 binary matrix.

Our program finds the chunk separation covering steps 2–36, in total 35 steps. The first chunk covers from step 4 to step 17L, and the second chunk covers from step 23R to step 36 and steps 2 and 3. The matrices W_1 and W_2 corresponding to two chunks have rank 15, and ker W_1 and ker W_2 have the following non-zero vectors u and v, respectively.

$$\begin{cases} u = [1\ 0\ 0\ 0\ 1\ 0\ 0\ 0\ 0\ 0\ 0\ 0\ 0\ 0\ 0\ 0]^T, \\ v = [1\ 0\ 0\ 0\ 0\ 0\ 0\ 0\ 0\ 0\ 0\ 0\ 1\ 0\ 0\ 0]^T. \end{cases} \tag{7}$$

Since W_1 and W_2 are not independent, we construct a 16×16 invertible binary matrix R satisfying

$$\begin{cases} [m'_0 \ \cdots \ m'_{15}]^T = R^{-1} M^T, \\ m'_0 \oplus m'_1 = m_0, m'_1 \oplus m'_{12} = m_{12}, m'_0 = m_4, \\ m'_j = m_{j-1} \ \text{ for } j = 2, 3, \text{ and } 4, \\ m'_j = m_j \ \text{ for } j = 5, ..., 11, 13, ..., 15. \end{cases} \tag{8}$$

The transformed message expansion WR, described in the previous section is shown in Fig. 2. As shown in Fig. 2, the first chunk includes m'_1 but not m'_0, and the second chunk includes m'_0 but not m'_1. Hence, by fixing m'_2 to m'_{15}, the meet-in-the-middle attack can be performed.

4.2   Partial-Matching Technique for Skipping 6 Steps

In the meet-in-the-middle attack, results of two chunks must be compared efficiently. Although 6 steps between two chunks are skipped in the employed attack as shown in Fig. 2, a part of the results of two chunks can be compared by using the partial-matching technique.

For simplicity, we omit the Feedforward$_1$, the message words except m'_0 and m'_1, and the constants in the skipped steps because essentially, they do not affect on the attack at all. Let $\text{state}^*_{23} = (x_0, x_1, x_2, x_3, x_4, x_5, x_6, x_7)$, and let the most left two words of state^*_{17} be y_0 and y_1. Then, The backward partial computations from state^*_{23} reach y_0 and y_1 as follows (See Fig. 4).

$$\begin{aligned}
y_0 = {}& G(G(G(G(G(G(G(x_0) \oplus x_1) \oplus G(x_0)^{\lll 13} \oplus x_2) \oplus G(G(x_0) \oplus x_1)^{\lll 13} \oplus G(x_0)^{\lll 23} \\
& \oplus x_3) \oplus G(G(G(x_0) \oplus x_1) \oplus G(x_0)^{\lll 13} \oplus x_2)^{\lll 13} \oplus G(G(x_0) \oplus x_1)^{\lll 23} \oplus x_4) \oplus \\
& G(G(G(G(x_0) \oplus x_1) \oplus G(x_0)^{\lll 13} \oplus x_2) \oplus G(G(x_0) \oplus x_1)^{\lll 13} \oplus G(x_0)^{\lll 23} \oplus \\
& x_3)^{\lll 13} \oplus G(G(G(x_0) \oplus x_1) \oplus G(x_0)^{\lll 13} \oplus x_2)^{\lll 23} \oplus x_5) \oplus G(G(G(G(G(x_0) \oplus \\
& x_1) \oplus G(x_0)^{\lll 13} \oplus x_2) \oplus G(G(x_0) \oplus x_1)^{\lll 13} \oplus G(x_0)^{\lll 23} \oplus x_3) \oplus G(G(G(x_0) \oplus \\
& G(x_0)^{\lll 13} \oplus x_2)^{\lll 13} \oplus G(G(x_0) \oplus x_1)^{\lll 23} \oplus x_4)^{\lll 13} \oplus G(G(G(G(x_0) \oplus x_1) \oplus \\
& G(x_0)^{\lll 13} \oplus x_2) \oplus G(G(x_0) \oplus x_1)^{\lll 13} \oplus G(x_0)^{\lll 23} \oplus x_3)^{\lll 23} \oplus G(x_5) \oplus x_6, \\
y_1 = {}& G(G(G(G(G(G(G(x_0) \oplus x_1) \oplus G(x_0)^{\lll 13} \oplus x_2) \oplus G(G(x_0) \oplus x_1)^{\lll 13} \oplus G(x_0)^{\lll 23} \\
& \oplus x_3) \oplus G(G(G(x_0) \oplus x_1) \oplus G(x_0)^{\lll 13} \oplus x_2)^{\lll 13} \oplus G(G(x_0) \oplus x_1)^{\lll 23} \oplus x_4) \oplus \\
& G(G(G(G(x_0) \oplus x_1) \oplus G(x_0)^{\lll 13} \oplus x_2) \oplus G(G(x_0) \oplus x_1)^{\lll 13} \oplus G(x_0)^{\lll 23} \oplus \\
& x_3)^{\lll 13} \oplus G(G(G(x_0) \oplus x_1) \oplus G(x_0)^{\lll 13} \oplus x_2)^{\lll 23} \oplus x_5)^{\lll 13} \oplus G(G(G(G(\\
& G(x_0) \oplus x_1) \oplus G(x_0)^{\lll 13} \oplus x_2) \oplus G(G(x_0) \oplus x_1)^{\lll 13} \oplus G(x_0)^{\lll 23} \oplus x_3) \oplus G(\\
& G(G(x_0) \oplus x_1) \oplus G(x_0)^{\lll 13} \oplus x_2)^{\lll 13} \oplus G(G(x_0) \oplus x_1)^{\lll 23} \oplus x_4)^{\lll 23} \oplus G(\\
& G(x_5) \oplus x_6) \oplus G(x_5)^{\lll 29} \oplus x_7 \oplus m'_0.
\end{aligned}$$

Step	0	1	2	3	4	5	6	7	8	9	10	11	12	13	14	15	
																	Converted message index
2L			*														2nd chunk
2R				*													
3L	○																
3R					*												
4L						*											
4R							*										
5L			*		*	*	*										
5R		●	*		*												
6L								*									
6R									*								
7L										*							
7R											*						
8L		●										*					
8R													*				
9L														*			
9R															*		
10L		●								*					*		1st chunk
10R			*					*				*	*				
11L				*													
11R					*												
12L								*									
12R		●									*						
13L															*		
13R				*													
14L					*												
14R							*										
15L		●	*			*	*				*						
15R				*	*				*						*		
16L										*							
16R														*			
17L			*														
17R	○																
18L						*											
18R								*									
19L												*					
19R	○	●															skip
20L			*		*								*		*		
20R	○					*		*		*							
21L		●									*						
21R					*												
22L														*			
22R							*										
23L	○	●															
23R									*								
24L				*													
24R										*							
25L					*		*		*	*							
25R	○		*										*	*			
26L	○																
26R													*				
27L						*											
27R															*		
28L								*									
28R			*														
29L										*							2nd chunk
29R				*													
30L	○						*				*		*				
30R			*		*						*				*		
31L						*											
31R				*													
32L														*			
32R								*									
33L				*													
33R														*			
34L									*								
34R	○																
35L	○		*				*						*				
35R				*			*		*				*				
36L															*		
36R									*								

Fig. 2. Chunks for the 35 steps (Steps 2 to 36) of ARIRANG

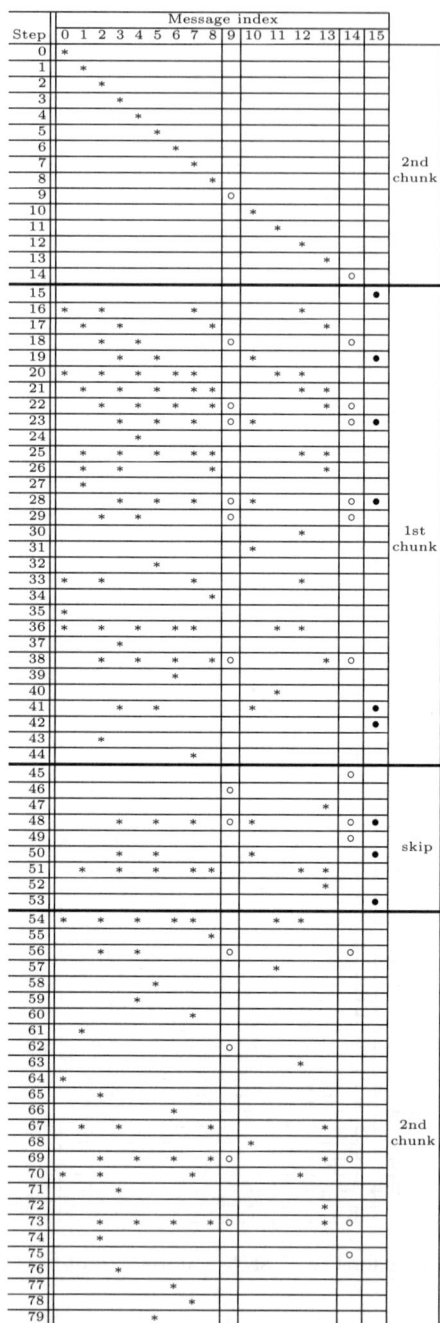

Fig. 3. Chunks for the 80 steps (Steps 0 to 79) of PKC98-hash

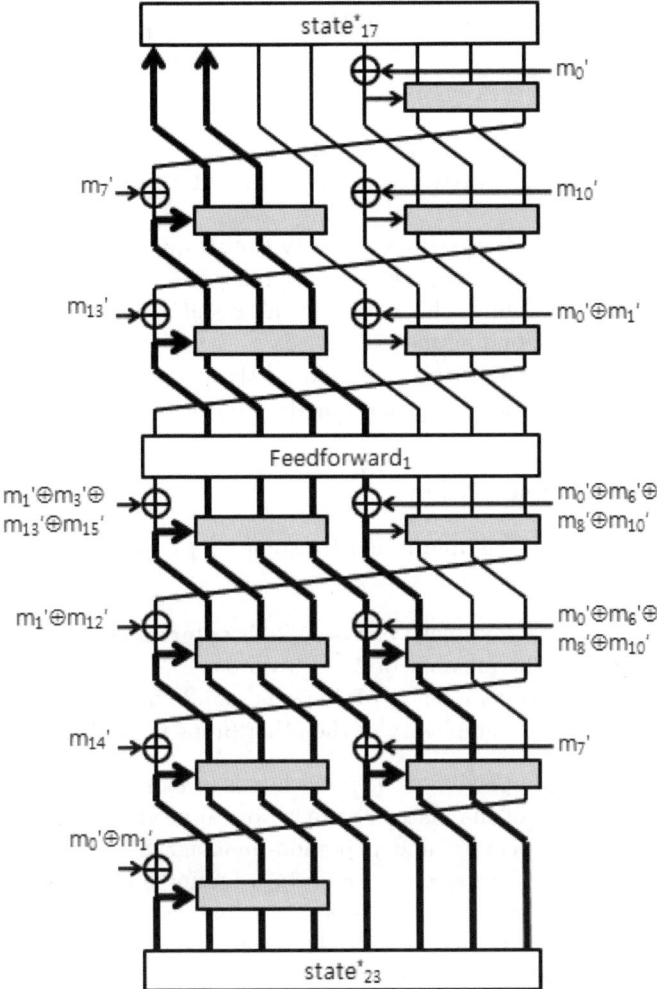

Fig. 4. The partial-matching technique for attacking 35 steps of ARIRANG. The bold lines denote the partial computations from state$^*_{23}$).

4.3 Attack Procedure for 35-Step ARIRANG

Let w'_j's be the messages words assigned by the converted message schedule WR. For a given hash value H_2, the attack pseudo-procedure is as follows.

1. Fix state$_4$ and $m'_i (i = 2, ..., 12)$ to randomly chosen values. Set m'_{13}, m'_{14}, and m'_{15} such that they satisfy the padding rule of ARIRANG.
2. For all possible 2^{32} candidates of the neutral word m'_1,
   (a) Compute $\begin{cases} \text{state}_{j+1} \leftarrow \text{step}(\text{state}_j, w'_{2j}, w'_{2j+1}) \text{ for } j = 4, ..., 16, \\ \text{state}^*_{17} \leftarrow \text{step}_L(\text{state}_{17}, w'_{34}). \end{cases}$
   (b) Make a table of $(m'_1, \text{state}^*_{17})$.

3. For all possible 2^{32} candidates of m'_0,

(a) Compute
$$\begin{cases} \text{state}_j \leftarrow \text{step}^{-1}(\text{state}_{j+1}, w'_{2j}, w'_{2j+1}) \text{ for } j = 3, 2, \\ \text{state}_{37} \leftarrow H_2 \oplus \text{state}_2, \\ \text{state}_j \leftarrow \text{step}^{-1}(\text{state}_{j+1}, w'_{2j}, w'_{2j+1}) \text{ for } j = 36, ..., 24, \\ \text{state}^*_{23} \leftarrow \text{step}_R^{-1}(\text{state}_{24}, w'_{47}). \end{cases}$$

(b) Compute the left two words y_0 and y_1 from state^*_{23} as explained in Section 4.2.

(c) Check whether there exists an entry $(m'_1, \text{state}^*_{17})$ in the table such that (y_0, y_1) is matched with the most significant 64 bits of state^*_{17}.

(d) If a match is found, check whether all results from both chunks match for the corresponding message words.

(e) If all bits match, output the pair of the corresponding message block $M^T = RM'^T$ and state_2 as a pseudo-preimage.

4.4   Complexity Estimation

The complexity for the computation of a $\text{step}(\cdot, \cdot, \cdot)$ is around $\frac{1}{35}$ 35-step ARI-RANG compression function.

- The computational complexity of Step 2a is approximately $2^{32} \cdot \frac{13.5}{35}$.
- Step 2b requires the memory of $2^{32} \times 9$ words.
- The computational complexity of Steps 3a and 3b is at most $2^{32} \cdot \frac{15.5+4}{35}$.
- The computational complexity of the other Steps is negligible.

The computational complexity of the procedure is at most $2^{32} \cdot \frac{12.5+19.5}{35} \cong 2^{31.87}$. The expected number of the matched pair by one procedure is $2^{32} \cdot 2^{32} / 2^{-256} = 2^{-192}$. So, we can expect to find a pseudo-preimage by repeating the above procedure 2^{192} times. Consequently, the attack finding a pseudo-preimage of 35 steps of ARIRANG-256 using the above procedure requires the computational complexity of $2^{223.87}$. The attack is converted to the preimage attack by ysing the algorithm described in Section 3.1 with the computational complexity of $2^{240.94}$ and the memory of $2^{32} \times 9$ words.

We can construct the similar procedure for finding a pseudo-preimage of 35 steps of ARIRANG-512. One procedure requires the computational complexity of $2^{63.87}$ and the memory of $2^{64} \times 9$ (64-bit) words, and we can expect to find a pseudo-preimage by repeating that procedure 2^{384} times. So, the attack finding a pseudo-preimage of 35 steps of ARIRANG-512 using the procedure requires the computational complexity of $2^{447.87}$. The attack is converted to the preimage attack by using the algorithm described in Section 3.1 with the computational complexity of $2^{480.94}$ and the memory of $2^{64} \times 9$ words.

5   Preimage Attack on PKC98-Hash

This section describes the detailed description of the attack on PKC98-hash reduced to 80 steps.

5.1   Chunk Separation for 80-Step PKC98-Hash

We omit the rotations and the constant XORs in the message schedule. Then, we can regard the message schedule as a 96×16 binary matrix.

Our program finds a chunk separation covering steps 0–79, in total 80 steps. The first chunk covers from step 15 to step 44, and the second chunk covers from step 0 to step 14 and from step 54 to step 79. As shown in Fig. 3, if we set $m_9 = m_{14}$, m_9 and m_{14} do not affect the first chunk. The second chunk does not include m_{15}. So, the first chunk uses m_{15} as a neutral word, and the second chunk uses $m_9 = m_{14}$ as a neutral word. Since m_{14} and m_{15} are related to the padding rule, we will mention how to adjust the padding problem.

5.2   Partial-Fixing Technique for Skipping 9 Steps

Fig. 5 shows how the results of two chunks are partially computed by the fixed bits of the message words. We choose and fix the bits of the related words to the data-dependent rotation number $s(45)$, $s(46)$, and $s(47)$ such that $s(45) = 0$, $s(46) = 10$, and $s(47) = 22$. The bits 15–0 of $m_{14}(= m_9)$ and m_{15} are fixed. We explain how the results of two chunks are partially compared at state_{49} as follows.

– Forward computation for b_{46}: we obtain $\mathsf{state}_{45} = (a_{45}, b_{45}, c_{45}, d_{45}, e_{45})$ as the result of the computation of the first chunk. Let τ_{45} be the output of the boolean function $f(\mathsf{state} + 45)$. Since we set $s(45) = 0$, $b_{46} = (\tau + K_1) + m_{14}$. Although m_{14} is the neutral word of the second chunk, bits 15–0 of m_{14} are fixed. So, we can compute bit positions 15–0 of b_{46}, uniquely.
– Forward computation for b_{47}: since we set $s(46) = 10$, the equation for b_{47} is as follows.

$$b_{47}^{\ggg 10} = f(\mathsf{state}_{46}) + m_9 + K_1.$$

$\tau_{46} = F(\mathsf{state}_{46})$ and m_9 are fixed in bits 15–0. So, we can compute the bit positions 15–0 of $b_{47}^{\ggg 10}$ uniquely.
– Forward computation for b_{48}: since we set $s(47) = 22$, the equation for b_{48} is as follows.

$$b_{48}^{\ggg 22} = f(\mathsf{state}_{47}) + (m_{13} + K_1).$$

$\tau_{47} = f(\mathsf{state}_{47})$ is fixed in bits 25–10 by b_{47} and $b_{46}^{\lll 10}$. So, we can compute the bit positions 25–10 of $b_{48}^{\ggg 22}$ by guessing the carry bit from bit position 9 to 10. Therefore, we obtain two candidates of bit positions 15–10 of c_{49} because $b_{48}^{\lll 10} = c_{49}$.
– Backward computation: in the similar way, we can compute the bits 15–0 of c_{49}, d_{49}, and e_{49} from a state_{54}. In the backward computation, we do not need to care for the carry bits.
– Matching check: the partially computed results from both chunks are compared at chaining variable c_{49}, d_{49}, and e_{49}. We check whether the bits 15–0 of c_{49}, the bits of 3–0 of d_{49}, and the bits 15–10 of e_{49} are matched.

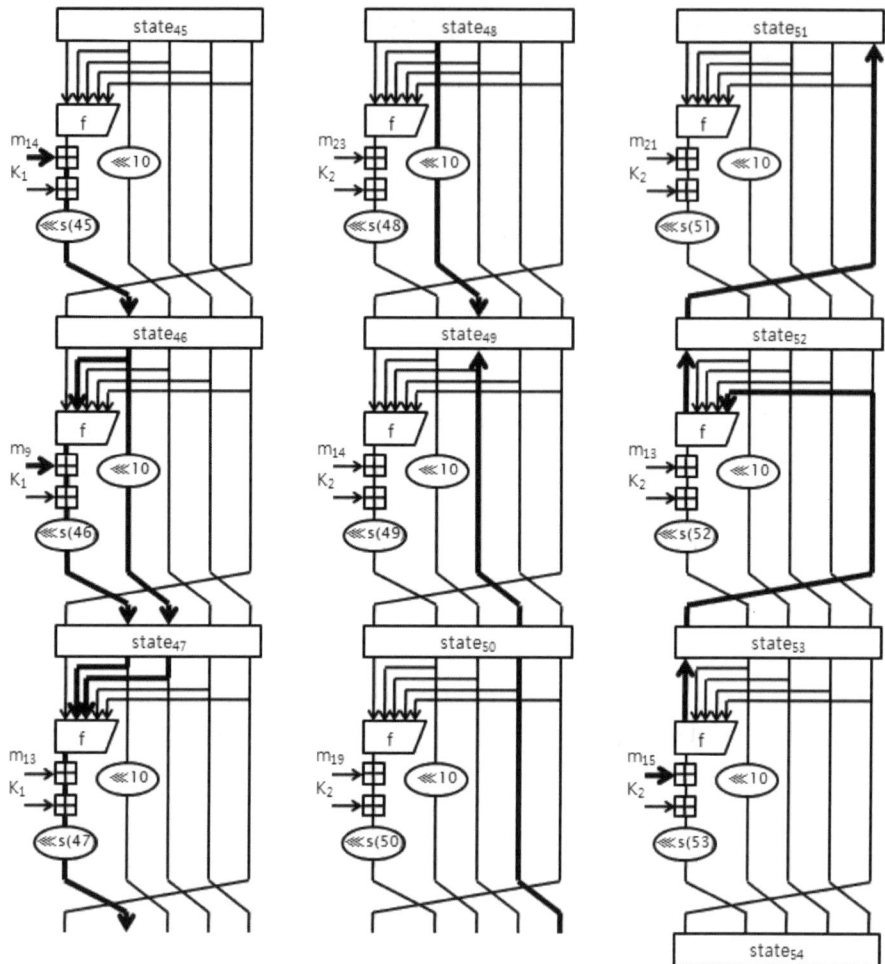

Fig. 5. The partial-fixing technique for attacking 80 steps of PKC98-hash. The bold lines denote the partial computations from state$_{45}$ and state$_{54}$.

5.3   Attack Procedure for 80-Step PKC98-Hash

For a given hash value H_N, the pseudo-preimage attack procedure is as follows.

1. Fix state$_{15}$ to randomly chosen value. Fix m_i's ($i \neq 9, 14, 15$), the bit positions 31, 30, and 13–0 of m_{14}, and the bit positions 31–16 of m_{15} considering the padding rule.
2. For all possible 2^{16} candidates of unfixed bit positions in $m_{14}(= m_9)$,
   (a) Compute state$_{j+1} \leftarrow$ step(state$_j, w_j$) for $j = 15, ..., 44$.
   (b) Compute the forward computation for the partial-fixing technique.

(c) For each m_{14}, keep two candidates of (m_{14}, state$_{45}$, bits 15–0 of c_{49}, bits 3–0 of d_{49}, bits 15–10 of e_{49}) and guessed carry bit in a table.

3. For all possible 2^{16} candidates of unfixed bit positions in the neutral word m_{15},

(a) Compute $\begin{cases} \text{state}_j \leftarrow \text{step}^{-1}(\text{state}_{j+1}, w_j) \text{ for } j = 14, ..., 0 \\ \text{state}_{80} \leftarrow H_N - \text{state}_0, \\ \text{state}_j \leftarrow \text{step}^{-1}(\text{state}_{j+1}, w_j) \text{ for } j = 79, ..., 54. \end{cases}$

(b) Compute bits 15–0 of c_{49}, d_{49}, and e_{49}.

(c) Compare the values of bits 15–0 of c_{49}, bits of 3–0 of d_{49}, and bits 15–10 of e_{49}, in total 26 bits, with those of entries stored in the table.

(d) If a match is found, check whether the all result from both chunks match for the corresponding message words and whether all guessed carry bits are correct.

(e) If all bits match and all guessed carry bits are correct, output the pair of the corresponding message block M and state$_0$ as a pseudo-preimage.

5.4 Complexity Estimation

The complexity for the computation of a step($\cdot, \cdot$) is around $\frac{1}{80}$ 80-step PKC98-hash compression function.

- The computational complexity of Step 2a and 2b is $2^{16} \times \frac{30+7}{80}$.
- Step 2c requires the memory of $2^{16} \times 7$ words.
- The computational complexity of Step 3a+3b is at most $2^{16} \times \frac{41+2.5}{80}$.
- The other Steps require negligible complexities.

The computational complexity of the procedure is at most $2^{16} \cdot \frac{37+43.5}{80} \cong 2^{16}$. The expected number of the matched pair by one procedure is $2^{16+1} \cdot 2^{16} / 2^{160+1} = 2^{-128}$. So, we can expect to find a pseudo-preimage by repeating the above procedure 2^{128} times. Consequently, the attack finding a pseudo-preimage of 80 steps of PKC98-hash using the above procedure requires the computational complexity of 2^{144}. The attack is converted to the preimage attack by using the algorithm describe in Section 3.1 with the computational complexity of 2^{152} and the memory of $2^{16} \times 7$ words.

5.5 Padding Problem

The neutral words m_{14} and m_{15} are the 64-bit binary encode of the bit-length of the hashed message in the padding rule. We fix the bits 8–0 of m_{14} as 110000000_2, such that the message length is guaranteed to be $512r+448$ for an positive integer r. It allow us to choose m_{13} freely. Then, we can use an expandable message [10] to perform the preimage attack with the estimated computational complexity and memory.

6   Conclusion

We proposed the preimage attacks on the reduced steps of ARIRANG and PKC98-hash. We applied recently developed techniques of the meet-in-the-middle preimage attacks. As a result, we attacked 35 steps of ARIRANG and 80 steps of PKC98-hash. Our attack for ARIRANG-256/512 is the best result and our attack for PKC98-hash is the first result in the analysis of preimage resistance. Our attacks can be used as second preimage attack with the same complexity.

References

1. FIPS 197: Advanced Encryption Standard (AES), November 26 (2001)
2. U.S. Department of Commerce, National Institute of Standards and Technology, Announcing the SECURE HASH STANDARD (Federal Information Processing Standards Publication 180-2) (2002)
3. U.S. Department of Commerce, National Institute of Standards and Technology, Fedral Register 72(212), November 2 (2007) Notices, http://csrc.nist.gov/groups/ST/hash/documents/FR_Notice_Nov07.pdf
4. Aoki, K., Sasaki, Y.: Previous Attacks on One-Block MD4, 63-Step MD5 and More. In: Avanzi, R., Keliher, L., Sica, F. (eds.) SAC 2008. LNCS, vol. 5381, pp. 82–98. Springer, Heidelberg (2008)
5. Aoki, K., Sasaki, Y.: Meet-in-the-Middle Preimage Attacks Against Reduced SHA-0 and SHA-1. In: Halevi, S. (ed.) CRYPTO 2009. LNCS, vol. 5677, pp. 70–89. Springer, Heidelberg (2009)
6. Chang, D., Hong, S., Kang, C., Kang, J., Kim, J., Lee, C., Lee, J., Lee, J., Lee, S., Lee, Y., Lim, J., Sung, J.: ARIRANG: SHA-3 Proposal, http://csrc.nist.gov/groups/ST/hash/sha-3/Round1/
7. Chang, D., Sung, J., Sung, S., Lee, S., Lim, J.: Full-Round Differential Attack on the Original Version of the Hash Function Proposed at PKC 1998. In: Nyberg, K., Heys, H.M. (eds.) SAC 2002. LNCS, vol. 2595, pp. 160–174. Springer, Heidelberg (2003)
8. Guo, J., Matusiewicz, K., Knudsen, L.R., Ling, S., Wang, H.: Practical Pseudo-Collisions for Hash Functions ARIRANG-224/384. ePrint Archive 2009/197 (2009)
9. Hong, D., Kim, W.-H., Koo, B.: Preimage Attack on ARIRANG. ePrint Archive 2009/147 (2009)
10. Kelsey, J., Schneier, B.: Second Preimages on n-bit Hash Functions for Much Less Than 2n Work. In: Cramer, R. (ed.) EUROCRYPT 2005. LNCS, vol. 3494, pp. 474–490. Springer, Heidelberg (2005)
11. Menezes, A.J., van Oorschot, P.C., Vanstone, S.A.: Handbook of Applied Cryptography. CRC Press, Boca Raton (1997)
12. Rivest, R.L.: The MD5 Message Digest Algorithm. Request for Comments 1321, The Internet Engineering Task Force (1992)
13. Sasaki, Y., Aoki, K.: Preimage Attacks on Step-Reduced MD5. In: Mu, Y., Susilo, W., Seberry, J. (eds.) ACISP 2008. LNCS, vol. 5107, pp. 282–296. Springer, Heidelberg (2008)
14. Sasaki, Y., Aoki, K.: Preimage Attacks on 3, 4, and 5-Pass HAVAL. In: Pieprzyk, J. (ed.) ASIACRYPT 2008. LNCS, vol. 5350, pp. 253–271. Springer, Heidelberg (2008)

15. Sasaki, Y., Aoki, K.: A Preimage Attack for 52-Step HAS-160. In: Lee, P.J., Cheon, J.H. (eds.) ICISC 2008. LNCS, vol. 5461, pp. 302–317. Springer, Heidelberg (2008)
16. Sasaki, Y., Aoki, K.: Finding Preimages in Full MD5 Faster Than Exhaustive Search. In: Joux, A. (ed.) EUROCRYPT 2009. LNCS, vol. 5479, pp. 134–152. Springer, Heidelberg (2010)
17. Shin, S., Rhee, K., Ryu, D., Lee, S.: A New Hash Function Based on MDx-Family and Its Application to MAC. In: Imai, H., Zheng, Y. (eds.) PKC 1998. LNCS, vol. 1431, pp. 234–246. Springer, Heidelberg (1998)

Improved Preimage Attack for 68-Step HAS-160[*]

Deukjo Hong[1], Bonwook Koo[1], and Yu Sasaki[2,3]

[1] The Attached Institute of ETRI
{hongdj,bwkoo}@ensec.re.kr
[2] NTT Information Sharing Platform Laboratories, NTT Corporation
sasaki.yu@lab.ntt.co.jp
[3] The University of Electro-Communications

Abstract. In this paper, we improve previous preimage attacks on hash function HAS-160, which is standardized in Korea. We show that the last 68 steps out of 80 steps of HAS-160 can be attacked, while a previous attack works for only intermediate 52 steps. We also show that the first 67 steps of HAS-160 can be attacked. These attacks are based on the meet-in-the-middle attack, which is also used in the previous attack. Recently, various techniques of preimage attacks have been proposed on other hash functions. We show that these techniques can also be applied to HAS-160 and the number of attacked steps can be improved. For the attack on 68 steps, we first generate pseudo-preimages with a complexity of $2^{150.7}$, and then convert them to a preimage with a complexity of $2^{156.3}$. This attack uses a memory of $2^{12} \times 7$ words. To the best of our knowledge, attacking 68 steps is the best of all attacks on HAS-160 hash function.

Keywords: HAS-160, hash function, preimage, meet-in-the-middle.

1 Introduction

Hash functions are important cryptographic primitives. They are used for various purposes all over the world, so their security deserves to be carefully analyzed, especially if they are used in practice. Hash functions are required to satisfy several properties such as preimage resistance, second-preimage resistance, and collision resistance. Let n be the bit length of hash values. Regarding the preimage resistance, it is obvious that if 2^n different messages are hashed, one of them matches the given target hash value with high probability. Therefore, finding preimages faster than 2^n computations is an undesired property. In fact, in the SHA-3 competition, National Institute of Standards and Technology (NIST) requires all candidates to guarantee the n-bit security for this property [1].

---

[*] Our attack target is the last 68 steps, but not the first 68 steps. Hence some may say 68-step HAS-160 is not broken yet. However, based on the discussion at the conference and the description in previous work, we determined to use this title.

D. Lee and S. Hong (Eds.): ICISC 2009, LNCS 5984, pp. 332–348, 2010.

HAS-160 is a hash function developed in Korea, and was standardized by Korean government in 2000 [2]. The design of HAS-160 is similar to SHA-0 and SHA-1 [3], in particular, the step function of HAS-160 is very similar. However, the message expansion is different. Hence, security analysis of HAS-160 is interesting and useful to know the security contribution of its design. At ICISC 2008, Sasaki and Aoki presented a preimage attack on HAS-160 reduced to 52 steps [4]. On the other hand, at CRYPTO 2009, Aoki and Sasaki presented a preimage attack on SHA-0 reduced to 52 steps [5]. So far, the number of attacked steps is the same. Hence, improving the attack is an interesting issue to compare their security.

The first cryptanalysis on HAS-160 was presented by Yun et al. [6] at ICISC 2005. They found that a collision for HAS-160 reduced to 45 steps could be generated in a very small complexity. This was improved by Cho et al. [7] at ICISC 2006, which reported that a collision attack could be theoretically applied until 53 steps. This was further improved by Mendel and Rijmen [8] at ICISC 2007, where a real collision until 53 steps was generated and a differential path yielding 59-step collisions was shown. After that, a preimage attack on 52 steps was proposed at ICISC 2008 [4]. Compared to the collision resistance, the preimage resistance has not been enough considered, hence more analyses on the preimage resistance are necessary.

Related Work

Our attack is based on the previous preimage attack on 52 steps of HAS-160 [4], which used the framework of meet-in-the-middle preimage attacks on other hash functions [9,10,11,12,13]. This framework has also been applied to the recently designed hash function ARIRANG [14] by Hong et al. [15,16]. Hence, developing techniques in this framework is important. Recently, various techniques for preimage attacks on MD4-based hash functions have been improved. For example, *initial-structure* and *partial-fixing technique for unknown carry behavior* were proposed for MD5 [17], and *linear algebra* such as finding *kernel* was introduced to analyze the message schedules of reduced SHA-0 and SHA-1 [5]. Whether or not these techniques can be applied to HAS-160 is not clear.

There is another hash function named HAS-V [18], which has the similar structure to HAS-160. A preimage attack on HAS-V was discovered by Mendel and Rijmen at ICISC 2007 [19]. Therefore, the preimage resistance of HAS-160 needs to be evaluated by recent attack techniques.

Our Results

In this paper, we show improved preimage attacks on step-reduced HAS-160. Our attacks are based on the previous meet-in-the-middle attack [4]. First, we revisit the initial structure technique. As a result, we found that up to 4 steps can be skipped by the initial structure while the previous work skipped only 3 steps. Besides, we point out that the initial structure can be constructed with much less memory than the previous work. This can reduce the memory complexity of the previous attack on 52 steps from 2^{48} to 2^{16}. Next, we consider extending the number of steps skipped by the partial-fixing technique for unknown carry behavior, while only the partial-fixing technique without carry was used in the previous work. As a result, we succeed in skipping 13 steps, while the previous work skipped only 8 steps. Finally, when we search for independent message words for the meet-in-the-middle attack, we apply the linear algebra to maximize the number of steps attacked.

By using these improvements, we can attack the last 68 steps (Steps 12 to 79) or the first 67 steps (Steps 0 to 66) of HAS-160. Both of our attacks first generate pseudo-preimages, and then convert them to a preimage. The complexity of these attacks for finding pseudo-preimages are approximately $2^{150.7}$ and 2^{154} respectively, and for finding preimages are approximately $2^{156.3}$ and 2^{158} respectively. The required memory is $2^{12} \times 7$ words and $2^{10} \times 7$ words respectively.

The comparison of the previous work and our attacks is summarized in Table 1. To the best of our knowledge, attacking 68 steps is the best of all attacks including collision attacks on the HAS-160 hash function. Due to the slight improvement of the attack complexity from the brute force attack and considering that HAS-160 has 12 steps more, HAS-160 is still secure. However, because the security margin is significantly reduced, we need to be very careful for future attack improvements on HAS-160.

Table 1. Comparison of preimage attacks on HAS-160

Reference	Step number	Time complexity		Memory use
		Pseudo-preimage	Preimage	
[4]	intermediate 48	2^{128}	2^{145}	$2^{32} \times 6$ words
[4]	intermediate 52	2^{144}	2^{153}	$2^{48} \times 9$ words
This paper	intermediate 52	2^{144}	2^{153}	$2^{16} \times 9$ words
This paper	first 65	$2^{143.4}$	$2^{152.7}$	$2^{16} \times 6$ words
This paper	first 67	2^{154}	2^{158}	$2^{10} \times 7$ words
This paper	last 68	$2^{150.7}$	$2^{156.3}$	$2^{12} \times 7$ words

Organization of this paper is as follows. In Section 2, we describe the specification of HAS-160. In Section 3, we summarize techniques in the previous work. In Section 4, we explain how to search for attacked steps using improved techniques. In Section 5, we propose preimage attacks on the last 68, the first 67, and the first 65 steps of HAS-160. Finally, we conclude this paper in Section 6.

2   Description of HAS-160

HAS-160 [2] is a hash function that produces 160-bit hash values. HAS-160 has the Merkle-Damgård structure, which uses a 160-bit (5-word) chaining variable and a 512-bit (16-word) message block to compute the compression function.

First, an input message M is processed to be a multiple of 512 bits by the padding procedure. A single bit 1 is appended followed by 0s until the length becomes 448 modulo 512. Finally, the 64-bit binary representation of the length of M is appended at the end.

The padded message is separated into 512-bit message blocks $(M_0, M_1, \ldots, M_{N-1})$. Let $CF : \{0,1\}^{160} \times \{0,1\}^{512} \to \{0,1\}^{160}$ be the compression function of HAS-160. A hash value is computed as follows.

1. $H_0 \leftarrow IV$,
2. $H_{i+1} \leftarrow CF(H_i, M_i)$ for $i = 0, 1, \ldots, N-1$,

where H_i is a 160-bit value and IV is the initial value defined in the specification. Finally, H_N is output as a hash value of M.

Compression Function

HAS-160 iteratively computes a step function 80 times to compute a hash value. Steps 0-19, 20-39, 40-59, and 60-79 are called the first, second, third, and fourth rounds, respectively. Let (H_i, M_i) be the input of the compression function.

Message expansion. First, M_i is divided into sixteen 32-bit message-words $m_0, \ldots, m_{15}$. The message expansion of HAS-160 is a permutation of 20 message words in each round, which consists of $m_0, \ldots, m_{15}$ and four additional messages $m_{16}, \ldots, m_{19}$ computed from $m_0, \ldots, m_{15}$. The computation of $m_{16}, \ldots, m_{19}$ is shown in Table 2. Let $X_0, X_1, \ldots, X_{79}$ be message words used in each step. The message word m_j assigned to each X_j is also shown in Table 2.

Table 2. Message expansion of HAS-160

Computation of m_{16} to m_{19} in each round

	Round 1	Round 2	Round 3	Round 4
m_{16}	$m[0,1,2,3]$	$m[3,6,9,12]$	$m[12,5,14,7]$	$m[7,2,13,8]$
m_{17}	$m[4,5,6,7]$	$m[15,2,5,8]$	$m[0,9,2,11]$	$m[3,14,9,4]$
m_{18}	$m[8,9,10,11]$	$m[11,14,1,4]$	$m[4,13,6,15]$	$m[15,10,5,0]$
m_{19}	$m[12,13,14,15]$	$m[7,10,13,0]$	$m[8,1,10,3]$	$m[11,6,1,12]$

$m[i,j,k,l]$ denotes $m_i \oplus m_j \oplus m_k \oplus m_l$

Message index order in each step

Round 1: $X_0, X_1, \ldots, X_{19}$	18	0	1	2	3	19	4	5	6	7	16	8	9	10	11	17	12	13	14	15
Round 2: $X_{20}, X_{21}, \ldots, X_{39}$	18	3	6	9	12	19	15	2	5	8	16	11	14	1	4	17	7	10	13	0
Round 3: $X_{40}, X_{41}, \ldots, X_{59}$	18	12	5	14	7	19	0	9	2	11	16	4	13	6	15	17	8	1	10	3
Round 4: $X_{60}, X_{61}, \ldots, X_{79}$	18	7	2	13	8	19	3	14	9	4	16	15	10	5	0	17	11	6	1	12

Step update function. Let $p_j, 0 \le j \le 80$ be 160-bit intermediate variables. The output of the compression function H_{i+1} is computed as follows.

1. $p_0 \leftarrow H_i$.
2. $p_{j+1} \leftarrow R_j(p_j, X_j)$ for $j = 0, 1, \ldots, 79$,
3. Output $H_{i+1}(= p_{80} + H_i)$, where "+" denotes 32-bit word-wise addition. In this paper, we similarly use "−" to denote 32-bit word-wise subtraction.

R_j is the step function for Step j. Let a_j, b_j, c_j, d_j, e_j be 32-bit values that satisfy $p_j = (a_j \| b_j \| c_j \| d_j \| e_j)$. $R_j(p_j, X_j)$ computes p_{j+1} as follows:

$$\begin{cases} a_{j+1} = (a_j \lll s1_j) + f_j(b_j, c_j, d_j) + e_j + X_j + k_j, \\ b_{j+1} = a_j, \\ c_{j+1} = b_j \lll s2_j, \\ d_{j+1} = c_j, \\ e_{j+1} = d_j, \\ p_{j+1} = a_{j+1} \| b_{j+1} \| c_{j+1} \| d_{j+1} \| e_{j+1} \end{cases}$$

where f_j, k_j, and $\lll s2_j$ represent bitwise Boolean function, constant number, and $s2_j$-bit left rotation defined in each round, and $\lll s1_j$ represents $s1_j$-bit left rotation depending on the value of $j \bmod 20$. These values are shown in Table 3.

Table 3. Function f, constant k, and rotations $s1$ and $s2$ of HAS-160

Round	Function $f_j(X, Y, Z)$	Constant k_j	Rotation $s2_j$
Round 1	$(X \wedge Y) \vee (\neg X \wedge Z)$	0x00000000	10
Round 2	$Z \oplus Y \oplus Z$	0x5a827999	17
Round 3	$Y \oplus (X \vee \neg Z)$	0x6ed9eba1	25
Round 4	$X \oplus Y \oplus Z$	0x8f1bbcdc	30

Rotation $s1_j$

$j \bmod 20$	0	1	2	3	4	5	6	7	8	9	10	11	12	13	14	15	16	17	18	19
$s1_j$	5	11	7	15	6	13	8	14	7	12	9	11	8	15	6	12	9	14	5	13

We show a diagram of the step function in Fig. 1. We assume that both addition and subtraction have the same complexity, as well as both left and right rotations, hence $R_j^{-1}(p_{j+1}, X_j)$ can be computed in almost the same complexity as R_j.

3   Related Work

3.1   Converting Pseudo-preimages to a Preimage

For a given hash value y, a pseudo-preimage is a pair of $(x, M), x \ne IV$ such that $CF(x, M) = y$. For the Merkle-Damgård hash functions, there is a generic algorithm that converts a pseudo-preimage attack to a preimage attack [20, Fact9.99]. Let the complexity of a pseudo-preimage attack be 2^k and the hash length be n.

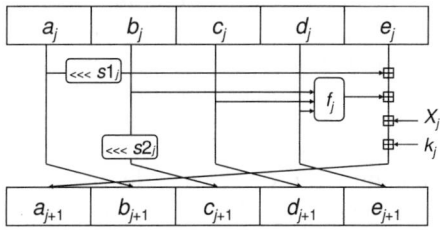

Fig. 1. Step function of HAS-160

1. Generate $2^{(n-k)/2}$ pseudo-preimages with a complexity of $2^k \cdot 2^{(n-k)/2}$.
2. Generate $2^{(n+k)/2}$ 1-block messages, and compute their hash values.

One of these hash values are expected to match. The complexity of this attack is $2^k \cdot 2^{(n-k)/2} + 2^{(n+k)/2} = 2^{1+(n+k)/2}$. Therefore, a pseudo-preimage attack with a complexity less than 2^{n-2} can be converted to a preimage attack.

In this attack, so called *Tree approach* proposed by Leurent [10] and *P^3-graph* proposed by de Cannière and Rechberger [21] cannot be used because these techniques require several special properties such that partial-pseudo-preimage must be computed very rapidly.

3.2   Meet-in-the-Middle Preimage Attack on 52-Step HAS-160

Sasaki and Aoki proposed a meet-in-the-middle preimage attack on 52-step HAS-160 [4]. First, *splice-and-cut*, *partial-matching*, and *partial-fixing* techniques, which were originally proposed for analyzing MD5 [11], were considered. In this framework, they first consider the first and last steps as consecutive steps, and divide the attack target into two *chunks* of steps so that each chunk includes several message words that appear only in one of two chunks[1]. These are called *neutral words*. Then, a pseudo-preimage is computed by the meet-in-the-middle attack. The partial-matching and partial-fixing techniques enable the attacker to ignore several steps at the end of chunks. They concluded that up to 9 steps can be skipped by using these two techniques.

Second, they showed an observation that additional 3 steps can be skipped at the beginning of two chunks. For this observation, they showed only the results. The generalization of this observation was later summarized as *initial structure* technique, which is explained in the next section.

3.3   Initial Structure and Partial-Fixing for Unknown Carry Behavior

Initial structure and partial-fixing for unknown carry behavior were proposed by Sasaki and Aoki to attack full MD5 [17]. Initial structure is a technique for skipping several steps at the beginning of chunks. Ref. [17] defined it as follows:

---

[1] In this paper, we call a chunk including the first and last steps of the compression function *first chunk* and a chunk consisting of only middle steps *second chunk*.

> *Initial structure is a few consecutive steps including at least two neutral words denoted by m^{2nd} and m^{1st}, where steps after the initial structure (2nd chunk) can be computed independently of m^{1st} and steps before the initial structure (1st chunk) can be computed independently of m^{2nd}.*

For HAS-160, only skipping 3 steps has been considered in [4].

Partial-fixing for unknown carry behavior deals with the modular addition of two partially known values. With this technique, more steps can be attacked though the attack becomes less efficient. Assume that we add two word-size variables A and B, where the upper half bits of A and B are known but the lower half bits are unknown. We obtain two candidates of the upper half bits of $A+B$ because of an unknown carry from the lower half bits. Ref. [17] summarized that the increase of S candidates can be filtered out without paying a significant cost, where S is the number of steps in the compression function. For HAS-160, this technique has not been considered by the previous work.

3.4   Computing Kernels of each Independent Chunk

Since HAS-160 has a linear message expansion, we can efficiently search for a chunk separation and neutral words by applying the kernel computing approach proposed for SHA-0 and SHA-1[5].

Let w_j be the message word used in the j-th step for $j = 0, ..., 79$, expanded from a message block $M = [m_0 \cdots m_{15}]$. For simplicity, we assume that $w_0, w_1, ..., w_{t-1}$ are used in the first chunk and $w_t, w_{t+1}, ..., w_{s-1}$ are used in the second chunk. Since the message expansion of HAS-160 is linear, we can regard it as a 80×16 binary matrix W satisfying $[w_0 \cdots w_{79}]^T = WM^T$, and have two sub-matrices W_1 and W_2 satisfying $[w_0 \ w_1 \cdots w_{t-1}]^T = W_1 M^T$ and $[w_t \ w_{t+1} \cdots w_{s-1}]^T = W_2 M^T$, respectively. We assume that rank $W_1 = \kappa_1 < 16$ and rank $W_2 = \kappa_2 < 16$. Then, W_1 and W_2 have non-trivial kernels ker W_1 and ker W_2, respectively. If we find a pair of binary vectors in ker $W_1 \times$ ker W_2 which do not share any nonzero bit position, we can set neutral words according to the vectors. Consider the example explained in [5]. Assume that we are given k_1 and k_2 as follows.

$$\begin{cases} k_1 = [1\ 0\ 1\ 1\ 0\ 0\ 0\ 0\ 0\ 0\ 0\ 0\ 0\ 0\ 0\ 0]^T \in \ker W_1, \\ k_2 = [0\ 1\ 0\ 0\ 1\ 0\ 0\ 0\ 0\ 0\ 0\ 0\ 0\ 0\ 0\ 0]^T \in \ker W_2. \end{cases}$$

Then, $W_1 k_1 = 0$ and $W_2 k_2 = 0$ hold. It implies that m_0 can be used as a neutral word for the second chunk if we set $m_0 = m_2 = m_3$, and that m_1 can be used as a neutral word for the first chunk if we set $m_1 = m_4$. If both W_1 and W_2 do not have full rank but there exists no such a pair of $(k_1, k_2) \in \ker W_1 \times \ker W_2$, we can easily construct an invertible matrix R such that $R^{-1}k_1$ and $R^{-1}k_2$ do not share any nonzero bit position for a $(k_1, k_2) \in \ker W_1 \times \ker W_2$. If such a matrix is constructed, we have $WM^T = (WR)(R^{-1}M^T)$, and we use $W' = WR$ and $M'^T = [m'_0 \cdots m'_{15}]^T = R^{-1}M^T$ as the message expansion and the message block converted by R.

4 Chunk Separation Search Using Improved Techniques

This section explains how to find chunks and neutral words that can attack long steps. To find them, the following two parameters need to be considered.

1. How many steps can be skipped at the beginning of chunks?
2. How many steps can be skipped at the end of chunks?

We first explain how to determine the parameters, then show the result of chunk separation search.

4.1 Initial Structure

The first parameter of the chunk separation search is achieved by the initial structure technique. So far, only the initial structure for 3 steps, which uses a large amount of memory, has been considered. We found that the length of the initial structure can be chosen from 2 steps to 4 steps, and we could save the memory to construct it. Our attack on 68-step HAS-160 uses a 3-step initial structure. Hence we show the memoryless 3-step initial structure in Fig. 2.

In Fig. 2, p_j is included in the first chunk and X_{j+2} is the neutral word for the first chunk. Similarly, p_{j+3} is included in the second chunk and X_j is the neutral word for the second chunk. Hereafter, we denote neutral words in the first and second chunks by NW^{1st} and NW^{2nd}, respectively. The goal is to guarantee that the change of X_{j+2} does not affect to p_{j+3} and the change of X_j does not affect to p_j. In Fig. 2, impacts of changing X_j and X_{j+3} are shown by bold and dotted lines, respectively. As shown in Fig. 2, in both chunks, the value of t_j, t_{j+1}, and t_{j+2} can be set to given constant values. This enables us to compute each chunk independently.

In the previous initial structure [4], the probability that p_j and p_{j+3} are correctly connected was 2^{-32}. Hence, we need to increase the free bits in each chunk by 32 bits. This increases the required memory by a factor of 2^{32}. Different from the previous one, this structure always correctly connects p_j and p_{j+3}. This prevents the increase of the required memory by a factor of 2^{32}. Finally, by replacing the initial structure used in [4] with this memoryless one, the memory use of the previous attack on 52 steps could be reduced from $2^{48} \times 9$ words to $2^{16} \times 9$ words.

We also show how to construct the memoryless 4-step initial structure in Fig. 4 in Appendix A.

4.2 Result of Chunk Separation Search

The second parameter of the chunk separation search depends on how many steps we can skip by the partial-fixing technique. Unfortunately, it depends on the message expansion and rotation numbers $s1$ and $s2$ of skipped steps. Hence, we cannot determine the number of steps skipped without considering the actual location of chunks. From our by-hand experiment, around 13 steps could be skipped.

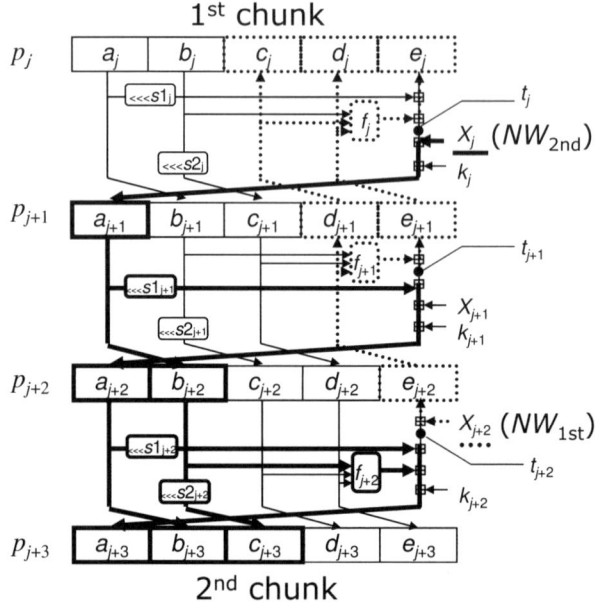

The order of addition is changed by the equivalent transformation

Fig. 2. Memoryless initial structure skipping 3 steps

Finally, we exhaustively search for the maximum number of attacked steps under chosen two parameters. Results of the chunk separation search are shown in Table 4. Assumption that we can skip up to 4 steps by the initial structure and 13 steps by the partial-fixing technique is reasonable. However, to observe what will happen if the attack techniques are improved, we also analyze the cases where 5 or 6 steps are skipped by the initial structure and up to 18 steps are skipped by the partial-fixing technique. Table 4 indicates that attacking 68 steps would be possible. Table 4 also indicates that even if the attack techniques are

Table 4. Results of chunk separation search

		# skipped steps by partial-fixing technique										
		7	8	9	10	11	12	13	14	15	16	17	18
	0	65	65	65	65	65	65	65	65	65	65	68	68
# skipped	2	65	65	65	65	65	65	67	67	68	68	68	68
steps by	3	65	65	65	65	65	68	68	68	68	70	70	70
initial	4	65	65	65	65	65	68	68	68	68	70	70	70
structure	5	65	65	65	66	66	68	68	68	68	70	71	71
	6	65	65	66	66	66	68	68	68	68	70	71	71

Skipping 3 and 8 steps by the initial structure and partial-fixing techniques, respectively, is the previous best result [4]. Our new attack skips 3 and 12 steps, respectively, with linear algebra analysis.

Step	Message word index 0-15																NW^{1st} $m[3,6,8,15]$	NW^{2nd} $m[2,8]$	
	0	1	2	3	4	5	6	7	8	9	10	11	12	13	14	15			
12									*										first chunk
13										*									
14											*								
15			*	*	o	*											✓		
16												*							
17													*						
18														*					
19															o		✓		
20	*			*						*				*					
21			*														✓		
22					o												✓		
23									*										
24												*							
25	*						*			*			*				✓		
26																o	✓		↑
27		•																✓	IS
28				*															
29							⊙										✓	✓	
30			o			o			*			*							↓
31										*									second chunk
32													*						
33	*																		
34				*															
35		•				*			⊙							o			
36							*												
37										*									
38													*						
39	*																		
40				*			o						*			o			
41											*								
42				*															
43														*					
44							*												
45	*		o				⊙		*									✓	
46	*																		
47									*										
48		•																✓	
49										*									
50				*		*						*		*					
51				*															
52												*							
53						o											✓		
54																o	✓		
55	*		•						*		*						✓	✓	skip
56							⊙										✓	✓	
57		*																	
58										*									
59			o														✓		
60	*				*					*						o	✓		
61							*												
62		•																✓	
63														*					
64							⊙										✓	✓	
65	*				o					*		*					✓		first chunk
66			o														✓		
67														*					
68									*										
69				*															
70		•				*	⊙					*					✓		
71																o	✓		
72										*									
73					*														
74	*																		
75				o	*					*					*		✓		
76											*								
77					o												✓		
78	*																		
79												*							

* denotes message words used in each step. o and • denote message words used as neutral words in the first and second chunks, respectively. ⊙ denotes m_8, which is a neutral word in both chunks. In the column of NW^{1st} and NW^{2nd}, we put a tick if $m_3 \oplus m_6 \oplus m_8 \oplus m_{15} \neq 0$ and if $m_2 \oplus m_8 \neq 0$, respectively.

Fig. 3. Selected chunks for the 68 steps

improved, the number of attacked steps is at most 71, hence the full HAS-160 would be secure against this approach.

5   Preimage Attack on 68 Steps HAS-160

In Fig. 3, we show the details of chunks obtained by the analysis in Section 4. We skip 3 steps (Steps 27–29) by the initial structure and skip 12 steps (Steps 53–64) by the partial-fixing technique. When we compute the first chunk, we change values of m_3, m_6, m_8, and m_{15} so that $m_3 = m_6 = m_8 = m_{15}$ is always satisfied. Similarly, when we compute the second chunk, we change values of m_2 and m_8 so that $m_2 = m_8$ is always satisfied. It is easy to check that changing m_2 and m_8 does not affect the first chunk as long as $m_2 \oplus m_8 = 0$ is satisfied. Independence of the second chunk can also be checked easily. m_8 is involved in both chunks. But this does not cause problems. In fact, we can apply the linear algebra to the message schedule so that $m_3 \oplus m_6 \oplus m_8 \oplus m_{15}$ is regarded as m_0' and $m_2 \oplus m_8$ is regarded as m_1' using the method shown by [5,6,7,8]. Then, $m_2', \ldots, m_{15}'$ will be represented by linear combinations of $m_0, \ldots, m_{15}$.

5.1   Initial Structure

The initial structure we use is basically the same as the one shown in Fig. 2 for $j = 27$. However, X_{29} is m_8 which needs to change to compute both chunks. In order to maintain the independence of two neutral words, we separate m_8 into two parts, *i.e.* $m_8 = m_8^H \| m_8^L$. Then, we change only m_8^L to compute the first chunk, and only m_8^H to compute the second chunk.

To compute the initial structure, we first fix the value of t_{29} to 0. Then, in forward, we compute $a_{30} \leftarrow t_{29} + (a_{29} \lll s1_{29}) + (m_8^H \| 0) + f_{29} + k_{29}$. In backward, we compute $e_{29} \leftarrow t_{29} - (0 \| m_8^L)$. Finally, computations for two chunks become independent.

By considering the partial-fixing technique explained in Section 5.2, length of both m_8^H and m_8^L should be 10 bits. Hence, strictly speaking, the representation of m_8 becomes $m_8^H \| 0 \| m_8^L$.

5.2   Partial-Fixing Technique

For the partial-fixing technique, we carefully consider the message order and rotation numbers in each step to analyze how many bits can be compared by the meet-in-the-middle. How the results of two chunks are compared is explained in Table 5. In the followings, we explain how the computations in Table 5 are processed.

Forward computation for a_{54}: We know all bits of $a_{53}, b_{53}, c_{53}, d_{53}$, and e_{53}. Because bit positions 31–10 of NW^{1st} are fixed, we can compute the same bit positions of a_{54}. However, we cannot know the carry from bit position 9 to 10. Therefore, we guess the possible two patterns of carry value denoted by C_{53}, and compute two candidates of bit positions 31–10 of a_{54}.

Table 5. Number of known bits in partial-fixing technique

j	$s1_j$	$s2_j$	a_j	b_j	c_j	d_j	e_j	NW^{1st}	#cands of a_j	
53	15	25	All	All	All	All	All	31–10		Forward
54	6	25	31–10	All	All	All	All	31–10	2^1	Forward
55			31–16	31–10	All	All	All	All	2^2	Forward
55	12	25	28–22	28–22	?	?	?	skipped		
56	9	25	28–14	28–22	21–15	?	?	skipped		
57	14	25	28–9	28–14	21–15	21–15	?	skipped		
58	5	25	28–7	28–9	21–7	21–15	21–15	All	2^4	Backward
59	13	25	23–2	28–7	21–2	21–7	21–15	All	2^3	Backward
60	5	30	23–2	23–2	21–0	21–2	21–7	All	2^2	Backward
61	11	30	All	23–2	21–0	21–0	21–2	All	2^1	Backward
62	7	30	All	All	21–0	21–0	21–0	21–0	1	
63	15	30	All	All	All	21–0	21–0	All	1	
64	6	30	All	All	All	All	21–0	21–0	1	
65			All	All	All	All	All			
j	$s1_j$	$s2_j$	a_j	b_j	c_j	d_j	e_j	NW^{2nd}	#cands of e_j	

Numbers denote the known bits of each chaining variable. Underlined variables in $j = 55$ are the variables where we compare the results of two chunks.

Forward computation for a_{55}: The equation for a_{55} is as follows:

$$a_{55} = \underline{a_{54}^{\lll 5}}_{31-16} + f_{20} + e_{20} + \underline{X_{20}}_{31-10} + k_{20} = \underline{a_{54}^{\lll 5}}_{31-16} + \underline{X_{20}}_{31-10} + Con,$$

where, subscripts besides underlines denote the positions of partially known bits. When we compute $X_{20} + Con$, we do not know the carry from bit position 9 to 10. However, if bit position y, $10 \le y \le 15$ of both X_{20} and Con are 0, the carry to $y + 1$-th bit is 0 regardless of the carry from $y - 1$-th bit to y-th bit. Similarly, if both values are 1, the carry to $y + 1$-th bit is always 1. Hence, we can know the carry from bit position 15 to 16 of $X_{20} + Con$ with high probability. Finally, due to the addition of $\underline{a_{54}^{\lll 5}}_{31-16}$ and ($X_{20} + Con$), we will obtain two results of bit positions 31–16 of a_{55}.

Backward computation: The basic process in the backward computation has already explained in [4], and computations for dealing with the unknown carry are the same as the forward computation. Hence, we omit the detailed explanation.

Match of two chunks: Finally, results from both chunks are compared at bits 28–22 of a_{55} and bits 28–22 of b_{55}, in total 14 bits.

5.3 Attack Procedure

Attack procedure

0. Apply the linear transformation for the message expansion matrix $[M]$ so that $(m_3 \oplus m_6 \oplus m_8 \oplus m_{15})$ and $(m_2 \oplus m_8)$ are regarded as m'_0 and m'_1 respectively, where $(m'_0, \ldots, m'_{15})$ are transformed message words.
1. Fix $m'_i, (2 \le i \le 15)$ and bit positions 31–10 of m'_0 and bit positions 21–0 of m'_1 to randomly chosen values. Fix a_{27}, b_{27}, t_{27} and t_{28} in the initial structure to randomly chosen values. Fix t_{29} to 0.
2. For all 10 free bits (bit positions 31–22) of m'_1 in Step 27,
   (a) Compute the initial structure and second chunk in forward to obtain the value of p_{53}.
   (b) Process the partial-fixing technique in forward to obtain values shown in Table 5 with guessing carry values C_{53} and C_{54}.
   (c) Make a table of $(m'_1, p_{53},$ bits 28–22 of $a_{55},$ bits 28–22 of $b_{55}, C_{53}, C_{54})$. Since we have 10 free bits in m'_0 and we guess two carry values, we obtain 2^{12} items in the table.
3. For all 10 free bits (bit positions 9–0) of m'_0 in Step 29,
   (a) Compute the initial structure and first chunk in backward to obtain the value of p_{65}.
   (b) Process the partial-fixing technique in backward to obtain bits 28–22 of a_{55} and b_{55} with guessing carry values $C_{62}, C_{61}, C_{60},$ and C_{59}.
   (c) Compare bits 28–22 of a_{55} and b_{55}, in total 14 bits, with those stored in the table.
   (d) If matched, compute $p_{j+1} \leftarrow R_j(p_j, X_j)$ for $j = 53, 54$ with matched m'_0 and m'_1, and check the correctness of C_{53} and C_{54}. Similarly, compute $p_j \leftarrow R_j^{-1}(p_{j+1}, X_j)$ for $j = 64, 63, \ldots, 55$ and check the correctness of $C_{62}, C_{61}, C_{60},$ and C_{59} and match of 146 other bits of p_{55}.
   (e) If all bits match, compute $m_0, \ldots, m_{15}$ from $m'_0, \ldots, m'_{15}$ by the linear transformation. Finally, $m_0, \ldots, m_{15}$ and p_{12} is a pseudo-preimage.

5.4 Complexity Estimation

We assume that the complexity for computing 1 step is equivalent to $\frac{1}{68}$ compression function operation of HAS-160 reduced to 68 steps.

The complexity of step 2a is $2^{10} \cdot \frac{26}{68}$ and the complexity of step 2b is $2^{10} \cdot (2^1 \cdot \frac{1}{68} + 2^2 \cdot \frac{1}{68}) = 2^{10} \cdot \frac{6}{68}$. The complexity of step 3a is $2^{10} \cdot \frac{33}{68}$. The complexity of step 3b is $2^{10} \cdot (1 \cdot \frac{3}{68} + 2^1 \cdot \frac{1}{68} + 2^2 \cdot \frac{1}{68} + 2^3 \cdot \frac{1}{68} + 2^4 \cdot \frac{1}{68}) = 2^{10} \cdot \frac{33}{68}$. In step 2c, 2^{12} items are stored in the table and in step 3b, $2^{14} (= 2^{10} \cdot 2^4)$ items are generated. Therefore, in step 3c, 14 bits of 2^{26} items are compared and $2^{12} (= 2^{26} \cdot 2^{-14})$ pairs will remain. In step 3d, forward computation of p_{54} costs $2^{12} \cdot \frac{1}{68} = 2^{10} \cdot \frac{4}{68}$ and the number of remaining pairs will be $2^{11} (= 2^{12} \cdot 2^{-1})$ by checking the correctness of C_{53}. Hence, computation of p_{55} costs $2^{11} \cdot \frac{1}{68} = 2^{10} \cdot \frac{2}{68}$ and the number of remaining pairs will be $2^{10} (= 2^{11} \cdot 2^{-1})$ by checking C_{54}. Backward computation up to p_{61} costs $2^{10} \cdot \frac{4}{68}$ and the number of remaining pairs will be $2^9 (= 2^{10} \cdot 2^{-1})$ by checking C_{62}. Computation of p_{60} costs $2^9 \cdot \frac{1}{68} = 2^{10} \cdot \frac{0.5}{68}$

and the number of remaining pairs will be $2^8(= 2^9 \cdot 2^{-1})$ by checking C_{61}. Computation of p_{59} costs $2^8 \cdot \frac{1}{68} = 2^{10} \cdot \frac{0.25}{68}$ and the number of remaining pair will be $2^{-18}(= 2^8 \cdot 2^{-1} \cdot 2^{-25})$ by checking the correctness of C_{60} and the match between bits 31–29, 21–0 of $a_{55} \lll s2_{56}$ and e_{59}. Since the number of remaining pairs is enough reduced, the complexity after this step is negligible. Finally, in step 3d, match of other 121 (=160-14-25) bits and correctness of C_{59} are checked and the number of remaining pair will be $2^{-140}(= 2^{-18} \cdot 2^{-121} \cdot 2^{-1})$. Therefore, by repeating the above procedure 2^{140} times, a pair matches for all bits, namely, a pseudo-preimage is found. The complexity of one iteration is $2^{10} \cdot \left(\frac{26}{68} + \frac{6}{68} + \frac{33}{68} + \frac{33}{68} + \frac{4}{68} + \frac{2}{68} + \frac{4}{68} + \frac{0.5}{68} + \frac{0.25}{68}\right) = 2^{10} \cdot \frac{108.75}{68} \approx 2^{10.690}$. Hence the total complexity is approximately $2^{150.7}(\approx 2^{10.690} \cdot 2^{140})$. Finally, pseudo-preimages are converted to a preimage with a complexity of $2^{156.3}(\approx 2^{(150.690+160)/2+1})$ by using the conversion algorithm described in Section 3.1.

In this attack, we use a memory to store 2^{12} items of (m'_1, p_{53}, 7 bits of a_{55}, 7 bits of b_{55}, C_{53}, C_{54}) in step 2c. Therefore, we need less than $2^{12} \times 7$ words of memory to generate a pseudo-preimage.

5.5 Message Padding

To find preimages, we need to satisfy the message padding rules. Because we use m_{15} as a neutral word, the value of m_{15} cannot be fixed in advance. This means that the length of preimages will be long and cannot be determined in advance. This problem can be solved by using *expandable message* [22] constructed with *fixed point* [23]. Note that when we generate second-preimages by using this preimage attack, we do not have to satisfy the message padding rules.

5.6 Preimage Attacks on the First 67 Steps and the First 65 Steps

The framework of the attacks on the first 67 and 65 steps are the same as the one for 68 steps. Due to the limited space, we only show the chunk separation for these attacks in Appendix B.

The attack on 67 steps skips 2 steps by the initial structure and 13 steps by the partial-fixing technique. We confirmed that the complexity of the attack is slightly higher than that of 68 steps. This is because the partial-fixing technique in this attack skips longer steps than the attack on 68 steps. Finally, pseudo-preimages can be found with approximately 2^{154} computations and preimages can be found with approximately 2^{158} computations. This attack uses $2^{10} \times 7$ words of memory to find a pseudo-preimage. The attack on 65 steps does not use the initial structure and skips only 7 steps by the partial-fixing technique. In this attack, pseudo-preimages can be computed with approximately $2^{143.4}$ computations and preimages can be found with approximately $2^{152.7}$ computations. This attack uses at most $2^{16} \times 6$ words of memory to find a pseudo-preimage.

6 Conclusion

This paper proposed improved preimage attacks on step-reduced HAS-160. We considered various techniques on meet-in-the-middle preimage attacks. Using these techniques, we succeeded in attacking the last 68 steps and the first 67 steps. The complexities for finding pseudo-preimages with these attacks are $2^{150.7}$ and 2^{154}, respectively. The complexities for finding preimages are $2^{155.6}$ and 2^{158}, respectively. The required memory are $2^{12} \times 7$ and $2^{10} \times 7$ words, respectively.

References

1. U.S. Department of Commerce, National Institute of Standards and Technology: Federal Register/Notices Vol. 72(212), November 2 (2007),
   http://csrc.nist.gov/groups/ST/hash/documents/FR_Notice_Nov07.pdf
2. Telecommunications Technology Association.: Hash Function Standard Part 2: Hash Function Algorithm Standard, HAS-160 (2000)
3. U.S. Department of Commerce, National Institute of Standards and Technology: Secure Hash Standard (SHS) (Federal Information Processing Standards Publication 180-3) (2008),
   http://csrc.nist.gov/publications/fips/fips180-3/fips180-3_final.pdf
4. Sasaki, Y., Aoki, K.: A preimage attack for 52-steps HAS-160. In: Lee, P.J., Cheon, J.H. (eds.) ICISC 2008. LNCS, vol. 5461, pp. 302–317. Springer, Heidelberg (2009)
5. Aoki, K., Sasaki, Y.: Meet-in-the-middle preimage attacks against reduced SHA-0 and SHA-1. In: Halevi, S. (ed.) Advances in Cryptology - CRYPTO 2009. LNCS, vol. 5677, pp. 70–89. Springer, Heidelberg (2009)
6. Yun, A., Sung, S.H., Park, S., Chang, D., Hong, S., Cho, H.S.: Finding collision on 45-step HAS-160. In: Won, D.H., Kim, S. (eds.) ICISC 2005. LNCS, vol. 3935, pp. 146–155. Springer, Heidelberg (2006)
7. Cho, H.-S., Park, S., Sung, S.H., Yun, A.: Collision search attack for 53-step HAS-160. In: Rhee, M.S., Lee, B. (eds.) ICISC 2006. LNCS, vol. 4296, pp. 286–295. Springer, Heidelberg (2006)
8. Mendel, F., Rijmen, V.: Colliding message pair for 53-step HAS-160. In: Nam, K.-H., Rhee, G. (eds.) ICISC 2007. LNCS, vol. 4817, pp. 324–334. Springer, Heidelberg (2007)
9. Saarinen, M.J.O.: A meet-in-the-middle collision attack against the new FORK-256. In: Srinathan, K., Rangan, C.P., Yung, M. (eds.) INDOCRYPT 2007, vol. 4859, pp. 10–17. Springer, Heidelberg (2007)
10. Leurent, G.: MD4 is not one-way. In: Nyberg, K. (ed.) FSE 2008. LNCS, vol. 5086, pp. 412–428. Springer, Heidelberg (2008)
11. Aoki, K., Sasaki, Y.: Preimage attacks on one-block MD4, 63-step MD5 and more. In: Avanzi, R.M., Keliher, L., Sica, F. (eds.) SAC 2008. LNCS, vol. 5381, pp. 103–119. Springer, Heidelberg (2009)
12. Aumasson, J.P., Meier, W., Mendel, F.: Preimage attacks on 3-pass HAVAL and step-reduced MD5. In: Avanzi, R.M., Keliher, L., Sica, F. (eds.) SAC 2008. LNCS, vol. 5381, pp. 120–135. Springer, Heidelberg (2009)
13. Sasaki, Y., Aoki, K.: Preimage attacks on 3, 4, and 5-pass HAVAL. In: Pieprzyk, J. (ed.) ASIACRYPT 2008. LNCS, vol. 5350, pp. 253–271. Springer, Heidelberg (2008)
14. Chang, D., Hong, S., Kang, C., Kang, J., Kim, J., Lee, C., Lee, J., Lee, J., Lee, S., Lee, Y., Lim, J., Sung, J.: ARIRANG. Available at NIST home page,
    http://csrc.nist.gov/groups/ST/hash/sha-3/Round1/submissions_rnd1.html
15. Hong, D., Kim, W.H., Koo, B.: Preimage attack on ARIRANG. Cryptology ePrint Archive, Report 2009/147 (2009), http://eprint.iacr.org/2009/147

16. Hong, D., Kim, W.H., Koo, B., Kwon, D.: Preimage attacks on reduced steps of ARIRANG and PKC 1998-Hash. Number 8A-2 in USB memory distributed at ICISC 2009 (2009)

17. Sasaki, Y., Aoki, K.: Finding preimages in full MD5 faster than exhaustive search. In: Joux, A. (ed.) EUROCRYPT 2009. LNCS, vol. 5479, pp. 134–152. Springer, Heidelberg (2010)

18. Nan Kyoung Park, J.H.H., Lee, P.J.: HAS-V: A new hash function with variable output length. In: Stinson, D.R., Tavares, S. (eds.) SAC 2000. LNCS, vol. 2012, pp. 202–216. Springer, Heidelberg (2001)

19. Mendel, F., Rijmen, V.: Weaknesses in the HAS-V compression function. In: Nam, K.-H., Rhee, G. (eds.) ICISC 2007. LNCS, vol. 4817, pp. 335–345. Springer, Heidelberg (2007)

20. Menezes, A.J., van Oorschot, P.C., Vanstone, S.A.: Handbook of applied cryptography. CRC Press, Boca Raton (1997)

21. Cannière, C.D., Rechberger, C.: Preimages for reduced SHA-0 and SHA-1. In: Wagner, D. (ed.) CRYPTO 2008. LNCS, vol. 5157, pp. 179–202. Springer, Heidelberg (2008)

22. Kelsey, J., Schneier, B.: Second preimages on n-bit hash functions for much less than 2^n work. In: Cramer, R. (ed.) EUROCRYPT 2005. LNCS, vol. 3494, pp. 474–490. Springer, Heidelberg (2005)

23. Dean, R.D.: Formal aspects of mobile code security. Ph.D Dissertation, Princeton University (January 1999)

A   Construction of 4-Step Initial Structure

We explain how to compute the first chunk step by step. Note that to construct this structure, bit positions we change in X_j and X_{j+3} must be different so that we can compute the f_{j+2} function in each chunk independently. In Fig. 4, we assume that free bits of X_j are bits 31 to L and free bits of X_{j+3} are bits $L-1$ to 0. First, we show that the change of X_{j+3} does not impact to p_{j+4}.

0. Fix values of $a_j, t_j, t_{j+1}, t_{j+3}$ to randomly chosen values, and fix t_{j+2} to 0.

1. Compute $e_{j+3} \leftarrow t_{j+3} - X_{j+3}$ so that the value of t_{j+3} does not change regardless of the value of X_{j+3}.

2. Compute free bits ($L-1$ to 0) of f_{j+2} to obtain corresponding bits of f_{j+2} denoted by f_{j+2}^L. Then, Compute $e_{j+2} \leftarrow t_{j+2} - X_{j+2} - (0\|f_{j+2}^L)$.

3. Compute f_{j+1}, then compute $e_{j+1} \leftarrow t_{j+1} - f_{j+1}$.

4. Compute f_j, then compute $e_j \leftarrow t_j - f_j - (a_j \lll s1_j)$.

Finally, we can guarantee that changes of X_{j+3} do not impact to p_{j+4}. By the similar analysis, we can also guarantee that changes of X_j do not impact to p_j.

B   Selected Chunks for the First 67 and the First 65 Steps

Chunks for the first 67 steps is as follows.

- The attack target is from Steps 0 to Steps 66 (the first 67 steps).
- 2-step initial structure is applied to Step 12 and Step 13 (skip 2 steps).

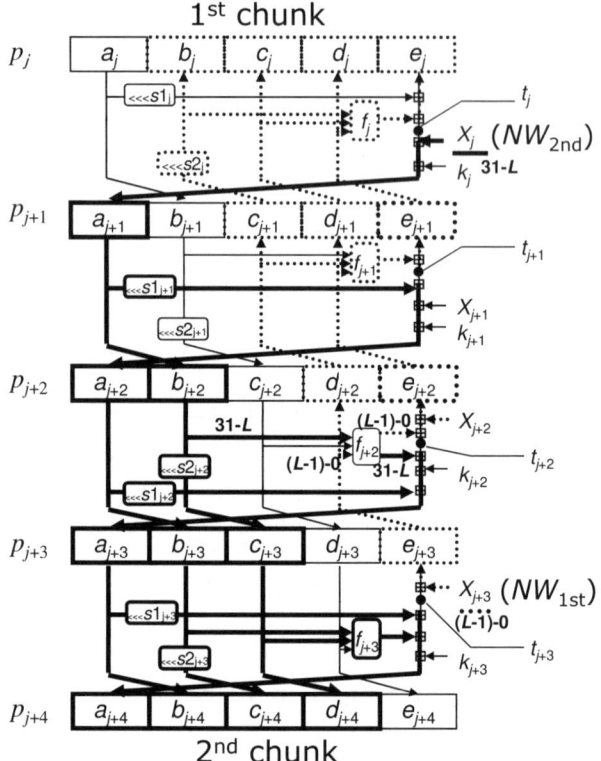

Fig. 4. Memoryless initial structure for skipping 4 steps

- Partial-fixing technique is applied from Step 37 to Step 49 (skip 13 steps).
- The first chunk is from Step 50 to Step 66 and Step 0 to Step 11. We use $m_0 = m_{10}$ as neutral words.
- The second chunk is from Step 14 to Step 36. We use $m_9 = m_{11} = m_{12} = m_{14}$ as neutral words.

Chunks for the first 65 steps is as follows.

- The attack target is from Steps 0 to Steps 64 (the first 65 steps).
- Partial-fixing technique is applied from Step 37 to Step 43 (skip 7 steps).
- The first chunk is from Step 44 to Step 64 and Step 0 to Step 15. We use $m_{12} = m_{14}$ as neutral words.
- The second chunk is from Step 16 to Step 36. We use $m_0 = m_{10}$ as neutral words.

Distinguishing Attack on Secret Prefix MAC Instantiated with Reduced SHA-1*

Siyuan Qiao[1], Wei Wang[2,1], and Keting Jia[1]

[1] Key Laboratory of Cryptologic Technology and Information Security,
Ministry of Education, Shandong University, Jinan 250100, China
sy_qiao@mail.sdu.edu.cn, weiwangsdu@sdu.edu.cn, kejia@mail.sdu.edu.cn
[2] School of Computer Science and Technology, Shandong University,
Jinan, 250100, China

Abstract. In this paper, we present a new distinguishing attack which works for secret prefix MAC based on 65-step (12-76) SHA-1. By birthday paradox, we first guarantee the existence of an internal collision at the output of the first iteration, then identify it by choosing the second message block smartly, and finally distinguish the specific MAC from a random function by making use of a near-collision differential path. The complexity of our new distinguisher is $2^{80.9}$ queries with success probability 0.51. In comparison, we also present a distinguisher on secret prefix MAC instantiated with 63-step (8-70) SHA-1 according to Wang's method introduced at FSE 2009 [21], which needs about 2^{157} queries with success probability 0.70.

Keywords: Cryptanalysis, MAC, Distinguishing Attack, SHA-1.

1 Introduction

A Message Authentication Code (MAC) algorithm, accepts as input a secret key and an arbitrary-length message to be authenticated, and outputs a fixed-length MAC value. The MAC algorithm guarantees both data integrity and data origin authenticity, where the verifiers can detect who send the message and whether the message is tampered during the transformation. It is important in internet communication and is widely used in security protocols such as SSL, SSH, IPsec, etc. Recent collision attacks on hash functions have undermined the confidence in the most popular hash functions such as MD5 and SHA-1 [2,3,16,17,18,20], thus the security of MAC constructions built on these hash functions needs to be reconsidered[4,6,8,12,13,15,19].

MACs are keyed hash functions, so it is natural to use hash functions in a way that uses secret keys. The secret prefix method is a MAC construction which prepends the secret key k to the message before the hashing operation, and it is a basic design unit for HMAC/NMAC [1]. The original secret prefix MAC

* Supported by National Natural Science Foundation of China (NSFC Grant No. 60525201) and 973 Project (No. 2007CB807902).

D. Lee and S. Hong (Eds.): ICISC 2009, LNCS 5984, pp. 349–361, 2010.

is defined as $MAC_k(m) = H(k\|m)$, but this is not secure because we have $H(m_1\|m_2) = H(H(m_1)\|m_2)$ when applied in iterated chaining hash structures such as Merkle-Damgård structure[11]. Then if the adversary obtains the MAC value of the message m_1, he is able to obtain the MAC value of the message $m_1\|m_2$ without knowing the key. One suggestion to guarantee a secure secret prefix MAC is to prepend the message length to the message before hashing, which is called LPMAC[21], the secret prefix MAC we analyzed in this paper belongs to this version.

There are three type of attacks on MACs, named distinguishing attack, forgery attack, and key recovery attack. Distinguishing attack can be divided into distinguishing-R and distinguishing-H attack[8]. Distinguishing-R attack means distinguishing a MAC from a random function, and distinguishing-H attack detects an instantiated MAC (by an underlying hash function or block cipher) from a MAC with a random function. This paper focuses on distinguishing-H attack, and we call it distinguishing attack for short.

Collision or near-collision differential paths for the underlying hash functions are often used to build distinguishers of MAC algorithms, and many cryptanalysis of MACs based on hash functions have been proposed [4,6,8,11,12,13,15,19,21]. For MACs based on SHA-1, Kim et al. proposed a distinguishing attack on HMAC/NMAC-43step-SHA-1 with data complexity $2^{154.9}$. They also described two kinds of distinguishers for HMAC, named as Differential Distinguisher and Rectangle Distinguisher where both come from the popular methods in the cryptanalysis of block cipher. The differential distinguisher utilizes a collision differential path with probability higher than 2^{-n}, and the rectangle distinguisher needs a near-collision differential with probability higher than $2^{-n/2}$[8]. Rechberger and Rijmen improved their attack to 50-step with data complexity $2^{153.5}$, who also proposed a related-key distinguishing attack on 62-step (17-78) HMAC-SHA-1, and a full key recovery attack on 34-step NMAC-SHA-1 in the related-key setting[12]. All these attacks require a collision or near-collision differential path with probability higher than 2^{-n}. Wang et al. presented a new distinguishing attack on LPMAC with 61-step SHA-1, which requires $2^{152.5}$ table lookups and $2^{154.5}$ queries with success rate 0.70[21]. Because there are too many sufficient conditions in the differential path to construct a distinguisher with complexity lower than 2^n, the authors neglected the exact differential path in the first round, replaced it with an inner near-collision, and explored new techniques to detect the inner near-collision. In this way, they only need to find differential path with high probability for the last three rounds. This work is motivated by the first distinguishing attack on HMAC/NMAC-MD5 without related-key settings, which detects an inner near-collision in the first iteration[19]. Their work introduced totally different methods to distinguishing attack.

We research into this new method[21] and present a distinguishing attack on LPMAC with 63-step (8-70) SHA-1. The complexity of the attack is 2^{157} queries with success probability 0.70. Then we build another distinguisher which works for LPMAC based on 65-step (12-76) SHA-1 with $2^{80.9}$ queries and success probability 0.51. For messages composed of 2 blocks, we denote the collisions occurring after the first block as internal collisions, and collisions at the final output as external collisions. It is obvious that the internal collision must lead to external collision. Thus, the internal collision can be identified easily. Since the output of the first block are used as IV of the second block, once an internal collision is detected, the IVs of the second blocks are the same. Then the second block follows a near-collision differential path with high probability if the LPMAC is based on reduced SHA-1.

This paper is organized as follows: Section 2 gives brief descriptions of SHA-1, LPMAC and Wang et al's distinguishing attack on LPMAC-SHA-1. In section 3, we present our results on 63-step SHA-1 using Wang's method, and then build a new distinguisher and compare it with the former one in section 4. Finally, section 5 concludes our paper.

2   Backgrounds and Definitions

In this section, we define the notations used in this paper, and give brief descriptions of SHA-1, LPMAC and the distinguishing attack proposed by Wang et al[21].

2.1   Notations

H	:	a hash function
$\overline{H}$	:	a hash function without padding and length appending
n	:	the length of the hash output
b	:	the length of one message block
IV	:	the initial chaining value
$x\|y$	:	the concatenation of the two bitstrings x and y
$x_{i,j}$	:	the j-th bit of x_i, where x_i is a 32-bit word, $j = 1, \ldots, 32$, and 32 is the most significant bit
$+, -$	:	the addition and subtration modular 2^{32}
$\Delta^- x$	:	the modular difference $x - x'$, where x and x' are two 32-bit words
$\wedge, \neg, \vee, \oplus$	:	the bitwise AND, NOT, OR and exclusive OR
$\lll s$	:	the left-rotation by s-bit

2.2   Brief Description of SHA-1

The hash function SHA-1 was issued by NIST in 1995 as a Federal Information Processing Standard[10]. It follows Merkle-Damgård iterative construction, takes a message M with the bit-length less than 2^{64} as input, and produces a 160-bit digest. Each 512-bit block M_i is divided into sixteen 32-bit words, denoted as $(m_0, m_1, \cdots, m_{15})$, and expanded to eighty 32-bit words $(w_0, \cdots, w_{79})$:

$$w_j = \begin{cases} m_j, & \text{for } j = 0, \ldots, 15, \\ (w_{j-3} \oplus w_{j-8} \oplus w_{j-14} \oplus w_{j-16}) \lll 1, & \text{for } j = 16, \ldots, 79. \end{cases}$$

The compression function of SHA-1 takes a 160-bit chaining value $h_i = (a_0, b_0, c_0, d_0, e_0)$ and a 512-bit message block M_i as inputs, and produces another 160-bit chaining value h_{i+1}, where h_0 is the initial value IV , and $M = M_0\|\cdots\|M_{t-1}$. By iterating all the message blocks M_i, we obtain the final 160-bit output value h_t.

The compression function consists of 4 rounds, and each round includes 20 steps. The details for the compression function are as follows:

1. Input: $w_0, \ldots, w_{79}$ and $h_i = (a_0, b_0, c_0, d_0, e_0)$, where h_i is a 160-bit chaining value.
2. Step update: For $j = 1$ to 80,

$$a_j = (a_{j-1} \lll 5) + f_j(b_{j-1}, c_{j-1}, d_{j-1}) + e_{j-1} + w_{j-1} + k_j,$$
$$b_j = a_{j-1}, \; c_j = b_{j-1} \lll 30, \; d_j = c_{j-1}, \; e_j = d_{j-1}.$$

Here, the Boolean function f_j and constant k_j are defined as:

round	steps	f_j	k_j
1	1-20	IF : $(x \wedge y) \vee (\neg x \wedge z)$	0x5a827999
2	21-40	XOR : $x \oplus y \oplus z$	0x6ed6eba1
3	41-60	MAJ : $(x \wedge y) \vee (x \wedge z) \vee (y \wedge z)$	0x8fabbcdc
4	61-80	XOR : $x \oplus y \oplus z$	0xca62c1d6

3. Output: $h_{i+1} = (a_0 + a_{80}, b_0 + b_{80}, c_0 + c_{80}, d_0 + d_{80}, e_0 + e_{80})$.

2.3   Brief Description of LPMAC

The secret prefix method is to append a message M to a secret key k before the hashing operation:

$$\mathrm{MAC}_k(M) = H(k\|M).$$

This method was proposed in the 1980's[7], but the original secret prefix MAC is insecure because we have $H(m_1\|m_2) = H(H(m_1)\|m_2)$ when applied in iterated chaining structures such as Merkle-Damgård structure. Then if we obtain the MAC value c_1 of the message m_1, we are able to obtain the MAC value c_2 of the message $m_1\|m_2$ without knowing the key k from

$$c_1 = MAC_k(m_1) = H(k\|m_1),$$
$$c_2 = MAC_k(m_1\|m_2) = H(k\|m_1\|m_2) = H(H(k\|m_1)\|m_2) = H(c_1\|m_2).$$

Prefixing the message length to the message before hashing is one suggestion to avoid the above attack[13], which is denoted as:

$$LPMAC_k(M) = \overline{H}(k\|length\|pad\|M) = \overline{H}_{k'}(M),$$

where $k\|length\|pad$ is a full block. Such kind of secret prefix MAC is called LPMAC[21], and we focus on it in the rest of this paper.

2.4   Wang et al.'s Distinguisher on LPMAC Based on 61-Step SHA-1

In this part, we describe the distinguisher proposed by Wang et al, which works on LPMAC with 61-step SHA-1 started from the first step[21]. Assume the LPMAC algorithm is either LPMAC-61-step-SHA-1 or LPMAC-RF (LPMAC with a random function).

For 61-step SHA-1, consider a differential path with two message blocks. Assume $(P\|M_0\|M_1, P'\|M_0'\|M_1')$ is one message pair, which produces a target differential path. P and P' are one-block messages, M_0 and M_0' are 448-bit (14 words) truncated messages of the second block, while M_1 and M_1' are the corresponding 64-bit messages left. Then select a target differential path, such that the first iteration can be any differential path, and the second leads to a near-collision. The second differential path is divided into two parts, where the first part consists of the first 14 steps which involves most conditions, and the second part is the last 47 steps with only 34 conditions. In order to make sure the truncated differential path of the last 47 steps with higher probability, choose a certain disturbance vector, which produces the near-collision for the second iteration. Neglect the special differential path in the previous 14 steps and only consider the output difference of the 14th step, it can be regarded as an inner near-collision. Then, if the inner near collision occurs, replace (M_1, M_1') with another $(\overline{M_1}, \overline{M_1'})$, and $(P\|M_0\|\overline{M_1}, P'\|M_0'\|\overline{M_1'})$ follows the differential path with probability 2^{-34}. If two pairs $(P\|M_0\|M_1, P'\|M_0'\|M_1')$ and $(P\|M_0\|N_1, P'\|M_0'\|N_1')$ result in the near-collision differential path:

$$H_k(P\|M_0\|M_1) - H_k(P'\|M_0'\|M_1') = H_k(P\|M_0\|N_1) - H_k(P'\|M_0'\|N_1') = \delta,$$

there will be

$$H_k(P\|M_0\|M_1) - H_k(P\|M_0\|N_1) = H_k(P'\|M_0'\|M_1') - H_k(P'\|M_0'\|N_1') = \delta'.$$

Based on these facts, the distinguisher can be constructed as follows: Select four messages $M_0\|M_1$, $M_0\|N_1$, $M_0'\|M_1'$ and $M_0'\|N_1'$ such that

$$\Delta(M_0\|M_1) = (M_0\|M_1) \oplus (M_0'\|M_1') \quad \text{and} \quad \Delta(M_0\|N_1) = (M_0\|N_1) \oplus (M_0'\|N_1')$$

follow certain differential path, and $M_0\|M_1$, $M_0\|N_1$ satisfy the sufficient message conditions. The distinguishing attack includes the following four steps:

1. Randomly choose a structure S, which consists of enough different one-block messages P. For 61-step SHA-1 it needs $2^{84.5}$ different P, because the total sufficient conditions for the near-collision is 169.
2. For all $P \in S$, query the MAC values of $P\|M_0\|M_1$, $P\|M_0'\|M_1'$, $P\|M_0\|N_1$ and $P\|M_0'\|N_1'$ respectively, and compute the differences of the following two structures:

$$S_1 = \{LPMAC(P\|M_0\|M_1) - LPMAC(P\|M_0\|N_1)|P \in S\},$$
$$S_2 = \{LPMAC(P\|M_0'\|M_1') - LPMAC(P\|M_0'\|N_1')|P \in S\}.$$

Search all the collisions between two structures by birthday attack.

3. For each collision, compute $LPMAC(P\|M_0\|M_1) - LPMAC(P'\|M_0'\|M_1')$, and denote it as δ. Then for the message pair $(P\|M_0, P'\|M_0')$, choose 2^{34} different message pairs $(\overline{M_1}, \overline{M_1'})$ such that $M_0\|\overline{M_1}$ satisfies the message sufficient conditions for the near-collision path. Query the MAC values for $(P\|M_0\|\overline{M_1}, P'\|M_0'\|\overline{M_1'})$. Check whether the difference $LPMAC(P\|M_0\|\overline{M_1}) - LPMAC(P'\|M_0'\|\overline{M_1'})$ is equivalent to δ. If the difference of a pair $(P\|M_0\|\overline{M_1}, P'\|M_0'\|\overline{M_1'})$ matching δ is found, we conclude that the LPMAC is based on 61-step SHA-1, and break.

4. Repeat steps 1-3. If the number of structures exceeds 2^{68}, conclude that the LPMAC is constructed from a random function.

This attack needs $2^{68} \times 2^{84.5} = 2^{152.5}$ table lookups and $2^{154.5}$ queries, and the success rate is about 0.70.

3 Distinguishing Attack on LPMAC Based on 63-Step (8-70) SHA-1

3.1 Discussion about Wang et al.'s Attack

The core of this attack is to explore some mathematical properties that can be used to distinguish the inner near-collision after the $14th$ step. For LPMAC, there are two obstacles to do this:

1. In the first iteration, the output difference of the first is unknown, which conceals the difference of the near-collision of the second block. Hence, the birthday attack can not be applied directly to the second iteration like the distinguishing attacks on MACs based on MD5.

2. How to choose messages, and fulfill the birthday attack to detect the inner near-collision.

Wang et al.'s distinguisher solved these problems by constructing two structures S_1 and S_2, but this leaves a problem that the probability of the differential path of the last 47 steps should be higher than 2^{-40}. In other words, the number of conditions on the near collision differential path of the last 47 steps should be less than 40. This narrows the choice of disturbance vectors and makes it tough to obtain further improvement of the attack. Consider the relationship between the disturbance vector and number of conditions of SHA-0: in the first round, each '1' leads to 5 conditions; 2 for the second round; 4 for the third one; and the last is the same as the second round[20]. Certain type of compound disturbance can decrease the total number of conditions, for example two consecutive '1's disturbances in the third round will lead to 6 conditions, while two inconsecutive ones will lead to 8 conditions. But since there are not many disturbance vectors to choose, it is hard to find proper disturbance vectors. We try this method on reduced SHA-1 started from the second round, and see how many steps we can reach.

Consider the restriction of 40 conditions, we search for best disturbance vectors with least conditions within certain rounds, using the similar method as[9].

Table 1. Start Point of the Disturbance Vector

number	value
0	0x00000000
1	0x00000000
2	0x00000002
3	0x00000000
4	0x00000002
5	0x00000000
6	0x00000000
7	0x00000000
8	0x00000000
9	0x00000000
10	0x00000000
11	0x00000000
12	0x00000000
13	0x00000000
14	0x00000000
15	0x00000000

At last we choose the start point of the disturbance vector as described in Table 1, and the rest are calculated forward and backward from the message expansion function. It is the same start point as[21], but we use it from different step of SHA-1. From the $22nd$ step to the $70th$ step, we built a 49-step near collision differential path for SHA-1 with 37 conditions, and we neglect the special differential path in the previous 14 steps, replacing it with an inner near collision. Table 2 shows the differential path selected.

3.2 Distinguishing Attack on LPMAC-63-Step-SHA-1 Using Wang's Method

First we should make clear how many chosen messages are needed to guarantee the existence of the inner near collision. The number of sufficient conditions for the inner near-collision is 162, where 160 conditions are from the output difference of the $22nd$ step, and 2 conditions are needed for the cancelation of step 22-23. So we need $2^{162/2} = 2^{81}$ messages to guarantee an inner near collision according to the birthday attack. Then select four messages $M_0\|M_1$, $M_0\|N_1$, $M_0'\|M_1'$ and $M_0'\|N_1'$ such that $\Delta(M_0\|M_1)$ and $\Delta(M_0\|N_1)$ follow the message difference as shown in Table 2, and $M_0\|M_1$, $M_0\|N_1$ satisfy the conditions in Table 3.

Then Wang et al.'s distinguishing attack can be applied to LPMAC based on 63-step SHA-1, as described in section 2.4, and we omit the details here. The complexity and success rate are computed as follows:

- Complexity: we need to choose $4 \cdot 2^{74} \cdot (2^{81} + 2^{37}) \approx 2^{157}$ messages in total, thus the complexity is 2^{157} queries and $2^{74} \cdot 2^{81} = 2^{155}$ table lookups.

Table 2. A Differential Path for SHA-1 Reduced to 63 Steps (8-70)

step i	disturb. vector	XOR difference of the input to step i Δw_{i-1}	Δa_i	Δb_i	Δc_i	Δd_i	Δe_i	conditions
8	80000003	-	-	-	-	-	-	-
9	80000000	-	-	-	-	-	-	-
10	3	-	-	-	-	-	-	-
11	2	-	-	-	-	-	-	-
12	80000001	-	-	-	-	-	-	-
13	2	-	-	-	-	-	-	-
14	3	-	-	-	-	-	-	-
15	2	-	-	-	-	-	-	-
16	80000003	-	-	-	-	-	-	-
17	0	-	-	-	-	-	-	-
18	80000000	-	-	-	-	-	-	-
19	2	-	-	-	-	-	-	-
20	80000001	-			-		-	-
21	0	2,5,6,31,32	32,1	2	30		30,31,32	$a_{19,2}=a_{18,2}+w_{19,32}+w_{20,32}+1$, $a_{19,3}=a_{18,3}+w_{19,1}+w_{20,1}+1$
22	0	1,30		32,1	32	30		
23	2	2,31,32			30,31	32	30	$a_{23,2}=w_{22,2}$
24	2	2,7,30,31,32	2			30,31	32	$a_{24,2}=w_{23,2}$, $a_{22,4}=a_{21,4}+w_{22,2}+w_{23,2}+1$
25	0	2,7,30,31	2	2			30,31	$a_{23,4}=a_{22,4}+w_{23,2}+w_{24,2}+1$
26	0	2,32		2	32			
27	0				32	32		
28	0					32	32	
29	0	32					32	
30	2	2						$a_{30,2}=w_{29,2}$
31	0	7	2					$a_{29,4}=a_{28,4}+w_{29,2}+w_{32,7}+1$
32	2			2				$a_{32,2}=w_{32,7}+1$
33	0	7,32	2		32			$a_{31,4}=a_{30,4}+w_{32,7}+w_{34,7}$
34	2	32		2		32		$a_{34,2}=w_{34,7}+1$
35	0	7	2		32		32	$a_{33,4}=a_{32,4}+w_{34,7}+w_{35,7}$
36	3	1,32		2		32		$a_{36,1}=w_{35,1}+1$
37	0	6,7	1		32		32	$a_{35,3}=a_{34,3}+w_{35,1}+w_{37,1}+1$
38	0	1,32		1		32		$a_{37,31}=a_{35,1}+w_{35,1}+w_{38,31}$
39	2	2,31,			31		32	$a_{39,2}=w_{38,2}$, $a_{38,31}=a_{37,1}+w_{35,1}+w_{39,31}+1$
40	0	7,31	2			31		$a_{38,4}=a_{37,4}+1$
41	0	2,31		2			31	$a_{40,32}=a_{38,2}+1$
42	0	32			32			$a_{41,32}=a_{40,2}+1$
43	0	32				32		
44	2	2,32					32	$a_{44,2}=w_{43,2}$
45	0	7	2					$a_{43,4}=a_{42,4}+1$
46	0	2		2				$a_{45,32}=a_{43,2}+1$
47	0	32			32			$a_{46,32}=a_{45,2}+1$
48	0	32				32		
49	0	32					32	
50	2	2						$a_{50,2}=w_{49,2}$
51	0	7	2					$a_{49,4}=a_{48,4}+1$
52	2			2				$a_{52,2}=w_{51,2}$, $a_{51,32}=a_{49,2}+1$
53	0			2	32			$a_{51,4}=a_{50,4}+1$, $a_{52,32}=a51,2+1$
54	0			2		32		$a_{53,32}=a_{51,2}+1$
55	0				32		32	$a_{54,32}=a53,2+1$
56	0					32		
57	0						32	
58	0							
59	0							
60	0							
61	0							
62	0							
63	0							
64	4	3						$a_{64,3}=w_{63,3}$
65	0	8	3					$a_{63,5}=a_{62,5}+w_{63,3}+w_{65,3}+1$
66	0	3		3				
67	8	4,1			1			$a_{67,4}=w_{66,4}$
68	4	3,9,1	4			1		$a_{68,3}=w67,3$, $a_{66,6}=a_{65,6}+w_{66,4}+w_{68,4}+1$
69	0	8,4,1	3	4			1	$a_{67,5}=a_{66,5}+w_{67,3}+w_{69,3}+1$
70	10	5,3,2			3	2		$a_{70,5}=w_{69,5}$

- Success rate: when the LPMAC is constructed from 63-step SHA-1, the attack succeeds if another collision is detected in step 3. An inner near-collision exists with probability:

Table 3. Conditions on Messages

$w_{23,7} = w_{22,2} + 1, w_{24,7} = w_{23,2} + 1, w_{30,7} = w_{29,2} + 1, w_{36,6} = w_{35,1} + 1,$
$w_{36,7} = w_{35,1}, w_{37,2} = w_{37,1} + 1, w_{39,7} = w_{38,2} + 1, w_{40,31} = w_{35,1} + 1,$
$w_{44,7} = w_{43,2} + 1, w_{50,7} = w_{49,2} + 1, w_{52,7} = w_{51,2} + 1, w_{53,2} = w_{49,2} + 1,$
$w_{64,8} = w_{63,3} + 1, w_{67,9} = w_{66,4} + 1, w_{68,8} = w_{67,3} + 1, w_{70,10} = w_{69,5} + 1$

$$1 - (1 - \frac{1}{2^{74} \cdot 2^{162}})^{2^{74} \cdot 2^{162}} \approx 1 - e^{-1} \approx 0.63.$$

If the first collision is captured in step 2, the probability of the second collision searched in step 3 is:

$$1 - (1 - \frac{1}{2^{37}})^{2^{37}} \approx 1 - e^{-1} \approx 0.63.$$

So, if the LPMAC is constructed from 63-step SHA-1, the distinguishing attack succeeds with probability $0.63^2 \approx 0.40$.

When the LPMAC is constructed from a random function, the attack succeeds if there is no collision found in step 3, and the probability is:

$$((1 - \frac{1}{2^{160}})^{2^{37}})^{2^{162+74-160}} \approx 1.$$

Therefore, the success rate of the attack is $(0.40 + 1)/2 = 0.70$.

4   New Method to Distinguish LPMAC Based on 65-Step (12-76) SHA-1

The above attack restricts the number of conditions involved in the differential path to be less than 40, which prevents cryptanalyzing more steps. However, we find another way to construct distinguishers that looses the requirements on the disturbance vectors. Consider the start point shown in Table 4, and the full differential path for 65-step (12-76) SHA-1 is shown in Table 5.

We assume that the MAC algorithm is either a LPMAC-65-step-SHA-1 or LPMAC-RF, then build another distinguisher as follows:

1. Generate a structure of $2^{80.5}$ one-block random messages x randomly, and append a fixed one-block message y to each x. Query the MAC values for all $x\|y$.
2. Search all the colliding messages $(x\|y, x'\|y)$ satisfying $LPMAC(x\|y) = LPMAC(x'\|y)$ by birthday attack. Denote the collisions happening at the output of the first iteration as internal collisions, while the collisions at the final output as external collisioins.

Table 4. Start Point of the Disturbance Vector

number	value
0	0x00000002
1	0x00000000
2	0x00000000
3	0x00000000
4	0x00000000
5	0x00000000
6	0x00000000
7	0x00000000
8	0x00000000
9	0x00000000
10	0x00000000
11	0x00000000
12	0x00000000
13	0x00000000
14	0x00000000
15	0x00000000

3. For all the collisions collected in step 2, we append another $y' \neq y$ to x and x', respectively, ask for $(x\|y', x'\|y')$, and check if they still collide. In this way, we can figure out the internal collisions.

4. Append 2^{78} one-block message pairs (y_1, y_2), which satisfies the difference and conditions on message block, to the internal collision pair (x, x'), respectively. Query with $(x\|y_1, x'\|y_2)$, and check whether there is at least one pair follows the differential path selected. Once a message pair whose output difference is the same as shown in the differential path is found, we conclude that the MAC algorithm is LPMAC-65-step-SHA-1. Otherwise, the MAC is a LPMAC with a random function.

The data complexity of the attack is $2^{80.5} + 2 \cdot 2^{78} \approx 2^{80.9}$ chosen messages. Since we can use the birthday attack to search colliding pairs, the time complexity is about $2^{80.9}$ queries. For two random messages x and x', according to the birthday paradox and Taylor series expansion, among the $2^{80.5}$ messages, we can find an internal collision with probability:

$$1 - (1 - \frac{1}{2^{160}})^{2^{160}} \approx 1 - e^{-1} \approx 0.63.$$

While for LPMAC-SHA-1, the collision in step 4 happens with probability 2^{-78} instead of the average probability 2^{-160}. So, when the LPMAC is based on 65-step SHA-1, we can find a collision in step 4 with probability:

$$1 - (1 - \frac{1}{2^{78}})^{2^{78}} \approx 1 - e^{-1} \approx 0.63.$$

Table 5. A Differential Path for SHA-1 Reduced to 65 Steps (12-76)

step i	disturb. vector	XOR difference of the input to step i						conditions
		Δw_{i-1}	Δa_i	Δb_i	Δc_i	Δd_i	Δe_i	
12	2	2	2					
13	0	7		2				$a_{12,2}=0$
14	0	2			32			
15	1	1,32				32		$c_{14,2}=0,\ d_{14,2}=1$
16	6,32	6,32	1				32	$a_{15,1}=0,\ a_{15,32}=1$
17	80000002	1,2		1				$a_{16,32}=0$
18	2	2,5,7,31	2,32		31			$a_{17,2}=0,\ a_{17,32}=0,\ c_{17,1}=0,\ d_{17,1}=1$
19	80000002	7,31	2	2,32		31		$a_{18,2}=0,\ a_{18,31}=1$
20	0	2,5,7,30,31,32	2,32	2	32,30		31	$a_{19,2}=0,\ a_{19,32}=0,\ c_{19,2}=0,\ d_{19,2}=1,$ $c_{19,32}=0,\ d_{19,32}=1,\ a_{19,31}=0$
21	2	30,32		2,32	32	32,30		$c_{20,2}=d_{20,2},\ c_{20,32}=d_{20,32}$
22	0	7,32	2		32,30	32	32,30	$a_{21,2}=0$
23	3	1,30		2		32,30	32	$c_{22,2}=d_{22,2}$
24	0	6,7,30	1,2		32		32,30	$a_{23,1}=0,\ a_{23,2}=0$
25	2	1,32		1,2		32		$c_{24,1}=d_{24,1},\ c_{24,2}=d_{24,2}$
26	2	2,7,31	2		31,32		32	$a_{25,2}=0$
27	1	1,2,7,31,32	2	2		31,32		$a_{26,2}=0,\ c_{26,2}=d_{26,2}$
28	0	2,6,31	1	2	32		31,32	$a_{27,1}=0,\ c_{27,2}=d_{27,2}$
29	2	1,2		1	32	32		$c_{28,1}=d_{28,1}$
30	2	2,7,31	2		31	32	32	$a_{29,2}=0$
31	1	1,2,7,31,32	2	2		31	32	$a_{30,2}=0,\ c_{30,2}=d_{30,2}$
32	0	2,6,31,32	1	2	32		31	$a_{31,1}=0,\ c_{31,2}=d_{31,2}$
33	0	1		1	32	32		$c_{32,1}=d_{32,1}$
34	2	2,31			31	32	32	
35	3	1,2,7,31,32	2			31	32	$a_{34,2}=0$
36	0	2,6,7,31	1,2	2			31	$a_{35,1}=0,\ a_{35,2}=0,\ c_{35,2}=d_{35,2}$
37	2	1,32		1,2	32			$c_{36,1}=d_{36,1},\ c_{36,2}=d_{36,2}$
38	2	2,7,31	2		31,32	32		$a_{37,2}=0$
39	0	2,7,31	2	2		31,32	32	$a_{38,2}=0,\ c_{38,2}=d_{38,2}$
40	0	2,31		2	32		31,32	$c_{39,2}=d_{39,2}$
41	2	2			32	32		$c_{40,32}=-d_{40,32}$
42	0	7	2			32	32	$a_{41,2}=0,\ b_{41,32}=-c_{41,32}$
43	0	2,32		2			32	$c_{42,2}=-d_{42,2}$
44	0	32			32			$b_{43,32}=-d_{43,32}$
45	2	2,32				32		$b_{44,32}=-c_{44,32}$
46	0	7,32	2				32	$a_{45,2}=0$
47	2			2				$c_{46,2}=-d_{46,2}$
48	0	7,32	2		32			$a_{47,2}=0,\ b_{47,32}=-d_{47,32}$
49	2	32		2		32		$c_{48,2}=-d_{48,2},\ b_{48,32}=-c_{48,32}$
50	0	7	2		32		32	$a_{49,2}=0,\ b_{49,32}=-c_{49,32}$
51	2	32		2		32		$c_{50,2}=-d_{50,2},\ b_{50,32}=-c_{50,32}$
52	0	7	2		32		32	$a_{51,2}=0,\ b_{51,32}=-c_{51,32}$
53	0	2,32		2		32		$c_{52,2}=-d_{52,2},\ b_{52,32}=-c_{52,32}$
54	0				32		32	$b_{53,32}=-d_{53,32}$
55	0	32				32		$b_{54,32}=-c_{54,32}$
56	0	32					32	
57	0							
58	0							
59	0							
60	0							
61	0							
62	0							
63	0							
64	0							
65	0							
66	0							
67	4	3						
68	0	8	3					$a_{67,3}=0$
69	0	3		3				$c_{68,3}=d_{68,3}$
70	8	4,1			1			
71	0	9,1	4			1		$a_{70,4}=0$
72	0	4,1		4			1	$c_{71,4}=d_{71,4}$
73	10	5,2			2			
74	0	10,2	5			2		$a_{73,5}=0$
75	8	4,5,2		5			2	$c_{74,5}=d_{74,5}$
76	20	6,9,3	4		3			$a_{75,4}=0$

For LPMAC-RF, the attack succeeds if there is no collision found in step 4. There are 2^{78} pairs in total, so the probability that there is no collision among them is:

$$(1 - \frac{1}{2^{160}})^{2^{78}} \approx 1.$$

Hence, the success rate of this attack is:

$$0.63 \times (0.63 \times \frac{1}{2} + 1 \times \frac{1}{2}) \approx 0.51.$$

The success rate can be increased by repeating the attack several times.

Compared with Wang et al.'s attack, this attack requires less chosen messages. So we can see that if we apply a distinguishing attack on reduced SHA-1 but don't start from the first round, Wang's attack does not show advantage. Otherwise, because their method can ignore the conditions in the first 14 steps of the complicated differential path of the first round, it has advantage. While for the latter distinguisher we presented in section 4, it is hard to find a suitable differential path start from the first step, because there are too many conditions in the first round.

5   Conclusion

We first introduce Wang et al.'s distinguishing attack presented at FSE 2009 which can distinguish LPMAC based on 61-step SHA-1[21], and apply it to LP-MAC with 63-step (8-70) SHA-1. Then we built another new distinguisher which works for LPMAC instantiated with 65-step (12-76) SHA-1. The complexity of the former one is 2^{157} queries with success rate 0.70, while for the latter one, it only needs $2^{80.9}$ queries, and the success probability is 0.51. The success rate can be increased by repeating the attack several times.

References

1. Bellare, M., Canetti, R., Krawczyk, H.: Keying Hash Functions for Message Authentication. In: Koblitz, N. (ed.) CRYPTO 1996. LNCS, vol. 1109, pp. 1–15. Springer, Heidelberg (1996)
2. Biham, E., Chen, R.: Near-Collisions of SHA-0. In: Franklin, M. (ed.) CRYPTO 2004. LNCS, vol. 3152, pp. 290–305. Springer, Heidelberg (2004)
3. Biham, E., Chen, R., Joux, A., Carribault, P., Lemuet, C., Jalby, W.: Collisions of SHA-0 and Reduced SHA-1. In: Cramer, R. (ed.) EUROCRYPT 2005. LNCS, vol. 3494, pp. 36–57. Springer, Heidelberg (2005)
4. Contini, S., Yin, Y.L.: Forgery and Partial Key-Recovery Attacks on HMAC and NMAC Using Hash Collisions. In: Lai, X., Chen, K. (eds.) ASIACRYPT 2006. LNCS, vol. 4284, pp. 37–53. Springer, Heidelberg (2006)
5. den Boer, B., Bosselaers, A.: Collisions for the Compression Function of MD5. In: Helleseth, T. (ed.) EUROCRYPT 1993. LNCS, vol. 765, pp. 293–304. Springer, Heidelberg (1994)

6. Fouque, P.A., Leurent, G., Nguyen, P.Q.: Full Key-Recovery Attacks on HMAC/NMAC-MD4 and NMAC-MD5. In: Menezes, A. (ed.) CRYPTO 2007. LNCS, vol. 4622, pp. 13–30. Springer, Heidelberg (2007)

7. Galvin, J.M., McCloghrie, K., Davin, J.R.: Secure Management of SNMP Networks. Integrated Network Management II, 703–714 (1991)

8. Kim, J., Biryukov, A., Preneel, B., Hong, S.: On the Security of HMAC and NMAC Based on HAVAL, MD4, MD5, SHA-0, and SHA-1. In: De Prisco, R., Yung, M. (eds.) SCN 2006. LNCS, vol. 4116, pp. 242–256. Springer, Heidelberg (2006)

9. Matusiewicz, K., Pieprzyk, J.: Finding Good Differential Patterns for Attacks on SHA-1. In: Ytrehus, Ø. (ed.) WCC 2005. LNCS, vol. 3969, pp. 164–177. Springer, Heidelberg (2006)

10. NIST. Secure Hash Standard. Federal Information Processing Standard. FIPS-180-1 (1995)

11. Preneel, B., van Oorschot, P.: MDx-MAC and Building Fast MACs from Hash Functions. In: Coppersmith, D. (ed.) CRYPTO 1995. LNCS, vol. 963, pp. 1–14. Springer, Heidelberg (1995)

12. Rechberger, C., Rijmen, V.: On Authentication with HMAC and Non-random Properties. In: Dietrich, S., Dhamija, R. (eds.) FC 2007 and USEC 2007. LNCS, vol. 4886, pp. 119–133. Springer, Heidelberg (2007)

13. Rechberger, C., Rijmen, V.: New Results on NMAC/HMAC when Instantiated with Popular Hash Functions. Journal of Universal Computer Science 14(3), 347–376 (2008)

14. Tsudik, G.: Message Authentication with One-Way Hash Functions. ACM Comput. Commun. Rev. 22(5), 29–38 (1992)

15. Wang, L., Ohta, K., Kunihiro, N.: New Key-Recovery Attacks on HMAC/NMAC-MD4 and NMAC-MD5. In: Smart, N.P. (ed.) EUROCRYPT 2008. LNCS, vol. 4965, pp. 237–253. Springer, Heidelberg (2008)

16. Wang, X., Lai, X., Feng, D., Chen, H., Yu, X.: Cryptanalysis of the Hash Functions MD4 and RIPEMD. In: Cramer, R. (ed.) EUROCRYPT 2005. LNCS, vol. 3494, pp. 1–18. Springer, Heidelberg (2005)

17. Wang, X., Yu, H.: How to Break MD5 and Other Hash Functions. In: Cramer, R. (ed.) EUROCRYPT 2005. LNCS, vol. 3494, pp. 19–35. Springer, Heidelberg (2005)

18. Wang, X., Yin, Y.L., Yu, H.: Finding Collisions in the Full SHA-1. In: Shoup, V. (ed.) CRYPTO 2005. LNCS, vol. 3621, pp. 17–36. Springer, Heidelberg (2005)

19. Wang, X., Yu, H., Wang, W., Zhang, H., Zhan, T.: Cryptanalysis on HMAC/NMAC-MD5 and MD5-MAC. In: Joux, A. (ed.) EUROCRYPT 2009. LNCS, vol. 5479, pp. 121–133. Springer, Heidelberg (2010)

20. Wang, X., Yu, H., Yin, Y.L.: Efficient Collision Search Attacks on SHA-0. In: Shoup, V. (ed.) CRYPTO 2005. LNCS, vol. 3621, pp. 1–16. Springer, Heidelberg (2005)

21. Wang, X., Wang, W., Jia, K., Wang, M.: New Distinguishing Attack on MAC Using Secret-Prefix Method. In: Dunkelman, O. (ed.) Fast Software Encryption. LNCS, vol. 5665, pp. 363–374. Springer, Heidelberg (2009)

Cryptanalysis of a Message Recognition Protocol by Mashatan and Stinson

Madeline González Muñiz and Rainer Steinwandt

Department of Mathematical Sciences, Florida Atlantic University,
777 Glades Road, Boca Raton, FL 33431, USA
{mgonza29,rsteinwa}@fau.edu

Abstract. At CANS 2008, Mashatan and Stinson suggested a message recognition protocol for ad hoc pervasive networks. The protocol provides a procedure to resynchronize in case of a (possibly adversarial) disruption of communication. We show that this resynchronization process does not provide the functionality intended and in fact enables an adversary to create selective forgeries. The computational effort for the attack is negligible and allows the insertion of arbitrary messages.

Keywords: Cryptanalysis, message recognition, ad hoc network.

1 Introduction

In [MS08], Mashatan and Stinson propose *a new message recognition protocol for ad hoc pervasive networks*, aiming at scenarios with resource restricted devices. Their protocol relies on the use of a cryptographic hash function providing suitable guarantees, and the protocol avoids the use of asymmetric cryptography. In informal terms, the scenario in [MS08] can be summarized as follows: during an initialization phase, two parties A and B are connected through an authentic channel of low bandwidth. While this narrow-band channel can be eavesdropped, the adversary is confined to be *passive*; i. e., no messages can be altered, deleted or inserted. Later on, A and B are connected via a public broadband channel that is completely controlled by the, now *active*, adversary. The protocol in [MS08] tries to make sure that messages sent over this public insecure channel by A are only accepted by B if they indeed originate from the party A with which the initialization phase was performed. Further, according to [MS08], the proposed protocol *provides a practical procedure for resynchronization in case of any adversarial disruption or communication failure*.

Mashatan and Stinson's proposal can be be seen in the same line of research as, for instance, Anderson et al.'s *Guy Fawkes protocol* [ABC+98], Stajano and Anderson's *resurrecting duckling* [SA00], Mitchell's scheme for remote user authentication [Mit03], Weimerskirch and Westhoff's *zero common-knowledge authentication* [WW04], and Lucks et al.'s *Jane Doe protocol* [LZWW08].

Our contribution. Below, we show that the resynchronization mechanism suggested by Mashatan and Stinson unfortunately does not work as intended, but

D. Lee and S. Hong (Eds.): ICISC 2009, LNCS 5984, pp. 362–373, 2010.
© Springer-Verlag Berlin Heidelberg 2010

actually enables an attack: an adversary can abuse the resynchronization process to send forged messages that are accepted as legitimate. The computational effort for the attack is negligible, and there is no restriction on the contents of the messages that can be inserted.

2 The Proposal from CANS 2008

This section recalls Mashatan and Stinson's proposal from CANS 2008 to the extent necessary for describing our attack. The protocol splits into three components, which we discuss in the next three subsections. For more details, we refer to the original paper [MS08], which elaborates on the underlying assumptions on the hash function H (*pre-image resistance, paired second pre-image resistance, paired collision resistance, binding pre-image resistance*, for instance). We denote *passwords*[1] for party A by x_i and for party B by y_i. Writing H for the underlying hash function, we set $X_i := H(x_i)$, $Y_i := H(y_i)$ and refer to the X_i and Y_i as *committing hash values* of the passwords. Finally, the *binding hash values* are denoted by $\mathcal{X}_{i(i+1)}$ and $\mathcal{Y}_{i(i+1)}$ for A and B respectively, where $\mathcal{X}_{i(i+1)} := H(x_i, X_{i+1})$ and $\mathcal{Y}_{i(i+1)} := H(y_i, Y_{i+1})$.

At any given time, the internal state of A is given by an 8-tuple $(x_i, x_{i+1}, X_i, X_{i+1}, \mathcal{X}_{i(i+1)}, y_{i-1}^*, Y_i^*, \mathcal{Y}_{i(i+1)}^*)$ with y_{i-1}^*, Y_i^*, $\mathcal{Y}_{i(i+1)}^*$ being B's most recent password, committing hash value, and binding hash value accepted by A. Likewise, the internal state of B is given by an 8-tuple $(y_i, y_{i+1}, Y_i, Y_{i+1}, \mathcal{Y}_{i(i+1)}, x_{i-1}^*, X_i^*, \mathcal{X}_{i(i+1)}^*)$ with x_{i-1}^*, X_i^*, $\mathcal{X}_{i(i+1)}^*$ being A's most recent password, committing hash value, and binding hash value accepted by B.

Adversarial model. During the initialization phase of the protocol, the involved parties A and B exchange information through an authenticated channel which we will denote by $\Longrightarrow$. The adversary is restricted to passive eavesdropping of this channel; no delaying, deleting, inserting, or altering of messages is allowed. During the execution of the protocol and in the resynchronization process, A and B communicate over an insecure channel which we denote by $\longrightarrow$. The adversary has full control over the insecure channel, and in particular can delete and insert messages. The goal of the adversary is to create a forgery; i.e., to provoke a situation where B accepts a message-recipient pair (A, m) where the message m has never been sent by A.

2.1 Initialization Phase

Figure 1 shows the steps performed by A and B in the initialization phase. In summary, during the initialization phase A, does the following:

---

[1] Here we follow the terminology in [MS08] and stress that exhausting all possible passwords is assumed to be infeasible. In particular, this use of the term *password* differs from the common use in the context of password authenticated key establishment.

A	B
Choose random x_0 and x_1 and form $\xrightarrow{X_0, \mathcal{X}_{01}}$ Receive $X_0, \mathcal{X}_{01}$. $X_0 := H(x_0)$, $X_1 := H(x_1)$, and $\mathcal{X}_{01} := H(x_0, X_1)$.	
Receive $Y_0, \mathcal{Y}_{01}$. $\xleftarrow{Y_0, \mathcal{Y}_{01}}$	Choose random y_0 and y_1 and form $Y_0 := H(y_0)$, $Y_1 := H(y_1)$, and $\mathcal{Y}_{01} := H(y_0, Y_1)$.
Let $y^*_{-1} := \perp$, so A's initial state is $(x_0, x_1, X_0, X_1, \mathcal{X}_{01}, \perp, Y_0, \mathcal{Y}_{01})$.	Let $x^*_{-1} := \perp$ so B's initial state is $(y_0, y_1, Y_0, Y_1, Y_{01}, \perp, X_0, \mathcal{X}_{01})$

Fig. 1. Initialization phase of [MS08]

- Choose random x_0 and x_1.
- Compute $X_0 := H(x_0)$, $X_1 := H(x_1)$, and $\mathcal{X}_{01} := H(x_0, X_1)$.
- Send $X_0, \mathcal{X}_{01}$ to B over the authenticated channel.
- Receive Y_0, and $\mathcal{Y}_{01}$ from B over the authenticated channel.
- Set $y^*_{-1} := \perp$, $Y_0^* := Y_0$, $\mathcal{Y}_0^* := \mathcal{Y}_0$.

Similarly, B performs the following steps:

- Choose random y_0 and y_1.
- Compute $Y_0 := H(y_0)$, $Y_1 := H(y_1)$, and $\mathcal{Y}_{01} := H(y_0, Y_1)$.
- Send $Y_0, \mathcal{Y}_{01}$ to A over the authenticated channel.
- Receive X_0, and $\mathcal{X}_{01}$ from A over the authenticated channel.
- Set $x^*_{-1} := \perp$, $X_0^* := X_0$, $\mathcal{X}_0^* := \mathcal{X}_0$.

The values $X_0, \mathcal{X}_{01}, Y_0, \mathcal{Y}_{01}$ which are interchanged by A and B over the authenticated channel can be eavesdropped—but not altered—by the adversary.

2.2   Execution of the Protocol

Once the initialization phase has been completed, the actual protocol execution can take place as described in Figure 2.

Summarizing, on input a message-recipient pair (m, B), A does the following during a protocol execution:

- Choose a random x_2 and form $X_2 := H(x_2)$, $\mathcal{X}_{12} := H(x_1, X_2)$.
- Compute $h := H(m, x_0)$.
- Send (m, h) and wait to receive $y_0', Y_1', \mathcal{Y}_{01}'$ from B. Resend if B does not respond.
- If $H(y_0') = Y_0^*$ and $H(y_0', Y_1') = \mathcal{Y}_{01}$, send $x_0, X_1, \mathcal{X}_{01}$ to B and update the internal state to $(x_1, x_2, X_1, X_2, \mathcal{X}_{12}, y_0', Y_1', \mathcal{Y}_{12}')$; else initiate resynchronization.

A's internal state:	B's internal state:
$(x_0, x_1, X_0, X_1, \mathcal{X}_{01}, y^*_{-1}, Y^*_0, \mathcal{Y}^*_{01})$	$(y_0, y_1, Y_0, Y_1, \mathcal{Y}_{01}, x^*_{-1}, X^*_0, \mathcal{X}^*_{01})$

A	**B**

Receive input (m, B). Choose a random x_2 and form $X_2 := H(x_2)$, $\mathcal{X}_{12} := H(x_1, X_2)$. Compute $h := H(m, x_0)$. $\xrightarrow{\ m,h\ }$ Receive m', h'.

Receive $y'_0, Y'_1, \mathcal{Y}'_{12}$. $\xleftarrow{\ y_0, Y_1, \mathcal{Y}_{12}\ }$ Choose a random y_2 and form $Y_2 := H(y_2)$, $\mathcal{Y}_{12} := H(y_1, Y_2)$.

If $H(y'_0) = Y^*_0$ and $H(y'_0, Y'_1) = \mathcal{Y}^*_{01}$, then send x_0, X_1, $\mathcal{X}_{12}$ and update your internal state as follows: $(x_1, x_2, X_1, X_2, \mathcal{X}_{12}, y'_0, Y'_1, \mathcal{Y}'_{12})$ else initiate resynchronization. $\xrightarrow{\ x_0, X_1, \mathcal{X}_{12}\ }$ Receive x'_0, X'_1, $\mathcal{X}'_{12}$. If $H(x'_0) = X^*_0$, $H(x'_0, X'_1) = \mathcal{X}^*_{01}$, and $h' = H(m', x')$, then update your internal state as follows: $(y_1, y_2, Y_1, Y_2, \mathcal{Y}_{12}, x'_0, X'_1, \mathcal{X}'_{12})$ and output (A, m') else initiate resynchronization.

Fig. 2. Protocol execution of [MS08]

After receiving (m', h'), B does the following:

- Choose a random y_2 and compute $Y_2 := H(y_2)$, $\mathcal{Y}_{12} := H(y_1, Y_2)$.
- Send $y_0, Y_1, \mathcal{Y}_{12}$ to A and wait to receive $x'_0, X'_1, \mathcal{X}_{12}$. Resend if A does not respond.
- If $H(x'_0) = X^*_0$, $H(x'_0, X'_1) = \mathcal{X}_{01}$, and $h' = H(m', x'_0)$ then update the internal state to $(y_1, y_2, Y_1, Y_2, \mathcal{Y}_{12}, x'_0, X'_1, \mathcal{X}'_{12})$ and output (A, m'); else initiate resynchronization.

Note that all messages are sent over an insecure channel, where the adversary can delete, modify, and insert messages at will. Further, it is possible for A to update its internal state after sending x_0, X_1, $\mathcal{X}_{12}$ without B updating its state. Therefore, the resynchronization process that follows is not symmetric.

2.3   Resynchronization Process

In the case of adversarial intrusion or communication failure, either A or B can initiate the resynchronization process in Figure 3. As shown in this figure, B has two sets of conditions that can update its internal state, whereas A has only one.

We can summarize the resynchronization process as follows:

- A and B respectively choose random x_2, y_2 and form $X_2 := H(x_2)$, $Y_2 := H(y_2)$, $\mathcal{X}_{12} := H(x_1, X_2)$, and $\mathcal{Y}_{12} := H(y_1, Y_2)$.

A's internal state:	B's internal state:
$(x_0, x_1, X_0, X_1, \mathcal{X}_{01}, y^*_{-1}, Y^*_0, \mathcal{Y}^*_{01})$	$(y_0, y_1, Y_0, Y_1, \mathcal{Y}_{01}, x^*_{-1}, X^*_0, \mathcal{X}^*_{01})$
A	**B**
Choose a random x_2 and form $X_2 := H(x_2)$, $\mathcal{X}_{12} := H(x_1, X_2)$.	Choose a random y_2 and form $Y_2 := H(y_2)$, $\mathcal{Y}_{12} := H(y_1, Y_2)$.
Receive $y'_0, Y'_1, \mathcal{Y}'_{12}$. $\xleftarrow{y_0, Y_1, \mathcal{Y}_{12}}$ Send $y_0, Y_1, \mathcal{Y}_{12}$.	
Send $x_0, X_1, \mathcal{X}_{12}$. $\xrightarrow{x_0, X_1, \mathcal{X}_{12}}$ Receive $x'_0, X'_1, \mathcal{X}'_{12}$.	
If $y^*_{-1} = y'_0$ and $Y^*_0 = Y'_1$, then $\mathcal{Y}^*_{01} := \mathcal{Y}'_{12}$, else initiate resynchronization.	If $x^*_{-1} = x'_0$ and $X^*_0 = X'_1$, then $\mathcal{X}^*_{01} := \mathcal{X}'_{12}$, otherwise if $H(x'_0) = X^*_0$ and $H(x'_0, X'_1) = \mathcal{X}^*_{01}$, then $x^*_{-1} := x'_0$, $X^*_0 := X'_1$, $\mathcal{X}^*_{01} := \mathcal{X}'_{12}$ else initiate resynchronization.

Fig. 3. Resynchronization process of [MS08]

- B sends $y_0, Y_1, \mathcal{Y}_{01}$ to A.
- A sends $x_0, X_1, \mathcal{X}_{01}$ to B.
- If $y^*_{-1} = y'_0$ and $Y^*_0 = Y'_1$, then A sets $\mathcal{Y}^*_{01} := \mathcal{Y}'_{12}$; else A initiates resynchronization.
- If $x^*_{-1} = x'_0$ and $X^*_0 = X'_1$, then B sets $\mathcal{X}^*_{01} := \mathcal{X}'_{12}$, else if $H(x'_0) = X^*_0$ and $H(x'_0, X'_1) = \mathcal{X}^*_{01}$, then B sets $x^*_{-1} := x'_0$, $X^*_0 := X'_1$, $\mathcal{X}^*_{01} := \mathcal{X}'_{12}$; else B initiates resynchronization.

During resynchronization, A can only refresh the value $\mathcal{Y}^*_{01}$, whereas B can either refresh the value $\mathcal{X}^*_{01}$ or update $x^*_{-1}, X^*_0, \mathcal{X}^*_{01}$.

3   Provoking an Unrecoverable Situation

If A or B suspects a communication failure or a possible adversarial intrusion, it can initiate the resynchronization process. Here we show that

- an adversary can create a situation where A keeps on initiating the resynchronization process, but the protocol does not recover, and
- an adversary can create a situation where B keeps on initiating the resynchronization process, but the protocol does not recover.

It is worth noting that in both cases, modification of a single message on the public channel is sufficient; i. e., the adversary does not have to stay "online" for achieving this type of denial of service: these attacks are qualitatively different from simply blocking communication between A and B. Section 4 builds on these observations to create a successful forgery.

A's internal state:
$(x_0, x_1, X_0, X_1, \mathcal{X}_{01}, \perp, Y_0, \mathcal{Y}_{01})$

B's internal state:
$(y_0, y_1, Y_0, Y_1, \mathcal{Y}_{01}, \perp, X_0, \mathcal{X}_{01})$

execution of the protocol

A	**B**

Receive input (m, B). Choose random x_2 and form $X_2 := H(x_2)$, $\mathcal{X}_{12} := H(x_1, X_2)$. Compute $h := H(m, x_0)$.

$\xrightarrow{m,h}$

Receive m', h'.

Receive y_0', Y_1', $\mathcal{Y}_{12}'$.

$\xleftarrow{y_0, Y_1, \mathcal{Y}_{12}}$

Choose a random y_2 and form $Y_2 := H(y_2)$, $\mathcal{Y}_{12} := H(y_1, Y_2)$.

Suppose that $H(y_0') \neq Y_0^*$ or $H(y_0', Y_1') \neq \mathcal{Y}_{01}^*$, hence initiate resynchronization.

A's internal state:
$(x_0, x_1, X_0, X_1, \mathcal{X}_{01}, \perp, Y_0, \mathcal{Y}_{01})$

B's internal state:
$(y_0, y_1, Y_0, Y_1, \mathcal{Y}_{01}, \perp, X_0, \mathcal{X}_{01})$

resynchronization process

A	**B**

Choose a random x_2 and form $X_2 := H(x_2)$, $\mathcal{X}_{12} := H(x_1, X_2)$.

Choose a random y_2 and form $Y_2 := H(y_2)$, $\mathcal{Y}_{12} := H(y_1, Y_2)$

Receive y_0', Y_1', $\mathcal{Y}_{12}'$.

$\xleftarrow{y_0, Y_1, \mathcal{Y}_{12}}$

Send y_0, Y_1, $\mathcal{Y}_{12}$

Send x_0, X_1, $\mathcal{X}_{12}$.

$\xrightarrow{x_0, X_1, \mathcal{X}_{12}}$

Receive x_0', X_1', $\mathcal{X}_{12}'$.

Since $y_{-1}^* \neq y_0'$ and $Y_{0*} \neq Y_1'$, initiate resynchronization.

Fig. 4. Unrecoverability after a resynchronization initiated by A

A's internal state: B's internal state:
$(x_0, x_1, X_0, X_1, \mathcal{X}_{01}, \bot, Y_0, \mathcal{Y}_{01})$ $(y_0, y_1, Y_0, Y_1, \mathcal{Y}_{01}, \bot, X_0, \mathcal{X}_{01})$

execution of the protocol

A   **B**

Receive input (m, B). Choose $\xrightarrow{m,h}$ Receive m', h'.
random x_2 and form $X_2 :=$
$H(x_2)$, $\mathcal{X}_{12} := H(x_1, X_2)$. Compute $h := H(m, x_0)$.

Receive y_0', Y_1', $\mathcal{Y}_{12}'$. $\xleftarrow{y_0, Y_1, \mathcal{Y}_{12}}$ Choose a random y_2 and form
                                                $Y_2 := H(y_2)$, $\mathcal{Y}_{12} := H(y_1, Y_2)$.

Suppose that $H(y_0') = Y_0^*$ $\xrightarrow{x_0, X_1, \mathcal{X}_{12}}$ Receive x_0', X_1', $\mathcal{X}_{12}'$. Suppose
and $H(y_0', Y_1') = \mathcal{Y}_{01}^*$. Then $H(x_0') \neq X_0^*$, or $H(x_0', X_1') \neq$
send x_0, X_1, $\mathcal{X}_{12}$ and up- $\mathcal{X}_{01}^*$, or $h' \neq H(m', x_0')$; then ini-
date the internal state to   tiate resynchronization.
$(x_1, x_2, X_1, X_2, \mathcal{X}_{12}, y_0', Y_1', \mathcal{Y}_{12}')$.

A's internal state: B's internal state:
$(x_1, x_2, X_1, X_2, \mathcal{X}_{12}, y_0', Y_1', \mathcal{Y}_{12}')$ $(y_0, y_1, Y_0, Y_1, \mathcal{Y}_{01}, \bot, X_0, \mathcal{X}_{01})$

resynchronization process

A   **B**

Choose a random x_3 and form   Choose a random y_2 and form
$X_3 := H(x_3)$, $\mathcal{X}_{23} := H(x_2, X_3)$. $Y_2 := H(y_2)$, $\mathcal{Y}_{12} := H(y_1, Y_2)$

Receive y_0', Y_1', $\mathcal{Y}_{12}'$. $\xleftarrow{y_0, Y_1, \mathcal{Y}_{12}}$ Send y_0, Y_1, $\mathcal{Y}_{12}$

Send x_1, X_2, $\mathcal{X}_{23}$. $\xrightarrow{x_1, X_2, \mathcal{X}_{23}}$ Receive x_1', X_2', $\mathcal{X}_{23}'$.

                                                Since $x_{-1}^* \neq x_1'$ and $H(x_1') \neq$
                                                X_0^*, initiate resynchronization.

Fig. 5. Unrecoverability after a resynchronization initiated by B

3.1 Unrecoverability with Resynchronization Initiated by A

As depicted in Figure 4, assume that after a successful initialization phase, A has internal state $(x_0, x_1, X_0, X_1, X_{01}, \perp, Y_0, \mathcal{Y}_{01})$, and B has internal state $(y_0, y_1, Y_0, Y_1, Y_{01}, \perp, X_0, \mathcal{X}_{01})$. Now A starts executing a protocol as specified in Section 2.2, sending a message m along with matching h-value to B. In response to this, B sends y_0, Y_1 and $\mathcal{Y}_{12}$.

The adversary can replace y_0 with a (random) value such that A's validity check $H(y_0') = Y_0$ and $H(y_0', Y_1') = \mathcal{Y}_{01}^*$ fails. Following the protocol specification, now A initiates the resynchronization process (see upper part of Figure 4). Note that so far A never updated its internal state and still has stored the values $y_{-1}^* = \perp$, $Y_{0*} = Y_0$, and $\mathcal{Y}_{01}^* = \mathcal{Y}_{01}$.

Now, in the resynchronization phase, B sends to A the values y_0', Y_1', and $\mathcal{Y}_{12}'$. These values do not match the values stored by A, however. Consequently, A initiates resynchronization again. Re-running the resynchronization will not help the situation, so the protocol becomes unrecoverable. Figure 4 summarizes the sequence of events.

3.2 Unrecoverability with Resynchronization Initiated by B

Consider a second scenario as in Figure 5. Assume that after a successful initialization phase A has internal state $(x_0, x_1, X_0, X_1, \mathcal{X}_{01}, \perp, Y_0, \mathcal{Y}_{01})$, and B has internal state $(y_0, y_1, Y_0, Y_1, \mathcal{Y}_{01}, \perp, X_0, \mathcal{X}_{01})$ as before. As before, A initiates an execution of the protocol in [MS08] by sending a message m along with matching h-value to B. In response, A receives y_0', Y_1', and $\mathcal{Y}_{12}'$ from B. Our adversary faithfully transmits these messages, so that A's validity check succeeds, and A updates its internal state to $(x_1, x_2, X_1, X_2, X_{12}, y_0', Y_1', \mathcal{Y}_{12}')$. Further, A sends x_0, X_1 and $\mathcal{X}_{12}$ to B. Our adversary can replace x_0 with a (random) value so that the values x_0', X_1', and $\mathcal{X}_{12}'$ received by B from A do not verify. Consequently, following the protocol specification in Section 2.2, B will initiate the resynchronization process. Note that so far B never updated its internal state and has stored $x_{-1}^* = \perp$, $X_0^* = X_0$, and $\mathcal{X}_{01}^* = \mathcal{X}_{01}$.

In the resynchronization process, A sends x_1, X_2, and $\mathcal{X}_{23}$ to B. Even if the values x_1', X_2', and $\mathcal{X}_{23}'$ received by B are identical to the values sent by A, $x_1' \neq x_{-1}^*$ and $H(x_1') \neq X_0^*$ cause B to initiate resynchronization again. Re-running the resynchronization will not resolve the situation, and analogously, as in the previous section the protocol becomes unrecoverable. Figure 5 summarizes the sequence of events.

4 Creating a Forgery

To describe the attack, in subsequent figures we denote the adversary by F. Messages delivered faithfully by F are denoted by $\rightharpoonup$ and the messages created by F are denoted by $\rightarrow$. To begin our attack, we assume that A and B have successfully completed the initialization phase of the protocol. From here on, the attack unfolds in four steps:

1. executing the message recognition protocol
2. first resynchronization (unsuccessful)
3. second resynchronization (successful)
4. executing the message recognition protocol a second time

The subsequent four subsections elaborate on each of these steps.

4.1   Execution of the Recognition Protocol

In this first step, the goal of F is to learn the initial password x_0 from A. For this, F proceeds as shown in Figure 6.

A's internal state:
$(x_0, x_1, X_0, X_1, \mathcal{X}_{01}, \perp, Y_0, \mathcal{Y}_{01})$

B's internal state:
$(y_0, y_1, Y_0, Y_1, \mathcal{Y}_{01}, \perp, X_0, \mathcal{X}_{01})$

A	F	B

Receive (m, B) as input. Choose a random x_2 and form $X_2 := H(x_2)$, $\mathcal{X}_{12} := H(x_1, X_2)$. Compute $h := H(m, x_0)$.
  $\xrightarrow{m,h}$ Receive m, h.

Receive y_0, Y_1, $\mathcal{Y}_{12}$.
  $\xleftarrow{y_0, Y_1, \mathcal{Y}_{12}}$ Choose a random y_2 and form $Y_2 := H(x_2)$, $\mathcal{Y}_{12} := H(y_1, Y_2)$.

Since $H(y_0) = Y_0$ and $H(y_0, Y_1) = \mathcal{Y}_{01}$, send x_0, X_1, $\mathcal{X}_{12}$ and update the internal state to $(x_1, x_2, X_1, X_2, \mathcal{X}_{12}, y_0, Y_1, \mathcal{Y}_{12})$.
  $\xrightarrow{\tilde{x}, X_1, \mathcal{X}_{12}}$ Since $H(\tilde{x}) \neq X_0$ initiate resynchronization.

Fig. 6. First step of the attack: execution of the protocol

Summarizing, in this first step of the attack F does the following:

- Forward m, h faithfully from A to B.
- Forward the values y_0, Y_1, $\mathcal{Y}_{12}$ sent from B faithfully to A.
- Choose a (random) $\tilde{x} \neq x_0$ so that that $H(\tilde{x}) \neq X_0$.
- Send $\tilde{x}$, X_1, $\mathcal{X}_{12}$ to B, i.e., replace the value x_0 sent by A with $\tilde{x}$.

Since $H(\tilde{x}) \neq X_0$, B initiates resynchronization after A has already updated its internal state to $(x_1, x_2, X_1, X_2, \mathcal{X}_{12}, y_0, Y_1, \mathcal{Y}_{12})$, and we are in similar situation to that discussed in Section 3.2.

4.2 First Resynchronization (Unsuccessful)

In this second step of the attack, F extracts the value x_1 from A, using the resynchronization process as shown in Figure 7.

Thus F's actions in this step of the attack can be summarized as follows:

- Forward the values y_0, Y_1, $\mathcal{Y}_{12}$ sent by B faithfully to A.
- Receive x_1, X_2, $\mathcal{X}_{23}$ from A.
- Send $\widetilde{x}$, X_1, $\mathcal{X}_{12}$ to B, i.e., the same values as above.

Since y_0 and Y_1 match what A has stored, A refreshes the value $\mathcal{Y}_{12}$ with the new one sent by B. Recall that B has two sets of conditions to check, as shown in Figure 3. As B has not accepted a password from A yet, we clearly have $x_{-1} \neq \widetilde{x}$ and the first condition is not met. Further, we have $H(\widetilde{x}) \neq X_0$, so the second condition is not met either. Hence the resynchronization is unsuccessful and B initiates resynchronization a second time. Note that at this point, F knows both x_0 and x_1.

A's internal state: $(x_1, x_2, X_1, X_2, \mathcal{X}_{12}, y_0, Y_1, \mathcal{Y}_{12})$		B's internal state: $(y_0, y_1, Y_0, Y_1, \mathcal{Y}_{01}, \perp, X_0, \mathcal{X}_{01})$
A	**F**	**B**
Choose a random x_3, and form $X_3 := H(x_3)$, $\mathcal{X}_{23} := H(x_2, X_3)$.		Choose a random y_2 and form $Y_2 := H(y_2)$, $\mathcal{Y}_{12} := H(y_1, Y_2)$.
Receive y_0, Y_1, $\mathcal{Y}_{12}$.	$\xleftarrow{\;y_0, Y_1, \mathcal{Y}_{12}\;}$	Send y_0, Y_1, $\mathcal{Y}_{12}$.
Send x_1, X_2, $\mathcal{X}_{23}$	$\xrightarrow{\;\widetilde{x}, X_1, \mathcal{X}_{12}\;}$	Since $x_{-1}^{*} \neq \widetilde{x}$, and $H(\widetilde{x}) \neq X_0$, initiate resynchronization.

Fig. 7. Second step of the attack: unsuccessful resynchronization

4.3 Second Resynchronization (Successful)

During this second resynchronization, B will update its internal state. In preparation of the subsequent forgery, F binds the x_1-value received from A to F's own value $\widetilde{x}$. Figure 8 delineates the sequence of events during this second (successful) resynchronization.

Summarizing, F does the following:

- Forward the values y_0, Y_1, $\mathcal{Y}_{12}$ sent by B faithfully to A.
- For the random $\widetilde{x}$ from the first step of the attack, form $\widetilde{X} := H(\widetilde{x})$ and $\widetilde{\mathcal{X}} := H(x_1, \widetilde{X})$.
- Send x_0, X_1, $\widetilde{\mathcal{X}}$ to B.

A's internal state: $(x_1, x_2, X_1, X_2, \mathcal{X}_{12}, y_0, Y_1, \mathcal{Y}_{12})$		B's internal state: $(y_0, y_1, Y_0, Y_1, \mathcal{Y}_{01}, \perp, X_0, \mathcal{X}_{01})$
A	**F**	**B**
Receive y_0, Y_1, $\mathcal{Y}_{12}$.	$\xleftarrow{y_0, Y_1, \mathcal{Y}_{12}}$	Choose a random y_2 and form $Y_2 := H(y_2)$, $\mathcal{Y}_{12} := H(y_1, Y_2)$. Send y_0, Y_1, $\mathcal{Y}_{12}$.
Choose a random x_3 and form $X_3 := H(x_3)$, $\mathcal{X}_{23} :=$ $H(x_2, X_3)$.	$\xrightarrow{x_0, X_1, \tilde{\mathcal{X}}}$	Verify that $H(x_0) = X_0$, $H(x_0, X_1) = \mathcal{X}_{01}$, then updates internal state.

Fig. 8. Third step of the attack: successful resynchronization

Since y_0 and Y_1 match what A has stored, A refreshes the value $\mathcal{Y}_{12}$ with the new one sent by B once again. As $H(x_0) = X_0$ and $H(x_0, X_1) = \mathcal{X}_{01}$, the second set of B's conditions is met, and B updates its internal state to $(y_0, y_1, Y_0, Y_1, \mathcal{Y}_{01}, x_0, X_1, \tilde{\mathcal{X}})$. Hence, the second resynchronization is successful, and F can initiate an execution of the message recognition protocol with B.

4.4 Executing the Message Recognition Protocol a Second Time

In the final step of the attack, F uses x_1 and the committing hash value $\tilde{X}$ with the $\tilde{x}$ chosen earlier. As seen in Figure 9, only F is communicating with B at

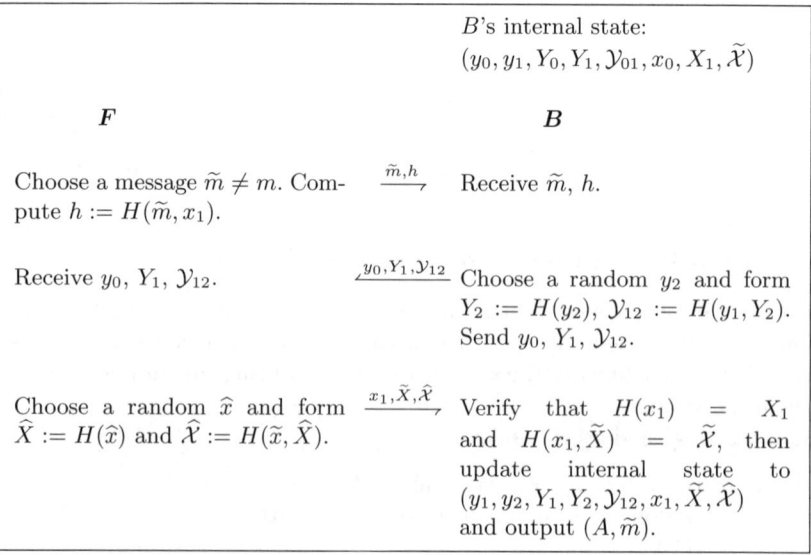

	B's internal state: $(y_0, y_1, Y_0, Y_1, \mathcal{Y}_{01}, x_0, X_1, \tilde{\mathcal{X}})$
F	**B**
Choose a message $\tilde{m} \neq m$. Compute $h := H(\tilde{m}, x_1)$. $\xrightarrow{\tilde{m}, h}$	Receive $\tilde{m}$, h.
Receive y_0, Y_1, $\mathcal{Y}_{12}$. $\xleftarrow{y_0, Y_1, \mathcal{Y}_{12}}$	Choose a random y_2 and form $Y_2 := H(y_2)$, $\mathcal{Y}_{12} := H(y_1, Y_2)$. Send y_0, Y_1, $\mathcal{Y}_{12}$.
Choose a random $\hat{x}$ and form $\hat{X} := H(\hat{x})$ and $\hat{\mathcal{X}} := H(\tilde{x}, \hat{X})$. $\xrightarrow{x_1, \tilde{X}, \hat{\mathcal{X}}}$	Verify that $H(x_1) = X_1$ and $H(x_1, \tilde{X}) = \tilde{\mathcal{X}}$, then update internal state to $(y_1, y_2, Y_1, Y_2, \mathcal{Y}_{12}, x_1, \tilde{X}, \hat{\mathcal{X}})$ and output $(A, \tilde{m})$.

Fig. 9. Fourth step of the attack: inserting a forged message

this stage, and the message $\widetilde{m}$ can chosen arbitrarily (with $m \neq \widetilde{m}$ to achieve indeed a forgery).

The actions of F in this last part of the attack can be summarized as follows:

- Choose a message $\widetilde{m} \neq m$ and compute $h := H(\widetilde{m}, x_1)$.
- Send $\widetilde{m}$, h to B.
- Receive y_0, Y_1, $\mathcal{Y}_{12}$ from B.
- Choose a random $\widehat{x}$ and form $\widehat{X} := H(\widehat{x})$ and $\widehat{\mathcal{X}} := H(\widetilde{x}, \widehat{X})$.
- Send x_1, $\widetilde{X}$, $\widehat{\mathcal{X}}$ to B.

5 Conclusion

The above discussion shows that the message recognition protocol suggested by Mashatan and Stinson in [MS08] does not provide the intended security guarantees: the resynchronization procedure can be abused to provoke a situation where the protocol does not recover and enables a successful forgery attack. Consequently, the protocol from [MS08] should not be used in the present form.

Acknowledgments

We would like to thank the Fields Institute in Toronto and the organizing committee of the Fields Cryptography Retrospecive Meeting in 2009: the financial support for attending this meeting enabled us to meet Atefeh Mashatan who made us aware of the work in [MS08]. We are indebted to Atefeh for helpful discussions.

References

[ABC+98]   Anderson, R., Bergadano, F., Crispo, B., Lee, J.-H., Manifavas, C., Needham, R.: A New Family of Authentication Protocols. Operating Systems Review 32(4), 9–20 (1998)

[LZWW08]   Lucks, S., Zenner, E., Weimerskirch, A., Westhoff, D.: Concrete Security for Entity Recognition: The Jane Doe Protocol. In: Chowdhury, D.R., Rijmen, V., Das, A. (eds.) INDOCRYPT 2008. LNCS, vol. 5365, pp. 158–171. Springer, Heidelberg (2008)

[Mit03]   Mitchell, C.J.: Remote User Authentication Using Public Information. In: Paterson, K.G. (ed.) Cryptography and Coding 2003. LNCS, vol. 2898, pp. 360–369. Springer, Heidelberg (2003)

[MS08]   Mashatan, A., Stinson, D.R.: A New Message Recognition Protocol for Ad Hoc Pervasive Networks. In: Franklin, M.K., Hui, L.C.K., Wong, D.S. (eds.) CANS 2008. LNCS, vol. 5339, pp. 378–394. Springer, Heidelberg (2008)

[SA00]   Stajano, F., Anderson, R.: The Resurrecting Duckling: Security Issues for Ad-hoc Wireless Networks. In: Malcolm, J.A., Christianson, B., Crispo, B., Roe, M. (eds.) Security Protocols 1999. LNCS, vol. 1796, pp. 172–182. Springer, Heidelberg (2000)

[WW04]   Weimerskirch, A., Westhoff, D.: Zero Common-Knowledge Authentication for Pervasive Networks. In: Matsui, M., Zuccherato, R.J. (eds.) SAC 2003. LNCS, vol. 3006, pp. 73–87. Springer, Heidelberg (2004)

Analysis of the Propagation Pattern of a Worm with Random Scanning Strategy Based on Usage Rate of Network Bandwidth

Kwang Sun Ko, Hyunsu Jang, Byuong Woon Park, and Young Ik Eom

School of Information and Communication Engineering, Sungkyunkwan Univ.,
Suwon 440-746, Republic of Korea
kwangsun.ko@gmail.com, {jhs4071,bwpark,yieom}@ece.skku.ac.kr

Abstract. There have been many studies on modeling the propagation patterns of Internet worms since the advent of Morris worm. Among them, there is a well defined propagation model, which is generally called random constant spread (RCS) model. However, there are some limitations to model the propagation patterns of new emergent Internet worms with the RCS model because the model uses the only number of infected hosts as the factor of a worm's propagation. The new worms have several considerable characteristics: *utilization of a faster scanning strategy, miniaturization of the size of a worm's propagation packet, denial of service by network saturation*, and *maximum damage before human-mediated responses*. These characteristics make it difficult to notice much harder than before whether a worm propagates itself or not. Therefore, a basic factor instead of the number of infected hosts, which is used by the RCS model, is required to model the propagation patterns of new worms. In this paper, only analysis and simulation results based on usage rate of network bandwidth, which can be considered as a basic factor, are presented about the propagation pattern of a worm with random scanning strategy. *Miniaturization of the size of a propagation packet* and *utilization of a faster scanning strategy* are related to the size of worm's propagation packet and its propagation rate, respectively. It is presented that the latter is more sensitive than the former.

Keywords: Propagation pattern of a worm, random scanning strategy, usage rate of network bandwidth.

1 Introduction

On November 2, 1988, a self-propagating program, called Morris worm, was released, and it is considered as the first computer worm on the Internet. The results of this worm are reported that about 6,000 major Unix machines were infected, and the cost of the damage was $10M ∼ $100M announced by the Government Accountability Office (GAO) in U.S. [1].

After this dramatic event, there have been the incidents of the infection by various worms, such as Code Red I/II, Nimda, Melissa, Slammer, and so on.

D. Lee and S. Hong (Eds.): ICISC 2009, LNCS 5984, pp. 374–385, 2010.

Until now, there have been many studies conducted to model these kinds of worm's propagation patterns because it is reported to need to be preceded in order to detect the advent of worms in early stage and then to prevent worms from spreading. Basically, to model the propagation pattern of a worm means to explain how it chooses its victims like modeling human diseases. (e.g. the biological model, [2], the classic susceptible and infected epidemic model [3]).

In general, various mathematical and analytical models have been presented for this because each worm has a different propagation pattern. Among them one of the most well-defined model (especially for worms using random scanning strategy) is the random constant spread (RCS) model explained in [4][5].

However, there are some limitations to model the propagation patterns of new emergent Internet worms with the RCS model because the RCS model uses the only number of infected hosts as the factor of a worm's propagation. The new worms have several considerable characteristics:

- Utilization of a faster scanning strategy
- Miniaturization of the size of a propagation packet
- Denial of service by network saturation
- Maximum damage before human-mediated responses

These characteristics make it difficult to notice much harder than before whether a worm propagates itself or not. So, a basic factor, instead of the number of infected hosts which is generally used by many propagation models as well as the RCS model, is required to clearly explain the propagations of new worms.

In this paper, only analysis and simulation results based on usage rate of network bandwidth, which can be considered as a basic factor, are presented about the propagation pattern of a worm with random scanning strategy. The remainder of this paper are organized as follows. Section 2 describes characteristics of new emergent Internet worms, and Section 3 explains the RCS model, which is based on the only number of infected hosts and is reported to be a major propagation model of worms using random scanning strategy. Section 4 and Section 5 describe the analysis and simulation results of the propagation pattern of a worm with a random scanning strategy in the perspective of usage rate of network bandwidth, respectively. Finally, this paper is concluded in Section 6.

2 Characteristics of New Emergent Internet Worms

Kienzle and Elder [6] presented a broad overview of recent worm activities. They extracted a number of trends subjectively from their study of past and present worms, and these trends in a qualitative perspective are as follows: commoditization, convergence, social engineering, additional propagation vectors, technology/vulnerabilities, speed of propagation, countermeasure awareness, and common platforms and software. More descriptions are in [6].

Qing and Wen also presented several characteristics in [7]. According to the analysis of function structure of Internet worms, there are four stages in worm's execution: collection information, probing, attacking, and propagating. Among them, the last propagating is reported to be a very important stage to worms' outbreak, and this stage of each worm may be different as which scanning strategy is chosen by the worm. Also, they categorized scanning strategy into six: random scan, sequential scan, hit-list scan, routable scan, DNS scan, and divide-conquer scan.

There are further researches [8][9][10] on this, but only random scan can be explained by mathematical and analytical models even though it is not always faster than any others. This is the main reason to choose in our paper. So, which features of new emergent Internet worms should be considered? Especially, which characteristics of them may be derived from these in terms of propagation? Four characteristics can be inferred from [6][7][11][12][13], and more descriptions are as follows:

Utilization of a faster scanning strategy. A scanning strategy used by a worm is reported to be a very important factor than others (such as the total number of susceptible hosts, the threaded number of a worm in an infected host, etc.). It is considered that new emergent worms will choose a faster scanning strategy to cause much damage without effort (however, this is not always agreed to). ([6][7] can be referred to.)

Miniaturization of the size of a worm's propagation packet. Generally, as the size of a worm's propagation packet is smaller, as more packets can be generated within an unit time and then be used to propagate under limited network bandwidth or system resources. As an example, the size of Code Red is 4 Kbytes, and that of Slammer is 404 bytes. It is reported that Slammer was two orders of magnitude faster than Code Red. (Code Red spreads so fast to infect more than 359,000 hosts on July 19, 2001 [14]).

Denial of service by network saturation. Generally a denial of service attack is defined as a behavior to make a host abnormal, so the host cannot do its proper jobs. It also includes one to exploit vulnerabilities of computer systems or to exhaust system or network resources. Recently, denial of service attacks mainly saturate resources of networks (or systems), or overflow the workload of them in short period, so they do not provide normal service any more. The characteristics of a worm's propagation are similar to that of recent denial of service attacks. ([6][7] can be referred to).

Maximum damage before human-mediated response. Code Red I in 2001 is reported to infect almost 360,000 hosts over 14 hours [14]. Slammer in 2003 is also done to infect more than 90% of vulnerable hosts within 10 minutes, and about 75,000 distinct IP addresses sending its propagation packets are monitored in the first 30 minutes of its early stage. This evidence shows that new emergent worms' propagation cannot be limited or defeated by human-mediated response any more.

Needless to say, there may be some differences depending on the main characteristics of a worm such as which network is used, which propagation strategy is used, and so on.

3   Random Constant Spread (RCS) Model

This is a model based on the epidemiology in which the propagation pattern of a worm is similar to that of a disease in human being. That is, in RCS model, a worm generally spreads its propagation packet using random scanning strategy; it randomly selects IP addresses based on random number generator effectively seeded, sends its propagation packet, and eventually infects all susceptible hosts on the Internet. Finally, the number of infected victims increases exponentially until there is no susceptible host or all hosts are infected. But actually it does not do because during the worms' propagation there may be some removal processes to affect the propagation: human countermeasures, system or network failure, security patches, and so on. For the explanation of this, there are two fine models: Kermack-Mekendrick model [15] and Two-factor model [16].

However, the RCS model cannot explain all propagation patterns of detected or undiscovered worms. Code Red II spreads its propagation packets based on the local strategy. An infected host gives consequence to send propagation packets to destination ones belonging to the same local network because in general most of hosts in same local network adopt a homogeneous security policy. Nimda or Melissa worms move in other susceptible hosts based on the specific lists, such as email lists or connected network drives. For these reasons, the RCS model cannot explain the propagation patterns of all worms, and there are no exact propagation models until analyzing worm's source code that is publicly addressed or reverse engineering of its binary code is done.

3.1   Traffic Analysis of Code Red I

The worm's propagation pattern which uses random scanning strategies may be explained by the RCS model and has great concerns of many researchers. In this paper, the analysis results of raw data of Code Red I are presented. This data is acquired from the Cooperative Association for Internet Data Analysis (CAIDA) [17] and is handled into a few types of data which include the number of new infected hosts and the cumulative number of infected hosts after the advent of the worm. This is shown in Figure 1.

As seen in Figure 1, during the first time interval $(0 < t < 3,500)$, the worm starts finding susceptible hosts necessary to spread until the number of infected hosts increases enough to be as a stepping-stone. The time required by this interval is variable as network environments and is taken until it is assured that the number of infected hosts reaches the value confirmed to exponentially spread. During the second $(3,500 < t < 4,500)$, based on the amount of previously infected hosts, the cumulative number of infected hosts increases exponentially until it reaches about 60% of total susceptible hosts. During the third $(4,500 < t < 7,000)$, the cumulative number of infected hosts increases linearly. The reasons why this phenomenon exists are explained later. During the last $(7,000 < t)$, the propagation of the worm becomes slower and stops due to a few reasons that most susceptible hosts are infected, removal processes such as human countermeasure and network failure have been done, or its own

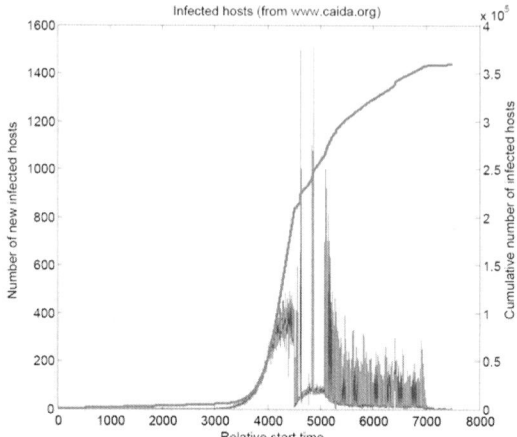

Fig. 1. Graph drawn based on both the number of new infected hosts and the cumulative number of infected hosts by Code Red I. The raw data come from CAIDA [18]. The x-axis shows relative start time monitored; the left y-axis shows the number of new infected hosts, and the right y-axis shows the cumulative number of infected hosts.

expiration mechanism is activated. (ex. Code Red I stops its propagation 00:00 UTC of July 20, 2001 by its own expiration mechanism).

From the perspective of the cumulative number of infected hosts, it can be seen that there are four phases in the results of traffic analysis of Code Red I : slow start, exponential spread, linear spread, and slow finish. In the first phase, the worm's propagation starts slowly until the number increases enough to be as a stepping-stone of propagation. The worm's clones spread exponentially and spread linearly. (Detailed descriptions are explained later.). Lastly, the worm's propagation finishes slowly until entire susceptible hosts are infected. A previous research [12] however has three phases in simple epidemic model: *slow start*, *fast spread*, and *slow finish*. Furthermore, in Figure 1 there is an important phase-transition around 4,500 of the x-axis in the aspect of the cumulative number of infected hosts. That is, the rate of exponentially increased cumulative number of infected hosts suddenly becomes linear. In addition, two more facts can be found.

- *Increasing rate of new infected hosts is stable within* $4,000 < t < 4,500$
  The numbers of new infected hosts within this interval are less than those within $5,100 < t < 5,200$ even if it is temporary, and the increasing rate of new infected hosts is stable, while the total numbers of infected hosts increase exponentially. For these reasons, it cannot be recognized for human countermeasures, such as security patches or removal processes, to be done against the propagation. In addition, during exponentially increasing in the aspect of the cumulative numbers of infected hosts, the worm's propagation does not need to be stable.

– *Numbers of new infected hosts suddenly drop within* $4,600 < t < 5,100$
The numbers of new infected hosts within this interval are a little more than those in *slow start* phase, and there are two short intervals in which the numbers of new infected hosts are suddenly higher than other intervals. For these, human countermeasures have been done especially during the interval to stop the propagation of Code Red I, and it cannot be explained why the numbers of new infected hosts suddenly become high?

As these facts, we can think why there is a transition from *exponential spread* phase to *linear spread* phase. Is there any particular reason? For this, analytic point of view in two aspects may be considered. First is that, as previous research results [12][16][18] presented, human countermeasures like security patches and the removal of susceptible or infected hosts stop worms from spreading. The other is that, as [19] expounded, worms propagation packets spread so rapidly that network saturations seem to be occurred in many bottleneck network nodes. The key reason of the transition can be based on the latter rather than the former; that is, it can be inferred that huge propagation packets of Code Red I produces denial of network service and continues until human reactions or no propagations with several reasons. The basis for it is reasonable through previous research results. In this situation, to monitor usage rate of network bandwidth may make it possible to detect a worm's propagation because network bandwidth is one of limited resources in the Internet and can be a sensitive factor to determine whether something wrong occurs or not. In $7,000 < t$ of Figure 1, the cumulative numbers of infected hosts do not increase anymore because of major two reasons: the overall infection of susceptible hosts, the propagation stop.

3.2 Previous Studies of Slammer

There is an another example, Slammer, to show that network bandwidth can be an important factor to detect worms' propagation. According to the previous research result [19] by Moore *et al.* using Dshield data set, in principle a host infected by Slammer can send propagation packets at 300,000 scans per a second through 100 Mbps. However, in practice the host can send propagation packets at the maximum 26,000 scans per a second because of limited network bandwidth and packet overhead in intermediate network nodes. These show that Slammer can send its propagation packets at 4,000 scans per a second in early spreading phase over the Internet. The propagation phase of Slammer is reported to change from *exponential spread* phase to *slow finish* phase without *linear spread* phase due to the limitation of network bandwidth as [19] expounded.

Two cases, Code Red I and Slammer, show that network bandwidth is the most important and sensitive factor to affect worms' propagations. Usage rate of network bandwidth can make it possible to determine whether a worm sends propagation packets or not.

4   Usage Rate of Network Bandwidth

The RCS model illustrates how a worm propagates itself over the Internet. In this model, two factors are used; a susceptible host and an infected host. The former is a host which is vulnerable to the worm attack. The latter is a host which has been infected by the worm and sends propagation packets. Let N denote the number of susceptible hosts in a network, and β is the propagation rate of a worm. At time t, the increasing rate of infected hosts dI_t/dt is defined as follows:

$$dI_t/dt = \beta I_{t-1}(N - I_t) \tag{1}$$

Eq. 1 is the basic one of the RCS model, and the increasing rate of infected hosts continuously rises until all susceptible hosts are totally infected. In this paper, Eq. 1 is used to define usage rate of network bandwidth by propagation packets of a worm, and additional notations have to be defined as follows.

At time t, let WB_t and NB_t denote usage rate of network bandwidth used by worm traffic and one by normal traffic, respectively. Total usage rate of network bandwidth TB_t can be defined as $TB_t = WB_t + NB_t$, however, during the propagation of a speedy worm in a short period, usage rate of normal traffic may be considered as a constant value, that is, $NB_t \cong C$ (ex. Slammer can send its propagation packets at 26,000 scans per a second.). Therefore, total usage rate of network bandwidth, TB_t, can be defined as $TB_t = WB_t + C$. Usage rate of network bandwidth used by a worm is reported to be proportional to worm's propagation rate as well as the size of its propagation packet. Ultimately, usage rate of network bandwidth during the propagation of a worm can be derived from Eq. 1 as follows:

$$dWB_t/dt = \epsilon_{IPv4} I_t \beta P_{size}(B - WB_t) \tag{2}$$

In Eq. 2, an effective value, ϵ_{IPv4}, is a constant value that means the portion of IPv4 addresses which is assigned by Internet Assigned Numbers Authority (IANA) [20] as public IP addresses. According to the research results, the portion is about 65.2% except reserved or private IP addresses; only 21.2% has not been allocated, and 13.7% is reserved. Actually, the reserved and unallocated portions can not have a worm's propagation packets. Even though valid addresses are not geographically and hierarchically distributed, various mechanisms like Classless Inter-Domain Routing (CIDR) or using private IPv4 address can make the distribution of IPv4 addresses uniformed on the Internet in terms of network bandwidth. In addition, only random scan among scanning strategies is concerned in our paper.

The value P_{size} means the size of a worm's propagation packet, and B means the rate of allocated network bandwidth. Using Eq. 2, the simulation results are presented later with usage rate of network bandwidth which is explained as an important factor to detect whether a worm propagates or not as a worm's propagation rate or the size of its propagation packet.

5   Simulation and Results

One of popular network simulators, NS-2 [21], is used to draw concretely numerical values, and reliable results are presented using MATLAB [22] based on the drawn numerical values. That is, because it is difficult to define usage rate of network bandwidth over the Internet as specific values, reliable parameters are simulated and drawn using a method that an abstract network is configured. The abstract network organized using NS-2 is shown in Figure 2.

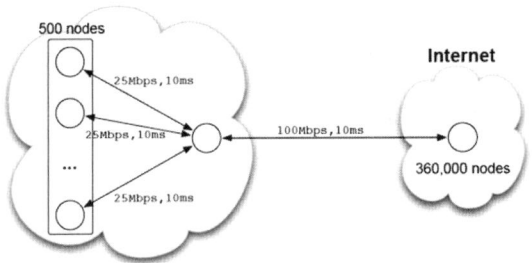

Fig. 2. Abstract network organized using NS2

As seen in Figure 2, the left side represents a protected network, and the right side does the Internet constituted by 360,000 nodes which number is drawn from previous research results. Firstly, a worm propagates in the Internet within the right side of the figure. Secondly, the number of infected hosts increases as time goes, and lastly the worms send propagation packets to the left side of the figure, the protected network. In this case, when the allocated network bandwidth at the gateway of the protected network is 100 Mbps (delay time is 10ms), it is monitored the number of propagation packets passing through the network link during an unit time. The reason why the network bandwidth is 100 Mbps is because the propagation rate of an abstract worm is presented by previous research results to be 4,000 scans per a second.

All parameters are identical to that of Slammer; the size of a propagation packet is 404 bytes, the worm's propagation rate is 4,000 scans per a second, and UDP protocol is used to propagate. After several simulations, about 13,200 propagation packets per an unit time pass through the network link shown in Figure 2, and about approximately 42.8% of network bandwidth is used. Based on these results, the ratio between a propagation packet and the number of propagation packets, which saturate allocated network bandwidth, is 1 to 13,200. To simulate correlation between usage rate of network bandwidth and either a worm's propagation rate or the size of a propagation packet using MATLAB, several research results [12][16][18] are used. Additional parameters of previous studies are also used.

Firstly, the simulation environment is configured, being similar with the propagation pattern of a worm based on the RCS model. All hosts in this network are susceptible, and the four phases are also appeared. Several parameters for simulation are as follows:

- Number of susceptible hosts: 5×2^{16}
- Propagation rate: 1.4 / (*the number of susceptible hosts*)
- Size of a propagation packet: 1

Next, as described in Eq. 2, ϵ_{IPv4} (=0.6758), β (=1.4/(5×2^{16})), and P_{size} (=32) are set regardless of simulation time t. Based on these data, simulation result is shown in Figure 3.

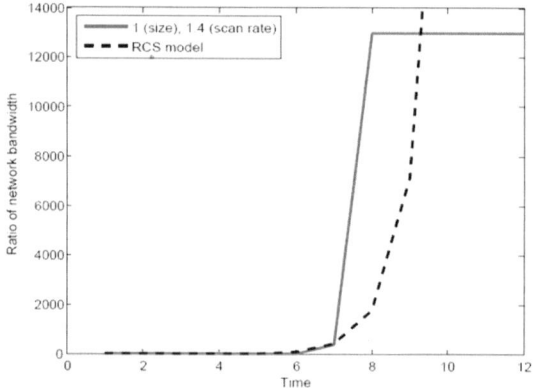

Fig. 3. Simulation result of usage rate of network bandwidth compared with the RCS model (The x-axis shows simulation time, and the y-axis shows the relative ratio of network bandwidth occupied by our model)

In Figure 3, the reason why the ratio of network bandwidth on the y-axis is used is to prove that it is more sensitive, compared with the number of infected hosts used by the RCS model. Because this factor can not be described with numerical values, the relative ratio to the factor of the RCS model needs to be presented explicitly. That is to say, the metric is used to show proportional values between our factor, usage rate of network bandwidth, and that of the RCS model. Based on these data, the correlation result between the size of a worm's propagation packet and usage rate of network bandwidth is illustrated in Figure 4.

As seen in Figure 4, when the ratio of a worm's propagation packet and the number of propagation packets which saturate the allocated network bandwidth (100 Mbps) is 1 to 13,200, it is shown the required time to saturate the allocated network as the size varies. Even though the size of a propagation packet becomes larger four times, it takes just only one simulation time to saturate the network. In addition, even though the size of a propagation packet becomes larger forty times from 0.1 to 4 on simulation, it takes just about three simulation time to saturate the allocated network bandwidth. However, a worm's propagation rate

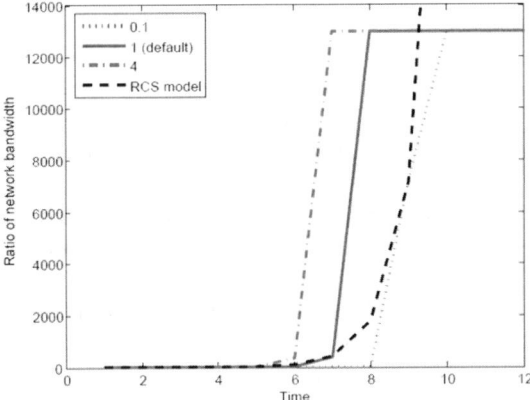

Fig. 4. Correlation between usage rate of network bandwidth and the sizes of a propagation packet (The x-axis shows simulation time, and the y-axis shows the relative ratio of network bandwidth occupied by our model)

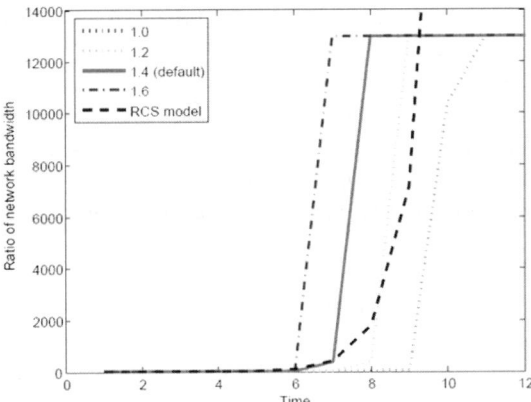

Fig. 5. Correlation between usage rate of network bandwidth and the worm's propagation rates (The x-axis shows simulation time, and the y-axis shows the relative ratio of network bandwidth occupied by our model)

requires a considerable change rather than the size of a propagation packet, even though the difference is very small. This simulation result is shown in Figure 5.

As seen in Figure 5, when the ratio of a propagation packet and the number of propagation packets which saturate the allocated network bandwidth (100 Mbps) is 1 to 13,200, it is shown the required time to saturate the allocated network as the propagation rate varies. When the propagation rate increases about 60% from 1.0 to 1.6, it is reduced approximately by four simulation time to saturate the network. In addition, even though a worm's propagation rate increases about 14.2% from 1.4 to 1.6 on simulation, it takes just about one simulation time to saturate the allocated network bandwidth.

In addition, the simulation results shown in Figure 5 and Figure 6 explain that a worm's propagation packet to saturate allocated network bandwidth. That is, among several characteristics of new worms, described before, *miniaturization of the size of a propagation packet* and *utilization of a faster scanning strategy* can be related to the size of worm's propagation packet and its propagation rate, respectively. It is presented that the latter is more sensitive than the former. This simulation is done assuming that normal traffic is considered as C where $TB_t = WB_t + C$. So it may take short time to saturate real networks because normal traffic always exists. Consequently, there is a sudden change of usage rate of network bandwidth at the start part of a worm's propagation, so that it can be possible to decide whether a worm propagates or not. On the other hand, there is one problem, a false-positive phenomenon, to decide which kind of traffic results in the sudden change. This issue is left for future work.

6   Conclusions

There have been many research results and studies on modeling the propagation patterns of various kinds of worms, and a well defined propagation model is the RCS model based on the only number of infected hosts. However, in terms of new emergent Internet worms, there are some limitations to model the propagation patterns of these worms with the RCS model because the advent of a worm should be detected in early stage. In addition, new worms have several considerable characteristics: *utilization of a faster scanning strategy, miniaturization of the size of a worm's propagation packet, denial of service by network saturation,* and *maximum damage before human-mediated responses.* These characteristics make it difficult to notice much harder than before whether a worm propagates itself. Therefore, a basic factor instead of the number of infected hosts is required to detect new worms.

In this paper, only analysis and simulation results were presented about the propagation pattern of a worm with random scanning strategy based on usage rate of network bandwidth, which can be considered as the factor to detect worms' appearances. The simulation results explained that a worm's propagation rate is a sensitive factor rather than the size of a propagation packet to saturate allocated network bandwidth. That is, *miniaturization of the size of a propagation packet* and *utilization of a faster scanning strategy* are related to the size of worm's propagation packet and its propagation rate, respectively. It is presented that the latter is more sensitive than the former.

References

1. Morris worm, http://en.wikipedia.org/wiki/Morris_worm
2. Bailey, N.T.J.: The Mathematical Theory of Epidemics, New York, Hafner (1957)
3. Hethcote, H.W.: The Mathematics of Infectious Diseases. SIAM Review 42(4), 599–653 (2000)

4. Moore, D., Shannon, C., Voelker, G.M., Savage, S.: Internet Quarantine: Requirements for Containing Self-Propagating Code. In: Proc. of IEEE INFOCOM 2003 Conference, IEEE Press, Los Alamitos (2003)
5. Staniford, S., Paxson, V., Weaver, N.: How to Own the Internet in Your Spare Time. In: Proc. of the 11th USENIX Security Symposium, pp. 149–167 (2002)
6. Kienzle, D.M., Elder, M.C.: Recent worms: a survey and trends. In: Proc. of the 2003 ACM Workshop on Rapid Malcode, pp. 1–10 (2003)
7. Qing, S., Wen, W.: A survey and trends on Internet worms. In: Computers & Security, vol. 24, pp. 334–346. Elsevier Ltd., Amsterdam (2005)
8. Zou, C.C., Towsley, D., Gong, W., Cai, S.: Advanced Routing Worm and Its Security Challenges. Simulation 82(1), 75–85 (2006)
9. Zou, C.C., Towsley, D., Gong, W.: Modeling and Simulation Study of the Propagation and Defense of Internet Email Worm. IEEE Transactions on Dependable and Secure Computing 4(2), 105–118 (2007)
10. Provos, N., McClain, J., Wang, K.: Search Worms. In: Proc. of the 4th ACM Workshop on Recurring Malcode, pp. 1–8 (2006)
11. Kargl, F., Maier, J., Weber, M.: Protecting Web Servers from Distributed Denial of Service Attacks. In: Proc. of the 10th international conference on World Wide Web, pp. 514–524 (2001)
12. Zou, C.C., Gong, W., Towsley, D., Gao, L.: The monitoring and early detection of internet worms. IEEE/ACM Transactions on Networking (TON) 13(5), 961–974 (2005)
13. Weaver, N.C.: Warhol Worms: The Potential for Very Fast Internet Plagues, http://www.iwar.org.uk/comsec/resources/worms/warhol-worm.htm
14. Moore, D., Shannon, C.: Code-Red: a Case Study on the Spread and Victims of an Internet Worm. In: Proc. of the 2002 ACM SIGCOMM Internet Measurement Workshop, Marseille, France, pp. 273–284 (2002)
15. Frauenthal, J.C.: Mathematical Modeling in Epidemiology. Springer, New York (1980)
16. Zou, C.C., Gong, W., Towsley, D.: Code Red Worm Propagation Modeling and Analysis. In: Proc. of CCS 2002 (2002)
17. CAIDA (Cooperative Association for Internet Data Analysis), http://www.caida.org
18. Zou, C.C., Gao, L., Gong, W., Towsley, D.: Monitoring and early warning for Internet worms. In: Proc. of 10th ACM Conf. Comput. Commun. Security, Washington, DC (2003)
19. Moore, D., Paxson, V., Savage, S., Shannon, C., Staniford, S., Weaver, N.: Inside the Slammer Worm. IEEE Security & Privacy 1(4) (2003)
20. IANA (Internet Assigned Numbers Authority), http://www.iana.org
21. The network simulator: NS-2, http://www.isi.edu/nsnam/ns
22. The MathWorks, http://www.mathworks.com

Author Index